Praise for *The Baffin Handbook*

"*The Baffin Handbook* . . . is an excellent new travel guide to the eastern Arctic."

— The New York Times

"Don't go north without *The Baffin Handbook* . . . packed with information essential to planning any trip in the region."

— The Globe and Mail

"Written by local residents or experienced Arctic hands . . . plus lists of outfitters, maps of parks and communities, and lots of colour photographs . . . the first ever tourist guide to Canada's Eastern Arctic."

— Canadian Geographic

"Precisely the kind of information first-time travellers to Baffin and environs need to plan successful vacations."

— Yukon News

"Visiting the fabulous Bylot Island bird sanctuary across Eclipse Sound from Pond Inlet or travelling from Pangnirtung to nearby Auyuittuq National Park requires not only a fat outfitter's fee but also the benevolence of the weather gods . . . *The Baffin Handbook* is an indispensable guide."

— Winnipeg Free Press

"The first-ever tourist guide to Canada's Eastern Arctic."

— Canadian Geographic

Praise for *The 1998 Nunavut Handbook* web site

"Celebrate the Earth with a trip north . . . *The Nunavut Handbook* is a nicely packaged guide to the people and wildlife of Canada's Eastern Arctic, one of the last great untouched wilderness areas on our shrinking planet."

— *USA Today*

"The web site alone is a great resource, both for travel information and historical accounts of life in the Arctic."

— *The Globe and Mail*

"*The Nunavut Handbook* — Discover the people and wildlife of Canada's Eastern Arctic, one of the last untouched wilderness areas."

— *The Eisenhower National Clearinghouse for Mathematics and Science Education*

"New on the Internet is a comprehensive travel guide to the Canadian Arctic. Check out *The Nunavut Handbook*, at www.arctic-travel.com."

— *The Ottawa Citizen*

"Overall, the guide appears to be up-to-date, clear and realistic . . . an excellent handbook for anyone contemplating travel in that all-day, all-night world."

— *Explore Magazine*

THE 1998 Nunavut HANDBOOK

Travelling in Canada's ARCTIC

Printed and bound in Canada.

Canadian Cataloguing in Publication Data

Main entry under title:
The 1998 Nunavut handbook

ISBN 1-55036-574-6

1. Nunavut (N.W.T.) — Guidebooks. I. Soublière, Marion
II. Title: Nunavut handbook.

FC4195.N8A3 1997 917.19'2043 C97-900609-0
F1060.4.N55 1997

Published by Nortext Multimedia Inc., Box 8, Iqaluit NT X0A 0H0, Canada

For ordering information:
Nortext Multimedia Inc.
Box 8
Iqaluit NT X0A 0H0
Canada
Tel.: 1-800-263-1452 (in North America)
1-613-727-5466 (outside North America)
Fax: 1-613-727-6910
E-mail: tinak@nortext.com
Web site: www.arctic-travel.com

Cover photo of iceberg shot during spring in Pond Inlet, Nunavut.

FOREWORD

A few years ago, as I was packing for a late June trip to Sanikiluaq, I had the foresight to throw in a copy of *The Baffin Handbook* along with the sweaters, socks and bug juice. I was glad I did. In small arctic settings where it seems to the untrained eye that there isn't a lot to do, it's good to be apprised of absolutely *everything* there is to do. My *Baffin Handbook* had tipped me off to a well-hidden eiderdown duvet and outerwear manufacturer. I made contact with the shop manager. She opened up the outlet for me, and within 25 minutes, about a half dozen of my travelling companions trooped in behind me to check out the action.

When *The Baffin Handbook* was published in 1993, it became the first travel guidebook to the eastern Arctic, filling the void for comprehensive, straight-shooting travel information for those venturing north. *The Nunavut Handbook* does the same for the new territory of Nunavut, and this time there's a twist: a companion web site (**www.arctic-travel.com**) that continues to update content, introduce new features, post questions and answers from travellers to Nunavut and residents living there, and further the northern storytelling tradition with a corner for travellers' tales.

Nunavut is rapidly changing these days in the countdown to April 1, 1999, the day Canada's newest territory officially comes aboard. Sometimes the pace of change feels chaotic. *The Nunavut Handbook* plans to publish yearly, and we hope that helps travellers keep abreast of some of the changes transforming the North. They can also stay tuned for changes via the web site.

Producing this book required an enormous amount of work and dedication from an enormous number of people, from a crack editorial team and hard-working editorial advisory board to the talented in-house design and production crew, marketing minds, administrative staff, sales representatives and company owners who envisioned all this.

We also thank the many individuals and organizations who helped in the research and fact-checking of this book. Special thanks go to Nunavut Tourism and GNWT Resources, Wildlife and Economic Development, in particular Rick Hamburg, Susan Makpah and Marion Glawson.

But most of all, this book is the collective gift of more than 40 talented writers who have experienced Nunavut in their hearts, minds and souls, because for the majority of them, it is their home. Too many travel guidebooks deliver the viewpoint of a stranger in a strange land. The words on the pages of *The Nunavut Handbook* are made-in-Nunavut. Our writers offered up anecdotes, insights, and opinions in addition to intimate accounts of their communities and northern lifestyle. If our book inspires you to head to Nunavut, it is because our storytellers have etched a picture of Nunavut from the inside, looking out.

I encourage *Handbook* readers and Internet surfers to fax or e-mail me their comments, suggestions for new travel angles to explore, or criticisms of the book. We want to make *The Nunavut Handbook* an essential part of your backpack, too.

Marion Soublière, Managing Editor

Fax: 1-613-727-6910
E-mail: marions@nortext.com

INTRODUCTION

Arctic Canada has been home to Inuit and earlier inhabitants for thousands of years. Throughout history, Inuit and their predecessors travelled in step with the seasons, inland across barren tundra and back to the coastline. They hunted the wildlife that would nourish their families: caribou, seal, fish, walrus, whales.

Our traditional lifestyle is here to stay, even if we spend as much time surfing the Internet as checking the fishing nets, or any other land-based analogy that comes to mind. We can thank the very modern Nunavut Land Claims Agreement for that. It protects and enshrines Inuit traditional values and culture. While a new public government readies itself for the territory of Nunavut in 1999 and Inuit rise to the educational challenges forced by the managerial needs of the new government — in all this busyness, we remember where we came from.

I saw a television documentary some years ago about the Alaska land claims settlement act and the Inuit desire to continue to harvest bowhead whales. In one part, the documentary showed senators or congressmen questioning some Alaskan Inuit about their land claim settlement. The line of questioning went something like this:

"Do you live in wooden houses?" they asked.

"Yes," replied the Inuit.

"Do you drive cars and trucks?"

"Yes."

"You're not real Eskimos anymore, are you?"

Here in Canada, we have had the same problem with some people who thought that just because we no longer live in igloos or travel only by dogteams, that we are no longer "real Inuit." We live in wooden houses, drive Jeep Cherokees, and fly in jumbo jets all over the world. But we are still Inuit. It is our spirit, our inner being, that makes us Inuit.

I predict that sometime within the next hundred years — perhaps 50 years from now — an Inuk will be elected prime minister of Canada. That prime minister will live at 24 Sussex, fly in jets, and hobnob with world leaders. But that prime minister will still be an Inuk.

I also predict that in the next thousand years, Inuit will become world leaders, starship captains, and travel to the far corners of our galaxy. But they will still be Inuit.

Sometimes it's hard to believe the future. It's such a contrast to the cultural upheaval of the past 35 years or so. Government policies that took nomadic hunters and their families away from the land and forced them into communities, that took the families' children away from their parents and punished them for speaking their mother tongue while attending residential schools — these colonial scars still hurt many Inuit. And their children, whose parents trade away childhood memories for drugs and booze. Time is a slow healer, but endless years spent surviving in an arctic environment have taught Inuit to be patient.

The years ahead are exciting for all northerners living in the central and eastern Arctic, but especially for Inuit. The trip into the future is a return to the best of the traditional past.

John Amagoalik

Map of Nunavut

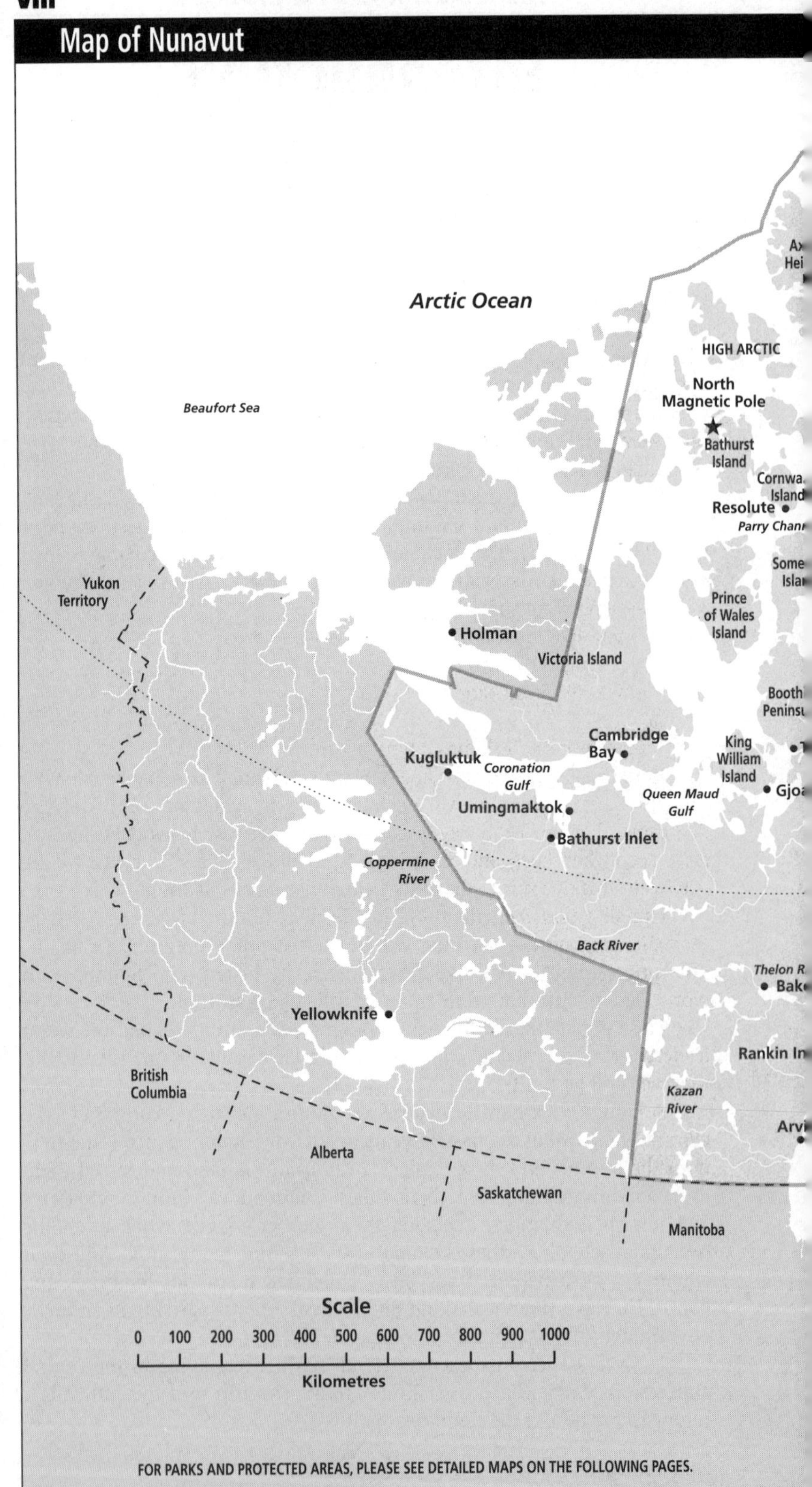
Arctic Ocean
Beaufort Sea
HIGH ARCTIC
North Magnetic Pole
Bathurst Island
Resolute
Prince of Wales Island
Yukon Territory
Holman
Victoria Island
Cambridge Bay
King William Island
Kugluktuk
Coronation Gulf
Queen Maud Gulf
Umingmaktok
Bathurst Inlet
Coppermine River
Back River
Yellowknife
Kazan River
British Columbia
Alberta
Saskatchewan
Manitoba
Scale
0 100 200 300 400 500 600 700 800 900 1000
Kilometres
FOR PARKS AND PROTECTED AREAS, PLEASE SEE DETAILED MAPS ON THE FOLLOWING PAGES.

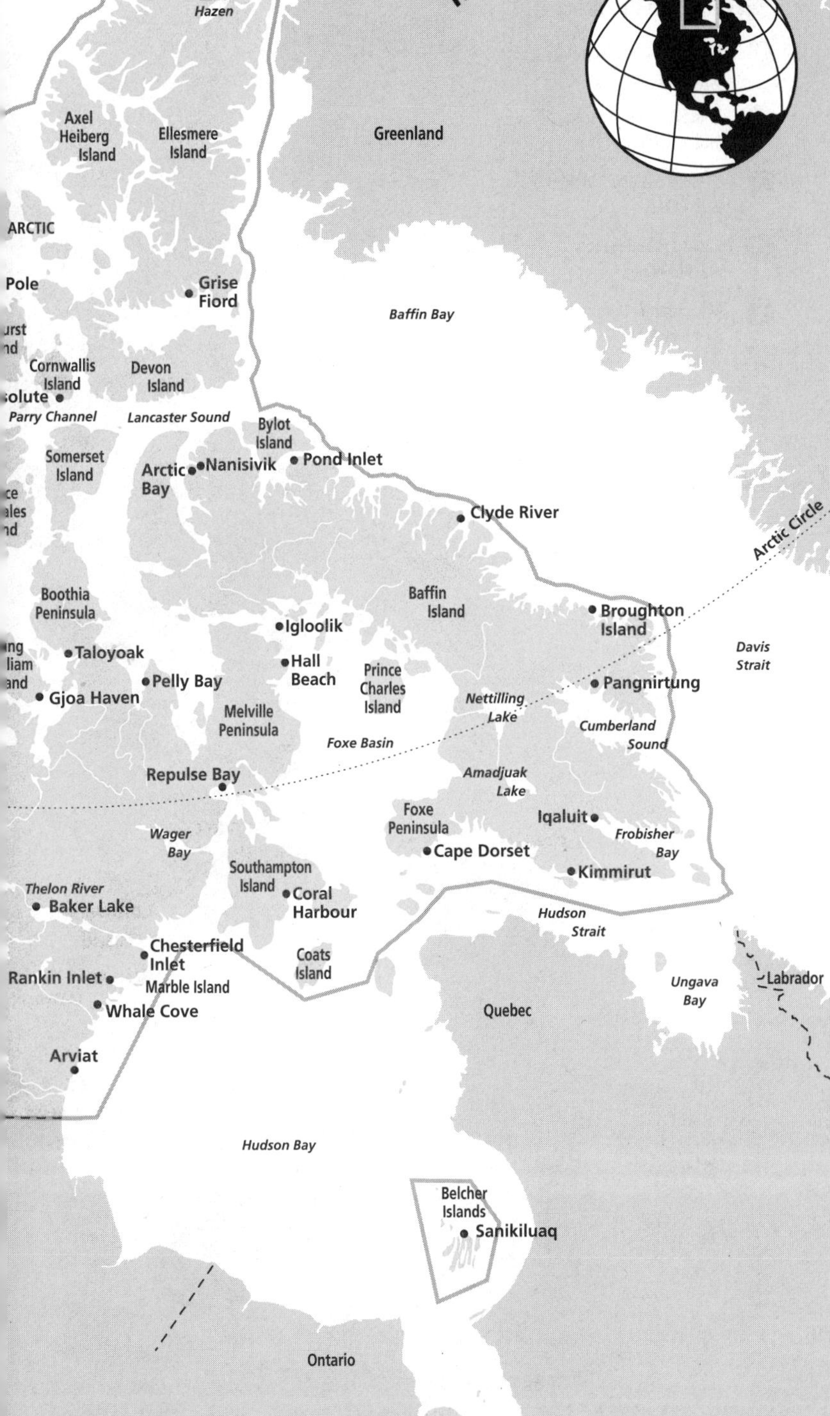
N
Lake Hazen
Axel Heiberg Island
Ellesmere Island
Greenland
ARCTIC
Pole
Grise Fiord
Baffin Bay
Cornwallis Island
Devon Island
Parry Channel
Lancaster Sound
Bylot Island
Somerset Island
Arctic Bay
Nanisivik
Pond Inlet
Clyde River
Arctic Circle
Boothia Peninsula
Baffin Island
Broughton Island
Igloolik
Davis Strait
Taloyoak
Hall Beach
Pelly Bay
Gjoa Haven
Prince Charles Island
Pangnirtung
Nettilling Lake
Melville Peninsula
Cumberland Sound
Foxe Basin
Repulse Bay
Amadjuak Lake
Foxe Peninsula
Iqaluit
Wager Bay
Frobisher Bay
Cape Dorset
Southampton Island
Kimmirut
Thelon River
Coral Harbour
Baker Lake
Hudson Strait
Chesterfield Inlet
Coats Island
Rankin Inlet
Marble Island
Ungava Bay
Labrador
Whale Cove
Quebec
Arviat
Hudson Bay
Belcher Islands
Sanikiluaq
Ontario

High Arctic and North Baffin Island

Axel
Heiber
Islar

Arctic Ocean

1

Bathurst Island

Cornwallis Island

Resolute

Beech

Parry Channel

2

Somerset Island

Prince of Wales Island

Victoria Island

Boothia Peninsula

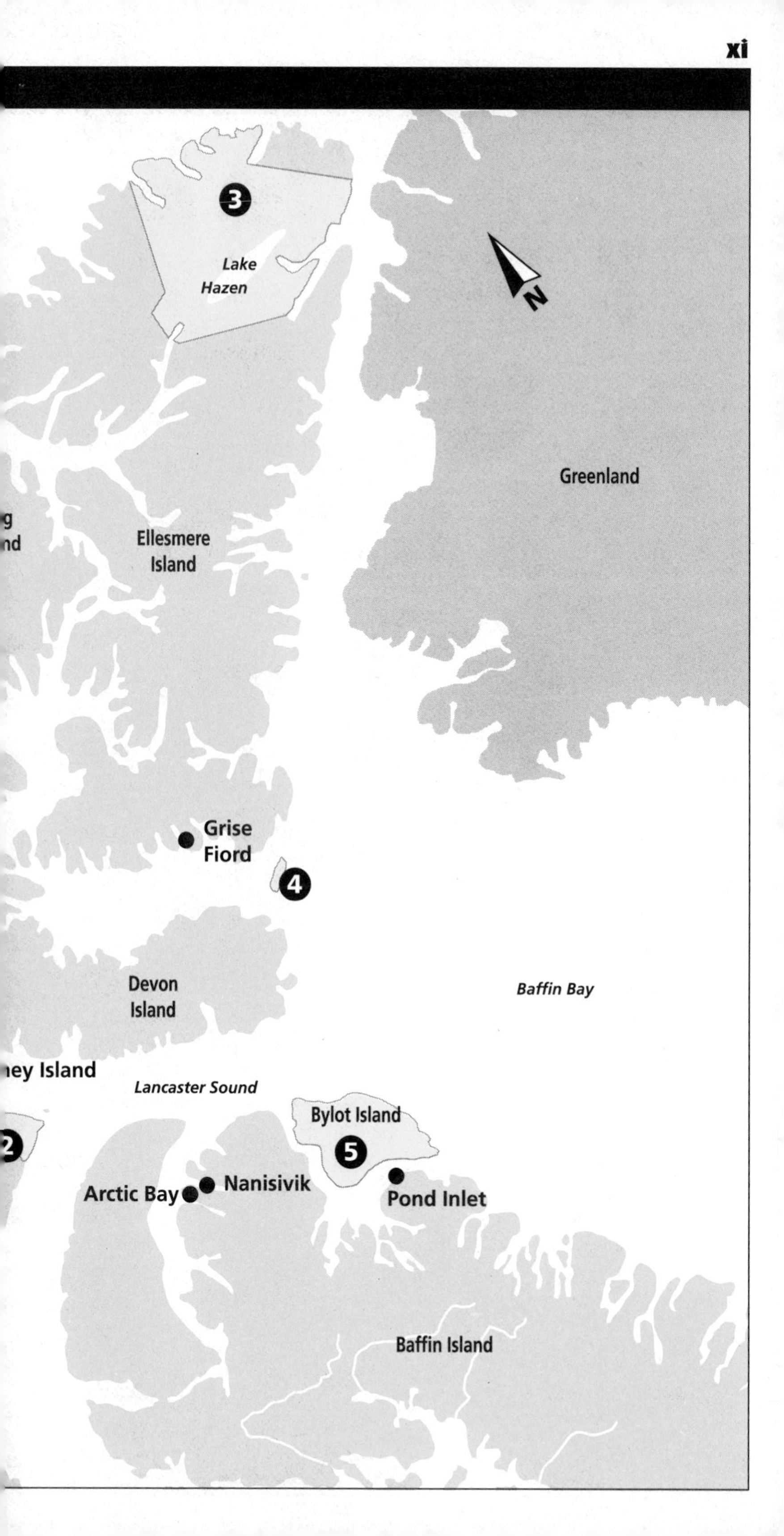

Lake
Hazen
N
Greenland
g
nd
Ellesmere
Island
Grise
Fiord
Devon
Island
Baffin Bay
ey Island
Lancaster Sound
Bylot Island
Arctic Bay
Nanisivik
Pond Inlet
Baffin Island

Arctic Coast, King William Island, Boothia Peninsula, Melville

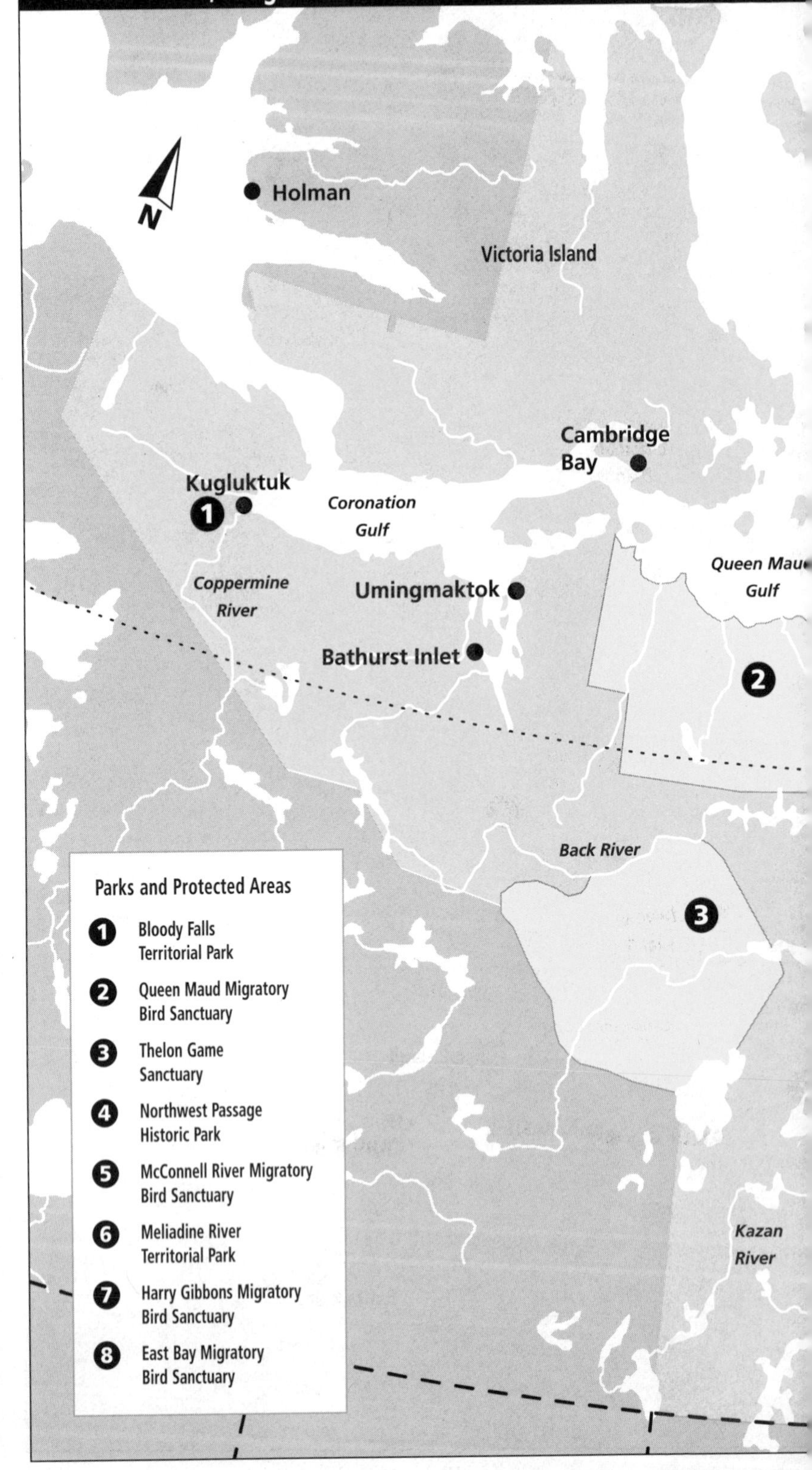

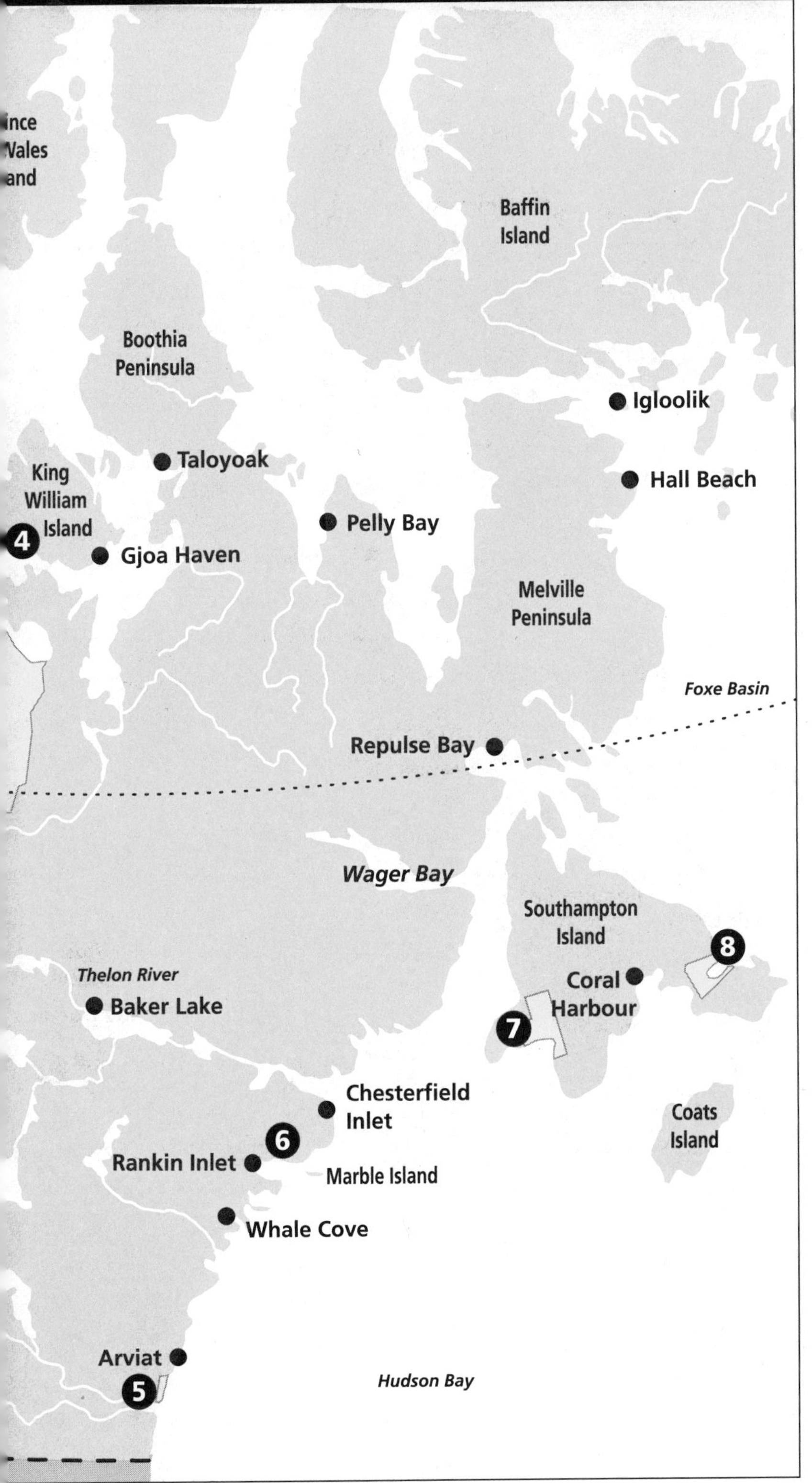
eninsula Area and West Coast/Hudson Bay
ince
Vales
and
Baffin
Island
Boothia
Peninsula
Igloolik
Hall Beach
Taloyoak
King
William
Island
4
Gjoa Haven
Pelly Bay
Melville
Peninsula
Foxe Basin
Repulse Bay
Wager Bay
Southampton
Island
8
Coral
Harbour
7
Thelon River
Baker Lake
Chesterfield
Inlet
6
Rankin Inlet
Marble Island
Coats
Island
Whale Cove
Arviat
5
Hudson Bay

North, Central and South Baffin Island, Southampton Island and

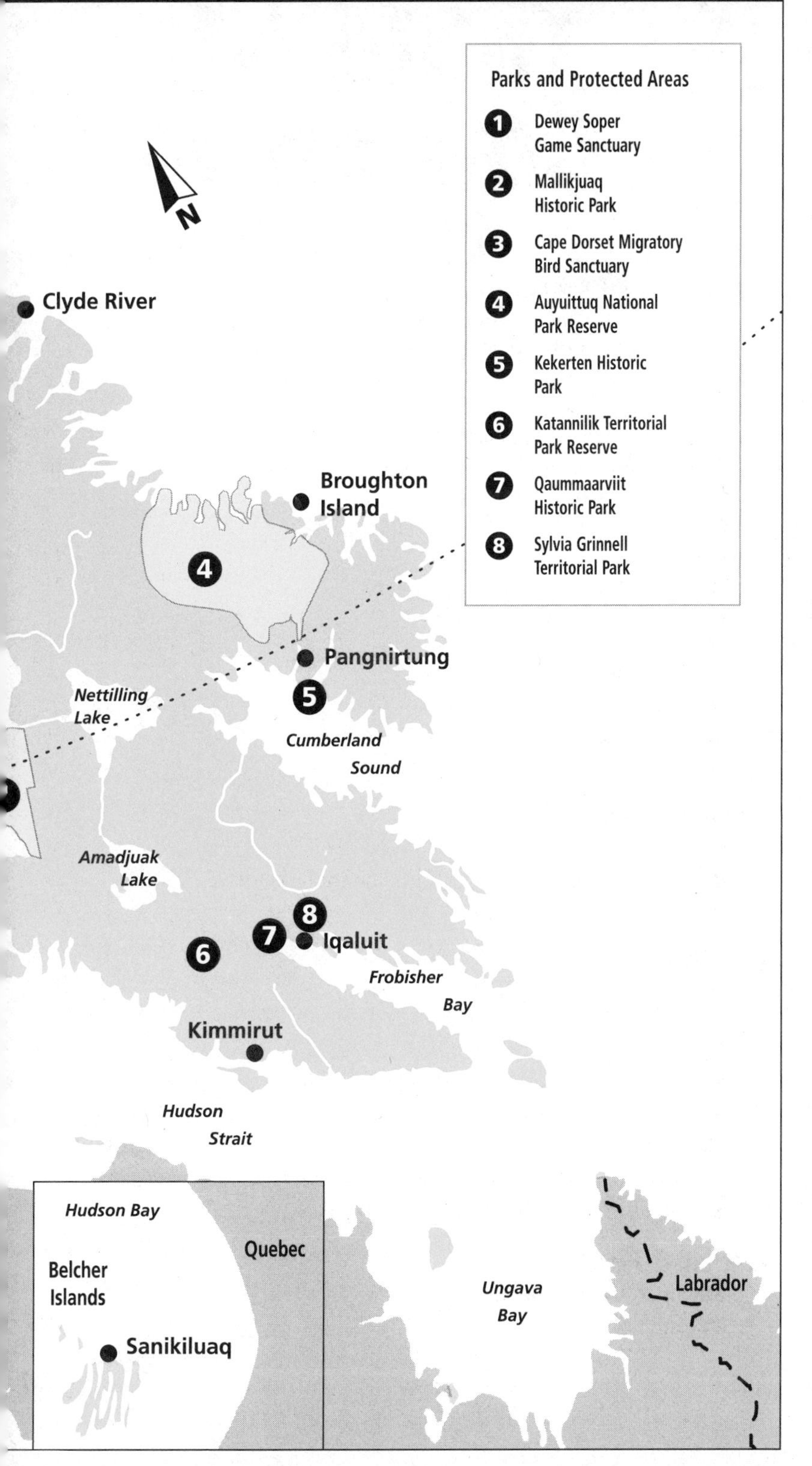
elcher Islands
Parks and Protected Areas
1 Dewey Soper Game Sanctuary
2 Mallikjuaq Historic Park
3 Cape Dorset Migratory Bird Sanctuary
4 Auyuittuq National Park Reserve
5 Kekerten Historic Park
6 Katannilik Territorial Park Reserve
7 Qaummaarviit Historic Park
8 Sylvia Grinnell Territorial Park
N
Clyde River
Broughton Island
Pangnirtung
Nettilling Lake
Cumberland Sound
Amadjuak Lake
Iqaluit
Frobisher Bay
Kimmirut
Hudson Strait
Hudson Bay
Quebec
Belcher Islands
Sanikiluaq
Ungava Bay
Labrador

Table of Contents

Planning Ahead

Getting Around

The People

Art and Music

Land and Wildlife

Activities

Destinations

West Coast/Hudson Bay

Southampton Island

Melville Peninsula Area

Boothia Peninsula and King William Island

Arctic Coast

High Arctic

North Baffin Island

Central Baffin Island

South Baffin Island

Belcher Islands in Hudson Bay

Planning Ahead

TRAVEL INFORMATION AND TOURS

by Carol Rigby, with contributions from Jennifer Bernius

Everyone's first trip to Nunavut is memorable, in one way or another. Take, as an example, the experience of two of the contributors to this guidebook.

In January 1986, they moved north to Frobisher Bay (now called Iqaluit), before the advent of daily jet service between Iqaluit and Ottawa. So they flew in a Hawker-Siddeley 748, eight hours of turboprops rumbling through the icy air with a refuelling stop in what is now called Kuujjuaq.

He was looking forward to research work with a local Inuit organization. She was wondering what her life would be like as an at-home mother with a three-year-old and a five-month-old.

True to form, the flight itself was eventful. Shortly after takeoff, the flight attendant announced that the ovens recently installed in the plane didn't work, so there would be no hot meals. Everyone snacked on unheated portions of their meals and cold pizza left over from somewhere. The five-month-old didn't mind, nor did the three-year-old, who was sick with some bug and running a fever by mid-flight. Mother did not take this to be an auspicious start to a new life in the North!

Yet, later in the flight, the feverish child lulled to sleep by the roar of the turboprops, a spectacular display of northern lights appeared, covering the entire sky. Those green and purple lights seemed to be a sign of greeting.

Today, more than a decade later, those children have grown up in Nunavut and consider it their home. They have welcomed many visitors to homes in which they have lived. Other travellers will tell other tales, but almost everyone will have something to relate about a trip that proves unique, whether it is about adventures on the land, about the hospitality of the people they meet, or about the sheer beauty of the landscape. Welcome to Nunavut.

Watching Nunavut Grow

One thing is certain over the next few years in Canada's Arctic, and that is that change will be constant. Although the new territory of Nunavut only officially comes into effect April 1, 1999, people are already calling the central and eastern Arctic "Nunavut" (pronounced "new-na-voot"). It's a word that means "our land" in the language of its aboriginal people, the Inuit, who make up the majority of Nunavut's residents at 85 per cent of the population.

Until the government of Nunavut is in place in 1999, the central and eastern Arctic must still abide by the legislation of the government of the Northwest Territories (GNWT), and that is why readers will see references to GNWT regulations throughout this book. As *The Nunavut Handbook* is updated, watch for changes that reflect the rapid evolution of Canada's newest territory, Nunavut.

How to Hire an Outfitter or Guide

To choose wisely among an ever-growing number of tour operators, outfitters and guides for your trip to Nunavut, you'll need to understand the kinds of service they offer. Some definitions might help you here.

Tour Operators, which are based in the North or South, generally offer packages that include any or all of the following: transportation to and within Nunavut, accommodation, meals, and excursions. They may refer you to an outfitter who will organize tours for you and supply you with the equipment and guidance you need for your stay in the region.

Outfitters are individuals or companies, based in the North or South, that provide varying levels of service. This service may include tours, guides, transportation, accommodation, clothing and equipment. Some locally based outfitters and guides provide only basic services, such as transportation to or from a national or territorial park. Others offer complete packages: dogsledding tours, for example, or fishing trips to local outpost camps, with meals included.

Guides usually work for outfitters, although some are self-employed. They accompany you on your travels in the North, and may offer naturalist, cultural or historical interpretation.

Currently, all guides and outfitters operating in Nunavut must be licensed under the Travel and Tourism Act, and as such, carry liability insurance.

Before you pay a deposit to a guide or outfitter, however, check that they're indeed licensed. If they assure you they are, but have no proof, verify with one of the **tourism licensing officers** listed in the directory at the end of this section. In the event that you hire a licensed guide or outfitter who's later unable to deliver the tour you agreed upon, the government, under the NWT Tourism Deposit Assurance Program, will reimburse you for your deposit. (Licensed tourism businesses have the right to display the seal of this Tourism Deposit Assurance Program in their brochures and advertising.)

Although tourism officers can't promote one operator over another, they're satisfied that all are safety-minded and generally provide excellent service. They say they rarely receive reports from unhappy clients.

You can obtain listings of licensed guides and outfitters by contacting a tourism licensing officer. Each officer's jurisdiction covers one of the administrative regions within the central and eastern Arctic — the Baffin Region, the Kivalliq (formerly called the Keewatin) Region or the Kitikmeot Region.

In 1969, the fledgling GNWT took a cue from the federal government and decided to carry on with administrative regions in order to manage the North's huge land mass. The Keewatin and Baffin regions were set up first, and years later, so was the Kitikmeot. People throughout Nunavut still widely refer to these regions, although at least one organization, **Nunavut Tourism**, pegs communities more closely to geographic features, where possible. For the purposes of this travel guidebook, the references to Nunavut's three regions have been retained in the chapters to follow, although our maps and index of destinations group communities according to common geographic denominators. Here's how both systems mesh:

The Kivalliq Region includes the communities of Rankin Inlet, Arviat, Whale Cove, Chesterfield Inlet, and Baker Lake (roughly along the west coast of Hudson Bay, except for inland Baker Lake). The Kivalliq also includes Coral Harbour (on Southampton Island) and Repulse Bay (in the Melville Peninsula area). According to the 1996 Census of Canada, the Kivalliq's population is 6,868.

The Kitikmeot Region includes another Melville Peninsula area community, Pelly Bay. Taloyoak (on Boothia Peninsula), Gjoa Haven (on King William Island), and Umingmaktok, Bathurst Inlet, Kugluktuk, and Cambridge Bay, all along the Arctic Coast, account for the remainder of the Kitikmeot communities. The Kitikmeot's population is 5,067.

The Baffin Region includes Arctic Bay, Nanisivik, Pond Inlet and Clyde River on North Baffin Island; Pangnirtung and Broughton Island on Central Baffin Island; and Iqaluit, Kimmirut and Cape Dorset on South Baffin Island. The High Arctic is home to two settlements, Grise Fiord and Resolute. So is the Melville Peninsula area: Igloolik and Hall Beach. And far to the south, on the Belcher Islands in Hudson Bay, is Sanikiluaq. The Baffin's combined population is 12,948.

One thing that binds communities throughout Nunavut is the growing interest in tourism, and the growing numbers of guides and outfitters. Many are members of Nunavut Tourism, an organization formed in 1995 to represent tourism operators in Nunavut. Nunavut Tourism will provide you with listings of their member operators and up-to-date information packages for all areas of Nunavut.

Still, to find the outfitter or guide who will best meet your needs, do your research. Make sure you know what you want. If you plan to view bowhead whales, then don't go with an outfitter to a location where there are no whales! Whomever you choose, be sure your tour guide or outfitter is familiar with local conditions. Your safety and comfort depend on it! Ask how long an operator has been in business, and talk to anyone who has travelled to Nunavut. Word-of-mouth may be your most reliable source.

Ask lots of questions. Be sure that what you're paying for is what you really want. Outfitters provide varying levels of service. One may transport you to a park, for example, and interpret for you while you're there. Another may only guide you to the park. A third may offer you transportation, interpretation and accommodation. What types of service do *you* want?

How about equipment? Will the operator supply you with tents and fishing rods? Northern clothing and emergency gear for poor weather? Hiking boots?

Communicate your needs. Inuit outfitters won't necessarily tell you everything they offer if you don't ask questions, because they may assume you already know. So ask, for example: "When and where will I be going? What will I do while I'm there? Where will I stay? What exactly am I paying for?"

You'll also need to inquire about provisions for your safety. Your safety is imperative.

Adventure travel in the North is exciting, but can turn life-threatening if you don't have the right safety equipment, the right training to pull yourself out of a dire situation, or a properly trained guide or outfitter to watch out for you. If you're travelling on open water, a licensed guide or outfitter must provide you with a survival suit — a flotation device that covers you from head to toe. Find out, as well, the kind of communications equipment they carry and whether they have a first-aid kit and training.

And, of course, be sure that a prospective outfitter speaks your language! A telephone conversation with him or her should clarify that. Some outfitters speak little English and rely instead on a son or daughter to provide interpretation for them.

Outfitters usually operate between the months of April and October only, since Nunavut's peak travel season is summer. You can still contact them in the off months to do advance planning.

A final thought: If you're already visiting a northern community and feel like taking a tour of the tundra, say, or a fishing trip, check in with the hamlet office or Hunters and Trappers Organization (HTO). They'll gladly refer you to a local licensed guide or outfitter. Staff at the HTOs are highly skilled on the land and water and they too may provide an outing for you. However, not all HTOs in Nunavut are licensed tourism operators. Make sure you check with the individual HTO.

Outfitter Charges

Many visitors are startled by the high cost of outfitter services. If you use the services of a reputable outfitter, you won't be gouged, but it's still wise to compare prices. In some communities, such as Pangnirtung, outfitters have formed associations that calculate typical costs for specific trips and then set standard fares. It's a good idea to compare prices with those in communities where no "set prices" exist.

Remember, however, that in many cases rates that are high by southern standards are fair in the North, giving outfitters a reasonable economic return for their labor and investment. If you find a cut-rate bargain, be warned that you may get cut-rate service. If you run into bad weather or other hazardous conditions, your life can literally depend on the skill of your outfitter, so don't skimp on outfitter costs.

While the outfitters, guides and tour operators providing services in Nunavut change frequently, you will find among them many operators that have been in business for years and have a wealth of experience.

Package Tours

Generally, southern tour operators offer more complete packages, though they may be less flexible in their options. If you want maximum flexibility or have unusual requirements — a scientific field party, for example — you're best to book with a local outfitter. But if you prefer a more conventional package tour, you'll likely find what you're looking for with a southern tour operator. Although many tourists like to organize their own trips, package tours are often the wise choice when travelling in Nunavut. Many of the smaller communities are unaccustomed to travellers and may lack facilities to support visitors who are on their own. A reliable tour operator with a proven track record, however, would give you a range of options that would be hard for you to organize.

If you're visiting Nunavut with a package tour, most of your itinerary will have been planned in advance. Contact your tour operator if you have questions about what the tour includes. If you're planning your own trip, it's essential to collect as much material as you can. Contact Nunavut Tourism for up-to-date information on packages, outfitters and other options. Read the chapters in this guidebook on periodicals and Internet resources to find more material on Nunavut.

If you plan to hike, camp, or travel extensively on the land, remember that by southern standards, most of Nunavut is a wilderness. Northern solitude may bring considerable risk, so be prepared and healthy if you plan to move off the beaten track. Read "Adventure Travel," Chapter 11, if you're planning such a trip. You can also ask Nunavut Tourism to put you in touch with knowledgeable local contacts who can advise you about travelling in their area. You can also speak to elders, who have years of wisdom, by approaching a community elders' society or an office of a regional Inuit birthright association for a referral.

Northern travel agencies can be very helpful in planning trips to and within Nunavut. As a rule, these agencies are more familiar with flight schedules, accommodations and other arrangements than are southern agents, particularly if you choose not to go with a package tour.

Visitor Information Centres

Several communities and parks have **visitor information centres** that are helpful when orienting yourself to a local area. In the smaller communities, these are usually located in or with libraries, museums or other institutions. Rankin Inlet's visitor centre is located in the Siniktarvik complex. The Arctic Coast Visitors Centre is in Cambridge Bay, while Kugluktuk is home to the Kugluktuk Heritage Centre. Iqaluit has a large information centre, Unikkaarvik, that serves as the regional centre for the Baffin. It also houses the Iqaluit library and is next door to the town's museum. Pangnirtung has two visitor centres, located side-by-side, for the town and for **Parks Canada**. An interpretive centre/library has been completed recently in Pond Inlet, and a visitor centre for Katannilik Territorial Park Reserve was due for completion in Kimmirut by June, 1997. Where no visitor centre or library exists, the best place to find community information is from a lodge, hotel, or government liaison officer.

Maps

If you're planning an adventure trip with canoeing or extensive hiking, you'll want to order maps well in advance of your trip. This way, you'll be assured of having the maps, and they'll help you in planning. You can't count on obtaining maps once you're in Nunavut because supplies are quickly exhausted in busy summer months. Contact Nunavut Tourism to determine if they have maps available. They'll suggest those that are appropriate for your trip and will give you addresses of suitable map outlets elsewhere in Canada. A 1:50,000 scale map is usually the scale required to give you sufficient detail. If you're planning to stray from the more frequently used routes, be forewarned that many areas of Nunavut haven't yet been mapped to this level of detail. For lists of available maps, check out **Geomatics Canada's** web site, or contact the **Canada Map Office** in Ottawa. For boaters, hydrographic charts are available from **Canadian Hydrographic Services**.

When planning a trip involving extensive adventure travel such as hiking, canoeing, or kayaking, you might consider purchasing a global positioning system (GPS). This hand-held receiver — ranging in price from around $250 to $400 — uses satellite information to identify your current location and to allow you to follow the route you have planned. A GPS won't replace your maps, but it will tell you where you are on the map and the distance you have travelled. If you have radio contact with an organization that deals with emergencies and you're in an emergency, you can then pinpoint your location exactly.

NATURALIST, CULTURAL, AND SCIENTIFIC RESEARCH TOURS

by Jennifer Bernius

As time luxuriously stretches ahead of you in Nunavut, you may prefer to chart your own agenda and explore this wilderness on your own terms.

But you may also want to take advantage of the rich bounty of naturalist and cultural tours provided by licensed guides and outfitters stationed in almost all Nunavut communities. The experience provides a unique and personal education. Moreover, what the tourism market offers here is continually diversifying. "Scientific outfitting," a concept still in its infancy as of early 1997, could become among the most cerebrally satisfying vacation packages that Nunavut provides.

A naturalist or cultural tour led by a trained interpretive guide will deepen your understanding and appreciation of Nunavut. A well-informed guide could take you to interesting places that might either be inaccessible, or hazardous if you travelled there on your own: to muskoxen on the shores of the Kazan and Thelon Rivers, for example; or to seals and narwhals at the floe edge along Baffin Island; or to a traditional Inuit outpost camp. A guide also interprets sights that otherwise might escape you.

The kind of tours you'll discover throughout Nunavut are as varied as the new territory's communities. A visitors centre, for example, may organize an afternoon stroll through a community, with stops at local points of interest.

An HTO or outfitter may arrange a day's trek on the tundra to view migrating caribou. Or they could take you on the trip of a lifetime: a 10-day, guided, customized journey by dogteam or snowmobile to an Inuit outpost camp where you can photograph whales and polar bears at the floe edge and stay in an igloo and heated cabin.

Nunavut Tourism, in tandem with the GNWT, has published a vacation planner called *The Arctic Traveller*, and it contains a directory of outfitters plus a brief description of their offerings. You'll find excursions to suit a broad range of interests: tours that appeal to adventurers, to history buffs, rockhounds, photographers, lovers of wildlife, wildflowers, Inuit art, legends and other cultural lore.

Some tours begin and end in a community, allowing you the freedom to explore the North your way. Others are packaged tours originating in southern Canadian cities. They include transportation, accommodation, meals, excursions and interpretation.

Several factors will influence your choice of tour. For a start, what interests you? Do you want to see wildlife? Marine mammals, inland grazing animals, migratory birds? If you love history, what cultures and periods fascinate you? Ancient Thule? Modern Inuit? European whalers and explorers? Hudson Bay traders? What regions attract you: the mountains and fiords of Baffin's spectacular Auyuittuq National Park Reserve? The rugged marsh country of the Hudson Bay lowlands? The richly varied terrain of the Arctic Islands? The magnificent Bloody Falls of the Coppermine River in the Kitikmeot Region? You'll find tours geared to all these interests and regions. Some expose you to several aspects of northern life at once, combining ecotourism with an interpretation of Inuit culture and lifestyle as well as an account of prehistoric or modern historical sites.

Time and money? A day of hiking with a guide around a settlement or out on the land could cost you about $70 to $150. For a tour by dogteam, snowmobile or all-terrain vehicle, or a cruise along a river or coastline by motorboat, increase that amount significantly. A typical three-day guided tour of the tundra, with two nights spent in a community hotel and another night in a tent, could amount to about $1,000. (That includes tent and all other equipment except sleeping bags.)

Add more days and you'll have to add a lot more dollars: that 10-day "total immersion" experience of a traditional Inuit camp at the mouth of a south Baffin fiord, which includes transportation by snowmobile or dogteam, meals (a combination of "country food" and southern fare, plus drinking water from 1,000-year-old icebergs), traditional Inuit clothing (caribou parkas), and accommodation (tents, cabins, igloo and a night in a hotel) will run up to $2,500. That doesn't include air transportation into Nunavut.

If you prefer greater comfort, however, your choice may be to take scenic and historical tours of the tundra from an ecotourism lodge. A week in one such establishment in Bathurst Inlet, including room, meals, tours and airfare from Yellowknife, comes to about $3,400.

Choosing when to go on a tour, of course, will have to take into consideration prevailing weather conditions. An outfitter in the Coral Harbour area of Hudson Bay, for instance, will take you by boat to the vast walrus colonies of Bencas and Walrus Islands, and to the thousands of thick-billed murres that nest along the cliffs of Coats Island. But the business operates only from the end of July through August. By early September, storms begin. The weather can be unpredictable even sooner. (So travel schedules may be unpleasantly affected.)

On the other hand, another outfitter in an inland Baffin region is open for business from March through to the end of August, with an array of tours and vehicles to get you to the best spots at just the "right" times. From July to August, you could travel by boat from Iqaluit to see huge populations of migratory birds — loons, geese, ducks, terns, falcons, owls — that nest along the shorelines of southern Baffin. Or, if you prefer to travel by snowmobile over land or ice, you could be escorted to the home turf of caribou, fox, seals and the occasional polar bear anytime between April and June. In summer, you could fly by Twin Otter over that same terrain to view the wildlife.

Most guides and outfitters are flexibile and informal in their approach to business. While they may offer pre-packaged tours for individuals and groups, they'll also customize a tour for you. Are you backpacking with friends and want to go sightseeing? No problem. The folks at the local hamlet office or HTO will gladly refer you to a licensed local guide or outfitter who will arrange a tour of your choice. Are you a naturalist who also loves Inuit art and culture? Visit Cape Dorset, Inuit art capital of the world. An outfitter there will guide you through the world-famous studios of the West Baffin Eskimo Co-operative where you'll meet renowned printmakers, sculptors and needleworkers. Tours are timed to fit your schedule: they could be a one-hour town walkabout, or they may be intensive week-long archeological and naturalist excursions to Foxe Peninsula. (These would show you, for example, the sites of ancient Thule dwellings and the largest collection of *inuksuit* — rock cairns in the shape of humans — in the world.)

Generally, naturalist and cultural tours are less physically demanding than adventure excursions. Many educational tour operators create a relaxed, unhurried atmosphere so that visitors appreciate the serenity and purity of a northern environment. Still, you'd be wise to ask an operator how much physical activity, such as hiking, will be required in a tour. Some educational adventures are planned specifically for older adults. In the summer, at Nunavut Arctic College in Iqaluit, **Elderhostel Canada** offers several courses on Inuit language, history and traditions, and northern flora and fauna.

As for accommodation, a wide variety of options exists. If you're the hardy sort, you might feel at home sleeping overnight in an igloo or camping on the tundra in a prospector's tent supplied by your outfitter. As mentioned earlier, some operators combine several forms of accommodation in one tour: on a five-day outing on the land, as an example, you might camp for three days and stay in a community hotel for the other two. Some outfitters encourage you to stay with local Inuit families to truly experience northern life.

At the other end of the spectrum, you may prefer the comfort of an ecotourism lodge. Bathurst Inlet in the Kitikmeot Region, for example, is home to a former Hudson's Bay Co. trading post and Oblate mission that's been converted into a retreat for naturalists. Some of the lodge's guided tours include outings to the central barren lands to view muskoxen, caribou, nesting birds and wildflowers. There are also visits to ancient Inuit stone houses and caches, as well as an excursion to a camp site used during Sir John Franklin's expedition through the Northwest Passage.

Be sure to check with outfitters about clothing and equipment for your tour. Many operators provide tents and other camping gear, as well as wilderness clothing. Ask them for a list of other items you should bring.

"Scientific Outfitting"

Ecotours and scientific research tours (in which travellers tag along with a crew of scientists and technicians as they head out to do fieldwork) haven't really developed as a homegrown industry in Nunavut yet, but the potential exists and wheels are starting to grind into motion. The **Nunavut Research Institute**, one of the first GNWT agencies to split in preparation for the coming of Nunavut, urges the use of traditional knowledge, science, research and technology as a resource for the new territory. It is brainstorming with Nunavut Tourism and community groups to figure out ways Nunavut's substantial scientific community can work with local outfitters and organizations in order to create "scientific outfitting." Qualifying agencies will be recognized and marketed by Nunavut Research Institute and Nunavut Tourism.

Travellers may be strictly observers on certain field trips, but on others they would do hands-on work in summer field projects.

Nunavut Tourism is aware of some companies that already bring ecotourism groups into Nunavut to experience wildlife science in the field. These camps involve scientific experts in their packages.

ENTERING CANADA

by Carol Rigby

All visitors from outside Canada, except those from the United States, must present a valid passport to enter the country.

Some visitors also require a visa and/or papers certifying that they've had a recent medical examination or inoculations. Be sure to inquire at the Canadian Embassy, High Commission, or Consulate serving your country to determine what papers are required to enter Canada.

Visitors to Canada may stay in the country for between three and six months, depending on their country of origin, purpose of entry, and port of entry. Again, check with your local Canadian immigration office to determine what rules cover your country. Foreign visitors are responsible for supporting themselves with regard to health, food, lodging and so forth. Foreign visitors are not covered by any Canadian government programs.

Sport hunters should check in advance with the Royal Canadian Mounted Police (RCMP) to determine any restrictions on the importation of firearms. Recently revised gun control legislation affects how guns are handled at entry points. Hunters should also check with the RCMP at their point of entry.

Nunavut is an excellent place for travelling with children, as they are widely accepted at almost all functions. Be aware, however, that as a result worldwide of cases of abduction and missing children, travellers with children come under heightened scrutiny. To avoid unpleasant grilling by Customs officers, follow these tips recommended by **Our Missing Children**, a program jointly run by the RCMP, Revenue Canada, Canada Customs, and Citizenship and Immigration Canada.

- Always carry identification for yourself and your child or children.
- If you're a single parent, have copies of relevant legal documents, such as custody rights.
- If you are not the legal guardian of the child or children, carry a letter of permission or authorization for you to have custody when entering Canada. A letter would also facilitate entry for any one parent travelling with their child or children. If possible, this permission should contain contact telephone numbers for the legal guardian or parent.
- If you're travelling as part of a caravan, be sure you're in the same vehicle as your child or children when you arrive at the border.
- Have your children memorize your home and office telephone numbers and teach them how to reach you in an emergency situation.

For more information, contact the national office of Our Missing Children. The program asks that if you're travelling with children, be patient if you encounter more questions than usual at Customs. The process is intended to prevent child abductions and runaways.

When entering Canada, be aware that non-residents of Canada are entitled to a Goods and Services Tax (GST) refund on goods and accommodation, as long as they stay less than one month at that accommodation. The GST is seven per cent. Ask Customs officials about this when you arrive. They should give you the necessary literature and forms, so you'll know which receipts to keep to claim a refund upon departure.

Restrictions exist on what you can bring into and take out of Canada and the Northwest Territories — such as alcohol. You should also consult with the **Customs, Excise and Taxation** office at your point of entry and departure to determine restrictions that apply to goods you're bringing in or taking out of the country. Some items considered souvenirs within Canada, such as jewelry made from walrus ivory, might be affected by restrictions under the Convention on International Trade in Endangered Species. Contact Customs, Excise and Taxation offices for information.

It's best to know before you arrive what you can and can't remove from the country. Avoid the heartbreak of having to forsake a valued souvenir because it's illegal to import into your home country.

ALCOHOL, TOBACCO, AND DRUG RESTRICTIONS

by Carol Rigby

In the Northwest Territories (NWT), regulations on importing and consuming alcohol differ greatly from those in southern Canada.

The rules are complex, vary from community to community, and seem to change frequently, as any community can change its status by plebiscite.

Alcohol can't be sold or given away by individuals visiting Nunavut. It is also illegal to trade alcohol for carvings or anything else. All of these are considered bootlegging and constitute a serious offence in the NWT.

A permit is required to bring into the NWT more than the following amount of alcohol (per visit):

- 750 ml of liquor
- 750 ml of wine
- 12 355-ml beers.

Permits can be obtained from the **NWT Liquor Commission** office in Iqaluit. A fee applies, determined by the amount of alcohol being imported. Visitors are not allowed to import home-made wine or beer.

In the Northwest Territories, each community has one of three policies on alcohol, confirmed by community plebiscite. These are "prohibition," "restricted," and "unrestricted." Individuals can be charged under the NWT Liquor Control Act for breaching these policies. The fine for unlawful possession of alcohol is $230.

Prohibition, or "dry," communities do not allow any alcohol to be imported or made within a 20-kilometre radius. You may not bring alcohol into these settlements except if you are in transit and it then must stay on the plane. Any liquor in transit must be sealed during the time you are travelling through the prohibited area. Prohibition communities include:

- Kimmirut
- Arviat
- Gjoa Haven
- Pangnirtung
- Coral Harbour
- Pelly Bay
- Sanikiluaq
- Whale Cove.

Restricted communities regulate the use of alcohol. For the majority of them, permission is required from the community's Alcohol Education Committee to bring alcohol into town.

Orders are usually approved, except in cases where the applicant has demonstrated he or she cannot drink responsibly. If you intend to bring alcohol into a community so restricted, you must contact the Alcohol Education Committee or other licensing body in advance (see telephone numbers in community chapters in the "Destinations" section). The following communities fall into this category:

- Arctic Bay
- Clyde River
- Pond Inlet
- Broughton Island
- Hall Beach
- Resolute
- Cape Dorset
- Igloolik
- Repulse Bay.

In a few communities that are called "restricted," the restrictions are of a slightly different nature. These include:

- Rankin Inlet
- Iqaluit
- Cambridge Bay.

In Rankin Inlet, possession of alcohol is restricted. There are licensed establishments in the hotels, but liquor consumption there is restricted to hotel guests. If you are not staying at the hotels, you cannot walk in and obtain a drink. In Cambridge Bay, the restriction applies to individuals. If you are found to have misused liquor, your eligiblity to place orders for it may be withdrawn. Otherwise it is unrestricted. In Iqaluit, restaurants generally serve alcohol as they do in southern Canada, and there are bars and lounges in hotels, and a number of private clubs. However, there is no local liquor or beer store. As is also the case for Rankin Inlet and Cambridge Bay, alcohol for personal consumption must be ordered from Yellowknife or brought in under permit. There is a Liquor Warehouse in Iqaluit, but it is only to supply the requirements of licensed establishments and special occasion permit holders. The restrictions on importing liquor still apply.

Unrestricted communities are governed only by the provisions of the NWT Liquor Control Act; they have no additional rules on consuming alcohol. Unrestricted communities include:

- Baker Lake
- Chesterfield Inlet
- Nanisivik
- Bathurst Inlet
- Kugluktuk
- Taloyoak
- Umingmaktok
- Grise Fiord.

If you know you will be travelling to open or controlled communities and wish to take alcohol with you, you may place an order with the Iqaluit Liquor Warehouse. This will save you the cost and trouble of importing the alcohol into the Northwest Territories. The liquor will be sent collect to the community via air freight (you must pay freight charges upon receipt). If you are travelling through a controlled community, the Alcohol Education Committee must approve your order ahead of time.

If you are visiting Iqaluit, you will not be able to purchase alcohol through the warehouse. By having it flown in from Yellowknife, you will save the cost and trouble of importing it into the Northwest Territories. Please note that both the Iqaluit and Yellowknife Liquor Warehouses only accept cash or debit cards, not credit cards.

The rules are complicated, so it is always worthwhile to consult the NWT Liquor Commission/Iqaluit Liquor Warehouse for up-to-date information if you want to bring alcohol into the Northwest Territories.

Tobacco

There are also restrictions on the amount of tobacco you can bring into the Northwest Territories with you. If you are a smoker, you may wish to contact the GNWT's **Department of Finance** to determine how much you can bring in, or to obtain a tobacco import permit. Tobacco use is widespread in the North so cigarettes are usually available in most stores, but they bear the same inflated price as most other northern commodities. Because of the heavy impact of tobacco use on the health of the local population, regulations are being implemented with regard to smoking in public places. The final form of these is still under discussion, so smokers should inquire if smoking is permitted in any public building. There is a bylaw in Iqaluit against smoking while in a taxi, as well.

Illegal Drugs

As in most countries, the possession or sale of opiates, narcotics and hallucinogens is illegal in Canada. Possession of illegal drugs is a serious offence, carrying a maximum penalty of seven years of imprisonment. Possession includes having a small quantity intended for personal use. People from outside Canada who use non-medical steroids should also be aware that these are illegal in Canada.

Drug trafficking is the giving, selling or receiving of any narcotic, opiate or hallucinogen.

Even though drug trafficking is an indictable offence — carrying a maximum penalty of life imprisonment — it is still a problem within Nunavut. The regional centres of Iqaluit, Rankin Inlet and Cambridge Bay, as major transportation hubs with direct connections to southern sources, are at the centre of much of this illegal activity. A common technique among traffickers is to ask someone travelling to one of the smaller communities to carry a package containing illegal drugs to a friend there. If the package is inspected by the RCMP and found to contain illegal substances, the carrier can be convicted of drug trafficking.

Never carry packages or parcels for someone you do not know well without verifying the contents, and avoid leaving your baggage unattended at any airport. You and your luggage may be searched by the RCMP if they have reasonable grounds to suspect you are carrying illegal substances (which in prohibited communities includes any form of alcohol). This does not mean that visitors are generally searched. The RCMP must have prior information about you that gives them grounds for suspicion. Respect community standards, and you should encounter no difficulties whatsoever.

HEALTH CARE AND MEDICAL INSURANCE

by Carol Rigby

Almost every Nunavut community has some form of health facility. Iqaluit has a hospital, while other communities have a health centre staffed by nurses equipped to treat minor emergencies and illnesses.

Nurses are on duty at health centres daily and on call for emergencies 24 hours a day. Patients requiring more serious medical attention are flown to the nearest regional medical centre: Iqaluit for the Baffin Region, Rankin Inlet for the Kivalliq Region, and Cambridge Bay for the Kitikmeot Region.

To learn more about what to expect in the event of medical emergencies while hiking and camping, please be sure to read the section on "search and rescue" in Chapter 11, "Adventure Travel."

Regional Centres

The **Baffin Regional Hospital** in Iqaluit handles most local health-care needs and also serves patients brought in from smaller Baffin communities. For more specialized treatment, patients are flown to Montreal. Those needing medical attention in Iqaluit should go to the Baffin Regional Hospital, which is open 24 hours a day. Iqaluit also has a dental clinic and an optical outlet. The dental clinic is equipped to handle most dental emergencies; patients must cover the cost of the visit themselves or through an accepted dental insurance plan. The optical outlet can make minor repairs to glasses and dispense new ones, provided you have a prescription and the time to wait for them, which may take two weeks or more. If the dispensing optician is visiting another Baffin community, the outlet may be closed.

Rankin Inlet has a health centre and a birthing centre, but no complete hospital facility. In serious medical emergencies, patients are flown first to a hospital in Churchill, Manitoba and if that isn't sufficient, to a hospital in Winnipeg, Manitoba. Rankin Inlet also has a **dental clinic** and a part-time **optical outlet**, which is staffed and open for business only once every three months. Call in advance to verify operating hours.

Serious cases that can't be treated at the **Cambridge Bay health centre** are flown to the Stanton Regional Hospital in Yellowknife. Cambridge Bay also has a **dental office**.

Communities Outside the Regional Centres

If medical needs can't be met by the local health centre, patients in the Baffin are flown to Iqaluit, or if specialized treatment is required, to Montreal. In the Kivalliq, patients are flown to Churchill or to Winnipeg. In the Kitikmeot, Yellowknife's Stanton Regional Hospital provides full medical facilities.

Doctors and dentists visit smaller communities periodically, but in emergencies, their presence isn't guaranteed. The community health centres don't offer a full 24-hour medical service, although nurses are on call around the clock for real emergencies.

Health Insurance

Visitors, students, and transient and temporary workers from elsewhere in Canada aren't eligible to enrol in the **NWT Health Care Plan**. Their provincial or Yukon health plan will cover most medical costs incurred in the Northwest Territories. But if they've been billed personally for health services, they should keep their documentation and seek reimbursement from their provincial or Yukon health care plan within six months. Visitors not covered by the NWT Health Care Plan must pay up front for services.

The NWT Health Care Plan doesn't cover non-residents for ground or air ambulance (medevac) services. Ambulance services used while in the Northwest Territories will be billed at their full cost. Travel on scheduled flights for medical services will also be charged to non-residents, even if ordered by a physician. In an emergency, the NWT plan will cover the bill, but the costs will be charged back to the patient or the patient's insurance plan. Air ambulance services are very expensive. Some non-residents may have full or partial coverage under private, employer or government health insurance plans. It's best to check your coverage before you leave home and purchase supplemental coverage where necessary.

Regular or Special Medication

Visitors who require regular medication should carry enough with them to last the length of their stay, plus an allowance for unexpected delays. Community health nurses recommend a month's supply for a two-week visit. Medication should be carried on your person, not packed in luggage. The only commercial pharmacy in the Baffin Region is in Iqaluit. Rankin Inlet also has a pharmacy. The nearest pharmacies to Kitikmeot communities are in Yellowknife. Health centres in the communities carry basic drugs, but they can't be counted on to have specialized medication.

Generally, visitors to the North don't require any immunizations other than those needed to get into Canada from other countries. Parks Canada recommends, however, that visitors to Ellesmere Island National Park Reserve obtain precautionary vaccinations against rabies and tetanus before coming to the park, due to its extreme isolation. It's also a good idea to make sure all your normal immunizations are up-to-date before coming north.

TIME AND COSTS

by Carol Rigby

When planning a northern itinerary, consider two things above all else: time and cost.

As most travel in Nunavut is by air, it's expensive and living costs are high. Allow yourself more time and money for almost every part of a trip here than you would when visiting less remote areas.

Air flights are often delayed by bad weather. Allow yourself ample time — preferably a whole day — to make connections between communities. A missed flight in some places can mean a wait of two or three days, depending on flight schedules. Three extra days of hotel and meal expenses could cost you another $500 or more. Budget for the unexpected.

Activities that take you outside the communities, such as hiking or canoeing, require a few extra days built in to cover the possibility of bad weather. Remember that life proceeds at a slower pace in the North. Don't expect everything to move quickly or on a precise schedule. If you bring a relaxed and flexible attitude, you'll have the time of your life.

Transportation and General Costs

Due to the great distance of Nunavut from major commercial centres, the cost of living here is high. Remoteness is part of the appeal of the North, but it does mean that nearly everything is more expensive than in southern Canada. Food, fuel and consumer goods from southern Canada are generally shipped in by sealift or barge. A sealift is cheaper but must be planned carefully to coincide with a short period in the summer when shipping lanes are ice-free. Waiting for an annual sealift means goods have to be purchased long before they're used in the North, adding to the expense. The further north you go, the more you can expect to pay for most items, especially food. The climate also plays a role in raising prices. Everything from building costs to utility charges are higher because of the cold.

One way to save money is by camping and cooking for yourself, rather than staying in hotels or lodges. Expect cool, wet weather, though, and be prepared to really "rough it." There are no campgrounds with showers and electrical hookups here!

ACCOMMODATION

by Carol Rigby

Most Nunavut communities have at least one hotel or lodge, although neither Nanisivik nor Umingmaktok has one.

Accommodation can range from the relatively sophisticated hotels of larger communities, with their conference facilities and restaurants, to more modest lodges in smaller communities, often operated by community co-operatives. Bed and breakfast establishments, called "tourist homes" in Nunavut, are becoming more widely available. You'll find these in Iqaluit and in a few other communities. Camping is the most economical way to go, but educate yourself beforehand so that you are safe while out on the land.

If you plan to stay in hotels and lodges during your visit, be prepared to pay high prices — often between $150 to $200 per person per night — for modest accommodation. Many community hotels or lodges include meals with the price of a room. (Details on individual hotels and tourist homes are listed within the community profiles in the "Destinations" section.) In most communities, space is booked by the bed, not by the room. Hotels can become suddenly busy when bad weather grounds an airline flight and passengers need a place for the night. So if you're travelling alone and space is limited, you'll have to share a room. In some cases, that may mean sleeping in a bunk room with several other people. Guests of the opposite sex, however, aren't expected to double up.

Sharing your room with a stranger also brings up the issue of the security of your valuables — although in smaller communities, where one is more likely to end up having to bunk in with a stranger, people are more insulted by the implication of dishonesty. Some hotels have locked storage space for valuables; others don't. If security is a concern, the best advice is to take your wallet with you to the bathroom, and try not to bring anything too valuable on your trip north.

Most accommodation is *not* luxurious — but it's clean and comfortable, and the local artwork on the walls might make southern luxury hotel owners envious! Generally, decor in northern hotels is slightly worn or shabby. Hotel rooms often have TV sets but may not always have phones. Fax service may be available at the front desk. Conventional plumbing is usually available, but water use is restricted in some communities at certain times of the year, or because it's delivered by truck. This may mean that showers have to be brief or taken every other day. You might also encounter shared bathrooms. And be aware that it's difficult to find smoke-free accommodation.

Some hotels have curfews, although your room key will usually get you in the front door. Check at the hotel's front desk if there isn't anything posted on this.

Visitors are encouraged to book well in advance. In summer particularly, accommodation fills up with workers who are in town for the short summer construction period.

Tourist Homes and Home Stays

A few communities offer licensed tourist homes, the equivalent of bed and breakfasts. A bona fide tourist home must meet specific criteria set by the GNWT to ensure guests of a certain standard of service. Since proprietors must own their tourist home, most of these lodgings aren't operated by Inuit, who are still gradually entering a wage economy.

A stay in a tourist home in a small community will give you the feeling of what it's like to live in the North. Bed and breakfasts in Iqaluit, on the other hand, are like small inns. You'll be certain to get a bed, washroom facilities and breakfast if you stay in one of these establishments. You will want to check out restaurants or lodge dining rooms for your other meals, or ask the tourist home proprietor whether they will prepare meals for you or allow you to use facilities to prepare your own meals.

Tourist homes are marginally less expensive than hotels or lodges. When you factor in the costs of meals, though, there isn't a significant difference. The main advantage to a tourist home is its personal service and low level of noise and activity. A hotel full of construction workers isn't always quiet!

If you really wish to billet with a local family in a community instead of a licensed tourist home, then investigate a "home stay." Check with the local hamlet office for information on residents who accommodate this type of request. Hamlets are the ones that decide who may carry on such a business. Home stays aren't licensed by the GNWT, however. If you do choose this option, you're on your own, so "caveat emptor."

Be sure you have determined clearly the following before agreeing to a home stay: What am I paying for? A bed? A bed and a room? How many people live in the house? (Housing conditions in the North are notoriously crowded.) Is there plumbing? (Many homes in the smallest communities still use "honey buckets.") Are any meals provided? Can facilities be used for cooking if no meals are provided? Have you provided this service to others before? Inuit families can be extremely hospitable and helpful, but northern living conditions are different, and can often be a shock to people raised in urban settings.

MONEY

by Carol Rigby

There are very few bank branches in Nunavut, although the increasing presence of debit card facilities in stores allows visitors to withdraw funds from their own accounts, provided the stores have enough cash on hand.

In Iqaluit, the Royal Bank of Canada and the Bank of Montreal have branches conveniently located across the street from each other. These are the only banks on Baffin Island. In Rankin Inlet, you'll find branches of the **Canadian Imperial Bank of Commerce (CIBC)** and the Royal Bank. Cambridge Bay has a branch of the Royal Bank.

Iqaluit also has two automated teller machines: a Royal Bank machine located in the Brown building/highrise complex and one in the Bank of Montreal. The Royal Bank also has automated teller machines in Rankin Inlet and Cambridge Bay. Whale Cove has an automated teller machine in its Co-op store.

In other communities, the local Northern store or Co-operative usually cashes recognized traveller's cheques in Canadian funds. But because cash shortages often occur in the communities, it's a good idea to carry Canadian money. The currency used here is the Canadian dollar. Money consists of notes — $5, $10, $20, $50, $100 — and coins — 1¢, 5¢, 10¢, 25¢, $1, $2.

You should also conduct significant banking transactions in Nunavut's largest communities — Iqaluit, Rankin Inlet or Cambridge Bay — before travelling to the smaller communities. If you're coming from outside Canada, it's best to exchange your currency before you arrive in Nunavut.

Credit and Debit Cards

Many retailers in Iqaluit, Cambridge Bay and Rankin Inlet accept credit cards, but hotels and stores in smaller communities are only beginning to accept them. Don't rely on credit cards in smaller communities, though, unless you have checked in advance with the local store or hotel. Generally, outfitters accept only cash, but always ask.

Debit cards are accepted at all Northern and Co-op stores in Nunavut now, and funds can be withdrawn from your own account if cash flow permits. The Co-op also accepts debit cards from outside Canada. At the Northern stores, Interac service is provided by the CIBC. Check with the bank to see which international cards they accept. In Nunavut, some places accept personal cheques if you have proper identification. Smaller communities don't accept them, so don't count on using them. Traveller's cheques are more widely accepted.

Sunday shopping is permitted in the Northwest Territories, although the practice may differ from community to community. In Nunavut's smaller communities, stores will sometimes close during the lunch hour.

Visitors from outside Canada should be aware that they're entitled to a Goods and Services Tax refund of seven per cent on goods and accommodation. For more information on this, see "Entering Canada," Chapter 3.

FOOD

by Carol Rigby

Many Nunavut restaurants offer delicious, well-prepared "country foods," the name for the kind of foods traditionally eaten by Inuit.

Arctic char, a fish with a taste that lies between salmon and trout, is one of the most popular. Scallops gathered from Cumberland Sound are sometimes available at restaurants and retail outlets in Iqaluit and other northern communities. Greenland shrimp is also a local favorite. Turbot from Pangnirtung may be available in season, in the Baffin. Caribou is a northern staple. It is very nutritious and low in fat, so it's a good choice for the diet-conscious, and widely available. Muskox, largely available in the Kitikmeot, is very much like well-marbled beef and well worth trying.

Many restaurants offer some kind of "northern" appetizers or combination entrées on their menus. These may include *maktaaq*, the outer layer of skin and blubber from whales. An Inuit delicacy, this food is very warming due to its high caloric content. But don't try to chew it — the longer you chew, the more it becomes like eating a rubber eraser! Cut small bits and swallow whole.

For the more adventurous palate, community feasts offer traditional fare such as raw and boiled caribou, seal and raw frozen char. Everyone is welcome at community feasts, but for those who have always lived an urban lifestyle, be prepared to experience culture shock: you will see whole seals laid out on the floor, being butchered and consumed raw as Inuit have done for centuries. Local shellfish such as mussels in Rankin Inlet and clams from Frobisher Bay near Iqaluit are also popular fare in some communities. But these are almost never available on a commercial basis — you will have to be lucky enough to have someone invite you to join them.

If photographing while at a community feast, it is courteous to ask permission before snapping someone's shot.

Hotel and Lodge Food in the Smaller Communities

Oddly, in the smaller communities you are likely to find less traditional food on hotel or lodge menus, and more standard North American fare, most of it not enhanced by the distance it has travelled before being prepared. Many lodges cater primarily to construction workers, so their food is usually hearty and plentiful, but uninspired. It is also expensive due to the high costs of importation. In many small communities there are no restaurant facilities outside the lodge. Check individual community listings for the food outlets available.

Campers and other visitors planning to prepare their own meals should come well supplied with food, particularly if specialized products like dehydrated camping food are required.

The availability of fresh food like dairy products or fruits and vegetables is a function of flight schedules and weather delays. Although supplies are reliable in the communities with daily airline service, it is not uncommon for fresh milk, eggs or bread to be completely unavailable in a small community. Be prepared to pay up to $2 for a single apple or orange in the more remote villages, and more than $5 for a litre of milk. If you are coming to visit friends or family in Nunavut, among the best gifts you can bring are supplies of fresh fruit, vegetables and dairy products. These should be carried in hand luggage to protect them from freezing.

Exporting Food

Many "country foods" can be easily transported, so you may want to share the taste of northern food with friends and family back home. Frozen food is almost always available at retail outlets and can usually be obtained through local hunters and trappers organizations as well. In some communities there are local businesses that specialize in providing country food. For example, you can take home vacuum-packed frozen locally smoked char from Iqaluit Enterprises, or vacuum-packed muskox chops from Kitikmeot Foods in Cambridge Bay, or caribou sausage from Keewatin Meat and Fish in Rankin Inlet. Some plants supply retail outlets as opposed to selling directly.

Visitors don't need a permit to take home arctic char, but special arrangements must be made to ship out caribou, muskox, seal or maktaaq. For permits or information about export amounts and restrictions, contact any community **Department of Resources, Wildlife and Economic Development** office. A wildlife officer from the department can also give you an idea of whether you will have difficulty importing the food into your own province, territory or country. It's also a good idea to check on this point before you head to Nunavut, if you think you'll be bringing food back with you. Slightly different regulations apply to hunters removing their catch. Again, consult a wildlife officer for details.

When carrying food in your luggage aboard an airline from the North, you may be asked to sign a waiver saying that if it spoils it is not insured by the airline. If you prefer, you can ship food home by cargo fridge/freezer. Check with your airline. However, unless you have extended travel plans with layovers in warm areas, food will usually stay quite well frozen if wrapped in several layers of newspaper, since the cargo hold is not heated while in the air.

COMMUNICATIONS

by Carol Rigby

Nunavut is linked to the rest of the world by satellite, telephone, television and radio.

Many individuals and businesses in the North use facsimile machines, computer modems and the Internet to communicate with other regions of Canada and abroad. Northerners have made a virtue of necessity by using sophisticated modern technology to link communities separated by long distances.

Telephones

Telephone service exists in every community but Bathurst Inlet and Umingmaktok. Pay phones aren't widely available except in some hotels, airport terminals and a few stores in larger communities. Visitors who aren't staying at a hotel or lodge with telephone service can usually get permission to use a phone in any building that serves the public. It's a good idea to have a calling card number to which you can charge long-distance calls. As telephone service is by satellite, you may hear the echo effect of "satellite bounce" during your phone calls, or a delay during conversations. Some communities also have very slow telephone line speeds, so if you're trying to use a portable computer modem, you may find the baud rate is too slow for some transmissions. All calls made to numbers outside the community of origin must include the area code in the number dialed, even if the number being called is within the same area code. Nunavut's area codes change to 867 on Oct. 21, 1997.

Television

The Canadian Broadcasting Corporation (CBC) North transmits television to Iqaluit and other communities. The Inuit Broadcasting Corporation (IBC) delivers programming in Inuktitut (the language of the Inuit), including news and entertainment. Television Northern Canada (TVNC) is devoted to programming by and for northerners and native people. Cable satellite TV is widely available, offering a range of commercial programming from across North America.

Radio

The radio is the lifeline of small communities, broadcasting personal messages and community news. It also helps save lives.

High frequency (HF) radio is the main communications tool for emergencies and other situations. The radiotelephone, or more formally the Spillsbury SBX-11, is used by all HTOs in monitoring land travellers and families living on the land.

The CBC, as the only local station that's easily receivable in every Nunavut community, broadcasts on the FM band in all communities except Iqaluit. Shortwave radio enthusiasts can receive many stations from around the world. Batteries aren't always available in local stores, so bring an adequate supply. An alternative is to get a small solar-powered charger and two sets of rechargeable batteries. This system works well during the long periods of daylight in summer.

Mail

As there's no door-to-door mail delivery in the North, all correspondence must be picked up at the post office. Mail is flown into all communities, so service can be delayed by bad weather or missed planes, particularly in the smaller communities. If you expect to be in Nunavut long enough to receive mail, have it addressed to you care of "general delivery" in a community convenient to you. Mail should be marked "hold for pickup" and carry a note with a forwarding address in case it isn't picked up by a specified date. In smaller communities, post offices are located in the local

Northern store or Co-op and other establishments. Ask post offices about their hours of operation because they're highly variable, especially outside Iqaluit, Rankin Inlet and Cambridge Bay. Don't be surprised to find the post office closed while the postmaster is taking a coffee break!

Newspapers and Magazines

Not so long ago, northerners regarded it as a great treat to get their hands on a daily newspaper. Now, in communities serviced by daily flights, it's easy to obtain copies of several Canadian dailies, including *The Globe and Mail* and a wide variety of magazines. Check at local retail outlets. In smaller communities, don't count on finding a daily paper, though you'll likely find copies of northern weekly papers such as *Nunatsiaq News, News/North* or *The Kivalliq News.*

E-mail and the Internet

Nunavut is wired! Despite complications caused by slow line speeds and satellite bounce, local Internet servers in Cambridge Bay, Rankin Inlet and Iqaluit have Nunavut plugged in and loving it — there's a very high rate of Internet users among residents. If you're looking for public access to the Internet, check at the Nunavut Research Institute's Research Centre in Iqaluit. It's also a high priority on Nunavut schools' curricula. Many schools already have Internet access, and several have their own web sites. In Rankin Inlet, the community access site is at Leo Ussak School. Several projects are under way throughout Nunavut to set up other public access stations, although at the time of writing, none was confirmed as up and running. In Rankin Inlet, check with the public library for more information about the community access site, if school staff can't be reached. If you're travelling with a computer (on business, for example), and have your own Internet server and account, you can access it through the phone lines in the major centres. Connections may be trickier in smaller communities that haven't yet upgraded their phone lines.

ADVENTURE TRAVEL

by Carol and Bruce Rigby

When travelling in Nunavut, take great care to protect yourself from natural hazards and to minimize disturbance to the very fragile arctic environment.

Don't underestimate the challenges of travelling on the land or sea. It's important to be self-sufficient. Natural hazards, from extreme weather to polar bears, can test your physical endurance, wilderness experience, and equipment to their limits. (Even for day trips, precautions should be taken. Please read the chapters on camping and hiking for more information.)

Because of 24-hour darkness in many areas and extreme cold almost everywhere, it's very uncommon for visitors to travel on the land in winter in most of Nunavut. Only those with specialized skills and equipment should attempt such travel.

ACCESS RESTRICTIONS

A little more than 350,000 square kilometres of Nunavut's 1.9 million square kilometres became Inuit-owned lands under the 1993 Nunavut Land Claims Agreement. Although their boundaries are not physically marked, these lands are private property and certain access restrictions apply.

If you're travelling with a licensed guide or outfitter, it is that person's responsibility to make the necessary arrangements to cross Inuit-owned lands. If travelling on your own (or conducting research or any commercial endeavor), first check a map to see whether your route takes you over Inuit-owned land. Maps are available from Nunavut Tunngavik Inc., the organization set up to see Nunavut's land claims agreement carried out.

If your travels take you over Inuit-owned lands, contact the appropriate Nunavut Land Administration Office for restrictions on the area. For recreational purposes, individuals are allowed access to a strip along a shoreline of any navigable body of water within Inuit-owned lands, extending either 30.5 metres (100 feet) into the water or 30.5 metres (100 feet) on to the land. However, there are also cases where Inuit have exclusive possession of land, such as Marble Island in the Kivalliq Region, which removes public right to use that land.

Visitors can obtain guidelines to access restrictions from one of the three land administration offices. To obtain clearance to travel on Inuit-owned lands, fax your itinerary, a map and the number of people in your party to the land administration office closest to the area where you'll be journeying. Allow two weeks for approval to be processed.

Maps
Nunavut Tunngavik Inc. (There is a nominal fee for maps.)
P.O. Box 1041, Cambridge Bay NT, X0E 0C0, Canada
Tel.: (403) 983-2517
Fax: (403) 983-2723
E-mail: ntilands@polarnet.ca

Nunavut Land Administration Offices
Baffin Region:
Tel.: (819) 979-5391
Fax: (819) 979-3238
E-mail: taudla@nunanet.com

Kivalliq Region:
Tel.: (819) 645-2810
Fax: (819) 645-3855
E-mail: rstjohn@arctic.ca

Kitikmeot Region:
Tel.: (403) 982-3310
Fax: (403) 982-3311

A little more than 350,000 square kilometres of Nunavut's 1.9 million square kilometres became Inuit-owned lands under the 1993 Nunavut Land Claims Agreement. Although their boundaries are not physically marked, these lands are private property and certain access restrictions apply (see sidebar on facing page).

Clothing and Equipment for Summer Travel

Summer weather in the Arctic can be very pleasant, but can change rapidly and dangerously. Freezing temperatures and snow are possible even in midsummer. Hypothermia — the inability of the body to maintain its vital core temperature — is insidious, painless and lethal. Be prepared. Layered clothing is essential. Sweating should be avoided since drying can be difficult and damp garments don't provide warmth when it may be needed most.

In the Kivalliq and Kitikmeot regions, temperatures can get quite hot for about three weeks starting in mid-July. Kugluktuk even saw temperatures reach 43° C in 1991 once. As a rule, however, dress for spring or fall temperatures, with long sleeves and full trousers. If you're going out on the land, avoid wearing blue jeans; an unexpected dunk in a river will have you freezing in your jeans in no time. Even if you're just taking a short hike out of town, dress warmly. We speak from experience! T-shirts and shorts may be fine on warmer days, but be prepared for cold weather. A sweater and long johns or other warm undergarments will guard against hypothermia should the weather turn foul. At least one complete change of clothes is necessary, should you get wet. Polypropylene or pile undergarments are a good investment because they "wick" moisture away from the skin while keeping you warm.

A good set of rain gear, including pants, is also required. You'll want a suit that keeps you dry in cold, driving rain. Windproof jackets and pants, preferably made from Gore-Tex or an equivalent "breathable" fabric, are also essential, not only to keep you warm, but to allow moisture to wick away when it's not raining. Winds can be constant in many areas and very chilling if not counteracted.

Dress in layers that can be easily added or removed as required. This will keep you comfortably warm while alternating between periods of exercise and rest. Avoid getting sweaty, for this can cause chilling when physical exercise stops. Synthetic pile or wool garments are excellent as they stay warm even when damp. On active days, avoid cotton clothes that can get damp and cold. And be prepared for insects in certain places — they abound even at these latitudes!

Bring windproof mitts or gloves, a warm knitted hat or tuque, and a scarf or balaclava to protect your face. Neck gaiters also protect the face. You'll probably also want a peaked cap or hat with a brim to keep the sun away from your eyes, neck and ears. Sturdy, well broken-in hiking boots will keep your feet comfortable most of the time, although running shoes are fine for wearing around camp. If you plan to cross any rivers during your trip (hiking through Auyuittuq National Park Reserve, for example), neoprene booties are highly recommended. If you do have to cross a river and don't have neoprene booties, remove your hiking boots and wear your sneakers, which will dry out faster if they're of lighter construction than your hiking boots. Any water you cross will be icy and can cause foot or leg cramps. Pile or wool socks are good for hiking as they'll stay warm even when slightly damp. Pile can be wrung out and will dry quickly.

If you'd like to take in some skiing while in Nunavut, please read "Skiing," Chapter 46, for important information about clothing and equipment.

Dressing for Boat Trips

When you travel by boat with an outfitter, be sure to dress very warmly. The air may seem relatively mild in summer, but the water is icy cold. (Sea water is 4° C at best, and glacier runoff is even colder.) Pay special attention to your feet, for they will be in contact with the hull, which is usually close to freezing. Those who spend lots of time on the water favor either heavily insulated rubber boots, or regular rubber boots worn a size or two larger, with duffel cloth socks and layers of wool or pile socks inside. These will keep your feet warm and dry. Be sure to have a warm hat, gloves or mitts, and wear windproof clothing.

Licensed outfitters who run boat tours are required by the GNWT to supply full flotation suits for everyone aboard the boat. Wear them — these suits have saved lives. Life-jackets are inadequate for arctic waters; normally, the life expectancy of someone wearing a life-jacket in arctic waters is about 20 minutes.

Don't take any unnecessary risks while in a boat; that's where accidents tend to happen.

Water

Flowing water outside the communities is generally safe to drink. There have been no recorded cases of giardia infestation, for example. As when camping anywhere, always draw water from running sources rather than from stagnant ponds or pools, but a special consideration in the North is to avoid consuming too much water from silt-laden glacial streams, which can cause digestive upset. Let water from a glacial stream settle before using it. Otherwise, water treatment is required only for peace of mind, or for people with very sensitive digestion. Be sure to carry plenty of water with you to avoid dehydration — especially problematic in cold conditions. Adopting the Inuit tradition of frequent tea breaks, or drinking some other warm beverage, is recommended.

Search and Rescue

Don't take any unnecessary risks when travelling on the land or water in Nunavut. Be sure to plan your routes carefully. Carry adequate maps and if possible, a GPS receiver. A search and rescue evacuation may be difficult or impossible under certain weather conditions and could be very costly. If your travels take you as far north as Grise Fiord, remember that a compass is of limited use this close to the North Magnetic Pole.

Ground search and rescue operations in the Baffin Region are co-ordinated out of Iqaluit by the Emergency Measures Office, in conjunction with the RCMP, local community authorities, the GNWT Department of Resources, Wildlife and Economic Development, Parks Canada, and others. When regional emergency measures offices send an alert for missing boats, marine searches are made by the Canadian Coast Guard. Searches for downed aircraft are co-ordinated by the federal Department of National Defence through a rescue centre in Edmonton, Alberta.

In the Kivalliq Region, the RCMP in conjunction with Iqaluit's Emergency Measures Office co-ordinates virtually all search and rescue efforts with the same type of community and government agencies that the Baffin Region does. Neither the Canadian Coast Guard nor the Department of National Defence has offices in the Kivalliq. When an alert is sent for missing boats, the RCMP joins forces with Iqaluit's Canadian Coast Guard office. The RCMP also heads search and rescue efforts for downed civilian aircraft; National Defence takes command when military aircraft are involved.

In all Kitikmeot communities, local groups of highly trained Rangers — civilian members of the Department of National Defence — work in search and rescue efforts, and RCMP detachments become involved when their services are called upon. The Kitikmeot deals with the Emergency Measures Office in Yellowknife. The Canadian Coast Guard heads marine searches for missing boats on the Arctic Ocean while National Defence is involved in the hunt for downed aircraft. In the event of oil spills and other environmental incidents, an early response team (trained municipal staff members) is first on the scene.

Those who plan climbing, skiing, glacier travel, or advanced mountaineering trips in Auyuittuq National Park Reserve, Ellesmere Island National Park Reserve or Katannilik Territorial Park Reserve should know that the rescue capability of the parks is restricted to basic evacuation only. The parks' warden service is geared towards resource conservation, not rescue operations, and recent budget cuts have limited the number and availability of park staff.

High-angle technical mountain rescue services are not provided by any agency in Nunavut. Visitors planning on doing mountaineering, glacier travel, climbing or other hazardous activities must realize that the responsibility for their safety lies solely with themselves.

Search and rescue must be discussed with park staff before you set off on any expedition. During registration on entering a park, staff will provide specific information about their rescue capabilities and your responsibilities.

Registration, Orientation and Emergency Supplies

For public safety reasons, registration and orientation are mandatory before entering a national or territorial park. Wardens and their staff will bring you up-to-date on the condition of local routes and will advise you of any specific hazards. You might also contact them prior to your arrival to help you select routes suitable for your skill level.

When travelling elsewhere on land or water, it's imperative that a responsible person be aware of your intended route and date of return. If you're planning to go out on the land or sea, you should register with the RCMP. While this is not mandatory, police and other experienced northerners agree that adventure travellers would be extremely foolish *not* to register with the RCMP. A second choice is to register with the local search and rescue group. You can get in touch with them through the hamlet office.

Be sure to supply yourself adequately for your trip. In Auyuittuq National Park Reserve, emergency supplies are kept in each of the emergency shelters. In Ellesmere Island National Park Reserve, emergency supplies are kept only at the Tanquary Fiord and Lake Hazen warden stations. Otherwise, emergency supplies aren't generally available for those out on the land.

Emergency Radios and Personal Locator Beacons

In Nunavut, HF radio is the main means of communication for both emergency and other purposes. The most common of these is the Spillsbury SBX-11, known to some as a radiotelephone. These radios can have up to four frequencies or channels, two of which are usually assigned to the HTOs in the communities. These frequencies are common across Nunavut. Individual agencies such as Parks Canada, Nunavut Research Institute, Polar Continental Shelf Project and others all have their own frequencies.

Channel 5031 is an open frequency used across Nunavut, and it's constantly monitored by Inuit hunters. Don't hesitate to break into the conversation to broadcast your message.

When available, HF radios may be rented or borrowed from outfitters or community organizations such as HTOs. The problem with bringing your own HF radio is that the manufacturer must install the correct crystal for the channel in question, as well as an intact wire dipole antenna tuned for frequency.

Within Auyuittuq National Park Reserve, HF radios are stationed in each of the emergency shelters. Sometimes the batteries need to be warmed up first. Cover them under your jacket, if that's the case. In Ellesmere Island National Park Reserve and Katannilik Territorial Park Reserve, it's recommended that each group rent and carry an HF radio as part of its communal gear. Radio "blackouts" — intense solar disturbances that prevent radio reception — are a serious communications problem in the Arctic. In some cases, radio communication is impossible for hours or even days. When an emergency coincides with a radio blackout, you're on your own.

Personal locator beacons are also commonly used and available for sale, rent or loan. When triggered, these beacons emit a radio distress signal to a satellite, which then transmits to emergency measures organizations. The beacons are to be used only in an emergency. Once triggered, they can't be turned off. When one of these signals is received, the receiving agency assumes that immediate rescue or evacuation is required. If a beacon is triggered by mistake, you may bear the cost of the emergency response. These beacons are particularly recommended for those travelling in extremely remote areas, in the off-season, or in areas where dangers (such as large numbers of polar bears) are known to be present.

Wildlife and Plants

Polar bears can be encountered throughout Nunavut, including at all parks. As they're marine mammals, they spend most of the year roaming the sea ice. In summer, they travel along the shoreline and occasionally venture great distances inland. Visitors aren't allowed to carry firearms, even for personal protection, within national parks. Several spray deterrents have been developed but they have yet to be proven effective against polar bears. To avoid polar bears — and barren-ground grizzly bears on mainland Nunavut — choose routes that don't pass through their habitat. Also be scrupulous in your management of food and waste. The pamphlet, *Safety in Bear Country*, is available from the Department of Resources, Wildlife and Economic Development, Nunavut Tourism, and some community visitor information centres.

It can be dangerous to approach too closely to muskoxen, particularly if they're lone bulls. Be extra careful. In Ellesmere Island National Park Reserve, muskoxen, when threatened, have been known to charge and gore people.

Rabies is present throughout Nunavut, especially in the fox population. Some animals, such as wolves and foxes, are very curious and may come right up to you. Avoid contact with all wildlife. Feeding wildlife is prohibited in parks and isn't wise in any case. Feeding also results in the "habituation" of wildlife. Once accustomed to human food, many species quickly become troublesome and can cause extensive damage to personal equipment and food stores.

Respect the need of the region's wildlife for undisturbed territory. When approaching wildlife to take a photograph or a closer look, stay downwind. Respect their need for distance, and don't make sudden movements. Never chase or harass animals. Respect for them is especially critical in calving, nesting and feeding areas, or when they are already stressed.

Travel quietly. You'll be more aware of your environment, and wildlife will be less disturbed. In fact, you'll increase your chances of observing wildlife. If you're travelling in a park, during your mandatory registration with park staff, learn as much as you can about those species that are easily disturbed. Inquire about places and times when disturbance is most likely so you can avoid travelling there during critical periods.

There are a few edible plants in Nunavut, notably several varieties of berries and others such as mountain sorrel. No known poisonous plants exist in the area. Don't eat any edible plants, however, unless you find yourself in an emergency. Much of Nunavut's vegetation is sparse, and some species, such as arctic blueberry in Ellesmere Island National Park Reserve, are rare, existing here only marginally at the most northern extent of their range. If a local outfitter takes you to a traditional berry-picking spot, though, it's usually okay to sample a few.

Artifacts, Archeological Sites and Cairns

Allow others a sense of discovery by leaving rocks, plants, and other natural objects, such as muskoxen skulls and caribou antlers, as you found them. Not only does collecting degrade the experience for others, but you may be breaking laws protecting archeological artifacts.

If you use rocks to secure your tent, return them to their original location before you leave. Don't remove rocks from any feature that looks, even remotely, like an archeological site. Partially buried symmetrical arrangements of stone may be all you see on the ground surface in the area of a prehistoric site. Archeological sites include tent rings, fox traps, and food caches. Some, particularly the older paleoeskimo sites in Ellesmere Island National Park Reserve, may be almost indiscernible to the untrained eye. These rare sites, however, are important cultural resources containing valuable information about life in the area 4,000 years ago! Please don't even touch any of these features. The exact arrangement and location of artifacts is crucial in determining what occurred at the site. Moreover, archeological sites in Nunavut are protected by law, and the unauthorized disturbance or removal of artifacts or other cultural specimens from any site is prohibited.

In some Nunavut parks, you can visit excavated prehistoric camp sites. Check with the park staff. If you find an archeological or historical artifact while travelling in a park, mark its location on your map and report it to staff when you leave the park. If you find what appears to be an undiscovered site outside a park, you're encouraged to report it either to the **Inuit Heritage Trust** in Iqaluit, which will ensure that the information is sent to the appropriate regulatory authority, or to the **Prince of Wales Northern Heritage Centre** in Yellowknife (a GNWT agency, this contact will no longer be valid once the new territory of Nunavut starts in 1999).

Don't build cairns or other markers or leave messages in the soil. These signs may be confusing to others and they detract from other visitors' sense of discovery and feeling of wilderness. Don't disturb or destroy any cairns that you find, because some are of great historical importance.

Glaciers

Glaciers abound in the Baffin Region. All members of groups planning glacier travel, such as ski-mountaineering, must be well versed in the techniques of such travel. When travelling on a glacier, ski-mountaineering groups should be properly roped together at all times. This means while in camp, as well. Even among experienced glacier travellers, deaths have occurred when someone has stepped outside the camp and fallen unroped into a crevasse. All team members must be capable of crevasse rescue techniques such as the Z-pulley and drop-loop systems. Harnesses, crampons, ice axes, carabiners, pulleys, ice screws, prusiks, jumar ascenders, and ropes that are nine millimetres in diameter or thicker are among the recommended equipment for hiking parties planning to cross glacier tongues along their routes. (Look for the UIAA stamp of approval on ropes and other climbing gear that the international mountaineering association deems acceptable.) Hikers must know how to use all equipment.

Those planning extended trips onto an ice cap should wear plastic double mountaineering boots, and carry a HF radio. If you're travelling within a park, before you set out, discuss with park staff possible drop-off and pickup points and escape routes. (If travelling outside a park, discuss this with another responsible person.) Don't be lulled into a false sense of security by the deceptively flat terrain of ice caps. They can harbor enormous hidden crevasses.

Avalanches and Rock Falls

It's essential that all members of parties travelling in areas where an avalanche may occur be well versed in avalanche avoidance and self-rescue techniques. Each party member should carry a dual frequency (227.5 kHz and 457 kHz) avalanche beacon that is switched on and set always to transmit (for example, Pieps DF, Ortovox FZ, Avalrt). They should also carry an avalanche probe, as well as a shovel. Practise self-rescue techniques beforehand. A pre-trip battery check is also recommended.

In many areas of Nunavut, rock falls are a serious hazard. Prolonged periods of rain greatly increase the frequency of rock falls. There's also an increased hazard of falling rock during periods of daily freezing and melting. Take particular care in selecting routes along steep slopes. Camp sites should be set up in protected areas away from the immediate base of mountains or cliffs. A growth of lichen on rock surfaces is a good sign of a protected area. Avoid areas of bare, clean rock.

Crossing Streams, Rivers and Lake Ice

Many streams and rivers in Nunavut are glacier-fed. Even with continuous daylight, their depth and speed change throughout the day. The ice-cold water is frequently opaque from glacial silt, and currents can be deceptively strong. If in doubt about your ability to ford a stream, wait until late at night or early morning to cross, as water levels are usually lower at these times of day. Unfasten your waist belt and loosen the shoulder straps on your pack. A hiking staff used as a third leg adds stability in stream crossings. Groups may wish to use buddy techniques, such as chains, wedges, or the people pivot, with arms linked and with the strongest members upstream. Wet suit, "reef boots" or windsurfing-type neoprene boots and pants are recommended to aid in fording the extremely cold glacier-fed rivers and streams, notably in Auyuittuq and Ellesmere Island National Park Reserves. Once committed to the crossing, you should be resolute and unfaltering, with eyes fixed on a point on the opposite side to prevent visual disorientation by moving water on all sides.

In a few lakes in Nunavut, ice lasts late into the summer. Although this persistent ice sometimes looks like a tempting shortcut compared with more gruelling land routes, lake ice should be considered unsafe and avoided from around June 1 through September 15.

Although the sea ice almost always breaks up around communities in the summer, year-round sea ice does occasionally occur. "Ice pans" floating in and out on the tides are common during the summer. Never attempt to walk on an ice pan, as it can carry you out to sea. Even worse is to be stuck on one with a polar bear. It has happened!

Tides

Tides in parts of Nunavut are among the highest in the world. Tides ebb and flow very quickly and can be dangerous when exploring tidal flats. To be stranded by the tide is not an adventure you want to experience! Tides have a considerable effect on boat travel. It's difficult to get in and out of Auyuittuq National Park Reserve at low tide, for example, because of the long, shallow flats that develop. Canadian Hydrographic Services has tide tables for various areas of Nunavut. It's also a good idea to consult the **Department of Fisheries and Oceans** before scheduling any boat trips. Tides vary by about an hour a day, so a high tide that comes at noon one day will arrive several hours later at the end of the week.

WEATHER

by Carol Rigby

Nunavut is a huge territory, and the weather can vary widely.

As a rule, in July and August, inland areas are warmer than coastal ones, while western regions are definitely warmer than the Baffin Region.

Summer highs can differ widely. The warmest day on record in Iqaluit was a balmy 24.4° C, whereas Baker Lake once experienced a torrid 33.6° C day in July. (The highest temperature recorded in the Arctic was 43° C in Kugluktuk. But this is the exception, not the rule!) If the temperature is right, visitors can even swim at some sandy beaches in Nunavut — there are several in Rankin Inlet and one in Kugluktuk. Broughton Island, on the other hand, has never seen a day warmer than 19° C.

Spring temperatures are more consistent throughout Nunavut, with average daytime highs between –20° C and –10° C. Cool days are tempered by lots of sunshine. From late March to the end of May, sun reflected off snow and ice can cause severe sunburn.

Daylight

In winter, visitors should be prepared for cold temperatures and short days. On the shortest days of winter in Iqaluit, the sun rises and sets within four hours. The further north you go, the shorter the winter days get. Communities north of the Arctic Circle don't see the sun at all for stretches at a time, although the sky may lighten a bit at midday. Conversely, at the summer solstice, the sun shines for up to 21 hours a day in Iqaluit and many Kivalliq communities. The further north you go above the Arctic Circle, the more days you'll experience 24-hour daylight. Unsuspecting visitors, wishing to sleep in the open under the stars at night, have been known to wake up with lovely sunburns!

Winter Cold

Low humidity reduces the impact of the cold, making a –20° C day feel more like –5° C in southern Canada. Winds, however, can cause frostbite, so it's wise to have a parka with a ruff around its hood for wintertime visits. January, February and March are the coldest months, with an average high in Iqaluit of –22° C and a low of –30° C. The record low was –46° C. Cambridge Bay is even colder: January averages are –30° C for high and –37° C for low. But the coldest day on record anywhere in Nunavut was in Pelly Bay where the temperature, combined with the windchill, reached –92° C!

Precipitation

As most of the Arctic is a polar desert, long stretches of almost cloudless days without precipitation are common. Total annual precipitation in Iqaluit, converted to a water equivalent, is 43 centimetres. (Ottawa gets more than twice this amount in an average year, and despite its much shorter winter, gets about the same amount of snow.) However, throughout most of Nunavut, cool temperatures mean that snow cover generally doesn't finish melting until

June. On most of the land, the only months without snow are June, July and August. Sea ice doesn't finish melting until later. Most rain falls just after the sea ice breaks up, usually between mid-July and the end of August.

Winds

The wind always seems to blow in the Arctic! In all regions of Nunavut, many communities have steady average winds of 15–20 km/h almost daily. Some communities are notorious for occasional extreme winds. In Pangnirtung, for example, many of the older houses have cables fastening their roofs to the ground to protect them against gusts of more than 100 km/h. Precipitation tends to fall sideways, as it's almost always accompanied by winds of 30–60 km/h. If you plan to spend extended time out on the land or water, you *must* consider the wind as a factor — it will magnify any chilling effects of the weather. The windchill factor is often more significant than the actual air temperature.

Weather Delays

Blizzards are most common during autumn — especially in October and November — and early spring, February through April. Travel to the smaller communities can be severely affected at these times, because pilots must rely on good visibility to approach airstrips that don't have instrument landing systems. In the summer, weather delays can also be caused by strong winds, unpredictable cloud cover, and along a coastline, fog. Build time into your schedule to allow for the possibility of being "weathered in" or "weathered out" of a community by poor visibility or strong winds. If outdoor activities such as hiking or boating are on your agenda, make allowances in your plans for days when you'll choose to stay put, rather than travel in terrible, hypothermia-inducing weather.

Length of Midnight Sun and Arctic Night in Select Nunavut Communities

Community	24 Hours of Sunshine	24 Hours of Darkness
Grise Fiord	April 22 to August 20	October 31 to February 11
Resolute	April 29 to August 13	November 6 to February 5
Nanisivik	May 6 to August 6	November 11 to January 30
Arctic Bay	May 6 to August 6	November 11 to January 30
Pond Inlet	May 5 to August 7	November 12 to January 29
Clyde River	May 13 to August 9	November 22 to January 20
Broughton Island	May 29 to July 15	December 16 to December 26
Pangnirtung	June 8 to July 4	no 24-hour darkness
Repulse Bay	June 4 to July 9	no 24-hour darkness
Hall Beach	May 21 to July 22	December 2 to January 10
Igloolik	May 18 to July 26	November 26 to January 15
Pelly Bay	May 21 to July 22	December 4 to January 7
Taloyoak	May 17 to July 27	November 25 to January 16
Gjoa Haven	May 22 to July 21	December 3 to January 9
Cambridge Bay	May 20 to July 23	November 30 to January 11
Kugluktuk	May 27 to July 17	December 10 to January 2

SOURCE: ENVIRONMENT CANADA

The limits of 24-hour sunlight and 24-hour darkness are not coincident, but extend approximately 50 nautical miles north and south of the Arctic Circle. This is due to a combination of effects: the "radius" of the solar disk accounts for approximately one-third of the shift, while the effects of refraction for the other two-thirds. Along the Arctic Circle, half the solar disk remains visible on the northern horizon at sunset on the longest day, and half the solar disk appears on the southern horizon during the shortest day.

CLOTHING AND PERSONAL EFFECTS

by Carol Rigby

Your choice of clothing and personal effects can make or break your arctic holiday.

If you're properly dressed and equipped, you'll find few obstacles to enjoying yourself. But if you're ill-equipped, you may be miserable. The clothing and equipment you need when visiting the North depends on when you're coming and what you're planning to do. A trip involving hiking, camping or some other outdoor summer activity will have different requirements than a dogsledding trip.

In most of Nunavut, summer weather is equivalent to cool spring or fall conditions in most of southern Canada, the northern United States, or Europe. However, the climate can vary dramatically from one region to another. Coastal sections of the Kivalliq and Baffin regions occasionally experience days that are warm enough for short sleeves and pants. The air is usually chilly, though, and nights can be downright cold. Kugluktuk in the Kitikmeot, on the other hand, can have hot spells of up to 30° C; in this case, it's worthwhile bringing along a swimsuit.

Expect conditions near the water to be cold all summer, with warmer weather possible in the interior. T-shirts may be comfortable on many days and come in handy as undershirts in cooler weather. Judge your need for shorts by your tolerance for cool temperatures and insect bites.

Check on the weather for the region you're planning to visit. If you love swimming, bring a bathing suit. Some communities have swimming pools and you might join the few hardy souls who take dips in nearly freezing waters. For example, the Duval River in Pangnirtung has a swimming hole of sorts, where brave teens like to go. It's not for the faint-hearted or easily chilled!

For summer travel to the communities, you'll want a good breathable set of rain gear, top and bottom. Don't bother to bring an umbrella, though, because it will just blow inside out and won't protect you against the rain, which often blows sideways in the Arctic! Make sure your jacket has a good hood that's sewn in or zipped on rather than snapped on.

Arctic dress is casual. Usually only elderly Inuit ladies wear skirts, and then with trousers underneath. Nearly everyone wears pants, sweatsuits or tights, usually with T-shirts, casual shirts and sweaters. Foot gear should be low-heeled and sturdy, as most roads are gravel and have no sidewalks. Footwear with ankle support is excellent for walking on the tundra; heavy leather hiking boots are necessary only if you plan to walk extensively on the land. Rubber boots with heavy felt or duffel liners and/or heavy wool socks are crucial for those planning fishing or sightseeing trips on freighter canoes. Even if you plan to stay within a community, be sure to bring warm wool or pile sweaters for cool summer days and nights.

If you plan to visit a community in winter, it's essential to bring a warm coat or parka with a good hood and a face-protecting ruff. Warm, low-heeled boots, a scarf, a close-fitting knitted hat, and windproof mitts are other essentials. Long underwear, turtlenecks, sweaters and warm trousers are all necessary if you plan to go outside. If you like to walk even in winter, windproof outer pants or pile-lined wind pants are indispensable. You can expect central heating in virtually all buildings. If you can rent well-fitting caribou clothing for a winter trip outside the communities, great. They are sometimes available from outfitters. Otherwise, conventional gear for extremely cold weather is a must. Goggles are also great for winter snowmobile trips.

You should also bring good sunglasses with UV (ultraviolet) filters, unless you're visiting above the Arctic Circle at Christmas, when the sun doesn't rise. The sun is up at least 20 hours a day in the summer; in the spring, reflection off the snow can be intense. Anyone without sunglasses who is out on the land in the spring risks snow-blindness. A cap with a brim is essential in spring and summer, as well. Baseball caps are a sure bet for visitors who like to trade!

Spring sunburns from forehead to neck are very common in the Arctic, so bring a good sunblock. (An "arctic tan" is very brown face and hands, and pale skin everywhere else.) Since the climate is dry, it's also a good idea to bring moisturizing lotion and lip salve. Make sure you bring all the personal toiletries you'll need, especially if you plan to travel beyond the larger communities of Iqaluit, Rankin Inlet or Cambridge Bay.

Most hotels and lodges have outlets for razors and hair dryers that operate on the standard 120-volt North American system.

INSECTS

by Carol Rigby

Parts of Canada's North are infested with insects for several weeks in the summer — somewhere between July and August — although the problem varies from one area to another.

Mosquitoes can be especially annoying, but they are a necessary nuisance within the Arctic's ecosystems, since they are breakfast, lunch and dinner for many of Nunavut's birds, and also help in the pollination of beautiful arctic flowers. Other than mosquitoes, blackflies and bumblebees, there are no biting insects or snakes of any kind in the North.

The Kivalliq Region has many shallow tundra lakes and is ideal for breeding mosquitoes. Blackflies are found inland during the last two weeks of August (Baker Lake is the Kivalliq's only inland community). Visitors will also encounter lots of blackflies and mosquitoes along the rivers and lakes in the Kitikmeot Region, and wasps and bumblebees around Kugluktuk. However, the more mountainous terrain and almost constant winds of the Baffin Region mean that fewer insects breed there.

If you plan to be outdoors for long in the Baffin, be sure to use a good insect repellent in case the wind drops or you find yourself hiking through a sheltered valley or along a pond or river bed where mosquitoes breed. When they do come, they can be thick. Generally, however, a bug hat or jacket shouldn't be necessary unless you're extremely sensitive to bites. You're more likely to encounter great numbers of mosquitoes in communities surrounded by flat terrain. There are no blackflies in most of the Baffin.

In the Kivalliq, good bug protection is essential. One of the new lightweight, all-in-one bug jackets with hood and face mask is ideal. The visitors centres sell these for around $65.

People have been known to tape shut sleeves and pant cuffs to keep bugs out of clothes. If you're camping, good screening on your tent is also essential. And carry lots of repellent!

Here are a few other tips from officials in Nunavut's tourism industry.

- Wear light-colored clothing. Insects are not as attracted to these as they are to dark clothing. Teal and green are the worst colors to wear.
- Forget the hype about Avon's Skin-So-Soft™ moisturizing lotion — despite it's reputation for doubling as an insect repellent, it doesn't work very long in the Arctic.
- Use a repellent containing the chemical DEET, a deterrent to bugs. According to the Drug Information Centre with the Faculty of Pharmacy, University of Toronto, 30 per cent DEET is acceptable for adults and 10 per cent DEET for children under five. High concentrations of DEET have proven toxic to some people. Its effect varies on individuals; generally, the younger you are and fairer your skin, the greater the toxic effect.
- Try bug hats, an inexpensive alternative. They come in several styles, from the hoop kind to caps with netting inside.
- Check the netting and door zippers on your tent before bringing it north. Buy a tent first-aid kit with netting patches for repairs.
- If you are allergic to bees, bring appropriate medication with you. There are very few pharmacies in Nunavut.
- When bugs are bad, do as the caribou do and head for the high ridges where the wind will blow bugs away! Or take up the Inuit practice of burning moss to smoke away mosquitoes.

PERIODICALS AND BOOKS

by Carol Rigby, with contributions from Dave Sutherland

When planning a trip to Nunavut, you may want to check out the following periodicals.

Above and Beyond
Box 2348, Yellowknife NT, X1A 2P7, Canada
Tel.: (403) 873-2299. Fax: (403) 873-2295
E-mail: abeyond@internorth.com

First Air's in-flight magazine carries general interest articles on life in the North.

Inuit Art Quarterly
2081 Merivale Rd., Nepean ON, K2G 1G9, Canada
Tel.: (613) 224-8189. Fax: (613) 224-2907
E-mail: iaf@inuitart.org
Web site: www.inuitart.org

Published by the Inuit Art Foundation, this magazine is for the serious art enthusiast.

Inuktitut
Suite 510, 170 Laurier Ave., Ottawa ON, K1P 5V5, Canada
Tel.: (613) 238-8181. Fax: (613) 234-1991
E-mail: itc@magi.com

A quarterly published by the Inuit Tapirisat of Canada, *Inuktitut* is a cultural magazine serving Canadian Inuit. It features both historical pieces on traditional ways of life, and articles on current issues of interest to Inuit. It is published in English and Inuktitut, the language of Inuit.

Nunatsiaq News
P.O. Box 8, Iqaluit NT, X0A 0H0, Canada
Tel.: (819) 979-5357. Fax: (819) 979-4763
E-mail: nunat@nunanet.com
Web site: www.nunanet.com/~nunat

An Iqaluit-based weekly newspaper that focuses primarily on current political events.

The Arctic Traveller: Nunavut vacation planner
P.O. Box 1450, Iqaluit NT, X0A 0H0, Canada
Tel.: 1-800-491-7910 or (819) 979-6551. Fax: (819) 979-1261
E-mail: nunatour@nunanet.com
Web site: www.nunatour.nt.ca

This publication is probably essential for planning your visit; contains listings of outfitters, trip packages, etc. Although obviously a promotional tool (it's published by Nunavut Tourism and the GNWT), it's one of the best print sources of current tourism information.

Up Here: Life in Canada's North
P.O. Box 1350, Yellowknife NT, X1A 2N9, Canada
Tel.: (403) 920-4652. Fax: (403) 873-2844
E-mail: outcrop@internorth.com

Another general interest magazine focusing on the North.

Books

Once in Nunavut, you may find it worthwhile to visit local branches of the public library system. There are regional library offices in Rankin Inlet (for the Kivalliq) and Iqaluit (for the Baffin), and local libraries in the following communities: Arviat, Baker Lake, Cambridge Bay, Igloolik, Iqaluit, Kugluktuk, Nanisivik, Pangnirtung, Pond Inlet and Rankin Inlet. Collections are small, except in Iqaluit and Rankin Inlet, which house regional collections. However, even the small libraries contain northern materials and often, items of local interest. Many are located either in visitor centre/museum complexes or in local schools. Hours are limited but should be clearly posted. Visitors are welcome to use materials in the local libraries, but may not borrow materials unless they are staying long enough (up to six months, for example) to warrant a temporary membership. The Iqaluit

Centennial Library also houses the Thomas Manning collection of polar books. The personal collection of respected biologist Thomas Manning, it contains many rare items and would be of interest to antiquarians, book lovers, and scientists.

Before coming to Nunavut, though, you might find the following books enlightening. Most are currently in print, though some older titles might only be available from a library. Many stores in the North may carry some books of local interest, but the only wide selection is in the bookstore section of Arctic Ventures in Iqaluit.

Anthropology and General Interest

Alexander, Bryan and Cherry. *The Vanishing Arctic.* Markham, Ontario: Fitzhenry and Whiteside, 1997. New York: Facts on File, 1997. An excellent pictorial overview of all arctic regions of the world, supported by a solid text.

Boas, Franz. *The Central Eskimo*. Lincoln, Nebraska: University of Nebraska Press, 1964. A classic of anthropology describing what is now a nearly vanished lifestyle.

Boult, David (editor). *The Inuit Way*. Ottawa: Inuit Women's Association of Canada, 1991. A booklet published by Pauktuutit, the Inuit Women's Association, with the express intent of explaining traditional Inuit attitudes to a non-Inuit audience. It deals with the social values of Inuit today.

Brody, Hugh. *Living Arctic: Hunters of the Canadian North*. Vancouver: Douglas and MacIntyre, 1987.

Brody, Hugh. *The People's Land: Eskimos and Whites in the Eastern Arctic*. Harmondsworth, England: Penguin, 1975. The "nature and consequences of native-white interactions are at the heart of this book" (introduction). Brody's books have stirred up a certain amount of controversy; he takes a very critical look at the effects of modern values on the traditional Inuit lifestyle and value systems.

Bruemmer, Fred. *Seasons of the Eskimo: A Vanishing Way of Life*. Toronto: McClelland and Stewart, 1971. Available in French as *Les Saisons de l'Esqimau: un mode de vie qui disparaît*. Montreal: Cercle du livre de France, 1994.

Bruemmer, Fred. *The Arctic*. Montreal: Optimum Publishing International, 1982.

Bruemmer, Fred. *The Arctic World*. Toronto: Key Porter, 1985. Bruemmer's books all feature his photography, which is stunning.

Hall, Ed (editor). *A Way of Life*. Yellowknife: Government of the Northwest Territories (Department of Renewable Resources), 1986. Describes the traditional tools and techniques that have helped aboriginal peoples of the Northwest Territories cope with life. One fascinating chapter describes the making of sealskin *kamiit* (boots).

Hancock, Lyn. *Nunavut*. Minneapolis: Lerner Publications Company, 1995. Aimed at schoolchildren, this recently released book provides a strong overview of Nunavut that benefits adults, too.

Jenness, Diamond. *The Life of the Copper Eskimos.* Ottawa: S. A. Acland, Printer to the King, 1922. The New Zealand-born anthropologist's work is considered by many scholars the best description of an Inuit group.

Kusugak, Michael and Robert Munsch. *A Promise is A Promise.* Toronto, New York: Annick Press Ltd., 1988. This children's book, beautifully illustrated by Vladyana Krykorka, is a tale of the *Qallupilluit,* imaginary creatures living underwater who snatch children straying too close to cracks in the ice.

Lopez, Barry. *Arctic Dreams: Imagination and Desire in a Northern Landscape.* New York: Charles Scribner's Sons, 1986. A meditative look at arctic ecology, and the relationships between humans and the land in the Arctic.

Pitseolak, Peter & Dorothy Harley Eber. *People from our side: a life story with photographs and oral biography.* Montreal & Kingston: McGill-Queen's University Press, 1993 (reprint edition). Pitseolak, born in 1902, is considered Baffin's first Inuk photographer. This is his account of changes brought to the nomadic lifestyle of the Inuit by fur traders, government schools, missionaries and alcohol. It's filled with photos from the 1940s on, capturing a historic time of transition.

Steltzer, Ulli. *Inuit. The North in Transition.* Vancouver: Douglas and McIntyre, 1982. An evocative photo essay on the changes taking place in the North.

Wilkinson, Douglas. *The Arctic Coast* (The Illustrated Natural History of Canada series). Toronto: Jack McClelland, 1975. One volume in a larger series, this gives an excellent overview of the physical geography and ecology of the Arctic coastline.

Arts, Crafts, Inuit Writing

Gedalof, Robin (editor). *Paper Stays Put: A Collection of Inuit Writing.* Edmonton: Hurtig, 1980. An anthology of essays, stories and legends by Inuit authors.

Houston, James. *Confessions of an Igloo Dweller.* Toronto: McClelland & Stewart, 1996. A very readable account of the Canadian art advocate who helped bring Inuit art to the world stage.

Ipellie, Alootook. *Arctic Dreams and Nightmares.* Penticton, BC: Theytus Books, 1993. Twenty short stories accompanied by drawings and an introductory essay, all by Ipellie, who has a distinctive artistic style and writing voice.

Larmour, W. T. *Inunnit: The Art of the Canadian Eskimo.* Ottawa: Government of Canada (Department of Indian Affairs and Northern Development), 1967. Available in French as *Inunnit: L'art des Esquimaux du Canada.*

Markoosie. *Markoosie: Harpoon of the hunter.* Montreal & London: McGill-Queen's University Press, 1970. This powerful little novella, the first work of Inuit fiction to be published in English, tells the story of a young man who reaches manhood during the hunt for a wounded polar bear, and his long journey home alone. Also available in Inuktitut.

Meyayer, Maurice (editor and translator). *Tales from the Igloo.* Edmonton: Hurtig, 1972. Traditional Inuit tales illustrated by Holman artist Agnes Nanogak.

Nanogak, Agnes. *More Tales from the Igloo.* Edmonton: Hurtig, 1986. As told by Nanogak.

National Museum of Man. *The Inuit Print: A Travelling Exhibition of the National Museum of Man.* National Museum of Man, Ottawa, 1977. A catalogue of the travelling exhibition that provides a retrospective of the first 20 years of Canadian Inuit prints.

Oakes, Jill E. and Rick Riewe. *Our Boots: An Inuit Women's Art.* Vancouver: Douglas & McIntyre, 1995. A definitive reference book examining the relationship between the arctic environment, Inuit culture, and footwear.

Petrone, Penny (editor). *Northern voices: Inuit writing in English.* Toronto: University of Toronto Press, 1988. A wide-ranging anthology with selections from different Inuit culture groups (such as Copper Inuit, Iglulik Inuit).

Roch, Ernst and Patrick Furneaux. *Arts of the Eskimo: Prints.* Montreal: Signum Press (in association with Oxford University Press, Toronto), 1974. Text by Furneaux and Leo Rosshandler.

Seidelman, Harold and James Turner. *The Inuit Imagination: Arctic Myth and Sculpture.* Vancouver: Douglas & McIntyre, 1993. New York: Thames and Hudson, 1994. Combines contemporary Inuit sculpture with traditional stories, songs, and oral reminiscences.

Strickler, Eva and Anaoyok Alookee. *Inuit Dolls: Reminders of a Heritage.* Toronto: Canadian Stage and Arts Publications Limited, 1988. For doll lovers and those interested in the Inuit way of life.

Swinton, George. *Sculpture of the Inuit,* revised edition. Toronto: McClelland and Stewart, 1992. This classic survey of the field has been recently re-published in a new and updated edition (former title was *Sculpture of the Eskimo*); the older edition may still also be available.

Flora and Fauna

Banfield, A.W.F. *The Mammals of Canada.* Toronto: University of Toronto Press, 1974. A standard in descriptive biology. Also available in French as *Les mammifères du Canada.* Laval, Quebec: Les Presses de l'Université Laval, 1974.

Bruemmer, Fred. *Arctic Animals: A Celebration of Survival.* Toronto: McClelland and Stewart, 1986. More stunning photographs from Bruemmer.

Chung, In-Cho. *Eastern North America as Seen by a Botanist: Pictorial I (The Arctic Region).* Daytona Beach, Florida: Samhwa Printing Co., 1989. An excellent pictorial survey of the grasses and wildflowers of the region. Makes it easy to identify specific plants.

Forsyth, Adrian. *Mammals of the Canadian Wild.* Camden East, Ontario: Camden House, 1985.

Godfrey, William E. *Birds of Canada.* Ottawa: National Museum of Natural Sciences, 1986. Also available in French as *Les oiseaux du Canada.*

Graves, Jonquil and Ed Hall. *Arctic Animals.* Yellowknife: Government of the Northwest Territories (Department of Renewable Resources), 1985. Illustrated by well-known Inuit artist Germaine Arnaktauyok in her trademark pointillist style, this is a concise but thorough survey of animal species found in the Canadian Arctic. Although more restricted in content than the larger mammal and bird books, it covers virtually all wildlife a visitor is likely to encounter on a trip to Nunavut, along with the Inuktitut name or names for each species.

Mech, L. David. *The Arctic wolf: Living with the Pack.* Toronto: Key Porter, 1988. Stillwater, Minnesota: Voyageur Press, 1988. Beautifully illustrated with the photos taken by Mech in the course of his studies of the arctic wolf, an authoritative text.

Peterson, Roger Tory. *A Field Guide to the Birds East of the Rockies.* Boston: Houghton Mifflin, 1984. The standard; what can you say?

Pielou, E. C. *A Naturalist's Guide to the Arctic.* Chicago and London: The University of Chicago Press, 1994. A well-written, non-technical overview of arctic animals, birds, fishes, plants and insects, illustrated by hand drawings.

Stirling, Ian. *Polar bears.* Toronto: Fitzhenry & Whiteside, 1988. Also Ann Arbor, Mich.: University of Michigan Press, 1988. An authoritative work by one of the world's foremost polar bear biologists, this also contains many amazing photographs collected during Stirling's years of studying the beautiful and dangerous animal known to the Inuit as *nanuq*.

History

Alia, Valerie. *Names, Numbers and Northern Policy: Inuit, Project Surname and the Politics of Identity.* Halifax: Fernwood, 1994. A look at the federal government program that changed Inuit history by assigning family names to Inuit.

Berton, Pierre. *The Arctic Grail: The Quest for the Northwest Passage and the North Pole, 1818-1909.* Toronto: McClelland & Stewart, 1988. New York: Viking, 1988. A readable, if lengthy, overview of the age of arctic exploration.

Copeland, A. Dudley. *Coplalook: Chief Trader, Hudson's Bay Company 1923-39.* Winnipeg: Watson & Dwyer, 1989. The autobiography of Dudley Copeland, describing his postings in various parts of the Arctic in the '20s and '30s. A firsthand view of the early interactions between the Hudson's Bay Co. and the Inuit.

Crowe, Keith J. *A History of the Original People of Northern Canada.* Montreal: McGill-Queen's University Press, 1991, revised edition. Originally intended for classroom use by northern native students, this book presents an alternative view of the history of the North, focusing on its indigenous peoples. The revised edition includes discussion of land claims and current issues in the relationship between native peoples and the federal and territorial governments.

Eber, Dorothy Harley. *When the Whalers Were Up North: Inuit Memories from the Eastern Arctic.* Kingston: McGill-Queen's University Press, 1989. Noted oral historian Eber has produced a fascinating view of the whaling era as passed down in the stories of Inuit elders.

Francis, Daniel. *Discovery of the North: the exploration of Canada's Arctic.* Edmonton: Hurtig, 1986. For those who don't want all the in-depth detail provided by Berton and Mowat, here is a more concise synopsis of arctic exploration.

Grant, Shelagh D. *Sovereignty or security: Government Policy in the North, 1936–1950.* Vancouver: University of British Columbia Press, 1988. Carefully researched, this book provides an overview of government policy during a critical period in the development of the North. Grant also addresses the issue of the "Arctic exiles," Inuit from Northern Quebec who, as part of a government program, were relocated to the remotest parts of the High Arctic.

McGhee, Robert. *Canadian Arctic Prehistory*. Toronto: Van Nostrand Reinhold, 1978. A classic on Inuit prehistory and the archeological record. Also available in French as *La préhistoire de l'Arctique canadien*. Montreal: Fides, 1984.

McGhee, Robert. *Ancient People of the Arctic*. Vancouver: University of British Columbia Press with the Canadian Museum of Civilization, 1996. The newest work by the eminent archeologist.

Mowat, Farley. *The Top of the World series: Vol. 1, Ordeal by Ice. Vol. 2, The Polar Passion: The Quest for the North Pole. Vol. 3, Tundra: Selections from the Great Accounts of Arctic Land Voyages*. All three books published by both Toronto: McClelland and Stewart, 1973 and Salt Lake City: Peregrine Smith Books, 1989. Mowat's selection and compilation of classic accounts of arctic exploration. A good overview, as long as one keeps in mind that the accounts have been edited and condensed by Mowat, who is known not to let the truth get in the way of a good story.

Schledermann, Peter. *Crossroads to Greenland: 3,000 Years of Prehistory in the Eastern High Arctic*. Calgary: The Arctic Institute of North America, 1990. With its high level of technical content, this is geared to archeological buffs, although Schledermann's book is of interest for the controversy it's stirred up regarding the migration and settlement patterns of the ancestors of today's Inuit.

Life with the Inuit/Eskimos

Almost another sub-genre of arctic writing is the group of books written by explorers, scientists, bureaucrats and just plain folks describing their time spent living among the Inuit (once known by outsiders as Eskimos). Many of these, especially the older titles, are available in different editions and are most likely to be found at a library.

Freuchen, Peter. *Peter Freuchen's Book of the Eskimos*. Greenwich: Fawcett Publications, 1961. Several editions published. Dates from the early part of the century.

Georgia. *Georgia: An Arctic Diary*. Edmonton: Hurtig, 1982.

Rowley, Graham S. *Cold Comfort: My Love Affair with the Arctic*. Montreal and Kingston: McGill-Queen's University Press, 1996.

Stefansson, Vilhjalmur. *My life with the Eskimo*. New York, Collier Books, 1962. Various editions. A classic.

Wilkinson, Douglas. *Land of the Long Day*. Toronto: Clarke, Irwin, 1966.

Inuit columnists and writers such as John Amagoalik, Peter Ernerk and Mark Kalluak also convey the Inuit perspective firsthand in northern newspapers.

And of course, if one is interested in adventure travel, there are innumerable accounts of people's trips and explorations, from Sir John Franklin and Sir Charles Francis Hall to modern-day explorers like Will Steger and Paul Schurke, Mike Beedell and Ed Struzik, and many others. Chances are if someone has done a trip to the North Pole, they've written a book about it!

INTERNET RESOURCES

by Marion Soublière

In a land one-fifth the size of Canada, where almost no roads link the 28 settlements separated by hundreds of kilometres of tundra, the information highway stands to pull northerners together unlike anything before.

The Internet is far more than just a plaything for inhabitants of remote northern Canada. It is already a vital resource tool for school and government-driven networks, and will become the backbone of Nunavut's new decentralized government structure. By relaying information digitally for everything from medical services to business conferences, Nunavut could recoup enormous costs that, until now, have been poured into expensive and necessary air travel.

Each of Nunavut's regions has an Internet service provider now; communities are gradually and eagerly going online. Usenet discussion groups, like **rec.travel.usa-canada**, **rec.backcountry**, **soc.culture.native** or **can.politics**, are good places to get feedback on other adventure travel experiences in the Arctic, learn what's new in the Inuit art world, or sense the political momentum as the world watches Nunavut prepare to take its place on the international stage.

Here are some web sites that virtual and real travellers to the Arctic may want to check out.

Travel

Nunavut Tourism — **www.nunatour.nt.ca**
Representing tourism operators across the territory, Nunavut Tourism provides travellers with lists of member operators and up-to-date information packages for all areas of Nunavut. Their newly revamped web site now also boasts a searchable services database so arctic travellers can get a headstart on the planning process.

First Air — **www.firstair.ca**
Check out seat sales on the web site of Canada's third largest scheduled airline, with more cargo/passenger routes than any other northern airline.

NWT Air — **www.nwtair.ca**
The regional carrier of Air Canada features a flight timetable database.

Air Canada — **www.aircanada.ca**
A content-crammed site that includes Air Canada reservation phone numbers worldwide.

Canadian Airlines — **www.cdnair.ca**
Canadian Airlines International owns Canadian North and is a partner with another frequent flyer to Nunavut, Calm Air (**www.calmair.com**). This sophisticated site has flights, schedules and Web airfare specials posted Wednesdays for travel on the upcoming weekend.

NWT Explorers' Guide — **www.edt.gov.nt.ca/guide/index.html**
This 1996 tourism guide, geared to all of the Northwest Territories, includes an extensive alphabetical listing of tourism operators for the eastern and western Northwest Territories. Since this is a 1996 guide and tourism operators must renew their licences yearly, check with tourism licensing officials in Nunavut for the most recent status of outfitters and others mentioned.

Environment Canada, Atmospheric Environment Services — **www.tor.ec.gc.ca/forecasts/index.html**
Weekly weather forecasts for a trio of communities: Baker Lake, Iqaluit and Resolute.

Geomatics Canada **www-nais.ccm.NRCan.gc.ca/wwwnais/sales/english/html/base_m.html**
Maps galore that you can order on line.

Canadian Tourism Information Network **xinfo.ic.gc.ca/Tourism/index-e.html**
Sponsored in part by the Canadian Tourism Commission, this site is a central source of Canadian tourism information.

Technology

Nunanet **www.nunanet.com**
First on the scene in Nunavut, the Internet service provider for the Baffin Region has lots of local users pages, background info on Nunavut, and a searchable database.

Sakku Arctic Technologies **www.arctic.ca**
The Kivalliq Region's Internet service provider features, among other things, an arctic mall where you can pick up that polar bear hide you've been looking for.

PolarNet **www.polarnet.ca**
Still skimpy on content, the Kitkmeot Region's newly arrived Internet service provider promises to deliver more stuff soon.

NorthwestTel Inc. **www.nwtel.ca**
Brush up on the history of telecommunications in the North.

Government and Politics

Nunavut Implementation Commission (NIC) **www.nunanet.com/~nic**
From the body that's drafting Nunavut's new government comes a content-packed site with some of the most authoritative information anywhere on Nunavut, plus press releases and many downloadable NIC reports. Links to other Nunavut and aboriginal sites.

Nunavut Planning Commission (NPC) **npc.nunavut.ca**
One of the first sites on Nunavut, the NPC is responsible for planning land use in the new territory. A researcher's delight, with an environmental database (11,000 entries), a digital database list (110 environmental datasets on Nunavut) and an experts database (650 entries). Coming soon is interactive mapping.

Department of Indian Affairs and Northern Development **www.inac.gc.ca/index_e.html**
A very thorough site that includes a section on Inuit art and a native e-zine. The frequently asked questions (FAQs) page is especially useful for those who wish to learn much more about Canada's Indians and Inuit.

Government of the Northwest Territories **www.ssimicro.com/~xpsognwt/Net**
A gateway to a series of government departments and services, including a link to the Bureau of Statistics where you'll find detailed statistical profiles of all communities in Nunavut and the western Northwest Territories.

Environment Canada **www.doe.ca/envcan/eng_ind.html**
Within this site is a hinterland who's who with loads of background on arctic wildlife, plus national wildlife migratory bird sanctuaries and other protected areas in Nunavut.

Natural Resources Canada **GeoNames.NRCan.gc.ca**
Plug in an official geographical name, get its latitude and longitude, see what else is within a 20-kilometre radius, or calculate distances between any two points in Nunavut and the rest of Canada.

Political Discussion Forum **ujuk.nunanet.com/discuss**
Iqaluit Internet service provider Nunanet has a cherished online political forum that gives keyboard critics the chance to let off a little steam.

Aboriginal Organizations

Nunavut Tunngavik Incorporated **nti.nunavut.ca**
This is Nunavut's land claims organization, responsible for seeing that promises made in

the land claims agreement are carried out. The web site focuses mostly on the Cambridge Bay lands management office. Download part or all of the Nunavut Land Claims Agreement.

Inuit Circumpolar Conference (ICC) **www.inusiatt.com**
This is a non-governmental organization that represents the 125,000 Inuit of Russia, Alaska, Canada and Greenland at the international level, promoting environmental and social initiatives. Although their web site is still under construction, you can download in-depth ICC documents here.

The Assembly of First Nations **www.afn.ca**
This national organization monitors changes made to The Indian Act, and has lots of great links to other native sites.

Art and Culture

Northern Country Arts **natsiq.nunanet.com/~northart**
Features Inuit and other northern artists. Visitors can order jewelry and other products on line.

Isaacs' Gallery of Inuit Art **www.novator.com/UC-Catalog/Isaacs-Catalog**
The upscale Toronto-based gallery features prints from Cape Dorset artists, and a massive calendar about aboriginal art exhibitions on the go.

Iqaluit Artists' Showcase **www.nunanet.com/art/iq-art.html**
See the works of Iqaluit artist Craig Clarke and others.

L'Association francophone d'Iqaluit **www.nunanet.com/~afi**
This web site, en français, looks at Iqaluit's French-speaking community.

THE ARCTICMAN **www.colourlab.com/arctic.htm**
Beautiful, haunting black-and-white portraits of Cape Dorset carvers by photographer Jerry Riley. Even more compelling, though, are the elders' thoughts on life.

Polar Pilots **www.nunanet.com/~tbert/polar_pilots.html**
The escapades of six enthusiastic pilots who promote recreational flying across the southern half of Baffin Island.

Education

The Northern Learning Network **www.learnnet.nt.ca**
In Nunavut and the western Northwest Territories, this is still the best place to go to check out all things northern and educational.

Inuuqatigiit **siksik.learnnet.nt.ca/Inuuqatigiit/TitleoPage.html**
Find out more about the Northwest Territories' new Inuit school curriculum.

Leo Ussak Elementary School **www.arctic.ca/LUS**
The first school in Canada's Arctic to hit the Web, this site has earned lots of kudos for forward thinking. Check out the extensive new student gallery where you can e-mail Rankin Inlet youngsters, or draw up your own plans for Nunavut in the "Countdown to Nunavut" project headed by computer teacher Bill Belsey, and e-mail your blueprint to the official body doing just that — the Nunavut Implementation Commission.

Joamie Elementary School **www.nunanet.com/~joamie**
Young Web handlers from Iqaluit tackle weighty subjects, including the North's cost of living, culture, politics and the economy.

Journey North **www.learner.org/content/k12/jnorth/www**
An excellent US-based interactive educational site that tracks migratory species like the Qamanirjuaq caribou via field observations and satellite collaring data, then e-mails updates to students across North America. A good way to become better acquainted with biologists, students, and others in Nunavut for whom wildlife is an integral part of life.

Media

Nunatsiaq News **www.nunanet.com/~nunat**
The site for Nunavut's leading weekly newspaper is updated every Friday. Download special reports on current issues confronting Nunavut.

News North **www.nnsl.com**
A weekly newspaper published from Yellowknife that's been serving the Northwest Territories for half a century. Also includes a guide to events and other tourism matters in the western Northwest Territories.

CBC North **www.netnorth.com/cbc/cbcnorth.html**
Information on television and radio programming for northerners.

Science and The Arctic

Nunavut Research Institute **www.nunanet.com/~research**
The new territory's premier science and technology institute promotes the use of traditional knowledge, science, research and technology as ways to help Nunavut flourish.

Arctic Circle **www.lib.uconn.edu/ArcticCircle/index.html**
A highly acclaimed site featuring a virtual classroom that teaches the world about the Arctic.

Arctic Perspectives **www.arcticpersp.org**
This non-profit organization builds awareness of the arctic North. The diary of a dogsled trip in communities through the Kivalliq and Kitikmeot makes great reading.

Canadian Arctic Resources Committee **www.carc.org**
A 5,000-member "citizen's organization" dedicated to bridging the gap between southern and northern Canada. Includes back issues of their newsletter *Northern Perspectives.*

Canadian Polar Commission **www.polarcom.gc.ca**
The Canadian government's national advisory agency on polar affairs.

PLANNING AHEAD: DIRECTORY

The 819 and 403 area codes change to 867 on Oct. 21, 1997.

Government Departments and Services

Customs, Excise and Taxation

Automated Customs Information System (ACIS): 1-800-461-9999 (within Canada). Contact offices at port of entry, Customs, Excise and Taxation:
Ottawa (613) 993-0534
Montreal (514) 283-9900
Toronto (416) 973-8022
Vancouver (604) 666-0545
Iqaluit (819) 979-6714
Yellowknife (403) 920-2446
Winnipeg (204) 983-6004
Calgary (403) 292-8750
Edmonton (403) 495-3400
Quebec City (418) 648-4445

Department of Finance, Government of the Northwest Territories

Tel.: 1-800-661-0820
Tel.: (403) 920-3470
Fax: (403) 873-0325

Department of Fisheries and Oceans

Tel.: (204) 983-5108
Fax: (204) 984-2401
E-mail: info@www.ncr.dfo.ca
Web site: www.ncr.dfo.ca

Inuit Heritage Trust

P.O. Box 2080, Iqaluit NT,
X0A 0H0 Canada
Tel.: (819) 979-0731
Fax: (819) 979-0269
E-mail: dstenton@nunanet.com

Nunavut Research Institute
Tel.: (819) 979-6734
Fax: (819) 979-4681
E-mail: lynnp@nunanet.com
Web site: www.nunanet.com/~research

Parks Canada
P.O. Box 353, Pangnirtung NT,
X0A 0R0 Canada
Tel.: (819) 473-8828
Fax: (819) 473-8612
E-mail: PNWT_Info@pch.gc.ca

Prince of Wales Northern Heritage Centre
P.O. Box 1320, Yellowknife NT,
X1A 2L9 Canada
Tel.: (403) 873-7551
Fax: (403) 873-0205
E-mail: richard_valpy@ece.learnnet.nt.ca
Web site: tailpipe.learnnet.nt.ca/pwnhc

Resources, Wildlife and Economic Development (RWED)
Tel.: (819) 979-5011
Fax: (819) 979-6791
In addition to bear safety reading material, one-day safety courses geared to travellers on the land are available from some local RWED offices. Enquire before arriving in Nunavut.

Health-Care Services

Baffin Regional Hospital in Iqaluit
Tel.: (819) 979-7300
To order an ambulance, call 979-4422.

Cambridge Bay Dental Office
Tel.: (403) 983-2285
Fax: (403) 983-2168

Cambridge Bay Health Centre
Tel.: (403) 983-2531
Fax: (403) 983-2262

NWT Health Care Plan
Health Services Administration
GNWT Department of Health and Social Services, Bag 003, Rankin Inlet NT,
X0C 0G0 Canada
Tel.: 1-800-661-0833 or (819) 645-5002
Fax: (819) 645-2997

Rankin Inlet Dental Clinic
Tel.: (819) 645-3322
Fax: (819) 645-3330

Rankin Inlet Health Centre
Tel.: (819) 645-2816
Fax: (819) 645-2688

Rankin Inlet Optical Outlet
Tel.: (819) 645-2327

Maps

Canada Map Office
130 Bentley Ave., Nepean ON,
K1A 0E9 Canada
Tel.: 1-800-465-6277 or (613) 952-7000
Fax: 1-800-661-6277 or (613) 957-8861

Canadian Hydrographic Services
For tide and current tables.
P.O. Box 6000,
9860 W. Saanich Road, Sidney BC,
V8L 4B2 Canada
Tel.: (250) 363-6358
Fax: (250) 363-6841

Geomatics Canada
Web site: www-nais.ccm.NRCan.gc.ca/wwwnais/sales/english/html/base_m.html

Northern Travel Agencies, Organizations and Programs

Elderhostel Canada
Tel.: (613) 530-2222
Fax: (613) 530-2096
Web site: www.elderhostel.org

Northcott Tour Planning and Consulting for the Eastern Arctic
P.O. Box 1272, Iqaluit NT,
X0A 0H0 Canada
Tel.: (819) 979-6261
Fax: (819) 979-1499 or (819) 979-6493

NorthWinds Arctic Adventures
P.O. Box 820, Iqaluit NT,
X0A 0H0 Canada
Tel.: 1-800-549-0551 (for Canada and United States)
Tel.: (819) 979-0551
Fax: (819) 979-0573
E-mail: plandry@nunanet.com
Web site: www.nunanet.com/~plandry

Nunavut Tourism
P.O. Box 1450, Iqaluit NT,
X0A 0H0 Canada
Tel.: 1-800-491-7910 (for Canada and the United States)
Tel.: (819) 979-6551
Fax: (819) 979-1261
E-mail: nunatour@nunanet.com
Web site: www.nunatour.nt.ca

Qamutik Travel
P.O. Box 158, Iqaluit NT,
X0A 0H0 Canada
Tel.: 1-800-642-8597 (only for callers from Canada's 819 and 403 area codes)
Tel.: (819) 979-0707
Fax: (819) 979-1265

Qamutik Travel
P.O. Box 190, Rankin Inlet NT,
X0C 0G0 Canada
Tel.: 1-800-642-8619 (only for callers from Canada's 819 and 403 area codes)
Tel.: (819) 645-2932
Fax: (819) 645-2113

Top of the World Travel
Enokhok Centre, Cambridge Bay NT,
X0E 0C0 Canada
Tel.: (403) 983-2031
Fax: (403) 983-2340

Special Services

Canadian Imperial Bank of Commerce
International debit cards currently accepted at Northern stores include Plus, and Cirrus in addition to Interac. VISA, MasterCard also accepted.
Tel.: (416) 980-4523
Fax: (416) 363-5347

NWT Liquor Commission/Iqaluit Liquor Warehouse
Tel.: (819) 979-5918
Fax: (819) 979-5836

Our Missing Children
Tel.: (613) 993-1525
Fax: (613) 993-5430

Tourism Licensing Officers

Baffin Region
Tel.: (819) 979-5001
Fax: (819) 979-6791
E-mail: rhamburg@nunanet.com

Kitikmeot Region
Tel.: (403) 983-7219
Fax: (403) 983-2802

Kivalliq Region
Tel.: (819) 645-5067
Fax: (819) 645-2346

Visitor Information Centres

Akumalik Visitors Centre, Baker Lake
Tel.: (819) 793-2456
Fax: (819) 793-2175/or (819) 979-2509

Angmarlik Visitors Centre, Pangnirtung
Tel.: (819) 473-8737
Fax: (819) 473-8685

Arctic Coast Visitors Centre, Cambridge Bay
Tel.: (403) 983-2224
Fax: (403) 983-2803

Clyde River Visitors Centre, Clyde River
Tel.: (819) 924-6034
Fax: (819) 924-6268

Katannilik Territorial Park Interpretive Centre
Tel.: (819) 939-2084
Fax: (819) 939-2406
E-mail: rjaffray@nunanet.com

Kugluktuk Heritage Centre, Kugluktuk
Tel.: (403) 982-3232
Fax: (403) 982-3229

Margaret Aniksak Visitors Centre, Arviat
Tel.: (819) 857-2698
Fax: (819) 857-2499

Nattinnak Centre, Pond Inlet
Tel.: (819) 899-8225
Fax: (819) 899-8175

Parks Canada Interpretive Centre, Pangnirtung
Tel.: (819) 473-8828
Fax: (819) 473-8612
E-mail: nunavut_info@pch.gc.ca

Regional Tourism Office, Rankin Inlet
Tel.: (819) 645-5067
Fax: (819) 645-2346

Unikkaarvik Visitors Centre, Iqaluit
Tel.: (819) 979-4636
Fax: (819) 979-1261
E-mail: nunatour@nunanet.com

Getting Around

FLYING TO NUNAVUT AND ITS COMMUNITIES

by Carol Rigby, with contributions from Jennifer Bernius

Most people visiting Nunavut arrive by air. There are no road links from the South and, with the exception of a 21-kilometre stretch between Arctic Bay and Nanisivik, no roads between communities.

Although cruises are sometimes available, there's no ferry or scheduled passenger ship service. Nunavut isn't linked either internally or to the South by rail.

In Nunavut, Iqaluit is the "gateway" city to the Baffin Region, while Rankin Inlet is the gateway to the Kivalliq. There are direct flights from Yellowknife (the capital of the Northwest Territories in the western Arctic) to five of the Kitikmeot's seven communities. There is no scheduled service to either Umingmaktok or Bathurst Inlet.

Greenland, a country that shares with Nunavut the same arctic climate and Inuit culture, is a gateway from Europe. **First Air** flies once a week between Kangerlussuaq, Greenland and Iqaluit in the winter, and twice weekly in the summer.

The Iqaluit Airport, a modern international facility, is the transportation hub of the Baffin Region. It also serves as an entry point to Canada for flights from Greenland. One airline, First Air, offers direct jet service to Iqaluit from Montreal or Ottawa in southern Canada. The flight generally takes from three to six hours, depending on whether a stop is made in Kuujjuaq (a community in northern Quebec). Schedules, departure points and the frequency of flights can change considerably from season to season, and this contributor's experience has been that southern travel agents aren't always aware of northern connections. Check with **Nunavut Tourism** or a northern travel agency if you're making travel arrangements yourself. If you're travelling with a tour, your best airline connections should be arranged with the tour company.

From Eastern Canada, flights to Iqaluit originate in Montreal and Ottawa. Connections can be made from Toronto and Quebec City. Contact a travel agent or First Air for up-to-date schedules and fares. From the Kivalliq, Kitikmeot and Western Canada, connections can be made to Iqaluit through Yellowknife and Rankin Inlet. Contact a travel agent, **NWT Air**, **Canadian North** or First Air for up-to-date schedules and fares.

Air Inuit flies to Sanikiluaq and Cape Dorset from the northern Quebec communities of Kuujjuarapik and Kuujjuaq.

Travellers to the Kivalliq usually arrive via Rankin Inlet. Its airport accommodates jet aircraft and has a new terminal. If you're coming from the east, the routing to Rankin Inlet is through Iqaluit. From the west, the routing is through Yellowknife. There are also flights to Rankin Inlet from Winnipeg, Thompson and Churchill, Manitoba. Rankin Inlet is served by First Air, Canadian North, **Calm Air**, NWT Air and **Skyward Aviation**.

To get to Cambridge Bay, you'll have to pass through Yellowknife, which also has direct flights to Taloyoak, Pelly Bay, Gjoa Haven and Kugluktuk. There is daily service with First Air; Cambridge Bay is also served by Canadian North and NWT Air. You can reach Cambridge Bay from Rankin Inlet or Iqaluit if you pass through Yellowknife. If your point of origin is due south, a connection to Edmonton and the Edmonton-Yellowknife flight is probably the least complicated option. Another option for larger groups is to charter a flight directly from Iqaluit or Rankin to Cambridge Bay. If a group is large enough, a charter can be economical.

Getting to the Communities

Regular scheduled air services link most Nunavut communities. Many flights to the smaller communities operate two or three times a week. Some of the intermediate-sized communities have daily service, although not by jet aircraft. If you can't find a scheduled flight to your destination, a charter service can probably get you there (see the directory at the end of this section).

Air Nunavut offers regularly scheduled flights serving Iqaluit, Pangnirtung, Cape Dorset, Sanikiluaq and Broughton Island.

Canadian Airlines flies Boeing 737 jet aircraft to Resolute from Edmonton through Yellowknife and Cambridge Bay.

First Air serves Broughton Island, Cape Dorset, Clyde River, Hall Beach, Igloolik, Kimmirut, Pangnirtung, Pond Inlet, Resolute, Grise Fiord, Nanisivik, Arctic Bay, Sanikiluaq, Rankin Inlet, Kugluktuk, Pelly Bay, Taloyoak, Gjoa Haven and Cambridge Bay. Kenn Borek Air also serves Pangnirtung and Cape Dorset.

In the High Arctic, **Kenn Borek Air** offers scheduled air service from Resolute to Grise Fiord, Arctic Bay, Nanisivik and Pond Inlet. Calm Air has scheduled flights from Rankin Inlet to Repulse Bay, Arviat, Whale Cove, Chesterfield Inlet, Baker Lake and Coral Harbour. Skyward serves Arviat, Whale Cove and Baker Lake from Rankin Inlet.

Whatever airline you use, it's best to make arrangements in advance through a travel agent. They'll design a package to fit your needs and will make reservations for you at no charge. Flights within Nunavut are frequently delayed by bad weather, and there are instances when aircraft are taken off scheduled service to fly as air ambulances. Be sure to check with your air carrier for up-to-date information.

Charter Services

Charter aircraft are the usual way to reach destinations in Nunavut not serviced by scheduled airline flights. They're also the only way to reach many fishing camps and parks.

If you're taking a package tour, the charter cost will probably be included, but check to be sure. If you're planning a trip on your own, you or your travel agent will have to make charter aircraft arrangements.

Airports, Security, Baggage

Airport facilities at many of the smaller communities are limited to a ticket counter, a baggage office, a small waiting area and washrooms. As the result of a recent building program launched by the government of the Northwest

Territories, several communities boast new airport buildings that are slightly larger and well laid out, although still modest in size. Iqaluit, Rankin Inlet and Cambridge Bay have more complete facilities.

In the small communities, standby passengers have lower priority than cargo, especially if they arrive at the last minute, so plan to get to the airport early if you don't have a seat reserved. A security check is performed on passengers leaving Iqaluit for the South and on passengers leaving Rankin Inlet. The RCMP in other communities will check your baggage if they have reason to believe you're bringing in an illegal substance such as drugs or, in some communities, alcohol.

It's illegal to carry hazardous goods in your luggage. If in doubt, check with the airline. The following items are restricted at all times: matches, lighters, flammable liquids or gases, fireworks, signal flares, bleaches, drain cleaners, aerosols, mercury and solvents. If you require camp stove fuel, buy it at your destination.

Cargo and luggage space may be unheated. In the winter and early spring, your luggage may get very cold, so don't pack anything that will be damaged by freezing. Small items that should be kept from freezing can be carried in the cabin of the aircraft. It's also advisable to use soft-sided luggage of reinforced fabric, rather than vinyl or plastic luggage, which is likely to crack in freezing temperatures. Luggage isn't at the mercy of automated baggage machines, but it can get thrown around a bit when transferred from trucks to luggage holds. Experienced northern travellers like duffel bags and frameless backpacks.

SPECIAL NEEDS TRAVEL, AND TRAVELLING WITH CHILDREN

by Carol Rigby

Travel in this part of Canada tends to be more difficult than in areas further south.

Weather conditions are often troublesome, health facilities are modest, specialized drugs or equipment may not be available, roads in communities are almost always gravel — when not snow-covered — and wheelchair access has only been enforced as part of the building code in the last four to five years. Special needs travellers should prepare well in advance if they intend to visit Nunavut.

Elderly or disabled people should make advance arrangements if they intend to travel to any communities outside Iqaluit, Rankin Inlet or Cambridge Bay, Nunavut's regional centres. Making travel plans through a tour operator who is aware of any special needs may be the best approach. The **Elderhostel** program frequently offers Nunavut destinations, and these trips are usually fully booked. (Elderhostel is a non-profit organization that provides cultural learning experiences by grouping travellers over 55 with their peers.) Special arrangements are made to accommodate the needs of those on Elderhostel trips.

People in Nunavut are helpful, and a lack of specific facilities should not dissuade travellers from visiting. There is a long-standing tradition in the North of including people with special needs in the daily lives and activities of the communities.

In the regional centres, most buildings constructed within the past few years are wheelchair accessible. In Iqaluit, **R. L. Hanson Construction Ltd.** has a Handi-Van that can be hired for transport around town or to and from the airport. **Emergency Services** also has a similar van that can be booked ahead of time through the Royal Canadian Legion.

The principal air carriers will also provide facilities and services both on and off the ground for passengers with special requirements. They ask only that they be informed at the time of booking of any special needs the traveller may have. This can include either the support of a flight attendant or the use of a wheelchair if mobility is a problem; people flying with children are regularly allowed to board in advance of other passengers and can obtain assistance with disembarking as well.

Travel with children is not especially difficult. People generally welcome children and are responsive to them. Parents should check ahead if they are worried about supplies for special needs and should carry a back-up supply of items like formula and baby food or any special medications.

When travelling on the land with kids, apply common-sense rules and monitor the children closely. They may be too young to tell you that something is wrong. Dress them in layers, keep them dry, change wet diapers as soon as possible, take frequent breaks for warm drinks, and have them wear good quality sunglasses and sunscreen. Bring warm wraps, like caribou skins, blankets or sleeping bags, for kids to sit on or under. Keep them moving, watch for frostbite if it's really cold or windy, and at the first sign of hypothermia, take immediate action by wrapping the child inside a blanket or sleeping bag next to another warm body. Make sure footwear and clothing are not too tight because that will cut off circulation. And bring lots of high-energy snacks!

by Carol Rigby

Don't plan to drive much while you're in Nunavut. Unlike the western part of the Northwest Territories, Nunavut is no place to tour by car.

In the Baffin Region, the only road connecting two communities is a 21-kilometre section linking Arctic Bay and Nanisivik. Most Kitikmeot communities are scattered over islands and archipelagos. There are no direct land connections between the Kivalliq and southern Canada, either. In some areas of the Kitikmeot, around communities such as Cambridge Bay, there's a network of roadways or tracks. People drive out of town along these roads to cottages and camps in outlying areas. Some communities and at least one Baffin community, Igloolik, have roads around town leading to local features of interest. Although there are a few stretches of pavement in towns like Iqaluit and Rankin Inlet, most roads are unpaved. To pave over permafrost is expensive and difficult.

Taxis

Many Nunavut communities offer taxi service. Taxis usually charge a flat rate per head, so more than one group can use the cab at the same time. Think of northern taxis as stop-at-your-door buses. Don't be surprised if the driver pulls up at other destinations to pick up or drop off passengers before getting to your stop. Don't pass up a taxi just because you see a passenger inside. There may be only one or two taxis in town, so hop in, if there's room.

Snowmobiles and All-Terrain Vehicles (ATVs)

All Nunavut communities are small enough for you to explore easily on foot. Most local people walk around town and use snowmobiles or ATVs to go longer distances or to carry loads. Contact your travel agent or an outfitter if you'd like an excursion on the land by ATV or snowmobile. These vehicles should only be driven by experienced operators, however. ATVs are also hard on the environment. When travelling by snowmobile, never travel alone. If your machine breaks down, a second can take you back home. It's also wise to carry a spare motor belt, spark plugs, extra gas, food, camp stove, tarp or tent, and even a sleeping bag for a winter day trip. Always tell someone where you're going and how long you expect to be gone. For more important safety information, read "Adventure Travel," Chapter 11.

Nunavut Tourism can give you an up-to-date list of firms that rent ATVs and snowmobiles. Several companies operate in Iqaluit and Rankin Inlet, and a few in other communities, such as Resolute.

Drivers of ATVs are required by territorial law to wear helmets. In Nunavut, individual communities decide whether a helmet, driver's licence, insurance and the like are required for snowmobile drivers. Most communities don't require that helmets be worn, although Baker Lake, Gjoa Haven and Cape Dorset do. Check with the local hamlet office for that community's policy.

Car, Truck and Bus Rentals

In the last few years, Iqaluit — and its traffic — have grown considerably. There are actually a couple of four-way stop signs in the town. If you think you need a vehicle to drive around Iqaluit, R. L. Hanson Construction Ltd., **Norwheels Enterprises**, Toonoonik Hotel and **Tower Arctic** rent cars, vans, etc. Rentals are about $80 per day. Communities in the Kivalliq and Kitikmeot regions rent an assortment of vehicles, too.

Motor vehicles are driven on the right side of the road in Canada. To rent a vehicle in the Northwest Territories, you should have an international driver's licence, which means first having a valid driver's licence from your home jurisdiction.

At least one firm, R. L. Hanson Construction Ltd. in Iqaluit, will charter bus tours for larger groups.

GETTING AROUND: DIRECTORY

The 819 and 403 area codes change to 867 on Oct. 21, 1997.

Airlines of Nunavut

Adlair Aviation 83 Ltd.

(charter service)

Yellowknife office:
P.O. Box 2946, Yellowknife NT,
X1A 2R3 Canada
Tel.: (403) 873-5161
Fax: (403) 873-8475

Cambridge Bay office:
P.O. Box 111, Cambridge Bay NT,
X0E 0C0 Canada
Tel.: (403) 983-2569
Fax: (403) 983-2847
Flies charters anywhere in Nunavut but best known in the Kitikmeot. Operates Lear 258, King Air 100, Twin Otter and Beaver planes.

Air Inuit

(scheduled and charter services)
1985 55th Ave., Dorval QC,
H9P 1G9 Canada
Tel.: 1-800-661-5850
Fax: (514) 633-5485
Flies charters to Nunavut from La Grande Rivière, Povungnituk and Kuujjuaq with a Twin Otter and HS748. Flies into northern Quebec from Montreal with a Dash 8.

Air Nunavut

(scheduled and charter services)
P.O. Box 1239, Iqaluit NT,
X0A 0H0 Canada
Tel.: (819) 979-2400
Fax: (819) 979-4318
Inuit-owned and based in Iqaluit. Charter flights cover Nunavut, western Northwest Territories, northern Quebec and Greenland. Operates twin-engine Super King Air 200, Navajo Chieftain and Navajo airplanes.

Air Tindi

(charter service)
P.O. Box 1693, Yellowknife NT,
X1A 2P3 Canada
Tel.: (403) 920-4177
Fax: (403) 920-2836
Flies charters anywhere in Nunavut with Husky, Cessna 185, Caravan, Beaver, Turbo Beaver, Turbo Otter, Twin Otter, King Air 200, King Air 90 and Dash 7.

Arctic Sunwest

(charter service)
P.O. Box 1807, Yellowknife NT,
X1A 2P4 Canada
Tel.: (403) 873-4464
Fax: (403) 920-2661
Flies charters anywhere in Nunavut with Beavers, Swearingen Metroliner II and Cessna 185.

Calm Air

(scheduled and charter services)
90 Thompson Drive, Thompson MB,
R8N 1Y8 Canada
Tel.: (204) 778-6471 or 1-800-839-2256
Fax: (204) 778-6954
E-mail: air@mts.net
Web site: www.calmair.com
Flies charters anywhere in Nunavut with three Saab 340Bplus, five HS748s, two Twin Otters and one Chieftain Navajo.

Canadian North, part of Canadian Airlines International

(scheduled service)
Tel.: 1-800-665-1177 or (416) 798-2211
Fax: (905) 612-2838
E-mail: comments@cdnair.ca
Web site: www.cdnair.ca

First Air

(scheduled and charter services)

Head office:
3257 Carp Rd., Carp ON,
X0A 1L0 Canada
Tel.: (613) 839-3340
Fax: (613) 839-5690
E-mail: reserv@firstair.ca
Web site: www.firstair.ca

For charter information:

Northern office:
P.O. Box 100, Yellowknife NT,
X1A 2N1 Canada
Tel.: (403) 873-4661
Fax: (403) 873-5209

Resolute office:
P.O. Box 150, Resolute NT,
X0A 0V0 Canada
Tel.: (819) 252-3981
Fax: (819) 252-3794

Iqaluit office:
P.O. Box 477, Iqaluit NT,
X0A 0H0 Canada
Tel.: (819) 979-5841
Fax: (819) 979-0746
Their charter aircraft, based in Yellowknife, Resolute, Iqaluit and Ottawa, fly anywhere in Nunavut. First Air operates four HS748s, 10 Twin Otters, one King Air, two Beavers, six 727s, one Gulf Stream and one Beech 99.

Keewatin Air
(charter service)
P.O. Box 38, Rankin Inlet NT,
X0C 0G0 Canada
Tel.: (819) 645-2992
Fax: (819) 645-2330

P.O. Box 126, Churchill MB,
R0B 0E0 Canada
Tel.: (204) 675-2086
Fax: (204) 675-2250
Based in Churchill and Rankin Inlet, their charters fly anywhere in Nunavut with twin-engine Merlins and King Air B200 pressurized turbine aircraft.

Kenn Borek Air
(scheduled and charter services)

Iqaluit office:
P.O. Box 1741, Iqaluit NT,
X0A 0H0 Canada
Tel.: (819) 979-0040
Fax: (819) 979-0132

Resolute office:
P.O. Box 210, Resolute NT,
X0A 0V0 Canada
Tel.: (819) 252-3845
Fax: (819) 252-3777
Flies charters anywhere in Nunavut with a Twin Otter; operates a King Air C90 and Beech 99 to communities with airstrips.

NWT Air
(scheduled and charter services)
Postal Service 9000, Yellowknife NT,
X1A 2R3 Canada
Tel.: 1-800-661-0789 or (403) 669-6606
Fax: (403) 669-6603
E-mail: nwtair@nwtair.ca
Web site: www.nwtair.ca
Charter service covers only Cambridge Bay, Rankin Inlet, Coral Harbour, Iqaluit, Resolute and Hall Beach with a Boeing 737 Combi.

Skyward Aviation Ltd.
(charter service)
P.O. Box 562, Rankin Inlet NT,
X0C 0G2 Canada
Tel.: 1-800-476-1873 or (819) 645-3200
Fax: (819) 645-3208
E-mail: skyward@arctic.ca
Based in Rankin Inlet, their charters fly anywhere in Nunavut with a wide range of single and multi-engine aircraft.

Travel Programs and Services

Elderhostel
Tel.: (617) 426-8056 or
(617) 426-5437 (TDD)
E-mail: webmstr@elderhostel.org
Web site: www.elderhostel.org

Emergency Services, Iqaluit
Advance booking of vans can be made through the Royal Canadian Legion.
Tel.: (819) 979-6215
Fax: (819) 979-4687

Norwheels Enterprises, Iqaluit
Tel.: (819) 979-0000 or (819) 979-6631
Fax: (819) 979-5804

Nunavut Tourism
P.O. Box 1450, Iqaluit NT,
X0A 0H0 Canada
Tel.: 1-800-491-7910 (for Canada and the United States)
Tel.: (819) 979-6551
Fax: (819) 979-1261
E-mail: nunatour@nunanet.com
Web site: www.nunatour.nt.ca

R. L. Hanson Construction Ltd., Iqaluit
Tel.: (819) 979-6004
Fax: (819) 979-4873

Tower Arctic, Iqaluit
Tel.: (819) 979-6465
Fax: (819) 979-6591

Travel Agencies
See the directory at the end of the "Planning Ahead" section.

The People

ARCHEOLOGY

by Sue Rowley

The cold, dry arctic climate of Nunavut often makes it a difficult place to live.

In fact, the Arctic was the last habitable region in the world occupied by people. However, this environment also makes Nunavut an archeologist's dream. Unlike most areas, where the remains of human occupation (sites) are quickly covered by vegetation and soil, in Nunavut they are often visible right on the surface. Also, because of the cold, dry climate, tools of antler, ivory and bone can be remarkably well preserved.

As you explore, please remember that these sites and artifacts are part of Nunavut's cultural heritage. They are fragile and irreplaceable. Nothing must be moved. Under the Nunavut Land Claims Agreement, every archeological artifact is owned jointly by the Inuit Heritage Trust (for the people of Nunavut) and by the government of Canada (for the people of Canada). It is illegal to buy, sell or remove archeological artifacts.

Research indicates Nunavut has been occupied continuously for more than 4,000 years (small pockets of the Kivalliq Region were occupied sporadically by Indian groups beginning 8,000 years ago). Archeologists divide Nunavut's inhabitants into two distinct but physically related groups: the Paleoeskimo people from at least 4,000 to 700 years ago; and the Neoeskimo people who entered Nunavut some 1,000 years ago.

The Paleoeskimo People

The Paleoeskimos emigrated from the west (Alaska) in small groups consisting of only a few families. Archeologists separate these original migrants into two groups: Pre-Dorset (in southern Nunavut) and Independence I (in northern Nunavut).

Pre-Dorset/Independence I people probably lived year-round in skin tents. Single walled in summer, in winter the walls were most likely doubled. A layer of heather or willow may have been placed between the skin layers and an exterior layer of snow added for extra insulation. Fires provided heat and soapstone oil lamps gave light.

These people wore skin clothing and made tools from bones, antlers, ivory, skins and rocks. They travelled mostly by foot, although they did have a few dogs and a small single-person boat similar to a *qajaq* (kayak). All animals except the massive bowhead whales were hunted.

Through time, the Paleoeskimo people adapted to minor fluctuations in climate, ice conditions, and resource availability. Then, around 2,700 years ago, the Nunavut climate became significantly cooler and the Paleoeskimo lifestyle underwent a period of rapid transition. The changes that occurred were so dramatic archeologists refer to these people by a different name: the Dorset culture.

At the beginning of the Dorset period several useful items of technology mysteriously disappeared, including the bow and arrow and the bowdrill. Dogs also disappeared.

New tools appeared, hunting techniques were modified and dwelling forms changed. Archeologists suggest that snowhouses were first built by the Dorset people as the earliest known snow knives are found in sites from this time period. The Dorset people also had a rich artistic tradition, carving miniature artistic masterpieces from ivory and antler for ceremonial and decorative use.

Despite the lack of dogs and little evidence they used large boats, the Dorset people travelled and traded materials over long distances. Copper from the Kugluktuk area and meteoric iron from northern Greenland have been recovered from Late Dorset sites in eastern Nunavut.

The Neoeskimos

About 1,000 years ago, life again changed dramatically in Nunavut, this time when the climate grew warmer and a new group of people emigrated from northern Alaska. These people were bowhead whale hunters. They had large *umiat* (skin-covered boats capable of carrying several families) and *qamutiit* (sleds) pulled by dogteams. They could cover distances at speeds unimaginable to Dorset people. Archeologists refer to these migrants as the Thule, the first of two Neoeskimo subgroups. The second subgroup is referred to as the Historic Inuit.

There is little archeological evidence of contact between the Dorset people and the Thule people. However, Inuit oral history identifies the Tuniit or Tunijuat as the people who occupied Nunavut before their own ancestors arrived. The Tuniit were regarded as a peaceful and shy people distrustful of the new arrivals. Although there were intermarriages between the two groups, there were also fights, and the Tuniit removed themselves from areas occupied by the Thule. Sightings of the Tuniit became rarer and eventually the Tuniit disappeared.

The Thule migrants brought a highly structured society with them based on the leadership of the whale boat captain. With time, their dependence on bowheads decreased. They adapted to regional variations in resource availability and modified their social organization accordingly. Some moved into the interior of the Kivalliq Region, becoming largely dependent on caribou. Others lived on the coast, hunting mostly marine mammals.

The Neoeskimo lifestyle was forever altered by the arrival of European explorers, traders, and whalers. The Historic Inuit period began with the voyages of Martin Frobisher to Baffin Island in the 1570s. Sporadic contact after this time period had little impact on Inuit culture. Then, in the 1820s, Europeans and Americans began whaling in eastern Nunavut. This whaling depleted bowhead stocks, concentrated Inuit into areas around whalers, and introduced both devastating diseases and new materials to Inuit society. This is the beginning of the modern period, a time marked by many rapid changes in material culture, religion, and social organization.

Archeological Sites

Nunavut is rife with evidence of human occupation, although many of these structures are difficult to date. Some of the most common features are *inuksuit* (rock cairns). These had many functions. The one on the horizon may be a route marker between two camping spots. Another by the side of the lake indicates where to find fish. A lone, long rock marks a nearby food cache. A row of inuksuit was used for driving caribou towards a river crossing or towards a group of hiding hunters.

Look closely at that pile of rocks at your feet. Is there a black stain on the rocks? Is there lichen growing on them? Are animal bones visible? If so, then this pile of rocks may be an old cache where hunters stored food.

On high ground you may come across rock graves. The deceased's belongings were often placed on or nearby the grave. Resist the temptation to touch these objects. Please treat graves with special respect.

You may also notice small rock boxes, *pullati*, that were used to trap foxes. The fox entered the trap to retrieve the bait and a rock or piece of ice dropped, blocking the entrance. Strange rock formations that look like stone igloos are *ullisauti*, tower fox traps. Bait was placed atop the trap and the fox would fall inside. Very large tower traps were even used for hunting polar bears.

Camp Sites

Camp sites are the places where people lived. By careful observation you can begin to determine both the time period and the season of occupation. In addition to the remains of homes, you may also see caches, outdoor fireplaces, box traps and inuksuit. Boys sat in rock outlines of *qajait* (kayaks) pretending to paddle and hunt. Girls built models of snowhouses and tents out of rocks to play house. There are many other interesting features to discover.

Both summer and winter Paleoeskimo camp sites consist of tent rings. The earliest Paleoeskimo dwellings were oval. Later Dorset dwellings vary in outline, but were frequently oval or rectangular. Oftentimes, all that remains of a Paleoeskimo dwelling is a few rocks, a small vegetated patch, or a slight depression along a beach ridge.

In contrast, Neoeskimo camp sites are more varied. Camps occupied in summer contain circular and oval tent rings. These are often bisected by a line of rocks separating the living area from the sleeping area.

Late fall/winter camps were often large. Today these sites are characterized by areas of lush vegetation and what appear at first to be large mounds. These mounds are actually semi-subterranean houses, constructed of whalebones, rocks and sod. Inside are sleeping platforms elevated for warmth. A layer of gravel, and then a mattress of heather, willow, or moss topped by heavy skins were placed on these platforms to provide insulation from both cold and rising damp. People slept on these beds in caribou skin sleeping bags. Soapstone lamps provided heat and light. When occupied, these houses were roofed with a skin cover supported by whalebone rafters. Sometimes heather or willow was sandwiched between two skin covers as insulation. This roof was held in place with rocks, sod and snow.

In winter and early spring, many Thule and Historic Inuit lived in snowhouses. Most were built on the sea ice but some were constructed on land and these can sometimes be identified. Snowhouse dwellers often threw the remains of their meals and the burnt blubber from their lamps just outside the door. This detritus left a semicircle of bones and blubber-blackened ground — all that is left of the long since melted snowhouse.

HISTORY

by Kenn Harper

In 1999 Canada's newest territory will become a reality. Yet it already has a history, rich and colorful.

It is the history of the Inuit who originally inhabited this land, by turns rich and sparse, and of the *qallunaat* who arrived in their changing quests — for a sea route westward, for whales, for furs and other natural resources, and finally to stay. It is a history of culture contact and cultural conflict. It is the history of the three regions of Nunavut.

Baffin Region

Historians identify the Baffin coast with Helluland of the Norse sagas and there may have been sporadic contacts between Norse and Inuit. But the recorded history of Baffin Island began in 1576 when Martin Frobisher, on an expedition in search of a Northwest Passage, discovered what he thought was gold in the bay that bears his name. The ore was worthless and Frobisher's encounters with the Inuit were not friendly. He seized four Inuit in 1576 and 1577 and took them to England where they quickly died. In 1585, John Davis, also in search of the Northwest Passage, explored Cumberland Sound; unlike Frobisher, his relations with Inuit were cordial.

Henry Hudson, in 1610, followed the south coast of Baffin Island into Hudson Bay, and five years later, William Baffin and Robert Bylot mapped that coast. But Baffin Island itself was, at best, only a landmark and, at worst, an obstacle in the path of those searching for a Northwest Passage. Its coastline remained largely unexplored.

In 1616 Baffin and Bylot sailed north as far as Smith Sound and discovered the entrances to Lancaster and Jones sounds. Returning south, they mapped a good deal of the Baffin coast, but after this voyage, northern Baffin Island was ignored for two centuries.

In the early 19th century, the search for a Northwest Passage came in vogue again. John Ross entered Lancaster Sound in 1818 and concluded erroneously that it was a bay rather than a strait. The next year his second-in-command, Lieutenant William Edward Parry, travelled through Lancaster Sound; the following summer he discovered the entrances to Admiralty and Navy Board inlets. In 1821, under Admiralty orders, Parry passed two winters exploring and mapping in the Igloolik area, and established good relations with the Inuit.

In 1845 John Franklin, commanding a large expedition in search of the passage, sailed through Lancaster Sound and into oblivion. His failure to return ushered in a new era in Arctic exploration, that of the Franklin searches. It lasted until 1880 but, again, explorers generally considered Baffin Island an obstacle. One notable exception was Charles Francis Hall, who explored Frobisher Bay from 1860 to 1862. Hall was one of the first to use Inuit clothing and travel methods. His Inuit friends, Tookoolito and her husband Ebierbing, accompanied him as interpreters and assistants for over a decade.

While the Franklin searches were under way, the last migration of Inuit from Canada to Greenland was also taking place. The shaman Qillaq (known later in Greenland as Qitdlarssuaq) led a group of Inuit from the Pond Inlet area to northwestern Greenland in the 1850s and 1860s, in search of new land and perhaps to avoid retribution for murders he had committed. Descendants of this group live there today.

British whalers reached northern Baffin Island by 1817, in their hunt for the bowhead whale, prized for its oil and baleen, which was used in corset stays, buggy whips, and other products requiring elasticity and flexibility. In 1840 William Penny, a whaling master from Peterhead, Scotland, with the help of a young Inuk, Eenoolooapik, rediscovered the entrance to Cumberland Sound, lost since Davis last entered it over two centuries earlier; it proved to be rich in bowhead whales. Its rediscovery marked a turning point in Baffin Island whaling. Whalers began wintering in Cumberland Sound in the 1850s to get an early start on whaling the following spring. American and Scottish companies established shore stations at Kekerten Island on the north shore of the sound and at Blacklead Island on its southern coast. The Americans sold their stations to the Scots in 1894, the same year that Reverend Edmund Peck established an Anglican mission at Blacklead. The mission remained open until 1926, by which time whaling had ended. A shore whaling station was also established by Scots at Albert Harbour near Pond Inlet in 1903. Everywhere, whaling had a profound impact on Inuit; it changed settlement patterns and provided Inuit with metal, tools, guns and whaleboats.

By the turn of the century, bowhead whale stocks were severely depleted and whaling had evolved into what was known as free trading. Small trading companies, all British, bartered with Inuit from shore stations or ships that called in summer. From 1900 until 1913 a Dundee company also operated a mica mine near Lake Harbour (now Kimmirut). In 1912 three expeditions, two Canadian and one from Newfoundland (then not part of Canada), visited Pond Inlet in search of gold. Each party subsequently returned to open a trading post. The Sabellum Company operated sporadically in southern Baffin from 1911 until 1926, using native traders and a small ship that arrived from Scotland in the summers. The only white employee of the company, Hector Pitchforth, died in 1924 at his lonely post near Clyde River.

Scientific research played a major role in Baffin history. In 1882–83 a German meteorological expedition overwintered at Sermilik Bay in Cumberland Sound as part of the International Polar Year. The following year the pioneer geographer and ethnographer, Franz Boas, passed one winter in the sound; the extensive report that he published, *The Central Eskimo,* was the first major ethnographic study of Canadian Inuit. In 1909, Bernhard Hantzsch, an ornithologist, travelled with Inuit to Foxe Basin, where he died in 1911, probably of trichinosis. The geologist, prospector and filmmaker, Robert Flaherty, overwintered at Amadjuak Bay in 1913–14. (His film, *Nanook of the North,* made in northern Quebec, is an ethnographic classic.) Between 1921 and 1924 Knud Rasmussen and his Fifth Thule Expedition conducted ethnographic research in the Igloolik area, and Peter Freuchen and Therkel Mathiassen explored much of northern Baffin Island, Freuchen accompanied by the Greenlander

Nasaitdlorssuarssuk and the Baffinlander Mala. Inland southern Baffin Island was explored and mapped by Burwash, Soper, Weeks and Haycock in the 1920s. Between 1936 and 1940 the British-Canadian Arctic Expedition completed most of the geographical investigation of Foxe Basin.

The Arctic Islands had been transferred from Britain to Canada in 1880, but it was not until 1897, when William Wakeham erected a cairn at Kekerten, that Canada took any active interest in exerting its sovereignty. In 1903 an official expedition under A. P. Low visited the High Arctic and Cumberland Sound. Between 1906 and 1911 the Canadian government dispatched Joseph Bernier on three official voyages to the High Arctic, to show the flag and collect Customs duties from whalers.

Canada became increasingly concerned over the activities of foreigners in the High Arctic — the Norwegian Sverdrup from 1898 to 1902, Robert Peary on his many attempts on the North Pole, Donald MacMillan's Crocker Land Expedition, and Rasmussen's interest in the Arctic Islands. Its response to these perceived threats was to establish Royal Canadian Mounted Police posts in the High Arctic. Pond Inlet was opened in 1921, and Craig Harbour on Ellesmere Island the following year. Dundas Harbour opened in 1924, Bache Peninsula in 1926, and Lake Harbour in 1927.

The Hudson's Bay Co. established its first post on Baffin Island at Lake Harbour in 1911. Cape Dorset was opened in 1913, Pangnirtung and Pond Inlet in 1921, Clyde River two years later and Arctic Bay in 1926. The Bay provided a more reliable supply of goods to hunters than had the earlier free traders, whom they displaced. The Bay trade was for fox pelts, later shifting to sealskins. In recent years, since the decline in the sealskin market, the trading posts have been transformed into modern department stores.

The Second World War and the Cold War which followed it forcibly opened the Canadian Arctic. The United States Air Force built an airfield at Frobisher Bay (now Iqaluit) during the war to handle aircraft transporting war materials to Europe. In 1955, construction began on the Distant Early Warning (DEW) Line, a joint project of Canada and the United States to create an early-warning radar chain across the Arctic to warn of any Soviet incursions. With this, Iqaluit became the supply and administrative centre for the Baffin Region. A weather station was established at Resolute in 1947, and in the early 1950s Inuit were relocated from northern Quebec to Resolute and Grise Fiord. In the late 1950s and the 1960s federal schools were built in most communities. A mammoth housing program was undertaken in the mid-1960s, and Inuit in general abandoned traditional camp life as a permanent lifestyle.

Keewatin Region

In 1610, in search of a Northwest Passage, Henry Hudson explored what others had thought was a gulf between Baffin Island and Labrador. Following its shores, Hudson reached the great inland sea that bears his name. Other explorers followed and the Hudson's Bay Co. established a fur trading post at Churchill in 1717, to open trade with Indians farther west. Inevitably, this led to contacts with Inuit in the Keewatin.

In 1719 James Knight's expedition in search of the elusive Northwest Passage disappeared north of Churchill. Nothing was known of its fate for almost 50 years until the remains of a house and two ships were found at Marble Island, near Rankin Inlet. The crew had perished of scurvy and starvation, despite the efforts of local Inuit to keep them alive.

As in Baffin, so in Keewatin, the whaling industry had a major impact on the lives of Inuit in the mid-19th century, attracting many to live near the whaling stations, providing trade goods which made life easier, but also introducing diseases to which the Inuit had no immunity. The first whalers to visit Hudson Bay wintered at Depot Island in 1860, losing many men to scurvy, but securing a fortune in baleen. In the remainder of that decade, over 40 American whaling voyages went to the Keewatin coast. The three most popular wintering sites for whalers were Repulse Bay, Depot Island and Cape Fullerton, and Marble Island, a place of legendary importance to the Inuit; when they visit they crawl the first few feet onto the island out of respect for an old woman whose spirit is said to reside there.

After 1870, the industry declined rapidly. As elsewhere, the whalers diversified into trading for "scraps" — whaler jargon for furs, skins, and ivory — and even mining. Scholars estimate that there were 146 whaling voyages to Hudson Bay between 1860 and 1915; 105 of these voyages over-wintered, trading with and employing Inuit. Between 1899 and 1903 a Dundee firm operated a shore station on Southampton Island, manned by three Scots and Inuit relocated from Baffin Island. In 1903 the company sent its vessel, the *Ernest William*, to Repulse Bay where it acted as a floating station until 1910. The decline of whaling quickened after the turn of the century; the last whaler into Hudson Bay, the *A. T. Gifford*, burned and was lost with its entire crew in 1915.

The most famous American whaling captain in Hudson Bay was George Comer, who made six whaling and trading voyages there. Aside from running profitable trips, Comer was an untrained scientist who, under the tutelage of the anthropologist Boas, made important contributions in anthropology, natural history, cartography and exploration.

While whaling activities dominated the Keewatin coast, other forces were at work in the interior. In 1893 Joseph and James Tyrrell, employed by the Geological Survey of Canada to survey the Keewatin interior, travelled from Lake Athabasca to the Dubawnt River and from there to Chesterfield Inlet and along the coast to Churchill. The following year Joseph Tyrrell explored and mapped more of the southern interior of the Keewatin.

In 1899 the naturalist David Hanbury travelled from Churchill north to Chesterfield Inlet and via Baker Lake to Great Slave Lake, making important contributions in geology, anthropology and natural history. The following year, James W. Tyrrell explored some of the same area. In 1901 Hanbury made an epic journey, from Great Slave Lake to Chesterfield Inlet and Marble Island, returning to Baker Lake to winter with Inuit. The next spring, he travelled to the mouth of the Coppermine River, where he sought information from the Inuit on copper deposits. He made contributions in geology, natural history, meteorology and anthropology.

In 1903, the Canadian government, concerned about Canadian sovereignty and the unchecked activities of whalers in Hudson Bay, established the first Arctic detachment of the Royal Canadian Mounted Police at

Fullerton Harbour, north of Chesterfield Inlet, intending to gradually enforce Canadian laws and exert "supervision and control."

In the forested areas to the south, the Hudson's Bay Co. faced increased competition from rival traders. So after 1912 the company made a concerted effort to move north and promote white fox trapping among the Inuit. They opened a post at Chesterfield Inlet in 1912 and an inland post at Ennadai shortly thereafter. In 1916 a post was opened on the south side of Baker Lake and another one at Repulse Bay, at Arviat (then known as Eskimo Point) in 1921, and at Southampton Island in 1924.

Father Arsène Turquetil, an Oblate priest, established a Roman Catholic mission at Chesterfield Inlet in 1912. From there, Catholicism spread to Eskimo Point, Southampton Island, Baker Lake, and even to Baffin Island. The RCMP relocated its Fullerton post to Chesterfield Inlet in 1922. A doctor was resident there by 1929 and the Oblates built a hospital and established a Grey Nuns convent in 1931 and an old folk's home in 1938. In 1951 they built the first school in the eastern Arctic; from 1954 until 1969 they also operated a large residential school. In 1970 the present government of the Northwest Territories assumed responsibility for education; by that time most communities had their own schools. That, combined with the rise in importance of Rankin Inlet, contributed to the decline of Chesterfield Inlet.

The Anglican Church also established missions in the region. Luke Kidlapik, a catechist from Blacklead Island, started a mission at Coral Harbour, and Donald Marsh established one at Eskimo Point in 1926, two years after the Roman Catholics had established there. Both churches were established in Baker Lake in 1927.

Knud Rasmussen's Fifth Thule Expedition, in the region in the early 1920s, was of profound importance to our understanding of traditional Inuit culture. Pioneering studies in ethnology, archeology, linguistics, botany and zoology were conducted in the Keewatin and other regions. Rasmussen's and Kaj Birket-Smith's monographs on the culture of the Caribou Eskimos are classics of modern anthropology.

In 1955 a nickel mine was developed at Rankin Inlet, an area previously of little importance and never a major site of Inuit occupancy. North Rankin Nickel Mines operated until 1962 and became a major employer of Inuit, resulting in the most major population shift since the whaling days. In 1958, at the height of the mining operation, the federal government established a settlement at Itivia, half a mile from the mine, as a rehabilitation project for Inuit from the interior, whose living conditions had deteriorated with major shifts in caribou migration patterns. In the 1970s the government of the Northwest Territories moved its administration offices out of Churchill and made Rankin Inlet the administrative centre of the Keewatin Region, a role it holds to this day.

Kitikmeot Region

In 1770 and 1771 Samuel Hearne, with a Chipewyan guide, Matonabbee, travelled overland from Churchill to the Coppermine River, becoming the first white man to reach the Arctic Ocean. To his horror, his Indian companions massacred a group of Inuit, their traditional enemy, near the mouth of the Coppermine River at the site known since as Bloody Falls. Hearne's amazing trek proved that no Northwest Passage would be found from the low latitudes of Hudson Bay.

The Arctic coast was mapped between 1819 and 1846. Franklin mapped 900 kilometres of coastline east from the Coppermine River to Coronation Gulf; in 1826 Dr. John Richardson mapped from the Mackenzie River to the mouth of the Coppermine. The British government's objectives were to promote geographical exploration, scientific research, and to confirm its territorial claims. Mapping was continued by George Back in 1834, by Thomas Simpson and Peter Warren Dease from 1836 to 1839, and finally by Dr. John Rae in 1845–46.

Important sea expeditions were also carried out. In 1819 Parry sailed through Lancaster Sound to Melville Island where he wintered. Ten years later Captain John Ross, in the *Victory*, became icebound in Prince Regent Inlet and remained there for three years. He and his crew got on well with local Inuit who hunted with them, supplied them with food and taught them Inuit travel techniques.

In 1846 the ships of the Franklin expedition got caught in the ice northwest of King William Island. The crews abandoned the ships after 18 months and made a futile effort to reach the South; all 105 men died of starvation and scurvy. Beginning in 1847, numerous search expeditions visited the Arctic, producing a wealth of information on the area. In 1854 John Rae, having heard Inuit tell stories of the expedition's fate, took the news back to England. Countless books have been written on the Franklin story and the subsequent searches, and the fate of Franklin has passed into northern mythology.

In 1903 the Norwegian, Roald Amundsen, seeking to locate the North Magnetic Pole, passed two winters on King William Island in the harbor that he named Gjoa Haven after his vessel. The *Gjoa* reached Nome, Alaska, in 1906, becoming the first ship to complete the Northwest Passage.

The westernmost reaches of Nunavut were the last to be explored by non-Inuit. Whalers based at Herschel Island gradually extended their whaling grounds east, and one, a Dane named Christian Klengenberg, passed the winter of 1905–6 trading off Victoria Island. Between 1908 and 1912, Vilhjalmur Stefansson, intrigued by Klengenberg's stories of fair-complexioned Inuit on Victoria Island (later sensationalized by newspapers as the "Blond Eskimos") explored in the area. In 1913–18 Stefansson returned to Coronation Gulf and Victoria Island with a large multi-disciplinary scientific party on the Canadian Arctic Expedition. A New Zealand-born anthropologist, Diamond Jenness, accompanied this expedition and in 1922 produced a classic of northern ethnographic literature, *The Life of the Copper Eskimos*, which many scholars considered the best description of a single Inuit group.

Independent fur traders wasted no time in establishing posts in the central Arctic. Christian Klengenberg established a post near the mouth of the Coppermine River in 1916 and in 1919, another one on Victoria Island. In 1920 he wintered his schooner at Bathurst Inlet. His descendants today live in Kugluktuk (Coppermine) and Holman Island. Other traders gradually moved into the area overland from Great Bear Lake, and were soon followed by geologists and trappers.

In November of 1913, two Oblate priests, Jean-Baptiste Rouvière and Guillaume LeRoux, were murdered by Inuit near Coppermine. The crime, caused by misunderstanding on the part of the Inuit and insensitivity on the part of the priests, was investigated and two Inuit were taken to Edmonton in 1917 for trial. They were sentenced to life imprisonment at Fort Resolution, but were released in 1919. An inevitable result of this case was the establishment of new police posts and the undertaking of regular patrols in the region.

The Hudson's Bay Co. opened a post at Bernard Harbour in 1916, Cambridge Bay in 1921, and King William Island in 1923. The Coppermine post was established in 1927 and Bathurst Inlet in 1934. The latter closed in 1964 and the buildings are now a naturalists' tourist lodge. Pelly Bay is the only place in the region where the Hudson's Bay Co. never established a post. In 1935 Father Pierre Henry built a famous stone church there. The community remained very isolated until 1961, when a school was built.

As elsewhere, missionaries arrived at about the same time as the traders. An Anglican mission was established in Coppermine in 1928, and both Anglicans and Roman Catholics built churches in Cambridge Bay in the 1920s.

Knud Rasmussen of the Fifth Thule Expedition travelled through the area in 1923 and 1924 with his Greenlandic assistants, Miteq and Arnarulunnguaq. Rasmussen produced detailed ethnographic monographs on the Netsilik and Copper Eskimos.

Spence Bay (now Taloyoak) has a curious history. In 1934, the Hudson's Bay Co. moved Inuit from Cape Dorset, Pangnirtung and Pond Inlet to Dundas Harbour on Devon Island to trap foxes. Two years later, the post was abandoned and the Inuit were moved to Arctic Bay and from there to Fort Ross. That post proved difficult to resupply because of ice conditions and in 1947 it closed. Most of the Inuit relocated to Spence Bay.

As elsewhere in the Arctic, Inuit largely abandoned camp life and moved into communities in the 1960s in conjunction with government housing programs and the construction of schools. In 1981 the territorial government designated Cambridge Bay as the regional administrative centre, and the community has grown steadily since.

Toward Nunavut

In this decade, the Nunavut land claim has been settled and the *Nunavut Act*, proclaiming the advent of a new territory of Nunavut, passed. Inuit are a majority in their homeland. Today Inuit and qallunaat approach the millenium determined to create a vibrant new territory, aware of both its past and the promise of its future.

INUIT CULTURE

An age-old hunting and trapping lifestyle has created a culture among Inuit that is largely universal throughout the central and eastern Arctic, although regional differences sometimes exist. Here, three Inuit writers from different corners of Nunavut — Ann Meekitjuk Hanson of Iqaluit, Peter Ernerk of Rankin Inlet and Joe Otokiak of Cambridge Bay — describe their culture.

The Baffin Region

by Ann Meekitjuk Hanson

Inuit "culture" and Inuit "ways" are difficult to distinguish because we don't have different words for them in our language. We use the word *illiqusiq* to mean "ways and habits." Illiqusiq includes all aspects of the Inuit way of life: survival skills, games, clothing, arts, medicine, the language, weather, the land, the sea, the way people are brought up — in short, life itself. In English, when I see the word "culture," I think of piano, ballet, opera, dance, poetry, theatre and anything that involves entertainment. I use the word *isomainaqiijutiit* to describe this kind of "culture" because it means "things to make us relax when chores have been completed." I use the word *sviilaqujutiit* to describe culture in the sense of "making fun."

Cultural Change

Cultures change with the times and Inuit culture is no exception. My grandmother, Koovianatukulook, and grandfather, Makivik, grew up in southern Baffin Island. In their time they enjoyed strength games, wrestling contests, throat singing, drum dances, storytelling, and even learning Scottish dances. In the winter, the games and celebrations took place in a *qaggiq* (a giant snowhouse); in summer, they were held outdoors. The songs were created specially for different occasions and were verbally "copyrighted"; no one was allowed to use them unless they were properly introduced and rightfully credited to their creator. The songs could be about anything: hunting experiences, humorous times, starvation, children, poems, mythical beings, or predictions of the future.

Pauta Saila, a well-known artist, statesman and elder from Cape Dorset, once shared the following prediction song created by a shaman named Atsiluaq. According to Pauta, Atsiluaq was alive "when the world was new." Atsiluaq, along with Enusiarajuk (another famous Inuk), were young men several generations before the *qallunaat* ("white people") came to the North. At a huge gathering in a qaggiq, Atsiluaq took the drum and began to sway back and forth, beating the circular instrument with a thick, rounded baton. He closed his eyes and continued to beat the drum to and fro. His feet firmly on the hardened snow floor, he was getting used to the rhythm. Finally, he was attuned to the movements of the drum and baton as if they were no longer controlled by him. He began his new song:

Atsiluaq
Angakunirataugajapuq
Hoooo... Hoooo... Hoooo... Hoooo... Hoooo...

Kananilak, kingaluni
Sangani kanani
Takujaupat
Qalunatapik
Aupalutapik
Atsiluaqli
Angakunirataugajapuq
Hoooo... Hoooo... Hoooo... Hoooo... Hoooo...

When he finished the song, there was silence in the crowded dome; the people were in absolute disbelief. By this time Atsiluaq was steaming and bare from the waist up. There was a new word in the song that the people had not heard before, it was qallunatuq. When he sensed the people's disbelief, he sang the song again and again:

Atsiluaq, this man
He would be called a great shaman
Hoooo... Hoooo... Hoooo... Hoooo... Hoooo...
There, over there
The high mountain
In the front, over there
You will see
A lovely cloth
A lovely red shade
Atsiluaq, this man
He would be called a great shaman
Hoooo... Hoooo... Hoooo... Hoooo... Hoooo...

Atsiluaq was one of the last well-known shamans who saw into the future. He saw this lovely red cloth fluttering in the wind. He was telling his people that the qallunaat were coming and they will fly a flag that contains red shades. The Hudson's Bay Co. flag and the Canadian flag both contain red colors. Atsiluaq was right. Today, with proper credit to Atsiluaq, people sing the song that predicted the coming of the lovely red cloth!

In my mother and father Josie and Meekitjuk's time, there were hardly any celebrations or rituals because the Inuit way of life was entering a new era. My mother and father were learning the new dances and music that came from Scotland. The Scottish and American whalers introduced a new type of culture that would live side by side with our Inuit ways. My mother and many others learned to play lively tunes on the "squeeze box" (accordion). They also learned dances that involved many people, unlike the Inuit drum dance, which is done by one person in the middle.

Our leaders created new steps according to the music. One dance practised today imitates harp seals. It is a wonderful dance to see because it is so much like the way the harp seals actually move. Some of the dances have been named after their creators. Each community has a favorite dance. A dance can last at least an hour and an evening of dancing can extend well into the early morning hours. The squeeze box musicians are revered for their talent, endurance, and their ability to play without repeating a tune all night. In some communities our young people are trained to dance for audiences. They wear traditional costumes as part of their performance, and as a symbol of their pride.

Storytelling is a most important element in our culture because it saves and enriches our language. The stories are often accompanied by a song that describes events and helps explain the purpose of the story. The story of Kaujajuk, an orphan boy who was badly mistreated, is a good example. Kaujajuk slept among the dogs on the porch to keep warm.

He sang this song as he nestled by his dogs and looked at the moon:

Moon, up there
My brotherlike, up there
You give me a little bit of warmth,
The window has become bright,
Moon up there, you are the only source of light,
I am trying to dry my clothes,
It is unlikely, it is hopeless, it will not...

The moon was like a brother to Kaujajuk. He gained his strength from it. A man from the moon came down and made Kaujajuk very strong. The man whipped him until he grew and grew. Although the song sounds bleak and hopeless, Kaujajuk becomes a very strong and powerful man. There was one woman in the village who showed a little bit of kindness and he saves her to be his wife. This is just a synopsis of the legend; the full story of Kaujajuk is very long with a lot of adventure, and mythical beings, and more songs. We have kept these kinds of stories alive by encouraging our elders to keep telling them. They are told on the radio and television, in schools, and lately our writers have been documenting them in their books.

Baffin Island is brimming with talented people who keep our culture alive by singing, carving, drawing, writing, producing radio and television programs, and just being here.

Cultural events have been making a strong comeback recently. They help us mark important occasions with prominence and they satisfy our need for relevance in our homeland.

Food

Food is the connector to everything that surrounds our culture. Each celebration includes a huge feast. We believe food tastes better when it is shared with family, relatives, and many other people. In my grandfather Makivik's time, all types of food were cached on the land, ready for a celebration. Back then there were many ways to prepare the foods, including different types of sauces and dips. I know of three sauces that are very good: *aalu*, *misiraq*, and *nirukkaq*.

Aalu is made from choice parts of caribou or seal. Here is the recipe. Make sure the meat is very lean and clean. Cut it up in tiny pieces and put it in a bowl. Add a few drops of melted fat. Then add a few drops of blood. Add *uruniq* (ptarmigan intestine) to taste. Stir everything very friskily with your fingers until the volume doubles and the mixture turns fluffy. This is one of the most popular dips for all kinds of meat.

Misiraq is another dip that is made all over the North today. It is made from blubber. Cut up pieces of seal blubber, whale, or *udjuk* (square flipper seal), making sure not to include any meat. Put the blubber in a safe container with a perforated top. Store it in a cool place where it can be slowly aged away from heat. When it ages properly the liquid ends up clear, like a fine white wine. The aroma is delicious and never bitter. All kinds of meats can be dipped in misiraq.

The third dip is called nirukkaq. It requires special care. Nirukkaq is the contents of caribou stomach. Here is my Uncle Annowalk's recipe. The hunter, when butchering the caribou, carefully removes the stomach contents and puts them into a container. The contents are frozen until ready to be used. When the time comes, the contents are thawed and a process called *siingijaijuq* is begun. This involves cleaning the contents very carefully with kneading motions. Undesirables like pieces of grass, leaves, lichen or lumps are removed. When smooth, it is ready. Caribou meat is used for dipping.

Our food is much more than just frozen or raw meats and sauces. We also enjoy different types of dried fish and meats, such as caribou. A traditional caribou stew made on the land using blackberry bush also makes a delicious meal that has a woody taste and a very refreshing smell. We have also developed recipes for caribou and fish dishes prepared the "new" way with spices.

When we feast on a seal we follow the traditions of our ancestors. One particular feast is called *alupajaq*. The men are around the seal, and two or three of them cut up the animal in a particular way. The women are grouped together in another area several feet away. The men's conversation is audible to the women. They tell hunting stories, pleasant stories. The women are talking about the seal, how nice it is to be so blessed with plenty.

The meat is then passed from the men to the women. The choice parts of the seal are for the women only. The first parts to come are the upper flippers. Two women are responsible for cutting up pieces for everyone. It is considered rude to leave anyone out. Next, the heart is cut up in small slivers and passed around, followed by the liver. The upper spine is then passed to the women while the men take the lower half. The ribs are cut into equal parts, with the women taking the front ribs and the men eating from the back ribs.

Guests are careful not to eat up every part of the seal. They must leave some for their kind hosts, unless they are urged to take some home. Some guests leave as soon as they have eaten, even before washing up. They feel they must not take up too much space and over-stay their welcome. Appreciation is expressed more than once before leaving. The remaining guests help clean up everything.

Stories and pleasantries are exchanged. There is much laughter. This kind of feast rotates throughout the community, with each home taking a turn. In a community feast where everyone gathers in a public place, all food is donated by families that have something to give. In bigger communities, much of the food is provided by designated hunters.

Feasts are very special because we believe sharing food is an important part of our culture and is an important link with our heritage. We believe food makes friends out of strangers. When we eat together, we feel more harmonious. And food doubles its volume when it is shared.

Staying with an Inuit Family

When we have a guest in our home it is a great honor because it means we are accepted as we are. We feel needed and humble that our home is good enough for other people. This includes parents, relatives, friends, visitors, or anyone who needs a place to rest. There are just a few guidelines you should know before staying with an Inuit family because sometimes we take it for granted people already know what to expect.

First of all, you are very welcome even if no one tells you so. You must feel at home at all times. Do not knock at the door before entering. Make normal noise. We don't like it when people try to be too quiet, it seems like they are sneaking behind our back.

In earlier times we never needed to lock any doors or secure any personal belongings because everything was shared. Our elders told us stealing was a very bad thing to do. As children, we were told that if we took something we were not supposed to have when no one was at home, a big hand would appear and grab us. Communities had different superstitions to discourage stealing. Today, it is still like that in some communities. When we enter a house where no one is home, we simply make tea and wait. This is considered one of the ways to become part of the family. The host feels esteemed and valued for her or his generosity. In bigger communities, locking doors has become a new custom, but this doesn't mean you are not welcome when your hosts are not at home.

It is important to take part in the household. This does not mean you have to do chores or take over. When guests are willing to try our country food, the host feels pride. At first, the host might be shy to offer any country food for fear of rejection. Sometimes we think our food will not be accepted by our guests because it has blood in it or it does not look clean enough. When we are feasting on a seal, caribou, ptarmigan or any other country food, we hate to be stared at and we don't like it when people take pictures of us eating. We would rather have you eat with us, or try a small piece and swallow fast. Please don't express any "yucks" or other words of ridicule. When our guests take interest in our food fare, we feel we are sharing our culture. If you don't like the meat raw, just ask your host to cook it for you.

Your hosts may take you for a trip on the land in any season. Do what they do and say; they know best. When we are getting ready to go on the land, it is often hot and it is very tempting to leave dressed as we are, but we know it will be a lot colder out there on the sea or land. Help with the grub, camping equipment, and children as much as possible. Everyone is expected to help as much as they can, no matter how big or little. Your hosts are doing their best to make you feel welcome and important.

There are three age groups of hosts that you will probably meet. First, there are the more mature Inuit who speak only Inuktitut. They were born on the land and lived the "real" nomadic Inuit way of life that existed before today's community-based wage economy. We look to them as experts on hunting, weather, directions, astronomy, plants, beliefs, ethics and anything else that has to do with the Inuit world. Please respect them as we do.

Then there is the 30 to 40 age group, the first bilingual generation. These people were born when transitions to a new wage economy were taking place. People in this group know both the Inuit and white worlds and are comfortable with both. The memories of those who grew up on the land are held dearly because this generation is the link between life on the land and life in a settlement. They are called the "in the middle" crowd.

Thirdly, there are the younger people who are in their early and late twenties. Most of them were born in a hospital. They are modern in just about everything they do, yet the elders have taught them ancient values such as respect for the land, the sea, the animals, and the weather. They have been taught to be good to other people, to share what they can, and to expect less.

Our young people, who have been in school most of their lives, have spent much less time on the land and sea than their parents and grandparents had by their age. To save our language, they had to be taught Inuktitut in school. They have gone through a lot of public scrutiny because they have been told over and over that they are our future and that they must carry on our "Inukness." This has been discussed on radio and television, in newspapers, and even in land claim negotiations. Sometimes this age group has heard unpleasant comments such as: our young people are not Inuk enough anymore, they are forgetting our language, they don't know the land well enough, or they are breaking the law too often. But in reality we know that our young people are still as Inuk as we are. They can be your most interesting hosts because they have gone through a lot of history in a short time and still maintain their Inukness.

No matter what age they are, Inuit hosts are family-oriented. We like to show our family and relatives to our visitors. If you stay with a family, there might be grandparents, aunts, uncles, cousins, and adopted children in the household. Some older children and young people might be sent to stay with other relatives to make room for you. This is very normal and readily accepted because a guest is so important and everything must be done to make him or her feel at home. No one feels rejected or unwanted. The guest need not feel that she or he is separating the family.

We welcome visitors in our homes for several reasons: you are visiting because you are interested, you are sharing our lives, you are receiving knowledge and spreading knowledge, you are gathering memorable times, and above all, we enjoy your company.

Most of all, be yourself. You do not need to lower or heighten your normal standards. Your Inuit hosts are themselves. Talk in a normal voice. Some people talk louder to us and use "pigeon English." This is so embarrassing to us. We are not hard of hearing. We want to be treated as equal human beings. It has been our experience that some visitors expect us to be historic pieces. They expect us to always be smiling. Their romantic notion is that we still live in snowhouses and have been frozen in time. Some people have been disappointed to see the modern side of our life. But we are still Inuit — in our hearts, minds, body and soul. Enjoy your visit!

The Kivalliq Region

by Peter Ernerk

For beginners, let's get one thing clear! Although myth has it that there are 100 ways of saying the word "snow" in Inuktitut, there is in fact only one word for it: *aput*. When men and women kiss each other, Inuit do not consider it "rubbing noses"; it is a kiss, filled with compassion, love, caring, and romance. It is called *kunik* in the Inuktitut language. And Inuit have always called themselves *Inuit* — the people. The name Eskimo, a Cree Indian word that means "eaters of raw meat," is a derogatory term that is no longer used in Nunavut.

Malingnga (follow me), I have some spiritual thoughts that I want to share with you. It's about Inuit language and culture, but let me say it my way! You know that the land and snow speak to us often, especially when there are lots of caribou footprints on the snow, or on the sandy lakeshores and on the soft moss in summer.

Inuit always had unwritten social laws that were extremely important to daily life. Most of them still apply today. The Inuit identity is that of kindness, compassion, giving, caring, helping, concern for others rather than oneself, laughing and joking, discipline, endurance, common sense, and most of all, responsibility.

Inuit culture and language are inseparable. The Inuit culture is oral and it's been passed on since time immemorial. We Inuit have one language with regional dialectical differences. We live in complete harmony with our environment and take our land and sea for granted. Nature is there for us, and we will leave the environment in good condition for our children. What's there is for us to take but we never abuse the animals and we treat them with great respect! The environment has a language of its own. Every notable landscape, lake and river has a name. We name them for the way they are shaped; for example, *Iviangiqnalik* (like a breast), *Kuugjuaq* (big river) and *Inuksulik* (having *inuksuit*, the Inuit rock cairns shaped like humans).

We are subsistence hunters and gatherers, and thus have survived for many thousands of years. We hunt to live and clothe ourselves, we gather vegetation, such as berries and seaweed to supplement our diet during spring and summer. We share what we have with our fellow Inuit, and through sharing we survive.

While growing up in the Kivalliq Region in the Naujaat-Repulse Bay area, we lived in *Nattiligaarjuk* (the lake that has seals) most of the time. We used to travel by dogteam to Naujaat for Christmas and Easter to participate in festive celebrations or to trade our carvings and fox furs. In the spring, when the days got longer, we would travel for many miles, then stop for tea and frozen caribou meat or fish. My father, who lived the stone-age, would look at the next hilltop, so far away on the horizon that it looked bluish. In Inuktitut he would say, "Far away! It's not moving, it will be reached." We did indeed reach the hill, but very slowly. From that I took our Inuit culture to mean patience!

Inuit life is a seasonal cycle. We look back to the past to plan our future. We vision seasons. Let me begin with the main fall activities. Fall meant moving inland as far as possible in an attempt to reach caribou country. If it was several nights' sleep, it didn't matter — just as long as there was enough caribou for us to catch so that we had food for the winter and good clothing for the entire family.

Caribou hunting was not an easy task, but not impossible. On some days it was easy to spot an animal, and that was good. But most other times we had to walk for many, many miles before we spotted one or saw a track or two of a caribou. As custom would have it, my father at times used to carefully cut around a caribou footprint with his pocket knife and place it backwards in the same spot. "Let the caribou return!" he would exclaim. This type of spiritual expression was used only as a last resort.

When we did catch caribou, we cached the meat and preserved it for the winter. The fishing season was also good during the ice freeze, especially in October. We would fish for arctic char through the ice by making holes. After eating caribou meat all summer, it was also a welcome change to start eating fish.

Days got shorter in December, January and February and it meant winter. There was hardly any hunting or fishing, except for occasional caribou hunts. Being inside a small *iglu* for an extended period of time was lonesome and frustrating. Nevertheless, people played games and sang traditional Inuit songs. Inuit songs were composed by hunters telling their experiences, mostly of hardships. Traditional Inuit songs were both powerful and entertaining. The drum dancer would also beat his/her drum to accompany a traditional song. On the other hand, spiritual or shaman's songs are sung only at rituals. They were set aside for special purposes, the same way as Christians do.

With the arrival of longer days in March and April, in spring, it became necessary to hunt seals through seal holes on the ice. This was very difficult work as we had to wait for seals to come up. The other hunters had their dogs sniffing for the holes through the thick snow. Seal holes are normally on the east side of ice ridges because of the prevailing westerly winds.

When the hunter caught a seal, it meant that we would have fresh meat for ourselves and our dogs, a welcome event. It also meant that we would have light from the oil fat of a seal for our *qulliq* (a soapstone oil lamp in the shape of a half-moon, its carved-out hollow contains the fat and wick). I remember, when my father or brother-in-law would bring home a seal, it was my mother's responsibility to butcher the animal. Before she skinned the seal, however, she would put out a small piece of freshwater ice — a message to all the other seals swimming under the ice that they would not be thirsty. Inuit respected all animals and cruelty was not accepted.

After a bit of a breather for about a month, we began hunting seals again. When all the snow had melted on the ice we looked for young mature seals, called *nattiaviniit*. The Hudson's Bay Co. clerks used to call them "silver jars." We traded these seals mostly for their coats, and this allowed us to obtain economic gains. It must be remembered that all animals we hunted were used for food for humans, for clothing, and for dog food.

We welcomed June and July, summer, with great excitement! This was and still is because the snow had melted. The month of June is *manniit* ("egg") month and people are out gathering eggs and the lakes and rivers are opening up. Arctic char swim downstream and people catch fish once again. Migratory birds such as geese and ducks arrive. For most, it's a welcome change to the diet. Inuit also carefully cut up caribou meat for drying. Arctic char, carefully filleted and hung to dry, provides the stomach with variety.

You know, Inuit are extremely terrified of bugs. It's guaranteed that bugs arrive each spring and summer. They usually come in great numbers. Most children are terrified of bugs, especially *iguttat* — bumblebees. They seem to want to stick around unless a person runs away from them.

Inuit named their people after various parts of the body, or animals. Sometimes *iguttaq* (a bumblebee) is used as a proper name of a person, such as the case with my older sister. There is some spiritual connection to this particular incident. In 1982 when my uncle (my father's younger brother) and his wife were out fishing in June on the ice, an iguttaq flew around them persistently most of the day. I was vacationing in Quebec at the time and on that particular day an iguttaq was flying around me, also persistently. I didn't think much of it, but a day or so later I learned that my sister had died. Our daughter's name is Iguttaq, named after my sister.

After fishing at a stone weir in mid to late August and catching lots of arctic char, we have enough fish for the winter. It is time to move inland again to hunt caribou. At this time there is good fat on the caribou. Inuit are great ones for wanting fat from caribou. No wonder; fat has many uses. To begin with, it is a good supplement to the meat that we eat. During the time that I was living a primitive and nomadic life with my parents, when we would move inland and catch caribou with lots of fat, we used the fat as candles. First we would chew the fat well to get rid of all the blood and moisture. Then we would find a piece of material from a flour bag, normally, and use that as a wick. It would light our tent brightly when days got dark. We also used to mix the fat with berries we had picked (we called this concoction "mixed"), and that tasted good!

This was also the time of year when the hair on the caribou skin was good for clothing, not too thin and not too thick. In the old days, Inuit used to catch as many caribou as we could. Whether we saw a herd of five or 30, we used to try and shoot them all. Food was always so scarce in those days that we had to have enough for our family and dogs. In order to preserve the meat, we would cache it in late summer and pick it up in the winter.

Even though all-terrain vehicles and snowmobiles have taken over as our means of transportation, we still follow the same seasons.

A new season is coming. Consider coming with me to experience the Inuit language and culture. You never know, it may speak to you in its own words. *Tukisiviitt?* (Do you understand?)

The Kitikmeot Region

by Joe Otokiak

Like other regions of the circumpolar world, Inuit culture in the Kitikmeot Region has gone through a cultural shock over a very short period of time. Its culture comprises bits of the western arctic flavor from Holman (which won't become part of Nunavut) and Kugluktuk; Cambridge Bay, Umingmaktok and Bathurst Inlet in the central region; and Gjoa Haven, Taloyoak and Pelly Bay in the east. In the Kitikmeot, there may be slight variations in style and time in all aspects of Inuit life — physical, mental and spiritual.

About 40 to 50 years took Inuit from a nomadic way of life to more permanent settings, as small communities evolved with the coming of other cultures into the Arctic. Much of Inuit life flowed in sync with the seasons, harvesting game and necessities to ensure survival for the future. Families travelling with others made the pursuit of game safer, and the chances of success more attainable. Over the generations, knowledge of what game was accessible during a specific time of the year was passed on among Inuit. The pursuit of game during the various seasons is still followed to some extent today in less vigorous ways.

In earlier times, during the winter months, Inuit travelled to areas where caribou was plentiful, and to coastal areas for seal.

In the spring, Inuit headed for the rivers along the coast where they'd fish for arctic char and hunt migrating birds. Fish were caught by jigging through the ice along the edge of lakes and coastal waters; as the ice melted, natural holes were used. Seals could be caught as they gathered to feed on the fish coming down the river. Birds were snared as they nested — much like snaring rabbits. The bird would get caught around the neck as it attempted to fly when scared off the nest.

When spring harvesting was done, Inuit would travel inland to caribou crossings and hunt them by kayak and bow and arrow. Caribou could be herded to an area where the men readied themselves to pursue them with kayaks. The places were carefully chosen and surveyed to ensure a good hunt. Another tactic used involved *inukhoks* (spelled elsewhere in Nunavut as *inuksuit*). Inukhoks were raised to help guide the animals along a route to men behind blinds, waiting with bow and arrow.

When fall approached, Inuit returned to the coast to do more fishing and caribou hunting.

Early winter is spent mostly seal hunting. Seal blubber is used to provide heat and cooking fuel for the *kulik* (also spelled *qulliq*). There were also caches of seal blubber in skin sacks which could be used in times of hardship.

All members of the Inuit family, with the exception of babies, had a part in carrying out responsibilities, whether large or small, in day-to-day life.

Elders were revered for the wisdom they gained over the years; their word was the unwritten law.

The young were taught at an early age to listen and obey those older than them because they knew better. Inuit children were taught to treat others in a way that they themselves would like to be treated, with respect. They were told never to talk back to an older person who may be correcting them out of concern for their own good and safety. Sometimes this is not adhered to, and the child learns by her or his mistake. Children were seldom hit when being corrected; rather, they were spoken to with love and assurance that this was done in their best interest.

Every human being was treated as an equal, regardless of his or her physical condition. Necessities of life were shared with those less fortunate to ensure survival. Inuit cared for each other and family ties were strong. If a difficult situation occurred, both the immediate and extended family would support each other and help in any way they could to bring about a solution. Inuit in smaller communities tend to have stronger family and community ties than those in larger settings.

The spirit of the Inuit was always that of contentment, even through hardship. It's reflected in the saying "*ayoknakman*" (pronounced "ah-yook-nuk-mun," this means "it can't be helped"). Inuit are quick to accept natural occurrences in life and move on. They had a great respect for their fellow man, the environment, and every living creature used for their survival. One would dare not say, "I'm going to catch that game," even if it seemed certain that the chances of catching the game were high. The only comment was "*Agunahoakneakaga*" (pronounced "ah-guu-na-hwak-nia-kah-gah," this means "I'll try and catch it"). Successful hunters were not boastful or proud; simply grateful and very fortunate. Inuit would not allow wounded animals to suffer unnecessarily. They were pursued, caught, and killed as quickly as possible.

Inuit believed that people's spirits lived on after death. As Inuit passed away, newborn babies were named after them by their close relatives and were treated as if the deceased person's spirit occupied the child. Children named after respected elders, in particular, were raised with great care, love, and gentleness.

The environment was respected and kept in its natural state as much as possible for others to use. Disposed material, not eaten by scavengers, soon disintegrates back into the ground with the help of the elements. Inuit were very much aware of weather conditions and could forecast the following day's weather.

Most food did not require extensive preparation. It was eaten raw, frozen, dried, boiled to make broth and aged while sitting in caches and in the animal's own fat. Boiled caribou was often accompanied by *kayuk* (pronounced "ka-yuuk," this is the animal's blood stirred into the broth after the meat has been taken out to form a thick soup). It warmed those who ate it.

Food left to age in caches is an acquired taste for those not accustomed to such food. Inuit savor these delicacies, especially elders. One such delicacy is seal flippers aged in seal blubber. When the fur can easily be removed, this is the time to enjoy them. Food was covered with a certain moss and cooked on flat rocks in an open fire in the summer. Hot stones were placed inside caribou stomachs filled with blood to make instant pudding. Dried food was usually eaten with different animal fats, solid or liquid. Various parts of game were eaten raw as they were being prepared for future use. Country food is still the main diet of Inuit today. It's more nutritious and less expensive than store-bought food.

Many Inuit traditions are practised, utilizing both past and present techniques, but there needs to be more of it as Inuit move toward their new role in the government of Nunavut. Inuit survived by their wits for thousands of years and will continue to do so with the wisdom of elders helping to build a strong foundation for future generations.

This glimpse into Inuit culture in the Kitikmeot Region is a very small piece of the iceberg, so to say. As the "people from the other side" will tell you, welcome to *Gelinikmeot* (pronounced "gee-li-nik-mewt" with a hard g sound) country.

by Ann Meekitjuk Hanson, with contributions from Joe Otakiak

Inuktitut, the language of the Inuit, is alive and growing. It is widely used throughout the North, and Inuit from across the Arctic can understand one another.

Dialects and accents vary from region to region, but Inuktitut is a single language.

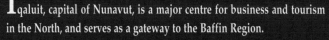

One of the first things a newcomer might notice is that a single word may be spelled many different ways. A white person is *qallunaaq, kabloona* — words that are spelled differently but sound roughly the same. The differences have come about because of our language's oral history. When a writing system was introduced for the first time more than 100 years ago, the words were written phonetically, and those phonetic versions varied from region to region. Today, Inuktitut is written in syllabics in the Baffin and Kivalliq regions, and in the eastern part of the Kitikmeot Region. In the western part of the Kitikmeot, it's written in Roman orthography. Since the mid-1970s, Inuit have made efforts to standardize Inuktitut so that the language becomes consistent throughout the circumpolar world. The "new orthography," the result of the standardization process, is gradually being used more, but the move to standardize Inuktitut is still ongoing.

In the Kitikmeot, the name given to the language of Inuit is "Innuinaqtun." Some phrases used in the Baffin and Kivalliq regions of Nunavut are fairly similar in sound and are recognizable to people living in western Nunavut. There are some similarities among words spoken in Gjoa Haven, Taloyoak and Pelly Bay and those spoken in the Baffin and Kivalliq regions, but the language structures are quite different.

A large portion of the population in the far western reaches of Nunavut speak English and are attempting to strengthen their Innuinaqtun in all areas, from schools to workplaces. As you move eastward, the Inuit language becomes more commonly used by Inuit. One difference visitors will notice in western Nunavut is that where Inuit from the eastern part of Nunavut use the "s" and "sh" sound, it is usually an "h" sound in the west. "Siksik," the ground squirrel, becomes "hikhik" in the western part of the Kitikmeot.

When she was a little girl, my great-grandmother Kalajuk's Inuktitut was pure, without a trace of any other tongue. Her language evolved out of nature and daily living. This was in the middle 1800s.

When the whalers came, they brought with them many things that would alter this way of life, including a new language. Words like tea, sugar, flour, waistcoat and paper became everyday Inuktitut words, but their pronunciation was distinctly Inuk: "tea" became *ti,* "sugar" was pronounced *sukaq, palaugaaq* meant "flour," "waistcoat" became *uasikuaq*, and "paper" was pronounced *paipaq*.

When the clergy came, more new words and phrases were added to our language. The people were taught a new way to communicate, called syllabics, which was the first "written Inuktitut." The syllabics system was developed by Rev. Thomas Evans for the Cree and was adapted for the Inuit by Anglican missionary Edmund Peck. Its symbols are fashioned after secretarial shorthand. My great-grandmother learned to read and write syllabics, but she had to do it mostly from memory because there was no paper!

When the Hudson's Bay Co. came, more terms and phrases were invented, all in Inuktitut. At the same time, my people were teaching the ministers and clerks Inuktitut, which secured our language. When the RCMP came, they too brought new words and expressions that broadened our language. They also had to learn Inuktitut.

I was born in 1946, at a time when my parents still depended on the land and sea for survival. Like generations before them, they were saving the language by oral traditions. I was brought up completely in Inuktitut but my parents used items for which no real Inuktitut word existed, like primus stoves, cups, teakettles, spoons, beads, plastic combs, rifles, tobacco, squeeze boxes, and a few other things. Words for all of these items were invented in our language.

I was 11 years old when I started formal classroom instruction. I learned by translating everything into Inuktitut. When I could not translate what I learned, it was very hard to understand. For example, when I learned about cows, horses and pigs, I couldn't understand why they didn't run away from the people. All the animals I had ever seen always ran away from people. The teacher did not explain that these were domesticated animals. A word quickly came to mind: *nujuataittut*, which means "animals that do not run away." After that, new things were easier to understand, but I had to form my own language to help me learn.

In 1964 I graduated from a secretarial school in Toronto. At the time I was one of very few fully bilingual Inuit. My services as an interpreter were in great demand by government departments. By this time all school-age children were receiving formal education in English only.

In 1965 I became aware that I did not know enough of my own culture — I mean the legends, songs, dances, myths, beliefs and histories of my people. I was working at the CBC at the time and my cousin Jonah Kelly and I started to tape the stories of our elders and air them on the radio. This was a new way to preserve both Inuktitut and our legends for all time. I like to think that we helped save a huge chunk of our language by taping the words of our people.

We have a huge language to keep alive. I say this because Inuktitut has the ability to grow without limit because it is a very descriptive language.

It is a good feeling to be able to carry on a conversation in Inuktitut without using a single word of English or any other language. That is why most imported items and concepts are given descriptive names and terms. I believe this method has enriched our language and made it grow.

The word *asujutidli* has been used in recent times as a greeting. Inuit traditionally didn't say anything when they greeted each other, preferring to communicate with a warm smile and a handshake. Conversation would begin after proper introductions, but words or expressions like "hello" or "how are you?" were historically uncommon in Inuktitut.

Asujutidli cannot be translated into a single English word; its closest meaning is something like: "it is truly you" or "you are truly you."

To say "I am from," first name your country or city and end it with *miungujunga*. For example: England-miungujunga or Toronto-miungujunga.

I want to learn to speak Inuktitut: *Inuktitut Uqariurumavunga*.

Uvanga means "Me," so to say "my name is," first say uvanga then say your name. For example: Uvanga Ann or Uvanga Peter. To say the same thing in the western part of Nunavut, you would say guyuga after the name: Ann-guyuga.

In order to learn useful Inuit phrases that might come in handy when travelling in the North, you should start by practising common Inuktitut sounds, like those listed in the facing sidebar.

COMMON INUKTITUT SOUNDS

i	(ee, long e)	**u**	(oo, u — long u)	**aa**	(ah)
pi	(pe)	**pu**	(poo)	**pa**	(pa)
ti	(tee)	**tu**	(too)	**ta**	(ta)
ki	(key)	**ku**	(koo)	**ka**	(ka)
gi	(ghee)	**gu**	(goo)	**ga**	(ga)
mi	(me)	**mu**	(moo)	**ma**	(ma)
ni	(nee)	**nu**	(noo)	**na**	(na)
si	(see)	**su**	(soo)	**sa**	(sa)
li	(lee)	**lu**	(loo)	**la**	(la)
ji	(jee)	**ju**	(joo)	**ja**	(ja)
vi	(vee)	**vu**	(voo)	**va**	(va)
ri	(re)	**ru**	(rue)	**ra**	(ra)

Guttural: **qi qu qa**

Nasal: **ngi ngu ngaa**

USEFUL PHRASES

English	Inuktitut	Pronunciation
How are you?	Qanuipit?	"Ka-nwee-peet?"
I am fine	Qanuingittunga	"Ka-nweeng-ni-toon-ga"
What is your name?	Kinauvit?	"Kee-nau-veet?"
I want to take your picture	Ajjiliurumajagit	"A-jee-lee-oo-roo-maa-ya-geet"
Thank you	Qujannamiik	"Coo-yan-na-mee-ick"
That's all	Taima	"Tie-ma"
You are welcome	Ilaali	"Ee-lah-lih"
I am hungry	Kaaktunga	"Kak-toon-ga"
I am cold	Qiuliqtunga	"K-o-lick-toon-ga"
It is cold (weather)	Ikkiirnaqtuq	"Ick-eang-nak-took"
Will the weather be good today?	Silasianguniapa?	"See-la-see-aang-un-ee-aa-pa?"
Help!	Ikajunga!	"Ick-a-yung-ga!"
Did you make this?	Una sanajait?	"Oo-na san-ai-yate?"
How much is it?	Qatsituqqa?	"Cat-see-to-kaw?"
How many?	Qatsiit?	"Cat-seet?"
Yes	Ii	"Ee"
No	Aakka or aagaa	"Ah-ka" or "Ah-ga"
Maybe (I don't really know)	Atsuuli or aamai	"At-soo-lee" or "Ah-my"
Expensive	Akitujuq	"Ah-kee-too-yuk"
I have to use the washroom	Quisuktunga	"Kwee-soot-toon-ga"
I am sick	Aaniajunga	"Ah-nee-a-yung-ga"
What is it?	Una suna?	"Oo-na soo-na?"
Where is the hotel?	Nau taima sinitavik?	"Naowk tie-ma see-nee-ta-vik?"
Where is the store?	Nau taima niuvivik?	"Naowk tie-ma new-vee-vik?"
Where is the church?	Nau taima tuksiavik?	"Naowk tie-ma took-see-aa-vik?"
Where am I?	Namiippunga?	"Nah-me-poon-ga?"
I want to go by dogteam	Qimuksikkuurumavunga	"Kim-mook-sick-koo-roo-mah-voon-ga"
I want to phone	Uqaalagumajunga	"Oo-ka-la-goo-ma-jung-ga"
I want to go fishing	Iqalliarumajunga	"Ee-ka-lee-aa-roo-ma-jung-ga"
Goodbye (to an individual)	Tavvauvutit	"Tah-vow-voo-teet"
Goodbye to you all	Tavvauvusi	"Tah-vow-voo-see"

LIFE IN NUNAVUT TODAY

by Ann Meekitjuk Hanson

Two days out of Iqaluit, the land looked like a black thread stretching out on the sea as we children scanned the horizon, urged by the adults to be the first to see shiny objects twinkling up to the skies.

To an 11-year-old, there was no name for these objects, yet they held a future that would alter my life forever.

In the summer of 1957, we were travelling from Kimmirut to Iqaluit by a whaling boat that held three families and several dogs. My Uncle Annowalk wanted to be closer to his wife and my mother who were in a Hamilton, Ontario, sanatorium with tuberculosis. In 1957, Iqaluit had airplanes once in a while. In Kimmirut we had air drops at Christmas. My uncle thought he might get a letter and that his letters might get to his wife. My uncle was looking for better ways to communicate, taking advantage of technology available at the time.

While we waited for my aunt and mother to come home from a place I did not know, I attended school for the first time. It was exciting, enticing and wondrous to learn another language! It was even more exciting to convert that new knowledge into my learned ways, for if I could not translate or interpret the newly gained knowledge, it was harder to learn and believe.

I remember families moving in from Pangnirtung and Cape Dorset. They came by dogteams in winter and by boats in summer. We were meeting relatives we had never met. When we were not blood relatives, we found a way to be related, by marriage or extended families.

In Kimmirut we had lived in small groups with one leader. In Iqaluit, there were many people with not one leader, but many! There were government administrators, the Hudson's Bay Co. manager, teachers, social workers, church ministers, Inuit leaders and doctors. Who were we to follow?

With many people in a whirl of new activities, employment, education, meetings, parties and travelling, it was easy to go unnoticed and stray away from generations-old traditions. We were learning English in school by day and hanging out in coffee shops, dancehalls, stores, pool halls, theatres, or visiting teachers at night. We talked about Elvis Presley, Bob Hope, Johnny Cash, Paul Anka, Sal Maneo, Audie Murphy. All this was painful for our elders because we were not speaking our language.

The traditional language in hunting terms, garment making, food, family terms, weather, land and seascapes, animals, shelter making, crafts making, was not being used anymore. Storytelling, drum dancing, singing old songs and poems were no longer practised. They were not forgotten but put aside while we were busy learning new things.

In the early 1970s I became aware I did not know enough about my language, culture, survival skills, garments, food and family anymore. I learned too, that I was not the only one.

Many young Inuit who'd gone away to residential schools had a difficult time readjusting to the Inuit way of life with their families. Children as young as five years old were taken from their families. They went to Chesterfield Inlet and later to Churchill and Yellowknife. Once they entered school, they were not allowed to speak Inuktitut. They were punished if they uttered one word of Inuktitut. I once had a wallet thrown at me. It missed my face by a few inches! Children did not come home until the next summer. I was away for over three years without ever coming home. Grandparents, parents, older siblings and aunts and uncles were strangers when we came home. We were strange to them too because we dressed differently, had haircuts, squeaky clean shirts and hair, a different language and altered manners. From that time on we, without knowing it, were in mourning for the loss of language, culture, skills and spirituality that is connected to nature. We turned to alcohol, drugs, substance abuse and self-destruction.

To learn and regain our language, culture, skills and arts, we formed education committees, alcohol and drug education groups, hunters and trappers organizations, social committees and other self-help groups that would help us to retrieve what we nearly lost. Today we may not use the traditional terms our fathers used when hunting, navigating, or creating new tools, but we have created new terms for the technology that is available to us. Our language is flourishing because we create names for computers, fax, satellite, telephone, television, HIV, primus stove, jet, hockey, Internet, religion, and other things. Our young people are taught in Inuktitut in our schools.

When we lived in our *ukkialivik* — a place to spend late autumn together with several families, usually relatives — activities were predictable and controllable. Social order was manageable. Everyone had a chore to do according to their talents. My mother knew how to manage the social order, deliver her neighbor's baby, clothe her family, care for the sick and tend the dying. My father hunted for his family and the village. Women and young people hunted the smaller game — ptarmigan, rabbit — fished, picked berries, and gathered berry bushes for insulation and bedding.

The children, the young people, and especially the orphaned were lectured on values, families, futures, beliefs, and generalities for a good life at every opportunity. We had to listen without ever talking back or arguing. We were yelled at, insulted or drilled purposely to strengthen our minds. This was our preparation for life.

Values were simple to follow: no telling lies, no stealing, be honest, be generous, be helpful in every way, be kind, think of others before oneself. All these we acknowledged by saying "yes, I understand," or nodding our heads.

All relatives from both sides have terms to distinguish which side they come from. For example, the grandmother from father's side is called *Anna*. The grandmother from the mother's side is *Annanasiaq*. By this term we understand right away which grandmother. Great-grandparents are called *illupiruq*. Aunts from mother's side are called *aja* and uncles *anga*. All their children have terms also, and in this way we know how we are related. There are terms for in-laws, their family members, all their children. All namesakes are treated with special respect and extra love.

Families, in the Inuit world, mean not only continuation of the blood line, but survival. Couples who cannot have babies are given babies so they will survive. The baby given away at birth is fully aware of his or her natural parents, siblings, aunts and uncles from the beginning. The child grows up with dual families.

As a young girl, suicide was unheard of with our youth. We were lectured that life is precious and a wonderful gift. We have to protect it and enjoy it. We only knew that elders, when they wanted the village to have enough to eat for survival, committed suicide with full blessing from families. Today, we are told suicide is the highest among our young people. I believe this is true. I have lost relatives. My friends have lost their children in their teens and early twenties. We cry and mourn together, not understanding why it happens. We have theories, maybe's, what if's, and guesses. To prevent further suicides, individuals and community groups have created workshops, crisis lines, healing groups and recreational activities. The young people have started to talk about responsibilities among themselves. They have created a board run by the youth, and take part in political talks with governments and Inuit organizations.

When I was growing up, marriage was scary and painful for some women.

When a girl child was born, she would be promised to a boy child, agreed by the families. When the young girl matured, a menstrual flow was an indication of maturity and her ability to have children. Then the young man took the girl, whether she was willing or not. She often struggled and cried. She was very frightened. If they had to travel, she was tied up and held by men. She would struggle and cry until she got used to her new husband. I saw my aunts and their friends crying for help and wrestling with the men they were to spend the rest of their lives with. I am told by my women friends that a kind, considerate man did not force his new wife to have sex with him. He waited until she was tamed! Some women were not so fortunate, they were raped! Today, those who married the old way are still together and manage to find humor in how they got to be together. Some say they cannot imagine life without each other. Rough beginnings and yet destined to sail along into new horizons today.

One of my great aunts talked about the elders of her time. She said her family had to obey the wishes of their elders. Once, they were travelling inland hunting for caribou, and were walking on their way back home, each carrying their load, including the dogs. The elder called for a family meeting. After talking about how grateful she was for everything, she said she wanted to be left alone to die. The family did everything to discourage the elder, but the elder said she wanted the family and the village to survive. The elder wanted the people to have more to eat, more skins for clothing, and to travel with ease. The family had to listen to the elder. The family left and never looked back.

We respect elders not because they are old and feeble, but because age is part of life. My friend Leah Nutara, who died at the age of 107 on Feb. 14, 1990, often talked about her mother lecturing her to respect and help the elders. There was one elder in the village Leah visited every day. She fetched her water from the river, gave her the cup of water by her side, emptied her urine pots, tidied her tent. When Leah finished, the elder would say "You will live a long life." Leah believed she lived for so long because she listened to her mother.

From snowhouses to modern housing — people from the South are often amazed how we have coped with the changes. It is not so hard, really. I have some friends from Perth, Ontario, who went to a little red schoolhouse, rode in horse and buggy, fetched water from the river, and churned butter. No one has a monopoly on material items that make us more comfortable or make living easier. No one has a monopoly on wanting to be more educated or using science to our advantage.

In the past, classroom education was foreign to our parents, aunts and uncles and the people before them, because there were no schools. They were educated on the land about the plants, seas, weather, animals, histories of people, biographies, song creation, natural laws, beliefs and endless ways of survival.

In the late 1950s and early '60s, formal classroom education was introduced and it was accepted as one of those "have to's" that crept into our lives without our involvement. Our parents understood it was important because they were told it was.

Even though formal education is relatively new, we are now starting to really understand why education is important. It is no longer just a word. Our relatives are on education committees and boards; our nieces and nephews, grandparents are writing books in Inuktitut. Our grandmothers and grandfathers are coming into our schools to tell stories, sing songs; our sons and daughters have become teachers and principals.

We know it takes educated people to run governments, to doctor and to nurse sick people, to determine what is right or wrong in the court of law, to pursue sciences for better living, to stay healthy and well, to preserve nature so humans may survive, to preserve histories for generations to enjoy.

When our elders talked about the future many years ago, they said, "you will live like the *qallunaat*." It was hard to believe because we knew of no life other than the one we had. Since we were taught not to talk back or ask too many questions, we just wondered how that would be. The elders said that a shaman had a vision long before that there were ships from the South and passed on the knowledge. We are the living proof today of that prediction.

We are nomads. We chase opportunity in order to survive. In the days before metal technology, we made tools to make hunting easier, shelter for comfort, arts for pleasure, wordsmithing by memory for stimulation and continuation of a language. All these have survived in spite of another dominant language imposed upon us without ever asking for it. Through our kindness and instinctively welcoming attitude, we nearly lost all. But we took action when everything was on the verge of becoming a memory.

We are still nomads, chasing opportunity by negotiating our way with words. We cope with changes by taking full advantage of a situation, by being completely involved in decision-making. We are no longer the subjects only, but contribute to making life in the North a living memory, mingling traditions with high technology!

I was not the first to see the shiny object on the horizon on Frobisher Bay that day in 1957, but my questions were answered before reaching the shores of Iqaluit. The shiny objects, part of the Distant Early Warning (DEW) Line radar system, were *nalagutiit* — listening devices from far away places. A new word was added to my vocabulary.

THE NUNAVUT LAND CLAIM

by John Amagoalik

When the $1.1 billion Nunavut Land Claims Settlement was proclaimed at a special ceremony in Kugluktuk on July 9, 1993, it was the culmination of two decades of hard work and negotiations that, in the end, gave birth to the most comprehensive settlement ever reached between a state and an aboriginal group anywhere in the world.

None of this would have transpired had Inuit not become politically organized. The roots of Inuit political organization go back to the late 1960s and early '70s, and the struggle for control of natural resources.

Inuit had just experienced the boom and bust of the '60s' High Arctic oil exploration. (By 1980, more than $800 million had been invested in oil and gas exploration in the Arctic Archipelago over 21 years of exploration activity. Only a few land-based sedimentary basins across the country produce oil or gas now. Today, Canada's greatest potential for future sources of hydrocarbons lies offshore in the Arctic and off the East Coast.)

In Canada, managing oil and gas development north of 60 N latitude is a federal government responsibility. The period of intense exploration in the 1960s made Inuit realize just how little control they had over their traditional lands. They discovered that governments and big business could do just about whatever they wanted in the homeland of Inuit. This was like a wake-up call for Inuit leaders.

Discovery of Oil in Arctic Alaska

The large oil discovery on the Alaskan North Slope and the Beaufort Sea in 1976 promised more exploration activity in the Canadian Arctic. There were proposals for tanker routes, pipelines, flying tankers, and giant submarines to transport the expected oil bonanza. Inuit in Alaska, the Northwest Territories, Labrador and Quebec started to express serious concerns about all these proposed mega-projects.

The oil was found, but by then, the energy crisis that began in the early 1970s was over and oil prices dropped. This made it economically unfeasible to transport the oil out of the Arctic. The question of who owned the land and its resources was also a key factor in creating uncertainty in the oil business.

Spurred on by the discovery of oil and the building of a pipeline from the North Slope to southern Alaska, the federal government of the United States and the state government of Alaska signed the first modern treaty with the aboriginal peoples of that state. Negotiating modern treaties was suddenly seen as a real possibility in northern Canada.

The Calder Case

British Columbia's landmark Calder Case in 1973 introduced the terms "land claims" and "aboriginal rights" into the everyday language of Canadians. The case, brought to court by Chief Calder of the Nishga Indians of northwestern British Columbia, reviewed the existence of "aboriginal title" claimed over lands historically occupied by the Nishga. In a split decision, the Supreme Court of British Columbia acknowledged the existence of aboriginal rights in Canada. The government of Canada, which had dismissed any suggestions of land and other rights of aboriginal peoples, suddenly found themselves having to take the issue much more seriously. It forced a reluctant government to the negotiating table.

A New Generation of Inuit Leaders

Around all these events, a generation of better educated and less timid young Inuit activists was emerging. They started networking among themselves. They travelled to all parts of the Inuit homeland within Canada — the Northwest Territories, Quebec, Labrador — to talk about Inuit rights and to provide forums to debate the issues of the day.

They organized, raised funds, and started research into land claims. Inuit political organizations were born. The Committee for the Original Peoples Entitlement (COPE) in the Beaufort Region, the Inuit Tapirisat of Canada, and the Northern Quebec Inuit Association were the first ones to be established. The first few steps towards Nunavut had been taken.

After its formation in 1971, the Inuit Tapirisat of Canada had the responsibility to pursue and negotiate land claims for the Inuit of Canada. One of the options debated at the time was to negotiate one claim for all Inuit living in Labrador, Quebec, and the Northwest Territories. But it quickly became apparent that this would not be possible. Bringing all the parties, the provincial governments, the territorial government, the federal government, and the Inuit from the three different jurisdictions, to the same table to negotiate one claim, was just too difficult. It was decided that regional negotiations were the way to go.

The James Bay and Northern Quebec Settlement

When the provincial government of Quebec decided to forge ahead with the James Bay hydroelectric project in 1971, it forced the Cree of James Bay and the Inuit of Nunavik (northern Quebec) to go to court to stop the project until aboriginal claims were settled in the area. They were successful in getting a temporary injunction, which forced the provincial government to the negotiating table. Two years later, the first modern land treaty in Canada involving the province of Quebec, the federal government, the James Bay Cree, and the Inuit of Nunavik was signed. The terms of that modern treaty became the starting point for all succeeding negotiations.

The Inuvialuit Settlement

Under pressure from oil exploration in the Beaufort Sea and an expected oil pipeline down the Mackenzie Valley, the Inuvialuit (Inuit) of the western Arctic felt it necessary to break away from the Nunavut land claim negotiations and settle quickly. The Inuit of Nunavut reluctantly gave them their blessing to pursue their own settlement.

The Inuvialuit settlement, which included some Dene tribes in the Mackenzie Delta, was modelled very much on the James Bay settlement. It was signed in June 1984.

The Nunavut Claim

No longer under pressure from oil or hydro development, the Inuit of Nunavut were now able to take the proper time to negotiate a comprehensive agreement. Negotiations had been off and on several times since 1974. By 1982, the Tungavik Federation of Nunavut was incorporated to pursue land claims negotiations on behalf of the Inuit of Nunavut, taking the mandate from the Inuit Tapirisat of Canada.

Thirteen years of intense and detailed negotiations followed. One reason why negotiations were so slow was because the federal government had no real land claims policy. This was a totally new area for them and they found themselves having to create new policy as they went along. They had never discussed such things as offshore rights, sharing of royalties, or self-governing institutions with real legal powers. The Nunavut Inuit claims negotiations are largely responsible for the much broader and liberal land claims policy that Canada now has, as opposed to the very narrow definition of aboriginal rights that existed in the 1970s. The nationally televised First Ministers Conferences on Aboriginal Rights of the early 1980s — even though they failed to reach agreement on the definition and broadness of aboriginal rights — did much to educate Canadians about aboriginal issues. This increased support from the general public for aboriginal rights, and as a result the federal government became more willing to discuss broader issues.

Finally, an agreement-in-principle was reached in 1990. Two more years of negotiations followed until a final agreement was signed in September of 1992. It was ratified by 84.7 per cent of Inuit beneficiaries in a plebiscite two months later.

The Nunavut treaty is seen around the world as an important benchmark in aboriginal matters. This modern comprehensive accord is structured to guarantee Inuit majority control over their future, giving them, for example:

- title to Inuit-owned lands measuring 355,842 square kilometres, of which 35,257 square kilometres include mineral rights
- capital transfer payments of $1.1 billion, payable over 14 years beginning in 1993
- a share of federal government royalties from oil, gas and mineral development on Crown lands
- the right to harvest wildlife on lands and waters throughout the Nunavut settlement area
- the right of first refusal on sport and commercial development of renewable resources in Nunavut
- a wildlife management board that is devising a wildlife management system to serve and promote the long-term economic, social and cultural interests of Inuit harvesters
- procurement preference policies that ensure federal and territorial government contracts awarded for Nunavut-destined projects will see increased participation of Inuit firms (providing training and education where needed). Also, the labor force hired must reflect the proportion of Inuit in Nunavut

- Inuit Impact and Benefits Agreements (IIBAs), negotiated in advance of major development projects (such as mining development) that could have a detrimental impact *or* provide benefits to Inuit.

The Nunavut Land Claims Agreement, having literally changed the map of Canada, is now profoundly changing the course of life for Inuit in Nunavut.

THE NEW TERRITORY OF NUNAVUT

by John Amagoalik

From the time land claims negotiations started between Inuit and the federal government, the idea of creating a new territory was always part of the proposal.

The Inuit of Nunavut were determined not just to settle their land claim, but to create a new political entity for themselves.

The federal government, on the other hand, informed the Inuit that political issues could not be discussed at the land claims negotiating table. The creation of a new territory, they insisted, had to be pursued through other forums. The Inuit reluctantly agreed, but told the government that a final agreement would not be signed unless it included a commitment to create a new territory. The two parties agreed to disagree on this point, but still began serious negotiations on a land claim settlement.

The idea to split the Northwest Territories into two new territories was first introduced as a bill in the federal House of Commons in 1965. Some eastern Arctic residents appeared before a House of Commons committee to oppose the bill because the population had not been properly consulted. As a result, the bill never got second reading and died on the order paper.

The federal government wanted the issue examined further, and created the Carrothers Commission to study political development in the North and to report back to Parliament. In 1966, after holding hearings in northern communities, the three-man commission recommended that the issue of dividing the Northwest Territories be further examined in 10 years.

It was almost a decade later when the Inuit started to force the issue of division onto the agenda of the Northwest Territories Legislative Assembly. The assembly was very hostile to the idea and wanted, instead, to devolve more power to the territorial government from the federal government. The Inuit opposed this devolution of powers, insisting that the issue of division be resolved first.

The territorial government finally agreed to put the question of division to the residents of the Northwest Territories in a plebiscite in April 1982. The Inuit leadership campaigned hard for division and the voter turnout in Nunavut's communities was very high. The campaign against division was much less committed and the voter turnout in western Northwest Territories was low. In Nunavut's communities, the yes vote for division was around 90 per cent. The overall result of the plebiscite was 53 per cent for division and 47 per cent against. Nunavut had cleared its first major hurdle.

Years of sometimes acrimonious negotiations on the boundary followed. Finally, in 1992, all interested parties had agreed on a line on the map. This was again put to voters in a Northwest Territories-wide plebiscite to ratify the negotiated boundary between Nunavut and the remainder of the Northwest Territories. Again, there was a high voter turnout in the east and a lower turnout in the west. The boundary was ratified and Nunavut cleared its second major hurdle.

By this time, the negotiations on a final land claims agreement were reaching the home stretch. Most of the major issues had been resolved — except for the territory of Nunavut. In a meeting between the Inuit leadership and Indian and Northern Affairs Minister Tom Siddon in September 1992, the federal government made a last attempt to exclude Nunavut from the final agreement. The Inuit stood their ground and informed the minister that they were prepared to delay the signing of a final agreement until after an expected federal election and a new government. They also informed the minister that they could not recommend ratification by the Inuit of a final agreement that did not include Nunavut. After some phone calls, the minister informed the Inuit leaders that the government would include a provision in the final agreement, committing the government of Canada to create Nunavut.

The final agreement was ratified by the Inuit and the *Nunavut Act* passed by Parliament in June 1993.

What Nunavut Will Be

On April 1, 1999, Nunavut becomes the first territory to enter the federation of Canada since Newfoundland joined in 1949. Nunavut, subject to the Canadian Constitution and the Charter of Rights and Freedoms, will be a public government with all of its citizens having the same rights. But because the population will be about 85 per cent Inuit, it will reflect that reality.

Nunavut voters have already selected their capital — Iqaluit, the territory's largest community. In 1995, the Nunavut Implementation Commission (NIC), a public body whose primary role is to advise how the government of Nunavut should be designed, released a comprehensive set of recommendations in its report *Footprints in New Snow*. About a year and a half later, *Footprints 2* added to the existing blueprint. The recommendations of both reports require federal cabinet approval.

An interim commissioner who will lead Nunavut to the world stage was chosen in 1997: former federal Member of Parliament Jack Anawak.

Also in 1997, Nunavut voters were asked to consider an NIC recommendation that Nunavut's legislative assembly be made up of two-member constituencies, with each constituency represented by a man and a woman. Voters rejected the proposal, which would have made Nunavut's legislature the first in the world to have guaranteed equal participation of both sexes. The gender parity idea, a controversial one that had its opponents, was seen as a way to help Nunavut regain the badly needed balance between men and women, once such an important part of Inuit culture.

DOING BUSINESS IN NUNAVUT

by Tracy Wallace

For the southern businessperson, doing business in Nunavut can be a unique, enlightening, and profitable experience.

But reaping the rewards of continuing developments in mining, telecommunications, and construction — hot growth areas in Nunavut these days — means understanding that things are sometimes done differently in a land where polar bears outnumber conference rooms and sealskin vests are more fashionable than Hugo Boss.

At the very least, southern businesspeople should begin a dialogue with their northern partners long before they arrive in Nunavut. These interactions will help southerners get a feel for the unique business environment into which they are venturing. Many individuals have said they would have saved a considerable amount of time and effort had they been aware of these differences beforehand.

The Business Environment

Two protectionist policies help northern and Inuit-owned businesses battle an exorbitant cost of living, lack of skilled labor, and other business obstacles: the government of the Northwest Territories' Business Incentive Policy, and Article 24 of the Nunavut Land Claims Agreement. Businesspeople coming to the North must understand how dramatically these policies tilt the economic playing field. A free market environment does not yet reign here.

Traditionally, the GNWT has played a very significant role in the economy of the territory. While many of these programs are being privatized, the GNWT remains the single largest employer in many communities.

The government's reach extends into the private sector as well. Its Business Incentive Policy favors qualified northern businesses vying for government contracts. So businesses receiving territorial grants are often obligated to use northern contractors, suppliers, and manufacturers whenever possible. This policy is beneficial for the northern economy, but there are disadvantages. Orders sometimes take exceedingly long to process; goods and services can bear inflated northern price tags.

You'll also find that Nunavut is not short on bureaucracy. In fact, there seems to be a board, department, or agency for virtually everything. Often, these groups need to approve major business deals, which can also slow transactions to a snail's pace.

For a hunting society that maintained a subsistence lifestyle for millenia, the addition of a wage economy is still relatively new to Inuit in Nunavut. Article 24 of the 1993 Nunavut Land Claims Agreement aims to see Inuit-owned businesses in Nunavut benefit from federal and GNWT contracts. Businesses must be at least 51 per cent Inuit-owned. The clause is meant to give fledgling Inuit-owned enterprises a leg up as business opportunities boom and construction of Nunavut's government infrastructure snowballs over the years leading up to 1999. It's also meant to benefit the people who, at 85 per cent, make up the majority of Nunavut's population.

Shoulds and Should Nots

Many businesspeople tend to live in a cultural vacuum, thinking that business is business, no matter where on Earth you go. This kind of attitude won't win you any friends in Nunavut, though, where your interests will be much better served if you take some time to learn about the people and the land with which you are interacting.

Check your "yesterday is too late" attitude at the door. Things in the North take time, and you must respect this above everything else. In addition to the various bureaucratic obstacles mentioned earlier, you'll find that northern businesspeople just don't have the same frenzied attitude as many southerners. The river runs the show, as they say; northerners understand that blizzards don't care about the importance of your deal. Remember: very rarely do things run like clockwork here. Accept this, and you'll save yourself a lot of stress. Remember, too, that with the exception of the construction and tourism sectors, the North virtually shuts down in the summer. Your business partners will likely be more interested in fishing, hunting, or camping on the land than dealing with you.

You'll also find in Nunavut that sometimes business deals are still sealed with a handshake as opposed to legal paperwork.

English is not the first language of Nunavut, so provide translation services for all meetings and correspondence. Most Inuit businesspeople speak English, but unilingual elders are often asked for their opinions in these matters. Failure to recognize the importance of Inuktitut, whether in written correspondence or verbal transactions, could spell business failure. The larger communities should have seasoned translators for hire; you may have to ask around in the smaller hamlets.

If your business takes you to Nunavut's smaller settlements, you must recognize the importance of the community and try to get involved. In the past, too many businesspeople have come to Nunavut with one thing in mind: make as much money as possible, then leave. This attitude has grown tiresome. Don't be a hermit. Start networking by contacting the hamlet office before you arrive. Once there, become a participant in the community, and you will be that much closer to gaining your business partners' respect and admiration. It'll also help you understand why things grind to a standstill when there's a big sale at the Northern store or Co-op. Also respect community bylaws, especially those prohibiting alcohol consumption.

Business Facilities

Business facilities in Nunavut run the gamut from cutting-edge technologies such as videoconferences and Internet access to hotels with a single rotary phone. Call beforehand to find out what they have or don't have. Some communities have more than one hotel, so you may have options.

Meeting facilities are generally restricted to the regional centres of Iqaluit, Rankin Inlet, and Cambridge Bay, although hotels in smaller communities — such as Gjoa Haven's new Amundsen Hotel — sometimes have facilities that belie their size.

The Astro Hill Complex in Iqaluit contains, for example, an elegant conference room for up to 30 participants and a theatre that seats 130; the Siniktarvik Hotel in Rankin Inlet has a translation booth in one of its boardrooms and the usual overhead projector, screens, televisions and video cassette recorder required for presentations. Arctic Islands Lodge also has audiovisual equipment, plus Internet access.

Such facilities are the exception rather than the rule. You may also find yourself conducting a conference in the community gym, provided it's not being used for a square dance.

Telecommunications are slowly becoming a greater reality throughout the territory. You may be able to save yourself the exorbitant airfare by conducting a meeting via teleconference or videoconferencing, available in the regional centres. In addition, more people are getting on line, but it seems to take forever to get the necessary equipment and expertise.

Bed and breakfast establishments are slowly becoming more commonplace in communities. Since these establishments are usually run out of a home, they won't have sophisticated business facilities. Your hosts may, however, offer some insight into the community and its people — knowledge that might ultimately foster your business dealings more than any fax machine could.

For a complete list of Nunavut's accommodation and business facilities, contact **Nunavut Tourism**.

Business Networks

Today, more business decisions in Nunavut are being made at the community level, so more initiative is being focused on job creation through the private sector and self-employment.

Nunavut has three regional chambers of commerce, and they make up the newly established **Nunavut Chamber of Commerce**, which currently operates from the Baffin Regional Chamber of Commerce in Iqaluit but plans to move into separate offices next year. The regional chambers of commerce are still the best contacts on regional endeavors, but for business projects with Nunavut-wide implications, get in touch with the Nunavut Chamber of Commerce.

Each of Nunavut's three regional Inuit birthright associations has an economic development arm interested in sound investments and joint venture prospects that promise good returns on the financial interests they are safeguarding for area Inuit. Business projects have ranged from mining, surveying, shrimp fishing, construction and heavy equipment sales, to electronic technology. For more information, contact the **Qikiqtaaluk Corporation** in Iqaluit, **Sakku Investments Corporation** in Rankin Inlet or the **Kitikmeot Corporation** in Cambridge Bay. There is also a Nunavut-wide Inuit development corporation — **Nunasi Corporation**.

The **Kivalliq Partners in Development**, based in Rankin Inlet, is a partnership between Sakku Investments Corporation, the **Keewatin Business Development Centre**, and the GNWT's Department of **Resources, Wildlife and Economic Development**. Contact Kivalliq Partners in Development for information on business and development opportunities.

Finally, the biggest networking event of the year is the **Nunavut Trade Show**, held annually in Iqaluit during the first week of March. The 1997 edition drew several thousand visitors.

THE PEOPLE: DIRECTORY

The 819 and 403 area codes change to 867 on Oct. 21, 1997.

Baffin Business Development Centre
Tel.: (819) 979-1303
Fax: (819) 979-1508

Iqaluit Chamber of Commerce
Tel.: (819) 979-4095
Fax: (819) 979-2929

Iqaluit Trade and Promotion Office
Tel.: (819) 979-3156
Fax: (819) 979-2929

Kitikmeot Corporation
Tel.: (403) 983-2458
Fax: (403) 983-2701
E-mail: brenda@polarnet.ca

Keewatin Business Development Centre
Tel.: (819) 645-2126
Fax: (819) 645-2567

Kivalliq Partners in Development
Tel.: (819) 645-2124
Fax: (819) 645-2170
E-mail: richc@arctic.ca
Web site: www.arctic.ca/kpd

Nunasi Corporation
Tel.: (403) 920-4587
Fax: (403) 920-4592
E-mail: nunasi@internorth.com

Nunavut Chamber of Commerce

Baffin Regional Chamber of Commerce:
Tel.: (819) 979-4653
Fax: (819) 979-2929

Keewatin Chamber of Commerce:
Tel.: (819) 793-2311
Fax: (819) 793-2310

Kitikmeot Chamber of Commerce:
Tel.: (403) 982-3232
Fax: (403) 982-3229

Nunavut Construction Corporation
Tel.: (819) 979-2600
Fax: (819) 979-2601

Nunavut Tourism
P.O. Box 1450, Iqaluit NT,
X0A 0H0 Canada
Tel.: 1-800-491-7910 (for Canada and the United States)
Tel.: (819) 979-6551
Fax: (819) 979-1261
E-mail: nunatour@nunanet.com
Web site: www.nunatour.nt.ca

Nunavut Trade Show
Tel.: (819) 979-4563
Fax: (819) 979-2929
E-mail: brcc@nunanet.com
Web site: nunanet.com/~brcc

Qikiqtaaluk Corporation
Tel.: (819) 979-4047
Fax: (819) 979-1486
E-mail: qc@nunanet.com

Resources, Wildlife and Economic Development, GNWT
Tel.: (819) 979-5071
Fax: (819) 979-6026

Sakku Investments Corporation
Tel.: (819) 645-2805 or (819) 645-2742
Fax: (819) 645-2063
E-mail: rdewar@arctic.ca

Art and Music

INUIT ART AND FINE CRAFTS

by Dave Sutherland

Nunavut's flourishing artistic output is a unique phenomenon, especially given the harsh environment, limited resources, and large volume of work of very high quality that issues from a relatively small population.

Yet it is the harshness of the environment and the limited resources that have contributed to the phenomenon.

Inuit are extremely resourceful and because of this, they have survived. Men developed a high degree of technical skill and ingenuity to fashion the tools necessary for survival. Women developed a high degree of technical skill to provide the clothing essential to survival. Along with the development of technical skill comes an intimate understanding of, and sensitivity to, the available materials. Also, people from a hunting culture develop strong powers of observation and a strong visual memory, valuable assets for any artist. Traditionally, carvings told a story. Today, many younger carvers have not been told the stories that accompanied carvings. More recently, social issues have become the theme of some artists' work. Self-expression, the common motivation of southern artists, is not considered appropriate by the older generation of Inuit artists, but is appearing occasionally in the work of young artists.

There is ample evidence that Inuit carved figurative objects long before contact with Europeans, and certainly women were fashioning garments for their families in those times. During early contact with Europeans, Inuit men created objects to exchange for goods brought by the new strangers, and Inuit women crafted clothing for them. This continued into the 20th century. However, the present phenomenon began with the visit of a young art school graduate, James A. Houston, to the Canadian Arctic in 1948. Houston was able to impress the Canadian government with the income earning potential of the small sculptures that he brought back from his arctic trip. The Hudson's Bay Co. and the government provided support, and the first exhibition of Inuit work was presented by the Canadian Guild of Crafts in Montreal.

If one is unfamiliar with Inuit art, or has only seen the little carved objects in souvenir shops and airport boutiques, a great surprise lies in store. Not only are there beautiful sculptures from miniature to monumental size, but also fine art prints, fabric art, jewelry, ceramics, and exquisite fur products. There is also great stylistic variety from community to community, and from artist to artist.

While the care of Inuit art follows the common-sense guidelines that go hand-in-hand with fine art, visitors planning to buy untanned fur products to take home should be aware these require special care. If not kept in a cool, dry place or in a freezer, fur products will rot.

Sculpture

The most common carving material is stone. One regularly hears it referred to as "soapstone." Soapstone or steatite was used for early carvings as it is

LAND, SPIRITUALITY, AND MYTHOLOGY IN INUIT ART

by Alootook Ipellie

Inuit culture, like aboriginal cultures from other parts of the world, has a long history of relating to and living off the land's natural resources — the flora and fauna indigenous to the circumpolar Arctic.

It is this long and often intimate relationship with the land that has inspired its craftsmen and artists from ancient to modern times. As evidenced by findings from known archeological excavations, the Dorset and Thule cultures — forebearers to the modern Inuit — were expert carvers and craftsmen who designed their own tools and weapons to make survival possible in such a harsh climate.

Many of their tools and weapons were decorated with images of animals that served as spirit helpers, aiding practising shamans in their search for game when famine and starvation invaded their camps. These intricate carvings were often done individually or in clusters on a piece of stone, driftwood, antler, bone or ivory. Some of these spiritual aids would end up on a shaman's clothing or became part of his amulet, which would be strung around his waist or around one or both shoulders with sealskin rope. On occasion, certain shamans would use waterfowl feathers, or skin or fur from different animals as charms to help evoke animal spirits.

Ancient Inuit had no means to write their people's history, and relied instead on an oral tradition to pass on the stories, legends and mythical tales to each succeeding generation over thousands of years. These same stories often end up depicted in various Inuit art mediums, interpreted in different ways by artists or carvers in each Nunavut community.

One reason so many Inuit become such good artists or carvers is that they come from a very visual culture. Their very livelihood depended solely on dealing with the landscape every day during hunting or gathering expeditions. They were always visualizing animals in their thoughts as they searched the land, waters and skies for game. It is not surprising, then, that their visual talents and imaginations were and are so easily manifested in their art.

Inuit children growing up on the land were exposed to the elements daily while being taught by their elders how to live off the land. They were learning a lifestyle from experts who knew the behavior of all seasons; experts who knew how to hunt each species in a particular way, with certain hunting tools and weapons. When the time came for them to become hunters and gatherers, they had to know how to make and use these same tools and weapons just like their elders.

The Inuit storytelling tradition was passed on to children the same way. That experience of living on the land, together with the knowledge of ancient stories and legends, results in the high standards one sees in Inuit art today.

Inuit have always respected the land. That high regard is still evident in the numerous themes they draw upon, whether these are realistic depictions of everyday life on the land, spiritual images of animals, or mythological interpretations of legends of long ago.

soft and easily worked. However, because it breaks easily, it is not a good carving material. Most artists now work in serpentine, a stone similar in chemical composition but harder. Argillite, quartzite, and marble are also used.

Most stone is obtained from quarry sites near each community, so it's generally possible to identify the community of origin by the appearance of the stone. For example, Kimmirut quarries an even textured grey-green stone and a brighter green stone that has the appearance of green marble. Cape Dorset uses similar stone quarried in the same area. Pangnirtung stone and that of many other communities is black. A smooth grey argillite is used by the artists of Sanikiluaq. Repulse Bay has a dark green stone. Arviat stone is very coarse grey that no doubt has influenced the type of work from that community. It does not lend itself to detailed work. Baker Lake stone is similar but darker in tone. There are, of course, exceptions to the rule. If a community finds its local stone difficult to get at, it may take stone from another area. Occasionally, stone has been imported from the South. In communities where stone is scarce, caribou antler, whalebone and ivory have been put to good use.

The quality of the carving material imposes some similarity in the style of work from each community and no doubt the stronger artists influence others as happens in every creative community. But within each community very individualistic styles exist and, with familiarity, one can begin to pick out the work of individual artists. In the whole of Nunavut, there is great variety from artist to artist.

Prints

It is important to first distinguish between commercially lithographed prints produced in editions of hundreds, and fine art prints produced by hand in a studio, usually in editions of 50 and often printed by the artist. It is the latter for which Nunavut artists have become famous.

Printmaking began in Cape Dorset. James Houston was inspired to try printmaking when an Inuk artist commented that Inuit could do it. The result is that Cape Dorset artists have produced annual editions highly prized by collectors for more than 35 years. Beautiful prints are also produced by artists in Pangnirtung.

Frequently, the drawings are done by older artists and given to others to print. In a number of cases the artist is the printmaker. In some communities (Cape Dorset, for example), the printmaker controls the final image. In other communities, the printmaker tries to produce a print that is as close to the original drawing as possible. A variety of processes are used: stone cuts (the image is cut in a stone block and the paper laid on the inked block), stencils, and lithography. In all cases, the finest quality paper and inks are used to ensure stability of the images.

Fabric Arts

Although many women work in stone, an attempt was made by the federal government to find activities in the art and fine craft field that would be more in keeping with women's traditional skills. A weaving project started in 1969 in Pangnirtung produces beautiful tapestries using European tapestry techniques. The designs are taken from drawings by elders and transformed by highly skilled weavers.

In Baker Lake, women began making garments for sale in the early '60s — winter parkas and vests cut from the heavy wool blanket called "duffel," originally imported from England by the Hudson's Bay Co. The garments were appliquéd and embroidered. The garment industry was not an easy one to master because of constant style changes and the remoteness of northern communities from fashion centres. It was found, however, that the skills used to decorate parkas could be put to use making beautiful cloth pictures. Baker Lake's appliquéd and richly embroidered wall hangings have been featured in public and private art gallery exhibitions in Canada and the United States.

There is evidence that Inuit women made dolls from the earliest times. The women of today have almost raised doll-making to an art form. Each community has women who make dolls on a casual basis. Some years ago, the women of Taloyoak organized production of what was referred to as the "packing dolls" — animal figures wearing an *amauti* or baby-packing parka containing a miniature of the mother animal. The women, who have achieved a reputation for exquisite workmanship, are now inventing variations on the theme under the name "Taluq," using new synthetic fabrics that are washable.

Another artisan who does similar work is Martina Anoee of Arviat. She makes very fine dolls from seal fur and hide, the faces of which are reminiscent of apple dolls.

Jewelry

The early inhabitants of the Arctic worked in ivory and bone. Their work was small in size, as necessitated by their nomadic lifestyle. It is natural, then, that people today readily take to the production of jewelry. Even before a jewelry workshop was established in Iqaluit in the late '60s, much was produced on an individual basis from local materials.

At the workshop, artists have been trained in the use of fine metals, predominantly silver. They also use local materials such as ivory, caribou antler and colored stones. Some artists have carried silversmithing into the realm of metal sculpture. Artist Looty Pijamini of Grise Fiord uses skills learned at the jewelry workshop to produce sculpture in silver.

Ceramics

In the 1960s and early '70s, artists in Rankin Inlet were encouraged to try their hands at working with clay. While the results achieved critical success, the project was not successful economically. Recently, a private gallery in Rankin has encouraged artists to return to the medium, inspiring younger people to try their hand. The new work shows a definite link with the past, but artists are also experimenting with new themes and techniques. A few pieces have been cast in bronze.

Prices

Should one wish to purchase objects to take home, a great range in size, quality and price can be found. The following is a rough guide.

Sculpture: small pieces can be found for $100. The prices rise with size and quality to monumental pieces of several thousand dollars.

Prints range in price from $100 to $800. The prices are set when the prints go to market and are the same at all galleries throughout the country.

Fabric Arts: Pangnirtung tapestries range in price from $450 to $5,000. Embroidered wall hangings can be had for $100 to $400 for those considered fine crafts. Those categorized as fine art are from $600 up to several thousand dollars. Dolls range from $150 to $400.

Jewelry: while it is possible to find small items for less than $50, most jewelry is in the $50 to $200 range.

Ceramic pieces are in the $250 to $400 range. Those cast in bronze range from $1,500 to $2,500.

INUIT MUSIC

by David Serkoak, with contributions from Ann Meekitjuk Hanson and Peter Ernerk

For centuries, music has been an important part of daily life in Nunavut. From traditional forms such as drum dancing and throat singing to contemporary stars such as Susan Aglukark and the singing duo Tudjaat, music has helped define Inuit culture through rapidly changing times.

Of all forms of traditional Inuit music, none was more popular than drum dancing, which played a part in almost every gathering, whether it be a celebration of birth, a marriage, the changing of the seasons, a successful hunt, a first kill, a greeting for visitors, or to honor someone who had died. In these instances, news of a special event would be spread by word of mouth; many people would travel long distances to attend. Some dances took place with just a few participants, others might fill the huge *qaggiq*, a special snowhouse where people gathered to socialize.

Drum dancing was enjoyed by people of all ages. In the traditional dance, singers — usually women — sat in a circle. Sometimes a man would volunteer to be the first dancer, at other times a group of men sitting behind the singers would coax someone to start. If no one came forward, the women would start singing, usually a personal song (*pisiit*) of a man in attendance, who would then be obligated to dance. Except for occasional tea breaks, drum dances continued unabated long into the night. Women and children usually participated in the drumming toward the end of the dance.

While drum dancing is not as important to Inuit life as it once was, it is still practised in communities such as Arviat, Baker Lake, Rankin Inlet, Repulse Bay, Gjoa Haven, Kugluktuk, Cambridge Bay, Pelly Bay, Taloyoak and Igloolik. Unfortunately, drum dancing is generally no longer practised for traditional reasons; in most places it is done for tourists. It is sometimes performed at symbolic celebrations such as opening ceremonies for conferences and festivals, at graduations, and in movie productions.

I grew up with the sound of the drum beating in my ears. It was always exciting to have other adults and children visit our home for a drum dance. When the children were invited to participate, we would say the drum was too heavy. My mother never accepted that excuse. She would hold one side of the drum for me and I would dance, my friends chuckling all the while.

Today, I enjoy drum dancing with my youngest daughter, Karla. My parents believed drum dancing enhanced your life, and it brings me joy to watch my daughter drum dancing beside me. The late Donald Suluk, a respected elder from Arviat, once said: "When I was a child I didn't know the meaning of the songs. I thought at the time they were just for fun and that they belonged to the shamans. Now I know they are not only for shamans, they are for the world to enjoy."

In the past, singing was also a very important part of Inuit culture. Almost every adult had their own personal song, of which there were many types: songs of contest, songs of satire, and occasionally, humorous songs with obscene lyrics. There were songs about hardship, happiness, loneliness, love, and hatred. There were also songs of legends that have been a part of Inuit music for centuries. Some songs were rivalry songs, where two "enemies" would insult each other through lyrics. One such song might go like this:

"Aijaa, una-ija-ija, how I think the little old squaw is foolish! Oh, how old squaw is foolish, ija-ija-ja-ji-ja-jaa!

Aijaa, why I think it is foolish that old squaw is moving on to the other side of the world, how I feel it is foolish."

Every song was a story in itself, a life experience of the composer. Some songs, however, had no ownership. These were sung to Inuit transients who attended a dance while passing through a camp, and were sometimes even sung to non-Inuit. Personal songs could also be given to another person. A song owner might give his song to show appreciation for help given in time of need, or to someone bearing the same name as himself.

Throat singing is a well-known form of Inuit music that is usually performed by two women. The singers stand face to face; it helps if one singer is taller than the other. Each singer repeats a different sound in a fast rhythm. The low-pitched sound that is the trademark of throat singing represents sounds made by different birds and animals. Sometimes, throat singing can be a contest to see who can sing the longest. Some women are able to throat sing by themselves, using a large bowl or kettle held near the singer's mouth to give resonance. This method is common in the Arviat area.

If you would like to try throat singing, here are the basics. Try to make a sound deep in your throat without making noise from your mouth. Make the sound as you exhale, then inhale quickly without making a sound. Repeat this, remembering to make sounds only when you exhale. The sounds can be long or short.

European music first came to the Inuit from whalers and traders of the Hudson's Bay Co. in the form of songs and instruments, especially the mouth organ, button accordion, fiddle, and Jew's harp. With the arrival of radio, country-western and bluegrass music also came to Nunavut. Many Inuit sent to southern hospitals also heard new tunes that they brought back to Nunavut.

Most of today's famous Inuit musicians are self-taught, and continue to be largely influenced by country-and-western music. Gospel music is another very popular style of singing. Inuit musicians, especially pioneers like Charlie Panigoniak, Simon Sigjariaq, Mary Atuat Thompson, Peter and Susan Aningmiuq, William Tagoona, and Itulu Itidlui are very popular with the general public here. Many combine aspects of traditional Inuit music with modern instruments.

Many Inuit musicians first became well-known across the North after being heard on CBC North radio. Today, the annual True North Concert and media coverage of regional music festivals bring these performers to an even wider audience.

Today's social gatherings and community celebrations are often highlighted by square dances. Bands play time-worn tunes from across the Atlantic that were introduced to the North long ago by homesick whalers and traders. Each region has a distinct style of square dancing.

Land and Wildlife

PHYSICAL GEOGRAPHY

by Olav Loken

Nunavut is a large territory covering 1.9 million square kilometres. This is about one-fifth of Canada, or an area close to half of Europe excluding Russia.

The distance from Nunavut's western boundary to Cape Dyer on the east coast of Baffin Island is approximately 2,400 kilometres; in the other direction, it is about 2,700 kilometres from the Manitoba border to the northern tip of Ellesmere Island. (For comparison, the distance from Toronto to Calgary is about 2,700 kilometres. In Europe, the distance between London and Istanbul is slightly more than 2,400 kilometres.) The territory also includes Sanikiluaq and other islands in Hudson Bay and James Bay, hundreds of kilometres south of the main part of Nunavut. This chapter gives a general overview of the physical geography of this large area; see the "Destinations" chapters for details on specific areas.

Approximately 45 per cent of the land area of Nunavut lies on the northern part of Canada's mainland. The rest is distributed throughout a large archipelago of hundreds of islands, including Baffin Island (Canada's largest), as well as Ellesmere, Axel Heiberg and Devon islands. Twelve of the 20 largest islands in Canada lie entirely within Nunavut. The Parry Channel, running from Lancaster Sound off Baffin Bay in the east to the Arctic Ocean in the west, separates the Queen Elizabeth Islands to the north from the rest of the territory.

Climate

Nunavut covers the northernmost and coldest parts of Canada. January mean surface temperatures range from around –20° C at the southern tip of Baffin Island, which is influenced by the Labrador Sea to the southeast, to less than –37° C around Lake Hazen on northern Ellesmere Island. As would be expected, the lowest winter temperatures occur in the northernmost part of the territory, but temperatures almost as low (below –35° C) are experienced in an area west of Wager Bay, almost 2,000 kilometres farther south. This is due to its continental location far from the major oceans.

July mean temperatures range from above 10° C in the southern part of the mainland to less than 2° C in the north. The maritime influence keeps the coastal areas relatively warm during the winter, but cool in the summer when the land is generally warmer than the sea. During the summer, inland locations such as the Tanquary Fiord-Lake Hazen area on Ellesmere Island, often enjoy temperatures well above the regional averages. Due to the low mean temperatures, there is continuous permafrost throughout the territory; only a rather shallow surface layer (15 to 150 centimetres) thaws every summer and refreezes during the following winter.

Annual precipitation ranges from more than 600 millimetres in an area on southern Baffin Island to less than 100 millimetres in the northern part; the area around Eureka on Ellesmere Island is the driest part of Nunavut.

Precipitation levels are generally low, and only a small part of the territory receives more than 300 millimetres per year. The highest precipitation occurs in the highlands along the eastern seaboard from southern Baffin Island to Ellesmere Island, due to a combination of topography and the maritime influence of the Labrador Sea and Baffin Bay. While the northwestern part of the archipelago is close to the Arctic Ocean, the continuous ice cover reduces evaporation and limits the maritime influence of this water body. This part of Nunavut receives less precipitation than parts of the Sahara Desert, and can be described as a polar desert.

Geology and Landforms

The southern part of the territory — the mainland and Baffin Island — is part of the Canadian Shield, consisting of rocks typically more than a billion years old. This rock formation extends to parts of Ellesmere Island. Younger, sedimentary rocks in largely horizontal layers cover the northern part of the Shield on Nunavut's western islands and along the Parry Channel, as well as smaller isolated areas further south, such as the islands in Foxe Basin and parts of Southampton Island. Except for their southern and eastern parts, the Queen Elizabeth Islands consist of still younger, and in part heavily folded, formations.

The highest mountains in Nunavut are found along the eastern part of the territory, where the land has risen in relatively recent geological time. A highland with many peaks reaching 1,500 metres to 2,000 metres above sea level extends from south of Cape Dyer on Baffin Island to Ellesmere Island. Northern Ellesmere is even higher and contains Nunavut's highest mountain: Mount Barbeau (2,616 metres). The mountains on Axel Heiberg Island reach about 2,200 metres above sea level. From the eastern Baffin highland, the Shield slopes gradually southwestwards to Foxe Basin and re-emerges on the west side of Hudson Bay, rising towards the west. The Boothia Peninsula, at the northern extreme of the mainland, reaches altitudes of about 600 metres and this higher ground extends southward, although most of the mainland is less than 300 metres above sea level. Farther north, along Barrow Strait, typical altitudes are between 400 to 500 metres above sea level, but the islands to the west of the Boothia Peninsula (such as Prince of Wales Island and the eastern part of Victoria Island) are mostly less than 150 metres above sea level. The islands to the west of Axel Heiberg Island are very low and the land rarely rises to more than 150 metres above sea level.

Most of Nunavut's landforms are shaped by ice sheets and glaciers. The Laurentide Ice Sheet extended north from its centre near Hudson Bay to the north side of Parry Channel, while the highlands of Ellesmere, Axel Heiberg and Devon islands supported separate ice centres with ice flowing in all directions, coalescing in many places. Except for Bathurst Island and Cornwallis Island, the low northwestern islands were not ice covered during the Wisconsin glaciation, some 18,000 years ago. However, previous ice sheets reached the Arctic Ocean coast. The spectacular valley and fiord landscape of parts of the archipelago was shaped during the glacial periods. On Baffin Island, the Laurentide ice spilled over the height-of-land and out toward Baffin Bay, carving out deep valleys and fiords, some reaching depths of more than 900 metres. The fiords are often separated by alpine landscapes, making this a favored area for climbers.

The ice sheets left large deposits of till (an unsorted mixture of clay, gravel and boulders), especially along the old ice margins, such as the distinct moraine features along eastern Baffin Island, and on the islands south of the Parry Channel, such as on Victoria Island. The last remnant of the Laurentide Ice Sheet is believed to have melted down over the shield area to the west of Hudson Bay, leaving large till deposits, often in the forms of drumlins. The area also has many eskers, long sinuous ridges of sand and gravel.

The earth's crust was depressed under the weight of the ice sheet, and when it melted, extensive low-lying areas were inundated by the sea. The land has since risen and marine deposits and old shoreline features can be found at altitudes of more than 200 metres above sea level.

Present Ice Caps and Glaciers

At present, ice caps and glaciers cover some 150,000 square kilometres of Nunavut; more than half of this is on Ellesmere Island where ice covers an area larger than the province of New Brunswick. Several outlet glaciers on Ellesmere, Devon and Bylot islands reach tidewater and calve off icebergs. Along the north coast, the ice streams form small ice shelves.

Baffin Island has mostly mountain glaciers, some reaching tidewater, but there are also two ice caps — the Penny and the Barnes. The former rests on the top of the high mountain region of the Auyuittuq National Park Reserve on the Cumberland Peninsula with ice tongues flowing in several directions. The latter lies west of Clyde River like an elongated loaf of bread on the sloping surface of the Shield, well to the west of the height-of-land. It has been suggested it is a remnant of the Laurentide Ice Sheet.

Hydrology and Lakes

The major rivers in Nunavut are on the mainland. The Back and the Coppermine flow toward the Arctic Coast, while to the east, the Thelon, Kazan and Dubawnt rivers flow to Hudson Bay. These rivers have generally gentle profiles. The irregular land surface and low relief provide for numerous lakes, particularly in the southern Kivalliq Region. The largest lake on the mainland is Dubawnt Lake.

On the islands, the distance to the sea is short and so are the rivers. The longest river and major watersheds are found on the west side of Baffin Island. Nettilling Lake, the largest lake in Nunavut, and Amadjuak Lake lie on southern Baffin. There are numerous lakes in the Shield area on Baffin Island. The eastern part of Victoria Island and the adjacent islands also have a large number of mainly small lakes.

Lakes are much less common on the Queen Elizabeth Islands, and many of those that do exist are glacier-dammed. The 72-kilometre-long and almost 10-kilometre-wide Lake Hazen on Ellesmere Island is the largest in the area.

All lakes and rivers freeze over during the winter, but are generally ice-free during the summer, except for some in the Far North that may retain their ice cover. Runoff peaks during the spring snowmelt, except where glacier meltwater contributes significantly to the discharge. Permafrost prevents infiltration of water into the ground and this contributes to rapid runoff.

The Offshore Area

The Nunavut archipelago separates the more than 3,500-metre-deep Arctic Ocean to the northwest from the 2,100-metre-deep Baffin Bay to the southeast. The channels in the archipelago are shallow by comparison, rarely reaching more than 500 metres and then only in areas where they have been over-deepened by glaciers. The channels along the Arctic Coast are very shallow. Only in Nares Strait between Ellesmere and Greenland does the sill depth between the two major water bodies exceed 200 metres. Water flows through the archipelago and into Baffin Bay, but only the relatively fresh and cold surface waters can pass through the shallow channels.

Sea Ice

The Arctic Ocean is perpetually ice-covered and a persistent current feature, the Beaufort Gyre, sweeps the sea ice southwestward along the northwest coast of Nunavut. Old (multi-year) ice from the Arctic Ocean penetrates into the Parry Channel and other channels opening toward the northwest. During the winter, sea ice forms in all the channels. Near shore and in the narrower channels, the ice is landfast; in other areas it shifts back and forth with the winds and tides. The sea ice facilitates travelling with dogteams and snowmobiles and during the winter and early spring the area is more like a continuous landmass than an archipelago.

Even during the winter, some small areas have regularly no, or very thin, ice covers. They are known as polynyas and are important for wildlife. The largest and best known polynya is the North Water at the north end of Baffin Bay. A combination of winds and upwelling ocean currents keeps the area relatively ice-free.

In the spring the North Water expands as the temperature rises, causing the northern part of Baffin Bay to become ice-free before the more southern parts. As open water expands south and west into Lancaster Sound, migration routes for whales and marine mammals are opened, the marine biota — plants and animals — flourishes and the sound becomes the feeding ground for millions of seabirds nesting in the adjacent cliffs. Sea ice distribution during the summer depends on weather conditions and varies from year to year; usually minimum ice cover occurs in September. By then Baffin Bay, Jones Sound, the eastern part of Parry Channel, and the channels along the mainland are normally free of ice, but extensive ice cover persists among the Queen Elizabeth Islands.

Icebergs are numerous in the coastal waters along the Baffin Bay coast. Some of them have calved off glaciers on Ellesmere and Devon islands, but the majority — including all the largest ones — stem from tidewater glaciers on Greenland. After breaking off from the glaciers, the icebergs drift north with the West Greenland current and, as it turns at the head of the Bay, flow south along the Canadian side. Some eventually reach the Grand Banks off Newfoundland more than 3,500 kilometres to the south.

FLORA

by Judy Farrow

For the flora of Nunavut, life is a precarious phenomenon. Winter wraps the land in an icy headlock for months on end, finally yielding to a spring where −30° C temperatures are not uncommon.

Summer, consisting of the months of July and August, is brief. Temperatures can still dip well below freezing, and dry winds often cause significant damage to plants. Arctic soils, which are usually acidic and low in nitrogen, are inhospitable hosts. Plants must eke out an existence in a few meagre centimetres of earth, their roots confined by unwieldy bedrock or permafrost that is never far from the surface. These rather uncivil factors combine to produce plants that are small, prostrate, and always straddling the tenuous line between wakefulness and dormancy.

Arctic plants endure these conditions through a series of adaptations. Most tundra plants are perennials, which helps ensure their long-term survival. So while even the hardiest species in more temperate latitudes easily succumb to freak frosts or storms, the flora of Nunavut can be completely frozen one minute and thawed the next as if nothing had happened. This physiological mystery still baffles scientists: arctic plants freeze with impunity!

Plants here also protect themselves against the elements by crowding together and creating small micro-climates. Temperatures in these micro-climates are significantly higher than that of the surrounding air, thereby promoting photosynthesis and metabolism that may otherwise be impossible. This is why you'll find Nunavut's plant life nestled in sheltered rock crevices or hugging the contours of the ground. Indeed, soil is rarely visible on the tundra because it is covered by a perpetual layer of mosses and lichens, through which other herbaceous and shrubby plants grow.

Botanists say that since arctic conditions have only existed for a few million years (a mere blink of an eye on the evolutionary time scale), there are no true arctic plant species; arctic conditions have not existed long enough for unique arctic species to have evolved. So you might be surprised at the number of plants you recognize: dandelions, chamomile daisies (look for them on the beach in Pond Inlet), harebells, and buttercups, to name a few. And while harsh arctic conditions can only support a relatively small number of species, all major categories of plants are represented in Nunavut. About 200 species of flowering plants are found above the tree line, and an even greater number of lichens and mosses.

On the Tundra Meadow

Even before the snow disappears, fluffy willow catkins have emerged, taking full advantage of Nunavut's abbreviated growing season. The hairs of the pussy willows are transparent, conducting sunlight down the hair shaft to the catkin body, warming it several degrees above air temperature. This warmth is then trapped by the insulating effect of the tiny hairs, allowing the willows to get a head start on summer. Similar devices are employed by other arctic plants.

As the snow melts, vibrant blooms of purple saxifrage begin to appear. Yellow cinquefoils peek out from between protective leaves at ground level; a delicate perfume carried on a cool breeze sends you combing the tundra for its source, Lapland rosebay.

Delicate white bells dress up the otherwise untidy-looking arctic heather, which was traditionally collected in great quantities by Inuit for use in sleeping mattresses in summer tents. The plant was also an important source of fuel, as a high resin content in the stems and leaves makes this shrubby material burn readily to produce a very hot flame. Arctic heather is still widely used as fuel by families spending time on the land in summer: two rocks and a pile of arctic heather will bring a teakettle to boil in no time. Look around for some Labrador tea to add to the kettle and treat yourself to a refreshing and soothing drink. Labrador tea features prominently in traditional Inuit medicine, and was often used as a calming agent for people undergoing potentially painful procedures.

While searching, observant visitors might notice that the pale cream flowers of the ubiquitous mountain aven always point toward the sun. The Inuit call them *malikkat* ("the follower") because they chase the sun across the sky. The cup-shaped dish formed by the petals acts as a solar collector, concentrating the sun's rays in the centre of the flower and directing heat to its reproductive structures, thus speeding seed production. Insects often use these flowers to warm themselves before flying off in the cool arctic air. In its fruiting stage, mountain avens develop long, fluffy plumes. Long ago, these spiralling plumes prompted a caribou hunt among Inuit, who knew the animals would soon start growing their winter coats, which were more difficult to sew into clothing than their summer coats.

The curious round leaves of wintergreen are tough and often have a slight reddish-brown tinge that enables them to absorb more heat from sunlight and photosynthesize even when the surrounding air temperature is cool. As the name of the plant suggests, the leaves maintain their color in winter, frozen and dormant. If conditions are right, moss campion grows in a perfectly round clump, which soon becomes covered with tiny pink flowers. Underneath these clumps is a substantial taproot, once eaten by Inuit in times of starvation.

In wetter areas of the tundra and lakeshores you'll find arctic cotton, a type of sedge whose flower heads develop beautiful white, silky plumes. Inuit once collected these cotton heads and used them with dried moss to make wicks for traditional seal-oil lamps known as *qulliq*. An 11-kilogram sack of cotton heads would supply one qulliq for a year. The silky cotton from willow catkins was also used.

With a protective helmet and a protruding lower lip, louseworts are curious plants, their tiny flowers somewhat reminiscent of garden snapdragons. They produce a good supply of nectar at the base of the flower tube and are frequently visited by large arctic bees. The plant's delicate leaves are often mistaken for small ferns, hence its other common name, the fernweed.

The Arctic even has its own version of fireweed, a prostrate variety that can turn whole hillsides or valleys bright pink. The young shoots also make a tasty salad. Prickly saxifrages are straggly plants with three-pronged leaves bearing sharp spikes. The plant's pretty white flowers form a bunch at the top of a flowering stem that grows a few centimetres above ground level. The plant makes a good strong tea that was once used by Inuit for upset stomachs and general aches and pains; the flowers may also be eaten.

If you happen across a patch of especially green, luxuriant growth during your wanderings across the tundra meadow, you can be sure you've come to an animal den, old human camp site, dump site, or bird roost. The arctic terrestrial environment is generally lacking in nitrogen, and plants take full advantage of nitrogen-rich areas such as these. Bladder campions, mountain sorrel, mouse-ear chickweed, and stitchwort are often found in these locations.

Black, plump crowberries are a favorite of the Inuit, but their many seeds give them a gritty taste. Blueberries are small, but sweet. Bright red cranberries are great for cooking, although they taste like sour apples when eaten raw. In late summer the foliage of alpine bearberry turns a brilliant scarlet, coloring entire hillsides. The berries become almost black when ripe. Despite their delicious appearance, though, the taste is very disappointing.

Lichens, while seemingly unspectacular, are nonetheless vital elements of the arctic environment. Lichens are not single plants, but rather, a symbiotic association of algae and fungi cells living together. The ubiquitous map lichen, named for its map-like growth pattern on rock faces, is used by scientists to date rocks. The rock tripe lichen that speckles tundra rocks saved many explorers from starvation. Caribou moss, which is actually a lichen, is a winter staple for caribou.

You are encouraged to enjoy the arctic flora, but treat it with the respect and tenderness it deserves. An eminent arctic botanist once reported that the woody stem of Lapland rosebay, which was no thicker than a man's thumb, showed no less than 400 annual rings!

LAND MAMMALS

by Marian and Mike Ferguson

The land mammals of Nunavut — models of adaptive perfection — have helped sustain arctic inhabitants for more than 4,000 years by providing raw materials for tools, food, clothing and shelter.

Each species is uniquely adapted to survive Nunavut's harsh, unstable terrestrial ecosystems and temperature extremes. These mammals are subjected to wider temperature extremes than their arctic marine counterparts.

Since the abbreviated arctic summer provides resident populations little opportunity to recover from harsh winters, the diversity of species in Nunavut is low compared with warmer parts of the world. Nevertheless, the adaptive success of these few species is witnessed in the massive numbers their populations sometimes reach, and the proven ability of remnant populations to recover after decades at low numbers. In turn, the peoples who have lived in the Arctic have proven *their* ability to adapt, prospering despite dependence on such wildly fluctuating environments and resources.

With some planning and luck, visitors to Nunavut will have ample opportunities to observe many of these unique species in their natural habitats. The sheer expanse of the territory makes it unlikely that you could view all species during one visit, but residents can advise you where, when and how to see wildlife of greatest interest to you. Although not all populations are migratory, most exhibit seasonal behaviors that make them difficult to observe at some times.

If seeing terrestrial wildlife is an important part of your visit, plan on using an experienced guide to maximize viewing opportunities. A variety of tours, lasting from a day to over a week, are available through outfitters or booking agents in most communities (see the individual community chapters in "Destinations"). Information can also be obtained from the Renewable Resources Officer (look in the phone book for the GNWT's **Department of Resources, Wildlife and Economic Development**) and the HTO in each community. Information on national parks is available from park staff.

Caribou

When Europeans arrived in North America, they encountered a species known to them as reindeer. American Indians called these animals caribou. In Nunavut they are known as *tuktut.*

More than 750,000 caribou — in two distinct ecological situations — live in Nunavut. On the mainland, caribou live on the tundra from spring to late summer, then migrate south into the vast boreal forest for the winter. Caribou that remain on the tundra throughout the year are, for the most part, restricted to relatively small islands. These animals are usually seen in smaller groups than the migratory caribou that winter among the southern trees. Nevertheless, caribou wintering on the tundra migrate between seasonal habitats within Nunavut. Most migrate over shorter distances than mainland caribou, but some on Baffin Island travel several hundred kilometres each spring.

Caribou can be seen near several communities in winter and spring. In summer and fall, bulls may be seen along the coast, but cows are usually farther inland near their June calving areas.

The caribou has always been the most important land mammal to the Inuit; until very recently the lives of Inuit were inextricably linked to these great wanderers. In times of scarcity the Inuit not only risked starvation, but faced winters of perpetual cold without the unsurpassed insulation of caribou-skin clothing. The unique structure of the caribou's hollow hair makes its fur extremely warm, yet easily worn. A hunter's caribou clothing needs to be replaced every few years because it will not retain its warmth.

In Nunavut, there are three subspecies of caribou. Barren-ground caribou is the most common, occupying the mainland and some southern arctic islands. Although caribou on Baffin Island are officially barren-ground caribou, recent genetic analyses suggest they may be distinct from other subspecies.

Peary caribou on the Queen Elizabeth Islands north of Barrow Strait and Lancaster Sound are recognized as "endangered" by the Committee on the Status of Endangered Wildlife in Canada. Peary caribou are naturally rare because the sparse vegetation in the High Arctic is often locked beneath snow and ice for up to 10 months each year. Many caribou on the mid-Arctic islands west of Baffin Island are interbreeds between barren-ground and Peary caribou.

A third subspecies, reindeer originally descended from Siberian stock, was introduced to the Belcher Islands in eastern Hudson Bay in 1978, about 100 years after native caribou had disappeared. Concerned that unrestricted growth of this free-ranging population could lead to overgrazing and potential future extinction, Inuit of Sanikiluaq have successfully stabilized their numbers at 600 to 800 animals.

Caribou bulls average 100 to 150 kilograms, while cows reach 75 to 100 kilograms. Subspecies differ in size, color and behavior. Peary caribou are the smallest. During summer, Peary and Baffin caribou are not known to form dense groups numbering in the thousands, as do the barren-ground caribou on the mainland, perhaps because they do not have to endure thick clouds of mosquitoes and other insects. Reindeer are typically seen in large, dense groups, even during winter.

Muskoxen

Should you be lucky enough to see the trademark shaggy coat of the muskox, you may feel like you've been transported back in time. Indeed, it's easy to imagine continental ice sheets covering much of North America — as they did some 18,000 years ago — when in the company of the "bearded one."

Unlike caribou, which prefer slow-growing lichens, muskoxen (*umingmait*) depend largely on grasses and sedges that recover relatively quickly from heavy grazing. In the summer, these herbivores may be seen in river valleys, along lake shores and near damp meadows. If grasses and sedges become unavailable in winter, muskoxen move onto ridges and hilltops to feed on willows and other plants. They are often seen in groups of 10 to 20, depending on season and location. When threatened, muskoxen form defensive circles with adults facing outwards and calves in the centre. This behavior, while effective against four-legged predators, makes muskoxen easy prey for human hunters.

Large numbers of muskoxen roamed the tundra of Nunavut before the arrival of European and Canadian traders. The subsequent market for meat and hides reduced their populations to dangerously low numbers until Canada protected them in 1917. Since then, muskoxen have recovered and recolonized most of their historic range so that closely regulated harvesting can be sustained. Today, Nunavut holds most of Canada's muskoxen with about 60,000 animals. The species occupies much of Nunavut, except for the eastern mainland and Baffin Island.

Inuit do not usually prefer muskoxen over caribou, although the meat can be delicious and the skins produce warm sleeping robes. Beginning in May, muskoxen shed large quantities of their underfur (*qiviut*), which can be spun into a luxurious wool. Bulls weigh about 350 kilograms, some 50 kilograms heavier than cows. Muskoxen mate in the summer; bulls can become unpredictable during this period. Do not approach muskoxen too closely, especially if you're not accompanied by an experienced guide. They can be aggressive. If you need to take refuge, quickly jump up onto a rock. Muskoxen are poor climbers.

Barren-Ground Grizzlies

The barren-ground grizzly is found on the mainland of Nunavut and is more common in the Kitikmeot Region than in the Kivalliq Region.

The barren-ground grizzly bear (*ak&a*) is smaller than its cousins elsewhere in North America; males weigh up to 215 kilograms, while females weigh up to 108 kilograms. Their hair, ranging from black to blond, is often flecked, or "grizzled," with white or grey. These bears exist on the margins of their range. Normally, grizzlies kill or scavenge animals, especially ungulates such as caribou, ground squirrels and insects, as well as garbage.

Wolves and Wolverines

Two types of wolves (*amaruit*) are found in Nunavut. Tundra wolves on the mainland are often brown or grey and weigh 30 to 40 kilograms, while arctic wolves on the islands are usually smaller and white. Tundra wolves prey mainly on caribou, while arctic wolves hunt either muskoxen or caribou. On Ellesmere Island, some wolves take muskoxen almost exclusively, even though much smaller caribou are available. Wolves will also eat hares, lemmings, birds, fish, foxes and garbage. Wolf packs tend to be small and widely scattered. Wolves are usually found wherever there is suitable prey, but these quick and secretive animals are never easy to spot. In winter and spring, your guide may show you fresh tracks. With some luck you may even see the wolves that made them. In summer, wolves are often at inland denning sites raising pups or hunting. You will need considerable perseverance, patience and luck to see signs of wolves once the snow melts.

Being a mammal of the Boreal forest, the wolverine (*qavvik*), the largest of weasels, is most common on the mainland of Nunavut, and is rarely seen on the Arctic Islands. The stocky body, short, powerful legs and large feet give the wolverine the appearance of a small bear. Its dark brown fur is streaked with two tan stripes running the length of the body. Wolverine fur is used for trimming parka hoods because frost slips off hairs easily. Weight ranges from about 14 to 28 kilograms; females are smaller than males.

Foxes, Hares and Lemmings

These smaller animals are relatively abundant throughout Nunavut, and can be seen near most communities. In 1919, red foxes (*tiriganiarjuat*) crossed Hudson Strait from Quebec to Baffin Island, and reached the Queen Elizabeth Islands by 1962. Red foxes go through phases of colors, including silver, black, brown and red. On average, they have litters of four to eight pups. The arctic fox (*tiriganiaq*) is white during winter, but changes to largely dark brown in summer. Arctic foxes usually bear only four to six young. As with the red fox, litter size increases significantly in years when lemmings are numerous.

Foxes travel extensively in search of food — they can be found almost anywhere. Although it's hard to predict if you will see any, foxes are curious and may approach your camp. However, a fox that approaches too closely and appears overly friendly could have rabies; play it safe and scare it away. The young become independent in September so you will probably see them in their quest for food. Foxes eat lemmings, hares, ptarmigan, bird eggs, decaying flesh from carcasses, and garbage.

Arctic hares (*ukaliit*) are widely distributed across Nunavut. They live among rocks on rough hillsides and mountains, where they have ready shelter from foxes, gyrfalcons and other predators. Hares eat grasses, sedges, willows and other plants. Across most of their range, they are seen in small family units, but on the Queen Elizabeth Islands you may encounter herds of 100 or more. From a distance, these groups look like white clouds flowing across the summer tundra. In southern parts of their range, they may moult to grey or brown in summer.

MARINE MAMMALS

by Mike Vlessides

Traditionally, few cultures in the world were more dependent on the creatures of the sea than the Inuit.

Indeed, in a land where resources were often scarce, the fertile waters of Nunavut and its vast populations of marine mammals provided the raw materials that helped Inuit society thrive in one of the world's harshest climates. Even today, as massive material changes continue to reshape Inuit society, the people of Nunavut use marine mammals as important sources of food, clothing, and increasingly, revenue.

Seals

While Canadian seas are home to nine species of seals, three of the most bountiful in the Arctic are the ringed, harp, and bearded seal.

Other marine mammals may garner more attention than the demure ringed seal, but few play as integral a role in Inuit society. For nearly four millennia, Inuit have relied extensively on *natsiq*, the smallest and most common marine mammal in the territory.

Traditionally, the ringed seal (which gets its name from the irregular, light-colored rings with dark centres that characterize adults) was the main staple of the Inuit diet; its skin was used as clothing, its blubber fuelled the soapstone lamps that provided both light and warmth, and its intestines, a delicacy to Inuit, were even used as containers and igloo windows. The skin also furnished harnesses for huskies, and soles for *kamiit* (boots). While the animal is no longer used to this extent, the ringed seal is still an important food source for the people of Nunavut, who also use the skin for boots and mitts, and less frequently, parkas, pants, and even artwork.

The ringed seal's importance in Inuit culture is largely the result of logistics. In addition to being the only seal that spends the entire year in the Arctic, ringed seal populations also number well into the millions. In spring, seals haul themselves through cracks and breathing holes in the ice to bask in the warmth of the sun. Often you'll spot several of them sleeping together, though you may find it difficult to get very close to them. They are fitful sleepers, rising every few minutes to scan the horizon for potential danger.

You'll find ringed seals far more daring in their aquatic element, however, often popping their inquisitive heads out of the water to observe passing boats. Still, they are somewhat difficult to spot in ice-free waters. The ringed seal is ubiquitous in Nunavut, populating arctic and subarctic waters. A few venture as far south as the Gulf of St. Lawrence.

Slightly larger than ringed seals, harp seals are distinguished by the black, harp-shaped saddle on their backs. Harp seals have never been as vital to Inuit as ringed seals, probably because they stay farther from shore. About 500,000 of them summer in Nunavut, migrating north when the sea ice finally yields in spring. They return south to warmer waters with the coming of autumn.

Inuit call harp seals *kairulik*, "jumping seals," a name derived from their penchant for porpoising and frolicking in arctic waters. They are found mostly in the eastern part of the territory, ranging throughout Foxe Basin, northern and eastern Hudson Bay, Hudson and Davis straits, and the northern parts of Baffin Bay.

The *udjuk*, or "squareflipper," as the bearded seal is sometimes called, is unique among Nunavut's seals in that it is a bottom feeder, eating crustaceans, mollusks, worms, hermit crab, and clams. Despite the energy the animal expends to attain its food, the bearded seal nonetheless grows to great proportions, maxing out at 350 kilograms.

Unlike more gregarious harp and ringed seals, bearded seals are usually found in pairs or small groups instead of large herds. These dark grey creatures spend most of their time on fields of drifting ice, diving 50 to 200 metres for food below. As their English name suggests, bearded seals are distinguished by the long, drooping whiskers around their mouths.

Despite their great girth, bearded seals are the most cautious of all Nunavut's seals. On the ice, they will head for safer pastures underwater long before humans get very close. In the water they are slightly braver. Often they'll allow your boat to get within several dozen metres; especially brazen individuals may even circle your vessel for a closer look before disappearing with a splash.

Bearded seals can be found throughout Nunavut, especially in shallow waters.

Walruses

Relaxed yet irksome, graceful yet clumsy, gentle yet ferocious, walruses (*aiviit*) are paradoxical animals that defy categorization. They can often be found packed like sardines on ice floes, but that doesn't stop one from occasionally rising up and jabbing his or her neighbor with a pair of ivory tusks. On land, these massive mammals (adult males can reach 3.5 metres and 1,400 kilograms) move with the grace of three-legged elephants, but in the water they are masterful swimmers.

Walruses dine extensively on clams, using their sensitive whiskers to detect the unfortunate mollusks on the sea floor. An adult walrus eats as many as 3,000 clams each day, although they also eat other bottom-dwelling creatures such as fish, crabs, worms and snails. Because they rarely dive deeper than 75 metres, walruses stay close to shallow waters.

The walrus's most distinguishing feature is its tremendous overbite. Both male and female walruses are blessed with these dentures. Despite their Latin name, *odobenidae* ("those that walk with their teeth"), walruses don't actually use their tusks for walking. Neither are the tusks used to dig up food. The tusks, serving as a symbol of dominance or social rank, are also used to help animals haul themselves from the water.

Walruses are restricted to Hudson Bay, the waters around Baffin Island, and the High Arctic.

Whales

Glorious to behold, belugas, bowheads, and narwhals are the three true arctic whales, although others are occasionally spotted here in summer. Of the three arctic whales, belugas are the most numerous and widely distributed. More than 60,000, and perhaps as many as 100,000, live in arctic and subarctic waters.

Snow-white belugas (*qinalugait*) stand out conspicuously in dark waters. Congregating in large numbers in the same areas every summer, these small-toothed whales are also the most gregarious and most vocal of the arctic whales, spending hours rollicking in shallow waters, chirping, trilling, and clicking to one another in apparent delight. Early whalers actually dubbed them "sea canaries."

Belugas, which reach about four to five metres in length, are found throughout Nunavut. They winter in areas of open water or shifting ice, where they have access to air, moving northward with spring.

Narwhals, the mysterious unicorns of the sea, also boast significant Nunavut populations, though their range is more restricted than belugas. The majority of *tuugaaliit* winter in northern Davis Strait and southern Baffin Bay. Toward the end of June they head for the fertile waters of Lancaster Sound and the deep bays and fiords of northern Baffin Island and beyond. A distinct population spends the winter in Hudson Strait, moving into northwestern Hudson Bay in spring.

Narwhals average four metres in length and weigh nearly two tonnes. Yet it is not this mottled whale's girth that gives the creature its reputation, but its unforgettable ivory tusk that twists from its upper jaw like the overgrown tooth it really is. Hundreds of years ago, reports of the existence of unicorns were fostered by serendipitous discoveries of narwhal tusks by imaginative European whalers.

The large majority of tusked narwhals are males, although females occasionally grow them as well. The purpose of this appendage is still unknown, although different theories have been championed for centuries. Most often, the tusk is used in displays of aggressive behavior; scientists believe they may be used to determine social rank, much like the tusk of the walrus.

Bowhead whales (*arviit*) are the giants of the arctic whales, reaching 18 metres in length and 100 tonnes. These gentle behemoths were hunted to near extinction in the 1800s and early 1900s; to this day their populations in the eastern Arctic remain dangerously low, thus their endangered status. There were once more than 11,000 bowheads in these waters; today, most biologists agree there are no more than 1,000. Nonetheless, the recently settled Nunavut Land Claims Agreement paved the way for the legal harvest of a bowhead for the first time in a generation; in August

1996, a group of hunters representing a cross section of Nunavut took part in this historic hunt.

Although not considered true arctic whales because they do not winter in the Arctic, killer whales are often associated with Nunavut because of their summer migrations. These carnivores are very deserving of their rather intimidating name, preying on fish, seals, and even small whales. It is believed that one of the reasons Nunavut's bowhead whales have not rebounded is because killer whales are preying on bowhead calves.

Killer whales tend to follow seal and whale populations north when the ice begins to break. They are found in Foxe Basin, Hudson Bay, Hudson and Davis straits, Lancaster and Eclipse sounds, and Admiralty Inlet.

Other whales visiting Nunavut's waters in summer are blue whales and sperm whales. Blue whales, the world's largest living mammals, can reach lengths in excess of 30 metres and weights of 100 tonnes. These endangered creatures sometimes venture into Davis Strait, the northernmost limit of their range in Canadian waters. Sperm whales, the largest of all toothed whales, are also occasional summer visitors to Davis Strait. Only bull sperm whales travel to arctic waters, however.

Polar Bears

More than any other creature, the world's largest land carnivore has come to symbolize the wild, rugged character of Nunavut. What may seem puzzling, however, is why the polar bear (*nanuq*) is considered a marine mammal at all. The reason is simple: polar bears, which are extraordinarily adapted for frigid arctic waters and are excellent swimmers, spend most of their lives on the sea ice and in the water. These abilities and adaptations allow the polar bear to successfully hunt and kill the staple of its diet, the ringed seal, which it hunts at breathing holes, at the floe edge, along cracks in the ice, and at polynyas.

The polar bears of Nunavut tend to be solitary creatures, generally travelling alone in winter. If you see more than one bear together, it is probably a mother and her cub or cubs. Cubs stay with their mothers for the first two or three years of life.

When the seemingly impenetrable shell of ice finally breaks up across Nunavut, polar bears are forced to concentrate somewhat in fiords and bays, where ice usually lasts longer. When this ice finally melts, the bears have few dietary options other than vegetation, small animals, and dead material that has been washed ashore. Occasionally, hungry bears wander into communities, drawn by the scents emanating from town dumps.

Polar bears are found throughout Nunavut, but they are especially common throughout Barrow Strait and Lancaster Sound, along the east and southeast coasts of Baffin Island, and north throughout Jones Sound.

BIRDS AND BIRDING

by Robin Johnstone

The drama from this distance is a faint blur of activity, but my binoculars convey a dramatic tale.

A horned lark is in the lead, streaking over the land, trying to gain some distance and some cover. Close behind, a female peregrine falcon, hungry after her long migration from coastal Brazil, matches every move of the fleeing appetizer. The distance between does not seem to close though, and the chances of escape begin to look good. Then, a sudden blur across my view, so fast my brain barely registers it. It is the tiercel, the female peregrine's mate. The hapless lark has been ambushed. Distracted by the peregrine in pursuit, the lark does not see its partner gaining height above it. The small male peregrine misses the lark in its first steep dive or stoop; but turns up, up, and completely over in a large loop that points him straight back down at his lunch. The second stoop is deadly accurate this time, and a cloud of lark feathers are left floating on the breeze. The dead lark is deftly passed in midair to his mate, and the pair returns triumphantly to their nesting cliff. One more meal in a summer of hunting to provide for a growing family.

– An excerpt from my field diary:
Rankin Inlet, Nunavut, Canada. May 27, 1995.

Birding opportunities in Nunavut are extensive and exciting, whether you are an expert birder hoping to add rare arctic species to your life list of birds, or someone who simply delights in watching birds going about their business. The Arctic is characterized by having few bird species, relative to temperate or tropical ecosystems. For instance, only two dozen or so species breed on Ellesmere Island, with another 10 to 20 species sighted. The lack of species number is made up for by the exotic nature of some of the species and the awe-inspiring sight of incredible numbers of others found in the large breeding colonies. Not all places harbor incredible densities of birds, but a long walk on the tundra may be very rewarding.

Tours or outfitters rarely cater specifically to birders in Nunavut; however, they provide excellent access to superb birding, as many destinations in Nunavut provide ideal opportunities for viewing birds, as well as other wildlife. For instance, a canoe trip down the Thelon River through the Thelon Game Sanctuary is a wilderness adventure that also includes excellent birding opportunities. Tree-nesting gyrfalcons, short-eared owls, snowy owls, rough-legged hawks, golden eagles and many other species may be seen.

Interpretive and birding skills among outfitters vary greatly. Novice through to expert birders will benefit from the world-class interpretive program at the long-running **Bathurst Inlet Lodge**, which sets an extremely high standard for the industry.

The best time for birding in Nunavut is mid- to late-May through August. There are excellent opportunities for birding throughout Nunavut in spring as the land begins to peek from beneath its heavy burden of snow and migrant species return in large numbers. By mid-August many birds have finished breeding and dispersed from their colonies or nest sites.

Storms can be very disruptive to any tour in August; especially when boat transportation is involved. Constant darkness and bitter cold leaves Nunavut almost devoid of bird life in winter, except for the hardiest of species — common ravens, gyrfalcon, ptarmigan.

A birding trip by snowmobile and *qamutik* (wooden sled) in late May or June can be very rewarding, and is recommended for anyone of a mildly adventurous nature. At this time birds tend to concentrate on patches of land free of snow, or areas of open water. On land, you may be entertained by sandhill cranes doing their graceful, though somewhat awkward, courtship displays. Magnificent flights of geese and tundra swans may be seen, and stunning aerial dogfights of peregrine falcons staking a territory and a mate may be observed from a safe distance. Long-tailed ducks (formerly known as oldsquaw), common and king eider ducks, black guillemots and many other seabirds may easily be found at leads — patches of open water — in the sea ice, or at the floe edge throughout Nunavut. Local outfitters can best advise when to visit their community to coincide with spring thaw and the appearance of leads. Dark sunglasses and sunscreen with an SPF 30 minimum are necessary at this time.

The following is a selection of highlighted species that characterize the Arctic, and some good places at which to observe them, in my opinion. Many excellent birding opportunities and exciting sightings may be gained by the self-reliant birder, though, at destinations that don't specify birding opportunities or interpretive programs.

Gyrfalcon, the largest of all falcons, rank highly on the wish list of keen birders, and seeing an individual of the white color phase is one of the biggest thrills any naturalist, amateur or professional, can experience. They prey mainly on ptarmigan and if their food supply is good, they may remain in the North through winter. They are not common birds but close proximity and relatively high densities may provide viewing opportunities at **Sila Lodge**, Wager Bay.

Ptarmigan are one of the true arctic species, adapted for year-round life in this harsh environment. Dense feathers on the top and bottom of their feet and long claws equip ptarmigan with an effective pair of winter boots that protect them from the bitter cold, and crampons for traction on ice. Rock ptarmigan are found throughout Nunavut, and willow ptarmigan are found through much of Nunavut except the eastern Baffin Island. They may be difficult to find close to communities because they are a country food item.

The snowy owl is a magnificent sight on the open tundra. Blatantly obvious perched upon the tundra, a snowy owl appears so white it is almost luminescent. Snowy owls are active during the day and may be seen throughout Nunavut when populations of lemmings peak. As lemming populations may vary among areas, check with local outfitters or the wildlife officers at the community Resources, Wildlife and Economic Development office as to whether they have been recently seen in the area you plan to visit.

Tundra peregrine falcons can be seen at many places across Nunavut. Peregrine falcon hot spots include Wager Bay, Bathurst Inlet, and Rankin Inlet. They also breed close to Coral Harbour. Surrounding Rankin Inlet is one of the densest and most easily accessible populations of peregrine falcons in the world. They are often seen at the airport, or you can take a taxi ride to the Meliadine River Territorial Park to observe a nearby nest. Peregrines may be observed hunting over colonies of black guillemots, flying almost at ground level over the tundra searching for fledgling passerines, and even lemmings — a prey item unusual for this species. The Rankin Inlet peregrine population has been studied for the last 15 years, and visiting biologists will happily answer any questions you may have. Unfortunately, the future of this program is uncertain, so check with the local Resources, Wildlife and Economic Development office for their activities. Your visit may coincide with one of their public slide presentations.

Keen birders seeking to lengthen their life list of birds may choose to visit Nunavut for a sighting of the ivory gull. Rarely venturing out of the Arctic, it is common in the eastern High Arctic. It spends the winter along the floe edge between Greenland and Canada and may be seen along the floe edge at Pond Inlet, especially during migration in late May/early June and later in October, as well as during the summer months in open coastal waters adjacent to colonies further inland. Occasional sightings are also made of the Ross's gull by lucky birders in the Baffin Region, although it seldom breeds in the Canadian Arctic. They have also been spotted on the Boothia Peninsula, Igloolik, Cornwallis, and McConnell River, so wherever you are, keep your head up, and your binculars handy.

Parasitic jaeger and long-tailed jaeger nest on the arctic tundra throughout Nunavut. A third species, the Pomarine jaeger, is limited to parts of the Kitikmeot, southern Baffin Island, and southern Southampton Island. Described as "dashing pirates" for their habit of robbing other birds of food, jaegers also prey on lemmings, the eggs and young of nesting songbirds and shorebirds. All three species may be seen around Kugluktuk, Cambridge Bay, Bathurst Inlet and Umingmaktok.

Few places in the world can match the sheer scale of seabird colonies in the Arctic. An incredible place to observe seabirds is the Prince Leopold Island Bird Sanctuary, which is accessible from Resolute. The steep cliffs of this small island are home to almost 375,000 seabirds, including thick-billed murres, northern fulmars, black-legged kittiwakes and black guillemots. Other places to enjoy the spectacle of such dense concentrations of seabirds are Bylot Island National Migratory Bird Sanctuary, accessible from Pond Inlet, and Coburg Island, accessible from Grise Fiord.

Few groups of birds herald the arrival of the warm months in Nunavut like waterbirds. Early June, when bodies of open water are limited, is one of the best times to observe them. Flocks of common eider and the gaudy king eiders are often seen skimming low over the sea ice and at meltwater ponds or leads. They are relatively numerous near Igloolik and Cape Dorset but may be seen from many coastal communities along the ice edge during migration. Males gather on the sea from early July before departing for the South. Rafts of females and young persist in northern regions through September and into November in southeastern Baffin Island. Long-tailed duck (oldsquaw) and northern pintail are probably the most common ducks throughout the region, but surf scoter and common scoter may be seen. The red-throated loon breeds throughout Nunavut, while Pacific loons may be seen on tundra ponds throughout most of Nunavut, except for the High

Arctic and northern Baffin Island. The yellow-billed loon breeds on tundra lakes and rivers throughout the Kitikmeot Region, northern parts of the Kivalliq Region and Baker Lake. It is replaced by the common loon in the southern Baffin and southern Kivalliq regions.

Many North American birders will be familiar with the species of geese that are found in Nunavut. A visit to Nunavut will give the opportunity, however, to see these species on their breeding grounds. Some 450,000 lesser snow geese, particularly those of the blue color phase, 50,000 Canada geese, and 1,600 Brant can be seen on the vast sedge lowlands and tidal flats of the Dewey Soper Bird Sanctuary. This is an excellent birding area and has been recognized by the United Nations Educational, Scientific and Cultural Organization (UNESCO) as "a wetland of international importance." Sabine's gulls and red phalaropes also nest here. Presently, the only way to get there is by air charter from Iqaluit. More easily accessible, and for less money, is the McConnell River Bird Sanctuary, just south of Arviat, where 300,000 lesser snow geese and Ross' geese nest. Northern pintail, black duck, common goldeneye, lesser scaup, and green-winged teal may also be seen here, and perhaps a short-eared owl. Harry Gibbons Bird Sanctuary on Southampton Island, accessible from Coral Harbour, is rich with waterfowl, nesting black-bellied plovers, and Brant. Brant may also be seen at Katannilik Territorial Park Reserve, near Kimmirut.

Shorebirds form one of the principal groups of arctic avifauna, with a variety of species nesting in Nunavut including black-bellied, semi-palmated, and lesser golden plovers; ruddy turnstones; dunlin, pectoral, Baird's, semi-palmated, and white-rumped sandpipers and two species of phalaropes — both red and red-necked. Arviat and Coral Harbour are prime locations for excellent views of shorebirds.

Responsible Birding and Photography of Birds

"Leave only footprints, and take only photographs" is a good adage for any ecotourist. For those wishing to observe or photograph nesting birds in any environment, however, a more stringent code of ethics and behavior is necessary. Nesting birds in the Arctic, like anywhere else, can be very sensitive to disturbances. Keeping an adult off the nest for a prolonged period may attract the unwelcome attention of predators, or result in the nest being abandoned, the lethal cooling of eggs, or death of nestlings due to exposure. For many species, the only indication of a nearby nest may be the raucous or seemingly bizarre behavior of the adult in attendance. Walk away and let the adult return to the daily grind of raising a family in a harsh environment. For some raptor species, this may entail walking even up to a couple of kilometres away from the nesting cliff. An undisturbed adult may treat the patient observer to intimate portraits of family life.

Equipment

The amount and expense of gear actually necessary for an enjoyable birding trip to Nunavut is pretty minimal. Bring your own binoculars to Nunavut as availability and selection are likely to be limited. Most birders will find the *Field Guide to the Birds of North America* — Second Edition, National Geographic Society, a useful reference in the field. Check on the Internet or at your local specialist birding store for this book and other specialist guides.

Stout waterproof footwear are necessary for hikes across the sometimes soggy tundra.

Don't leave home without a plentiful supply of mosquito repellent. In my experience, I've found repellents containing less than 95 per cent DEET are almost worthless for protection. However, according to the Drug Information Centre with the Faculty of Pharmacy, University of Toronto, 30 per cent DEET is acceptable for adults and 10 per cent DEET for children under five. High concentrations of DEET have proven toxic to some people. Its effect varies with individuals.

Unfortunately, DEET is as repellent to humans as it is to bugs! Make sure you don't get any on your fingers or in your eyes. DEET may also melt many plastics and rubbers, so take care with your cameras and binoculars! For more tips on battling bugs in the Arctic, read Chapter 14, "Insects."

LAND AND WILDLIFE: DIRECTORY

The 819 and 403 area codes change to 867 on Oct. 21, 1997.

Bathurst Inlet Lodge
P.O. Box 820, Yellowknife NT,
X1A 2N6 Canada
Tel.: (403) 873-2595 or
(403) 920-4330
Fax: (403) 920-4263
E-mail: bathurst@internorth.com
Web site: www.canadiana.com/vnorth/bathurst

Nunavut Tourism
P.O. Box 1450, Iqaluit NT,
X0A 0H0 Canada
Tel.: 1-800-491-7910 (for Canada and the United States)
Tel.: (819) 979-6551
Fax: (819) 979-1261
E-mail: nunatour@nunanet.com
Web site: www.nunatour.nt.ca

Resources, Wildlife and Economic Development
For grizzly bear safety course.
Tel.: (403) 982-7240
Fax: (403) 982-3701

Sila Lodge/Frontiers North Inc.
173 Ragsdill Rd., Winnipeg MB,
R2G 4C6 Canada
Attention: Lynda Gunter
Tel.: 1-800-663-9832 or (204) 949-2050
Fax: (204) 663-6375
E-mail: frontiers_north@mb.sympatico.ca

Activities

HUNTING AND FISHING

by Jerome Knap

Big-game hunting is a major component of Nunavut's tourism industry, with good reason.

Most Inuit are still active hunters, so there is always an ample supply of available guides. Nunavut also boasts some of the world's premier big-game animals. In addition to majestic polar bears, elusive barren-ground grizzlies and seemingly prehistoric muskoxen, hunters can set their sights on caribou, wolves, wolverines and, for the first time since the 1950s, walruses.

Nunavut Tourism has published the comprehensive *Nunavut Sport Hunting Guide*, which lists all hunting operators in Nunavut. When booking a hunting or fishing trip, make sure the outfitter is licensed, bonded, and has liability insurance. Any operator should also be able to provide references of past clients.

Polar Bears

The ice bear is arguably the planet's top big-game trophy. With 50 per cent of the world's population of polar bears, Nunavut is the premier place to hunt them. But venturing out in search of *nanuq* — the Inuktitut word for polar bear — is not for the faint of heart. By international agreement, these hunts must be conducted by traditional methods, utilizing dogteams. Each community in Nunavut controls an annual quota for polar bears through individual HTOs. Sometimes, HTOs also act as outfitters by hiring guides and organizing hunts.

Until very recently, polar bear trophies could not be imported into the United States (US) according to the US Marine Mammal Protection Act. This act has recently been amended, however, and American hunters are now permitted to take back trophies from approved polar bear populations in Canada. Check with the **Resources, Wildlife and Economic Development** office nearest your destination to determine if a quota has been approved for importation. Since this act seems to change periodically, it also might be a good idea for American hunters to check with the **US Fish and Wildlife Service** before entering Canada.

Muskoxen

With the exception of Baffin Island, muskoxen are found almost anywhere in Nunavut. The largest populations are found on Victoria Island, where there is an estimated population of 43,000. As with polar bears, all hunting and outfitting for muskoxen is subject to annual quotas, as allocated and organized through community HTOs.

In the Baffin Region, muskox hunting is restricted to the High Arctic: southern Ellesmere Island, Devon Island, Bathurst Island, and northern Prince of Wales Island. Hunts in these areas can be organized from Grise Fiord and Resolute. High Arctic muskoxen are generally smaller than those found farther south.

In the Kitikmeot Region, muskox hunting can be arranged from almost any community. Hunting takes place along both the Coronation and Queen

Maud gulfs, Victoria Island, King William Island, Boothia Peninsula, and southern Prince of Wales Island. The world's largest trophies are taken from mainland quotas in the Coronation Gulf and Queen Maud Gulf areas. In many communities, it is possible to take advantage of combination hunts, both for caribou and muskoxen, and to hunt opportunistically for wolves and wolverines.

Caribou

Nunavut has three races, or subspecies, of caribou, and an intergrade between the barren-ground and Peary caribou. Members of the smallest race, Peary caribou are near white and found most commonly on the High Arctic islands, although they can also be found on northwest Victoria Island and the northern portions of Prince of Wales Island, Somerset Island, and the Boothia Peninsula. Due to recent, drastic starvation events that have reduced some herds by as much as 80 per cent, Peary caribou are currently under intensive management scrutiny. Subsistence hunting has been voluntarily restricted, and sports hunting within the animal's range has been banned. The reindeer on the Belcher Islands are the private property of the people of Sanikiluaq and are not hunted.

Larger and more numerous barren-ground caribou are found on the Nunavut mainland and Baffin Island. These caribou form the large, well-known migrating herds, and include the Bathurst, Bluenose, Beverly, and Qamanirjuaq herds. Caribou can also be found on Southampton Island. In total, these herds now comprise more than 1.2 million animals in populations that are either stable or increasing slightly. Trophy hunting is done by intercepting the caribou during their autumn migration. Hunts can be arranged from many communities.

An intergrade or hybrid of these two races is found on southern Victoria Island, King William Island, and the Boothia Peninsula, where it is possible to hunt Peary-like caribou. Quotas are available in Pelly Bay, Taloyoak, Gjoa Haven, Cambridge Bay, and Kugluktuk. The status of these animals is currently under investigation.

Barren-Ground Grizzly

Extirpated over much of its range during the height of the fur trade, this relatively small but aggressive grizzly has made an amazing comeback in recent years.

Commercial quotas for sports hunts are only available in the Kivalliq and Kitikmeot regions. The most consistent hunts take place around the communities of Kugluktuk, Umingmaktok, and Bathurst Inlet, where close to 10 bears are taken annually. Hunts are conducted almost exclusively in early May, when bears come out of hibernation and there is still enough snow on the ground for tracking.

Wolves and Wolverines

Wolves are common in Nunavut, and can be separated into two types. On the mainland, wolves move seasonally with caribou, their main prey. In the High Arctic, wolves are more resident and tied to locally available prey species. Wolves are highly prized for their pelts, which are commonly used to trim traditional parkas. Wolf hunting is available upon request with some outfitters, and can be done opportunistically along with a grizzly or muskox spring hunt. Potential hunters should keep in mind that physical fitness is most important in hunting wolves, as tracking is done at high speeds by snowmobile.

Wolverines are prized everywhere in Nunavut as a source of superior parka trim and hood trim. Densities of these terrestrial scavengers are highest within the ranges of the major caribou herds. Most of the annual wolverine catch occurs in the western Kitikmeot Region.

Marine Mammals

Until three years ago, only individuals with a General Hunting Licence could hunt walrus in Nunavut. Now a very limited — and somewhat experimental — hunting season has been opened for non-resident hunters. Special quotas have been established to benefit communities with walrus populations. Non-resident hunters take the tusks; the walrus meat stays in the village. Hall Beach, Igloolik, and Coral Harbour are currently operating walrus hunts.

The only other marine mammals for which licences are available are ringed and harp seals.

Licences and Export Permits

Visitors wishing to hunt in Nunavut are required to use licensed outfitters; hunting licence applications are submitted upon booking a hunt. Hunting licences are processed and issued by the nearest office of the Department of Resources, Wildlife and Economic Development.

You currently need a Northwest Territories Export Permit to export all wildlife parts from Nunavut, including wildlife you have hunted. Permits can be obtained in all hamlets from local wildlife officers or other government personnel. No territorial permit is required to export fish or items manufactured from wildlife parts. Exporting marine mammal parts requires a separate Marine Mammal Transportation Licence. For details on export permits, licence fees, trophy fees, and hunting seasons, contact the Department of Resources, Wildlife and Economic Development.

Exporting certain wildlife products (polar bears, grizzlies, wolves, and walruses) from Canada requires an international export document called CITES (Convention on International Trade in Endangered Species). The regional offices of the Department of Resources, Wildlife and Economic Development in Iqaluit, Arviat, and Kugluktuk are the only places in Nunavut that issue CITES documents.

Before coming to Nunavut, hunters must learn the import regulations of their home countries. You may want to defer this responsibility to a Customs broker familiar with these requirements. Also note that hunters must often pay a fee for sports-hunted trophies that can cost hundreds of dollars.

Fishing

From huge lake trout lurking in the deep, cold lakes of the Kivalliq Region and the Arctic Coast, to battling arctic char cruising the pools and estuaries of arctic rivers, Nunavut is home to some of the world's best fishing.

Many Nunavut outfitters and tour operators specialize in fishing trips. Unless you are an experienced northern traveller, it's probably wise to start out with a package trip that provides a local guide. Some packages also provide visits to traditional Inuit outpost camps. There are a few fishing lodges in Nunavut, though not as many as in the western Northwest Territories.

Most arctic fishing is done with lures. Dedicated fly fishermen, however, will enjoy the thrill of arctic char and grayling. Check with your outfitter to determine the most appropriate equipment. Due to the slow rate of growth of arctic fish, catch-and-release fishing is encouraged for sport fishermen, although you are certainly allowed to keep and eat your catch, within limits. There is usually no difficulty in taking some of your catch home, but it will have to be frozen.

Of all the game fish found in Nunavut, none is as sought after as the legendary arctic char, considered by many fishermen to be one of the top game fish in the world. There are, however, only a few established char fishing camps in Nunavut, and only two lodges offer char fishing. Community outfitters and guides will be well versed in the best local char fishing spots.

Baffin Region

On Baffin Island, all the rivers in Steensby Inlet — including the Erickson, Nina Bang, Rowley, and Isortoq — have excellent char runs, but only the Rowley has an airstrip suitable for a Twin Otter. This is also true of the rivers on the isolated west side of Baffin Island, where only the Koukdjuak, flowing from huge Nettilling Lake, is accessible by aircraft. Nettilling Lake has several gravel bars suitable for airplane landings.

In north Baffin, the Robertson River, which flows into Milne Inlet near Pond Inlet, is excellent for char fishing but requires an expensive air charter. Two other outstanding char rivers in north Baffin are the Jungersen and Moffat, which offer superb fishing in late August and early September.

Several river estuaries on Cumberland Sound offer excellent char fishing in early and mid-summer, although stocks here have decreased somewhat in recent years due to commercial fishing in the area. There is also char fishing in the Tongait River, whose stunning scenery will appeal to all anglers. Clearwater Fiord is another popular char fishing spot in the sound.

Not all of the best char fishing in the Baffin Region is confined to Baffin Island itself, however. Near the community of Hall Beach, huge char inhabit the waters of Hall Lake (as do superb lake trout); on Melville Peninsula there is also an excellent gravel airstrip at the southwest end of the lake. The rivers that empty into Hall Lake offer exciting char runs, too.

The most unique fishing spot in Nunavut has to be Lake Hazen, the most northerly lake in North America, located in Ellesmere Island National Park Reserve. Char here are surprisingly abundant though smaller than their southern brethren. The problem is that in some years, the ice on the lake never melts completely. Nearby Ruggles River offers an excellent char run as well.

Kitikmeot Region

Two fishing lodges in the Kitikmeot currently specialize in char fishing: **Plummer's Lodge at Tree River in the Coronation Gulf**, and the **High Arctic Lodge**

on Victoria Island, at Surrey Lake. The Tree River once yielded a world-record char of 32.4 pounds and a fly-fishing record char of 21.6 pounds. Tree River is extensively managed, though, and only 700 char can be caught each year. High Arctic Lodge offers excellent wildlife viewing opportunities in addition to outstanding char fishing.

There are also many char runs available to those willing to charter planes or boats to remote locations. The Bathurst Inlet area offers more than five char runs and boasts some of the most stunning scenery in the entire region. These runs include the Nauyak, Ekalulia, Hiukitak, Burnside, Western, and Hood rivers.

From Cambridge Bay, char runs can be accessed at Ferguson Lake and Char Lake on Victoria Island. Char runs in the Queen Maud Gulf area (the Perry and Ellice rivers) are also accessible from here. **Adlair Aviation** of Cambridge Bay can arrange day trips to these locations.

What may be perhaps the world's largest char run takes place every year on the Coppermine River, where char can be taken in spawning grounds some 300 kilometres inland from the river mouth. This is one of the few places in the world char can be taken in sight of trees. Subsistence use of this river is high, though, limiting sport-fishing opportunities. The community of Kugluktuk stages an annual fishing derby that is gaining popularity among visitors.

Several char runs occur in the Chantry Inlet area, south of Gjoa Haven. Smaller runs are also accessible on King William Island. Taloyoak boasts fine runs on the Netsilik, Lord Lindsay, and Garry rivers.

Arctic char taken near Pelly Bay are renowned for their taste and distinctive deep crimson flesh, indicative of a diet high in crustaceans. These fish are often the preference of Kitikmeot residents.

The major sport fish of the Kitikmeot Region is the lake trout, found in every significant lake system in the region. These fish can be taken at almost any time of year, either by jigging through the ice, trolling on large lakes, or casting from shore.

North of Taloyoak, fishermen have the privilege of fishing the most northerly lake trout in continental North America, west of Lord Lindsay Lake. In some lakes it is possible to average 10-pound catches all day. Each lake system has its own type of trout, depending on stock genetics and available feed.

Taloyoak and Cambridge Bay are the gateways to the most accessible large lakes in the region. Near Taloyoak, lakes such as the Hansteen, Jekyll, Angmaluktuk, Ishluktuk, Lady Melville, and Netsilik offer excellent trout fishing. Legend says that trout have swamped kayaks in some of these lakes, pulling down hapless paddlers. This is not particularly unbelievable after viewing 60-pound catches. Out of Cambridge Bay, Kitiga and Ferguson lakes offer excellent trout fishing.

In Kugluktuk, try for lake trout in Emagyok and Imik lakes, both within 60 kilometres of town.

Lake whitefish are also common, and easily caught with a slower, deeper retrieve. Grayling are generally confined to the western portion of the region, and can be caught in most moving freshwater streams and rivers.

Kivalliq Region

Like other Nunavut communities, those in the Kivalliq Region all have access to char rivers. Of course, some have more than others, and the abundance of char varies with the season. There are some exemplary fishing spots, however.

Duke of York Bay on Southampton Inlet boasts a number of char rivers. Char spend much of the short arctic summer in the bay and can be caught by simply rough casting from rocky points. The problem here is access; it's a day's travel from Repulse Bay through a strait that frequently remains clogged with ice throughout the summer. Closer to Coral Harbour, Sixteen-Mile Brook and Rocky Brook offer excellent char runs.

Most of the rivers that flow into the west shore of Hudson Bay boast arctic char. The Maguse River near Arviat is a particularly good spot, as is Sandy Point, which is also accessible from Whale Cove. In Rankin Inlet, try the Dianne River and Corbet Inlet.

Chesterfield Inlet is also an outstanding place for char fishing. In fact, the fish run from Chesterfield Inlet to Baker Lake and on into the Thelon River system as far as Shultz Lake.

The major sport fish of the Kivalliq Region is the lake trout. Lakes in the southern part of the region also have huge northern pike; many streams are filled with arctic grayling.

The biggest lake in the region is Dubawnt Lake. Trout as big as 40 pounds lurk here; grayling fishing is outstanding. East and south of the lake are several lodges with excellent fishing. This may well be the best lake trout water in Nunavut. If interested, fishermen can also fly to the Kazan River for lake trout, grayling and northern pike.

Shultz Lake, in the Thelon River system, also has lake trout and arctic grayling.

Fishing Regulations

If you are between the ages of 16 and 65 and plan on fishing in Nunavut, you must first buy a sport fishing licence, which is readily available in most communities from the local office of Resources, Wildlife and Economic Development. You will receive a copy of the *Northwest Territories Sport Fishing Guide* when you get your licence, or get one in advance from Nunavut Tourism.

As the guide notes, "Sport fishing in the Nunavut Settlement Area may be subject to terms and conditions in accordance with the Nunavut Land Claim Agreement." Your tour operator should be aware of these access restrictions. If you're out fishing on your own, contact the Nunavut Land Administration Office responsible for the region you intend to visit in advance of your trip. The sidebar on access restrictions in Chapter 11, "Adventure Travel," provides more details.

Sport fishing is only allowed in **national parks** with a National Park Fishing Permit.

PHOTOGRAPHY

by Mike Beedell

Photography in the North can be one of the most exhilarating and rewarding experiences imaginable.

It's complicated by enormous seasonal variations in light and temperature. Severe cold and long winter nights evolve into the perpetual daylight of spring and summer, with a quality of light unsurpassed on Earth. This wide range of conditions creates special challenges; to make the most of your photographic journey, it's essential that you be prepared.

Cold

Most photographic equipment today is battery-operated. Be sure to take plenty of extras, especially if you'll be travelling in cold weather. I suggest you take three complete sets of rechargeable batteries and a few lightweight chargers. This way you'll be saving the environment and money, as well. You'll find some good small solar-powered chargers for AA batteries on the market. Remember that batteries lose power quickly in the cold, so try to keep a spare set warm in your pocket. Don't throw away cold batteries; they may work again once they're warmed up. Some northern photographers recommend that in cold weather you keep your camera inside your coat or parka, taking it out only to compose and shoot. This usually keeps the camera warm enough to function well all day without a battery charge. This approach can cause condensation to form on lenses and film, however, especially if you're sweating.

Manual cameras are best for extremely cold temperatures of –20° C and lower. If you have your gear under your coat, keep it in a zip-lock plastic bag to minimize the effect of moisture from your body. Then when you move from a cold to a warm environment, always put your equipment in a sealed plastic bag filled with cold air and allow your gear to warm up slowly. This will minimize condensation on your camera bodies and lenses. (Nothing is more annoying than that moment when you reach for a lens to capture a magnificent polar bear prowling along the pressure-ice, only to find that a frostsicle has formed inside your lens!) As film becomes very brittle when temperatures drop below –25° C, always try to keep some rolls warm inside your coat. Wind your film slowly so it doesn't shatter or cause static to build up. If you wear lightweight polypropylene or silk gloves inside your mitts, these will help you to change film or lenses and perform intricate zooms with your video camera in the cold.

An extension wire that clips on to your video or still camera is another handy item to carry; it allows you to keep your camera batteries on your body to avoid power drain from the cold. A good photography store should have one that's appropriate for your needs. A hand-warmer that runs on solid fuel or lighter fluid is also beneficial. You can even strap one to your motor-drive or video to keep it going in the cold!

Light

Illumination can be very intense during spring and summer days in the North. You may find that you take your best pictures on early spring mornings, late evenings, or during long luminous nights when the sun never sets. In winter and spring, much of this intensity comes from reflections off snow and ice, which are difficult for light meters to measure accurately. If your camera has a standard built-in meter, your exposures will usually be inaccurate and render your subject in underexposed greyish tones. To capture the beauty of a landscape and the whiteness and brilliance of snow, you'll have to increase exposure by 1.5 to 2 stops. If you're not sure what your meter tells you, then "bracket" your shots by overexposing and underexposing what your meter tells you is correct so you cover a number of exposures.

Generally, the light at midday is too harsh and intense for good photography. Morning and evening light is softer, gentler, and more pleasing. The low slanting light of an arctic night has a magical quality. Side-lighting, with the low sun either on your left or right, rather than directly behind you, accentuates contours and texture in snow, giving form and relief to a landscape. Back-lit pictures can also be dramatic. When you shoot directly into the sun just as it's rising above the horizon, however, you should, once again, bracket your exposures. To improve your imagery, study the angle of light and remember these light-awareness rules:

- front-lighting enhances light and color
- side-lighting enhances texture and form
- back-lighting enhances mood and silhouettes.

Nature and Photo Tours

Nunavut is a stunning photographic showcase of the arctic world. You can explore the northern landscape for years, yet still not fully capture the extraordinary variety of its natural and cultural life. You'll be awestruck when you photograph your first Titanic-sized iceberg glistening in the midnight sun. Or when you focus on a swift narwhal, its ivory tusk piercing mirror-calm waters. Or when you zoom in on a polar bear as it moves ghost-like over pack-ice in search of seal. If wildlife isn't your passion, then the magnificent tundra and Nunavut's hardy Inuit and other northerners will keep you enthralled. There never seems to be enough film!

Until recently, travel to many northern sites was difficult, even impossible, unless you had a lot of time, money and northern contacts. Today, photo tours can offer you wonderful experiences that suit your budget and time-frame. Whether you're an eager beginner, advanced amateur or seasoned professional, photography is now within reach of everyone who can afford it. Photo tour accommodation can be arranged at base camps, in the homes of Inuit, or at local hotels within most communities.

In spring and summer, your best times for shooting are during sunlit nights between 8 p.m. and 3 a.m. Shadows are long at this time of day, and color and texture are defined unlike anywhere else on the planet. A quality photo tour will recognize that your schedule will be upset and will allow you time to explore and photograph late at "night" and sleep during late morning or early afternoon. When booking a photo tour, ask how flexible the schedule will be. Many Inuit families and guides also like to travel during the luminous nights of summer.

Your stay at a base camp will help you to get good photographic results at a relaxed pace. Once your comfortable tents are set up in a wilderness area, you can venture out on your own or shoot with the group. On some tours, photo workshops are offered. You get to set the pace. You may have access to an Inuit freighter canoe, a small inflatable boat like a Zodiac, or a larger boat for travel on water. Or you may hike on the tundra, where you can photograph ancient Inuit sites, peregrine falcons and other wildlife, and dazzling displays of tiny wildflowers and colorful lichen.

Back at the base camp, your day winds down over a hot meal with new friends who share your interest in photography and adventure travel. Be aware, though, that group tours require compromise on your part; they offer you less privacy than you'd have travelling on your own or with a few friends. If this is a problem, you'll find that many tour companies arrange customized trips for individuals or private groups.

Point-to-point photo tours (unlike those where you stay in one community or base camp) offer the most variety; accommodation is in northern hotels or camping out on the land with Inuit families. During your tour, you may travel extensively to wildlife and cultural "hot spots." Expect to see everything from congregations of beluga whales to cliffside colonies of seabirds; from community festivals to intriguing historical sites. Serious shutterbugs may find such a tour a whirlwind, especially considering the leisurely pace of community life and the unpredictability of arctic weather.

A home stay with an Inuit family can be culturally and photographically rewarding. Before booking with a tour company, confirm with them that the family is comfortable with you documenting their daily life. If they are, you can ask permission to photograph them flensing sealskins, for example, or worshipping at a local church. The instant results provided by a Polaroid or video camera can help ease any discomfort, by enabling you to share the experience with your hosts. Be sure to respect the family's privacy. Remember, too, to follow through with your promise to send copies of photos to them after you return. That way, the experience will be happily remembered by everyone.

Find out, as well, how long the tour operator has been in business. Keep in mind, however, that experience doesn't necessarily equal excellence. Ask the company to give you phone numbers of previous clients who might tell you what they think of the operator. Nunavut Tourism will give you the names of licensed photo tour operators, although they won't recommend one over another. Obtain the name of the tour leader, and ask about his or her arctic expertise. Don't forget that an "expert" or "famous photographer" doesn't necessarily make a good leader. Such a leader may have poor social skills — and a penchant for too much single-malt whisky! The best leaders have a loyal clientele who return as much for them as for their tours. Beware the "famous photographer as guide" approach, a hook that's used on many photo tours. Be sure the person is a good teacher and pleasant travelling companion, not some pompous egotist whom you'll be stuck with for a week!

You should also ask the company for the number of participants on your tour, their ages, and their photographic experience. The operator should provide you with a list of suggested equipment to bring. As well, ask whether they will assist in transporting your gear; some companies will, others won't. They should describe the kind of terrain you'll be travelling and the level of physical fitness required to make the trip. Most photo tours involve light to moderate physical activity; some can accommodate the physically handicapped. In the event of bad weather, companies don't offer refunds because such conditions are a fact of life in the Arctic. Be patient — your safety is of foremost concern.

If you don't want to book with a photo tour company, but prefer to create your own customized trip, contact Nunavut Tourism for a list of licensed guides. These guides know the land and wildlife intimately, and should offer you a safe and fulfilling journey.

With planning and patience, you'll capture images to treasure for the rest of your life. Remember, however, that northern weather can change in an instant. Whether it is deadly or simply dramatic may depend on your attitude and level of preparedness.

Photographic Equipment and Supplies

Before you leave for the North, be sure you have enough film for your entire trip; you may have difficulty finding a particular film outside major centres. Take a camera, or cameras, that you're familiar with. A northern journey, where you're surrounded by unparalleled photographic opportunities, is no time to learn what your camera can or cannot do!

In Nunavut, summer travel in an open boat is usually a marvellous, safe way to see the territory. Boating has its hazards, however: you and your equipment can get very wet. A spray of salt water across your camera can damage it forever. If you're paddling a wild river — actually, if you're anywhere near water — a waterproof camera case, such as the Pelican Box, is excellent for carrying lenses. It can be a heavy, awkward load, though, to carry on long hikes. A cheaper, more versatile way to keep your gear dry is a waterproof bag that you can tuck inside your backpack. If you're not on a tight budget, I'd take both. The following is a list of equipment I carry on northern photographic trips:

- Lowe-Pro camera backpack
- waterproof Pelican Box
- sturdy, light tripod
- extra batteries
- camera bodies — one electronic, one manual
- video camera and monopod or shoulder-pod
- 20 millimetre lens 2.8, 28–75 zoom, 80–200 2.8, 100 macro, 300 millimetre, 500 millimetre
- flash with extension cable and reflective material for floral work (aluminum foil)
- filters — polarizer, warming filters, ultraviolet, skylight
- light meter
- cable release, lens tissue and fluid

- small umbrella, or heavy gauge plastic bag for shooting during rough weather
- duct tape, jeweller's screwdriver, leatherman stool.

Film

If you're a keen photographer, I'd take a minimum of five rolls a day. If you're a pro, go for 10 rolls a day. For slides, I recommend Fujichrome 50 Velvia and Provia 100, Kodachrome 64 and 200, Fujichrome 400, and Kodak Elite 400. For prints, choose similar ASA ratings. Black and white film is also very rewarding. Remember to take videotapes and extra nicad batteries, as well.

Light at high latitudes, and altitudes, tends to be bluish, especially on overcast days. An ultraviolet or skylight filter will eliminate some of the excess blue without your having to change your exposure. A filter will also protect your lens. A warming filter will balance out the cool tones of a bluish cast.

These suggestions should help you to appreciate and capture the exquisite beauty and clarity of the northern light and landscape. If you have patience and a keen eye, you'll return from your travels with photos that reveal the majesty of this extraordinary land.

by Carol and Bruce Rigby

Campers in Nunavut must be thoroughly self-sufficient. There are few specially designated camping spots and, for the most part, when camping you're generally on your own.

A few communities have a designated campground with outhouses and perhaps running water, but these are the exception rather than the norm. Chapters in the "Destinations" section indicate whether a community has a campground. But there are no trailer parks, electrical hookups, and the like. If you go camping, you must be prepared to "rough it." For important information about weather, search and rescue measures, proper clothing, water outside the communities, protecting yourself from natural hazards, minimizing damage to the fragile arctic environment and other travel advice, please read Chapter 11, "Adventure Travel," as well.

Most communities have a spot where they prefer campers to pitch their tents. This preference is usually based on protecting the hamlet's water supply, so inquire at the hamlet office before setting up in any community.

Under the 1993 Nunavut Land Claims Agreement, a portion of Nunavut's 1.9 million square kilometres became Inuit-owned land. Although their boundaries are not physically marked, these lands are private property and certain access restrictions apply.

Aside from these lands, campers are free to pitch a tent almost anywhere on the open tundra, but it's important to remember that the land you are camping on is probably part of the traditional territory of an Inuit family. Though you are welcome to use it, treat it with respect.

Choose camp sites in durable locations that will show no trace of being used. A durable site is especially important if you plan to use the site as a base camp or if you are travelling in a large group. Avoid vegetated sites or soil types that are sensitive to disturbance. Wearing "soft" shoes around camp is not only a great relief after a day spent in heavy hiking boots, but they also minimize your impact on the ground around your camp site. Avoid camping near sensitive wildlife areas such as grass-sedge meadows. Do not dig trenches around tents or build wind breaks from rocks. Always leave camp sites as clean or cleaner than you found them.

Most parks indicate preferred camping areas. Within Auyuittuq National Park Reserve, the areas near and around the warden stations and emergency shelters provide good camp sites. Around the Tanquary Fiord and Lake Hazen warden stations in Ellesmere Island National Park Reserve, camping is only permitted in designated areas to avoid expanding disturbance beyond sites that already show the heavy impact of visitors.

Camping Stoves, Tents and Sleeping Bags

Campers should bring their own gear with them to Nunavut even if they are booking through an outfitter (unless the outfitter says otherwise). General camping gear and supplies are sold in Nunavut's larger settlements and some other communities, but specialized backpacking or technical gear is not available here. Camping equipment, like everything else, is much more expensive in the Arctic than in other areas.

Nunavut is above the treeline, so a camp stove is required. Camp stove fuel must be purchased in the nearest community because it is illegal to pack it in luggage carried aboard aircraft. Camp stoves should be capable of burning either naphtha (white gas) or kerosene, which are generally available in small communities. There are few places where propane can be purchased in a convenient form for camping (Rankin Inlet and Iqaluit are two exceptions), and often there are local bylaws governing the safe storage of propane. A naphtha stove is highly recommended because kerosene supplies frequently run low in small communities in late summer before the year's supply arrives by sea lift.

Your camping stove *must* be capable of operating reliably in high winds. You should also test and practise using it before you arrive — there's nothing worse than trying to figure out how to use a new piece of equipment when your hands are freezing, the wind is howling and you're famished!

Lightweight tents designed for backpacking trips must be able to withstand high winds. Wind speeds in Auyuittuq National Park Reserve, for example, easily reach 100 kilometres per hour, and there are no trees to offer windbreaks. Low profile shapes are recommended.

Don't skimp on your tent. If caught in a heavy storm, your survival may depend upon it.

Heavy white canvas tents may be provided by an outfitter, but these are most frequently used as cook tents or mess tents. You are still well advised to have a small dome tent for your sleeping quarters. Fire-rated tents are important because accidents do happen when cooking in tents.

Unless you're an experienced cold-weather camper and know your tolerance for cold precisely, bring a warm sleeping bag. Even in midsummer, the nights can be very chilly, and rapidly changing weather means hypothermia is always a risk when camping for extended periods. Your sleeping bag should be rated to at least –15° C. Anyone planning a spring skiing trip in Nunavut should prepare as they would for a midwinter camping trip in more southern climates. A bag rated to –35° C is recommended.

You will be much warmer and more comfortable if you bring a sleeping pad to insulate you from the ground. Foam or Thermarest™ pads are effective, though air mattresses are not good (they're inclined to deflate, especially in cold temperatures). A bivy sack can also provide you with an extra layer of insulation. If you're going anywhere near the water, bring a waterproof covering (even a securely fastened garbage bag!) for your sleeping bag. A wet sleeping bag is useless.

Food

Be generous in estimating food requirements. Nunavut's generally cool environment and rugged terrain place heavy demands on the body's energy reserves, especially when backpacking or doing other activites out on the land.

Campers or others planning to prepare their own meals should come well supplied with food, particularly if specialized products like dehydrated camping food are required. Stores in larger communities offer a reasonable selection of food, and prices are competitive once you factor in shipping costs.

On the other hand, selection in the smaller communities can be extremely limited, especially during the peak visitor season in July and August, which is usually before the annual resupply by ship.

Water

As when camping anywhere, always draw water from running sources rather than from stagnant ponds or pools. A special consideration in the North is to avoid consuming too much water from silt-laden glacial streams, which can cause digestive upset. Let water from a glacial stream settle before using it. Be sure to carry plenty of water to avoid dehydration — especially problematic in cold conditions. Frequent breaks for warm drinks, such as the traditional Inuit tea break, are recommended.

Litter

Pick up and pack out all of your litter. Smokers, that includes your cigarette butts. You can help by picking up any litter left by others. Report any large accumulations of litter, or large items such as empty fuel drums, to local authorities. You can minimize litter and food scraps with careful planning and preparation. Food can be packaged in plastic bags instead of cans, bottles, or tin foil. Carefully measured meals help minimize leftovers and reduce both waste and weight.

If you burn garbage to reduce its volume, use an existing charred area or make the fire on rock or sand. Fire can easily be hidden in moss, and although there's no risk of forest fires, tundra fires have been known to happen — they spread insidiously and are very hard to put out. Take special care to ensure that any fires you light are completely extinguished before you break camp.

Human Waste

In low-use areas away from toilet facilities, feces should be left on the surface, well away from trails, camp sites, and all bodies of fresh water. Choose a dry, open exposure away from travel routes. Leaving feces exposed on the surface will maximize their exposure to the light and air and accelerate their decomposition. If you are travelling with a large group, particularly if you are using a base camp, it is advisable to dig a shallow communal latrine (15 centimetres) in dry soil at least 50 metres away from traffic routes, camp sites, and bodies of fresh water. Make sure the latrine is properly covered after use to hide its presence from those that follow and to discourage animals from digging it up.

If travelling along a body of salt water, it is acceptable to deposit your feces in a shallow pit below the tidal high-water mark.

Minimize the use of toilet paper. Burn it as completely as possible. Sanitary napkins or tampons should be packed out with other garbage, unless you are travelling in an area where encounters with bears are possible. In that case, they should be burned in a hot fire by soaking them in naphtha. Sanitary supplies should never be buried.

While camping in any national or territorial park at identified sites, such as the Sylvia Grinnell campground outside Iqaluit or the warden or emergency shelters in the national park reserves, use the toilet facilities provided and adhere to the instructions for their use.

Waste Water

Use soap sparingly — even the preferable biodegradable types. Leftover soap should not be dumped in lakes or streams. Take sponge or "bird" baths using a pot of water. Do this well away from bodies of water. This allows the biodegradable soap to filter through the soil and break down before reaching any body of water. Clothes can be cleaned by rinsing them thoroughly. Soap is not necessary and can cause skin irritation if not thoroughly rinsed out.

Waste water from washing dishes and excess cooking water should be poured into a shallow pit away from camp sites and bodies of water. Pick up food scraps and pack them out with other litter. If travelling in bear country, though, smelly garbage should be burned and any odorless residue packed out.

HIKING

by Carol and Bruce Rigby

You are probably well aware of the adage "take only pictures, leave only footprints."

In the Arctic, where the land itself is very sensitive to disturbance, we request that you "take only pictures, and leave as few footprints as possible." By hiking amid Nunavut's wild beauty, however, you'll also be taking home some indelible memories.

Before arriving in Nunavut, check to see whether your planned hiking trail takes you across Inuit-owned land. Under the 1993 Nunavut Land Claims Agreement, a portion of Nunavut's 1.9 million square kilometres became Inuit-owned land. Although their boundaries are not physically marked, these lands are private property and certain access restrictions apply.

For important information about this and stream and river crossings, rock falls, safeguarding archeological finds, search and rescue measures, proper clothing, and other travel advice, please read Chapter 11, "Adventure Travel," as well.

Some communities have marked hiking trails in their vicinities. Often there are brochures available locally or from Nunavut Tourism to indicate where these are. Within Auyuittuq National Park Reserve, most of the hiking trails are marked with *inuksuit*. But in other parks such as Ellesmere Island National Park Reserve, Katannilik Territorial Park Reserve and Sylvia Grinnell Territorial Park, there are no trail-marking systems (other than suggested routes marked on the park's photo-mosaic trail maps).

As you hike along, stay on the marked trails. Where these do not exist, plan your route ahead to include durable terrain that can withstand high traffic. Resistant routes include gravel stream bottoms and bedrock. Other hard, stable, plant-free surfaces and snow patches will provide paths with minimal environmental damage.

Avoid soft soil and vegetated areas, particularly grass-sedge meadows. Their drainage patterns can be disrupted by trails running through them. These grass-sedge meadows are critical feeding habitat for wildlife. If you remove or disturb vegetation, soils will be exposed to the elements, disturbing the critical balance of frozen and unfrozen ground, and resulting in erosion damage.

Parks Canada studies also show that low-lying wet areas and wind-deposited dunes are particularly delicate.

In steep terrain, it is least damaging to ascend or descend on rock outcrops or snow. On soil-covered surfaces, it is less damaging to ascend than to descend steep slopes. If slopes are so steep that it's necessary to dig your toes and heels into the soil to get a grip, you should use another route if possible.

If you come to an area in a park where the shape of the land forces you to hike over steep terrain in a place where marked trails do not exist, look for game trails such as those left by muskoxen or caribou. These usually provide the safest and best passage. Keep in mind, however, that most arctic wildlife are far more agile and capable climbers than the average hiker. When descending loose scree, move slowly and cautiously. Rapid descents can cause large quantities of scree to slide, leaving obvious scars and altering erosion patterns. They can also result in sprained ankles or worse.

BOATING AND CANOEING

by Carol and Bruce Rigby

Boating is a popular way to see Nunavut in summer, once the ice has broken up by mid-July.

A variety of vessels ply northern coasts and some rivers. However, boating in the region does require skills and preparation unique to the arctic environment. (Be sure to read Chapter 11, "Adventure Travel," for important information about clothing, safety, and search and rescue measures. Also be aware that there are access restrictions to Inuit-owned lands.) Many experienced outfitters and groups offer boating packages, particularly sea kayaking trips in northern Baffin and canoeing trips in the Kivalliq Region. If this is your first boating trip in the Arctic, you're wise to sign up with a group package.

Outfitters provide boat passengers with flotation suits. If boating on your own, be sure to rent a suit. Life jackets are just not good enough for frigid arctic waters.

Motorized freighter canoes and Lake Winnipeg boats, used by most outfitters, are common in Nunavut. These are six to seven metres long with large outboard motors, and are usually used to transport visitors to parks and other sites of interest. Because of the dangerous conditions that prevail in the North, though, when you rent any kind of motorboat here, you'll also have to hire a guide. If you think the additional cost is unnecessary, you'll probably change your mind once you experience the challenges of extreme tides, winds and rocky seacoasts. Even seasoned northern travellers won't set out on the water without a good local pilot.

Canoeing

The Kivalliq and Kitikmeot regions offer excellent canoeing opportunities on such rivers as the Back, the Coppermine, the Thelon, the Dubawnt and the Kazan. The Kazan and the Thelon are part of Canada's Heritage Rivers System. The Back, Dubawnt and Thelon flow through parts of the Thelon Game Sanctuary. Canoeing is an ideal way to experience the Sanctuary's majestic landscape and wildlife.

Canoeing these rivers shouldn't be undertaken lightly. As all rivers are far removed from most Kivalliq communities, safety should be your first priority when planning a canoe trip. Experienced Kivalliq trippers recommend that you go in a group of at least six canoeists, and use three canoes at least five metres long. This will give you a margin of safety, should damage occur to any one of the canoes. Spray decks for canoes are recommended, as the water will be cold and there may be patches of whitewater.

Weather may cause delays, so allow yourself plenty of time and calculate supplies accordingly. (One estimate is that 20 kilometres per day is a reasonable average distance to travel.)

Also be sure to carry a second set of maps, as they'll be essential to your safety. If you can obtain a global positioning system, you'll find it a valuable piece of equipment, because it will help you locate your position and destination through the use of satellite information. Before heading out, be sure to leave your itinerary with a responsible body, such as the RCMP or the local search and rescue group, in the nearest community. That way, if you're delayed, they'll know when and where to look for you.

In the Baffin Region, canoes are used on only one river — the Soper. Other Baffin rivers, where mountainous terrain has given birth to some of the wildest rapids in North America, are sometimes used by kayakers.

Rafting

Rafting has been tried on three rivers: the Sylvia Grinnell, outside Iqaluit; the Soper, near Kimmirut; and a single recorded descent of the McKeand, which drains from the Hall Peninsula into Cumberland Sound. Iqaluit's one experienced rafting operator runs tours primarily on the Soper. The Sylvia Grinnell provides some whitewater during late spring/early summer runoff. For most of the summer, though, that river is a float trip. The Soper River, too, isn't a demanding whitewater trip. Take suitable precautions, however, as the water will be cold.

Sailing

During the whaling era, Inuit used to sail extensively, but once motorboats became available, sailing fell out of favor. Although there are still a few dedicated sailors today, sailing small boats is uncommon in Nunavut because of the danger of hypothermia. Sailboats and sailboards aren't available for rent.

KAYAKING

by Renee Wissink, with contributions from Carol Rigby

Aside from a dogsled trip, what could be a more natural way to travel in Nunavut than by kayak?

After all, the kayak (*qajaq*) was an arctic invention, a mode of transport for which the Inuit are famous. Apart from the *umiaq*, a much larger open boat used to transport whole families and their possessions, the kayak was the main method of water transport, be it for hunting caribou on inland lakes, or hunting whales, walrus and seals on the sea. While styles of kayaks varied from region to region within Nunavut, they were generally a broader, more robust craft with a large cockpit — quite different from the stereotypical sleek, fast kayak of West Greenlandic design that most people assume all Inuit used.

Traditional kayaks were usually made from a driftwood frame and covered with sealskins. Hunters would generally wear a sealskin *annuraaq* that doubled as a cockpit cover. (This men's jacket, in addition to having drawstrings at the hood and wrists, also cinched at the waist, where the drawstring attached to the kayak cockpit.) Hunters also had to juggle an assortment of weapons and implements (harpoons, floats, lines, toggles, plugs) in order to hunt.

Imagine the bravery required to paddle this frail craft, armed only with a harpoon in quest of a 750-kilogram bull walrus, or even a bowhead whale! Many hunters were lost in the hunt or blown out to sea.

The advent of the kayaking tourism industry in Nunavut has brought the modern kayak back to its homeland. Kayaking venues are endless. Be aware, however, that there are access restrictions to Inuit-owned lands in Nunavut. To learn more about this as well as safe travel advice, read Chapter 11, "Adventure Travel."

For the river runner looking for the adrenaline high of whitewater, short, fast rivers like Baffin Island's Sylvia Grinnell River outside Iqaluit, or the Soper River near Kimmirut, are ideal. Outfitters and packages are available for both. Nunavut Tourism can provide names of outfitters and put you in touch with experienced northern kayakers.

Baffin Island can also provide a number of first descents for the real adventurer. In 1984, for instance, a small group from the Iqaluit Kayaking Club did the first descent of the McKeand River on south Baffin Island.

The river kayaker should not overlook the Kivalliq and Kitikmeot regions since their rivers, including the Thelon and Coppermine, accommodate most of the classic river trips that canoeists have been paddling for years. For the sea kayaker, Nunavut, with its thousands of kilometres of marine coastline, is a paddler's dream. To explore its myriad bays, fiords and inlets would take several lifetimes. Access to Nunavut's marine environment is excellent since almost all communities are located on the coast.

Kayaking in Nunavut has its special problems: cold water, unpredictable weather, sea ice, walruses, polar bears, and large tides are a few of them. Frobisher Bay, for example, has a tidal range in the 12 to 15 metre range, the third largest in Canada. Paddlers must come fully prepared in accordance with the difficulty of the trip they choose. In addition to the standard gear, a good wetsuit or drysuit is a must. Life jackets alone are inadequate. The ability to self-rescue — including being able to Eskimo roll — is desirable. Take the time to learn about local knowledge of prevailing winds, tides and currents. Get in touch with the local HTO. You could also contact Canadian Hydrographic Services for tide and current tables.

If you're looking for a safe, all-inclusive recreational trip, travel with one of the growing number of licensed tour operators offering kayak tours. Communities such as Pond Inlet offer pre-organized tours that save you the headache and expense of transporting boats and gear up north. Hire an outfitter to take you and your kayak to magnificent paddling areas like the territorial historic parks or the Bylot Island bird sanctuary near Pond Inlet.

If travelling on a self-guided tour, make sure your equipment and training are up to the task. Assume everything will take longer than on a southern trip and have contingency and emergency plans in place. River runners in the Arctic add one level to the whitewater classification because of the cold water. A rapid that would be Class 3 in the South is rated as Class 4 in Nunavut. Carry an HF radio and/or a global positioning system, and know how to use them. But above all, respect the land and water, and have fun.

CRUISES

by Mike Vlessides

The stark reality of a trip to Nunavut is that you are likely to suffer some sort of inconvenience during your visit.

The sheer size and remoteness of the place are enough to throw a monkey wrench into the best-laid plans. Add midsummer blizzards, shared accommodation and once-weekly fresh foods, and it's easy to understand why vacations here are rarely steeped in luxury. Unless, of course, you take to the water.

Every summer for the past 10 years, ice-breaking and ice-strengthened ships have been plying the seas between Siberia and Greenland, offering passengers a kinder, gentler northern experience. These ships offer a broad range of services, from basic accommodation and meals to amenities more typically associated with world-class hotels than the Arctic. But this kind of luxury does not come cheaply.

Cost

Cruise prices are as varied as Nunavut itself. The least expensive begin at about $3,000, which will get you five days or perhaps even a week at sea. You can expect clean, comfortable accommodation — similar to that of a three-star hotel — and simple yet hearty buffet-style meals. Just don't hold your breath waiting for someone in a tuxedo to offer you a piece of Baked Alaska.

The more luxurious end of the spectrum carries a much weightier price tag. For as much as $22,000, you can enjoy several weeks cruising the Arctic with European chefs whipping up international cuisine, fluted crystal glasses bubbling with champagne, saunas and indoor swimming pools. The most luxurious vessel now visiting the area is the *MS Hanseatic*, currently owned by Radisson Seven Seas Cruises. And while the *Hanseatic* may be long on luxury, it is still not immune to the vagaries of arctic travel. In the summer of 1996 the ship ran aground in shallow waters near Gjoa Haven, spurring a well-publicized removal of its passengers.

The average naturalist cruise (a cruise that showcases the destination's wildlife and environment) takes from 10 to 14 days and costs about $11,000.

Itineraries

Itineraries tend to change from year to year, so check with the tour company before setting your heart on one particular route. There seem to be more ships in Nunavut every year, though, so the chances of finding one that offers what you want are always increasing.

An especially popular route over the past decade has been the Northwest Passage cruise, which often begins in Russia and travels across the top of Alaska and Canada, usually terminating at the High Arctic community of Resolute, near the North Magnetic Pole. The problem with ending in Resolute, however, is that you never get to Baffin Island, which

ᑐᕌᒐᖓᑕ ᐅᖃᐅᓯᖓᑦ
Mission Statement

ᕿᑭᖅᑖᓗᒻᒥᐅᑕᓕᒫᑦ ᐃᓄᐃᑦ ᐅᖑᒪᖅᑲᑦᑕᑎᐊᕐᓗᒋᑦ, ᐱᓕᕆᔾᔪᐊᑎᖅᑲᑦᑕᕐᓗᒋᑦ ᑭᒡᒐᖅᑐᕐᓗᒋᑦ, ᐃᓄᐃᑦᓗ ᐱᔪᓐᓇᕐᓂᖏᑦ ᐃᑲᔫᓯᐊᕐᓂᓇᕙᒃᑕᖏᑦᓗ ᖃᓄᐃᑦᑐᑐᐃᓐᓇᐃᑦ ᐱᕚᓪᓕᕐᓂᖅᓴᐅᖁᓪᓗᒋᑦ; ᐊᒻᒪᓗ ᐊᑐᖅᑕᐅᓂᖅᓴᐅᖁᓪᓗᒋᑦ ᐃᓄᐃᑦ ᐅᖃᐅᓯᖓᑦ ᐱᖅᑯᓯᖏᓪᓗ, ᐃᓄᐃᑦ ᐊᕙᑎᒥᐅᑕᓄᑦ ᐅᒃᐱᓇᔭᑐᖅᑲᖏᓪᓗ, ᐃᓄᐃᑦᓗ ᐃᒻᒥᓂᖅᓯᓕᖅᐸᓪᓕᐊᓂᖅᓴᐅᖁᓪᓗᒋᑦ, ᑮᓇᐅᔭᑎᒍᑦ, ᐃᓅᓯᖏᑎᒍᓪᓗ ᐃᓅᑦᑎᐊᕐᓂᖅᓴ-ᐅᓕᖁᓪᓗᒋᑦᓗ ᐃᒻᒥᒃᑰᓂᖅᓴᐅᑦᑎᐊᓕᖁᓪᓗᒋᑦ ᓯᕗᓂᒃᓴᑦᑎᓐᓄᑦ ᐃᓄᐃᑦ ᑭᖑᕚᒃᓴᖏᓐᓄᑦ ᑎᑭᑦᓗᒍ. ᐃᓘᓐᓇᖏᓐᓂᓪᓗ ᐱᓕᕆᐊᖑᕙᖕᓂᐊᕐᓗᑎᒃ ᒪᑐᐃᖓᔪᒥᒃ ᑭᐅᒃᑕᕐᑎᐅᓂᖅᑲᕐᓗᑎᓪᓗ ᐱᓕᕆᐊᓕᒫᖏᓐᓄᑦ.

To safeguard, administer and advance the rights and benefits of the Inuit of the Baffin Region; and to promote the Inuit language and traditions, Inuit environmental values, as well as Inuit self-sufficiency, economic, social and cultural well-being through succeeding generations; all in an open and accountable forum.

P.O. Box 219, Iqaluit, NT X0A 0H0 • Tel: (819) 979-5391 • Fax: (819) 979-3238

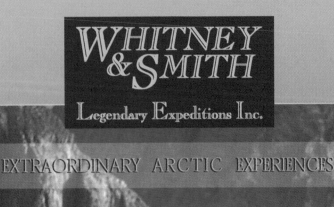

boasts some of the most spectacular scenery in Nunavut. Other popular routes travel between Canada and Greenland.

A Day in the Life

Once you get past the niceties of the vessel itself, most arctic cruises offer a similar combination of activities. These are all-inclusive affairs, so you won't have to worry about making separate arrangements with guides in individual communities. While on the boat you can look forward to interpretive slide shows on arctic natural history from experts in the field, entertaining stories from seasoned northern travellers, and the discerning eye of at least one staff naturalist who's always on the lookout for birds and marine mammals.

Wildlife and bird spotting is not limited to the ship itself, however. Most are usually equipped with smaller and far more agile, sturdy inflatable boats — such as Zodiacs — that are used to visit less-accessible areas where mammals roam and birds nest. These boats are also often used for trips to shore, whether to visit a community, an archeological site, a place of historical importance, or a simple day hike across the tundra. The bigger and more expensive icebreakers also make shore excursions via helicopter.

Community visits not only give you a chance to purchase art from local craftspeople, but also to get a more intimate feel for the people of Nunavut and their unique way of life, an experience most definitely absent on board the ship. Most shore visits are prefaced with an informative seminar; staff or local guides will also provide information and answer questions at the site itself. Sometimes, cruise lines will also book special guest speakers in different communities.

Many tours will also give passengers an opportunity to stretch their legs with a variety of tundra hikes, ranging from short interpretive trips to more vigorous undertakings, such as climbing small mountains. Several tour companies also have arrangements with remote lodges and camps, where there is typically an abundance of a particular bird or mammal.

When booking your trip, always inquire about trip leaders. Don't be impressed solely by a recognizable name. Make sure that the person you're relying on has ample arctic experience, especially with people. There's nothing worse than pulling into a community and finding that your trip leader has an unfavorable reputation there. Travelling with a leader who speaks Inuktitut is always a plus.

Protocol

Some years ago, residents of Broughton Island were shocked when a score of passengers from a cruise ship descended on their Baffin Island community and blatantly walked into homes, took snapshot after snapshot and left with little more than a 'thank you.' Apparently, the unwitting passengers had been told by their guides that the community was a sort of "living museum," and visitors were free to come and go as they pleased before shoving off for the next port of call.

The resulting din raised by residents was so loud that the now-defunct Baffin Region Tourism Association stepped in and drafted protocol guidelines for all cruise ships entering Nunavut. Cruise ships visiting Nunavut are still required to send copies of their itineraries to tourism licensing officers with the GNWT's Department of Resources, Wildlife and Economic Development which, in turn, advises communities of the ship's impending arrival. Individual communities will then inform the cruise director how passengers should conduct themselves while in the community. Ask your cruise director for a copy of these dos and don'ts.

If they are unavailable, rely on your common sense. Don't barge into someone's home unless invited, and don't stick a zoom lens in someone's face without first asking their permission.

Since you'll be entering the community by boat, there's a chance you may come across townspeople on hunting trips. These encounters, while an excellent opportunity to witness Inuit hunters in action, can also be quite gory, and therefore upsetting to the unprepared visitor. Inuit have been relying on marine mammals as a natural resource for countless years; be careful to respect this cultural difference.

Finding the Right Ship

There are only so many ice-breaking and ice-strengthened vessels floating around out there, so your choices are finite. And while there seem to be more companies operating in Nunavut every year, spaces do fill up quickly. Plan at least six months in advance — longer for novel trips that rewrite the record books. For example, a first-ever circumnavigation of Baffin Island taking place in the summer of 1997 has apparently been booked for over a year now.

As with any trip, it's never a bad idea to consult a travel agent. Just don't be surprised if the person on the other side of the desk looks at you bug-eyed when you tell them you want to take a trip through the Northwest Passage. These trips are surely not mainstream, and many travel agents will have no idea what you're talking about. Any travel agent worth their salt should be able to dig up the necessary data, however.

If you find yourself on the receiving end of a travel agent's blank stare, don't despair. In an age where worlds of information are just a mouse click away, there's always the Internet. You'll find that most arctic cruise lines have their own web site, replete with itineraries, amenities, costs and dates. And since most arctic cruises have a naturalist bent, you should find these companies advertising in nature-related magazines and periodicals. Nunavut Tourism will also field questions on arctic cruises.

WHALE WATCHING

by Mike Vlessides

The boat slips quietly through the molten-crystal waters of the frigid arctic sea. It seems as if I've been staring across this vast expanse for hours, with nary a whale in sight.

Perhaps, I begin to think, there's something wrong with me. An Inuk shipmate senses my edginess. "Just listen for the blow," he keeps telling me. "Listen for the blow."

Listen for the blow. Although I've never seen a whale in Nunavut, I know well what he's describing. The "blow" occurs when the whale surfaces to exhale through its blowhole, sending a pillar of mist metres into the air. I relax a bit. I know that when the whale does blow, it will not take me by surprise.

I should have known better. The whales I've seen in the past were breathtaking, regal creatures, but pedestrian compared to the leviathan we now seek: the bowhead, which maxes out at some 18 metres and 100 tonnes. For when the bowhead finally blows, it is like nothing I've ever heard. The hiss of an angry polar bear. The bellow of a distant foghorn. And a V-shaped tower of mist lingering in the air long after the whale has descended into its watery domain. For a brief moment, I am in the company of kings.

Although a relatively recent phenomenon, whale-watching trips in Nunavut are becoming increasingly popular both with tourists and outfitters. In fact, would-be whale watchers can book trips from many Nunavut communities, especially those conveniently located near prime whale habitats. As with any organized trip, though, you'll find that service varies widely between outfitters. Do your homework and you'll be amply rewarded.

The Hot Spots

Every spring and summer, the three arctic whales — ghostly snow-white belugas, unicorn-like narwhals and massive bowheads — migrate north along common avenues. Their destinations, however, are quite different. Narwhals head for deep fiords, bowheads for areas rich with plankton, and belugas for shallow river mouths.

In Nunavut, the best place to spot whales is around the Baffin Region. The coast of Baffin Island, with its countless inlets, fiords and bays, is bountiful whale habitat. Most communities in the Kivalliq Region sit on the shores of mammoth Hudson Bay, a good whale habitat; but you may have to travel further afield to find them in any concentrations. The Kitikmeot Region is not known for its whale populations.

The Baffin Region

Most communities here are in whale country. There are, however, a few spots that warrant particular attention because of nearby concentrations at certain times of year.

Lancaster Sound, the long finger of water that separates Baffin Island from Devon Island, is not only one of the best whale-watching spots in Nunavut, it is also one of the most fertile wildlife regions in the entire Arctic. Every spring and summer, these waters play host to thousands of whales, seals, and walruses, as well as countless birds. The waterways around Lancaster Sound, especially Admiralty Inlet and Eclipse Sound, are also prime whale habitats. The four closest communities are Pond Inlet, Arctic Bay, Nanisivik and Resolute. Nanisivik is a mining town with no outfitters. Resolute, at the west end of Lancaster Sound, doesn't have as great a view of the whales. Pond Inlet and Arctic Bay, where outfitters are keenly in touch with whale watching, are your best bets.

One of the most amazing spring whale phenomena occurs near the communities of Pond Inlet and Arctic Bay, where whales awaiting breakup congregate at the floe edge, in leads (wide cracks in the ice), or in polynyas (areas of water that remain ice-free throughout the year). Here you are virtually guaranteed to see whales, since they tend to return to the same spots every year.

Isabella Bay has long been known to residents of nearby Clyde River as bowhead country. In August and September, dozens of bowheads use these shallow waters to splash, court, and mate. In fact, a national wildlife area, the Igaliqtuuq (Isabella Bay) Biosphere, is in the process of being set up. But the issue of tourism has still to be finalized. Access to the bay is also difficult. However, at press time, the local HTO had agreed a few select group of tourists could enter the Isabella Bay area in late summer with a licensed outfitter, provided a cautious approach into the Bay is taken.

The waters around Clyde River and the Cape Christian area are fairly good for spotting bowhead whales as well.

Cunningham Inlet, on Somerset Island, is one of the best beluga habitats in all of Nunavut. Every summer, especially in August, hundreds of whales fill the inlet and the warm, shallow waters of a local river estuary. Visitors who have watched whales here say it is one of the most amazing sights in the natural world. Arctic Watch Limited maintains a tourist lodge at the inlet and offers a variety of visitor packages.

Other spots of note are: Cumberland Sound (bowhead, beluga, narwhal), Foxe Basin, especially around Igloolik (bowhead), and Sanikiluaq (beluga). Cumberland Sound and Igloolik/Foxe Basin are good for whales in either spring or summer; Sanikiluaq in summer.

The Kivalliq Region

With the exception of Baker Lake, every Kivalliq community is either on or close to Hudson Bay, where thousands of whales summer. The biggest problem is that unlike the Baffin Region, there are relatively few places in the Kivalliq where you are guaranteed seeing large concentrations of whales. On the other hand, belugas often congregate in river estuaries by the hundreds along the east coast of the bay in northern Quebec (known as Nunavik) and to the south near Churchill, Manitoba — a point of interest to cruise-bound visitors to Nunavut whose journeys take them to other waters as well. Coral Harbour is known for large populations of belugas, as is Arviat; Repulse Bay is good for all three arctic whales in summer.

The Kitikmeot Region

As noted before, the Kitikmeot is not as good as its sister regions. Nonetheless, small populations of whales do inhabit the waters of the Arctic Coast, and there's always the odd chance you'll see one if out on a boat. But unless you have an indeterminate amount of time to dedicate to whale watching, your best bet is to go elsewhere.

What to Expect

As with any kind of wildlife excursion, there are vast differences in outfitters' service and prices. At a minimum, though, you want to make sure your outfitter is safe, especially when heading out to sea with them, and currently licensed. If you are even the least bit skeptical, politely take your leave.

Your licensed guide or outfitter will provide a survival (flotation) suit for boat travel. These overall-type units not only keep you afloat, but preserve precious body heat in case of an accident.

Whale-watching trips also vary in their length. Some outfitters will take you out for an afternoon only, others overnight. Expect to pay anywhere from $75 per person for a half-day trip to around $150 per person for a full day (prices based on group rates). Also remember there's no guarantee you'll actually see anything, so don't think about trying to get your money back if you come home disappointed.

You'll enjoy your trip immensely if you take warm, waterproof clothing — more than you think necessary. Chances are, they will be necessary. You should also bring a pair of binoculars, a camera and/or video camera (both with a powerful telephoto lens), seasickness pills if travelling on water, insulated rubber boots, and some extra food, in case your taste differs from your guide's.

In addition to community-based outfitters, some of the larger non-Nunavut-based tour companies also organize spring and summer whale-watching excursions. Often, whale watching is a component of a larger eco-package, but companies sometimes offer whale-watching tours only. Amenities range from kayaks and tents to the luxury of a refurbished icebreaker. A few of the many companies offering these trips include: Marine Expeditions, Adventure Canada, Atlantic Marine Wildlife Tours and Canadian River Expeditions. See Chapter 41, "Cruises," for more information on extended boat trips through and around Nunavut.

When to Go

Most visitors to Nunavut come in the summer: July and August. At this time of year you can watch whales from the deck of a boat or the relative comfort of a land-based observation site. Nevertheless, it is possible to see these marvellous creatures in other seasons as well, especially spring. At this time of year, your mode of travel will be in a *qamutik*, pulled behind a snowmobile.

One last note: Inuit have hunted and eaten whales for millennia. If you would rather avoid witnessing a whale hunt, express this clearly to your guide, especially if your destination is the floe edge, a lead, or polynya.

DOGSLEDDING

by Peter Ernerk

Thirty years ago, in Naujaat-Repulse Bay, the Roman Catholic mission told us three people had drowned in a lake where they were doing spring char fishing.

Later we heard that the victims' *qimmiit* (husky dogs) had walked to a neighboring outpost camp, and that is how members of the other camp knew immediately that something had gone wrong.

Qimmiit, huskies, Eskimo dogs, or *canis familiaris borealis* are all names for these Inuit workhorses. For more than 2,000 years they pulled *qamutiit* (wooden sleds) and provided companionship, helped communicate messages, and guided explorers across the Arctic. As far back as I can remember my father, Athanasie Angutitaq, held these qimmiit in high regard. While snowmobiles have replaced dogsled teams in many parts of Nunavut today, the importance of these dogs remains visible. Nostalgic reminders of an earlier lifestyle, they are used for transportation, tourism, and in annual dog races such as Nunavut 200.

Huskies are built to live and work in the North. Their warm coats do not require protection even in the coldest winters; they think nothing of the meanest blizzards. The fish they eat gives them beautiful fur coats, while walrus and seal give them strength to pull heavy loads. In the past we fed our dogs mostly arctic char, caribou meat, and sometimes seal meat in *Nattiligaarjuk* ("a lake that has few seals"). Huskies are adaptable. They can continue to work even if they go without food for several days. I remember in olden days, when we were running low on food, sometimes we did not feed them for a week at a time, and yet they pulled the heavy qamutiit. No mercy!

In Nattiligaarjuk my family and I would fish at *saputit*, a stone weir, a dam built across the river to trap fish. After spearing fish with the leister (a two-pronged spear used by Inuit) in cold waters, my father and I used to cuddle under the warm caribou blankets with his dog Nakataq, especially in the evenings. Nakataq was the boss of our dogs. He became our *tasikuaq*, the sniffer of seal holes in the winter, and *isuraqtujuq* — the lead dog. During the years that I spent in Naujaat, we depended upon Nakataq for being a good leader.

Years ago, when we travelled inland from the coast in search of caribou, we would walk for many miles. Adults, both men and women, would carry a lot of belongings such as bedding, skin blankets, and a few extra clothes. Our dogs carried the rest of the load, including wooden sticks needed to set up the tent. While caribou hunting, we also depended upon our dogs to sniff the caribou tracks, especially when we were travelling downside of the wind. If conditions were right, our dogs would smell the scent and begin to run towards the herd. Soon, we would see caribou.

Going back to the coastal regions was more difficult as both people and dogs carried caribou meat from the land. *Tunnuq* (caribou fat) was particularly heavy to carry, but in the end we all managed.

In March, when the days were getting longer, we would go out to the sea to hunt seals through their breathing holes. The holes were covered with snow but we used the huskies to sniff out the seal holes. Depending where the wind was coming from, we would walk beside the ridges of snow. Breathing holes were normally on the east side of ice ridges; westerly winds would build up thick snowdrifts here, giving seals, especially their young pups, more protection. Once the dogs smelled a seal hole, they would run until they located the hole. Then we poked through the thick snow until the seal hole was revealed. My father would prepare to wait at the seal hole, while my sister, brother-in-law and I continued to look for other holes. While hunting for seals in the winter, dogs were also used to chase polar bears in case they came to the area. While the huskies fought the bear, it was easier for the hunter to kill the animal by harpooning it. Living in coastal areas can be dangerous at times. I remember two occasions when a polar bear came to our camp. And polar bears are dangerous! Our husky dogs barked and helped to keep the polar bear away from our tent. This gave my father time to load his rifle and kill the polar bear. When danger came, qimmiit alerted members of the camp by barking at dangerous animals.

Some lead dogs were trained to find their way home in the middle of a blizzard. I remember once when my brother-in-law and I were returning home to Nattiligaarjuk from a caribou hunt. The wind picked up and started to blow snow in every direction. Soon we could not see much ahead of us. After travelling a bit longer, we decided to camp for the night and tied up the dogs, so they wouldn't walk away. The next morning, after the blizzard had cleared up, we discovered to our great surprise that we were only about two miles away from home!

In the 1960s, huskies were declining so much that some people became concerned about their complete disappearance. Part of this concern was due to the high cost of snowmobiles (in Repulse Bay, for example, a snow machine was worth about $700) and a drop in demand for furs, one of the few sources of cash for hunters and trappers.

But between 1973 and 1974, Yellowknife's Bill Carpenter, who Inuit call *Qimmiliriji* — "a dog man" — established the Eskimo Dog Research Foundation and breeding kennels, developing a love for the kindly Eskimo husky. Because the Royal Canadian Mounted Police had introduced other types of sled dogs to many Arctic communities, and because snowmobiles and pet dogs were becoming more common too, the husky was no longer pure. Carpenter managed to find some huskies that he felt were pure, and began a breeding program. With help from the Canada Council, companies and all levels of government, he raised several thousand dogs and established a registered line of the Canadian Eskimo Dog. Often, for the price of transporting animals to their communities or outpost camps, he would donate surplus dogs to Inuit team owners. Carpenter has continued this tireless work over the years.

The community of Igloolik can also take credit for the continued existence of these beautiful qimmiit. In years past, Igloolik supplied other communities in Nunavut with these dogs. And in Iglulik Isuma Productions' documentary film *Nunavut*, which depicts Inuit life in the 1940s, real qimmiit are used to transport the actors.

In many communities, these dogs are back in a big way, but as a slightly different breed, smaller in size. They require doghouses, some even insulated, and nutritional southern dog food. What's more, they have shorter fur. However, one elder in Rankin Inlet still operates his dogs the way he did years ago, feeding them country food — uncooked, of course. Seventy-year-old dog musher Robert Tatty won the $10,000 first prize during the 1996 Nunavut 200 dog race from Arviat to Rankin Inlet, and finished first again in 1997.

Tourists can go dogsledding, too. Prices range from about $40 for a one-hour trek, up to $150 for a full-day outing. Dress warmly because weather conditions up here can get cold and wicked without warning. Also, while it's fine to photograph qimmiit from a distance, don't try to pat them as you would pets. These are working animals, and can be aggressive. If you follow this advice, however, you'll find dogsledding to be a lot of fun. Guaranteed!

FLOE EDGE TOURS

by Andrew Taqtu and Jennifer Bernius

In choice spots around Nunavut each spring, a fascinating world unfolds at the floe edge — the place where open water joins land-fast ice, where still waters meet waters propelled by currents.

Surrounded by a landscape of colossal icebergs and glacial valleys, waters come alive with migrating marine mammals and birds that have started their annual trek north in March. Expect to see bowhead whales, walruses, harp seals, bearded seals, narwhals, beluga whales, seagulls, white-fronted geese, thick-billed murres, black guillemots, ivory gulls, pintail ducks, and polar bears.

Camped in their backyard, visitors may see belugas and narwhals just 20 metres away. An underwater view is even more intimate, although diving isn't up-and-running yet in Nunavut as a tourism activity. Film crews shooting underwater footage have been able to get within about five metres of these magical creatures. On land, you may find yourself about 15 metres from a polar bear, if it's not running away. And that's probably the direction you'll hope it will take. Polar bears are dangerous. Your only security is your guide, armed with a rifle, who acts as a bear monitor while you drink in the panorama.

You can also inspect archeological camp sites while out on the land, or lie in wait for a seal at its breathing hole. (If the seal hasn't appeared after 20 minutes, that means it's getting some fresh air at another breathing hole!)

Tours often set out from Pond Inlet and Arctic Bay, with the intended destination being Lancaster Sound and its environs. It has some of the richest concentrations of wildlife anywhere in the North because of migration routes that open up for whales and marine mammals, thanks to its early ice-free conditions made possible by winds and upwelling ocean currents.

Around southern Baffin Island, Cape Dorset has tours to the nearby floe edge.

The best time of year to head out is between April and mid-July when the weather, though still chilly at night, is not so cold that people unaccustomed to an arctic climate won't enjoy it. Bring warm clothing, as well as sunglasses and sun lotion to survive spring's intense sunshine. Waterproof boots should also have warm insulation. Rainy weather clothing is also recommended for nasty wet weather that can pop up between May and July. Many outfitters will supply you with survival suits and winter boots anyway.

An experienced guide will tell you that even for first-time visitors, there's nothing to worry about at the floe edge as long as you're careful. Be on the alert when close to current-filled water. Stay away from the rim of the floe edge. People have been known to fall into the water after treading too close to the edge on unstable ice that hangs above the water; they don't realize the wind has worn it away.

Also be on the lookout when a northwest wind is blowing, something that can happen any time of year when the moon is full. The wind whips up waters, and as a result waves chip away at the floe edge.

Tours

Floe edge tours generally run between seven and nine days, and can range from about $2,000 to $4,000, depending on the length and degree of "luxury" factored into the package.

On most tours, travellers get to the floe edge via a *qamutik* pulled by a snowmobile, or in some cases, dogteam. Crossing frozen ocean and tundra through scenery of breathtaking beauty, this four- to six-hour trip can be a highlight in itself. Depending on ice conditions, the going is rough in places, smooth in others. There are breaks for lunch and tea, and opportunities to photograph a playful seal or two and enjoy the awesome silence.

One such tour, a week-long June-only event that heads from Arctic Bay to the floe edge at Cape Crawford on Lancaster Sound, includes transportation to and from the floe edge, tenting gear, meals, and flotation (survival) suits in its price tag. This rather rigorous tour, catering to groups of four, is designed for hardy adventurers who don't mind breaking camp each morning in order to reach the best spots for viewing wildlife. (Film crews from *National Geographic* and numerous TV networks have taken this tour.) Although there's no set itinerary, a spectacular feature of this trip is the bird sanctuary of Prince Leopold Island. Proposed as a United Nations World Heritage Site, the island is a nesting place for thousands of murres, kittiwakes, ivory gulls, gyrfalcons and jaegars.

Travellers sleep as a group in a large, heated, insulated tent and dine on camping fare. Guides are usually older local Inuit who may speak only Inuktitut. Often, they're accompanied by young family members who translate for them.

A less rigorous tour is another one-week expedition that flies groups of up to 20 by chartered Twin Otter from Nanisivik to a base camp at Cape Crawford. Travellers take daily outings from this fixed camp by snowmobile or dogteam to points of interest, including Prince Leopold Island. Sleeping in a heated, insulated tent with two to three others, the group dines on standard southern fare with some "country food" in a cook-tent. The bill here covers the flight to and from the floe edge, and a hotel room in Arctic Bay on the last night before flying home.

The floe edge experience from Pond Inlet — usually a mid-May to June trek — is likely to transport you to the extraordinary wildlife sanctuary of Bylot Island in Eclipse Sound, adjacent to Lancaster Sound. A photographer's dream, the island is renowned for the thousands of marine and land mammals that migrate here each summer. Its cliffs are also summer home to some 52 species of birds. Near the edge of the island are hoodoos, strangely contoured sandstone formations carved by wind and weather into columns that rise up to 23 metres. You'll also have the opportunity to stand on Sermilik Glacier and drink glacial water — the purest in the world! On Ikpiarjuk Glacier, on Baffin Island, you can visit an exquisite ice cave.

Travellers stay in warm, expedition-style tents (two people per tent) at the floe edge. Your guide may move your camp, due to shifts in the ice floe. Southern-style food is eaten in the guide's tent. All trips include transportation to and from the floe edge and tenting gear — warm sleeping bag, survival suit, winter boots, all meals while out on the land, and the services of a guide.

One final word of advice from an experienced guide: if the ice you're standing on happens to break away, stay on the ice floe till the wind takes you back to land-fast ice. Better yet, stay away from ice that's likely to break away!

MOUNTAIN CLIMBING

by Beverly Illauq

Mountain climbing is elevating Nunavut to new heights.

For years, climbers have been flocking to the tallest uninterrupted cliff face on the Earth — the 1,500-metre-high Mount Thor, located in the Auyuittuq National Park Reserve near Pangnirtung. The face of this giant is so clean that it overhangs slightly near its peak.

Recently, other parts of Nunavut have started to earn mountaineering acclaim, too. In 1995 and 1996, European, Japanese and American teams made major big wall climbs in the area of Sam Ford Fiord, close to Clyde River on north Baffin Island. In 1996, the American-Canadian Hollinger/Synott/Chapman team summited the difficult north face of Polar Sun Spire, which they established as one of the three highest sheer walls in the world at 1,338 metres.

Other fiords near Clyde River have been assessed for mountaineering and climbing potential. Although these areas remain virtually untouched, the number of walls and mountains of good quality rock and grade within a 160-kilometre radius of Clyde River is said to be limitless. Clyde Inlet, Scott Inlet, and Sam Ford Fiord are the closest big wall areas to Clyde River. All of the mountains in these areas are accessible by snowmobile and *qamutik* during the snowmobile season, and by boat in the summer. The sea ice provides a platform for access to the walls. (Climbers should first acquaint themselves with the rigors of Nunavut's unique environment by reading Chapter 11, "Adventure Travel." As when doing any activity on Nunavut's land or waterways, check first to see if there are any access restrictions to the area you plan to visit.)

The best time to climb in the Sam Ford Fiord/Clyde River area is May and June, even though ice conditions vary greatly during this period. Only by May is the weather warm enough to allow even uncomfortable climbing, and if climbers want to avoid being stranded for the six-week breakup period, they must be picked up by their outfitter by June 30. It can take from 10 to 36 hours by snowmobile and qamutik to reach your climbing destination, depending on the distance from the community and ice conditions.

In July and August, climbers must contend with tremendous winds and difficult water conditions. Access to climbing areas would be unpredictable, and the logistics of scaling walls rising directly from the sea very challenging. Summer climbs, for this reason, are usually not attempted.

Because of the harsh climate and the area's remoteness, it is essential to hire licensed guides for consultation about local conditions, for support throughout an expedition if needed, and for taxi services between the community and the climbing areas. Be advised, though, that there are no mountain-climbing guides in Clyde River and there is no means of rescue. Inuit guides, however, can provide invaluable support.

Climbing teams have written extensively about their Clyde River-area expeditions. Some of the best articles appear in *Climbing* magazine (nos. 147 and 158); its French counterpart, *Vertical* (numéro 81, août 1995), carried the same article. *The American Alpine Journal* and the *Canadian Alpine Journal* have also covered the subject.

SKIING

by Terry Pearce, with contributions from Carol Rigby

Springtime skiing in Nunavut is one of the best-kept secrets in Canada. There are open and often spectacular views wherever you go, and you don't have to climb 300 metres or so to reach treeline.

This, combined with about 18 hours of sunshine, create near perfect cross-country skiing. Exotic, too.

In a two-hour circuit outside Nunavut's capital, Iqaluit, you can ski in the company of caribou, sometimes hundreds of them, grazing in herds in the hills and valleys that surround the town.

In other locations you may be lucky enough to see muskoxen, white wolves, arctic hares or flocks of migrating birds. Some communities have parks or park reserves nearby, and it is usually not difficult to hire a local guide to take you and your gear by snowmobile to the starting point of your trip. Bring your own equipment. Ski rentals are not common, even for guided packages.

Another unique experience in Nunavut is skate skiing on the frozen ocean. In late spring the sea ice is an average of 160 centimetres thick along all coastlines, bays and fiords. When the snow has melted from the surface, usually in May, it is possible to skate ski on the ice for miles in any direction to visit islands and other places along the coast. It's a real blast!

At present, Nunavut has no downhill ski resorts (although tour operator Arctic Odysseys of Seattle, Washington started Twin Otter-based skiing in the mountains of Auyuittuq National Park Reserve and Cumberland Peninsula in 1996). The short ski season and limited traffic is compounded by the drawback of hard, ridged, wind-sculpted snow that can lead to loss of control when skiers encounter a chance soft patch.

Self-Guided Skiing

Any community in Nunavut can provide accommodation and serve as a good base for one-day or multi-day ski trips. Once outside a community, be aware that there are access restrictions to Inuit-owned lands. (See Chapter 11, "Adventure Travel.")

For the confident and physically fit, the 97-kilometre Akshayuk Pass can be the trip of a lifetime. Located in Baffin Island's Auyuittuq National Park Reserve, this awesome mountain valley runs north/south of the western edge of the Penny Ice Cap. Glaciers from the ice cap pour down into the pass, adding to the spectacular scenery. Glaciers in the vicinity of Summit Lake (the halfway point in the pass) can be accessed without too much difficulty. Excellent ski touring possibilities are unlimited on these glaciers.

But experience in glacier travel, with all appropriate safety and rescue equipment, is essential. Whether it's for a few hours or days, any wilderness activity is conducted at your own risk.

Guided Skiing

Currently only a few licensed outfitters in Nunavut cater to cross-country skiers. NorthWinds Arctic Adventures in Iqaluit provides guided ski trips (dogteam-supported, and no heavy pack to carry!) to a number of destinations, including Katannilik Park trail, where river valleys and the low mountains of the Meta Incognita Peninsula are traversed to reach the small community of Kimmirut. Another journey cuts across the land and sea ice to a cabin one day's travel from town. Or try the Akshayuk Pass, or even a trip to the North Pole!

Equipment

You'll need:

- warm, lightweight clothing with the ability to wick moisture away from your body
- windproof outer jacket with hood, and windproof pants
- a balaclava and warm headgear (an insulating headband enables you to release heat from your head while keeping your ears warm and wind-free during periods of physical exertion)
- several pairs of windproof mitts. Glove liners are handy for doing up bindings and tying knots without having to expose your hands to the wind, but gloves alone are not recommended because they won't keep your hands as warm as mitts
- steel edge skis

- heavy-duty, double ski boots or single boots with good insulated boot gaiters
- skins for use on glaciers.

In fact, bring all the equipment and clothing you would take on a back-country, above-treeline trip in the Canadian Rockies.

If you're doing a multi-day ski trip, remember that while daytime temperatures out on the snow can be very pleasant with the longer days and reflected sunlight, nighttime temperatures can easily dip below –20° C and windchills can make it seem even colder.

Bring a warm three-quarter length parka — not to wear when physically active, but as protection in case of a spring blizzard or for evenings sitting around camp. Ideally, the parka should have some kind of ruff around the face as protection against the wind (northerners wear fur around their faces for a very good reason).

In springtime, you'll need warm, well-insulated footgear with lots of room to layer on extra socks. A pair of down booties for wearing in the tent or when your feet get chilly is also a good idea.

by John MacDonald

To those who care to look up, the skies above the Arctic offer unique rewards.

Summer's midnight sun aside, the full wonder of the arctic sky is best seen during the dark months of winter when the dominant moon brilliantly illuminates the snow-clad landscape and the stars and planets glimmer eerily through animated curtains of lilac-colored northern lights. For winter travellers to Nunavut, the arctic sky could well be the highlight of their visit.

Due to the proximity of the polar regions to the Earth's axis, as one journeys into the higher latitudes, the visible portion of the celestial sphere decreases while its various luminaries — the sun, moon, stars and planets — appear to take on increasingly eccentric itineraries. Throughout spring and summer at the latitude of north Baffin Island, the sun never sets, the stars are masked, and the moon, if it can be seen at all, hangs pale and ineffective in the light-flooded sky. In winter, things are reversed and the sun retreats to the south, leaving the celestial stage to the moon, stars and planets.

If you are familiar with southern skies you will notice immediately that the stars and constellations, particularly above northern Nunavut, appear in unfamiliar positions. Orion will be lower, the Big Dipper unexpectedly higher, and Sirius, if it appears, will be seen only briefly, progressing slowly along the southern horizon, emitting its brilliant display of prismatic colors rarely seen in more southerly latitudes.

Tilting your head awkwardly backwards you'll be able to spot the North Star seemingly directly above you, its altitude above the horizon equalling the latitude of your position. In early spring and fall, twilight lingers interminably, seamlessly joining today's sunset with tomorrow's dawn. And, in some years, the midwinter moon (depending on the position of the plane of its orbit around the sun), will circle the sky for days on end without setting — winter's spectacular equivalent of summer's midnight sun.

A quest of many winter visitors to the Arctic is the unforgettable sight of the aurora borealis, the northern lights. These are caused by the glow of molecular gases in the atmosphere, activated by charged particles from the sun. The aurora normally occurs in a broad 500- to 1,000-kilometre-wide belt known as the "auroral oval," which is centred on the North Magnetic Pole. Rarely as colorful as auroral displays occurring along the 60th parallel, the northern lights seen across Nunavut are no less awe-inspiring infused with their subtle, shifting greenish hues. According to Inuit tradition, whistling at the northern lights makes them come nearer. Beware!

Over countless generations, Inuit developed an astronomy well-suited to a number of their practical needs, including time-reckoning and the prediction of the sun's return after the winter's dark period, an event heralded by the sighting of the stars Altair and Tarazed in December's morning sky.

Stars were also used for navigation, particularly when hunting on the moving ice floe, where they provided the only points of known reference. The moon provided their calendar, 13 lunations accounting for the seasonal year. Each moon was usually named for some significant event in the natural world coinciding with its appearance. In the Igloolik area, for example, the "moon of returning sun" corresponded to a period beginning approximately in mid-January. June was called the "egg moon" when migratory birds, particularly eider ducks, started nesting. Between mid-October and mid-November, the period when the sea ice freezes over, the moon was known as *Tusaqtuut* — "hearing" — because travel by dogteam was now possible and one could "hear" news from neighboring camps.

The arctic sky was an important focus for Inuit spiritual belief and mythology. Stars, in some areas, were said to be the spirits of the dead, particularly of those who in life had broken taboos. People who died through loss of blood went to the northern lights where, for eternity, they played an endless game of football using a walrus head as the ball. The occasional reddish tinge of the aurora symbolizes the manner of their death.

A widespread myth accounts for the sun and the moon. Abbreviated, the story tells of a sister's discovery of her brother's incest and their subsequent flight to the sky in shame, each carrying torches of flaming moss. She, with her bright flame, became the sun, while her brother, whose torch was soon reduced to smoldering embers, became the moon. The celestial pursuit continues. The sister-sun, however, still aggrieved at her brother-moon's treachery, alternates between feelings of pity and revenge, sometimes feeding him, sometimes not. Thus the moon is forever doomed to a cycle of feast and famine, waxing or waning each month in response to his sister's disposition.

Other myths imaginatively account for particular groupings of stars as well as for a number of other celestial and atmospheric phenomena including eclipses, meteor showers, sundogs and rainbows. During your visit, talk with an elder about these. Your appreciation of the arctic sky will be greatly enriched and you'll discover the remarkable talent Inuit have for observation, imagination and inventiveness.

Some Inuit Star and Constellation Names:

Altair and Tarazed	– *Aagjuuk* (no known meaning)
The Big Dipper (Ursa Major)	– *Tukturjuit* ("caribou")
Pollux, Castor, Capella and Menkalinan	– *Quturjuuk* ("collar bones")
Aldebaran	– *Nanurjuk* ("polar bear")
The Pleiades	– *Sakiattiak* ("the breast bone")
Sirius	– *Singuuriq* ("the flickering one")
Orion's "belt" stars	– *Ullaktut* ("the runners")
Three stars in the constellation Cassiopeia	– *Pituaq* ("the lamp stand")
The North Star	– *Nuutuittuq* ("does not move")
Betelgeuse and Bellatrix	– *Akuttujuk* ("far apart")

EVENTS AND FESTIVALS

by Jennifer Bernius

There are so many reasons to celebrate in Nunavut! At the end of a long, dark winter, what better way to welcome sunlight and warmer days than with a community festival?

Many northerners love a party and celebrate in ways unique to them — through traditional games and contests, music, dances and feasts that may last well into the night. You're welcome to join the festivities, by participating in such unique events as bannock-making or tea-boiling contests, or by cheering on competitors in fascinating traditional games.

In addition to the events listed in this chapter, communities mark several holidays and special occasions in a distinctively northern way.

On Canada Day, July 1, you'll find fun-filled events in most settlements, including parades, games and contests, dances and community feasts.

If you're visiting a community on Nunavut Day, July 9, celebrate the formation of Nunavut with local residents. Activities vary but usually include races, contests and traditional and modern games.

At Christmas, week-long festivities transform virtually every community. Caroling, school pageants, traditional games and races, and church services are some of the ways northerners honor this special time.

Easter celebrations might include dogteam and snowmobile races, and indoor and outdoor games. Feel free to join the events and to attend any church service.

During the Victoria Day weekend in May, most communities sponsor fishing derbies.

For information on these or other events, call the hamlet office (ask for the recreation co-ordinator) of the community you intend to visit. Be sure to verify as well the dates of these festivities, as they can change due to bad weather.

You can also check *The Nunavut Handbook* web site at **www.arctic-travel.com** for updates on events and festivals taking place in Nunavut.

In the meantime, here are brief descriptions of some annual celebrations that *Nunavumiut* (people of Nunavut) look forward to!

ARVIAT

For more information, contact the hamlet recreation co-ordinator, (819) 857-2841.

Arviat Day (June 1): Join local residents in traditional games and concerts as they commemorate the day when Eskimo Point became Arviat.

Inummarit Music Festival (Mid-August, 1997): This three-day annual event in Canadian singer Susan Aglukark's home town is not to be missed. It's a celebration of traditional and contemporary Inuit music, and features talents from across Nunavut performing in Inuktitut and English.

BAKER LAKE

For more information, contact the hamlet recreation co-ordinator, (819) 793-2862.

Hamlet Days (Mid-May): Celebrate the anniversary of Baker Lake's hamlet status and the arrival of spring, with dogteam races, a children's carnival, elders' tea and bannock, and a contest to judge the best traditional outfit.

Kivalliq Inuit Regional Games (June): These extraordinary games turned 20 in 1997 and brought together contestants from all seven Kivalliq communities. Contestants compete in traditional events such as the high kick, harpoon throw, hand and arms pulls, as well as other tests of strength and agility. The regional games are hosted by different Kivalliq communities yearly.

CAMBRIDGE BAY

For more information, contact the hamlet recreation co-ordinator, (403) 983-2337.

Omingmak Frolics (May): This 10-day celebration of spring offers a treat for everyone: snowmobile races, ice sculpting, arctic games, kids' games, bike race, parade, King and Queen, plus Prince and Princess contests.

Music Festival (July 9–13, 1997): Linked to Nunavut Day celebrations this year, this jamboree brings together artists from across Nunavut performing traditional and contemporary music. Fashion shows spotlighting traditional and modern clothing are also on the agenda.

GJOA HAVEN

For more information, contact the hamlet recreation co-ordinator, (403) 360-7141.

Qavvarrvik Carnival (Mid-May): This long weekend of traditional events includes *iglu*-building contests, dogteam and snowmobile races.

IGLOOLIK

For more information, contact the Igloolik Inullariit Elders Society at (819) 934-8910.

Return of the Sun (Mid-January): This traditional celebration, organized by the Igloolik Inullariit Elders Society, is full of Inuit symbolism and ritual, and is usually accompanied by traditional games and a fashion show of traditional dress.

IQALUIT

Toonik Tyme (Mid-April): For more information, contact Toonik Tyme

Committee. Contact the Iqaluit Trade and Promotion Office (tel.: (819) 979-3156; fax: (819) 979-2929) for current phone and fax numbers for the committee. Nunavut's largest week-long festival includes traditional and modern games, iglu-building, dogsled and snowmobile races, and plenty of entertainment. It's a memorable spring festival!

Nunavut Trade Show (First weekend of March): For more information, contact the Baffin Regional Chamber of Commerce, (819) 979-4653 or fax (819) 979-2929. E-mail: brcc@nunanet.com, or check their web site for an overview of the previous year's trade show (**nunanet.com/~brcc**). This is Nunavut's premier business event, and is pivotal for those who need to network. The 1997 edition drew several thousand visitors, with close to 100 exhibitors.

KUGLUKTUK

For more information, contact Simon Kuliktana, hamlet recreation director, (403) 982-4471.

Nattik Frolics (April): Traditional games, snowmobile races, seal hunt, King and Queen contest, square dances, community feast.

Iqalukpik Fishing Derby (Late August): A real family event that guarantees great prizes for young and old, plus great-tasting char.

NANISIVIK

For more information, contact Lois Sutherland or Dawn McConnell, Nanisivik Mines, (819) 436-7502. Fax: (819) 436-7435.

Midnight Sun Marathon (July 1st Long Weekend, 1997): This marathon, celebrating the longest day of the year, is organized by Nanisivik Mines and attracts runners from as far away as Europe and Australia. They compete in 10, 32, 42, and 84-kilometre races between Arctic Bay and Nanisivik along Nunavut's only stretch of road linking two communities. Due to limited hotel space, the marathon is open to only 100 runners.

PANGNIRTUNG

For more information, contact hamlet recreation co-ordinator Billy Etoongat, (819) 473-8953.

Summer Music Festival (Aug. 1–4, 1997): Join artists from across Nunavut as they play traditional and modern Inuit music.

PELLY BAY

For more information, contact the hamlet recreation co-ordinator, (403) 769-6281.

Kitikmeot Northern Games (July 25–27, 1997): Join competitors in these unique events: duck-plucking, seal skinning, tea-boiling, bannock-making, fish-fileting. Cheer the athletes as they compete in the high-kick, one-arm reach and other traditional games.

Midnight Sun Golf Tournament (Aug. 8–10, 1997): Where else but in Nunavut would you find an all-night golf tournament on an original, home-made golf course with rugs taken from the homes of local citizens?

RANKIN INLET

For more information, contact Rick Denison, Hamlet of Rankin Inlet, (819) 645-2895.

Nunavut 200 Dogteam Race (April): Competitors in this exciting annual event race the 200 kilometres along the sea ice from Rankin Inlet to Arviat. About 25 teams from across Nunavut participated in the 1997 version, averaging 30-50 kilometres a day.

Pakallak Time (May): Join in the merrymaking as Rankin celebrates spring. This annual event usually includes dogteam and snowmobile races, indoor and outdoor games, Inuit games, a fashion show and square dances.

UMINGMAKTOK

Kalvik Frolics (Easter Weekend): Each year, the highlight of this very traditional festival is the search for a beautiful wolverine pelt.

ACTIVITIES: DIRECTORY

The 819 and 403 area codes change to 867 on Oct. 21, 1997.

Cruising the Internet

www.cybercruises.com
Going by the name of *Tutto Crociere* — the *Cyberspace Cruise Magazine*, this site has loads of links to other cruise sites, cruise lines, cruise travel agencies, plus tidbits of cruise news in a "Seen and Heard" corner.

www.travelpage.com
Includes extensive profiles of all kinds of cruise lines.

Guides/Outfitters/ Tour Operators

Adventure Canada
Tel.: 1-800-363-7566 or (905) 271-4000
Fax: (905) 271-5595

Arctic Marine Wildlife Tours
Tel.: (506) 459-7325
Fax: (506) 453-3589

Arctic Watch Limited
Tel.: (403) 282-2268
Fax: (403) 282-2195
E-mail: info@arcticwatch.com

Canadian River Expeditions
Tel.: (604) 938-6651 or 1-800-898-7238
Fax: (604) 938-6621
E-mail: canriver@whistler.net
Web site: www.tginl.com/pages/bc/outadv/canre

Marine Expeditions
Tel.: (416) 964-9069 or 1-800-263-9147
Fax: (416) 964-2366
E-mail: marine_expeditions@sympatico.ca
Web site: netsys.syr.edu/~jslinder/fproj

Nunavut Tourism
P.O. Box 1450, Iqaluit NT,
X0A 0H0 Canada
1-800-491-7910 (for Canada and the United States)
Tel.: (819) 979-6551
Fax: 1-819-979-1261
E-mail: nunatour@nunanet.com
Web site: www.nunatour.nt.ca

Qullikkut Guides and Outfitters
For an information package on climbing in the Clyde River area, or a videotape of the 1996 ascent of Polar Sun Spire by the Hollinger/Synott/Chapman team.
P.O. Box 27, Clyde River NT,
X0A 0E0 Canada
Tel.: (819) 924-6268
Fax: (819) 924-6362

Hunting and Fishing

Adlair Aviation
Tel.: (403) 983-2569
Fax: (403) 983-2847

High Arctic Lodge on Victoria Island
P.O. Box 280, Penticton BC,
V2A 6K4 Canada
Tel.: (250) 493-3300
Fax: (250) 493-3900
E-mail: higharctic@vip.net

Nunavut Tourism
P.O. Box 1450, Iqaluit NT,
X0A 0H0 Canada
Tel.: 1-800-491-7910 (for Canada and the United States)
Tel.: (819) 979-6551
Fax: (819) 979-1261
E-mail: nunatour@nunanet.com
Web site: www.nunatour.nt.ca

Ottawa office:
1675 Russell Rd., P.O. Box 8080
Ottawa ON, K1G 3H6 Canada
Tel.: (613) 998-4931
Fax: (613) 998-1217
E-mail: chs_sales@chshq.dfo.ca
Payment required in advance (Arctic volume of tide and current tables is $6.50). VISA, MasterCard.

Plummer's Lodge at Tree River in the Coronation Gulf
Tel.: (204) 774-5775
Fax: (204) 783-2320

Resources, Wildlife and Economic Development
Iqaluit Office:
Tel.: (819) 979-5011
Fax: (819) 979-6791

Arviat Office:
Tel.: (819) 857-2941
Fax: (819) 857-2499

Kugluktuk Office:
Tel.: (403) 982-7240
Fax: (403) 982-3701

US Fish and Wildlife Service
Tel.: (703) 358-1949
Fax: (703) 359-2271
Web site: www.fws.gov/laws
E-mail: R9LE_wwwemail.fws.gov

Maps and Tide Tables

See map sources in "Planning Ahead" directory.

Canadian Hydrographic Services, Department of Fisheries and Oceans
British Columbia office:
P.O. Box 6000,
9860 W. Saanich Road, Sidney BC,
V8L 4B2 Canada
Tel.: (250) 363-6358
Fax: (250) 363-6841
E-mail: chart_sales@ios.bc.ca

Skiing

National Parks
Auyuittuq National Park Reserve
P.O. Box 353, Pangnirtung NT,
X0A 0R0 Canada
Tel.: (819) 473-8828
Fax: (819) 473-8612
E-mail: PNWT_Info@pch.gc.ca

Destinations

Nunavut Communities: Facilities									
Community	Hotels	Restaurant in Hotels	Restaurant outside Hotels	Guest House/Bed & Breakfast	Campground	Hiking Trails	Taxi	Arts/Crafts Workshop	Visitors Centre/Museum
Arctic Bay	•	•			•	•	•	•	
Arviat	•	•	•	•			•	•	•
Baker Lake	•	•	•		•	•	•	•	•
Bathurst Inlet	•			•	•	•			
Broughton Island	•	•		•	•	•		•	
Cambridge Bay	•	•	•		•	•	•	•	•
Cape Dorset	•	•	•	•	•	•	•	•	•
Chesterfield Inlet	•	•	•			•	•		
Clyde River	•	•		•	•			•	•
Coral Harbour	•	•					•		
Gjoa Haven	•	•	•			•	•	•	•
Grise Fiord	•	•			•				
Hall Beach	•	•	•				•		
Igloolik	•	•	•	•			•		•
Iqaluit	•	•	•	•	•	•	•	•	•
Kimmirut	•	•	•	•	•	•		•	•
Kugluktuk	•	•				•	•	•	•
Nanisivik						•			•
Pangnirtung	•	•	•		•	•	•	•	•
Pelly Bay	•	•	•			•			
Pond Inlet	•	•	•	•	•	•		•	•
Rankin Inlet	•	•	•			•	•	•	•
Repulse Bay	•	•	•			•		•	
Resolute	•	•		•	•	•	•	•	•
Sanikiluaq	•	•				•		•	•
Taloyoak	•	•							
Umingmaktok				•					
Whale Cove	•	•					•		

RANKIN INLET

by Jimi Onalik

Ask someone from Nunavut for their first impression of Rankin Inlet, and they may tell you about the wind.

* Population:	2,058 (Inuit: 79%, non-Inuit: 21%)
Telephone Area Code:	819 (changes to 867 on Oct. 21, 1997)
Time Zone:	Central Time
Postal Code:	X0C 0G0
How to Get There:	Possible routes:
	• Winnipeg-Rankin Inlet
	• Yellowknife-Rankin Inlet
	• Ottawa/Montreal-Iqaluit-Rankin Inlet
	• Kangerlussuaq (Greenland)-Iqaluit-Rankin Inlet
	Winnipeg to Rankin Inlet (1,470 kilometres north) is via Calm Air or
	Air Canada. First Air also serves Rankin Inlet
Banks:	The Royal Bank (which also has an automated teller machine) and the
	Canadian Imperial Bank of Commerce
Alcohol:	Controlled. Alcohol can be brought into Rankin Inlet only by permit.
	In the community, it's available only to those who register at a hotel.
	People can also order alcohol from the NWT Liquor Warehouse
Taxis:	Yes

They probably formed that impression the moment they arrived. Located on the western shores of Hudson Bay, the community is well known for its severe winter storms, which can make the walk from the airplane to the air terminal seem like one of the coldest on Earth. But just as there's more to New York than crime, there's more to Rankin Inlet than the wind.

Today, Rankin Inlet, or *Kangiq&iniq* as it is known in Inuktitut (meaning "deep bay/inlet"), is a bustling community that serves as both a government town and a transportation hub for the Kivalliq Region. It is Nunavut's second largest community and the self-described "business capital" of the territory. For the past 20 years, Rankin has been a regional centre for the government of the Northwest Territories, traditionally the largest employer here. Recent cutbacks and layoffs, however, have caused many people to rely less on government as a source of income. Instead, many Inuit have become entrepreneurs, and their stores, freight expediter services, electrical, plumbing and real estate companies are flourishing. Rankin Inlet has become a community of which its residents are immensely proud.

Originally, Rankin Inlet's roots were in mining, and the 1990s suggest the return of mining companies here. Rich mineral deposits in the region,

*Populations for all communities from the 1996 Census of Canada. At press time, 1996 population breakdowns by ethnic groups were not yet available. Percentages cited here are based on the 1991 Census.

Rankin Inlet Street Map

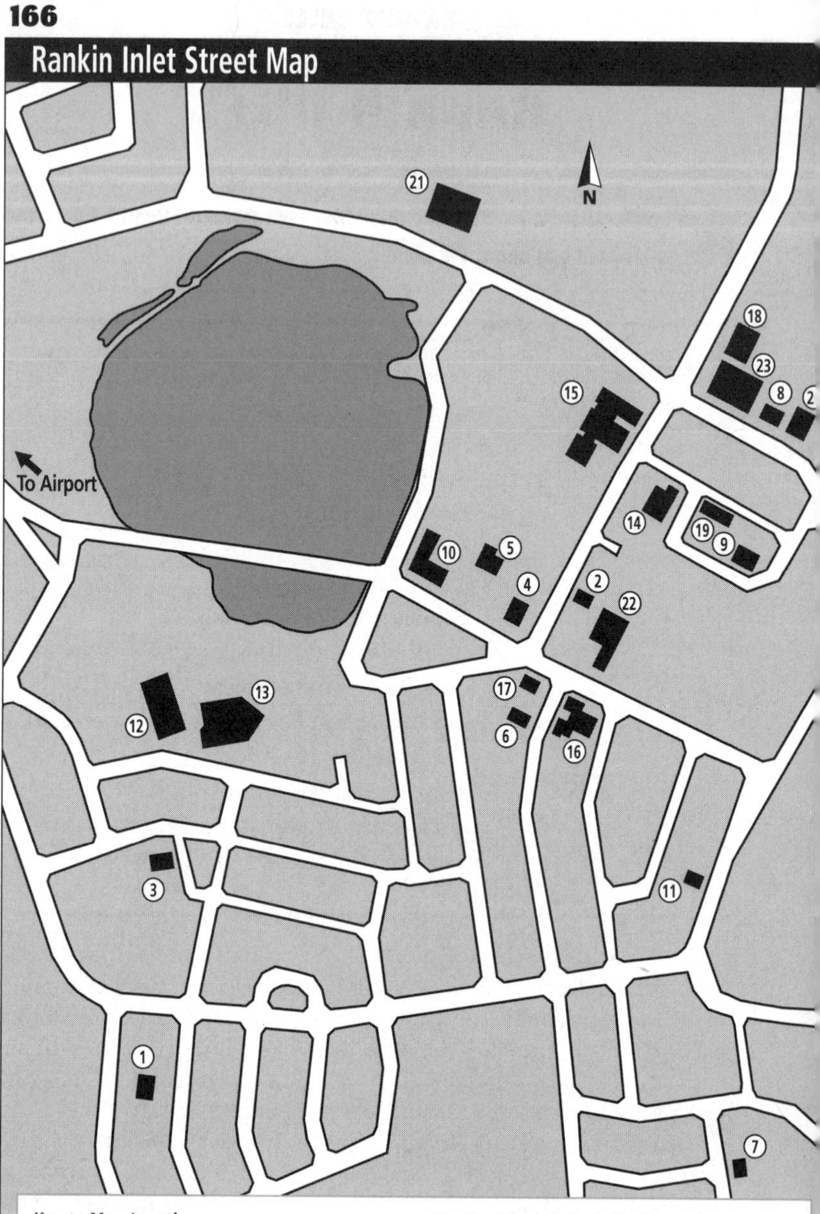

Key to Map Locations

1 C & H Rentals
2 Coffee Delights
3 Glad Tidings Fellowship Church
4 Hamlet Office
5 Health Centre
6 Holy Comforter Anglican Church
7 Hunters and Trappers Organization
8 Inuit Cultural Institute
9 Ivalu
10 Kissarvik Co-op Store and Bank
11 Kowmuk's
12 Leo Ussak Elementary School (includes Rankin Inlet Community Access Centre)
13 Maaniulujuk Ilinniavik High School (includes John Ayaruaq Library)
14 Nanuq Inn
15 Northern Store (includes Quick Stop fast food restaurant)
16 Nunavut Arctic College
17 Police
18 Post Office
19 Renewable Resources Office
20 Resources, Wildlife and Economic Development
21 Roman Catholic Church
22 Siniktarvik Hotel and Keewatin Regional Visitors Centre
23 Treasures Gift Shop, Kiguti Dental Clinic and Sakku Drugs

including gold, have led to a bit of a boom in exploration. The existence of several major exploration camps nearby hint that an operating mine may someday return.

Rankin Inlet, a gateway to the Kivalliq Region, also attracts tourists who visit to fish, hunt, canoe, or enjoy the land and wildlife. Each year, hundreds of travellers bound for other destinations spend some time in the community.

In 1993, with the signing of the Nunavut Land Claims Agreement, Rankin became a major political centre for budding land claims organizations. The head office of the **Kivalliq Inuit Association**, as well as regional offices for **Nunavut Tunngavik Incorporated**, are located here.

History

The history of Rankin Inlet is a story of a people who have triumphed over adversity. The vibrant nature of the community today attests to the determination of Inuit to overcome their hardships.

Although Inuit seldom used the actual town site of Rankin Inlet, they hunted and fished in the surrounding area for many years. Artifacts that reveal this use can be found throughout the region. In nearby Meliadine River Territorial Park, for example, generations of Inuit fished for arctic char during the spring and fall.

The Rankin Inlet area has also been an important meeting place for Inuit and outsiders. The mid-1800s saw the arrival of fleets of American and European whalers in Hudson Bay. To maximize their profits after long journeys to the whaling grounds, the whalers often spent a winter or two frozen into the ice. One of these overwintering locations was at Marble Island, about 70 kilometres from Rankin.

Archeological remains that may still be found on Marble Island paint a stark picture of the whalers' life here. Despite their best efforts, those men from warmer latitudes weren't fully able to deal with the arctic climate. Signs of their efforts to adapt — their cabins, storage shacks and even an amphitheatre where they performed plays for each other — are scattered across the island. If you're touring around Marble Island at low tide, you'll spot a ship underwater. On nearby Deadman's Island, whalers' graves are a silent reminder of those who could not adapt.

For Inuit, Marble Island also has legendary significance; even today, when they visit it, they crawl up to the tide level, out of respect for an old woman whose spirit is said to reside there. Legend has it that those who don't crawl will encounter bad luck on the anniversary of their visit.

The relationship between Inuit and whalers continued until the early years of the 20th century. By 1910, when whale stocks had severely declined, the whalers stopped coming to the Rankin Inlet area. During the first half of this century, Inuit contact with outsiders was limited to missionaries and Hudson's Bay Co. traders.

The 1940s and 1950s were grim times for the Inuit of the entire Kivalliq Region. A shift in the migration patterns of caribou led to widespread starvation among inland Caribou Inuit. To provide food and supplies to starving Inuit, the Canadian government established communities along the west coast of Hudson Bay. The communities of Arviat, Whale Cove and Baker Lake were created to serve the needs of the local people.

Rankin Inlet, however, was formed with a different goal in mind. The Canadian government of the 1950s believed that the subsistence economy was no longer viable and that modern technology would provide comfort to all. The Inuit must be brought into a wage-based economy. The discovery of large amounts of nickel at Rankin Inlet, and the high price of the mineral during the Korean War, convinced the government to do just that.

In 1955, the North Rankin Nickel Mine began production. Many Inuit hunters and trappers moved, with their families, to Rankin Inlet, and became miners, working for a wage underground and in the mill. Inuit were brought in from Repulse Bay, Coral Harbour, Chesterfield Inlet, and Arviat to take part in what was viewed as a bold new experiment. This experiment was to introduce Inuit to the necessary skills for hard-rock mining and to a lifestyle of shift work and paycheques.

The North Rankin Nickel Mine produced high-quality ore and plenty of work for seven years. The Inuit employees were very hard-working and much appreciated by the mine owners. In fact, many Inuit who worked here went on to other mines in southern Canada. Many residents of Rankin Inlet still have mementoes from friends and relatives who worked in towns such as Lynn Lake, Manitoba, and Sudbury, Ontario.

In 1962, the mine closed, bringing about another period of hardship that almost closed the hamlet. Families were now pressured to return to their home communities. Only after a period of negotiations with residents determined to keep their new home on the map did the government allow Rankin Inlet to stay open. By now, however, the several hundred people who remained were used to the wage economy; they needed to find a means to support their families. As a result, the mid-1960s were marked by a series of enterprising, sometimes bizarre, economic development schemes, not all as successful as the nickel mine.

In one venture, Rankin Inlet was briefly the site of one of the most northerly farms in Canada, producing chicken and pork for local use. After accounting for the costs of their accommodations, the chickens and eggs from this "farm" proved very expensive. Furthermore, the only affordable food available for the pigs was fish, leading, as you can imagine, to some pretty fishy-flavored pork.

In another case, a cannery was opened to preserve local foods. Apparently, though, the market for tinned seal meat and *maktaaq* in southern Canada was limited, because this project didn't last very long.

A successful, albeit short-lived, experiment was the creation of a ceramics studio in 1964. The fine pieces produced by the hunters, trappers, miners and artists have been collected by individuals and galleries around the world. Despite the project's artistic and commercial success, the newly formed GNWT never fully backed it; in the early 1970s, it died a slow death. Happily for art-lovers everywhere, this unique studio has been revived recently through the efforts of a local artist. Now a new generation of artists work here alongside their elders to produce exotic, eerily beautiful work.

By the early 1970s, the headquarters for the Kivalliq Region moved from Churchill, Manitoba, to Rankin Inlet. So Rankin was now a government town. The arrival of civil servants and their families revitalized the community. Elders who were born on the land and who became miners, farmers, and artists, could not make the transition into government jobs. Their children, however, did find work in the new bureaucracy. They, like their parents, had experienced enormous change. Today they hold positions of power in Rankin Inlet.

Many believe that the resilience of Inuit, born out of the intense necessity to adapt to enormous change over the past 50 years, will help the people of Rankin Inlet as they face even greater changes with the creation of Nunavut in 1999.

Rankin Inlet: Its Land and Wildlife

The land around Rankin Inlet possesses a subtle beauty. It's often said that its splendor can best be appreciated by seeing it as if through a wide-angle lens, or by viewing it up close, as if under a microscope. The huge expanse of rolling hills and sky gives a haunting feeling of closeness to the land. Intricate rock formations, tiny flowers, and natural wind-sculpted snowdrifts reveal the triumph of art over a harsh climate.

All this beauty is easily accessible. The relative flatness of the land and the many all-terrain vehicle (ATV) and walking trails nearby make it fairly easy to get out of town and enjoy the glories of the tundra. A five-minute hike from the edge of the hamlet will have you in a land that appears untouched by humans. You'll likely discover *siksiit*. In fact, summer and fall belong to these ground squirrels, who are everywhere, chattering incessantly from their perches on top of sandy bumps in the land. Overhead, majestic birds of prey, such as the peregrine and gyrfalcons, keep a watchful eye on the happenings below. Loons, geese, swans and sandhill cranes are other sights to keep your shutter-fingers busy.

Farther out on the land, you may see small herds of caribou jaunting across the tundra in their endless search for lichen and other food. Curious foxes and an occasional wolf may also appear, usually in the distance. Suntanning seals dot the sea ice nearby, or you may see the small heads of seals bobbing in waters close to shore. A complete description of all the animals in the area would take up an entire afternoon of sitting and drinking tea with local elders.

You may bump into some animals, however, that are best seen from afar. In the fall, it's not uncommon for polar bears to wander close to town; and in summer, wolverines and even grizzly bears sometimes appear. Unless you're willing to go down in local lore as the tourist who left town with fewer limbs than when you came, be sure that on your outings you're accompanied by someone who's familiar with local conditions.

The weather in Rankin? Okay, let's get this straight from the start. It can be damn cold here, especially from December to February. Average temperatures from the end of November to the end of March are –35° C, with some pretty ferocious Kivalliq winds averaging 15 to 25 kilometres an hour. To stay warm, you'll have to wear clothing that's at least as sophisticated as that worn by lunar astronauts!

Thankfully, though, the climate isn't always this harsh. Many days in spring and summer are calm and sunny. In fact, temperatures can rise above 30° C in July and August. The trick is to be prepared for a wide range of weather conditions.

Summer in Rankin lasts roughly from mid-June to the end of August. During this period, weather conditions vary the most. Every few years, Rankin experiences a snowstorm in mid-June. Generally, however, you can count on temperatures in the 10° C to 15° C range. There are stories, however, of tourists who complain because of midsummer heat, with temperatures climbing up past the 30° C mark. In weather like this, expect to find almost everyone swimming in one of the many small lakes nearby.

The season in Rankin that resembles autumn is brief. This usually lasts from the beginning of September to the end of October, and is marked by the return of chilly winds. You may actually feel colder at this time of year because of the high winds mixed with wet conditions. Expect weather similar to winter in northeastern United States or southern Ontario or Quebec.

Winter, which lasts from the end of October until mid to late March, is definitely an experience. The many blizzards wreak havoc with flight schedules. Expect an average temperature in the –30° C to –35° C range. It gets warmer during blizzards and a lot colder on clear days. Rankin residents are used to these conditions, but visitors tend to stay indoors and take a lot of taxis.

Spring is one of the best times to visit Rankin. Temperatures warm up to the –10° C to –20° C range. As days grow longer, visitors may enjoy brilliant sunshine, but will still experience frequent spring storms. Half of the annual snowfall occurs in March and April.

Tours

Located in the **Siniktarvik Hotel**, the **Keewatin Regional Visitors Centre** interprets the history of the region and its communities, as well as the cultural heritage and natural resources. A diorama illustrates the clothing and traditional tools used in the past. The helpful young staff will answer your questions and broaden your understanding of Nunavut. The Centre is open all year round.

The **Inuit Cultural Institute**, established in 1974 to protect the cultural heritage of Inuit, has an extensive 1,700-item collection that includes photographs, film and taped interviews with elders — but it's currently housed in Yellowknife at the Prince of Wales Northern Heritage Centre. The Institute will convert Rankin Inlet's old air terminal into Inuit Silattuqsarvingat — the Inuit University of the North. It plans, in part, to involve Inuit in learning processes consistent with Inuit culture.

While in Rankin, take a stroll over to the relics of the North Rankin Nickel Mine. The rusty old machinery on a promontory overlooking the inlet and the tidal flats are all that remain of the mine. (The old headframe burned down in a huge fire in 1975.)

From the road behind the **Matchbox Gallery**, an easy hike will take you to the south shore of the inlet and a view of the rocky Barrier Islands. Here you'll find a collection of small buildings, the remains of the old settlement of Itivia. In the 1950s, the federal government built a settlement at Itivia to aid inland Caribou Inuit who were suffering from starvation.

The road at Itivia ends at the barge dock. In summer, heavy equipment and supplies arrive here by barge. If a barge is in, walk down to the dock and watch the unloading.

Ten kilometres to the north of Rankin lies the Meliadine River Territorial Park. You can take a guided tour to this fascinating Thule site, where you'll find stone tent rings, meat caches, fox traps and the remains of semi-subterranean houses.

Another site worth visiting is an immense *inuksuk* on the rocks above Williamson Lake overlooking Rankin. This towering stone figure was built in 1991 by Joe Nattar.

You may also want to take an excursion to Marble Island, where Captain James Knight and his crew were marooned in 1721 while searching for minerals and the Northwest Passage. About 32 kilometres from Rankin is the site where Knight's two ships were wrecked and where the explorer and his crew of 60 disappeared.

Rankin is the jumping-off spot for a major ecotourist facility in the Kivalliq Region, **Sila Lodge**. Located on Wager Bay, the lodge attracts many naturalists who come to view polar bears, caribou and other wildlife, and to tour the tundra and archeological sites.

As the ease of travelling on the tundra may cause you to become complacent, it's always advisable to go out with an experienced, licensed guide. The weather can be very unpredictable and you can soon learn that during a storm, it's far better to be bored in a hotel room than to be panic-stricken on the land. Preparedness is essential.

Several licensed guides offer tours of the community and of other points of interest nearby, including **Kivalliq Consulting**, **Management and Training Services Ltd.**, **Sea Taxi**, and **Kivalliq Charter Boat Service**. For further information on licensed guides and tours, contact the Keewatin Regional Visitors Centre, the Rankin Inlet office of the Department of Resources, Wildlife and Economic Development, or the **Aqiggiak Hunters and Trappers Organization**.

Shopping

Rankin Inlet has a thriving arts and crafts community. In recent years, ceramics has made a comeback here. This stunning pottery, as well as more traditional carvings and wall hangings, provide a wide variety of treasures to choose from. You'll find several places where you can view or purchase the work of local artists.

The Matchbox Gallery, owned by local artist Jim Shirley, provides two services to local artists. It offers them a place where they produce spectacular pottery, and it exhibits their work. **Ivalu** is Rankin's fashion centre. Local seamstresses have sewn beautiful inner and outerwear in contemporary Inuit designs. The store has a great selection of hats, jackets, vests, and the like.

The Siniktarvik Hotel has a modest assortment of carvings and other local handiwork in their gift shop. **Treasures** sells a wide variety of local art and southern gifts. It's also a great place to buy jewelry.

Ask around. Many local artists sell their work privately. Inquire at your hotel or at the Keewatin Regional Visitors Centre for information on how to contact them.

Events

Like residents of other Nunavut communities, the people of Rankin love square dancing. Holidays and community celebrations are basically an excuse to hold a square dance. The Kivalliq style of dancing slightly resembles the Scottish variety, with movements that are very fast and tricky. From the vantage point of a spectator seated along the walls of a community hall, the dances appear impossible to learn. Have courage, though. Newcomers will find that Rankin residents are always willing to indoctrinate a first-timer. Just remember to bounce up and down a lot and keep your elbows out; the other dancers will hurl you in the right direction!

All Christian holidays, such as Christmas and Easter, as well as Canada Day, are celebrated in grand style. For several days, everyone joins in square dances, games for adults and children, dogteam and snowmobile races, Inuit games and hockey games. If you haven't seen a snowmobile race where drivers tow someone sitting on a plastic jerry can, you haven't lived a full life!

Each May, the community celebrates Pakallak Time. This festival offers many of the same activities as other holidays, but with something extra. After a long winter, it's a joyous celebration of the warmth and sunlight of spring. Pakallak Time is a great way to meet people from Rankin, as well as those who come from other communities to join in the fun.

Rankin Inlet is also home to a healthy and competitive population of dogsled mushers. For a real Nunavut experience, take a trip from Rankin by dogteam in winter or spring. Some enterprising mushers have organized tours ranging from half an hour to a day or longer. Ask the staff at your hotel or contact the **Aqiggiak Hunters and Trappers Organization** for more information. Remember to ask as well about the many exciting dogteam races held in and around Rankin.

At the community hall, located in the Singiittuq Complex, flea markets, craft sales and games are occasionally held. For details, ask local residents, call the hamlet recreation co-ordinator, or watch the community announcement channel on Cable 15. Actually, watching this station is entertainment in itself, as the Kissarvik Co-op, which operates the channel, is always on the lookout for new and improved ways to misspell the English language.

Accommodation and Dining

Of the two hotels in Rankin, the 45-room Siniktarvik is *the* business facility in town. The hotel, which can accommodate 94, provides rooms and services similar to those found at medium-priced southern establishments, including conference and catering services. During conferences, the hotel may be particularly busy; guests can also expect parties and dances at the hotel. Rooms are $156 per person per day for a single occupancy and $132 per person for a double. The restaurant features an à la carte menu and serves both hotel guests and the public. At 8 p.m., the restaurant closes and a licensed bar area opens at 9 p.m.

The **Nanuq Inn** offers less luxurious, though comfortable, lodging. The inn has nine rooms, five of which have showers. Guests staying in rooms without showers share four washrooms on the premises. Rooms are $125 per person per day for single occupancy and $95 per person for double. The restaurant has an extensive à la carte menu and a partitioned non-smoking area. It is licensed for hotel guests. The inn has conference and banquet facilities and holds community dances occasionally. It also now has the Anawak Theatre, where movies are shown.

In addition to these hotel restaurants, visitors can snack at two other spots in town. The **Northern Quick Stop**, located in the Northern store, sells Kentucky Fried Chicken and Pizza Hut fast foods. **Coffee Delights**, a smoke-free venue, offers desserts plus a wide variety of gourmet coffees.

And on the subject of snacks: how about caribou processed into sausage, pastrami, salami or jerky? Or smoked char or char jerky? You can buy these and other delicacies at the **Northern store** and the **Kissarvik Co-op**. Processed at the Keewatin Fish and Meat plant in Rankin, these tasty foods are available packaged or in bulk.

Services

The **John Ayaruaq Library** is shared by Rankin Inlet schools, as well as community residents. Visitors will find a fairly good selection of books on the history of the region and of the North in general. Call for library hours.

Located next to the Nanuq Inn, the Youth and Elders Centre is a popular meeting place for the young and old in Rankin. Although the Centre's hours are sporadic, it's well worthwhile to check out the activities offered here.

If you need a regular fix of time on the Internet, the **Rankin Inlet Community Access Centre** is for you. Located in the **Leo Ussak Elementary School**, the facility provides free access to the Internet. As the Centre has limited hours, call ahead for information.

Rankin Inlet has a fairly good local transportation system. The four taxi companies — **Airut Taxi**, **Ernie's Taxi**, **Jay's Taxi**, and **M & M Taxi** — charge $4 for trips in town and $5 for trips to or from the airport. Taxis usually take less than two minutes to appear at your door; sometimes before south-bound flights, however, the wait is a little longer. Be ready to hop in the van once you hang up the phone. But if you're headed for the airport, don't be surprised if it takes up to 10 minutes for the cab to arrive.

If you'd enjoy the freedom of your own vehicle while in town, you have two options. You can rent a truck for short- or long-term periods from Airut Taxi. Or, if you're the adventurous sort, you can rent ATVs from **C & H Rentals**. (The company also rents trailers and cars.)

The Bombardier is another interesting form of transportation available in Rankin Inlet. This is an overgrown, enclosed snowmobile that runs on tracks and skis. In winter and spring, there are regularly scheduled trips from Rankin Inlet to Arviat and other communities. To experience this new form of travel, call **Kowmuk's**.

DIRECTORY

The 819 and 403 area codes change to 867 on Oct. 21, 1997.

Accommodation and Dining

Nanuq Inn
VISA accepted.
Tel.: (819) 645-2513
Fax: (819) 645-2393

Siniktarvik Hotel
All major credit cards accepted, as well as Interac.
Tel.: (819) 645-2949
Fax: (819) 645-2999

Coffee Delights
Noon to 9 p.m., Monday to Saturday. Closed Sunday.
Tel.: (819) 645-2582

Northern Store Quick Stop
10 a.m.–9 p.m., Monday to Saturday; 1–5 p.m., Sunday.
Tel.: (819) 645-2055

Guides/Outfitters/Tour Operators

Aqiggiak Hunters and Trappers Organization
Tel.: (819) 645-2350
Fax: (819) 645-2867

Keewatin Regional Visitors Centre
Contact the following outfitters through the Visitors Centre:

Kivalliq Consulting, Management and Training Services Ltd., Sea Taxi, Kivalliq Charter Boat Service.
Tel.: (819) 645-2949
Fax: (819) 645-2999

Resources, Wildlife and Economic Development
Includes the regional tourism office.
Tel.: (819) 645-5067
Fax: (819) 645-2346

Sila Lodge
774 Bronx Ave., Winnipeg MB,
R2K 4E9 Canada
Attention: Lynda Gunter
Tel.: (204) 949-2050 or 1-800-663-9832
Fax: (204) 663-6375

Services

Airport
Tel.: (819) 645-3048 (Calm Air)
Tel.: (819) 645-3200 (Skyward)
Tel.: (819) 645-2961 (First Air)

C & H Rentals
Tel.: (819) 645-3162
Fax: (819) 645-2665

Churches

Catholic Church
Services: 11 a.m. Sunday, in Inuktitut and English. 5:30 p.m. mass from Monday to Saturday.
Tel.: (819) 645-2824

Glad Tidings Fellowship
Services: 11 a.m. and 7 p.m., Sunday; 7:30 p.m., Wednesday.
Tel.: (819) 645-2018

Holy Comforter Anglican Church
Services: 11 a.m. (in Inuktitut and English) and 7 p.m. (in Inuktitut), Sunday.
Tel.: (819) 645-2657

Hamlet Office
Tel.: (819) 645-2895
Fax: (819) 645-2146
E-mail: munri@arctic.ca

Health Centre
Tel.: (819) 645-2816
Fax: (819) 645-2688

Inuit Cultural Institute
Tel.: (819) 645-3010
Fax: (819) 645-3020

John Ayaruaq Library
Located in the Maaniulujuk Ilinniavik High School.
Tel.: (819) 645-5034
Fax: (819) 645-2889

Kiguti Dental Clinic
Tel.: (819) 645-3322
Fax: (819) 645-3330

Kivalliq Inuit Association
Tel.: (819) 645-2800
Fax: (819) 645-3848

Kowmuk's
Tel.: (819) 645-3034
Fax: (819) 645-2478

Nunavut Tunngavik Incorporated
Tel.: (819) 645-5400
Fax: (819) 645-3452/3451

Police (RCMP)
Tel.: (819) 645-2822
Fax: (819) 645-2568

Post Office
Located behind the mall housing Treasures Gifts and Sakku Drugs.
10 a.m.–5 p.m., Monday to Friday.
Tel.: (819) 645-2680

Radio Station (FM 105.1)
Tel.: (819) 645-2244

Rankin Inlet Community Access Centre
Located in the Leo Ussak Elementary School.
Tel.: (819) 645-2814
Web site: www.arctic.ca/LUS/CAC.html

Schools

Leo Ussak Elementary School
Tel.: (819) 645-2814
Fax: (819) 645-2333
E-mail: ussak@arctic.ca
Web site: www.arctic.ca/LUS

Maaniulujuk Ilinniavik High School
Tel.: (819) 645-2761
Fax: (819) 645-2209

Nunavut Arctic College
Tel.: (819) 645-2529
Fax: (819) 645-2387

Taxis

Airut Taxi
Tel.: (819) 645-2411

Ernie's Taxi
Tel.: (819) 645-3668

Jay's Taxi
Tel.: (819) 645-2420

M & M Taxi
Tel.: (819) 645-2892

Shopping

Ivalu
9 a.m.–5 p.m., Monday to Friday.
Closed weekends.
VISA accepted.
Tel.: (819) 645-3400
Fax: (819) 645-2115

Kissarvik Co-op
9:30 a.m.–6:00 p.m., Monday to Saturday. Closed Sunday.
VISA, MasterCard, Interac.
Tel.: (819) 645-2801
Fax: (819) 645-2280

Matchbox Gallery
10 a.m.–12 p.m., 1–4 p.m., Monday to Friday. Closed weekends.
VISA, MasterCard.
Tel./Fax: (819) 645-2674

Northern Store
10 a.m.–6 p.m., Monday to Wednesday;
10 a.m.–7 p.m., Thursday and Friday;
10 a.m.–6 p.m., Saturday. Closed Sunday.
VISA, MasterCard, Interac.
Tel.: (819) 645-2823
Fax: (819) 645-2082

Sakku Drugs
10 a.m.–6 p.m., Monday to Saturday.
Closed Sunday.
VISA, MasterCard, Interac.
Tel.: (819) 645-2811
Fax: (819) 645-2860

Treasures
10 a.m.–12 p.m., 1–6 p.m., Monday to Friday; 12–5 p.m., Saturday.
Closed Sunday. VISA accepted.
Tel.: (819) 645-3373
Fax: (819) 645-3374

MELIADINE RIVER TERRITORIAL PARK

by Karen LeGresley Hamre

Just inland from the west coast of Hudson Bay, about 10 kilometres northwest of Rankin Inlet, lies the beautiful Meliadine River Territorial Park, straddling the Meliadine River in the Meliadine River Valley.

In summer, visitors and residents of Rankin Inlet come to enjoy the park's magnificent scenery, pristine waters, good fishing, and abundant wildlife — including the endangered peregrine falcon. The park's most outstanding features, however, are its many excellent archeological sites.

Things to See and Do

The main attractions and facilities here lie on the south side of the Meliadine River, along a one-kilometre-wide by five-kilometre-long strip. The road from Rankin Inlet that runs through most of the park leads to Meliadine's major archeological site. It also winds its way up to a small, shallow lake above the river. Most summers, Sandy Lake is warm enough to provide delightful swimming. Nearby, you'll find change rooms, outhouses, picnic tables and tent pads. An elders/visitors cabin can be reserved for community events and camping. A small path leads through the primary archeological sites, some of which are marked with interpretive signs. (For more detailed information on the ruins, check with the **Hamlet of Rankin Inlet**.)

The history of land use by earlier inhabitants here spans some three millennia. The park has more than 45 archeological sites, some dating as far back as the Pre-Dorset period from 1000 BC to 500 BC. Although many features aren't yet dated, most appear to be of the Thule period, between 1300 and 1600. Archeological evidence indicates that ancient peoples used the lands for fishing and hunting caribou in summer and fall.

Of all the old sites, *Ijiralik*, situated on a small esker off the main road, is the most striking. (Like other ruins in the park, Ijiralik derives its name from an Inuit legend. Ijiralik is the name of one who turns into a caribou, or other spirit, that whistles.)

During Thule times, when sea levels rose as a result of glacial melting, the site lay closer to the shores of Hudson Bay than it does today. Referred to as simply "KfJm.3" by archeologists, Meliadine boasts many intriguing artifacts dating from the 1400s to modern times. In an area of about 100 metres by 150 metres, you'll find tent rings, caches, ingenious fox traps, graves, semi-subterranean houses, *inuksuit*, kayak stands and curious little structures believed to be puppy houses.

As the sites are precious historical records in stone and are protected under Northwest Territories legislation, visitors must not disturb them.

Flora and Fauna

The park's geology is noteworthy, too. On the south side of the Meliadine River stands a massive esker — a sand and gravel ridge that forms a spine along the park. The main road and trails run along the top of it, providing spectacular views of the Meliadine Valley and beyond. Because the tundra at the esker is covered by lichen-moss, which is highly sensitive to disturbance, visitors should walk on the roads and paths wherever possible. Most of the park is covered by a variety of glacial deposits. A bedrock outcrop that rises about 47 metres above sea level is the park's highest point.

At least 24 unusual species of plants may be found in the park, including the rare three-awned grass (*Trisetum triflorum*), which grows only in the rich soil at the Thule ruins. It is unknown elsewhere in the Kivalliq.

The best time to visit the park is during July and early August. Even then, the weather can be variable. Generally, summers here begin in June and last until September. Some years, however, the weather is cool and rather nasty throughout. So come prepared for sudden climate changes. When you walk through the lovely Meliadine Valley on a warm, sunny day, however, you may easily forget other dismal times.

Getting There

The hike to Meliadine is a long, though not uncomfortable, trek of about 10 kilometres. To reach the elders/visitors cabin, you'll have to go another four kilometres. Fortunately, though, the road along the top of the esker is well-drained, allowing for easy walking. And the breeze at this height keeps the hordes of mosquitoes at bay.

Kivalliq Tours, and Caroline Anawak, in particular, are the licensed guides to the park. Caroline, wife of Nunavut's interim commissioner, Jack Anawak, knows the archeological sites and other attractions intimately. If you want to join Kivalliq Tours for a half-day or day-long tour, you'll need to travel in a group of four to six people. Outfitters find that it's not worth the wear and tear on their vehicle from the bumpy road to take out only one or two visitors at a time. Check with Kivalliq Tours; they might put you in touch with other visitors wishing to tour the park.

You can also take a taxi to the park and around the sites, and arrange to be picked up later. But it will cost you a hefty $100 to get out to Meliadine. If you prefer to drive yourself, you can rent a "Honda," a four-wheel all-terrain vehicle. They're available from **C & H Rentals** in Rankin Inlet. Please remember, though, that driving off-road here is not permitted. Although the hamlet continues to extend and improve the road down to the river valley, road conditions to and within the park can vary in their state of repair. Road upgrading is expected within the next three years.

Crossing from the south to the north side of the Meliadine River is no easy feat. If you don't mind getting cold and wet, you can wade across in some locations. To date, there are no plans to build a road or trails across the river. Most visitors prefer to leave the north side of the river to the plants and wildlife, and to enjoy the view from the south.

Camping

You can reserve the elders/visitors cabin for overnight stays by calling Nunavut Tourism's **tourism development officer** for the Kivalliq, or by calling the hamlet office. The cabin is a simple affair, with six beds. Be sure to bring your own stove, cookware and other kitchen supplies, toiletries, and toilet paper. (There is an outhouse to the side of the cabin.) It's best to bring a large water container, too. The river, a source of fresh water, is about 200 metres away, a bit far if you're walking at midnight!

If you're camping, you'll find tent pads at Sandy Lake. With a permit, you may also camp at other locations. Don't stay at archeological sites, or in private cabins within the park boundaries. Call the tourism development officer for information on the best tenting sites.

Remember, too, that there are very few facilities in the park. There are no emergency services or park wardens to check on you. Have plenty of bug juice on hand and come equipped with a bug jacket/hat. That way, when the wind dies, you'll be protected. Generally, the Kivalliq is notoriously windy. But the rare summer evenings when the wind is still can be exceedingly unpleasant — unless you've come to study biting insects. Be prepared for all sorts of weather: rain, sun, and cool temperatures. Bring waterproof clothing, a warm hat and one to keep off the sun, sturdy waterproof hiking boots, sunglasses, and sunscreen for those long hours of sunlight.

DIRECTORY

The 819 and 403 area codes change to 867 on Oct. 21, 1997.

C & H Rentals
Based in Rankin Inlet.
Tel.: (819) 645-3162
Fax: (819) 645-2665

Hamlet of Rankin Inlet
Tel.: (819) 645-2895
Fax: (819) 645-2146
E-mail: munri@arctic.ca

Kivalliq Tourism Development Officer, Nunavut Tourism
Tel.: (819) 645-5067
Fax: (819) 645-2346

Kivalliq Tours
Tel.: (819) 645-2731
Fax: (819) 645-2362

ARVIAT

by Shirley Tagalik

If you are a visitor, you are to be welcomed; when visiting Arviat, expect people to smile, nod and say hello.

Population:	1,559 (Inuit: 94%, non-Inuit: 6%)
Telephone Area Code:	819 (changes to 867 on Oct. 21, 1997)
Time Zone:	Central Time
Postal Code:	X0C 0E0
How to Get There:	Possible routes:
	• Winnipeg-Arviat
	• Yellowknife-Rankin Inlet-Arviat
	• Ottawa/Montreal-Iqaluit-Rankin Inlet-Arviat
	• Kangerlussuaq (Greenland)-Iqaluit-Rankin Inlet-Arviat
	Winnipeg to Arviat (1,300 kilometres north) is via Calm Air
	Rankin Inlet to Arviat (200 kilometres south) is via Calm Air or Skyward Aviation
Banks:	None. Cash and traveller's cheques are preferable
Alcohol:	Alcohol and alcoholic beverages are prohibited
Taxis:	Yes

For centuries, Arviat (pronounced "ar-vee-at") has been a site that welcomed visitors to her sandy shores, and much of what makes Arviat an interesting place to visit today is rooted in this history.

Years ago, the industrious *Paallirmiut* were the original residents of this coastal area of western Hudson Bay. A self-sufficient group of Inuit, they were able to sustain large camps. They were joined by the traditionally isolated *Ahiarmiut* — inland Inuit who knew only caribou — and by sophisticated ex-whalers from the Repulse Bay and Coral Harbour areas. The way these three groups hunt, raise children, speak, build *igluit*, make tents, sew clothes, all differs. Each group has struggled to keep its traditional identity while uniting to build a community that can creatively solve its social challenges: 80 per cent unemployment, and a high birthrate that sees almost 60 children born yearly.

Today, the community is known as one particularly rich in traditional knowledge and values, where Inuktitut is spoken widely and valued highly, and where hunting traditions are maintained.

History

Still identified on many maps by its former name, Eskimo Point, Arviat comes from the Inuktitut name for bowhead whale, *arviq*.

Thule culture sites here date back to AD 1100. Many ancient *qajaq* stands found at traditional summer camp sites attest to the fact that hundreds of Inuit gathered in this area. Summer brought Pallirmiut families together to hunt sea mammals — whales, seals, walrus — for meat and oil. Two of these sites, *Arvia'juaq* (an island shaped like a big bowhead) and *Qikiqtaarjuk*, were designated national historic sites in 1995.

With the establishment of the Hudson's Bay Co. trading post in 1921, camp sites shifted into the vicinity while the local economy shifted to a rich trapping industry. Arctic fox were extremely plentiful and the harsh Keewatin (now called Kivalliq) climate ensured thick, full coats. A visit to *Nuvuk*, the site of the old Hudson's Bay Co. post, will introduce visitors to a real York boat, one of the last to ply the waters of Hudson Bay. It carried supplies in trade for furs.

The early church history of the Roman Catholic mission, established in 1924, can be viewed through pictures and documents at the **Mikilaaq Centre**, a diocese-operated community centre located in the original **Roman Catholic church** adjacent to its new counterpart. The **Anglican mission**, established in 1926, brought missionaries Donald and Winifred Marsh of England to the Arctic. Their books, including *Echoes from a Frozen Land* (Edmonton: Hurtig, 1987), provide a rich early history of the area.

Demand for furs later dwindled, and at the same time caribou migration patterns changed, creating hardship for many groups of Inuit. Hardest hit were the Ahiarmiut, described in Canadian author Farley Mowat's books *People of the Deer* and *The Desperate People*. Eventually they were relocated by the Canadian government to Arviat. The community's Federal Day School opened in 1959, marking the beginning of permanent settlement.

Meanwhile, 600 kilometres northeast, migrant Inuit from Repulse Bay and Cape Dorset moved onto Southampton Island after disease wiped out the island's residents, the *Tuniit* people. But the demand that their numbers placed upon the island caribou herd was too much. When the last caribou from that herd was shot a generation ago, another wave of people were drawn to Arviat in the early 1970s.

Arviat: Its Land and Wildlife

Dotted with shallow lakes, the land, rich in flora and fauna, is flat glacial terrain consisting of sandy low marsh, muskeg, and long tidal flats. Between June and August, it is the perfect nesting area for thousands of migratory birds. The McConnell River Bird Sanctuary, south of the community, is a good spot to view nesting pairs of geese, sandhill cranes, swans, ducks and loons. Nesting sites attract snowy owls, peregrine falcons and gyrfalcons. At any long tidal flat, swarms of sandpipers, plovers, phalaropes, arctic terns, gulls and jaegers can also be found, fiercely protecting their nests. Pods of belugas can be viewed in the bays. Many Inuit hunt whales at this time and trips can always be arranged with local outfitters.

Although a short walk from town will introduce you to the rich feathered world, the snow goose is particularly accommodating in August and September when the parents march their gaggles right into town and take over whatever grassy spots are left to nibble. Trips up rivers near the community provide rich fishing grounds, and also a certainty of seeing migrating caribou. The caribou hide is still extensively used for winter clothing, and family caribou camps spring up at this time of the year.

Tours

Late October and early November are the months to view the polar bear migration. Trips by dogteam or snowmobile provide a view of bears hunting seals along the edge of the newly forming ice. However, like the geese, the bears also tend to come to the dump looking for fast food. Sport hunts can be arranged through **Arviat Tundra Adventures**.

Lake trout, arctic grayling, white fish and cod are available throughout the year, but the arctic char runs that take place in June and again in September/October are special events. Outfitters can take you to the best fishing grounds, and small planes are available for charter during summer and autumn.

Outfitters can be arranged through the Arviat Tourism Office or Arviat Tundra Adventures (run by the Arviat HTO). The HTO also arranges the charter flights.

The **Margaret Aniksak Visitors Centre** is open mid-June to early September. An interesting interpretive display of traditional Inuit life and artifacts collected from archeological digs at the Arvia'juaq site can be seen. More information about guided visits to the national historical sites can be obtained by first visiting the **Parks Canada** web sites and through contacting the **Arviat Historical Society**.

The **Sivulinut Elders Society** sponsors cultural programs, drum dances, and interpretive events, staging them regularly in each other's homes. At times they set up open house in a caribou tent where, dressed in beaded *amautit* (women's parkas) and traditional costumes, they teach traditional string games, coach beginners in throat singing, and hold big cookouts featuring caribou heads, caribou hoofs, and other delicacies. The **Arviat Tourism Office** will help you track down information on the event; you can also pay for an open house to be arranged (again, contact the Arviat Tourism Office).

From February to March, elders, under the auspices of the Qitiqliq high school and **Levi Angmak Iliniavialaaq Elementary School**, organize the **Classroom in the Iglu**. Here you can experience life in a traditional camp where elders tell stories and plan traditional activities. Elders take turns staying in the iglu and teachers, students and visitors often ask to stay the night! There are usually several rooms to the iglu. Contact elementary school principal Elisapee Karetak for details.

Shopping

Arviat's vibrant artistic community has thrived since contact with newcomers in the 1920s. Winifred Marsh, a talented painter in addition to her role as a missionary, captured the wonderful beaded *amautit* in her book *People of the Willow*. This gave rise to many well-known fashion designers and artists specializing in wall hangings (local wall hangings are also characterized by intricate beadwork on caribou skin). Dolls with soapstone or dried sealskin faces, fashioned by artists such as Martina Anoee and Alice Akkamuk, are other local treasures. Many well-known dollmakers sell work from their homes. The Arviat Tourism Office (as well as almost anyone on the street) will steer you toward any artisan you'd like to contact. You can also phone in a request to the local noon hour radio show.

The Arviat style of carving, often described as minimalist, was introduced by Canadian author and academic George Swinton to the world by way of an exhibition at the Osaka Expo in the 1960s. It propelled carvers like Elizabeth Nuturaluk, Tasseor Tuksweetuk, John Pungnark, and Miki to world fame. Today, new generations of carvers explore their art in exciting and innovative ways, as one can see from a visit to the Ulimaut Carving Shop, a carver's workshop operated by the **Qitiqliq high school** in tandem with the local carvers' society at a nearby building. Mostly young carvers work here; it's a chance to see carving in progress and to enquire about other members of the carvers' society.

At **Nunavut Arctic College**, a new jewelry-making tradition is just taking root. An experimental mixture of metal, stone, ivory and bone, the craft is producing beautiful pins, pendants, earrings, bracelets, and even spoons.

Traditional seamstresses make clothing for hunting and northern living, but a number of Arviat designers are translating traditional design into modern fashion statements. Among them are Charlotte St. John (contact her through **Eskimo Point Lumber Supply**), and Jackie King (contact **Ralph's Bed and Breakfast**). Such items are sold privately and usually made-to-order. The Arviat Tourism Office can also put you in touch with clothing designers, along with artisans specializing in miniature artifacts, paintings, prints, weaving and pottery.

Some local artwork, dry goods, and produce are sold through the **Padlei Co-op** and the **Northern store**. Hardware, materials and groceries can be found at Eskimo Point Lumber Supply, which will also permit you to charter a small plane, helicopter or Bombardier.

Accommodation and Dining

Padlei Inns North has 10 beds in five rooms, each with a private bathroom and television. A lounge area, which has a telephone, adjoins the dining room, where good full-course meals are served. Prices are $175 per person per night (including meals) or $125 per person per night without meals. Visitors who aren't staying at the hotel can still eat in the hotel's dining room, if they book in advance. Meal prices vary.

Ralph's Bed and Breakfast, meanwhile, is really a nine-bed, six-room bed and breakfast/lunch/dinner ($175 per person per night) or, bed and breakfast ($125 per person per night). Group rates are also available. Located in a homey two-storey house with a shared bathroom on each floor, it has a common lounge stocked with a television and video cassette recorder. Like the Padlei Inns North, the place is lived-in, but in good condition. Non-guests should make reservations well in advance for lunch and dinner.

For special treats in northern eating, the **Arviat Meat and Fish Processing Plant**, close to the Northern store, produces excellent country food fare such as smoked and dried fish products, caribou sausage, caribou jerky, and so on. Tours of the plant can be arranged.

Confectionery and fast food are available from **Neevee's Coffee Shop**, **Jeannie's Bakery**, Ralph's Arcade, and the Mikilaaq Centre.

Events

Arviat has a strong musical tradition with well-known Inuit performers such as Charlie Panigoniak and Susan Aglukark. In late August, the

Inuumariit Musical Festival is a wonderful weekend of music, dancing and celebration. The Nunavut Dogteam Derby is usually held in March.

Services

Arviat's **Health Centre** has a walk-in clinic from 9 a.m. to 12 p.m. weekdays. In the afternoons (from 1 to 5 p.m.), it's by appointment only. A nurse is always on call for emergencies. The community also has an **RCMP** detachment.

DIRECTORY

The 819 and 403 area codes change to 867 on Oct. 21, 1997.

Accommodation and Dining

Padlei Inns North
VISA, Diners Club/enRoute.
Tel.: (819) 857-2919
Fax: (819) 857-2919

Ralph's Bed and Breakfast
Contact Ralph King.
Tel.: (819) 857-2653
Fax: (819) 857-2623

Neevee's Coffee Shop
9–12 a.m. daily.
Tel.: (819) 857-2999
Fax: (819) 857-2963

Jeannie's Bakery
1–11 p.m., Monday to Saturday.
Closed Sunday.
Tel.: (819) 857-2720

Outfitters/Guides/ Tour Operators

Arviat Cultural Tours
Contact Simeonie Mamgark.
Tel.: (819) 857-2941
Fax: (819) 857-2499

Arviat Tourism Office
Tel.: (819) 857-2941
Fax: (819) 857-2499

Arviat Tundra Adventures
Contact Angeline Suluk.
Tel.: (819) 857-2636
Fax: (819) 857-2488

Classroom in the Iglu
Ask for elementary school principal Elisapee Karetak.
Tel.: (819) 857-2547
Fax: (819) 857-2656

Margaret Aniksak Visitors Centre
Tel.: (819) 857-2698
Fax: (819) 857-2499

Services

Airport
Tel.: (819) 857-2997 (Calm Air)
Tel.: (819) 857-2424 (Skyward)

Angukak Snowmobile Rentals
Tel.: (819) 857-2941
Fax: (819) 857-2499

Arviat Historical Society
Contact Luke Suluk.
Tel.: (819) 857-2806
Fax: (819) 857-2806

Arviat Truck Rental and General Contracting
Tel.: (819) 857-2446
Fax: (819) 857-2446

Churches

Alliance Church
Services at 11 a.m. and 7 p.m., Sunday.
Tel.: (819) 857-2950
Fax: (819) 857-2608

Anglican Mission
Services at 11 a.m. and 7 p.m., Sunday; 7 p.m., Monday and Wednesday.
Tel.: (819) 857-2948
Fax: (819) 857-2252

Roman Catholic Church
Services at 11 a.m., Sunday;
7 p.m., Wednesday.
Tel.: (819) 857-2840

Health Centre
Tel.: (819) 857-2816
Fax: (819) 857-2980

Mikilaaq Centre
Community centre operated by
Roman Catholic diocese.
Tel.: (819) 857-2521
Fax: (819) 857-2787

Parks Canada
Web site: www.parkscanada.pch.gc.ca

Police (RCMP)
Tel.: (819) 857-2822
Fax: (819) 857-2691

Post Office
Located in the Centre of Arviat.
Tel.: (819) 2859

Radio Station (FM 105.1)
Tel.: (819) 857-2939 or (819) 857-2810

Resources, Wildlife and Economic Development
Contact the economic
development officer.
Tel.: (819) 857-2941
Fax: (819) 857-2499

Sally's ATV Rentals
Tel.: (819) 857-2657
Fax: (819) 857-2222

Schools

Levi Angmak Iliniavialaaq Elementary School
Tel.: (819) 857-2547
Fax: (819) 857-2656

Nunavut Arctic College
Tel.: (819) 857-2903
Fax: (819) 857-2928

Qitiqliq Secondary School
Tel.: (819) 857-2778
Fax: (819) 857-2669

Sivulinut Elders Society
Tel.: (819) 857-2064

Taxis

Paul's Taxi and Van Rentals
Tel.: (819) 857-2677

Tomas Taxi
Tel.: (819) 857-2222

Weather Office
Tel.: (819) 857-2802

Shopping

Arviat Meat and Fish Processing Plant
9 a.m.–5 p.m., Monday to Friday.
Closed weekends.
Tel.: (819) 857-2381

Eskimo Point Lumber Supply
VISA, Interac.
9 a.m.–5:30 p.m., Monday to Friday;
1–5 p.m., Saturday. Closed Sunday.
Tel.: (819) 857-2752
Fax: (819) 857-2883

Northern Store
10 a.m.–6 p.m., Monday to Thursday;
10 a.m.–8 p.m., Friday;
10 a.m.,–6 p.m., Saturday.
Closed Sunday.
VISA, MasterCard, Interac.
Tel.: (819) 857-2826
Fax: (819) 857-2925

Nunavut Arctic College Metalworks Jewelry-Making Program
Tel.: (819) 857-2903
Fax: (819) 857-2928

Padlei Co-op
From May 1 to Sept. 1: 9 a.m–10 p.m.,
Monday to Saturday. Closed Sunday.

From Sept. 1 to Apr. 30: 10 a.m.–10 p.m.,
Monday to Saturday. Closed Sunday.
VISA, Diners Club/enRoute, Interac.
Tel.: (819) 857-2933
Fax: (819) 857-2762

WHALE COVE

by Ulrike Komaksiutiksak

I will always remember our arrival in Whale Cove in 1995. My daughter was four at the time and previously had lived with us in some larger communities in the Northwest Territories.

Population:	301 (Inuit: 94%, non-Inuit: 6%)
Telephone Area Code:	819 (changes to 867 on Oct. 21, 1997)
Time Zone:	Central Time
Postal Code:	X0C 0J0
How to Get There:	Possible routes:
	• Rankin Inlet-Whale Cove
	• Winnipeg-Rankin Inlet-Whale Cove
	• Yellowknife-Rankin Inlet-Whale Cove
	• Ottawa/Montreal-Iqaluit-Rankin Inlet-Whale Cove
	• Kangerlussuaq (Greenland)-Iqaluit-Rankin Inlet-Whale Cove
	Rankin Inlet to Whale Cove (64 kilometres south) is via Calm Air or
	Skyward Aviation
Banks:	None, although there is a Royal Bank automated teller machine
	at the Co-op
Alcohol:	Alcohol and alcoholic beverages are prohibited
Taxis:	Yes

When we touched down, she looked around and saw only the landing strip, the small trailer that serves as airport terminal and some cabins in the distance. She glanced at me and asked, "Mom, are we going to live outside?"

Whale Cove's **airport** is a 15-minute drive out of town, unusually far for a small northern community. Visitors often ask why this is so. Some residents believe the rocky land was unsuitable for an airport to be built close to town. Others say it was a decision of the *kujjangajuq* ("upside-down person"), the Inuktitut name for the settlement managers of the old days. In any case, the taxi ride into Whale Cove — or *Tikirarjuaq*, meaning either "where a lot of people arrive," or "long point," according to a more traditional interpretation — gives you an excellent view of the tundra surrounding the settlement.

The community is on the west coast of Hudson Bay, just south of Rankin Inlet. The land around Whale Cove is rugged, with rolling hills and many small, pristine lakes. During winter, nearby Wilson Bay is covered by sea ice; in summer, huge waves from the bay crash onto the rocky shoreline, creating beautiful spectacles. The town itself is nestled in a cove facing the waters of Hudson Bay.

History

In the 1600s, explorers Thomas Button and later, Luke Foxe, sailed along the coastline near Whale Cove in search of the Northwest Passage. In the 1700s, Hudson's Bay Co. men moved into the area to ply their trade with the Inuit. About an hour and half by snowmobile from town lies the abandoned community of Tavani, a former Hudson's Bay Co. post.

Whale Cove was created during the Keewatin famine in the winter of 1957 to 1958, when many Inuit faced starvation as the caribou disappeared. Federal government officials chose this area to relocate survivors of the famine. They believed that the abundance of wildlife here would allow the Inuit to pursue their traditional lifestyle of hunting, fishing, and trapping. The proximity of the site to Rankin Inlet would make it easy for government to administer the community. Both inland and coastal Inuit were brought from areas in and around Baker Lake, Arviat, and Rankin Inlet.

Typical of government decision-making at that time, the site was chosen and the community planned without the input of Inuit. Little thought was given to kinship ties or the cultural skills of the Inuit. The settlement was formed of three distinctly different groups of people who spoke three different dialects. The inland Inuit had to adapt their hunting methods to coastal conditions. Later, other Inuit arrived when the nickel mine in Rankin Inlet closed in the early 1960s.

The economy of Whale Cove then was one of traditional subsistence supplemented by some commercial resource harvesting. For a brief time, a cannery operated in the community, producing canned *maktaaq* and seal that was shipped to the South. In 1967, the Whale's Tail Monument, a project honoring Canada's centennial, was built on a hill overlooking the settlement. Still today, tourists enjoy the splendid view from here.

Whale Cove: Its Land and Wildlife

Whale Cove's people are closely connected with nature. This predominantly Inuit community still follows the rhythms of the seasons. In spring, at the end of May, it is rare for many people to remain in town. Most are off camping on the land, fishing for arctic char or lake trout at favorite spots nearby. Hunting geese and gathering eggs are other traditional springtime activities.

In late June or July, the ice in Hudson Bay breaks up, and the waters sparkle in shades of deep blue-green. Many Inuit take to their boats to catch seal and walrus. By late August, the harvest of beluga whale begins. The maktaaq is a mainstay of the diet here. Maktaaq and arctic char may also be sold to the local fish plant. Arctic flowers bloom in profusion at this time of year, painting the tundra in vivid colors. Local residents who aren't out on the land can usually be found at Reagan's Lake or Old Water Lake, popular swimming holes just out of town.

Berry-picking is a favorite autumn activity, when *paungait* (blackberries) and *aqpiit* (type of raspberries) ripen to the delight of young and old. In October, polar bear hunting season begins, continuing until the community's quota is filled. This can be a dangerous time for the community; residents are kept on close alert in case a bear wanders through town. Fox-trapping and wolf-hunting begin now, too, continuing through the winter. Caribou is hunted year-round.

Throughout the year, women sew for their families, again reflecting the community's close ties to the seasons. During autumn, they get busy sewing parkas and wind pants in preparation for winter. Throughout winter, they prepare for months of travelling in spring, making hats, *kamiit* and mittens for family members. *Amautit* are made to carry new babies, and traditional Inuit hunting clothes are sewn from hides and fur.

The variety of traditional foods reflects the abundance of wildlife here. Travellers may want to sample such delicacies as *igunaq* (aged maktaaq), *pipsi* (dried char), *inaluaq* (seal intestine), *nipku* (dried caribou), and *quaq* (frozen caribou).

Visitors strolling through town may notice caribou hides hanging out to dry and men working on their snowmobiles, all-terrain vehicles, or *qamutiit*. A carver or two may be busy at work. Fishermen come and go on the beaches of Kisarvik or Itivia. The local Co-op is a meeting place for local people and for visitors who want to get to know residents and find out information. On the outskirts of the community you'll hear the sound of silence. Don't be surprised if a *siksik* (ground squirrel) pops up to greet you or an arctic hare darts across your path.

Tours

Although there are currently no licensed outfitters in town, both the local **Hunters and Trappers Organization** (HTO) and the Co-op are working to obtain that status. They are excellent contacts and sources of information for travellers who wish to take a tour, fish, or hunt outside the community. Visitors can enjoy day trips to good fishing spots at Long Lake, Solomon Lake, or Wilson River. All are located within an hour from the community by snowmobile. (Check with the HTO to find out the best spots for fishing, as this depends upon the season. Early fall, for example, is best for lake trout and char.) Those who want to camp for a few days may travel to Pistol Bay, White Rock, or Ferguson River. Before setting out, however, be sure to check with local people about weather conditions and the surrounding wildlife. Weather can change rapidly and without warning. And, of course, during summer, be prepared for lots of mosquitoes!

Events

Community gatherings include feasts, square dances and many indoor and outdoor games. Traditional arctic games, contests such as tea and bannock-making, igloo-building, *inuksuk*-building, snowmobile races and rabbit-hunting, are some of the activities visitors may enjoy. Watch for the annual fishing derby during Victoria Day weekend, plus Canada Day and Hamlet Day festivities in July. Christmas and New Year's celebrations and Easter festivities are joy-filled times, too. For more information, contact the Hamlet of Whale Cove's recreation leader.

Shopping

The two places to shop in town aren't always well stocked. Travellers are wise to phone ahead to check what supplies are available in the community. The **Issatik Co-op** sells groceries, clothes, hardware, souvenirs, arts and crafts, and some sports, fishing and gaming gear. **AT&T Enterprises**, better known as "The Shop," is a convenience store carrying some groceries and dry goods. It also has video rentals.

Sewing is a source of pride and income for many residents of Whale Cove. Visitors may buy clothes and wall hangings from local seamstresses or from the Co-op.

Accommodation and Dining

The **Tavani Inns North** is operated by the Co-op. It has six rooms, with two beds per room. Each room has a television and private bathroom. The price is $200 per night single occupancy, and $175 for double occupancy (rates include meals).

Arrangements may be made for dining without accommodation by contacting the Co-op manager. Check for meal prices. The hotel also has a public phone and laundry facilities.

Services

The Whale Cove **Health Centre** is open for walk-ins from 8:30 a.m. to noon, Monday to Friday. Emergencies are accepted at any time. The Centre has one nurse, who consults with doctors in Churchill or Rankin Inlet as needed.

The **post office**, located in the Issatik Co-op, is open from 1 to 5 p.m., Monday to Friday. There is no **RCMP** station in Whale Cove. Officers from Rankin Inlet are on call and visit the community monthly.

In winter, Bombardiers (large, enclosed snowmobiles) may be chartered from Rankin Inlet. **Kowmuk's Taxi** has scheduled rides to Whale Cove.

The Issatikpaluk Radio Society operates the local **radio station**. Programs with announcements and advertisements are broadcast in the morning, at noon, and in the evening.

DIRECTORY

The 819 and 403 area codes change to 867 on Oct. 21, 1997.

Accommodation and Dining

Tavani Inns North
VISA, MasterCard, Diners Club/enRoute.
Tel.: (819) 896-9252
Fax: (819) 896-9087

Services

Airport
Tel.: (819) 896-9973
Fax: (819) 896-9109 (hamlet office)

Church

Whale Cove Roman Catholic Church
Services at 10:30 a.m., Sunday.
Inuktitut only.
Tel.: (819) 896-9932

Hamlet Office
Tel.: (819) 896-9961
Fax: (819) 896-9109
For the recreation leader:
Tel.: (819) 896-9961

Health Centre
Tel.: (819) 896-9916
Fax: (819) 896-9115

Police (RCMP)
Based in Rankin Inlet.
Tel.: (819) 645-2822
Fax: (819) 645-2568

Post Office
Located in the Issatik Co-op.
Tel.: (819) 896-9956

Radio Station (FM 106.2)
Operated by the Issatikpaluk Radio Society.
CBC Yellowknife FM 106.1
Tel.: (819) 896-9903 (off air)
Tel.: (819) 896-9930 (on air)

School

Inuglak School
Tel.: (819) 896-9300
Fax: (819) 896-9005

Taxis

Kowmuk's Taxi
Based in Rankin Inlet.
Tel.: (819) 645-3034
Fax: (819) 645-2478

Sigininq Taxi
Tel.: (819) 896-9089

Weather Office

Hamlet office.
Tel.: (819) 896-9961
Fax: (819) 896-9109

Whale Cove Hunters and Trappers Organization
Tel.: (819) 896-9944
Fax: (819) 896-9143

Shopping

AT&T Enterprises
5:30–10 p.m., Monday to Thursday; 5:30–11 p.m., Friday; 1–11 p.m., Saturday; 1–6:30 p.m. and 8–11 p.m., Sunday. Cash, traveller's cheques only.
Tel.: (819) 896-9365
Fax: (819) 896-9358

Issatik Co-op
9 a.m.–5 p.m., Monday to Thursday;
9 a.m.–6 p.m. Friday.
Closed on weekends.
VISA, MasterCard, Diners Club/enRoute.
Tel.: (819) 896-9927 or (819) 896-9956
Fax: (819) 896-9087

CHESTERFIELD INLET

by Jennifer Bernius

About eight years ago, local resident Victor Samuurtok likes to recall, a huge polar bear wandered into town and ended up on his front porch. Samuurtok had only time to load his rifle and shoot the bear, right on his porch. It made for one of his shortest hunting trips ever.

Population:	337 (Inuit: 95%, non-Inuit: 5%)
Telephone Area Code:	819 (changes to 867 on Oct. 21, 1997)
Time Zone:	Central Time
Postal Code:	X0C 0B0
How to Get There:	Possible routes:
	• Winnipeg-Rankin Inlet-Chesterfield Inlet
	• Yellowknife-Rankin Inlet-Chesterfield Inlet
	• Ottawa/Montreal-Iqaluit-Rankin Inlet-Chesterfield Inlet
	• Kangerlussuaq (Greenland)-Iqaluit-Rankin Inlet-Chesterfield Inlet
	Rankin Inlet to Chesterfield Inlet (80 kilometres) is via Calm Air
Banks:	None. Cash and traveller's cheques are preferable
Alcohol:	Alcohol may be brought into Chesterfield Inlet, governed only by the provisions of the NWT Liquor Control Act. However, there's no place to buy alcohol in the community
Taxis:	Yes

Fortunately, polar bears in the community are a once in a blue moon occurrence. Chesterfield Inlet is known more for its glory days when it was a regional centre of power.

Some folks here like to remind visitors that their town is the oldest continuing community in the eastern Arctic. The old mission was built between 1911 and 1912, the first Roman Catholic building in the region. At the same time, the Hudson's Bay Co. established its first permanent post in the Arctic at Chesterfield Inlet. The venerable Hudson's Bay Co., chartered in 1670 with headquarters in London, England, is the English-speaking world's oldest incorporated joint-stock merchandising company, and is now headquartered in Winnipeg, Canada.

In 1914, the Northwest Mounted Police (now the RCMP) moved their base from Cape Fullerton to Chesterfield, setting up a station here.

Today, Chesterfield Inlet is a closely knit Inuit settlement of more than 300 people. Families are so intertwined, that just about everyone is related. There's a strong community spirit here and a comfortable blend of traditional and modern lifestyles.

You'll find many of the same modern structures in Chesterfield as in other northern settlements: houses, a nursing station, a school, a Co-op and a **Northern store**. But you'll also spot polar bear and caribou hides drying outside people's homes. Local women sew these into sleeping mats and make parkas from caribou calf skins that may also be drying outside. As for that pink fish drying over there — that's *pipsi* or dried arctic char. Some of the Inuit men may be working outside on snowmobiles and *qamutiit*. Out in the inlet in summer, you'll see men with nets fishing for char.

In winter, most people remain in the community. But in spring, they're off to the lakes nearby fishing for char and lake trout. In late June and July, they drive their snowmobiles to the floe edge about a half-hour away, to hunt ring, bearded and harp seals. In October and November, they quickly fill their quota of the polar bears that roam the region — that sometimes make unwelcome appearances in the community! Throughout the year, caribou are only about an hour or so outside of town, making the men's hunting easier.

History

The Inuit name for Chesterfield Inlet is *Igluligaarjuk*, meaning "place with a few houses." For thousands of years, the ancestors of modern Inuit, the Thule, inhabited the land around Chesterfield Inlet. These resourceful people travelled inland by dogteam in search of caribou, then returned to the inlet to hunt whales and other marine life from their skin boats. Over time, they established large settlements of sod houses in the region, one of which lies just outside Chesterfield Inlet.

In the 1700s, explorers in search of the Northwest Passage plied the waters of Chesterfield Inlet. Captains John Bean and William Christopher thought the inlet itself might be the route that would lead them to China. But though they didn't find their elusive Passage here, they did discover many whales in Hudson Bay.

From the mid-1800s to the beginning of this century, whalers visited the area regularly and often overwintered here. They counted on local Inuit to hunt caribou for them and to man their whaleboats. At Chesterfield Inlet, Inuit often gathered to trade and seek employment with the whalers.

Until the mid-1950s, the community was a major centre north of Churchill. It was the Hudson's Bay Co.'s main supply centre for other posts in the area. It was also the site of the largest RCMP barracks and the largest Roman Catholic mission in the eastern Arctic, as well as a medical and educational centre.

Yet people have predicted the death of Chesterfield Inlet. When the nickel mine opened in Rankin Inlet in 1955, many Inuit left their traditional lifestyle in Chesterfield for paid work underground. Some of those Inuit returned to the community when the mine closed in the early 1960s. Then in the early 1970s, when Rankin became prominent as a regional centre, people again feared the end of Chesterfield as residents left to seek work there.

But Chesterfield Inlet lives on, a community of people committed to their settlement and to their traditions.

In the long, often colorful history of the settlement, there is a tragic chapter. In 1953–1954, a residential school opened, operated largely by the Grey Nuns and several Roman Catholic priests. One purpose of the Turquetil Hall/Joseph Bernier Federal Day School was to instill in students the customs and values of the outsiders. Young children were taken from their camps and settlements by the RCMP and missionaries, and forced to attend the school, the first established in the Keewatin. Some 80 Inuit children from across the region came to spend 10 months a year at the hostel. Here they were forbidden to speak their language, Inuktitut; all their cultural and spiritual traditions were denied them. The school was taken over by the government in the mid-1960s, and remained in existence until the late 1980s, when a modern one was built. Years later, many former students publicly shared their experiences of physical and sexual abuse, suffered at the hands of school staff.

Despite everything, many former students of the Turquetil Hall/Joseph Bernier Federal Day School stress that the school produced the best and brightest of leaders in Nunavut. This, they say, was because there was commitment, endurance and discipline at the school.

Chesterfield Inlet: Its Land and Wildlife

Located at the mouth of Chesterfield Inlet is a picturesque setting overlooking Fish Bay, where you'll notice a few small fishing boats. (Chesterfield Inlet has a fish plant that processes arctic char for shipment to the South.) If you're in town in late August, you'll spot beluga whales cavorting right in the harbor. In the distance, you may even catch sight of an orca feeding on char in the waters of the inlet.

An easy ride by all-terrain vehicle will take you to several excellent fishing spots. For char and lake trout, local people travel to First, Second and Third Lakes, all within 25 kilometres of the settlement. In the inlet near the community are islands — *Pikiulaaqtuuq, Nanujumaaq*, and *Qikiqtaarjuk* — where Inuit go in June to gather eggs from geese, ducks, terns and seagulls. The people also hunt geese in this area. Other notable birds found in the rugged land around the town include eider ducks, king eiders, snowy owls, gyrfalcons and occasionally, peregrine falcons.

Tours

For a glimpse of the community's rich history, try the Chesterfield Inlet Historic Trail. This self-guided walking tour leads you through the early years of the settlement. It includes the original Hudson's Bay Co. trading post (now part of the Northern store), the oldest building in the town; the original **Roman Catholic mission**, completed in 1912; and the St. Theresa Hospital, built in 1931 by the **Grey Nuns**, who still run it as a facility for the severely handicapped. Although most of the tour is along gravel roads, sections cross rock and tundra, so be sure to wear sturdy boots. The tour takes two hours. Copies of the tour guidebook are available in the **hamlet office** in the community complex.

Just north of Chesterfield, within walking distance, lies a large Thule site believed to be about 300 years old. Here you'll see the remains of many ancient sod houses, fox traps and food caches. You'll need to go with a guide, though, as polar bears may prowl in the area. Find out more from the Hunters and Trappers Organization or hamlet office.

Another area worth visiting is the site of the first detachment of the Northwest Mounted Police, established at Cape Fullerton in 1903. The post was built to oversee the activities of American whalers. If you contact a local outfitter, they'll arrange a boat tour for you to the post — weather permitting! The boat trip takes four to six hours. Many visitors camp overnight at the area before returning to Chesterfield.

For information about these and other tours, contact: Steven Inukshuk, **Bluewater Outfitting** (for boat, wildlife, photography and historic site tours and fishing); Kamille Simik, **Qingak Outfitting** (for boat excursions, fishing and nature tours); and Andre Tautu, **North Wind Outfitting** (for boat tours and fishing). You may also contact the **Aqigiq Hunters and Trappers Organization** for information on tours. Although not currently licensed, the HTO plans to become licensed in the near future.

Shopping

The Northern store and **Pitsiulak Co-op** sell groceries, clothes, hardware, souvenirs and crafts, as well as some sporting goods. You might want to check before you visit Chesterfield, however, to ensure that the items you need are in stock. The Co-op also sells locally crocheted hats and jewelry carved from caribou antler. **L & C Taxi** operates a confectionery store where you can buy some outdoor clothing, fabrics and snack foods.

If you'd like to take carvings home with you, the outfitters listed above can suggest local artists.

Accommodation and Dining

The **Tangmavik/Inns North Hotel**, owned by the Pitsiulak Co-op, is located in the former Joseph Bernier School building. It accommodates 20 in seven rooms; bathrooms are shared. The hotel has a television, laundry facilities, informal dining room, small lounge, conference and banquet facilities. The price is $170 per person per night, meals included.

Services

Chesterfield Inlet's **health centre** is open for walk-ins from 8:30 a.m. to noon, Monday to Friday. A nurse is always on call for emergencies. An **RCMP** officer from Rankin Inlet visits Chesterfield Inlet monthly.

DIRECTORY

The 819 and 403 area codes change to 867 on Oct. 21, 1997.

Accommodation and Dining

Tangmavik/Inns North Hotel
VISA accepted.
Tel.: (819) 898-9975/9190
Fax: (819) 898-9056

Guides/Outfitters/Tour Operators

Aqigiq Hunters and Trappers Organization
Tel.: (819) 898-9063
Fax: (819) 898-9079

Bluewater Outfitting
(hamlet office)
Tel.: (819) 898-9031
Fax: (819) 898-9108

North Wind Outfitting
(hamlet office)
Tel.: (819) 898-9931
Fax: (819) 898-9108

Qingak Outfitting
General Delivery, Chesterfield Inlet NT, X0C 0B0 Canada
No telephone number.

Services

Airport
Tel.: (819) 898-9940

Church

Roman Catholic Mission
Services at 10:30 a.m., Sunday; 7 p.m., when priest is visiting Chesterfield.
Tel.: (819) 898-9933

Grey Nuns
Hospital for the handicapped.
Tel.: (819) 898-9917
Fax: (819) 898-9080

Hamlet Office
Tel.: (819) 898-9951
Fax: (819) 898-9108
Economic Development Officer
Afternoons only.
Tel.: (819) 898-9951

Health Centre
Tel.: (819) 898-9968
Fax: (819) 898-9122

Police (RCMP)
Monthly from Rankin Inlet. By-law officer can be contacted through the hamlet office.
Tel.: (819) 898-9923

Post Office
In Co-op store.
10:30 a.m.–12 p.m., 1:30–5 p.m., Monday to Friday.
Tel.: (819) 898-9975

Radio Station (FM 107.1)
Tel.: (819) 898-9934

Schools

Nunavut Arctic College
Tel.: (819) 898-9048

Victor Sammurtok School
Tel.: (819) 898-9913
Fax: (819) 898-9153

Taxi

L & C Taxi
Also vehicle rentals.
Tel.: (819) 898-9966

Weather Office
Tel.: (819) 898-9940

Shopping

L & C Taxi and Store
9 a.m.–12 p.m., 1–5 p.m., and 6:30–10:30 p.m., Monday to Friday; 6:30–10:30 p.m., Saturday and Sunday. Doesn't accept credit cards.
Tel.: (819) 898-9966
Fax: (819) 898-9103

Northern Store
10 a.m.–12 p.m., and 1–6 p.m., Monday to Friday. Closed Saturday and Sunday. VISA, MasterCard, Interac.
Tel.: (819) 898-9920
Fax: (819) 898-9160

Pitsiulak Co-op
9:30 a.m.–12 p.m. and 1–6 p.m., Monday to Friday. 9:30 a.m.–12 p.m., Saturday. VISA, MasterCard, Interac.
Tel.: (819) 898-9975 or (819) 898-9981
Fax: (819) 898-9056

BAKER LAKE

by Darren Keith

I'm on my way to Baker Lake. I know this because of my growing excitement, and because I am glued to the window of the plane searching for familiar landforms.

Population:	1,385 (Inuit: 91%, non-Inuit: 9%)
Telephone Area Code:	819 (changes to 867 on Oct. 21, 1997)
Time Zone:	Central Time
Postal Code:	X0C 0A0
How to Get There:	Possible routes:
	• Winnipeg-Baker Lake
	• Ottawa/Montreal-Iqaluit-Rankin Inlet-Baker Lake
	• Yellowknife-Rankin Inlet-Baker Lake
	• Kangerlussuaq (Greenland)-Iqaluit-Rankin Inlet-Baker Lake
	Rankin Inlet to Baker Lake (almost 300 kilometres northwest) is via Calm Air or Skyward Aviation
Banks:	None. Cash and traveller's cheques are preferable
Alcohol:	Alcohol is not restricted, governed only by the provisions of the NWT Liquor Control Act. However, alcohol cannot be purchased in Baker Lake, nor is it served at the hotels
Taxis:	Yes

The source of my excitement is the sheer vastness of the barren lands that surround me, and the opportunity to meet people who belong in that landscape. Warning. The power of this land can become a passion that will bring you back again and again.

Our flight path from Rankin Inlet has brought us over the great expanse of Baker Lake or *Qamani'tuaq*, meaning "huge lake adjoined by a river at both ends." Out the window to the south, I can see the serpentine form of the Kazan River stretching from the horizon to its mouth at Baker Lake where it ends its 850-kilometre journey through the heart of the barren lands. I wonder at the skill and knowledge of the Inuit whose lives have depended on the Kazan River for centuries. The abundant archeological sites along the river testify to the people's prosperity and hardship. In historic times, the river was used by explorers like J. B. Tyrell, and the members of the Fifth Thule Expedition. Recently, the river has become one of the premier routes for experienced wilderness paddlers. The Kazan well deserves its designation as a Canadian heritage river.

As we descend into Baker Lake, I look to the northeast and see the area's other Canadian heritage river, the Thelon River, curving out of the Half-Way hills in the distance. The Thelon River is also steeped in history. It was home to Inuit from its mouth up to the Beverly Lake area in what is now the Thelon Wildlife Sanctuary. J. B. Tyrell also explored this river in 1893, followed by David Hanbury in 1899 and 1901 to 1902. Many other modern-day explorers paddle the river each year.

Out the other window, I can see the community of Baker Lake. The sight of the community perched on the edge of this huge lake, surrounded on all sides by hundreds of kilometres of tundra, reinforces how remote this village is at the geographical centre of Canada. Nowhere else can one have such a deep experience of the barren lands and its people. My travels on water, snow and ice with Inuit friends have given me a glimpse into their world. To them, these are not "barren" lands, but named and understood places, where they and their ancestors have struggled and flourished as an integral part of this unique landscape. Their claim to this place as their homeland has been hard-earned. Their profound sense of belonging here is evident in their faces and their easy movement through the landscape.

At the tiny Baker Lake airport, we walk from the plane into a crowd of smiling faces. A proud family has come out to greet a mother and her newborn child. An elder addresses the child as "my mother," due to its name. Although born in southern Canada, this child's soul — in the Inuit belief system — has always lived here among them. Still bathed in the warmth of this scene, I meet an elderly friend and shake his hand. "*Tunngahugit,*" he says. Welcome to Baker Lake. I feel it, and you will, too.

History

When Captain William Christopher of the Hudson's Bay Co. sailed through Chesterfield Inlet in 1761 and gave Qamani'tuaq its English name, Baker Lake, the area had already been known to Inuit for centuries. In the channels of Chesterfield Inlet, today's visitor can see an abundance of inuksuit, tent rings and other archeological evidence of Inuit occupation. This is true of all waterways that feed into Baker Lake.

In some ways, the community of Baker Lake is a very young community. Until the mid-1950s, most Inuit still lived on the land in areas surrounding Baker Lake. The *Utkuhiksalingmiut* came from the Back River, the *Hanningajurmiut* from the Garry Lake area, the *Akilinirmiut* from the Thelon River area around Beverly Lake, the *Qairnirmiut* from the lower Thelon River, Baker Lake and Chesterfield Inlet, and the *Harvaqtuurmiut* from the Kazan River area. What all these groups share is a history of life lived almost exclusively inland away from the ocean. They all relied on the resources of the barren lands, mainly caribou and fish, ptarmigan and rabbit.

With the exception of the Back River, the area surrounding Baker Lake has only recently become known to European Canadians.

In 1834, George Back descended the river that today bears his name. Interestingly, Back heard about another major river in the region, the Thelon, but did not investigate. It was not until 1893 that the Thelon would be descended by Joseph and James Tyrell of the Geological Survey of Canada, via the Dubawnt River. The two brothers carried on through Baker Lake and Chesterfield Inlet and south along Hudson Bay to Churchill. James Tyrell continued exploring the next year by descending the Kazan River to a short distance below Yathkyed Lake, and then east via the Ferguson River to Hudson Bay and Churchill. The two expeditions helped

Baker Lake Street Map

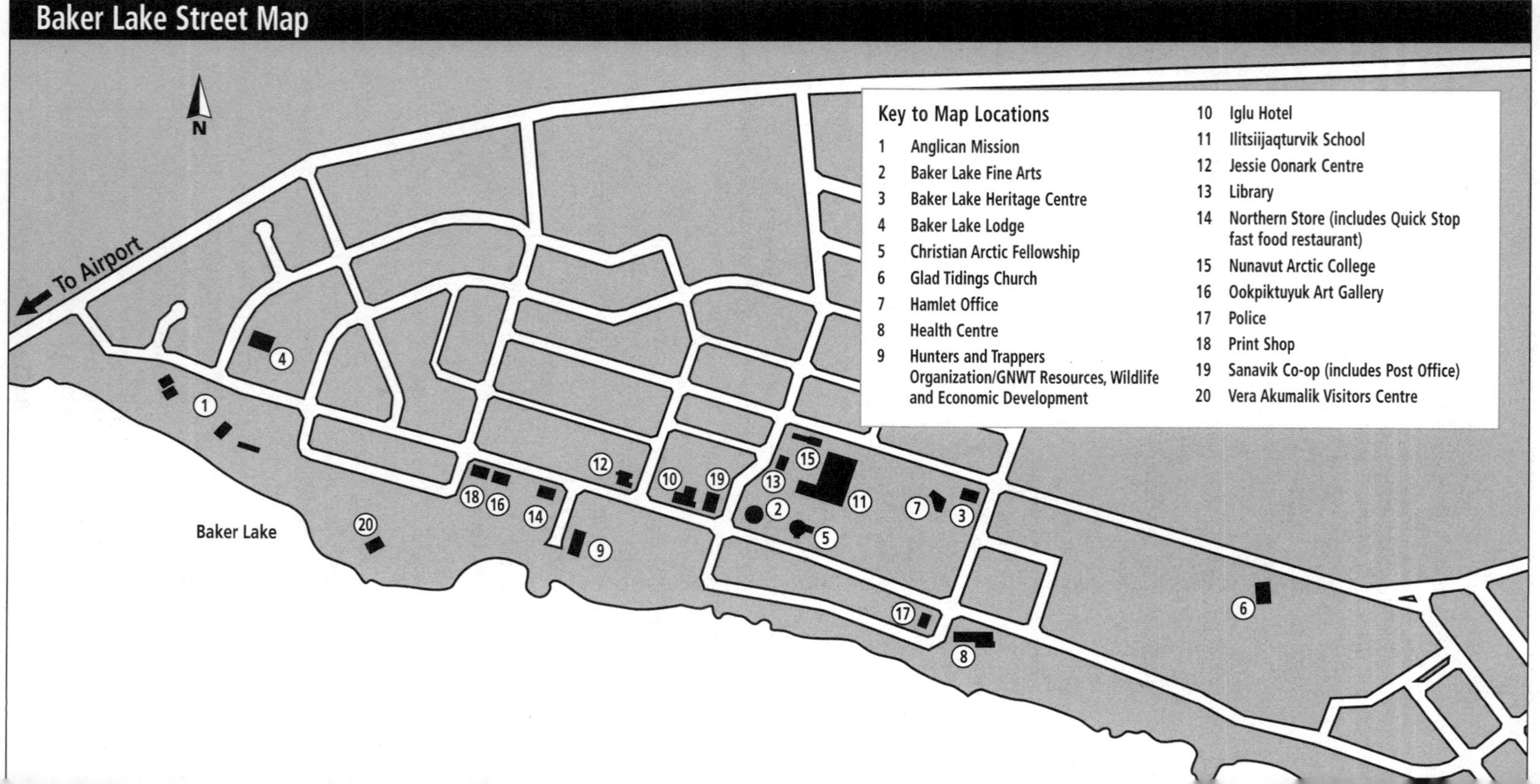
N
To Airport
Baker Lake
Key to Map Locations
1 Anglican Mission
2 Baker Lake Fine Arts
3 Baker Lake Heritage Centre
4 Baker Lake Lodge
5 Christian Arctic Fellowship
6 Glad Tidings Church
7 Hamlet Office
8 Health Centre
9 Hunters and Trappers Organization/GNWT Resources, Wildlife and Economic Development
10 Iglu Hotel
11 Ilitsiijaqturvik School
12 Jessie Oonark Centre
13 Library
14 Northern Store (includes Quick Stop fast food restaurant)
15 Nunavut Arctic College
16 Ookpiktuyuk Art Gallery
17 Police
18 Print Shop
19 Sanavik Co-op (includes Post Office)
20 Vera Akumalik Visitors Centre

garner some knowledge of the region's underlying rock formation, its natural features, and its native population.

In 1899, British explorer David Hanbury travelled by dogteam up the coast of Hudson Bay and through Chesterfield Inlet. From Chesterfield Inlet, Hanbury travelled by boat through Baker Lake and up the Thelon River, gaining access to Great Slave Lake via the Hanbury River and Artillery Lake. Hanbury returned again between 1901 and 1902, spending much time in the area between Chesterfield Inlet and Beverly Lake on the Thelon River, where he befriended many Inuit.

In the spring of 1922, anthropologists Kaj Birket-Smith and Knud Rasmussen travelled up the Kazan River and met with Harvaqtuurmiut and *Paallirmiut* along the river and at Yathkyed Lake. Their report stands as the earliest and most descriptive study of historic Inuit life in the area.

European Canadians didn't establish a permanent presence at Baker Lake until the Hudson's Bay Co. post was built at *Uqpiktujuq*, or Big Hips Island, in 1916. Competition arrived in the form of the Revillion Frères in 1924 when they set up a trading post at the mouth of the Thelon River. In 1926, the Hudson's Bay Co. also moved to the mouth of the Thelon near the present location of Baker Lake. Two men from Chesterfield Inlet, Naittuq and Singiittuq, played an important role in piloting supply ships through the narrows of Chesterfield Inlet and into Baker Lake. They were asked to help lead the ships because they knew where the shallow parts of the inlet lay. After years of competition the Hudson's Bay Co. bought out the Revillion Frères in 1936 and moved the operation into their building. The building survives to this day in the form of the Vera Akumalik Visitors Centre on the waterfront behind the Northern store.

In the fall of 1927, both the Anglican and Roman Catholic missions arrived to begin the competition for the souls of the Inuit. The original **Anglican mission**, St. Aiden's, was built in 1930 and still stands today.

Government arrived in force during the 1950s and '60s. The nursing station (or health centre) was built in 1956 and the Federal School in 1957. Children were brought into town to go to school. This, in combination with some hard years of starvation, brought Inuit into the settlement to stay. In 1962, houses were built for Inuit by the Department of Northern Affairs and National Resources. Although some Inuit families were still on the land in the '60s, it was only a matter of time before everyone lived in town.

Baker Lake: Its Land and Wildlife

The barren lands surrounding Baker Lake offer many and varied landscapes to explore. Many of these areas have been recognized as Canadian treasures through various designations.

In the west, in the area of the upper Thelon River, is the Thelon Wildlife Sanctuary. The Sanctuary was established in 1927 to save the dwindling muskoxen population here. The effort has been very successful. Muskoxen can now be seen near Shultz Lake on the Thelon River and as far west as the Kazan River, areas where they have not been seen in a century.

In being designated Canadian heritage rivers, Baker Lake's two major rivers, the Thelon and Kazan, have both been recognized for their rich natural and cultural heritage. Both are home to populations of caribou, muskoxen, barren-ground grizzlies, wolves, foxes, wolverines, peregrine falcons, lake trout and grayling. A section of the Kazan River has also been designated a national historic site. The Fall Caribou Crossing National Historic Site, which commemorates the history of the traditional fall caribou hunt, begins at the spectacular Kazan Falls, and ends in Thirty Mile Lake. It encompasses many archeological sites and was the location of camps where Inuit hunted migrating caribou. Hunters lanced the animals from *qajait* (kayaks) as they swam across the river. The success of this hunt determined the survival of Inuit over the long barren-land winter.

To the north of Baker Lake is the splendor of Wager Bay. This rich natural area boasts populations of polar bears, seals, beluga whales, wolves, caribou and other animals. Negotations are under way to turn the Wager Bay area into a national park, and Parks Canada predicts the park may be up and running by 1998 or 1999.

Tours

Tourist information is available at the **Vera Akumalik Visitors Centre**, right on the beach facing the water, behind the Northern store. The Centre is usually open June through Labor Day. Contact the Hamlet of Baker Lake's community economic development officer for details.

The inland way of life of the Baker Lake people is to be commemorated at the soon-to-be-finished Baker Lake Heritage Centre, situated beside the **hamlet office**. The Centre will offer visitors an opportunity to learn about the culture and history of all Inuit groups who now comprise the population of Baker Lake. There will also be exhibits interpreting the nearby Fall Caribou Crossing National Historic Site. For more information on the Heritage Centre, contact the community economic development officer at Baker Lake's hamlet office.

Outfitters and guides in Baker Lake can take you on tours of the community and the surrounding area. In the summer, you can travel by boat to hunt caribou, or fish for lake trout or arctic char. Many visitors also choose to explore this area by canoe. Some of the most challenging and remote barren-land rivers are located in the Baker Lake area: the Thelon, Kazan and Back rivers. At the same time you can glimpse wildlife, or visit historical and archeological sites.

Edwin Evo Outfitting and Naturalist Tours is a reputable outfitter that provides visitors with an entertaining and safe journey. Owner and operator Edwin Evo takes pride in organization and safety, and is very knowledgeable about travel in the area. In his brand-new 6.7-metre Zag-Fab aluminum boat, he will take visitors out for some sport fishing or wildlife viewing and photography, docking perhaps for a hike, or viewing archeological sites. Evo will also pick up customers at the end of their paddle down the Kazan, Thelon or Quoich rivers.

Sila Lodge is a well-established tourist lodge at Wager Bay that permits an organized and safe way to view arctic landscapes, wildlife, and Inuit and European historic sites. The Wager Bay area is well known for its polar bear population. These majestic animals, along with an abundance of wildlife, such as ringed and bearded seals, beluga whales, caribou, wolves, and many species of birds, make the area a photographer's dream. Visitors can see it all while boating or hiking under the watchful eye of trained guides. The lodge has five three-bedroom guest cabins and a main lodge with dining room. By all reports the dining here is excellent. A one-week stay at Sila Lodge plus one night in Baker Lake (airfare from Baker Lake included) is about $3,600.

The Baker Lake **Hunters and Trappers Organization** is licensed to outfit sport hunts for caribou and muskoxen. Caribou hunts are held in August and September and hunters are transported by boat. Muskoxen hunts run in the second or third week of March. Due to the season and the long distances that have to be travelled by snowmobile, muskoxen hunts are only for the adventurous few with very good winter clothing. The HTO uses only highly skilled guides like Jacob Ikinilik, Brian Ookowt and Philip Putumiraqtuq. All have excellent land skills and, if you're interested, you may even learn something about Inuit culture. **Canada North Outfitting Inc.** works in tandem with the HTO to provide these hunts.

In spring you can camp in an *iglu* and learn the ways of Inuit at a traditional camp. David Awksawnee has been successfully running the **Ahearmiut** Spring Traditional Camp for some time, employing other Inuit from Baker Lake to treat newcomers to a "life on the land" experience. Visitors can learn to build an iglu while dressed in hand-sewn caribou skin clothing, much like Inuit have done for centuries. Your Inuit hosts will demonstrate traditional technology made from local materials. Awksawnee can also design an outing to fit your interests.

Exploring the wilderness around Baker Lake can be exciting, but also challenging. This area can be very windy and the weather may change quickly, so don't be surprised if you have to spend some time sitting out the weather on your tour. In addition, mosquitoes can be very bad in the Baker Lake area. Take precautions by bringing a head net and/or bug jacket. Speak with your outfitter or tour operator about what clothing and other gear you should bring, and what conditions to expect during the trip.

Shopping

Ookpiktuyuk Art Gallery, located next to the **Northern store**, is run by Henry and his son David Ford. Henry's father Harry Ford operated the first Hudson's Bay Co. trading post at Baker Lake on Big Hips Island or Uqpiktujuq (Ookpiktuyuk is an old spelling of the word). The gallery specializes in the wholesale and distribution of carvings, wall hangings, tapestries and drawings to art galleries in southern Canada and around the world. Visitors can drop in to view the latest offerings from local Inuit carvers. Whether you buy something or not, you'll undoubtedly come away a little richer having heard a story or two from Henry and David.

Jessie Oonark was an artist who brought Baker Lake's art to the attention of the world. The staff of the **Jessie Oonark Centre**, across from the Northern store on Baker Lake's main street, do the same thing by producing quality clothing bearing the art of Baker Lake artists. You can stop in for a tour, and pick up a T-shirt or sweatshirt as a keepsake. Recently a Nunavut Arctic College jewelry program has been operating from the Centre; a jewelry guild may eventually be established in Baker Lake.

Baker Lake Fine Arts has recently changed hands. Previous owner Marie Bouchard has headed south after supporting the efforts of local artists and craftspeople for many years, but the tradition continues with new owner Sally Qimminunaaq Webster. Baker Lake Fine Arts carries carvings, wall hangings, crafts, traditional tools, and jewelry. The store is in the new dome-shaped building on the main street near the school and across from the Co-op.

In the past year, the world-renowned Baker Lake print tradition has been revived. Elder artists such as Victoria Mamnguqsualuk, Janet Kigusiuq, Magdalene Ukpatiku, Janet Ikuutqaq, Nancy Sevoga, and Thomas and Philippa Iksiraq share techniques with younger artists to produce unique prints. For the first time since 1990, a collection of 20 Baker Lake prints will be released on Sept. 12, 1997 in selected galleries in both Canada and the States. Prints for sale locally can be purchased by contacting either Kyra Fisher or Thomas Iksiraq. A major fund-raising campaign has been started to provide the printmakers of Baker Lake with a permanent studio. They are presently housed in an old building next to the Ookpiktuyuk Gallery.

The Northern store and **Sanavik Co-op** sell groceries, supplies, clothing, hardware — you name it. The Northern is brand new this year and has a fast food restaurant called the **Quick Stop** in the front. It also has a professional butcher on staff. Baker Lake's **post office** is located at the Co-op.

Flea markets are held from time to time at either the **Jonah Amitna'aq** school or the Recreation Centre ("the arena"). This is a good place to find traditional clothing such as caribou mitts, *kamiit*, parkas and *amautit*.

Events

Hamlet Days, a spring celebration usually held in mid-May, is a time for games, dogteam races and a children's carnival. The Hamlet of Baker Lake's recreation co-ordinator can supply more details.

Baker Lake is famous for its square dances. They happen often and seemingly without warning. When in town, ask anyone if they know when the next square dance is going to be held, or call the recreation co-ordinator. Dances are always staged at the Recreation Centre.

Accommodation and Dining

The **Iglu Hotel** can accommodate up to 56 people in 25 rooms, each with private bathroom, television, telephone and two or three single beds. There is a lounge with a television and pool table, a meeting room and a dining room that serves hearty meals. Rooms are $150 per night single occupancy, or $125 per night double occupancy (meals not included in either case). There's also one room with three beds; it's $100 per person per night. Meals are $15 for breakfast, $25 for lunch, and $30 for dinner.

At **Baker Lake Lodge**, guests choose from five sleeping cabins, which have a central bath-house, or four rooms, each with a private bath and television. Prices for cabins are $65 per person per cabin (each cabin sleeps three to four people). Prices for rooms are $100 per night single occupancy, or $165 per night double occupancy. Meals are not included in accommodation rates. The main lodge building has a lounge with a nice atmosphere and a dining room offering standard southern cuisine (breakfast is $10, lunch is $17, and dinner is $25). The lodge, located on the edge of town closest to the **airport**, is a short walk to the centre of Baker Lake and all attractions. Co-owner Boris Kotelewetz will come out to the airport to pick you up.

On the road to the airport is a **campground** intended for canoeists. It has four tent pads, a bathroom and cook shelter. There's also a campground operated by the hamlet at the mouth of the Kazan River where canoeists can wait out the weather, or wait for a pickup from Baker Lake. It's free to the public.

The Quick Stop at the Northern store is one of Baker Lake's gathering places — a good place to get fast food or have a coffee and chat.

Services

In addition to scheduled flights, charter service is available from Calm Air, Skyward Aviation and others out of Rankin Inlet. Over the past few years Ptarmigan Airlines has had a Twin Otter in Baker Lake.

Visitors must make appointments for the Baker Lake **Health Centre's** public sick clinic, held from 9 a.m. to noon, Monday through Friday. There is 24-hour emergency service.

DIRECTORY

The 819 and 403 area codes change to 867 on Oct. 21, 1997.

Accommodation and Dining

Baker Lake Lodge
VISA accepted.
Tel.: (819) 793-2905
Fax: (819) 793-2965

Hamlet Office
Tel.: (819) 793-2874
Fax: (819) 793-2509

Iglu Hotel
VISA, MasterCard, Interac.
Tel.: (819) 793-2801
Fax: (819) 793-2711

Quick Stop
In the Northern store.
10 a.m.–9 p.m., Monday to Saturday; 1–6 p.m. Sunday. Summer: 12–9 p.m., Saturday.
Tel.: (819) 793-2211

Outfitters/Guides/ Tour Operators

Ahearmiut
Tel.: (819) 793-2383
Fax: (819) 793-2965

Canada North Outfitting Inc.
Tel.: (613) 256-4057
Fax: (613) 256-4512
E-mail: cnonorth@istar.ca

Edwin Evo Outfitting and Naturalist Tours
Tel.: (819) 793-2293

Sila Lodge Ltd
Tel.: 1-800-663-9832 or (204) 949-2050
Fax: (204) 663-6375
E-mail: frontiers_north@mb.sympatico.ca

Vera Akumalik Visitor Centre
Open seasonally, usually June until Labor Day.
Tel.: (819) 793-2874
Fax: (819) 793-2509

Services

Airport
Tel.: (819) 793-2927

Churches

Christian Arctic Fellowship
Tel.: (819) 793-2580

Glad Tidings
Services at 11 a.m., and 7 p.m., Sunday; 7 p.m., Wednesday.
Tel.: (819) 793-2898

St. Aiden's Anglican Mission
Tel.: (819) 793-2433

Hamlet Office
Tel.: (819) 793-2874
Fax: (819) 793-2509

Health Centre
Tel.: (819) 793-2816
Fax: (819) 793-2812

Hunters and Trappers Organization
Tel.: (819) 793-2520
Fax: (819) 793-2034

Library
Adjacent to Ilitsiijaqturvik.
Tel.: (819) 793-2909

Police (RCMP)
Tel.: (819) 793-2922
Fax: (819) 793-2149

Post Office
Located at the Co-op.
Tel.: (819) 793-2912

Resources, Wildlife and Economic Development
Ask for the wildlife officer.
Tel.: (819) 793-2944
Fax: (819) 793-2514

Schools

Ilitsiijaqturvik School
Tel.: (819) 793-2842
Fax: (819) 793-2029

Jonah Amitna'aq Secondary School
Tel.: (819) 793-2842
Fax: (819) 793-2029

Nunavut Arctic College
Tel.: (819) 793-2971
Fax: (819) 793-2181

Taxi

D C Cabs Ltd.
Tel.: (819) 793-2558
Fax: (819) 793-2665

Shopping

Baker Lake Fine Arts
Tel.: (819) 793-2865
Fax: (819) 793-2000

Jessie Oonark Centre
9 a.m.–5 p.m., Monday to Friday; weekends by appointment. VISA, Interac.
Tel.: (819) 793-2428
Fax: (819) 793-2429

Northern Store
10 a.m.–6 p.m., Monday to Thursday; 10 a.m.–9 p.m., Friday; 1–6 p.m., Saturday. In winter, 10 a.m.–6 p.m., Saturday. VISA, MasterCard, Interac.
Tel.: (819) 793-2920
Fax: (819) 793-2565

Ookpiktuyuk Art Gallery
9 a.m.–noon, 1–5 p.m., Monday to Friday; weekends by appointment. VISA accepted.
Tel.: (819) 793-2534
Fax: (819) 793-2422

Print Shop
Contact Kyra Fisher at Tel./Fax: (819) 793-2366 or Thomas Iksiraq at (819) 793-2497 for prints.
Cash only accepted.
E-mail: fredyka@aol.com

Sanavik Co-op Association
10 a.m.–6 p.m., Monday, Friday, Saturday; 10 a.m.–8 p.m., Tuesday to Thursday. Closed Sunday. VISA, Interac.
Tel.: (819) 793-2912
Fax: (819) 793-2594

CORAL HARBOUR

by Ken Beardsall

When I first visited Coral Harbour as a teenager on a school exchange trip 20 years ago, the community left a lasting impression on me.

Population:	669 (Inuit: 94%, non-Inuit: 6%)
Telephone Area Code:	819 (changes to 867 on Oct. 21, 1997)
Time Zone:	Eastern Standard all year (Coral Harbour doesn't use Daylight Saving Time)
Postal Code:	X0C 0C0
How to Get There:	Possible routes:
	• Winnipeg-Rankin Inlet-Coral Harbour
	• Yellowknife-Rankin Inlet-Coral Harbour
	• Ottawa/Montreal-Iqaluit-Coral Harbour
	• Kangerlussuaq (Greenland)-Iqaluit-Coral Harbour
	Rankin Inlet to Coral Harbour (about 500 kilometres east) is via Calm Air or First Air. From Iqaluit (more than 700 kilometres west), it's via First Air
Banks:	None. Cash and traveller's cheques are preferable
Alcohol:	Alcohol and alcoholic beverages are prohibited
Taxis:	Yes

For the past nine years, I've been living and teaching here, and its appeal to me is as strong as ever.

Is it the wide-open, rocky tundra around the settlement that I value so much? The warmth of the local people? The intriguing history of the former inhabitants? The waters that abound with wildlife each spring? These must be why I live in Coral Harbour — excellent reasons, too, for tourists to travel here. When you arrive, expect lots of handshakes from the friendly people of Coral Harbour!

In Inuktitut, Coral Harbour is called *Salliq,* meaning a large, flat island in front of the mainland. The English explorer Sir Thomas Button named the land Southampton Island, to honor his benefactor, the Earl of Southampton, who promoted his voyage in 1604 in search of the Northwest Passage. There's nothing southern, however, about this island in northern Hudson Bay, except for the name of its only community, Coral Harbour.

Incredibly, in the icy waters near the settlement, you can find coral! I've discovered bits of it while picking mussels and jigging for arctic cod in the harbor. It's fossilized coral that once thrived when northern Canada had a warmer climate. Today, of course, the climate of Coral Harbour is not conducive to its growth.

Coral Harbour today is a thriving community where a healthy birthrate ensures visitors will see many young smiling faces over the next few years. The settlement is an interesting blend of the traditional and the modern.

While walrus meat sits on the dock for everyone to share, for example, a front-end loader nearby may be preparing a lot for construction. You'll see people busily carving soapstone, ivory, whalebone or the marvellous limestone from nearby Bear Island.

History

A fascinating aspect of Southampton Island relates to its original inhabitants, whom archeologists call *Sallirmiut.* (The Inuit refer to them as the *Tuniit.*) These reclusive people are believed to have been the last of the Thule Inuit, whose culture disappeared from other areas of the Arctic about 1750. Until the beginning of the 20th century, the Sallirmiut were isolated from other Inuit, hunting bowhead whales and other marine mammals, as well as caribou. In 1902, however, a Scottish whaling ship, the *Active,* sailed into Hudson Bay and set up a station at Cape Low, at the southern tip of Southampton Island. One of the ship's crew carried the deadly typhus disease. After a brief association with the whalers and other Inuit, the Sallirmiut, too, fell ill. The disease spread throughout their camps. With the exception of four children who had been adopted previously by Inuit families elsewhere, the entire population died.

You can visit a large Sallirmiut camp site at Native Point, about 64 kilometres southeast of Coral Harbour, by boat in summer or by snowmobile or dogteam in spring. (Tours to Native Point are available through **Kajjaarnaq Arctic Tours** and **Ningeocheak Outfitting**.) A winter visit isn't recommended because the site will be snow-covered. Here, on a high peninsula, you'll find the remains of 12 sod huts, many bones and animal parts, as well as a curious feature: Avaalak's rock. Legend has it that Avaalak, a Sallirmiut, carried a boulder up a hill from the beach to display his superhuman strength. He is also said to have killed bowhead whales by himself from a kayak. His people were known for their remarkable strength, short stature, strange hairdos and their ancient language. The Sallirmiut must have found Southampton Island attractive as it was — and still is — rich in wildlife.

Among those attracted by such riches were Scottish whalers. Between 1899 and 1903, Robert Kinnes and the Sons of Dundee operated a shore station on Southampton Island, run by three Scots; a group of Inuit relocated here from Baffin Island. In 1903, the firm sent its vessel, *Ernest William,* into Repulse Bay to act as a floating station there and in nearby waters; the ship returned to Scotland in 1910.

After the turn of the century, the whaling industry finally collapsed. The last whaler into Hudson Bay, the *A.T. Gifford,* burned and was lost with its crew off Coats Island, about 130 kilometres south of Coral Harbour, in 1915.

In 1925, the Hudson's Bay Co. established a trading post at the site of Coral Harbour by combining other posts from Chesterfield Inlet and Coats Island. The traders brought with them Inuit from Baffin Island, northern Quebec and the mainland Keewatin (now called the Kivalliq Region).

Just outside Coral Harbour, the Americans built a major military airbase to service thousands of aircraft ferried to Europe during the Second World War. They later used the airport as a depot during construction of

DEW Line stations further north. After the War, when they abandoned the site, they left behind much of their equipment, including thousands of oil drums. Many smaller items that had been long buried, such as tools and bottles, come to the surface occasionally — mementoes of Coral Harbour's role in the War. Today the base is protected under territorial legislation: artifacts are not to be removed.

In the 1950s and '60s, federal government presence in the region increased with the building of a school in 1955, a nursing station in 1963, and public housing. The government encouraged Inuit to move from their camps in the land to the community to receive health care and social services. An Anglican mission was started in Coral Harbour by Luke Kidlapik, an Inuit catechist trained at Blacklead Island in Cumberland Sound.

Coral Harbour: Its Land and Wildlife

Today, visitors come to Coral Harbour to experience the wonderful diversity of wildlife here. Offshore waters are alive with walrus, beluga whales and seals.

A large population of polar bears dwells on the island; if you're travelling by boat, you may spot these magnificent animals lumbering along the coastline. As well, the island is home to a large herd of caribou. During the 1950s, caribou were hunted to extinction; in 1967, however, they were airlifted here from Coats Island. Since then, their populations have grown so much that they are now hunted commercially by local people.

Bird watchers will be delighted by multitudes of migratory species on the island. Two areas worth visiting are the East Bay Bird Sanctuary, about 70 kilometres east of Coral, and the Harry Gibbons Bird Sanctuary, about 140 kilometres southwest of the community. Here you'll spot snow geese by the thousands, as well as tundra swans, sandhill cranes and many other species.

Tours

Boating is an ideal way to view marine mammals at close range, and the harbor here attracts a large fleet of crafts, including several fishing boats imported from Nova Scotia and Prince Edward Island. There are three-to-five-day guided tours to Coats, Bencas and Walrus Islands that can also include a stopover at Native Point. You'll travel by boat to see herds of walrus lounging on the rocks; you may even catch a glimpse of a polar bear or two. At the towering Akpa Cliffs, on Coats Island, you can observe flocks of thick-billed murres, glaucous gulls and black guillemots in their nests or wheeling about majestically. Coats Island is a particularly good vantage point for watching birds. Here you can observe their goings-on from a boat at the bottom of the cliffs or from perches at the top. The best time for viewing the birds is in June.

If boating isn't for you, you'll have plenty of opportunities to view wildlife by land. You can travel by snowmobile or by all-terrain vehicle to the beautiful Kirchoffer Falls only 24 kilometres away from the community. Here, gyrfalcons and peregrines soar to and from their nests on the cliffs beside the mighty Kirchoffer River. You might also spot caribou, snowy owls and many other species of breeding birds.

Shopping

Coral Harbour has many fine artisans who create treasures in walrus ivory, whalebone and sealskin. Of particular note are intricately carved ivory pieces, including rings and other jewelry. Visitors can buy these at the **Katudgevik Co-op** and Leonie's Place Hotel, or purchase them directly from the artist. Groceries and dry goods are also available at the **Northern store** and the Co-op.

Accommodation and Dining

Leonie's Place is a small, comfortable hotel with six double-occupancy rooms, all with private washrooms and a radio. There is a television in the lounge. The price is $120 per person per day without meals and $180 with meals. The hotel serves meals for registered guests only, and accepts only cash or traveller's cheques. Meals are as follows: $10, breakfast; $20, lunch; $30, supper.

The **Esungarq Motel**, owned by the Co-op, is undergoing renovations, but should be ready for guests by autumn of 1997. Call the Co-op for further information.

Services

The **Health Centre** is open to the public 8:30 to 11:30 a.m. weekdays, with 24-hour emergency service. There is also an **RCMP** detachment in Coral Harbour.

DIRECTORY

The 819 and 403 area codes change to 867 on Oct. 21, 1997.

Accommodation and Dining

Co-op Esungarq Motel
Renovations to be completed by autumn 1997.
Tel.: (819) 925-9926
Fax: (819) 925-8308

Leonie's Place Hotel
Cash, traveller's cheques accepted.
Tel.: (819) 925-9751 or (819) 925-8810
Fax: (819) 925-8606

Guides/Outfitters/ Tour Operators

Kajjaarnaq Arctic Tours
Tel.: (819) 925-8366
Fax: (819) 925-8593

Ningeocheak Outfitting
Tel.: (819) 925-9797
Fax: (819) 925-8445

Services

Airport and Weather Information
Tel.: (819) 925-9711

Aiviit Hunters and Trappers Organization
Tel.: (819) 925-8622
Fax: (819) 925-8300

Churches

Glad Tidings Church
Services: irregular hours.
Tel.: (819) 925-8875

St. Joseph's Roman Catholic Mission
Services: 11 a.m. and 7 p.m., Sunday.
Tel.: (819) 925-8277

St. Mark's Anglican Church
No minister currently.
Tel.: (819) 925-8397

How to be a well-outfitted Arctic traveller...

Arctic waters are fascinating, but they are also frigid. If you're planning to explore Arctic waters, there are a couple of things **you** should do to make sure you're on friendly and safe terms with our beautiful but challenging Arctic environment. First make sure your guide is licensed and also properly equipped with signalling devices, radios and first-aid equipment to handle any possible emergency. Second, as a well-outfitted Arctic traveller, **you** should make sure you have a floater suit for yourself and everybody else to wear in the boat. Once your personal safety is dealt with, then you can focus on having a great time!

Department of Resources, Wildlife and Economic Development

Hamlet Office
Tel.: (819) 925-8867
Fax: (819) 925-8823

Health Centre
Tel.: (819) 925-9916
Fax: (819) 925-8380

Police (RCMP)
Tel.: (819) 925-9954
Fax: (819) 925-8483

Post Office
Located at the Katudgevik Co-op.
Tel.: (819) 925-9909

Schools

Nunavut Arctic College
Tel.: (819) 925-9746
Fax: (819) 925-8410

Sakku School
Tel.: (819) 925-9923
Fax: (819) 925-8410

Taxis

Eleven Mile Trek Taxi
Tel.: (819) 925-9767

Veronica's Taxi
Tel.: (819) 925-8324

Shopping

Katudgevik Co-op
10 a.m.–9 p.m., Monday to Saturday.
Closed Sunday. VISA, Interac
Tel.: (819) 925-9969
Fax: (819) 925-8308

Leonie's Place Hotel Craft Shop
3–5 p.m., Monday and Wednesday;
3–6 p.m., Friday.
Cash, traveller's cheques.
Tel.: (819) 925-8626
Fax: (819) 925-8606

Northern Store
10 a.m.–6 p.m., Monday to Wednesday; 10 a.m.–7 p.m., Thursday and Friday; 10 a.m.–4 p.m., Saturday.
Closed Sunday. VISA, MasterCard, Interac.
Tel.: (819) 925-9920
Fax: (819) 925-8863

IGLOOLIK

by John MacDonald, with contributions from Louis Tapardjuk and George Qulaut

Situated amid the flat expanse of the Melville Peninsula's eastern coastal plain, the settlement of Igloolik has long been off the beaten track for tourists in the eastern Arctic.

Population:	1,174 (Inuit: 95%, non-Inuit: 5%)
Telephone Area Code:	819 (changes to 867 on Oct. 21, 1997)
Time Zone:	Eastern Time
Postal Code:	X0A 0L0
How to Get There:	Possible routes:
	• Ottawa/Montreal-Iqaluit-Igloolik
	• Winnipeg-Rankin Inlet-Iqaluit-Igloolik
	• Yellowknife-Rankin Inlet-Iqaluit-Igloolik
	• Kangerlussuaq (Greenland)-Iqaluit-Igloolik
	Iqaluit to Igloolik (about 800 km northwest) is via First Air
Banks:	None. Cash and traveller's cheques are preferable
Alcohol:	Alcohol and alcoholic beverages cannot be purchased in
	Igloolik. Visitors who want to bring alcohol into the community
	must first obtain a permit from the community's **Alcohol Education**
	Committee
Taxis:	Yes

Today, whether you come to see people, wildlife or a wilderness vastly different from Baffin Island's craggy peaks and fiords, you will find a region rich in its own treasures and well worth exploring.

A visit here takes you not only to the geographic centre of Nunavut but also to what is widely considered the cultural hub of Nunavut. Ancient ties to northern and southern Baffin Island, as well as the Kivalliq and eastern Kitikmeot regions, contribute to the distinct mix of Inuit cultural traditions practised in Igloolik today. The area has long been blessed with abundant natural resources that Inuit culture and identity thrive on: walruses, seals, whales, polar bears, caribou, fish and waterfowl. These resources continue to provide the economic, spiritual and intellectual basis for cultural continuity within Igloolik. People here take immense pride in nurturing Inuit heritage and traditions while embracing the inevitable changes brought on by modernization. The challenge in maintaining this balance is the very essence of Igloolik's vibrancy.

History

The fertile seas around Igloolik have attracted and sustained arctic hunting peoples for millennia. Information about the area's earliest inhabitants comes mainly from the numerous archeological sites on the island, some dating back more than 4,000 years. The island's history also lives in timeless

Inuit traditions about the legendary *Tuniit*, believed by archeologists to be the people of the Dorset culture who inhabited the region for almost 2,000 years.

Many Igloolik families are descended from members of the famed Qitdlarssuaq migration to Greenland in the mid-1800s. Then some 40 Inuit, including a number from the Igloolik area, embarked on an epic journey led by Qillaq, a renowned shaman who was said to be evading a blood feud. Qillaq and his companions eventually reached northwest Greenland, where they settled among Inuit already there. (Qillaq — spelled as Qitdlaq in Greenlandic form — later became known as Qitdlarssuaq, "the great Qitdlaq," after arriving in Greenland.)

First direct contact with Europeans occurred when British Navy ships *Fury* and *Hecla*, under the command of Captain William Edward Parry, wintered at Igloolik in 1822–1823. Parry's expedition failed in its main goal — the discovery of a northwest passage. However, with the help of Inuit (in particular Iligliuk and Ewerat, who drew accurate maps of the area for the expedition's officers), Parry added considerably to European knowledge of the people, lands and seas to the north of Hudson Bay. According to local accounts, Parry's ships were driven from Igloolik by a vengeful shaman who vowed that white men would never again return to the area by sea. Indeed, it was well over 100 years before another ship was seen in Igloolik waters.

The island was visited briefly in 1867 and 1868 by the American explorer Charles Francis Hall during his futile search for survivors of the lost Franklin expedition. In 1913, Alfred Tremblay, a French-Canadian prospector with Captain Joseph Bernier's expedition to Pond Inlet, extended his mineral explorations overland to Igloolik, and in 1921, members of Knud Rasmussen's Fifth Thule Expedition visited the island. Published reports of that expedition provide a detailed picture of traditional Inuit life just before "modernization" began.

The first permanent presence of outsiders on Igloolik Island came with the establishment of a Roman Catholic mission in the 1930s. By the end of the decade, the Hudson's Bay Co. had also set up a post on the island. Over the next 20 years, most Inuit continued to live in traditional camps in the nearby coastal areas of northern Foxe Basin.

During this time two individuals, Ittuksaarjuat and his wife Ataguttaaluk, emerged as highly respected leaders, caring for their people in times of hardship, sharing resources and ensuring co-operation among the region's camps. Igloolik's school is named in memory of Ataguttaaluk.

The present community of Igloolik dates from the late 1950s, with the federal government's increasing administrative interest in the Arctic. By the mid-1960s, a school, nursing station and **RCMP** detachment were permanently established, as well as the Anglican mission (1959) and the Igloolik Co-operative (1963). As with other settlements in the eastern Arctic, Igloolik grew rapidly as Inuit families from surrounding camps moved into the community to avail themselves of services offered by government agencies.

Throughout the changes brought about by growth and modernization, Igloolik has never lost sight of its cultural roots, a fact reflected in the day-to-day life of the community and in the activities of a number of local organizations. An active elders group, the Inullariit Society, teaches land skills and traditional sewing to the community's youth and, in co-operation with the Igloolik Research Centre, sponsors a major oral history project aimed at documenting the elders' rich traditional knowledge. In mid-January of each year, the Society also organizes a festival to celebrate the return of the sun after winter's dark period. Igloolik is also home to two video production organizations, Igloolik Isuma Productions Inc., an independent company specializing in Inuit cultural programming, and a local office of the Nunavut-wide Inuit Broadcasting Corporation.

Igloolik: Its Land and Wildlife

The island's flat, accessible terrain, in many parts blanketed with flowering tundra plants, makes bird watching, hiking and camping especially rewarding. Many species of birds nest locally, including loons, geese, eider ducks, terns, jaegers, plovers, snow buntings and snowy owls. Numerous migratory birds also visit the area in late spring and summer.

From late April until June, conditions are usually superb for dogteam trips through nearby valleys, lakes and bays, or out to the floe edge. Scattered herds of caribou, basking seals and even walruses can often be seen on these trips.

Breakup of the sea ice around Igloolik Island usually occurs in late July or early August. During the subsequent open-water season, which lasts until mid-October, boating excursions into Fury and Hecla Strait are frequently rewarded with the unforgettable sight of bowhead whales on their summer migration in northern Foxe Basin.

Tours

Igloolik offers a variety of activities based on the area's natural attractions and seasonal cycle. The best time to visit, however, is from mid-April to September, when the sky barely darkens and temperatures creep ever higher.

There is a good view of Igloolik and the surrounding landscape from atop the limestone bluff two kilometres north of town. Most of the island can be seen from this point. The low shoreline of Melville Peninsula fills the horizon to the west and south. With good visibility you can see north across Fury and Hecla Strait to the distant mountains of Baffin Island.

There are numerous archeological sites on Igloolik Island. These sites are best visited during the snow-free season (mid-June to mid-September) when they are fully exposed. Fine examples of Dorset and Thule dwellings, some recently excavated, are found in the vicinity of Arnaqquaksat Point, five kilometres from town and a pleasant walk by road and pathway. The impressive ruins of an old Thule settlement can be seen at Ungalujat Point, 18 kilometres from town by dirt road. Here there are more than 30 significant structures, including the walls and stone benches of a circular ceremonial house once used for festivities following a successful whale hunt. A drive to the site by taxi can be arranged when the road is passable, usually from July to mid-September. You can also arrange with a local outfitter to get there by snowmobile, dogteam or boat, depending on the season.

On the way to Ungalujat Point there is the grave of an English sailor who died here in 1823 during Parry's expedition. The spot is marked by a finely engraved headstone carved from local limestone. Further along the coast to the east is Igloolik Point, site of the old Inuit village for which the island is named. The area around Igloolik Point is still a favorite spot of Inuit residents for summer camping and for the community's summer walrus hunt.

A short distance off Igloolik's northwest shore lie the islands of Avvajjaq, one of them the site of a former Inuit settlement and an abandoned Roman Catholic mission house dating from the 1930s. The rolling granite hills and winding valleys of the Avvajjaq area offer excellent cross-country skiing from mid-April through May. Its maze of sheltered islands and narrow passageways would delight sea-kayaking enthusiasts in summer.

There is no fishing to speak of on Igloolik Island itself. Mogg Bay (*Nalukajarvik*), 24 kilometres southwest of Igloolik on the Melville Peninsula, is the nearest good fishing spot for arctic char. Lake trout and char can also be fished in adjoining lakes. August brings excellent open-water fishing along the shores and fiords of Baffin Island, but weather and ice conditions in Fury and Hecla Strait often make access to this area difficult.

Shopping

The **Igloolik Co-operative** and the **Northern store** are the community's main retail outlets, offering a wide variety of merchandise and groceries. Naphtha for camp stoves is sold only at the Co-op.

In season, frozen arctic char and caribou can be purchased from the local **Hunters and Trappers Organization** (HTO).

Igloolik is also a fine place to purchase Inuit art; artisans here most commonly produce sculptures. Carvings are sold mainly through the Co-op, though you may also buy them from individual artists. Wall-hangings and paintings by local artists are frequently displayed for sale in the Co-op restaurant.

Traditional skin clothing and hunting implements are occasionally sold at the HTO.

Accommodation and Dining

Igloolik's **Tujormivik Hotel** has eight rooms, seven of which are double or triple occupancy, depending on the number of guests. There are no private washrooms in the rooms. All rooms have color TVs, but none have phones. There's a phone in the lounge, which also has a TV. Generous meals often include local foods such as arctic char and caribou. Guests with particular dietary needs or preferences can, with sufficient notice, arrange to have special meals prepared at no additional cost.

The hotel rate (three meals included) is $185 per person per day. Without meals the room rate is $125. A new 20-room hotel is planned for 1998. A number of private homes in Igloolik offer bed-and-breakfast-type accommodation. A current list of these can be obtained from an officer with the GNWT's **Resources, Wildlife and Economic Development** department.

The Anglican mission is now operating **Dean's Bed and Breakfast**. The cost is $125 per person per night and includes three meals. Rates are reduced for six nights or more.

Igloolik's only **restaurant** is operated by the Co-op. Here they serve solid meals at reasonable prices (breakfast $5, lunch $10, dinner $25). The Tujormivik Hotel also serves meals to non-guests (breakfast $10, lunch $15, dinner $35); give them a few hours' notice. Snacks or light meals can be obtained at the **Co-op's coffee shop**.

Services

A number of organizations around town welcome visitors. The **Igloolik Hamlet Office** provides up-to-date information about the town and its services. The **Ataguttaaluk Elementary School** — which also houses the community's excellent **public library** — has a permanent gallery depicting the town's history.

Tours are given by the **Igloolik Research Centre**, a territorial government facility that supports scientific research in the area. The centre also runs a number of environmental monitoring programs, has a general reference library and houses a large collection of traditional knowledge and oral history materials contributed by members of the Inullariit society.

Igloolik's **health centre** is staffed by four resident nurses. Walk-in clinics are 9–11:30 a.m., Monday to Friday. There are special clinics every weekday afternoon. A nurse is on call 24 hours a day. Physicians from Iqaluit visit the community regularly.

DIRECTORY

The 819 and 403 area codes change to 867 on Oct. 21, 1997.

Accommodation and Dining

Co-op Coffee Shop
9 a.m.–11 p.m., Monday through Saturday; 1–6 p.m. and 8–11 p.m, Sunday.
Tel.: (819) 934-8948

Dean's Bed and Breakfast
Cheque or cash.
Tel./Fax: (819) 934-8586

Restaurant
10 a.m.–8 p.m., Monday to Wednesday;
10 a.m.–9 p.m., Thursday to Saturday;
12–7 p.m., Sunday.
Tel.: (819) 934-8595

Tujormivik Hotel
VISA accepted.
Tel.: (819) 934-8814
Fax: (819) 934-8816

Outfitters/Guides/ Tour Operators

Hunters and Trappers Organization
Tel.: (819) 934-8807
Fax: (819) 934-8067

Services

Airport
Tel.: (819) 934-8973

Alcohol Education Committee
Tel.: (819) 934-8905

Churches

Anglican Church
Services 11 a.m. and 7 p.m., Sunday; 7:30 p.m., Tuesday (Inuktitut only).
Tel./Fax: (819) 934-8586

Full Gospel Church
Phone number unavailable.

Roman Catholic Church
Services occasionally when the priest is in town.
Tel.: (819) 934-8846
Fax: (819) 934-8757

GNWT Resources, Wildlife and Economic Development
Tel.: (819) 934-8866
Fax: (819) 934-8757

Hamlet Office
Tel.: (819) 934-8830

Health Centre
Tel.: (819) 934-8837
Fax: (819) 934-8901

Igloolik Research Centre
Tel.: (819) 934-8836
Fax: (819) 934-8792
E-mail: igloonri@nunanet.com

Public Library
Located in Ataguttaaluk Elementary School.
Tel.: (819) 934-8812

Police (RCMP)
Tel.: (819) 934-8828
Fax: (819) 934-8723

Post Office
Located at Igloolik Co-operative.
Tel.: (819) 934-8727

Radio Station (FM 105.2)
Tel.: (819) 934-8824 (off air)
Tel.: (819) 934-8832 (on air)

Schools

Ataguttaaluk Elementary School
Tel.: (819) 934-8996

Nunavut Arctic College
Tel.: (819) 934-8876

Taxis

Qamaniq Taxi
Tel.: (819) 934-8942

Union Taxi
Tel.: (819) 934-8177

Weather Office
Tel.: (819) 934-8947

Stores

Igloolik Co-operative
9 a.m.–6 p.m., Monday to Wednesday and Saturday; 9 a.m.–9 p.m., Thursday and Friday. Closed Sunday.
VISA, traveller's cheques, Interac.
Tel.: (819) 934-8938
Fax: (819) 934-8740

Northern Store
10 a.m.–6:30 p.m., Monday to Wednesday and Saturday.
10 a.m.–9 p.m., Thursday and Friday.
Closed Sunday. VISA, MasterCard, traveller's cheques, Interac.
Tel.: (819) 934-8822
Fax: (819) 934-8978

by Lyn Hancock

Hall Beach is the kind of community you don't find featured in many tourist brochures.

Population:	543 (Inuit: 95%, non-Inuit: 5%)
Telephone Area Code:	819 (changes to 867 on Oct. 21, 1997)
Time Zone:	Eastern Time
Postal Code:	X0A 0K0
How to Get There:	Possible routes:
	• Ottawa/Montreal-Iqaluit-Hall Beach
	• Winnipeg-Rankin Inlet-Iqaluit-Hall Beach
	• Yellowknife-Rankin Inlet-Iqaluit-Hall Beach
	• Kangerlussuaq (Greenland)-Iqaluit-Hall Beach
	Iqaluit to Hall Beach (about 800 km northwest) is via First Air
Banks:	None. Cash and traveller's cheques are preferable
Alcohol:	Alcohol and alcoholic beverages cannot be purchased in Hall Beach. Visitors who want to bring alcohol into the community must first obtain a permit from the community's **Alcohol Education Committee**
Taxis:	Yes

Spread along a series of exposed sand and gravel beaches on the shore of Foxe Basin and backed by a soggy carpet of lakes and tundra ponds, the place can seem rather desolate.

Despite its relatively bleak facade, however, Hall Beach can be a rich experience for tourists. My most treasured moments in Nunavut took place here: drifting through a maze of ice sculptures at the floe edge, watching walruses and polar bears; trooping down to the beach to greet hunters bringing in belugas; and warming my hands in the body of a whale.

History

Whereas other communities in Nunavut traditionally developed around trading posts, whaling stations or seasonal hunting and fishing camps, Hall Beach was created instantly when a Distant Early Warning (DEW) Line site was built there in 1957 to help monitor Canadian air space in the Far North. Today the community is home to a North Warning System radar site, an advanced technological model of the DEW Line site.

Modern artifacts such as these are a powerful contrast to the extensive piles of stone and bone strewn over the gravel beaches at each end of town, evidence of Thule-culture Inuit and earlier Dorset peoples. Tent rings, food caches, grave sites, *qammait* (sod houses) and semi-subterranean houses are found to the north of the community at places called *Qimiqtuvik* and *Napakut*.

Resting on raised beaches at the southern end of town are numerous Thule winter houses. Still visible are the flagstone floors, stone sleeping platforms and massive bowhead whale skulls that formed doors and rafters or were wedged into walls. Blocks of sod that once covered roofs lie fallen on the ground.

Early contact between Inuit and non-Inuit was infrequent, but intense. Arctic explorers William Edward Parry and G. F. Lyon were the first Europeans to visit the area in 1822–1823 while wintering in their ships at Igloolik. In the 1860s, American explorer Charles Francis Hall lived and travelled with Inuit of the region; Hall Beach and Hall Lake are named after him. It wasn't until the 1920s that the next non-Inuit visited the area when members of the Fifth Thule Expedition documented the life of these Inuit in depth.

In the 1950s and 1960s, Inuit moved from surrounding camps to work and settle around the DEW Line site. (*Sanirajak*, meaning "along the coast" in Inuktitut, refers to the broad region encompassing Hall Beach.) And despite the rapid changes that have occurred since then, Hall Beach is still one of the most traditional communities in Nunavut.

Hall Beach: Its Land and Wildlife

Opportunities for bird watching in Hall Beach are endless. In late spring and summer, dozens of species of ducks, geese, swans and other waterfowl migrate north to nest on the innumerable tundra ponds behind the community. The most common species are common eiders, oldsquaws, brant, tundra swans, phalaropes, Sabine's gulls, and in high lemming years, snowy owls. Peregrine falcons can be found in hilly areas on the far side of Hall Lake.

The tundra is also a paradise for botanists and photographers. Though sparse, the soil produces carpets of moss, lichen and ground-hugging flowers such as arctic cotton, arctic heather, mountain avens, moss campion, and lots of louseworts and saxifrages. Residents rave about the spectacular sunsets of early spring and late fall, which are accentuated by the flatness of the landscape.

Tours

A visit to Hall Beach is a visit to the heart of Inuit tradition and hospitality. You can wile away the hours walking and talking along the shore, where residents camp in tents during the sunny days and nights of an all-too-brief summer. Here they tend fishing nets, stew cauldrons of walrus meat, slice *maktaaq* (the skin of the beluga whale) and hang crimson strips of arctic char to dry. With three months of endless daylight, people like to get out of their houses as much as possible.

Someone may be scraping blubber from the hide of a seal flipper for a pair of *kamiit* (boots). Another may be chiselling soapstone into a walrus or polar bear. Show an interest in the people and their activities and you may be invited for tea, bannock, this import courtesy of Scottish whalers and traders is a fried bread that remains a staple of the Inuit diet) or perhaps even a pot of walrus stew spiced with coiled intestines.

Hall Beach is also known for a traditional delicacy you may not want to eat. *Igunaq* is made by cutting raw walrus meat into large chunks, wrapping them in sausage-shaped bags of walrus hide and burying them under mounds of gravel. Six to 12 months later, people dig up the fermented meat and eat it raw. Elders say igunaq tastes like cheese. The younger generation describes it differently.

Contact the **Hunters and Trappers Organization** (HTO) for information on fishing and hunting. Fishing is best from mid-July through late August. Charter trips to popular fishing spots such as Hall Lake or *Nugsannarjuq* (Fisherman's Lake) can be arranged. See Chapter 17, "Flying to Nunavut and Its Communities," for airlines offering charter service. You can also fish from the shore of the community.

Mid- to late August is the best time for caribou hunting. Polar bear hunting is best done in late October and late April. Hall Beach is one of the few places in Canada where walruses are still numerous and walrus hunting is a common daily activity between July and September.

You can ask staff at the HTO, Co-op, **Co-op Hotel**, or **hamlet office** to recommend someone to take you.

Other sights worth noting are the remains of an old whale carcass on the edge of town (estimated to be between 350 and 800 years old and still of pungent odor); the wreckage of a World War II Lancaster bomber that crashed near Hall Lake in the mid-1950s while carrying supplies during the construction of the DEW Line station; and five waterfalls in a steep river canyon at Nunaparvik about 70 kilometres south of town near Roche Bay.

Events

A good time to visit Hall Beach is Hamlet Day — April 1 — when visitors can join a community feast, traditional games and square dancing. Hamlet Day celebrates the imminent return of continuous daylight from mid-April through mid-August.

Accommodation and Dining

The **Hall Beach Co-op** runs a small hotel that sleeps 15 people in five rooms. Be prepared to share your room, though. Rooms don't have televisions, phones, or private washrooms. There is a common area with a telephone, two bathrooms with showers, washer/dryer, TV and VCR with free videos. Rooms are $170 per person per night, including meals. Senior citizens get a 15 per cent discount.

A small canteen is open at the Co-op from 10 a.m. to 10 p.m. daily, except for Sundays when it is open from 1 to 10 p.m.

Shopping

There are two stores in Hall Beach, the **Northern store** and the new Co-op. Each sells general merchandise and groceries, including frozen meat and some fresh vegetables. You can also buy arctic char at the HTO.

Hall Beach doesn't have big-name artists, but Philomene Nattuq and Leah Anguilianuk are well known in the hamlet for their carvings and jewelry. The Co-op can provide names of other artists who welcome visitors into their homes to buy arts, crafts and sewing. Ask and you may be inundated, however. Many have something to sell; make sure it's something you want.

Services

There are two resident nurses at the Hall Beach **Health Centre**. Their hours are 8:30 a.m. to 12 p.m., Monday to Friday (general clinic); 1 to 5 p.m. (public health programs). For emergencies, call anytime.

First Air services Hall Beach from Iqaluit on Monday, Tuesday, Thursday and Friday.

DIRECTORY

The 819 and 403 area codes change to 867 on Oct. 21, 1997.

Accommodation and Dining

Co-op Hotel
VISA, MasterCard, American Express.
Tel.: (819) 928-8952 or (819) 928-8876
Fax: (819) 928-8926

Shopping

Hall Beach Co-op
10 a.m.–9 p.m., Monday to Friday; 1 p.m.–9 p.m., Saturday; 1 p.m.–6 p.m., Sunday (for coffee and snacks). VISA accepted.
Tel.: (819) 928-8876
Fax: (819) 928-8926

Northern Store
10 a.m.–6:30 p.m., Monday to Wednesday; 10 a.m.–8 p.m., Thursday and Friday; 1–6:30 p.m., Saturday. Closed Sunday. Interac accepted.
Tel.: (819) 928-8875
Fax: (819) 928-8874

Services

Airport
Tel.: (819) 928-8919

Alcohol Education Committee
Tel.: (819) 928-8880

Churches

St. Francis Roman Catholic Church
Priest comes to town every few months.
Tel.: (819) 928-8872

St. Silas Anglican Church
No phone.

Frontec Logistics
Runs the North Warning System radar site.
Tel.: (819) 928-8987

Hamlet Office
Tel.: (819) 928-8844
Fax: (819) 928-8355

Health Centre
Tel.: (819) 928-8827
Fax: (819) 928-8847

Hunters and Trappers Organization
Tel.: (819) 928-8994
Fax: (819) 928-8765

Police (RCMP)
Tel.: (819) 928-8930
Fax: (819) 928-8949

Post Office
Located at the Co-op.
Tel.: (819) 928-8821

Radio Station (FM 106.1)
Tel.: (819) 928-8829

School

Arnaqjuaq School
High school.
Tel.: (819) 928-8855
Fax: (819) 928-8810

Taxi

Co-op Taxi
Tel.: (819) 928-8876

Weather Office
Tel.: (819) 928-8807

by Peter Ernerk

Would you like to see an Inuk elder teaching Inuit youth how to drum dance and sing traditional Inuit songs?

Population:	559 (Inuit: 96%, non-Inuit: 4%)
Telephone Area Code:	819 (changes to 867 on Oct. 21, 1997)
Time Zone:	Central Time
Postal Code:	X0C 0H0
How to Get There:	Possible routes:
	• Winnipeg-Rankin Inlet-Repulse Bay
	• Edmonton-Yellowknife-Rankin Inlet-Repulse Bay
	• Ottawa/Montreal-Iqaluit-Rankin Inlet-Repulse Bay
	• Kangerlussuaq (Greenland)-Iqaluit-Rankin Inlet-Repulse Bay
	Rankin Inlet to Repulse Bay (about 500 km north) is via Calm Air
Banks:	None. Cash and traveller's cheques are preferable
Alcohol:	Alcohol and alcoholic beverages are not sold in Repulse Bay.
	Alcohol can only be imported if prior permission is obtained from the
	local **Alcohol Education Committee.** However, the Committee
	meets infrequently and has no contact phone number, so it is extremely
	difficult to bring alcohol into the community
Taxis:	No

You can when you reach the Arctic Circle and Repulse Bay, an Inuit community still steeped in tradition — and one of the last places in the Arctic to join the 20th century.

Repulse Bay thrives on hunting, fishing and trapping; many elders, like **Victor Tungilik**, have spent a lifetime doing so. This is a place where it's not unusual in the summer to see hunters returning home with fish, narwhals, belugas, seals and walruses.

Victor has almost always lived in *Naujaat* — the Inuktitut name for Repulse Bay. Born in 1924, this cultural performer is also the composer of several traditional songs, and is sometimes found at Repulse Bay's **Tusarvik School** where he teaches youth to drum and sing. Daughter Elizabeth Mapsalak can arrange for visitors to hear Victor's teachings about Inuit culture firsthand. Or those new in town may want to drop by **Nunavut Arctic College**, where elders Octave Sivanertok and Abraham Tagornak often lecture.

Repulse Bay residents are proud of their community, and of the beautiful surrounding landscape. The horizon is dotted with scenic inlets and hills of all shapes, some of which are snow-covered year round. When you land and enter the Repulse Bay air terminal, you'll be met by the smiles of local residents. If you're not sure how to find your way around, just ask anyone. Everyone in Naujaat is proud to share their history and culture with visitors.

In May 1964, I returned home after attending a high school in Yellowknife, and encountered a professor from Winnipeg, George Swinton of the University of Manitoba. He wanted to document Repulse Bay carvers for a book he was writing. I had learned to speak English a bit, and was now able to translate "pretty good" from English to Inuktitut. After George finished his work, he asked me what I wanted for helping. I liked, and got, the nice beige pants from the store.

Was there anything that my parents wanted? Some tea and tobacco. Before he departed, George came to take a picture of my family. My mother had an *ulu* (a woman's knife) that he liked very much and wanted to buy. My mother, always very generous with people, said because the professor had done so much already for us, he could have the ulu for free. That was how we showed our appreciation to this southern visitor and you know, we were happy doing it. As for the ulu, we've since learned it now resides at the Winnipeg Art Gallery.

History

Surrounding Repulse Bay are endless *inuksuk* landmarks. *Inuksuit* (the plural of inuksuk) are rocks piled on top of each other in the shape of a human, and they are referred to as stone cairns in English. Inuit built them thousands of years ago to show where they had travelled. These landmarks are built to be noticed.

Many years ago, the Inuit of Repulse Bay travelled back and forth by *qamutiit* and boat to the land of *Amitturmiut* — the people from *Iglulik* (Igloolik) and *Sanirajak* (Hall Beach). These travellers marked their way with inuksuit. For centuries there's been continuous contact with the people of *Arviligjuaq* (Pelly Bay), and many marriages have taken place between the Inuit of Iglulik, Naujaat and Arvilikjuaqmiut.

Whalers began making regular voyages to Repulse Bay in 1860, but by 1914 commercial whaling had all but stopped. The Hudson's Bay Co. opened a permanent trading post in 1919 (in 1987, the North West Company, which operates the Northern stores department chain, took over). In the 1940s and 1950s, the Inuit of Naujaat trapped mostly white foxes. Fur prices were considered very good then, and the price of goods affordable ($0.50 a gallon for kerosene for the primus stove). Many people traded their fox furs and sealskins with the Hudson's Bay Co., and then purchased whaling boats, canoes and outboard motors.

In the 1930s, missionaries came to this area and altered the course of Inuit life. The very name "missionaries" implies that we Inuit were to be saved. Not surprisingly, perhaps, religious affiliation matched tribal membership. The Amitturmiut converted to the Anglican religion, settling mostly near the Hudson's Bay Co. trading post on the west side of the community's small hill. Roman Catholics, consisting of *Nattilikmiut* (people who originally hailed from Pelly Bay) and *Aivilingmiun* (people whose ancestry can be traced to Repulse Bay), settled on the east side. On this unnamed hill is a traditional grave site. By the 1950s it was not uncommon to hear Inuit arguing among themselves as to whose religious faith was better. This was especially common among the children. This division, of course, was not an Inuit choice.

In the 1940s, people started carving in a big way, working largely in soapstone, ivory, and occasionally whalebone. This allowed Inuit to live well, providing them with additional income. It also freed them from their dependence on government support. The Inuit of Naujaat led the way in carving, as did the Inuit of *Kinngait* (Cape Dorset). Repulse Bay produced a good number of the best, including the late Marc Tungilik, who became very famous for carving miniature ivory carvings, and Irene Katak (the author's mother).

Many of Repulse Bay's famous carvers have since passed away: Lucy Agalakti Mapsalak, Celina Putulik, Paul Akuarjuk, Christine Aalu Sivaniqtuq, Madeline Isiqqut Kringayak, Athanasi Ulikattaq, Bernadette Iguttaq Tungilik. But others, such as John Kaunak and Paul Maliki, still practise their craft in Naujaat, while others, like Mariano Aupilardjuk and Bernadette Saumik, live in Rankin Inlet. Many of these carvers' pieces can be viewed at art galleries and museums in Canada. A large collection of Naujaat carvings is on permanent display at the Eskimo Museum in Churchill, Manitoba.

By 1968, when the Canadian government introduced the Eskimo Rental Housing Program, almost all of the area's Inuit settled in Naujaat. A new wage economy was helped along by the presence of government institutions that hired locally.

Repulse Bay: Its Land and Wildlife

About five kilometres north of the community is a cliff where seagulls nest every June. It is from this nesting place that Naujaat got its name: "fledgling," or baby seagull, in Inuktitut. The English name of Repulse Bay came in 1742 from a disgruntled Captain Christopher Middleton, sailing on behalf of the British Admiralty. Disappointed that he had journeyed so far north and had not found the elusive Northwest Passage, Middleton named the body of water he had sailed into "Repulse Bay."

During May and June, Naujaat comes alive with the arrival of migratory birds. The small birds, among them snow buntings, arrive first, a real sign of spring. Numerous species of larger birds follow. Chanting in their monotone voice late into the night, loons are particularly entertaining, especially when one is at an outpost and just beginning to fall asleep. Other notable birds are eider ducks, oldsquaw ducks, seagulls (*naujat*) and jaegers. The jaegers and seagulls often pick fights with one another, usually over a piece of meat. Visitors will also spot ptarmigan, tundra swans, peregrine falcons, gyrfalcons, rough-legged hawks and sandhill cranes. Geese, including the Canada, Snow and Greater species, are more abundant today than they were in the 1950s and 1960s, perhaps due to improved vegetation. Further out from the community, arctic terns and black guillemots can be seen.

In Naujaat, June is known for its *manniit*: "eggs." Arctic terns have some of the best-tasting eggs in the Arctic, but when walking along the small ponds where these birds lay their eggs, it's best to avoid them. Arctic terns are very protective, and swoop down so low that they've been known to knock a person's head with their beak. Be careful!

In fall and winter, ravens and white snowy owls can be seen further out from the community.

Marine wildlife around Repulse Bay is plentiful too: in addition to families of bearded, ringed, harp and harbor seals, the waters in this area are home to bowhead whales.

Tours

One can walk back in time and visit the historical ruins and sod houses just north of Naujaat. Inuksuit and old stone graves are all within walking distance.

In September 1991, Repulse Bay saw the return and reburial of 63 skeletal remains "stolen" from the community's traditional archeological site in 1922 by members of the Danish Fifth Thule Expedition, headed by crew member Therkel Mathiassen. Thousands of artifacts were taken to Denmark, along with these skeletal remains, used first for medical training and later displayed at a local museum. The community of Naujaat is still working to bring home the 3,500 artifacts that lie scattered now in museums throughout Denmark, Germany, the United States and elsewhere. But because of the red tape involved, the task promises to be a daunting one.

If boating or viewing marine life is your pleasure, contact chairman John Kaunak of the **Arviq Hunters and Trappers Organization** to arrange a boat outing. View seals, birds, walrus, caribou, or head about 18 kilometres southwest to the *Qikiqtat* (Harbour Islands) and *Niaqunguut* (North Pole River) to see the old stone house of early explorer Dr. John Rae of the Hudson's Bay Co. This journey is accessible by boat in the summer. Take your camera to record your own history of Naujaat.

Shopping

At the **Naujat Co-op**, you can buy a carving or two for your friends. If you're not from Canada, though, check with the local wildlife officer to see what you can and can't take home. United States residents, for example, can't import whalebone or ivory carvings.

Groceries and other everyday goods are available from the Co-op and the **Northern store**.

The **Nuksutet Sewing Group** will custom tailor anything from *kamiit* (boots) and mitts to *amautit* (women's parkas) and other clothing. Phone manager Elizabeth Kidlapik to place an order.

Events

Many festivals are annual occurrences in Naujaat. In January 1997, the community's first-ever dance festival drew the liveliest from Repulse Bay, Baker Lake, Rankin Inlet, Chesterfield Inlet, Coral Harbour, Arviat, Whale Cove, Igloolik and Hall Beach. Easter Games feature igloo-building, snow-mobile and dogteam racing, and indoor games. The Repulse Bay Fishing Derby usually drops anchor in May, and Canada's birthday on July 1 sets the scene for Hamlet Day celebrations. For more information on recreational and sports activities, contact recreational director Silas Tinashlu at the **Repulse Bay Hamlet Office**.

Accommodation and Dining

Inns North, operated by the Naujat Co-op, has 11 rooms, 10 with two twin beds and one with a double. All have private washrooms, and about half have color TVs. Rooms don't have phones, but there is a public phone near the lobby and a lounge with a television for guests. There is also one suite with a living room area, hot plate and fridge. Altogether, the hotel accommodates 23 people.

Rooms are $125 per person per day (without meals) or $180 with meals. The suite is $145 per person per day without meals, and $200 including meals. Meals are priced as follows: breakfast ($10), lunch ($20) and supper ($25), and are served at posted times. Visitors who aren't staying at Inns North can also make prior arrangements to eat there. Hotel guests can do their own laundry if they arrange it first with the hotel manager.

The recreation committee operates a year-round canteen facility at the Repulse Bay Community Complex (during the winter, there's also one at the Community Arena).

Services

With flights from Rankin Inlet to Naujaat running a minimum of four times weekly, air transportation is good.

If you have a medical emergency while visiting the community, a nurse can be reached by phoning the **Repulse Bay Health Centre**. There is 24-hour emergency service. Although there are no doctors in the community, nurses do consultations over the phone with an on-call doctor in Churchill. General clinics run from 8:30 a.m. to 12 p.m., Monday to Friday.

The community gymnasium (used for volleyball, basketball, soccer and public meetings), the **post office**, and local **radio** are all located at the Hamlet Office Complex, where employees and elected council members such as Mayor Steven Mapsalak toil for the municipality.

DIRECTORY

The 819 and 403 area codes change to 867 on Oct. 21, 1997.

Accommodation and Dining

Inns North
VISA, MasterCard, Diners Club/enRoute, Interac.
Tel.: (819) 462-9943
Fax: (819) 462-4152

Outfitters/Guides/ Tour Operators

Arviq Hunters and Trappers Organization
9 a.m.–12 p.m., Monday to Friday.
Tel.: (819) 462-4334
Fax: (819) 462-4335

Services

Airport
6:45 a.m.–5:15 p.m., Monday to Friday; 8:45 a.m.–3:15 p.m., weekends.
Tel.: (819) 462-9973

Churches

Glad Tidings Church
Phone number unavailable.

Repulse Bay Anglican Church
No telephone.

Repulse Bay Roman Catholic Church
Services 7 p.m., Monday to Sunday; 11 a.m., Sunday (Inuktitut only).
Tel.: (819) 462-9912

Hamlet Office
Contact hamlet manager Sheldon Dorey.
Tel.: (819) 462-9952
Fax: (819) 462-4144

Health Centre
Tel.: (819) 462-9916

Police (RCMP)
Call detachment in Rankin Inlet.
Tel.: (819) 645-2822

Post Office
Located in the Hamlet Office Complex.
1–5 p.m., Monday to Friday.
Tel.: (819) 462-4194

Radio Station (FM 107.1)
To place public information and announcements, call Friday from 6–10:30 p.m.
Tel.: (819) 462-4061

Resources, Wildlife and Economic Development, GNWT
Tel.: (819) 462-4002
If office closed, call Rankin Inlet office at (819) 645-5037.

Schools

Nunavut Arctic College
Tel.: (819) 462-4281
Fax: (819) 462-4293

Tusarvik School
Elementary and high school. Also provides library services.
Tel.: (819) 462-9920
Fax: (819) 462-4232

Victor Tungilik
(Cultural Performances)
Contact Elizabeth Mapsalak at (819) 462-4203 for arrangements. A fee applies.

Weather Office
Tel.: (819) 462-9973

Stores

Naujat Co-op
10 a.m.–7 p.m., Monday to Friday; 11 a.m.–7 p.m., Saturday. VISA, MasterCard.
Tel.: (819) 462-9943
Fax: (819) 462-4152

Northern Store
10 a.m.–6 p.m., Monday to Wednesday; 10 a.m.–7 p.m., Thursday and Friday; 10 a.m.–6 p.m., Saturday.
VISA, MasterCard, Interac.
Tel.: (819) 462-9923
Fax: (819) 462-4011

Nuksutet Sewing Group
1–5 p.m., Monday to Friday.
Tel.: (819) 462-4500

PELLY BAY

by Steven W. Metzger

In early April, the night sky is completely dark for only a few hours; by late May, the sun will be up for 24 hours.

Population:	496 (Inuit: 95%, non-Inuit: 5%)
Telephone Area Code:	403 (changes to 867 on Oct. 21, 1997)
Time Zone:	Mountain Time
Postal Code:	X0D 1K0
How to Get There:	Possible route:
	• Yellowknife-Pelly Bay
	Yellowknife to Pelly Bay (about 1,300 km northeast) is via
	First Air. All passengers coming from central or eastern Canada
	must stay overnight in Yellowknife
Banks:	None. Cash and traveller's cheques are preferable
Alcohol:	Alcohol and alcoholic beverages are prohibited in Pelly Bay
Taxis:	Yes

It should be getting warmer now, but winter's grip is strong this year. The men spend more hours than usual fishing, because there are no *tuktut* (caribou). The elders say this happens every few years. They hope the warmer weather will bring caribou, but for now, the people endure as they always have. They travel in the bitter cold to *Kuk* (Kellet River), or to one of the many other bountiful lakes and rivers in the area, to tend their fish nets. Arctic char and whitefish are in good supply, and occasionally a seal is caught near *Kurvigjuak* ("where the giant 'relieved' himself on top of the mountain"). Still, everyone longs for the caribou to return, to complete the group of animals — seal, caribou and fish — that are synonymous with life.

I moved here four years ago, and after countless journeys on the land, I'm still captivated by its stark beauty and isolation. I marvel at a culture that enabled the Inuit to thrive for centuries in this challenging environment using only animal products, stone and snow. Elders welcome visitors to the community, and relish the chance to retell the old stories, like the one about the giant at Kurvigjuak. As they talk, their warmth and joy fill my spirit. I sense their strong connection to the land, and I can't help but have a deep respect for the *Arviligjuarmiut* (those living in the area of *Arviligjuaq*, the "place with lots of bowhead whales"), which is the Inuit name for Pelly Bay. The English name came from early explorers who chose it to honor Sir John Pelly, a governor of the Hudson's Bay Co. The bowhead whales of the Inuktitut name ply these waters no more.

History

Completion of the local airstrip in 1968 allowed the Canadian government to transport 32 prefabricated houses into Pelly Bay. Until then, the

Arviligjuaqmiut lived a semi-nomadic lifestyle. Small family groups, living in *igluit* (igloos) and skin tents, followed the wildlife that sustained them. Occasionally, groups would come together to hunt and fish. In 1937, when the Catholic mission was established here, groups would meet for Christmas celebrations at *Kugaarjuk* (the mouth of the Kugajuk River), then separate again to pursue their nomadic cycle.

The first Catholic missionary, Father Pierre Henry, arrived in 1935. He built a small stone chapel/house, but soon learned that stone wasn't a good insulator in this harsh climate. Instead, he adopted Inuit ways, living in an iglu and wearing traditional Inuit clothing during the cold months. He and Father Franz Vanderbilt, who remained a powerful force in the community until 1965, built the stone church in 1941. Recently the Hamlet of Pelly Bay received a government grant to restore the deteriorating church as a historic site.

Until 1955, when the DEW Line site was built, people here had almost no contact with the outside world. In 1829, English explorer John Ross camped nearby, but no whalers or Hudson's Bay trading post ever came to Pelly Bay. That was due largely to the string of islands guarding the mouth of Pelly Bay. Ice jams in the bay's mouth made access impossible.

Traditions have remained strong; yet as the Inuit have encountered the modern world, this has led to an interesting blend of cultures. When you enter a home here, for example, it's not unusual to find family members watching the latest movie on a large-screen TV, while eating raw arctic char cut from a fish lying on a square of cardboard in the centre of the room.

By the early 1970s, most Arviligjuaqmiut had moved into town, drawn by the local store, school, health station, and houses with government-subsidized rent. Created by the Canadian government to help assert its sovereignty over the North, Pelly Bay is now a small settlement with a wage economy. Although it's changing rapidly — Internet is just around the corner — its heritage, built through centuries of life on the land, is still vibrant, and traditional activities remain very important.

Pelly Bay: Its Land and Wildlife

Between the bay to the west and the seemingly endless, flat tundra to the east, Pelly Bay is nestled in the coastal mountains at Kugaarjuk. The settlement's well-known landmarks — its stone church, set off by a group of large *inuksuit*, and its cross, built by hand atop the mountain across the river using 45-gallon drums — are distinctive features of the scene you discover when you arrive by air.

July to September marks a time of rapid change. The sea ice is melting and the tundra becomes a multi-colored carpet of wildflowers. Thousands of migrating birds arrive from the South, including falcons, rough-legged hawks, snowy owls, seagulls, ravens, terns, jaegers, ptarmigans, cranes, ducks, geese, and swans. By the end of September, the ice starts to form again. Travel by boat is ideal for arctic char fishing and exploring archeological sites. You can also hike and camp on the wide-open tundra or in mountain valleys. In early August, Inuit fish with *kakivait* (traditional spears) at an ancient *saputit* (stone weir) on the Kugajuk River. Insect repellent is a must during July.

Tours

For tours out on the land, contact the **Hunters and Trappers Organization**. While there are currently no licensed outfitters in Pelly Bay, residents are very friendly, willing to help you enjoy your visit, and happy to share their experiences with you. Although only a few all-terrain vehicles and snow machines are available for rent, you can arrange to take a trip on a *qamutik* pulled by dogs or snow machines.

Between October and November, visitors can camp with Inuit at the Kellet River for the fall arctic char run. Arrange an early-season dogsled or snow machine trip. Low light angles create a paradise for landscape photographers.

For those who want to experience an arctic winter, the time to do it is from December to February. Between early December and mid-January, the sun doesn't rise. While winter travel on the land is for seasoned adventure travellers, those who qualify may want to accompany Inuit on a traditional seal hunt. Enjoy the displays of northern lights.

Visitors can help celebrate spring from March to June, but remember: sunglasses are a must. Mid-April to May is especially great for touring the land and viewing wildlife by dogsled and snow machine. You can also see baby seals basking on the sea ice, or do some ice fishing.

If you plan to visit Pelly Bay between November and March, it's essential to wear clothing for extremely cold weather. Although some caribou clothing is available for rent, you're best to come prepared.

Events

On Easter weekend, cheer on the athletes at the Spring Games, where you'll see such contests as harpoon throwing. The community hosts a talent show in mid-November, and Christmas games are held during the last week of December.

Shopping

The **Koomiut Co-op** is the only store in Pelly Bay. Prices are high, but basic food, clothing and personal items are available.

Pelly Bay carvers work with ivory, whalebone, antler and stone. Many women make excellent traditional clothing, and accept orders from visitors. Depending on the time of year and the materials needed for clothing, waiting periods may be lengthy.

Accommodation and Dining

The **Inukshuk Inn** is operated by the Koomiut Co-op. The hotel has eight rooms (two ensuite, six with shared facilities) to accommodate 16 guests. Each room has a television and video casette recorder. Rates are $125 per day per person, and include complimentary airport pickup. Meals, served at scheduled times, are $10 for breakfast, $15 for lunch, and $25 for dinner.

Canteens run at the hamlet gym (part of the hamlet office building) and, between October and April, at the **Nattalik Ice Arena**.

Services

The Pelly Bay **Health Centre** is staffed by two nurses who handle routine and emergency medical needs. Hours are 8:30 a.m. to 5 p.m., Monday to Friday.

One of the nurses is always on call, while a doctor in Yellowknife is always on call for telephone consultations.

The hamlet recreation department offers programs at the hamlet gym; from October to April, it operates the Nattalik Ice Arena.

A one-man **RCMP** unit provides 24-hour service.

DIRECTORY

The 819 and 403 area codes change to 867 on Oct. 21, 1997.

Accommodation and Dining

Inukshuk Inn
VISA, Diners Club/enRoute.
Tel.: (403) 769-7211

Outfitters/Guides/ Tour Operators

Hunters and Trappers Organization
1–5 p.m., Monday to Friday.
Tel.: (403) 769-6071
Fax: (403) 769-6713

Services

Airport
10 a.m.–12 p.m., 1–4 p.m., Monday, Tuesday, Thursday and Friday; 1–4 p.m., Wednesday.
Tel.: (403) 769-7505
Fax: (403) 769-7302

Church

Roman Catholic Church
Services 7 p.m., Monday to Sunday; 11 a.m., Sunday.
Tel.: (403) 769-6261
Fax: (403) 769-6261

Executive Service Office
A government of the Northwest Territories liaison office.
Export permits, licences, documents.
1–5 p.m., Monday to Friday.
Tel.: (403) 769-7411
Fax: (403) 769-7706

Hamlet Office
Tel.: (403) 769-6281
Fax: (403) 769-6069

Health Centre
Tel.: (403) 769-6441
Fax: (403) 769-6059

Kitikmeot Inuit Association
An Inuit birthright organization.
8:30 a.m.–5 p.m., Monday to Friday.
Tel.: (403) 769-7948
Fax: (403) 769-6202

Nattalik Arena
October to April, hours vary.
Tel.: (403) 769-7969

Police (RCMP)
Tel.: (403) 769-7221
Fax: (403) 769-6807

Post Office
Located in the hamlet office.
10–11:30 a.m., 1–4 p.m., Monday to Friday.
Tel.: (403) 769-6011

Radio Station (FM 105.9)
Can be used for public announcements.
12–1 p.m., 5:30–6:30 p.m., daily.
Tel.: (403) 769-6099 (off air)
Tel.: (403) 769-6221 (on air)

Resources, Wildlife and Economic Development
8:30 a.m.–5 p.m., Monday to Friday.
Tel.: (403) 769-7011
Fax: (403) 769-6105

Schools

Kugaarjuk School
Tel.: (403) 769-6211
Fax: (403) 769-6116

Nunavut Arctic College
Call hamlet office for information.
Tel.: (403) 769-6281
Fax: (403) 769-6069

Taxi

Co-op Taxi
Tel.: (403) 769-6231

Weather Station
6 a.m.–5 p.m., Monday to Friday.
Tel.: (403) 769-6567

Shopping

Koomiut Co-op
9:30 a.m.–5:30 p.m., Monday to Friday. Only open on Saturdays between October and May, 12–3 p.m. Closed Sunday. VISA accepted.
Tel.: (403) 769-6231
Fax: (403) 769-6098

TALOYOAK

by George Bohlender

Sitting at the foot of a series of rocky hills on the shores of a small body of water known as Stanners Harbour, Taloyoak is the northernmost community on the North American mainland (69° 32' north latitude).

Population:	648 (Inuit: 92%, non-Inuit: 8%)
Telephone Area Code:	403 (changes to 867 on Oct. 21, 1997)
Time Zone:	Mountain Time
Postal Code:	X0E 1B0
How to Get There:	Possible route:
	• Yellowknife-Taloyoak
	Yellowknife to Taloyoak (about 1,200 kilometres northeast) is via First Air.
	All passengers, including those coming from central or eastern
	Canada, must stay overnight in Yellowknife
Banks:	None. Cash and traveller's cheques are preferable
Alcohol:	Alcohol is not restricted, and is governed only by the provisions of the
	NWT Liquor Control Act. However, there's no place to buy alcohol
	in the community
Taxis:	No. Guests of local hotels should arrange for airport pickup when
	booking their rooms

The word *taloyoak* means "large caribou blind" in Inuktitut, and refers to a stone caribou blind traditionally used by Inuit of the area to corral and harvest caribou.

History

The traditional inhabitants of the Taloyoak (pronounced "ta-low-ywak") area were the *Netsilik* Inuit, the *Netsilingmiut,* a people largely sustained by the abundance of seals in the region, which provided their main source of food and clothing.

The search for the Northwest Passage has played an important role in the contemporary history of the Taloyoak region. The first significant European exploration here occurred between 1829 and 1833, when Sir John Ross and his crew combed the area after their ship became trapped in ice. Between 1848 and 1860, the area was visited extensively by British and American sailors searching for the lost Franklin expedition.

The foundation of the modern community began in 1948, when poor ice conditions forced the Hudson's Bay Co. to close its trading post at Fort Ross on the south coast of Somerset Island, some 250 kilometres north of Taloyoak. The post was relocated to its present location at Stanners Harbour, and Taloyoak — then known as Spence Bay — was born.

Shortly after the establishment of the Hudson's Bay Co. post, the RCMP arrived. They were followed by Catholic and Anglican missionaries in the early 1950s. These entities formed the nucleus of the burgeoning community, which grew as the federal government encouraged Inuit to settle in Spence Bay. In Taloyoak today, traditional activities such as hunting and trapping remain a prominent part of everyday life. These activities are supplemented by carving, crafts production, and wage employment, which combine to provide a lifestyle balanced between old and new.

Taloyoak: Its Land and Wildlife

As with other Nunavut communities, plants burst to life every spring and summer on the tundra. Countless berries blanket surrounding hills; wild blueberries and bearberries are harvested by residents throughout the summer. Fields of arctic cotton are reminiscent of fluffy white dandelions, and fragrant, dried arctic heather is used as tinder for campfires in this treeless land.

Local bird life includes ravens, seagulls, jaegers, and ptarmigan. Gyrfalcons nest quite close to the community and snowy owls have been seen from the roadside between Taloyoak and nearby Middle Lake. Huge flocks of ducks and Canada geese also fly over the community on their migrations.

Animals encountered in and near the community include ground squirrels (*siksiit*), lemmings, weasels, arctic hares, and arctic foxes. Wolves are not usually found near town, and hunters must also travel some distance for caribou. Muskoxen are present further north on the Boothia Peninsula and Somerset Island, and on the barren lands to the south.

The waters around Taloyoak are rich with ringed seals. Whales are generally scarce, but are occasionally spotted further north. Polar bears are found in coastal areas to the north and west.

There are many outstanding fishing spots within walking distance of town. Arctic char can be caught during their autumn run in local lakes and rivers. Ice fishing for lake trout and whitefish is common during late winter and spring. Middle Lake, which is linked to Taloyoak by a seven-kilometre road, is a popular year-round fishing destination. It is also a favorite camping spot in summer, and many families have cabins there.

Tours

Several buildings still stand at Thom Bay, which was a Roman Catholic mission during the 1940s. The site, 80 kilometres northeast of town, is easily reached by snowmobile in late winter and early spring.

The shores of Netsilik Lake offer fine examples of previous habitation. The remains of dozens of stone and sod houses can be seen here, about 25 kilometres southeast of town. The lake can be reached by both snowmobile (in winter and spring) and boat (in summer). At present there are no licensed outfitters in Taloyoak, but the **Spence Bay Hunters and Trappers Organization** is a good clearinghouse for information about weather conditions and the surrounding land.

The history of the area is well represented within the community itself. The stone caribou blind for which Taloyoak is named is located on the southeast side of the harbor, near the **Northern store**. The original Hudson's Bay Co. warehouses and the stone church built by Catholic missionaries in the 1950s are also still standing.

Monuments in the community formally identify its diverse history. One is to John Stanners, the town's first Bay manager. It is located across from the Northern store's staff house. Two plaques commemorate the exploits of European explorers Sir John Ross and Sir James Clark Ross. But the most interesting monument in town commemorates a local hero, David Kootook. Kootook was aboard a bush plane that crashed in the western Northwest Territories during a medical evacuation flight in 1973. Kootook helped the pilot, Martin Hartwell, survive, but perished before help arrived. The monument is located across from the airport terminal.

Shopping

Taluq Designs Ltd. produces the famous Spence Bay 'packing dolls,' arctic animals carrying young in wool duffel parkas, in a modern facility across from the Co-op. Here you can also pick up other sewn crafts and garments, which are either created at the shop or imported from other Nunavut and western Northwest Territories communities.

Visitors interested in carvings will have no problem watching the artists in action, as most work outside their homes during the 24-hour sunlight of spring and summer. Carvers and craftspeople make regular visits to hotels to sell their latest works; a selection of carvings is also available at the Co-op.

Groceries and dry goods can be purchased at the Northern store and the **Paleajook Co-op**.

Accommodation and Dining

The **Boothia Inn** provides shared accommodation for up to 20 people in 10 rooms, some of which have private bathrooms. All rooms have cable TV. The cost is $170 per person per night, including all meals, or $125 without meals.

The **Paleajook Co-op Hotel** also accommodates 20 people in 10 rooms. Unlike the Boothia Inn, however, there are no private bathrooms. All rooms have cable TV. The cost is $160 per person per night, including meals, or $110 without meals.

There are no restaurants in Taloyoak. Both hotels can provide meals for non-guests and those with special dietary requirements, given sufficient notice. At the Paleajook breakfast costs $10, lunch, $15 and dinner is $25. Breakfast at the Boothia is $12.50, lunch $17.50 and dinner is $30.

Services

At Taloyoak's **health centre**, patients are seen mornings from Monday to Friday, and other times on an emergency basis.

DIRECTORY

The 819 and 403 area codes change to 867 on Oct. 21, 1997.

Accommodation and Dining

Boothia Inn
VISA, MasterCard, Diners Club/enRoute.
Tel.: (403) 561-5300
Fax: (403) 561-5318

Paleajook Co-op Hotel
VISA accepted.
Tel.: (403) 561-5803
Fax: (403) 561-5603

Services

Airport
Tel.: (403) 561-5400

Churches

Good Shepherd Anglican Church
Services at 11 a.m. and 7 p.m., Sunday.
Tel.: (403) 561-5710

Roman Catholic Church
Tel.: (403) 561-5161

Health Centre
Tel.: (403) 561-5111
Fax: (403) 561-6906

Police (RCMP)
Tel.: (403) 561-5201
Fax: (403) 561-5094

Post Office
Located at the Paleajook Co-op.
1:30–4:30 p.m., Monday to Friday.
Tel.: (403) 561-5221

Radio Station (FM 105.1)
Tel.: (403) 561-6808 (off air)
Tel.: (403) 561-6581 (on air)

Schools

Netsilik School
Tel.: (403) 561-5181
Fax: (403) 561-5036

Nunavut Arctic College
Tel.: (403) 561-5371
Fax: (403) 561-5202

Spence Bay Hunters and Trappers Organization
Tel.: (403) 561-5066
Fax: (403) 561-5066

Shopping

Northern Store
10 a.m.–12:30 p.m. and 1:30–6 p.m., Monday to Thursday; 1–6 p.m. and 7–8:30 p.m., Friday; noon–4:30 p.m., Saturday. Closed Sunday.
VISA, MasterCard, Interac.
Tel.: (403) 561-5121
Fax: (403) 561-5708

Paleajook Co-op
10 a.m.–12:30 p.m. and 1:30–6 p.m., Monday to Thursday; 10 a.m.–12:30 p.m. and 1:30–7 p.m., Friday; 1–5 p.m., Saturday. VISA, MasterCard, Diners Club/enRoute, Interac.
Tel.: (403) 561-5221
Fax: (403) 561-5603

Taluq Designs Ltd.
9 a.m.–noon and 1–5 p.m.,
Monday to Friday (September to May).
VISA accepted.
Tel.: (403) 561-5280
Fax: (403) 561-6500
Web site: www.ssimicro.com/xsevente/devcorp/taluq/index.html

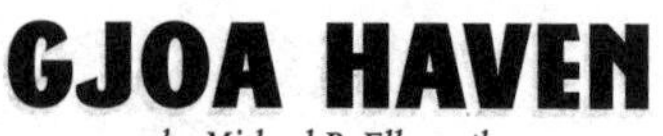

by Michael P. Ellsworth

Gjoa Haven was once dubbed "the finest little harbor in the world" by Norwegian explorer Roald Amundsen, and that probably explains why this inlet, nestled on the southeast coast of King William Island on the Northwest Passage, also became the namesake of the wooden ship that Amundsen sailed through the Northwest Passage between 1903 and 1906 — the *Gjoa*.

Population:	879 (Inuit: 96%, non-Inuit: 4%)
Telephone Area Code:	403 (changes to 867 on Oct. 21, 1997)
Time Zone:	Mountain Time
Postal Code:	X0E 1J0
How to Get There:	Possible route:
	• Yellowknife-Gjoa Haven
	Yellowknife to Gjoa Haven (about 1,100 kilometres northeast) is via First Air. All passengers, including those coming from central or eastern Canada, must stay overnight in Yellowknife
Banks:	None. Cash and traveller's cheques are preferable
Alcohol:	Alcohol and alcoholic beverages are prohibited
Taxis:	Yes

To local residents, the community is called *Uqsuqtuuq*, the "place of plenty of blubber," for the herds of seals that once flourished here. Today, you have to travel outside Gjoa Haven to find seals.

On Aug. 28, 1903, Amundsen, with his crew of six, arrived here on his sloop, the *Gjoa*, on his quest for the Passage. The deep narrow harbor offered a safe haven from treacherous pack ice so common in this area. Amundsen's successful navigation of the route may have been partly due to his willingness to adopt some of the traditional ways of the *Netsilik* people here, such as their methods of hunting, fishing and travelling.

Today, Gjoa Haven (Gjoa is pronounced as "Joe") is one of the fastest-growing communities in the Kitikmeot, with a population close to 900. (In 1961, only 100 people lived here.) In recent years, families from Back River (*Utkuhiksalingmiut*), Cambridge Bay, Parry River, and Spence Bay — now called Taloyoak — moved to the settlement for schooling, trading, health care, housing, and other services. Although the Netsilik seem to lead a modern lifestyle, they are very traditional people. Families spend a month or two out on the land each summer; many travel by dogteam. They hold drum dances often and enjoy throat singing. Many still wear traditional caribou clothing.

History

Many elders in Gjoa Haven are living histories of the time *qallunaat* came in their tall ships. Over a cup of tea, they may eagerly tell you stories of starving explorers such as Franklin's men, who are believed to have deserted their ice-locked ships in Terror Bay. That was in 1847, the year summer never came to the North. Those desperate men walked for miles pulling sleds filled not with supplies, but with books and fine china. You may even hear rumors that people here know the location of Franklin's grave. Out of respect for the dead, however, they refuse to tell outsiders.

Elders may also recall encounters with Amundsen and with Catholic and Anglican missionaries. They'll tell you about the early days of the Hudson's Bay Co. trading post. Back in 1927, the Hudson's Bay Co. took advantage of Gjoa Haven's excellent harbor by establishing a trading post here. White fox were abundant on the island then, and many Netsilik travelled far to trade. Although people forget the first manager's real name, they still think of him as *Putuguittuq* or No Big-Toe. The Hudson's Bay Co. here was one of the last to use round aluminum tokens in trading for furs. As late as the 1960s, store manager George Porter still used tokens, because local people didn't yet trust Canadian currency.

Gjoa Haven: Its Land and Wildlife

Gjoa Haven is built on sand and boulders covering limestone bedrock. In spring and summer, the rolling tundra outside the settlement blooms with a variety of lichen, moss, and arctic willow that cover the island. You'll find many lakes and ponds with water so pure you can drink directly from them. In fact, the community's water supply comes from Water Lake, about two kilometres northwest of town.

Although you may spot a caribou, muskox, wolf, fox, or snowy owl on the tundra, local people often have to travel far to hunt wildlife to supplement their diet. Other wildlife found here are geese, swans, falcons, eider ducks, and arctic hares. Marine life includes arctic char, found in the bay in June and July, seal, trout, and cod, which is used mainly as dog food. In spring, many families go to Back River for the whitefish that are plentiful there. When the char leave Gjoa Haven in early August, local people travel, as they have for generations, to *Iqalungmiut*, to fish in the Kakivakturvik River, a traditional weir 45 kilometres northeast of the settlement.

Tours

The Northwest Passage Historic Park, about 3.2 kilometres long, can be visited easily in an afternoon. (See Chapter 62, "Northwest Passage Historic Park.")

If you walk along the beach, you'll notice many narwhal and beluga bones that have washed ashore. To travel across the tundra, you can rent an all-terrain vehicle at the local **Kekertak Co-op** for about $75 a day. You may enjoy visiting lakes nearby and camp near others from the town. You may come across old Inuit camp sites, rock circles that were bases for sealskin tents. Or you may see caches, piles of rocks preserving fish or caribou. You might even stumble across the remains of early expeditions! As the ice in the bay lasts for about nine months, you can also travel by snowmobile to Honeymoon Island and Hovguard Island, about 15 kilometres south of Gjoa Haven, where you'll see old camp sites, *inuksuit* and possibly a caribou or two.

For a tour of the island to view caribou, muskoxen, seal or polar bears, you'll want to get in touch with a licensed outfitter and currently there's only one in Gjoa Haven — **Gjoa Haven Tours**. The local **Hunters and Trappers**

Organization is also a good source of information about the surrounding land and wildlife.

Shopping

Among Gjoa Haven's excellent carvers are Nelson Takkiruq, Paul Aaluk, Joseph Squkshaq, Uriash Pukiqnak; some, such as Judas Ullulaq, are world-renowned. You can buy their work at the local **Northern store** and the Kekertak Co-op or at their homes. A local women's group, **Quqmaq's**, sells finely crafted wall hangings and clothing such as *kamiit* (sealskin boots) and parkas.

Events

Each summer, an annual fishing derby is held at a lake near Gjoa Haven. In mid-August, golfers tee-off in the challenging 18-hole Sun Golf Classic at Canada's most northerly 18-hole golf course. For more information on recreation and sports activities, contact the recreation department at the Gjoa Haven **hamlet office**.

Accommodation and Dining

The **Amundsen Hotel**, built in 1995, can accommodate up to 26 people in 13 rooms (two of which have suites) and in 1997, the hotel is building another six rooms. Presently, each room comes equipped with cable TV and a washroom. Some also have a fridge and stove. Rooms rent for $210 a night (the suites are $250) and include breakfast, lunch and dinner. The hotel's restaurant also serves meals to outside guests priced as follows: breakfast $10, lunch $20, and dinner $30. A canteen in the hotel serves fries and drinks nightly. The hotel rents movies, too.

Mary's Inn, built in 1987 and now under new management, has four bedrooms priced at $110 per person per day without meals and $170 with meals. Up to five guests can stay at any one time. Meals are $15 for breakfast, $20 for lunch and $25 for dinner. Bathrooms are shared. Mary's Inn has plans to expand as well.

At the arena during hockey and curling matches, a canteen is open nightly.

Services

The **Health Centre**, staffed by four nurses, is open from 8:30 a.m. to 12 p.m. daily. Special clinics, such as prenatal classes, are offered each afternoon until 5 p.m. A nurse is always on call for emergencies.

The hamlet's recreation department uses facilities in the local school, **Quqshuun Ilihakvik**, for volleyball, wrestling, soccer, floor-hockey and badminton. A new **arena** in Gjoa Haven has a standard-sized skating rink and two curling rinks that are used from October to May. Sliders and brooms can be used without charge. You can skate for free most Saturdays and Sundays. Gjoa Haven also has a baseball diamond.

The **Post Office**, located in the Kekertak Co-op, is open daily from 10 a.m. to 5 p.m.

The George Porter **hamlet office** has a canteen, community hall, museum, local radio station, council boardroom, as well as offices for local government workers. An arcade in the community is open nightly and serves snacks.

DIRECTORY

The 819 and 403 area codes change to 867 on Oct. 21, 1997.

Accommodation and Dining

Amundsen Hotel
VISA, MasterCard, Diners Club/enRoute.
Tel.: (403) 360-6176
Fax: (403) 360-6018

Mary's Inn
VISA, MasterCard.
Tel.: (403) 360-6032
Fax: (403) 360-7313

Guides/Outfitters

Gjoa Haven Tours
General Delivery, Gjoa Haven NT,
X0E 1J0 Canada
No telephone or fax numbers.

Services

Arctic Airport
Tel.: (403) 360-6321

Arena
Tel.: (403) 360-6105

Churches

Anglican Mission
Tel.: (403) 360-6907

Catholic Church
Tel.: (403) 360-6071

Dental Therapist Office
Located at Quqshuun Ilihakvik School.
Tel.: (403) 360-7201

Hamlet Office
Tel.: (403) 360-7141
Fax: (403) 360-6309
Economic Development Officer:
Tel.: (403) 360-6008
Fax: (403) 360-6142

Health Centre/Dental Office
Tel.: (403) 360-7441
Fax: (403) 360-6110

Hunters and Trappers Organization
Tel.: (403) 360-6028
Fax: (403) 360-6913

Police (RCMP)
Tel.: (403) 360-6201
Fax: (403) 360-6147

Post Office
Located in the Kekertak Co-op.
Tel.: (403) 360-7271

Radio Station (AM 64)
Tel.: (403) 360-6075

Resources, Wildlife and Economic Development
Tel.: (403) 360-7605

Schools

Jr/Sr High School
Tel.: (403) 360-6505
Fax: (403) 360-6204

Nunavut Arctic College
Tel.: (403) 360-7561
Fax: (403) 360-6049

Quqshuun Illilakvik Centre
Tel.: (403) 360-7201

Taxi

Kekertak Co-op/Taxi
Tel.: (403) 360-7271
Fax: (403) 360-6018

Weather Office
Tel.: (403) 360-6321

Shopping

Gjoa's Smoke Shop
No set hours, and operates irregularly through the year, depending on business. Usually opens at 5 p.m.
VISA, MasterCard, Interac.
Tel.: (403) 360-6122

Kekertak Co-op/Taxi
VISA, MasterCard, Interac.
Tel.: (403) 360-7271
Fax: (403) 360-6018

Northern Store
VISA, MasterCard, Interac.
9:30 a.m.–6 p.m., Monday to Friday;
1–4 p.m., Saturday. Closed Sunday.
Tel.: (403) 360-7261
Fax: (403) 360-7905

Quqmaq
1–3 p.m. Operates irregularly throughout year. Does not accept credit cards.
Tel.: (403) 360-6316

NORTHWEST PASSAGE HISTORIC PARK

by Michael P. Ellsworth

Many explorers of the past searched for a northern sea route that would take them from the Old World to the Orient.

You may know them from the lands and waters that bear their names. Martin Frobisher and John Davis, of the 16th century; Henry Hudson, of the 17th; Edward Parry, John Ross, John Franklin, Robert McClure and Richard Collinson of the 19th century: despite terrible odds, these and other adventurers sailed into perilous waters, armed with the knowledge they'd gained from previous voyagers. Yet the successful navigation of the Northwest Passage occurred not only because of the contributions of these earlier expeditions, but because of the knowledge of the Inuit inhabitants of the North. Roald Amundsen was the first explorer to adopt some of the survival techniques, such as hunting, fishing and toolmaking, of the *Netsilik* people on King William Island. He was also the first to traverse the Passage.

At the Northwest Passage Historic Park, in Gjoa Haven on King William Island, you can make your own discoveries about the extraordinary quest for the Passage. Here you can "journey" on a historical route to learn about the land that was home to Amundsen and his six crewmen from 1903 until 1906. At locations around the community, you'll find six signs describing the historical significance of the area. Set in cement to protect them from harsh weather, the signs are written in both English and Inuktitut.

The route begins at the George Porter Hamlet Centre where you'll find a miniature replica (1:50) of Amundsen's ship, the *Gjoa*. Among the museum's artifacts, you can examine traditional tools such as *uluit* (woman's knives) and *kakivait* (spears), as well as caribou clothing and water containers, a kayak, and photos taken by one of Amundsen's crew during his stay in Gjoa Haven. You can also learn the history of explorers such as Franklin and Amundsen, plus that of the Netsilik people.

Your first stop will be at the "magnet," a shelter Amundsen used in his observations of the North Magnetic Pole. In 1903, the Pole was about 90 kilometres north of Gjoa Haven. The magnets and other instruments that Amundsen used here are on display in a museum in Norway.

To help him in this work, the explorer and his men constructed the shelter from packing crates filled with sand and covered with sailcloth. (Driftwood is a rare commodity in the North!) In their construction, they had to take care not to use copper nails in the crates, as these would interfere with magnetic observations. The crates also offered a space where crewmen could pursue leisure activities during long, dark winter months. Two crewmen stayed in this shelter, while the others lived aboard the ice-bound *Gjoa*.

The second site is the "observatory" Amundsen built to house his scientific instruments. In this refuge made of sailcloth, he spent many hours documenting his findings on the North Magnetic Pole. Perhaps, too, he reflected on his teacher and mentor, George Von Neumayer, for before leaving Gjoa Haven, Amundsen erected a cairn here to honor him. Below the cairn was a marble slab that supported Amundsen's scientific instruments. Years later, the Hudson's Bay Co. rebuilt the cairn; the marble slab remains intact to this day. Close to the observatory, a third site shows where Amundsen's crew collected fresh water from a lake nearby. Recently, the lake was filled in because its location next to the local school was hazardous to children. Ever the eager student, Amundsen learned from the Netsilik to hunt, fish, sew caribou clothing, and to travel over the land.

A key to Amundsen's discovery of the Northwest Passage may have been in his finding what he called "the finest little harbor in the world." At the fourth site, you'll note the geography of this natural harbor. On Sept. 9, 1903, the *Gjoa* entered a haven in this deep, narrow inlet that provided refuge from massive pack ice and stormy seas. Here, after their arduous journey, Amundsen and his crew found a peaceful place to pursue their scientific work and to learn about the land from the Netsilik.

The fifth site is a grim reminder of the challenges facing arctic expeditions. Here, high on a sandy plateau, it's believed the remains of Franklin's crew were brought to rest after they were discovered on the southwest coast of King William Island. Their grave site is one of many scattered across the North. You can also see the gravestone of William Harold, a Hudson's Bay employee, who was found frozen to death on Oct. 22, 1905. The young man had apparently perished while on his way out to hunt seals. On the chilly day of his death, his body was found without a hat or mitts.

As you walk to the Hudson's Bay Co. Complex, the final site along the trail, you'll see an old wooden ship docked along the sandy shoal nearby. No, it isn't the *Gjoa*! It's a supply ship, the *Kingalik*, that was hauled here by barge from Holman Island in 1993. Vessels like this were used to transport supplies to the Hudson's Bay Co. posts across the North. And the goods they brought, such as firearms, ammunition, southern food, clothing, tea and tobacco, transformed the nomadic lifestyle of the Netsilik forever. In 1927, both the Hudson's Bay Co. and Can Alaska trading companies moved to Gjoa Haven from a port near Douglas Bay, which is about 50 kilometres from Gjoa Haven. Their outbuildings were the first modern structures in Gjoa. Today they are used by the Northern store.

UMINGMAKTOK

by Joe Otokiak

On the Canadian map, the official spelling of this tiny outpost camp is "Umingmaktok."

Population:	51 (100% Inuit)
Telephone Area Code:	None. Telephone service does not exist yet. HF radio is the only method of communication (channels 5046, 5031). There is one satellite-powered telephone for emergencies only
Time Zone:	Mountain Time
Postal Code:	Write to Umingmaktok, General Delivery, c/o Cambridge Bay NT, X0E 0C0 Canada
How to Get There:	Charter air service from Cambridge Bay
Banks:	None. Bring cash or traveller's cheques
Alcohol:	Alcohol is not restricted, and is governed only by the provisions of the NWT Liquor Control Act. However, alcohol cannot be purchased in Umingmaktok
Taxis:	No

In the language of Inuit, Umingmaktok means "he or she caught a muskox." But Inuit call this settlement Umingmak*tuk* — "like a muskox." Located about 80 kilometres due north of the community of Bathurst Inlet on the eastern shore of its namesake inlet, the settlement was until recently called Bay Chimo, and I believe the English name originated from the ship that sailed through the area many years ago, the *Bay Chimo*. This chapter will refer to the community as Inuit refer to it — Umingmaktuk.

Nestled in a little bay, Umingmaktuk — pronounced "oo-ming-mak-tuk" — has a trading post (the **Co-op Store**), a couple of warehouses for perishable store supplies, a one-classroom school, and a smattering of homes in three locations near bays, each a few kilometres from the other. In outpost camps, Inuit live as they have for thousands of years, hunting and fishing to feed and clothe themselves and their families. Umingmaktuk, which is not even connected to the rest of the world yet by telephone, is one of the last examples in Nunavut of an almost completely self-sustained hunting community. The homes here would not be much more than cabins by southern standards, but for the Inuit, they're a little more comfortable than living in snowhouses, especially during the winter months.

The one-room school houses students from kindergarten to about Grade 8. Teacher Peter Kapolak is quite busy during school days. There is a generator that supplies electricity to the classroom and some other buildings close by. All heating is done by diesel fuel stoves and heaters, which are very quiet, compared to furnaces. In Umingmaktuk, one can even watch a little television — by watching videos on VCR machines.

Although aided by modern hunting tools such as snowmobiles, GPS receivers, boats, motors, guns and scopes, Inuit in Umingmaktuk continue to lead traditional lives. The head of each household still harvests the food

for the table, most of it from the land, and the wives tend to family needs in addition to their daily chores. Most days are busy ones, spent hunting for food and gathering pelts for trade in order to purchase gas to operate new equipment.

Evenings are filled by carving life's experiences into soapstone, which is plentiful in an area not too far from the community.

Families still call each other over for a cup of tea or coffee, and a chat. One would need a good set of lungs and others, a keen sense of hearing. It is polite to heed the call as soon as possible in order to fit socially into the small community. Here, everyone contributes to the survival of all, even in small ways. Country food is shared with those less fortunate or unable to go hunting. In fact, anything can be shared as long as there's enough to go around, knowing that kindness will be rewarded later on.

History

Umingmaktuk's roots go back to the 1960s. That's about the same time the store arrived, making trade for cash goods possible. In the years since, an airstrip has been constructed, and the local HTO has built wind turbines and solar generators to power the community's 10 food freezers.

Umingmaktuk: Its Land and Wildlife

There are many camp sites within a radius of about 120 kilometres from Umingmaktuk, mostly along the coastal areas. Such places include Parry Bay to the north, Brown Sound to the southwest, and Gordon Bay to the south. Certain families occupy these areas for the better part of the year.

The winter months are busy, but not as busy as spring and summer when the environment seems to come alive. Plants such as crowberries, blackberries and cranberries grow in and around the settlement. A variety of wildlife can be seen as birds migrate north to nest and animals have their young. Arctic char and caribou are both abundant in this area. Remember before coming to Umingmaktuk to obtain a fishing licence from the Cambridge Bay office of **Resources, Wildlife and Economic Development**.

Tours and Events

The local HTO, although not a licensed outfitter, conducts guided tours.

One of the biggest community events, the Kalvik Frolics held during Easter weekend, sees Umingmaktuk almost double in population with the influx of neighboring snowmobilers. The crowning touch is the search for a beautiful wolverine pelt.

More information regarding tourist attractions in the Kitikmeot Region is available from the **Arctic Coast Visitors Centre** in Cambridge Bay and Nunavut Tourism.

Shopping, Accommodation and Dining

The Co-op Store also doubles as a hotel for non-Inuit visiting the community. One must be ready to do a little home cooking and picking up after oneself as chores are shared amongst those using the facility.

Since it's not possible to phone to book reservations, write to store manager Gwen Tikhak (Manager, Co-op Store, General Delivery, c/o Cambridge Bay NT, X0E 0C0 Canada) at least a month in advance of your visit. Include your phone number. Tikhak will call back to confirm the reservation. Rates are $125 per person per night. While there is a fold-out bed and foam mattresses, you should bring a sleeping bag as well. The store can accommodate up to three people. Lodging can be paid for by cheque, and you can buy store items with cash or traveller's cheques only. The price for lodging doesn't include meals. If you have special food requirements that include frozen food items, let the manager know that in advance, too.

The little store is filled to overflowing after the summer barge arrives with the winter's supply of goods. During the late spring season in May and June, it can be practically bare, with the exception of food staples and a few dry goods. The store keeps regular hours but if one were in need of some item during a practical time of day, Tikhak — the store's sole operator — can open it for you. With Inuit coming and going in the community, the hours of operation are flexible.

Services

If someone should require medical care or if an emergency occurs, there is a liaison person who will contact medical personnel in Cambridge Bay for instructions. If you require special medication, bring the name of the drug with you so that information can be relayed to Cambridge Bay if necessary. Lately, there has been more air travel into the community via air charters from Cambridge Bay, as various organizations and government agencies conduct their business. Every summer, a Northern Transportation Co. tug brings in store supplies for the winter, building material, and fuel on barges.

Telephone service is due to arrive in Umingmaktuk once commercial power is installed, although when that will happen is still unknown. In the meantime, every household has an HF radio that allows radio users to reach others in Cambridge Bay to the northeast, and Kugluktuk to the west. In Umingmaktuk, HF radios are usually used from the time one gets up, approximately 6 a.m. or earlier during the spring, to about 10 or 11 in the evening, or whenever the reception deteriorates.

Visitors are always welcome in Umingmaktuk and you're sure to have an experience you'll remember for years to come. Pay us a visit. *Qakugulu* (kah-goo-goo-loo) — see you soon!

DIRECTORY

The 819 and 403 area codes change to 867 on Oct. 21, 1997.

Arctic Coast Visitors Centre
Tel.: (403) 983-2224
Fax: (403) 983-2802

Cambridge Bay Health Centre
Tel.: (403) 983-2531
Fax: (403) 983-2262

Co-op Store
Write to manager Gwen Tikhak, Co-op Store, General Delivery, c/o Cambridge Bay NT, X0E 0C0 Canada to make arrangements for lodging. Credit cards are not accepted. Bring cash, traveller's cheques, or for lodging, personal cheques.

Police (RCMP)
Detachment in Cambridge Bay.
Tel.: (403) 983-7219
Fax: (403) 983-2498

Resources, Wildlife and Economic Development
In Cambridge Bay.
Tel.: (403) 983-7219
Fax: (403) 983-2802

BATHURST INLET

by Lyn Hancock

If you can visit only one place in Nunavut, I would recommend Bathurst Inlet, an oasis of culture and wildlife on the mid-Arctic Coast where people live more traditionally than perhaps any other place in the territory.

Population:	18 (population breakdown by ethnic group not available)
Telephone Area Code:	No phone service
Time Zone:	Mountain Time
Postal Code:	No regular mail service. Mail sent to the Yellowknife office of
	Bathurst Inlet Lodge will be forwarded to the community
How to Get There:	Charter flights only
Banks:	None. Cash and traveller's cheques are preferable
Alcohol:	Alcohol may be brought into Bathurst Inlet, governed only by the
	provisions of the NWT Liquor Control Act
Taxis:	No

Statistics Canada pegged Bathurst Inlet's tiny population at 18 in the 1996 Census, but it's really 27 when everyone's at home.

Elsewhere in Nunavut, when Inuit were abandoning their traditional camps for the amenities of government-established settlements, the residents of Bathurst Inlet chose to remain on the land. Community members have only recently started taking temporary jobs in the wage economy to help support their traditional way of life.

The residents of Bathurst Inlet — located at the southern end of the inlet that bears the same name — are known as the *Kingaunmiut* or people of "the nose," the name of a hill behind the community. The community is best-known for the **Bathurst Inlet Lodge**, a naturalist facility that was once a Hudson's Bay Co. trading post and Roman Catholic mission. In fact, the lodge still bears the distinctive red-and-white colors that adorned all Hudson's Bay Co. buildings in years past.

History

Excellent interpretation by local guides brings the inlet's rich history to life. Whether you travel by boat, plane or foot, you'll see many signs of Inuit archeological heritage: stone traps and caches, tent rings, caribou-decoy *inuksuit*, and even the bleached bones and treasured possessions of the dead in open grave sites dotting the tundra.

Nadluq, "caribou crossing place," is a well-known site about 80 kilometres southwest of Bathurst Inlet on an island in the Burnside River. As many as 600 years ago, local Copper Inuit hunted caribou here, using the animals' antlers for the walls and roofs of their semi-subterranean homes. During an 1821 expedition, a group under British explorer Sir John Franklin travelled down Bathurst Inlet and the Hood River toward Fort Enterprise until thwarted by the 49-metre-high Wilberforce Falls, and forced to continue the trek on foot. Of the 20 men who started the journey, only nine survived.

Non-Inuit settlement of the inlet was not attempted until 1929, when a mining exploration camp was established. A Hudson's Bay Co. trading post and an Oblate mission soon followed. In 1964, the Hudson's Bay Co. abandoned its Bathurst Inlet post and moved north to better seal-trading opportunities in Umingmaktok, only to abandon that post in 1968. A year later, RCMP officer Glenn Warner and his wife Trish transformed the deserted buildings at Bathurst Inlet into Bathurst Inlet Lodge. Today, the Warners are partners in the lodge with the people of the community.

Bathurst Inlet: Its Land and Wildlife

Bathurst Inlet is truly splendor in the middle of the barren lands, a place of rolling tundra hills, snaking eskers, meandering rivers, and awesome gorges through which water spills picturesquely over ancient, twisted rock. Not far from here you'll find Wilberforce Falls, the highest arctic waterfall in the world, and the Quadyuk Islands, great pyramidal humps that run down the inlet like a dinosaur's backbone.

The mild climate at the southern end of the inlet encourages diverse and luxuriant vegetation, which provides prime wildlife habitat. More than 125 species of wildflowers have been identified here, as well as some 80 varieties of nesting birds and 13 types of mammals. The availability of canoes, boats, and planes at the lodge, and a reliable guiding staff, make it easy to see many of these splendid creatures.

Bathurst Inlet has one of the largest and healthiest populations of peregrine falcons in the world. The inlet is also an important staging ground for migratory waterfowl such as Canada geese, snow geese, and white-fronted geese. East of the inlet is the Queen Maud Gulf Bird Sanctuary, the nesting ground of more than 95 per cent of the world's population of once-threatened Ross's geese. Flights to this six million-plus hectare migratory bird sanctuary — Canada's largest — can be arranged through the lodge. Independent travellers must first obtain a permit from the **Canadian Wildlife Service**, which monitors human activity in the sanctuary. Allow at least 45 days for a reply.

Muskoxen and barren-ground caribou also breed at Bathurst Inlet. With a population of nearly 500,000, the Bathurst caribou herd is one of the largest free-roaming mammal herds in the world. Each spring, the caribou pass near the southern end of the inlet en route to calving grounds to the northeast. Other relatively abundant mammals include barren-ground grizzlies, wolves, foxes, and wolverines.

Fishing is not emphasized at this lodge, although there are good populations of land-locked arctic char, lake trout and grayling to provide anglers with a satisfying fishing experience.

Tours

Long before ecotourism became a trendy word, Inuit of Bathurst Inlet were sharing their land and lifestyle with visitors. The Warner family and the Kingaunmiut have lived and worked together for three generations. Their partnership is a remarkable success story in cross-cultural co-operation, working together in related companies such as Bathurst Arctic Services, Air Tindi, and Top of the World Travel. Bathurst Lodge began as a naturalist lodge but has grown to offer much more. With the flurry of mining exploration taking place these days in Canada's North and around Bathurst Inlet, the company also serves geologists, prospectors, miners, and surveyors.

The lodge generally runs naturalist programs from the last week in June until mid-July. A week's stay, which includes return airfare from Yellowknife, accommodation, and day trips (excluding special charters), costs $3,180. Alternatively, you may camp at one of the lodge's more affordable outposts in the central barren lands. A week of caribou viewing in a cabin at Pellatt Lake, about 200 kilometres south, costs $2,000 and includes transportation from Yellowknife.

Shopping/Accommodation and Dining/Services

There are few commercial facilities in the Bathurst Inlet settlement other than the lodge, which also supplies power to local homes from its generator. Guests of the lodge receive three home-cooked meals and an afternoon tea daily. The lodge, which can accommodate 25 guests, also boasts a lounge, conference room, library, and the only self-serve bar in Nunavut. Guests help themselves, make a notation in a log book, and pay when they leave. Community residents will occasionally sell arts and crafts to guests of the lodge.

There is no scheduled air service to Bathurst Inlet. Air Tindi and First Air in Yellowknife and Adlair Air in Cambridge Bay provide charter services. It costs about $2,500 to charter a plane between Bathurst Inlet and Cambridge Bay and from $2,000 to $5,000 to charter one between Yellowknife and Bathurst Inlet, depending on the type of plane.

There are no phones in Bathurst Inlet, so most people communicate via HF radio, channel 5446. The Yellowknife office of Bathurst Inlet Lodge will take calls for individuals in the community.

There's no health facility or RCMP detachment here either. The closest medical help is 100 kilometres away in Umingmaktok, where many people from Bathurst Inlet regularly shop.

DIRECTORY

The 819 and 403 area codes change to 867 on Oct. 21, 1997.

Bathurst Inlet Lodge
P.O. Box 820, Yellowknife NT,
X1A 2N6 Canada
VISA accepted.
Tel.: (403) 873-2595 or (403) 920-4330
Fax: (403) 920-4263
E-mail: bathurst@internorth.com
Web site: www.canadiana.com/vnorth/bathurst

Canadian Wildlife Service
Tel.: (403) 920-6056
Fax: (403) 873-8185
E-mail: enviroinfo@cpgsv1am.doe.ca
Web site: www.mb.ec.gc.ca

KUGLUKTUK

by Millie Kuliktana

Set between the banks of the mighty Coppermine River and the shores of Coronation Gulf on the Arctic Ocean, the name Kugluktuk (formerly known as Coppermine) was intended to reflect the meaning "the place of moving water" in Inuktitut.

Population:	1,201 (Inuit: 90%, non-Inuit: 10%)
Telephone Area Code:	403 (changes to 867 on Oct. 21, 1997)
Time Zone:	Mountain Time
Postal Code:	X0E 0E0
How to Get There:	Possible route:
	• Yellowknife-Kugluktuk
	Yellowknife to Kugluktuk (about 600 kilometres north) is via First Air.
	All passengers, including those coming from central or eastern Canada,
	must stay overnight in Yellowknife
Banks:	None. Cash and traveller's cheques are preferable
Alcohol:	Alcohol is not restricted, and is governed only by the provisions of the
	NWT Liquor Control Act. However, alcohol cannot be purchased in Kugluktuk
Taxis:	Yes

However, something was lost in the naming process and the proper spelling, *Qurluqtuq*, fell by the wayside. Kugluktuk actually means "two startled people"! The community's peaceful demeanor, though, is unlikely to startle newcomers.

The Inuit of this area are known as the Copper Inuit, a name born of the nearby Copper Mountains. Many hunters still use local copper to fashion tools, a valuable asset for a people that spend many months hunting and fishing. By spending so much time on the land, Inuit of Kugluktuk ensure their traditional skills are passed on to younger generations, whether it be sewing fur clothing, hunting wild game, carving soapstone, preparing traditional food, drum dancing, or enjoying good old-time fiddling.

History

Kugluktuk is not far from historic Bloody Falls, on the Coppermine River. In 1771, Bloody Falls was the site of a fierce battle between local Inuit families and a group of travelling Chipewyan.

The river is also the site of a well-known murder. In 1913, two hunters, Sinisiak and Uluksak, murdered two Oblate priests, Father Jean-Baptiste Rouvière and Father Guillaume LeRoux. The priests, en route to Dene Indian lands, were afraid they couldn't make it without these two Inuit men guiding them. The hunters, forced to lead the trip, feared for their lives and the welfare of their families back at home. Sinisiak and

Uluksak were taken to Edmonton in 1917 for trial. Although sentenced to life imprisonment at Fort Resolution, they were released in 1919.

The Hudson's Bay Co. built a trading post at Kugluktuk in 1927, and the following year the Anglican Church established a presence, too, joining the Catholic Church, which had already been there for more than a decade. The RCMP arrived in 1932. The arrival of these organizations in Kugluktuk forced traditional medicine men and shamans to cease their practices, hunters to work for wages, children to become formally educated, and traditional methods of discipline to be halted.

Kugluktuk's more contemporary history is highlighted by the final signing of the Nunavut Land Claims Agreement between Inuit leaders and the federal and territorial governments on July 9, 1993. Musicians, artists, Inuit leaders, dignitaries, adults, children and elders sang, laughed, cried and feasted together, celebrating this historic day under warm, sunny skies.

Kugluktuk: Its Land and Wildlife

In Kugluktuk, the activities of both people and wildlife are seasonal. With spring comes the return of geese and snow buntings, and the scurry of the squirrel. Residents spend more time outdoors in the ever-increasing sunlight; you'll see many making 'dry meat' by hanging strips of meat in the midday sun.

In summer, the glimmering tundra and the waters around the community come to life. The tundra, close to the treeline here, is home to a wide variety of wildlife, including moose, wolverines, wolves, foxes, muskoxen, barren-ground grizzlies, and caribou. All species bring an abundance of food and fur to the hunters and trappers of the community. The **Coppermine Hunters and Trappers Organization**, working in conjunction with outfitter **Fred Webb**, can also arrange sport hunts and fishing trips for visitors. Hunts zero in on muskoxen, caribou, grizzly bears, and wolf trophy sport hunting.

The animals can be nuisances, too, especially grizzlies, which tend to wreck cabins and tent frames, shredding the canvas tarps used for roofs. An interesting Inuit belief is that a foggy morning in the spring is a sign of a grizzly that's bellowed a blast of warm air into the cool morning air after waking from its long winter hibernation.

The rare visit of beluga whales excites local hunters. They seek the *maktaaq* of the beluga, the chewy outer layer of skin and fat considered a delicacy by Inuit. The most common marine mammal in the area is the ringed seal, which is an important part of the summer and autumn diet. Fishing for arctic char also plays a large role at these times.

The cliffs that erupt from the ground to the east and west of the community are havens for the peregrine falcons and ravens that crowd the southern faces of the cliffs to bask in the heat of the sun. Summer also means time for Kugluktuk's gardeners to exercise their green thumbs. Some successfully grow a variety of vegetables, including potatoes.

Tours

Many tourists come to Kugluktuk via the Coppermine River, a favorite waterway for northern paddlers. Among the many who have ventured down the broad, swift river are former Canadian prime ministers Pierre Trudeau and John Turner, England's Prince Andrew, and Canadian singer Gordon Lightfoot.

Bloody Falls Territorial Park is a great place for a walk through the history of our people. You can hike the 13-kilometre trail, drive an all-terrain vehicle, or ride in a boat with an experienced river navigator. While there you can stop for a picnic and some fishing.

A boat trip on the Arctic Ocean will take you north of Kugluktuk to Cape Krusenstern. Here you'll find the remains of an old trading post that once belonged to Slim Semmler, an early independent fur trader.

Despite its location north of the Arctic Circle, Kugluktuk is one of few communities in Nunavut where summer days get warm enough to let you wile away hours on the beach. In July and August, avid swimmers take advantage of the hamlet's Waterfront Beach Program where the Coppermine River empties into Coronation Gulf.

The warm temperatures also aid a longer boating season, which begins in late June and ends in early October. Northwest Passage Expedition Ltd. provides outings in the Coronation Gulf area in its 30-foot cabin cruiser, checking out old trading posts, abandoned DEW Line sites and historic reminders of earlier explorers along the way. Another licensed guide is **Aime Ahegona Arctic Tours**, specializing in river and coastal tours, and fishing trips.

A boat ride will get you to the **Coronation Golf Club**, an 18-hole course located on a sand bar between the community and the ocean. Summer is the best time to play there, since early autumn rain and high winds can flood the course.

The **MacDonalds Pool Hall** is an alcohol- and smoke-free centre for youth, located in the centre of Kugluktuk. There's pool, video games, movie rentals and fast food available.

Shopping

The **Kugluktuk Co-op**, here since 1960, sells groceries, dry goods, and local arts and crafts. The **Northern store** also sells groceries and dry goods.

The local **Kugluktuk Anguniaqtiit Association** offers a variety of country foods, including arctic char, caribou, and muskox jerky.

The **Kugluktuk Heritage Centre** on Coronation Drive displays arts and crafts that are usually for sale. Kugluktuk is the home of traditional *iglu* carvings. These soapstone igloos have removable tops and display a traditional Inuit family scene inside. The women of Kugluktuk are also well known for their prowess in making dolls, which you may be able to buy here. Some dolls are made with soapstone faces, others are made of fur.

Events

The annual Nattiq Frolics brings families from surrounding communities to Kugluktuk every April to visit and compete in a variety of contests. These contests include traditional seal hunting, sealskinning, snowmobile races, and Inuit games. There's also traditional feasting and lots of square dancing.

Early autumn brings lots of great fishing and expensive fishing rods to the annual Ikalukpik Fishing Derby. Anglers of all ages try for the heaviest char and best fishing story.

Accommodation and Dining

The **Coppermine Inn** can accommodate 26 people in 14 rooms (all but two are double occupancy). Four rooms have private bathrooms; the rest have shared bathrooms. All have televisions, and there is a pay phone in the lobby. Rates are $190 per person per night (including meals), or $125 without meals. The restaurant is open to non-guests, who should make reservations with sufficient notice. Meals are $15 for breakfast, $20 for lunch and $30 for dinner.

The **Enokhok Inn** takes up to six people in three rooms (two of which have shared bathrooms). All rooms have televisions. There's also a TV in the lobby, plus a public phone. Rates are $170 per person per night (including meals), or $125 without meals. Meals are $10 for breakfast, $15 for lunch and $20 for supper. The restaurant is open to hotel guests only, but non-guests may make reservations as long as plenty of notice is given.

There's also a **coffee shop** in the Co-op store.

DIRECTORY

The 819 and 403 area codes change to 867 on Oct. 21, 1997.

Accommodation and Dining

Co-op Coffee Shop
11 a.m.–8 p.m., Monday to Friday;
12:30–8 p.m., Saturday and Sunday.
Tel.: (403) 982-4231

Coppermine Inn
VISA accepted.
Tel.: (403) 982-3333
Fax: (403) 982-3340

Enokhok Inn
VISA accepted.
Tel.: (403) 982-3197
Fax: (403) 982-4291

Outfitters/Guides/ Tour Operators

Aime Ahegona Arctic Tours
P.O. Box 158, Kugluktuk NT,
X0E 0E0 Canada
No telephone.
Contact Kugluktuk community economic development officer instead.
Tel.: (403) 982-7242

Coppermine HTA-Webb Ltd.
Tel.: (403) 463-2035
Fax: (403) 463-2026
E-mail: 73204.2734@COMPUSERVE.COM
Web site: fordinfo.com/fredwebb

Coppermine Hunters and Trappers Organization
Tel.: (403) 982-4908
Fax: (403) 982-5912

Kugluktuk Heritage Centre
Tel.: (403) 982-3232
Fax: (403) 982-3229

Services

Airport
Tel.: (403) 982-5131

Hamlet Office
Tel.: (403) 982-4471
Fax: (403) 982-3060

Health Centre
Tel.: (403) 982-4531
Fax: (403) 982-3115

MacDonalds Pool Hall
No telephone. Try CB Radio channel No. 7.

Coronation Golf Club
Tel.: (403) 982-3071
Fax: (403) 982-3071

Library
Tel.: (403) 982-3098

Police (RCMP)
Tel.: (403) 982-4111
Fax: (403) 982-3390

Post Office
Centrally located in the community.
10 a.m.–5:30 p.m., Monday to Friday.
Tel.: (403) 982-5905

Schools

Kugluktuk School

Tel.: (403) 982-4406
Fax: (403) 982-3404

Nunavut Arctic College

Tel.: (403) 982-4491
Fax: (403) 982-4004

Taxi

AAA

Tel.: (403) 982-3280

Shopping

Kugluktuk Anguniaqtiit Association

Affiliated with Coppermine HTO.
Tel.: (403) 982-5902
Fax: (403) 982-5912

Kugluktuk Co-op

9 a.m.–6:30 p.m., Monday to Wednesday; 9 a.m.–8 p.m., Thursday and Friday. 12:30–5:30 p.m., Saturday. Closed Sunday. VISA, Interac.
Tel.: (403) 982-4231
Fax: (403) 982-3070

Northern Store

10 a.m.–6:30 p.m., Monday to Wednesday; 10 a.m.–8 p.m., Thursday and Friday; 1–6:30 p.m., Saturday. Closed Sunday.
VISA, MasterCard, Interac.
Tel.: (403) 982-4171
Fax: (403) 982-3607

by Joe Otokiak

Along the shores of the Queen Maud Gulf on the southeast coast of Victoria Island lies the regional centre for the Kitikmeot Region, Cambridge Bay.

Population:	1,351 (Inuit: 75%, non-Inuit: 25%)
Telephone Area Code:	403 (changes to 867 on Oct. 21, 1997)
Time Zone:	Mountain Time
Postal Code:	X0E 0C0
How to Get There:	Possible routes:
	• Yellowknife-Cambridge Bay
	• Winnipeg-Rankin Inlet-Cambridge Bay
	• Ottawa/Montreal-Iqaluit-Rankin Inlet-Cambridge Bay
	• Kangerlussuaq (Greenland)-Iqaluit-Rankin Inlet-Cambridge Bay
	Yellowknife to Cambridge Bay (almost 900 kilometres northeast) is via First Air, NWT Air or Canadian North (Canadian Airlines)
Banks:	Royal Bank of Canada, open from 10 a.m. to 4 p.m., Monday to Thursday and 10 a.m. to 5 p.m. Friday
Alcohol:	Alcohol is not restricted, and is governed only by the provisions of the NWT Liquor Control Act. Supplies are ordered from Yellowknife or brought in under permit. If individuals are found to have misused liquor, their eligiblity to place orders may be withdrawn
Taxis:	Yes

The Inuktitut name for Cambridge Bay, *Iqaluktuutiak,* means “fair fishing place,” for the excellent fishing to be found in lakes and rivers nearby.

As in other northern settlements, there's a strong sense of expectancy these days among the Inuit of Cambridge Bay. In less than two years, the Nunavut government will be created and people here are preparing for momentous change. Many Inuit are busily educating themselves so that on April 1, 1999, they will be ready to administer their own territory.

In the meantime, the GNWT continues to employ most Inuit here. Nunavut Tunngavik Inc., the organization implementing the Nunavut Land Claims Agreement, however, also employs many local people. Increasingly, too, an entrepreneurial spirit fills the air, as Inuit venture into business for themselves or work for others, such as the Inuit-owned **Ikaluktutiak Co-operative**. Mineral deposits near Cambridge Bay and throughout the Kitikmeot mean many Inuit are working for southern-based mining companies in the region.

Despite this activity, the people of Cambridge Bay still value their traditional lifestyle. Many elders depend on the abundant wildlife here for their food. Others, who are educated in southern ways and work in 9 to 5 jobs, leave town when they can to hunt and fish nearby. Even young people, who rely on the goods and services of outsiders, are becoming conscious of the importance of protecting their cultural heritage.

History

In the early 1950s, the community of Cambridge Bay grew with the establishment of a DEW Line station and a military airstrip. The little bay here offered an excellent harbor where the Hudson's Bay Co. could set up a post nearby and offload supplies. Services typical of most northern towns were soon provided: an administrator's office, an **RCMP** station, federal day school, nursing station, Anglican and Roman Catholic churches, and a Ministry of Transport office. The Inuit came to the community from areas to the west, and many still have relatives and close ties in settlements as far away as Tuktoyaktuk in the western Arctic. Those who had formerly lived in makeshift shanties of wood scraps and discarded materials from work sites, now moved into tiny "matchboxes" — plywood one-room structures with a washroom. Life as the people had known it would never be the same.

Increasingly, those Inuit who still lived on the land were drawn to the community to trade their furs for hunting supplies. Gradually, as employment opportunities increased, especially at the DEW Line site, families began to settle down in permanent homes. But then the fur trade declined, and some who had come here expecting to find work, now became dependent on government handouts. At this time, as well, families had to move into town so their children could attend the local school. The men, who had counted on their wives' assistance while out on the land, now travelled alone to the hunting grounds or in the company of other men. Wives remained at home to raise their school-aged children. Other children, whose parents still lived on the land away from Cambridge Bay, were rounded up by plane and sent to boarding schools in Inuvik and Fort Simpson in the western Arctic.

For many years, a commercial char fishery, operated by the Ikaluktutiak Co-Operative, provided seasonal employment and additional income for some hunters and trappers. Later, however, as aquaculture of salmon and trout reduced prices, the fishery was a less lucrative source of

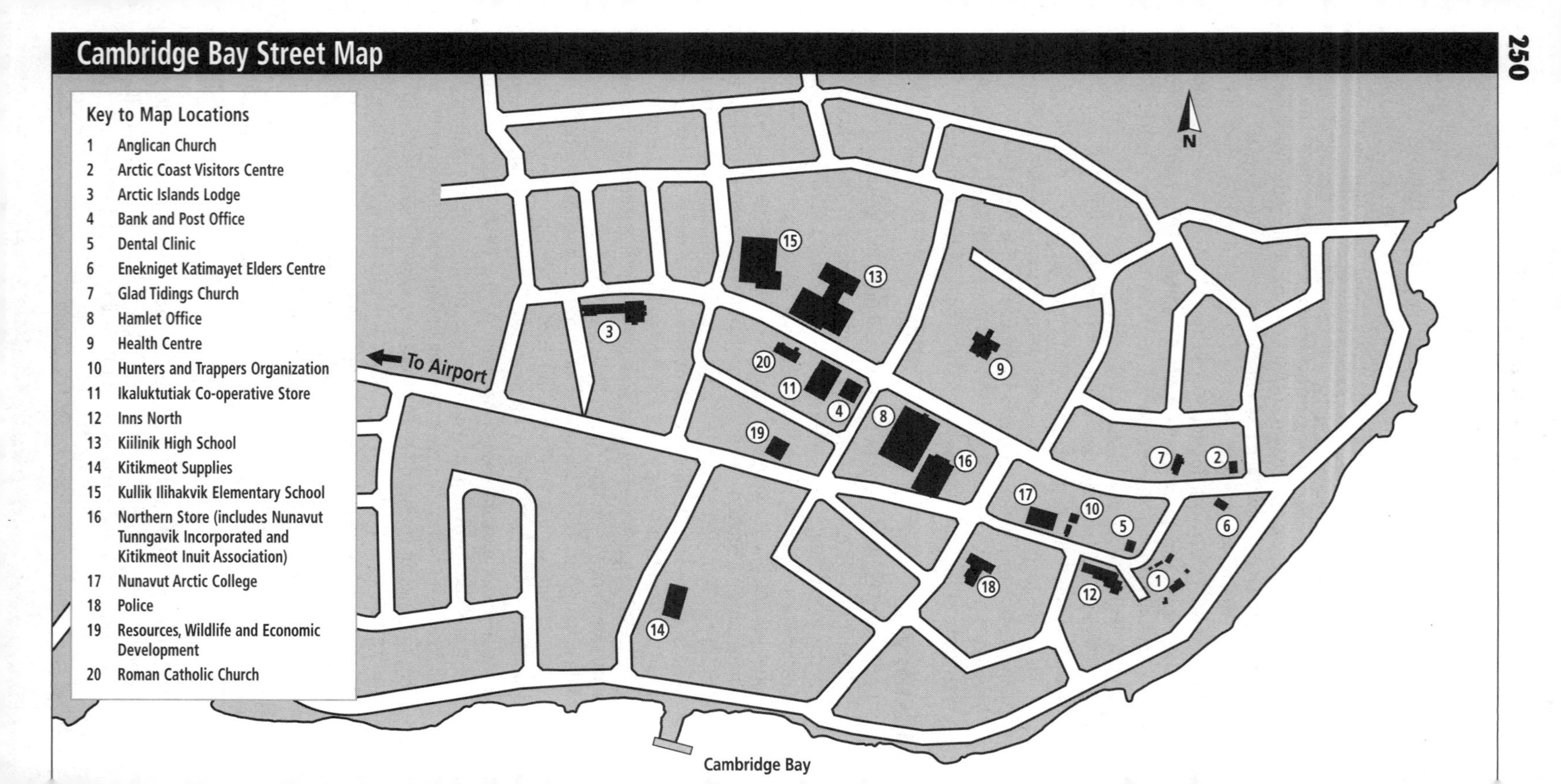
Cambridge Bay Street Map
Key to Map Locations
1 Anglican Church
2 Arctic Coast Visitors Centre
3 Arctic Islands Lodge
4 Bank and Post Office
5 Dental Clinic
6 Enekniget Katimayet Elders Centre
7 Glad Tidings Church
8 Hamlet Office
9 Health Centre
10 Hunters and Trappers Organization
11 Ikaluktutiak Co-operative Store
12 Inns North
13 Kiilinik High School
14 Kitikmeot Supplies
15 Kullik Ilihakvik Elementary School
16 Northern Store (includes Nunavut Tunngavik Incorporated and Kitikmeot Inuit Association)
17 Nunavut Arctic College
18 Police
19 Resources, Wildlife and Economic Development
20 Roman Catholic Church
N
To Airport
Cambridge Bay

employment. At about the same time, the fur industry nearly collapsed when international animal rights activists protested the inhumane capture of animals — in particular, the hunting of seals in Eastern Canada and the trapping of other animals for their fur. The territorial government offered a few manual jobs to the Inuit until they could attain higher education or work experience and assume jobs in management.

Cambridge Bay: Its Land and Wildlife

Throughout the year, trout remain in the lakes, while char migrate to coastal areas in spring and summer, then return upstream to the lakes for the winter.

Of the many interesting stories local elders like to tell, one in particular explains the existence of the high hills that lie to the north of the community. Mount Pelly (*Uvayok*), the largest landmark in the area, is said to be a male giant; Baby Pelly (*Inuhoktok*), standing just behind it, is next; while furthest away is Lady Pelly (*Amaktok*). The hills were believed to be a family that travelled through the area from sea to sea in search of food. Eventually, they perished of starvation. As they waded across the sea onto Victoria Island, the man was first to die, as he faced southeast. The young lad behind him, as indicated by the name, Inuhoktok, died next. Lastly came the mother, Amaktok, who was carrying her baby. For miles around this rocky barren land of tiny ground-hugging plants and gently rolling hills, these landmarks can be seen.

On the outskirts of the community, the land is home to caribou, muskoxen, foxes, wolves, lemmings and weasels. Further afield, you'll find polar bears, wolves, wolverines, grizzly bears and ground squirrels. If you look into the harbor, you'll spot the gleaming heads of ringed seals bobbing about, while further offshore towards the mainland, you'll notice bearded seals.

In spring and summer, the tundra bursts into life with the arrival of migratory birds. First on the scene are snow buntings and whistling swans. Soon they are joined by sea gulls, Canada geese, Ross's geese, black Brants, snow geese, king and common eiders, pintails, oldsquaws, jaegers, peregrine falcons and many other species. Throughout the year, snowy owls, rock and willow ptarmigan and ravens can be seen.

One concern you may face when you travel by land or on water is foul weather and the possibility that you may get lost in winter or swamped while boating. But you learn to be patient and to wait out bad weather. As the saying goes "It'll calm down sometime cause it won't blow forever." It's like pursuing game: you have to be very patient if you're to survive in the North. There are always delays.

Tours

Within walking distance of the community, you'll discover many archeological sites near the river to the northeast and the Mount Pelly area. (The land here is being developed as a territorial park.) Historic sites have interpretive signs along the dirt roads that wind around the bay and up to Mount Pelly. At the end of the road, you can hike wherever your heart desires or fish for char or trout in the lakes that dot the area. For information on tours to the sites, contact the **Arctic Coast Visitors Centre**. And while you're out on the land, be sure to bring warm clothing and insect repellent.

For tours of the community and points of interest nearby, you have several options available. Some tours are organized as part of big game sport hunting or fishing packages offered by **High Arctic Lodge** and other licensed outfitters.

Events

The highlight of the year's events is the Omingmak Frolics, a festival held in the third weekend of May that features a competitive seal hunt, a talent show, snowmobile races, children's games, cooking and tea boiling, ice chiselling and fishing contests.

Another not-to-be-missed occasion this year is the music festival to be held from July 9 to 13 as part of Nunavut Day festivities. Artists from across Nunavut will perform traditional and contemporary music. Other activities will include displays of traditional and modern northern fashion.

Shopping

The modern **Northern store** and the local Co-op usually stock everything from fresh produce to camping equipment. **Kitikmeot Supplies** sells hardware, lumber, office supplies, household goods, snowmobiles and petroleum products for trucks and other vehicles. At the **Enekniget Katimayet Elders Centre**, you can ask the local women to sew you traditional garments. You may also find a few items for sale, such as parkas and footwear.

To purchase works of art by local carvers, ask around to see who has pieces available. Also, try the Northern store and Co-op.

Visitors with a taste for "country foods" won't want to miss the local meat and fish processing plant, **Kitikmeot Foods**, owned and operated by the territorial government and the local Hunters and Trappers Organization. Here you'll find caribou, muskox and a variety of fish products prepared and packaged in many ways.

Accommodation and Dining

The **Ikaluktutiak Co-op Hotel/Inns North** accommodates 46 guests in 23 rooms with double occupancy. The hotel has a non-smoking restaurant and a coffee shop that are also open to local residents. Rooms have a TV and radio. Bathrooms are shared. Other facilities include laundry services, phones in some rooms, a fax machine and a conference room that can host up to 100 people. Rooms are $115 per person per day, not including meals. Cost of meals is as follows: breakfast, $10; lunch, $15; and dinner, $25.

Arctic Islands Lodge has 25 luxurious rooms, of which 17 are single occupancy and eight are double occupancy. Some are non-smoking rooms. All have a private washroom, telephone, and cable TV. The lodge has a restaurant and coffee shop with designated non-smoking areas, which are open during regular working hours. Laundry facilities, fax, and photocopying are also available to guests. In spring and summer, nature and wildlife tours are conducted, weather permitting. A conference room accommodates up to 125 people. Rooms are $165 per night for single occupancy and $190 per night for double occupancy. Meals cost about $40 per day.

On Hadley Bay at the north end of Victoria Island is the High Arctic Lodge. Operating from early July to mid-September, this hunting and fishing lodge accommodates 12 guests in five cabins. A gift shop is located in the main lodge. A week-long fishing adventure at the lodge costs $3,295. This includes the flight from Cambridge Bay, meals, and fishing trips to outpost camps. The lodge also organizes naturalist, canoeing and hunting packages, and outings to ancient Inuit camps. Call the lodge for prices.

The Northern store sells fast foods such as pizza and Kentucky Fried Chicken at its Quick Stop snack bar. You may also rent videos here. Over at the arcade, you can play some pool or pinball and stock up on snack food; the arcade is open until about 11 p.m.

Services

Cambridge Bay provides residents and visitors with a **health centre**, **dental clinic**, **post office**, RCMP detachment, public **library**, weather information centre, visitors centre, and recreational activities such as hockey, curling, and a fitness centre.

The Co-op provides **taxi** service for airport arrivals and departures from 9 a.m. to 7 p.m. during weekdays and after hours. You'll need to order a taxi in advance. Local schools teach students from kindergarten to Grade 12 and **Nunavut Arctic College** offers training to adults in many areas.

Commercial airlines fly regularly into Cambridge Bay. NWT Air, Canadian and First Air provide scheduled flights, while Adlair Aviation Ltd. offers charter service to the community. Northern Transportation Ltd. (NTCL) provides shipping to the region in summer.

Telecommunications are increasingly used by local residents, including telephones, computers and fax machines and now the Internet, via Internet service provider Polarnet. Radio broadcasting is provided by CBC Radio in Inuvik.

DIRECTORY

The 819 and 403 area codes change to 867 on Oct. 21, 1997.

Accommodation and Dining

Arctic Islands Lodge
VISA, MasterCard, American Express, Diners Club/enRoute, Interac.
Tel.: (403) 983-2345
Fax: (403) 983-2480
E-mail: ailfr@polarnet.ca

Ikaluktutiak Co-op/Inns North
VISA, MasterCard, American Express, Diners Club/enRoute.
Tel.: (403) 983-2215
Fax: (403) 983-2649

Guides/Outfitters/ Tour Operators

Arctic Coast Visitors Centre
For references to licensed outfitters.
Tel.: (403) 983-2224
Fax: (403) 983-2302

High Arctic Lodge
Cash, traveller's cheques.
Tel.: 1-800-661-3880 (USA only)
Tel.: (250) 493-3300/3900
Fax: (250) 493-3900
E-mail: higharctic@vip.net

Services

Airport
Tel.: (403) 983-2501

Churches

Glad Tidings Church

Services: 11 a.m., 7:30 p.m., Sunday; 7:30 p.m., Wednesday; 7:30 p.m., Friday, (English and Inuktitut).
Tel.: (403) 983-2387

Roman Catholic Diocesan Centre

Tel.: (403) 983-2521

St. George's Anglican Church

Services: 9:30 a.m. (English), 11 a.m., (Inuktitut), Sunday.
Tel.: (403) 983-2440

Dental Clinic

9 a.m.–12 p.m., 1–5 p.m., Monday to Friday. Call first, as the clinic travels to other communities.
Tel.: (403) 983-2285
Fax: (403) 983-2165

Hamlet Office

Tel.: (403) 983-2337
Fax: (403) 983-2193

Health Centre

Walk-in Clinic:
8:30 a.m.–12 p.m., 1–5 p.m., Monday and Friday; 8:30 a.m.–12 p.m., Tuesday to Thursday.
24-hour emergency service.
Tel.: (403) 983-2531
Fax: (403) 983-2262

Library

Tel.: (403) 983-2406
Fax: (403) 983-2455

Enekniget Katimayet Elders Centre

Tel.: (403) 983-2912

Police (RCMP)

Tel.: (403) 983-2111
Fax: (403) 983-2498

Post Office

Located across from firehall.
8:30–11:30 a.m., 12:30–5 p.m., Monday to Friday.
Tel.: (403) 983-2243

Royal Bank of Canada

Tel.: (403) 983-2007
Fax: (403) 983-2754

Schools

Kiilinik High School

Tel.: (403) 983-2726
Fax: (403) 983-2455

Kullik Ilihakvik Elementary School

Tel.: (403) 983-2510
Fax: (403) 983-2515

Nunavut Arctic College

Tel.: (403) 983-7234
Fax: (403) 983-2384

Taxi

Ikaluktutiak Taxi

Tel.: (403) 983-2201

Weather Office

Tel.: (403) 983-2254

Shopping

Ikaluktutiak Co-operative Ltd.

10 a.m.–7 p.m., Monday to Friday; 12–5 p.m., Saturday; 1–5 p.m., Sunday.
VISA, MasterCard, Interac.
Tel.: (403) 983-2201
Fax: (403) 983-2085

Kitikmeot Foods

VISA accepted.
Tel.: (403) 983-2881
Fax: (403) 983-2801

Kitikmeot Supplies Ltd.

8 a.m.–5 p.m., Monday to Saturday.
VISA, Interac.
Tel.: (403) 983-2227
Fax: (403) 983-2220

Northern Store

10 a.m.–6:30 p.m., Monday to Friday; 12–5 p.m., Saturday; 1–4 p.m., Sunday.
VISA, MasterCard, Interac.
Tel.: (403) 983-2571
Fax: (403) 983-2452

BLOODY FALLS TERRITORIAL PARK

by John Laird

Bloody Falls Territorial Park in the central Arctic is one of Nunavut's few parks with a shared history between the Inuit and the North's other primary aboriginal group, the Dene Indians.

Unfortunately, this history has not always been amiable. In fact, the falls got their English name in 1771, when European explorer Samuel Hearne witnessed the massacre of unsuspecting Inuit by the group of Chipewyan warriors with whom he was travelling. (Chipewyan was an earlier name for Dene.) Today, Bloody Falls is recognized as a national historic site. The Inuit enjoy sharing their heritage with visitors, but ask that you respect the land of their ancestors.

Despite its gory contemporary moniker, northern peoples have gathered at this special place on the Coppermine River for thousands of years. Here, age-old volcanic rock forces the broad, swift-flowing river into a narrow channel of boiling rapids and twisting eddies. The roar of Bloody Falls calls out as you approach across the broad, silent tundra. Inuit refer to the camp site below the falls as *Onoagahiovik*, the place where you "stay all night," a name that recalls a time when fishing was an integral part of their nomadic lives. Even today Inuit camp there to fish, and some have cabins, too.

This region has most recently been inhabited by the Copper Inuit, a people known for making tools from copper found in the Copper Mountains, about 80 kilometres south of the park. Many explorers, including an early expedition of doomed arctic explorer Sir John Franklin, have travelled through the area.

Things to See and Do

Located on the west side of the river, Bloody Falls Territorial Park covers a 7.5-square-kilometre tract of land centred on the falls. The park landscape is typical of the area, with rolling tundra occasionally interrupted by escarpments and rocky outcrops. Closer to the river, steep cliffs and sandy hills descend in plateaus to the valley below. From the park's highest hill, you can barely make out the community of Kugluktuk and the Arctic Ocean, about 13 kilometres to the north.

The ancestors of both the Inuit and Dene fished and hunted at Bloody Falls. At the falls you'll find stone remnants of winter houses used more than 500 years ago by people of the Thule culture. Other archeological evidence indicates earlier inhabitants, the Pre-Dorset, camped at the falls more than 3,500 years ago.

The remains of early caribou-hunting camps dating back some 1,500 years have also been found in the park and are linked with the Taltheilei tradition, a prehistoric Dene people. These camps are scattered on sand plateaus along the west bank, downstream from the falls, but may be difficult to spot since they have been somewhat obscured by blowing sand.

Bloody Falls is a great fishing spot, popular with local people and visitors alike. In spring, arctic char migrate down the Coppermine River to the Arctic Ocean; some people say they taste best at this time of year. In late August, when the char begin to travel upstream again, the nearby community of Kugluktuk holds its annual fishing derby, an event enjoyed by many visitors.

Both Kugluktuk residents and Coppermine River travellers camp at Bloody Falls. The area is generally not heavily used, however, so you may have the park to yourself. There is a wonderful camp site near the falls that is somewhat sheltered by waist-high willows. There are a few picnic tables and an outhouse at the camp site, but no other services. Drinking water can be obtained from the river and nearby lakes.

Flora and Fauna

The golden eagles that soar above the river throughout the summer nest along the steep cliffs at the falls, as well as other locations along the river. Also watch for rough-legged hawks, peregrine falcons, and gyrfalcons. Other avian cliff dwellers include countless swallows, which nest under rock ledges at the falls.

Watch for animal tracks as you walk along the muddy shore above and below the falls. Barren-ground caribou migrate nearby in spring and autumn. Caribou have also been known to occasionally appear within the park or along the trail from Kugluktuk in summer.

The barren lands, a general reference to the tundra, are also home to barren-ground grizzly bears. Although your chances of encountering one are rare, you should still take precautions. When camping, store food well away from your tent, pack out all garbage when you leave the park, and keep fire pits clean and free of food. For more information on bears, contact the government of the Northwest Territories' **Department of Resources, Wildlife and Economic Development** in Kugluktuk.

Wildflowers jump into bloom in late June, dotting the tundra with bright colors for three to four weeks. One of the more interesting plants found at Bloody Falls is the black-tipped groundsel, which was described here in 1821 by John Richardson, a surgeon-naturalist on the Franklin expedition. The plant's black tips inspired Richardson to name it *senecio lugens*, derived from the Latin word *lugeo* ("to mourn"), a name that recalls the slaughter that once occurred at the site. By late August, the bright greens of summer give way to golden yellow, the tundra's last hurrah before winter begins.

Getting There

A rough, 13-kilometre trail stretches across the tundra from Kugluktuk to Bloody Falls. You can hike to the park in four or five hours, but be prepared for wet, spongy ground and a few stream crossings. Despite these minor obstacles, it's a beautiful hike, taking you past many little lakes. Keep an eye out for grizzly bears! You can also rent an all-terrain vehicle (ATV) in Kugluktuk and drive to the park in two hours. ATV rentals cost about $75 to $100 per day; contact the economic development officer in Kugluktuk for more information.

Licensed outfitters will also take you on a 45-minute trip to the park by motorboat. Trips cost around $70 per person, slightly less per person for groups of up to four people. Bring a picnic lunch if your guide isn't supplying one. Note that the river is sometimes shallow, especially in August and September, so you may have to hike the last one or two kilometres to Bloody Falls. Contact the **Kugluktuk Heritage Centre** for more information on licensed outfitters in the community.

Many outfitting companies offer rafting and canoeing trips down the Coppermine River. Typically, these companies fly groups from Yellowknife to various points on the river for one- to two-week adventures that usually terminate at Kugluktuk. If you take one of these trips, Bloody Falls should be a scheduled stop along the way, but check with your trip leader. For more information on companies that offer such trips, contact **Nunavut Tourism**.

You can also visit the park in winter, although it is highly recommended you do so with an outfitter who is familiar with the area, since blowing snow can obliterate landmarks in a frighteningly brief period of time. The falls and the river will be frozen, although water continues to run below the ice.

DIRECTORY

The 819 and 403 area codes change to 867 on Oct. 21, 1997.

Resources, Wildlife and Economic Development
Located in Kugluktuk.
Tel.: (403) 982-7206
Fax: (403) 982-3701

Kugluktuk Heritage Centre
Tel.: (403) 982-3232
Fax: (403) 982-3229

Nunavut Tourism
P.O. Box 1450, Iqaluit NT,
X0A 0H0 Canada
Tel.: 1-800-491-7910 (for Canada and the United States)
Tel.: (819) 979-6551
Fax: (819) 979-1261
E-mail: nunatour@nunanet.com
Web site: www.nunatour.nt.ca

ULTIMA THULE, AND THE NORTH POLE

by Renee Wissink

From Sir James Lancaster's namesake sound at 74 N to Ward Hunt Island at 83 N latitude, the High Arctic (or Queen Elizabeth Islands, as they appear on maps) is the world's most northerly region.

For those who inhabit gentler climates, the High Arctic is the ultimate conquest — a landscape of inspiration, a land of extremes, of abused superlatives, reserved in imagination as an untouched place.

The Quest for Adventure

In 330 BC the Greek explorer Pytheas sailed north from the Mediterranean and became the first recorded voyager to cross the Arctic Circle. He had learned of a mysterious archipelago called Thule (pronounced "too-lee"), somewhere to the north. Thule became an irresistible attraction to the human imagination, but also an elusive goal. As the frontiers of arctic exploration moved north, so did Thule, until it took on mythical proportions, becoming in poetry "Ultima Thule" — the land farthest north.

The affliction was not just ascribed to non-aboriginal peoples. The renowned Inuit shaman Qillaq (who later became known as "Qitdlarssuaq," meaning the great Qitdlaq) also thirsted for the undiscovered. He led the last great Inuit migration from the Lancaster Sound district to northwest Greenland, home of the Polar Inuit. The world's most northerly populated region has since been named Thule. It appears that Qillaq's motives were no more pragmatic than others, as he is quoted around 1858 as having said: "Do you know the desire to see new land? Do you know the desire to see new people?"

For centuries the quest for Ultima Thule became the pursuit of the geographic North Pole, the most coveted of all polar prizes. The geographic North Pole, situated permanently in the Arctic Ocean, is the rotational axis of the earth in the Northern Hemisphere. It should not be confused with the much more southerly North Magnetic Pole near King Christian Island — the point from which the Earth's magnetic field radiates. The North Magnetic Pole is in constant lateral motion, having moved several hundred kilometres from the point where it was originally located in 1831. A magnetic compass points to the North Magnetic Pole, not the geographic North Pole, so is almost totally useless to trekkers to the true geographic North Pole.

The dream of reaching Ultima Thule became reality when Robert E. Peary reached the area near the North Pole on April 6, 1909. Completing one of the most arduous chapters in polar history, he exclaimed: "The Pole at last! The prize of three centuries, my dream and ambition for 23 years, mine at last."

Still, the dream did not die for other explorers. Just as mountain climbers did not stop attempting to conquer Mount Everest after Edmund

Hillary and Tenzing Norgay stood on the summit, so too have many attempted to follow in Robert Peary's footsteps. All who have stood at the North Pole have realized that the goal was not the slab of ice upon which they stood — indeed, the area of the Pole is indistinguishable from all the rest of the ice in the nearly six-million-square-kilometre expanse of the Arctic Ocean.

Rather, the goal was within themselves, their personal Ultima Thule, their quest for adventure.

The Easy Way

Several tour operators organize North Pole trips from Resolute on Cornwallis Island. Most itineraries are for a week to 10 days. This provides a "weather window" for the polar flight and allows visitors to see other High Arctic sites, such as the Polaris mine on Little Cornwallis Island, the North Magnetic Pole, the fossil forest on Axel Heiberg Island, the Inuit community of Grise Fiord, and the Fort Conger Historic Site in Ellesmere Island National Park Reserve. Only two airlines fly to the Pole — Kenn Borek Air and First Air, each using Twin Otters on skis. Both airlines depart from Resolute and use the Environment Canada weather station at Eureka as their staging point.

Once at Eureka, you await your weather window. Weather reports are checked and double checked and when all looks good, you're off on your assault of the Pole. Like a major mountain expedition using supply camps at different elevations, your next stop is at a fuel cache in the vicinity of 86 N latitude, some 120 nautical miles north of the most northerly land in the world. A homing beacon placed with the cache allows your pilot to find this most northern of fuel stations out on the moving polar pack ice. After refuelling, you begin the final leg. Below is a seemingly endless scene of white with only the plane's global positioning system (GPS) navigating you to that point that Robert Peary christened the "Big Nail."

Once over the Pole, your pilots will search for a suitable stretch of ice to land on, a procedure not without risk — at least one Twin Otter lies at the bottom of the Polar Basin. As you circle, the latitude readings on the plane's GPS change wildly and with each loop you circle all the world's time zones. Your stop at the Pole will be approximately one hour, just enough time to feel the magic, take a few photos, and toast your success. You will have reached your Ultima Thule: as you stand at the North Pole, north itself is no more and south lies in every direction.

If you are contemplating an arctic adventure, start by contacting **Nunavut Tourism**, **Parks Canada**, the GNWT's Department of **Resources, Wildlife and Economic Development**, and local licensed outfitters.

First Air and Kenn Borek Air, as well as Nunavut Tourism, can tell you which tour operators offer North Pole tours. Expect to part with between $8,500 and $14,000, depending on the package.

The Hard Way

The North Pole remains the ultimate polar challenge. For this "horizontal Everest," Ward Hunt Island just off the north coast of Ellesmere Island is the base camp, as each year a new crop of "pole vaulters" sets out from this small island on the gruelling 772-kilometre journey to the Pole. Sadly, like Everest base camp, Ward Hunt Island is strewn with piles of equipment and garbage abandoned by expeditions from many countries. A walk through the flotsam and jetsam on Ward Hunt — now administered by Parks Canada as part of Ellesmere Island National Park Reserve — is a walk through a field of dreams, shattered and realized. Each new expedition establishes its own particular challenge: the first by ski, the first by ultralight aircraft, by hot air balloon, helicopter, motorcycle, and the list continues to grow.

Northerners have serious concerns about polar trekkers, and some involve search and rescue. While the Baffin Region has a Search and Rescue Program administered by the Emergency Measures Organization in Iqaluit and supplemented by National Parks Public Safety Plans, the cost for search and rescue could become burdensome to the taxpayer. For example, the cost of a search for one overdue North Pole trekker topped the $250,000 mark. Full-cost recovery and mandatory expedition insurance are two avenues being explored by the territorial and federal governments to offset these costs.

Protection of wildlife is also a concern. Arctic wolves and polar bears have been killed by expeditions. Northerners want to ensure that expedition members are properly instructed on how to avoid and deter aggressive polar bears. While such encounters are dangerous, not all need end in the death of a bear. There is also concern about how expeditions cache fuel and food, and how they dispose of their waste.

DIRECTORY

The 819 and 403 area codes change to 867 on Oct. 21, 1997.

Nunavut Tourism
P.O. Box 1450, Iqaluit, NT,
X0A 0H0 Canada
Tel.: 1-800-491-7910 (for Canada and the United States)
Tel.: (819) 979-6551
Fax: (819) 979-1261
E-mail: nunatour@nunanet.com
Web site: www.nunatour.nt.ca

Parks Canada
Tel.: (819) 473-8828
Fax: (819) 473-8612
E-mail: Nunavut_info@pch.gc.ca

Resources, Wildlife and Economic Development
Tel.: (819) 979-5070
Fax: (819) 979-6026

ELLESMERE ISLAND NATIONAL PARK RESERVE

by Renee Wissink

Encompassing Canada's northernmost lands, Ellesmere Island National Park Reserve (NPR) is an enclave of sedimentary mountain ranges, ice caps, glaciers, fiords and fertile arctic oases.

At 37,775 square kilometres, it is Canada's second largest national park, and six-and-a-half times the size of Canada's smallest province, Prince Edward Island. It covers half of that portion of Ellesmere Island north of Greely Fiord, and a third of the island's northern coastline. Seven major fiords indent its coast, and ice shelves along its northern coasts feature predominantly, abutting the Arctic Ocean. The scale of the land is immense and at the same time, intimate. Patterns of rock, frost-cracked ground, willows and wildflowers form intricate networks that extend to vistas of mountains and glaciers which, in the clear, dry air, seem near enough to touch.

Animal Life

Much of Ellesmere Island NPR, including the Hazen Plateau, is a polar desert, with some areas receiving less annual precipitation — about 2.5 centimetres — than the Sahara. Still, there is enough water from snow and glacial melt to support a broad network of vegetated areas, including highly productive grass-sedge meadows, and some of the most productive wildlife habitats in the High Arctic. The park's thermal oases — including the Lake Hazen basin and the Tanquary Fiord region — spring to life each summer and are home to herds of muskoxen and small roaming bands of endangered Peary caribou. About 30 species of birds, including several Old World migrants, like the Red Knot, can be found here. Arctic wolves roam over huge territories and den at sites they've been reusing for up to three millennia. Arctic hares are ubiquitous and have been seen in herds numbering in the thousands — heaps of hares! Other species include arctic fox, ermine, collared lemming, ringed seals, walrus, and occasionally whales and polar bears in coastal areas.

Due to their inexperience with humans, animals in the park often appear innocent around people, in a Galapagos-like manner. In one instance, a pack of 11 arctic wolves visited a camp, disconcerting the backpackers as they circled closely with quizzical stares. Avoid the temptation to touch or feed wolves or foxes that approach closely, however. It is against the law, and wolves and foxes on Ellesmere Island have been known to carry rabies.

The Park's Northern Region

Ellesmere Island NPR contains most of the major ice shelves within North America. Ice shelves are ancient deposits of very thick freshwater ice (up to 60 metres in depth), tightly frozen to the land and extending several kilometres seaward as a rigid cover over the Arctic Ocean. In summer, the surface of these shelves is covered with a series of low, white ice ridges and shallow blue water troughs running parallel to the coast for many miles. Sometimes huge pieces of these shelves, many square kilometres in extent, break away and float free for years, propelled by ocean currents — particularly the Polar Gyre. During their travels they have been used by scientists as bases for floating research stations, complete with aircraft landing strips.

The northern coast of the park, only 720 kilometres from the North Pole, is rugged with medium-sized sedimentary mountains and deeply incised glacial valleys and fiords. Glaciers spill down the sides of some valleys (Piper Pass, for example), spreading out on the valley floors like giant pancakes.

To the south lie the vast Grant Land Mountains and Ice Cap, comprised of two nearly parallel ranges (the British Empire Range and the United States Range). Mount Barbeau, at 2,616 metres, is the highest mountain east of the Rockies in North America. Most of the mountains are partially "submerged" *nunataks* ("pieces of land"), their peaks sticking through a vast ice cap up to 900 metres thick. From the air, the austere beauty of this landscape resembles a mini-Antarctica. This enormous reservoir of ice covers about a third of the park reserve, and its glaciers flow north toward the Arctic Ocean, and south toward the Hazen Plateau.

Lake Hazen

The Henrietta Nesmith Glacier overlooks a broad basin called the Hazen Plateau to the south and ends only a short distance from Lake Hazen, the core of the park reserve. Because of the slope of the land in the Lake Hazen basin and its orientation toward the sun, this thermal oasis provides an ecosystem during the warmest years with a frost-free season rivalling Schefferville, Quebec — 3,200 kilometres southeast.

The Lake Hazen warden station, located on the site of the old Defence Research Board camp (established in 1957), is on the north shore of Lake Hazen. A small cluster of modest buildings and wall tents, located on a flattened knoll, house the warden station and a tent site for visitors. Many interesting side trips are accessible from the Hazen camp, including a number of short hikes into the Garfield Range. As at the Tanquary Fiord warden station, visitors to Hazen camp must register with park staff upon arrival — providing information on their travel routes, equipment, supplies, southern contacts and expected departure date. They must also close their registration when leaving to confirm departure.

Lake Hazen is the largest freshwater lake in the High Arctic (500-square-kilometre-plus surface area) and one of the largest in the circumpolar world. The only fish here are arctic char, joined by sparse populations of zooplankton and phytoplankton. Limited sport fishing (four "keepers" per angler) is possible.

To the southeast is Lady Franklin Bay where visitors can find Fort Conger, a historic site of worldwide significance. The remaining buildings have the same protective status as the Parliament Buildings in Ottawa. Fort Conger played a pivotal role in the early voyages of explorers and scientists to the area, and was a base for those seeking the North Pole. Visitors to this relic-strewn site are asked to follow the special precautions outlined in the park's Fort Conger information brochure, available at registration.

Tanquary Fiord

The southwestern boundary of the park encloses the upper end of the exquisite Tanquary Fiord. An airstrip, staff buildings, visitor shelter and camp site are located near the head of the fiord, and many scenic features can be seen within a day's hike.

The terrain is relatively easy and the local flora and fauna are a good cross section of High Arctic species.

A small scenic kettle lake lies in a depression a short distance from the Tanquary warden station. Its margins are well vegetated with many species of flowering plants. Nearby are the stone ruins of an early Inuit occupation, including two kinds of stone foxtraps and a muskox ambush structure. Park staff are on hand during the summer to discuss local attractions, travel plans, safety measures and conservation tips.

Visitors hiking the Tanquary-to-Lake Hazen corridor should start their trek at the Lake Hazen warden station. This is because the length and condition of the Lake Hazen airstrip limits aircraft takeoff weight. Landings other than at the Tanquary Fiord and Lake Hazen warden stations require a permit from the park. Make arrangements as far in advance as possible.

As in all arctic parks, visitors must arrive fully equipped and self-reliant. There is no local source of equipment or supplies, and search and rescue capability in the region is very limited. In the event of a personal emergency, it will take considerable time and expense to perform an air evacuation. There are no standby rescue aircraft in the area and the only civil airbase in the High Arctic is at Resolute, about 960 kilometres from the park.

Planning a Trip

Entry to the High Arctic is through the community of Resolute, served several times a week by scheduled airlines with connections to Edmonton, Montreal and Ottawa. Prudent visitors will have previously made plans for accommodation in Resolute and travel to and from the park. Last-minute shopping and return travel arrangements must be completed before leaving Resolute, because civilization will lie behind you once you depart for the park.

Parks Canada recommends that visitors to Ellesmere Island NPR obtain precautionary vaccinations against rabies and tetanus before coming to the park, due to its extreme isolation.

Air travel, the only way of getting to the park, is by Twin Otter, a rugged and reliable Canadian-built turboprop aircraft that has made a name for itself as the workhorse of the Canadian Arctic. The charter cost from Resolute to the park and back is high — between $17,000 and $18,000 (includes pickup trip). The plane carries about 10 people and their gear.

There are two ways to substantially reduce the cost of the trip. The first is to travel with a pre-arranged group (this could drop your cost to under $4,000 if at least six people are making the trip). The second is to split your charter with another group. If the airline can fly another group out after dropping you off, the plane doesn't fly an empty leg, thus cutting costs in half. You may wish to make a side trip to the tiny picturesque Inuit hamlet of Grise Fiord but be aware that this will add to the cost of your charter.

The *Visitor Handbook*, available at registration, has sections on polar bears, conservation practices (trail etiquette), species lists, a guide to sport fishing, and information on Fort Conger. Tour operators are well-prepared to handle problems, and visitors planning a trip to the High Arctic should use the services of a licensed tour operator or outfitter with experience in the area. Make arrangements well in advance, and check with **Nunavut Tourism** as well as the Parks Canada office in Pangnirtung for up-to-date information on outfitters and other services such as HF radio rental.

You'll need four map sheets at a scale of 1:250,000 to cover the entire park:

- Clements Markham Inlet 120F & 120G-67
- McClintock Inlet 340D-67
- Tanquary Fiord 340D-67
- Lady Franklin Bay 120 C&D-67

Sections of the park are currently being mapped at 1:50,000. Groups entering the park can get a 1:64,000 air photo mosaic of the Tanquary-to-Lake Hazen corridor with some recommended travel routes. Obtain one beforehand by writing to the Parks Canada office in Pangnirtung, or upon registration.

Due to cutbacks within Parks Canada, the future management of the park is in question. Services such as orientation, registration and emergency response may be discontinued. Check with the office in Pangnirtung before departure to see if either the Tanquary Fiord or Lake Hazen warden stations will be staffed and how and when to obtain orientation and registration.

DIRECTORY

The 819 and 403 area codes change to 867 on Oct. 21, 1997.

Canada Map Office
Tel.: 1-800-661-6277 or (613) 952-7000
Fax: (613) 957-8861

Nunavut Tourism
Tel.: 1-800-491-7910 (for Canada and the United States)
Tel.: (819) 979-6551
Fax: (819) 979-1261
E-mail: nunatour@nunanet.com
Web site: www.nunatour.nt.ca

Parks Canada, Pangnirtung
(c/o Senior Warden, Ellesmere Island National Park Reserve)
For a copy of the *Visitor Handbook* or the park's information brochure, *Canada at the Top of the World.*
Tel.: (819) 473-8828
Fax: (819) 473-8612
E-mail: Nunavut_info@pch.gc.ca

by Terry Jesudason

A popular T-shirt in Resolute once boasted: "Resolute is not the end of the world, but you can see it from here."

Population:	198 (Inuit: 74%, non-Inuit: 26%)
Telephone Area Code:	819 (changes to 867 on Oct. 21, 1997)
Time Zone:	Central Time
Postal Code:	X0A 0V0
How to Get There:	Possible routes:
	• Ottawa/Montreal-Iqaluit-Resolute
	• Winnipeg-Rankin Inlet-Iqaluit-Resolute
	• Calgary/Edmonton-Yellowknife-Cambridge Bay-Resolute
	• Kangerlussuaq (Greenland)-Iqaluit-Resolute
	Iqaluit to Resolute (about 1,500 kilometres north) is via First Air. Passengers must stay overnight in Iqaluit. Cambridge Bay to Resolute (about 700 kilometres northeast) is via Canadian North (Canadian Airlines International)
Banks:	None. Cash and traveller's cheques are preferable
Alcohol:	Alcohol and alcoholic beverages cannot be purchased in Resolute. Visitors who want to bring alcohol into the community must first obtain a permit from the community's **Alcohol Education Committee**
Taxis:	No. Drivers will usually offer a ride to anyone walking the seven kilometres between the airport and town

Indeed. Located on the south coast of Cornwallis Island at almost 75 N latitude, Resolute is the gateway to the High Arctic.

In this, Canada's second most northerly community, looks can often be deceiving. First-time visitors may see only an endless sea of grey shale rocks, but between those rocks grow the small, colorful arctic flowers that burst to life for a short period each summer. Winter travellers are greeted with countless miles of snow and ice, but across that white expanse you can go forever.

Excellent jet service from eastern and western Canada, as well as two local charter airline companies, make Nunavut's northernmost reaches easily accessible from here. Whether you're planning a trek to the geographic or North Magnetic poles, a hiking excursion in Ellesmere Island National Park Reserve, Canada's most northerly national park, a season of scientific research or a simple visit to the land of the midnight sun, Resolute is often the first chapter in an adventure.

History

Though Inuit have travelled and camped on the shores of Resolute for many hundreds of years, the area is steeped in a European history matched by few other Nunavut communities. The site was a critical juncture along the Northwest Passage, the famed route to Asia sought so desperately by European explorers in the 18th and 19th centuries. The community bears the name of the *HMS Resolute*, one of the vessels that came in search of the lost British expedition under Sir John Franklin.

After the Second World War, when many parts of the Arctic were becoming strategically important, a weather station was established at Resolute. Two years later an airstrip was opened and the community became a focal point for arctic transportation. In 1953 the first Inuit families to live in the modern community of Resolute arrived when they were moved here by the federal government from Pond Inlet and the northern Quebec community of Inukjuak.

A contentious and highly emotional point in Nunavut's history, the reasons for the move have been interpreted differently by the federal government and the 17 families who were moved to either Resolute or Grise Fiord. The Canadian government says Inuit from Inukjuak were going hungry because caribou and other resources were scarce, and so the Inuit families voluntarily agreed to move to an area where game was more plentiful.

Members of the Inuit families, however, felt they were forced to abandon their homes for a harsh and alien land, and were used by the Canadian government to help assert sovereignty in the High Arctic. The debate resulted in hearings by the Royal Commission on Aboriginal Peoples, and in the spring of 1996, the surviving "High Arctic exiles" (as the Inuit relocatees and their family members are called) were awarded $10 million in compensation from the federal government. The government did not admit any wrongdoing, however, and did not extend an apology as exiles had requested.

Since the 1950s Resolute has also been a centre for scientific research in the High Arctic with a logistics support base provided by the federal government at the Polar Continental Shelf Project. A federal school was opened and a major housing program initiated in the 1960s. In 1975 the community was relocated to the present townsite.

Resolute: Its Land and Wildlife

Resolute springs to life for a brief but fertile period every summer. In June, thousands of birds — including ivory gulls, arctic terns, snow buntings, jaegers and red-throated loons — nest on nearby islands. Arctic wildflowers begin to bloom near the end of the month, peaking by late July. Arctic poppies, purple saxifrages, mountain avens, chickweeds and buttercups are among the more visible species.

Travellers who venture out on the sea ice with local guides in April and May have a very good chance of seeing seals, and perhaps polar bears, in their natural habitat. In the summer you can go beluga watching and char fishing on Somerset Island. Air charters are organized through First Air or Kenn Borek Air Ltd. Fishing is best done in late June and early July.

Tours

The waters of Resolute Bay are frozen most of the year, so visitors can walk on the famous Northwest Passage, which passes directly in front of the village. Hiking is good in summer; the area is an old seabed, rich with fossils dating back 400 million years. Near the village, the Mecham River forms small rock pools of clear, cold meltwater where children swim the long days of summer away.

If not already booked with sport-hunting trips, local guides with dogteams can also be hired for short trips. **Amagoalik Outfitters** organizes day trips by snowmobile and sledge in spring, or by boat in summer.

Archeology buffs can visit the sites of Thule tent rings about five kilometres from the airstrip. Two sites have been reconstructed with stones and whalebone to illustrate living conditions more than 500 years ago.

From Resolute there is air charter access to many nearby attractions. Beechey Island, the wintering site of Sir John Franklin's ill-fated 1845 expedition, is about 100 kilometres from town. You can also access Ellesmere Island National Park Reserve, or the limestone cliffs of Prince Leopold Island Migratory Bird Sanctuary where hundreds of thousands of thick-billed murres, northern fulmars, black-legged kittiwakes and black guillemots nest.

Another attraction that can be reached by air charter is Polar Bear Pass National Wildlife Area, 120 kilometres northwest of Resolute on Bathurst Island. Polar Bear Pass is an unusually productive habitat in the midst of a polar desert. Some 54 species of birds have been identified here, but mammals are the most significant feature of the area. In addition to the many polar bears that travel through the pass, Polar Bear Pass also has the largest concentration of muskoxen on Bathurst Island. Endangered Peary caribou can also be found here, although their numbers are diminishing.

A new park is currently being proposed for the northern part of Bathurst Island. If approved, the park — which will shelter a major calving area for endangered Peary caribou — will cover about one quarter of the island. Similarly, a national wildlife area is also being proposed at Creswell Bay on Somerset Island, south of Resolute. The lowlands around Creswell Bay are an important habitat for nesting and staging shorebirds and waterfowl; marine mammals such as belugas and narwhals feed in the bay's fertile waters.

The North Magnetic Pole is approximately 500 kilometres from Resolute; the geographic North Pole is 1,700 kilometres away. Both are accessible by air charter in spring by ski-equipped aircraft. Several companies offer tour flights to both poles in April.

Visitors can see the base station of the **Polar Continental Shelf Project** by contacting the camp manager.

Shopping

Groceries can be purchased at the **Tudjaat Co-op**. Souvenirs and handicrafts are available at the **Co-op Gift Shop** in the airport terminal building. These items are sometimes available directly from local carvers, who work mainly in soapstone, ivory and whalebone.

Accommodation and Dining

The **Narwhal Inn**, near the airport, accommodates 45 people in 30 rooms with single and double occupancy. Cafeteria-style meals are served in a spacious dining room. Bathrooms and a television room are shared. The rate is $235.40 per person per night and includes all meals, airport transportation and GST. Accommodation without meals is $155.15 (including GST) per person per night.

Tudjaat Inns North is located in the village and accommodates 10 people in seven rooms with single and double occupancy. Family-style meals sometimes include northern foods. Bathrooms and TV/reading rooms are shared. Rates start at $185 per person per night including all meals and airport transportation.

Some Inuit families are willing to board visitors. Arrangements vary and meals may not be included, although guests are allowed use of the kitchen. Personnel at the **hamlet office** will be able to point you in the right direction.

There are several good places to camp, all of which are close to sources of fresh drinking water. One is near Resolute Lake, about one kilometre from the airport. Another good area is near the Mecham River, not far from the village. Keep in mind that camping areas are exposed and Resolute weather is often a fickle phenomenon, so bring a sturdy tent and stake it well. Campers are expected to respect the land and remove their garbage.

There are no restaurants in Resolute but visitors can buy meals at either the Narwhal Inn (breakfast $15, lunch $25, dinner $35) or Tudjaat Inns North (dinner $35, breakfast and lunch vary) through prior arrangement with the managers.

Services

In addition to jet service from both eastern and western Canada, Resolute is serviced regularly by Kenn Borek Air Ltd., with weekly flights to Grise Fiord, Pond Inlet and Arctic Bay.

The **Health Centre**'s walk-in clinic is Monday to Friday from 9 a.m. to 12 p.m. Public health clinics take place in the afternoon, from 1 to 5 p.m. Resident nurses are also on call for emergencies. There is an **RCMP** detachment in town; trekkers and expeditions would be well advised to check here before setting out, to fill out a Wilderness Travel Registration form.

Vehicles can be rented from **Narwhal Arctic Services**, **Kheraj Enterprises** or **Diane Guy**.

DIRECTORY

The 819 and 403 area codes change to 867 on Oct. 21, 1997.

Accommodation and Dining

Narwhal Inn
VISA, MasterCard.
Tel.: (819) 252-3968
Fax: (819) 252-3960

Tudjaat Inns North
VISA, MasterCard, Interac.
Tel.: 1-888-866-6784 (in North America)
Tel.: (819) 252-3900 or (819) 252-3901
Fax: (819) 252-3766

Outfitters/Guides/Tour Operators

Amagoalik Outfitters
Tel./Fax: (819) 252-3800

High Arctic International Explorer Services Ltd.
Tel.: (819) 252-3875
Fax: (819) 252-3766

Services

Airport
Manager
Tel.: (819) 252-3923

Alcohol Education Committee
Tel.: (819) 252-3660
Fax: (819) 252-3201

Church

St. Barnabas Anglican Church
No phone.

Diane Guy
Vehicle rentals.
Tel.: (819) 252-3747
Fax: (819) 252-3611

Hamlet Office
Tel.: (819) 252-3616
Fax: (819) 252-3749

Health Centre
Tel.: (819) 252-3844
Fax: (819) 252-3601

Kheraj Enterprises
Tel.: (819) 252-3701
Fax: (819) 252-3663

Narwhal Arctic Services
Tel.: (819) 252-3925
Fax: (819) 252-3649

Polar Continental Shelf Project
Tel.: (819) 252-3872
Fax: (819) 252-3605

Police (RCMP)
Tel.: (819) 252-3817
Fax: (819) 252-3775

Post Office
Located at the Tudjaat Co-op.
Tel.: (819) 252-3959
Fax: (819) 252-3618

Radio Station (FM 105.1)
Tel.: (819) 252-3683

Schools

Nunavut Arctic College
Tel.: (819) 252-3782
Fax: (819) 252-3778

Qarmartalik School
Tel.: (819) 252-3888
Fax: (819) 252-3690

Weather Office
Tel.: (819) 252-3824

Shopping

Co-op Gift Shop
12–4 p.m., Monday; 3–7 p.m., Tuesday; closed Wednesday; 1–4 p.m., Thursday and Friday; 3–7 p.m., Saturday. Closed Sunday. VISA, MasterCard, Interac.
Tel.: (819) 252-3718

Tudjaat Co-op
10 a.m.–noon and 1–5:30 p.m., Monday to Friday; 1–5 p.m. Saturday. Closed Sunday. VISA, MasterCard, Interac.
Tel.: (819) 252-3854
Fax: (819) 252-3618

by Kenn Harper

This is the island of lost souls. A rocky morsel of land off the southwest coast of Devon Island, Beechey is steeped in the lore of the search for the Northwest Passage.

Of the hundreds of European and American explorers who have walked the shores of Beechey, though, none are more closely associated with this desolate place than the lost Franklin expedition, which sailed into Lancaster Sound in 1845 and disappeared forever.

After sailing up Wellington Channel in his undying quest to find a northern route to the riches of the Orient, British argonaut Sir John Franklin and his crew of 129 men were stopped by ice and returned to spend the winter of 1845–1846 at Beechey. His ships, the *Erebus* and *Terror*, moored safely in the harbor to the east of the island that now bears their name.

The following spring, Franklin and his men continued to the southwest on their fatal quest. They most likely sailed along the ice-choked waters of Peel Sound and the strait that now bears his name. In September 1846, the two ships were beset by ice to the north of King William Island. There they remained until April 1848, when the vessels were finally abandoned. The remaining men trekked south along King William Island toward the mainland. Not one lived to tell the tale.

Traces of Franklin's winter on Beechey were found by other explorers in 1850: the remains of three storehouses, workshops, a wash house, large numbers of empty meat tins and three graves. No written records were found. Nonetheless, Beechey became an important depot and meeting place for Franklin searchers for a few years in the 1850s.

In 1852–1853, Commander W.J.S. Pullen, of the Belcher expedition, built Northumberland House on Beechey. Constructed from the masts and spars of a wrecked whaling ship, Northumberland House was intended as a supply depot for members of the Franklin expedition, should they return to Beechey. They never did. In the late 19th and early 20th centuries, Northumberland House was used by Canadian and British sailors as a winter refuge and site for securing messages and stores.

In recent years, Joseph MacInnis and Owen Beattie have brought the island renewed prominence. In 1980, MacInnis located the *Breadalbane*, a British vessel sent out in 1853 to resupply Franklin search ships in the area. On Aug. 21, 1853, the *Breadalbane* was nipped in the ice off Beechey Island and sank in 15 minutes. All 21 crew members were saved, however.

In 1998, **Arctic Watch Limited**, which now operates a naturalist lodge on Somerset Island, plans to run submarine tours under eight feet of ice, on to the wreck of the *Breadalbane*.

Forensic anthropologist Beattie conducted a well-publicized exhumation of three seamen buried in 1845–1846 by Franklin at Beechey: John Torrington, John Hartness and William Braine. Beattie's 1987 best-seller, *Frozen in Time*, attracted particular attention to the island; few who have seen the book will easily forget the garish photo of Torrington's frozen and wizened face on the cover. Beattie, along with co-author John Geiger, concluded that the men probably died from poisoning caused by the lead used to seal meat tins at the time. In the last two decades, a few eccentric history buffs have chosen to be buried on Beechey, near the remains of Franklin's unlucky cohorts.

Beechey is only an island at high tide. At low tide it is joined to Devon Island by a sandbar. It has never been permanently inhabited, nor have Inuit traditionally camped there.

Relatively inaccessible, Beechey Island can be reached most easily from Resolute by chartered Twin Otter aircraft. However, the island has no tourist facilities. For more information, contact First Air or Kenn Borek Air in that community.

DIRECTORY

The 819 and 403 area codes change to 867 on Oct. 21, 1997.

Arctic Watch Limited
Tel.: (403) 282-2268
Fax: (403) 282-2195
E-mail: info@arcticwatch.com

GRISE FIORD

by Larry and Laisa Audlaluk

On the southern coast of Ellesmere Island, in a landscape of stunning grandeur, lies Canada's most northerly community, Grise Fiord.

Population:	148 (Inuit: 92%, non-Inuit: 8%)
Telephone Area Code:	819 (changes to 867 on Oct. 21, 1997)
Time Zone:	Eastern Time
Postal Code:	X0A 0J0
How to Get There:	Possible routes:
	• Ottawa/Montreal-Iqaluit-Resolute-Grise Fiord
	• Kangerlussuaq (Greenland)-Iqaluit-Resolute-Grise Fiord
	• Yellowknife-Cambridge Bay-Resolute-Grise Fiord
	Iqaluit to Grise Fiord (almost 2,000 kilometres north) is via First Air.
	Yellowknife to Grise Fiord (about 1,900 kilometres northeast) is via Canadian, and requires three nights in Resolute before heading to Grise Fiord on Kenn Borek Air. From Iqaluit, it's either a one-night stay in Resolute or change planes immediately to proceed aboard Kenn Borek Air to Grise Fiord
Banks:	None. Cash and traveller's cheques are preferable
Alcohol:	Alcohol is not restricted, and is governed only by the provisions of the NWT Liquor Control Act. However, there's no place to buy alcohol in the community
Taxis:	No

Visitors to this tiny hamlet in the High Arctic are often awestruck by the vista of magnificent mountains, icebergs and glaciers they discover here. There is good reason for its Inuktitut name, *Aujuittuq* — "the place that never thaws out."

Grise Fiord owes its English name to the Norwegian explorer Otto Sverdrup, who charted the south and east coasts of Ellesmere Island from 1899 to 1903. Among the many names he gave to fiords in the area, he called this particular one Grise Fiord, which means "pig fiord" in Norwegian. It seems that the sounds made by many walrus here reminded him of the grunting of pigs!

History

Ellesmere Island is rich in prehistoric Inuit sites. In historic times, however, no Inuit lived here except those who passed through as part of the great migration of Baffin Inuit from the Igloolik/Pond Inlet area to northern Greenland, led by Qillaq (later called Qitdlarssuaq) in the mid-1800s.

In 1922, the RCMP established a post at Craig Harbour, 55 kilometres west of Grise Fiord. Between 1926 and 1940, the post closed and reopened several times. Then in 1951, the post opened once again, after a detachment at Dundas Harbour on Devon Island was closed.

In 1953, the federal government resettled eight Inuit families from Inukjuak (formerly known as Port Harrison) in northern Quebec, and Pond Inlet, to Craig Harbour.

As in Resolute, the move of the "High Arctic exiles" remains a controversial one. (See Chapter 70, "Resolute" for more details.)

In 1956, the RCMP post moved from Craig Harbour to Grise Fiord. At the same time, some relocated Inuit who had been living at Lindstrom Peninsula eight kilometres across from Grise Fiord started trading here at the government store. In the 1960s, once a federal school was built and a housing program begun in Grise Fiord, the families from Lindstrom Peninsula were moved to the community.

Grise Fiord: Its Land and Wildlife

Many visitors find that the land surrounding Grise Fiord is among the most strikingly beautiful in the North. And with endless daylight from May to late August, there's lots of time to explore it! The South Cape Fiord, 40 kilometres west of the community, is an ideal spot for viewing and photographing towering icebergs. If you want to see walrus, beluga whales, guillemots, murres, seals and even polar bears, you can arrange a trip to the floe edge where the sea ice meets open water, about 50 kilometres east of the community. To do so, you're best to make travel arrangements before you arrive in Grise Fiord.

By late May, many birds return from the South to nest in the area of Grise Fiord. Along the fiords eight kilometres north of the community, you'll find seagulls by the thousands at this time. In June, snow geese, king eiders, and eider ducks, among others, arrive on the scene; by late June, most of the snow geese are nesting. From April right through the summer, you'll spot snow buntings and rock ptarmigan throughout southern Ellesmere Island.

About 100 kilometres southeast of Grise Fiord is Coburg Island, a national wildlife area that is considered one of the most important nesting areas for seabirds in the Canadian Arctic.

Tours

You'll find archeological sites as close as two kilometres from the airport; others further away from town you can visit by boat or snowmobile. A 30-minute ride across the fiord will take you to a polar bear trap of the Thule culture. Another area to visit is the site of three Inuit camps from the time of the 1953 relocation, at Lindstrom Peninsula, 11 kilometres from Grise Fiord. This is a popular picnic spot for local people. About 45 kilometres west of the community, at Harbour Fiord, you'll see a cross erected to the memory of a sailor, one of Otto Sverdrup's men, who died here.

You might also take an excursion to Goose Fiord, roughly 70 kilometres west of Grise Fiord. That's the location where Sverdrup was forced by ice to stay an extra year in the narrows of the fiord that didn't break up one summer. If you head over to Fram Fiord, about 50 kilometres east of the community, you may encounter muskoxen grazing on the tundra. This is the fiord where Sverdrup, in his ship, the *Fram*, sought shelter during a storm.

For 10 months of the year, the sea around Grise Fiord is frozen; break-up usually isn't complete until mid-August. By mid-May, the sun shines for 24 hours a day in the High Arctic, so expect to see people on the move at all hours of the day and "night." In mid-August, the sun is lower on the horizon and evenings are chilly.

At present there are no licensed outfitters in Grise Fiord, although a relatively new outfitter that is a subsidiary of the local HTO — Qutsittumiut Outfitting — says it plans to become licensed. Still, local people will arrange snowmobile trips for you to archeological sites or to view the wildlife, to be part of a dogteam ride or to stay overnight in an igloo you've helped to build.

Shopping

Grise Fiord is noted for miniature ivory carvings, traditional clothing and other arts and crafts such as the arctic tuque. Raw narwhal tusks are sometimes available, but you must also have an export permit to remove them from the area. You can buy arts and crafts from the **Grise Fiord Inuit Co-op Ltd.**, which also sells groceries and assorted dry goods.

Accommodation and Dining

The **Grise Fiord Lodge**, operated by the Grise Fiord Inuit Co-op Ltd., is a nine-room facility with a daily rate of $195 per person, meals included. Each room has a television, but bathrooms are shared. There's a pay telephone, plus a TV and video cassette recorder in the lounge. Airport transportation can be arranged through the hamlet. Several camp sites in the area close to running creeks are open, at no charge, from spring through summer.

Grise Fiord has no restaurants. Visitors can buy a meal at the Grise Fiord Lodge by prior arrangement with the Co-op.

Services

Grise Fiord's **health centre** is open from 9 a.m. to 12 p.m. on weekdays for walk-in traffic. Public health sessions run from 1 to 5 p.m. There is also a nurse on call for emergencies at all times. There is an **RCMP** detachment here, too.

DIRECTORY

The 819 and 403 area codes change to 867 on Oct. 21, 1997.

Accommodation and Dining

Grise Fiord Lodge
VISA, Diners Club/enRoute, Interac.
Tel.: (819) 980-9913/9135
Fax: (819) 980-9954

Outfitters/Guides/ Tour Operators

Iviq Hunters and Trappers Organization
Tel.: (819) 980-9063
Fax: (819) 980-4311

Services

Church

Anglican Church
Call minister, Aksajuk Ningiuk.
Tel.: (819) 980-9929

Hamlet Office
Tel.: (819) 980-9959
Fax: (819) 980-9052

Health Centre
Tel.: (819) 980-9923
Fax: (819) 980-9067

Police (RCMP)
Tel.: (819) 980-9912
Fax: (819) 980-9095

Post Office
Located in the Co-op Store.
11 a.m.–12 p.m., 1–5 p.m., weekdays only.
Tel.: (819) 980-9913

Radio Station (FM 107.1)
Broadcasts: 10–11 a.m., 5–6 p.m., 10–11:30 p.m.
Tel.: (819) 980-9951

Schools

Nunavut Arctic College
Tel.: (819) 980-9081

Ummimak School
Tel.: (819) 980-9921
Fax: (819) 980-9043

Weather Office
Tel.: (819) 980-9946

Store

Grise Fiord Inuit Co-op Ltd.
11 a.m.–12 p.m., 1–5 p.m., Monday to Friday; 3–4 p.m., Saturday. Closed Sunday.
VISA, Diners Club/enRoute, Interac.
Tel.: (819) 980-9913
Fax: (819) 980-9954

by Kenn Harper

Arctic Bay is called *Ikpiarjuk* — "the pocket" — because of the high hills that surround the almost landlocked bay from which the community gets its name.

Population:	639 (Inuit: 94%, non-Inuit: 6%)
Telephone Area Code:	819 (changes to 867 on Oct. 21, 1997)
Time Zone:	Eastern Time
Postal Code:	X0A 0A0
How to Get There:	Possible routes:
	• Ottawa/Montreal-Iqaluit-Resolute-Arctic Bay
	• Kangerlussuaq (Greenland)-Iqaluit-Resolute-Arctic Bay
	• Yellowknife-Cambridge Bay-Resolute-Arctic Bay
	Resolute to Arctic Bay (350 kilometres southeast) is via First Air from Ottawa or Montreal, and via Canadian from Yellowknife. Passengers must stay in Resolute two nights on the Ottawa/Montreal route; one night on the Yellowknife route. Visitors already in Resolute can fly to Arctic Bay via Kenn Borek Air
Banks:	None. Cash and traveller's cheques are preferable
Alcohol:	Alcohol and alcoholic beverages cannot be purchased in Arctic Bay. Visitors who want to bring alcohol into the community must first obtain a permit from the hamlet's **Alcohol Education Committee**
Taxis:	Yes

As you look southward from the community toward Adams Sound, Uluksan Point is on your right, while Holy Cross Point is at the end of the long peninsula to your left. Arctic Bay is connected by a 21-kilometre road to Nanisivik, a mining town developed in the mid-1970s.

History

Captain William Adams seems to have been the first non-Inuk to see Arctic Bay; he entered the bay in 1872 with his whaling ship, the *Arctic*. A Hudson's Bay Co. post was established here in 1926 but closed the following year. The post was re-established in 1936, when relocated Inuit from Pangnirtung and Cape Dorset moved here from the unsuccessful Hudson's Bay post at Dundas Harbour.

The Anglican church built a mission at Moffet Inlet, south of Arctic Bay, in 1937. It closed 10 years later after the accidental shooting and subsequent death of Canon John Turner. A Roman Catholic mission operated in Arctic Bay for a short time in the 1930s. As with most other Baffin Island communities, the present town developed as a result of government housing initiatives in the 1960s.

Arctic Bay: Its Land and Wildlife

Arctic Bay is on the Borden Peninsula, an uneven, undulating plateau dissected by numerous river valleys. In the northern part of the peninsula, where the community is located, mountains reach as high as 1,300 metres. Flat-topped King George V Mountain dominates the view from the community to the southeast.

Terrestrial wildlife around Arctic Bay is minimal. In the last few years, caribou have come close to the community, but sightings are more common farther south near Admiralty Inlet. Polar bears also frequent the area.

Every summer, Admiralty Inlet plays host to a variety of marine mammals. Narwhals frequent the waters and occasionally come into Arctic Bay itself. Narwhals are hunted for their ivory tusk and *maktaaq*. Killer whales are often present along the west coast of Admiralty Inlet. Bowhead sightings, like the whales themselves, are rare. Walruses are often seen in western Admiralty Inlet. Ringed seals are ubiquitous.

Tours

Near the old airstrip on the western end of town stands the original Department of Transport house, which served as a weather station between 1942 and 1952 and is still used as a dwelling. Also located in this area is the residence of the Northern store manager and some 50-year-old outbuildings. The store and its large warehouse were built more recently. Locals recall the legend of Jimmy Bell, a former Hudson's Bay Co. manager whose ghost was said to have haunted the residence until the death of his former best friend, Amagoalik. The Taqqut Co-op building, in the centre of town, originally came from Blacklead Island to serve the Hudson's Bay Co. in the 1920s.

At Uluksan Point, a low promontory with surprisingly lush vegetation in the summer, there are the remains of many stone houses, some at the very edge of the water and some that were occupied in recent times. The cairn that dominates Holy Cross Point was erected by Captain Joseph E. Bernier, who wintered here in 1910-1911 with the Canadian government steamship *Arctic*. Uluksan is a pleasant walk from the community and a favorite picnic site in late spring and summer.

A summer road stretches northwest from Arctic Bay over the hill and then along the shores of a lake known locally as Dead Dog Lake. The road continues on to Victor Bay, where many Inuit pitch tents in summer, both for holidays and hunting. This road is also an excellent hiking route.

Niglasuk Company, owned by the local HTO, provides outfitting and guide services. Dogteam or snowmobile trips are available in spring, and boat trips can be taken during summer and early autumn. In summer you may be lucky enough to observe a narwhal hunt. The company's main offerings are a floe edge trip in June and a week-long caribou hunt in late August. They also offer polar bear hunts in late winter, but these must be booked a number of years in advance. Local people may also be interested in taking visitors out on trips by snowmobile and *qamutik*, dogteam or boat. Arrangements can be made after your arrival in the community, but it is advisable to make them beforehand.

King George V Mountain is a challenge for hikers and climbers alike. Allow a day to reach the top and return to the community. A spectacular view awaits those who attain the summit.

Shopping

Arctic Bay is noted for miniature ivory carvings, traditional clothing and other arts and crafts. Stone used here is grey argillite, similar to that used in Sanikiluaq far to the south, but with brownish blotches and streaks. Carvings made from this stone are often very small, and pieces are sometimes made so that the brown markings stunningly enhance their features. Unfortunately, the carving of this stone has declined in recent years. The **Taqqut Co-op** offers a selection of locally made soapstone carvings, and both the Co-op and the **Northern store** sell northern souvenirs. Narwhal tusks are often available in summer and autumn.

Groceries and hard goods are sold at both the Northern and Co-op.

Events

The most important tourist event of the year in both Arctic Bay and neighboring Nanisivik is a gruelling set of runs of various lengths between the two communities, the Midnight Sun Marathon. Often billed as one of the world's toughest foot races, it takes place on the weekend closest to Canada Day, July 1. The race, which attracts experienced marathoners the world over, starts in front of Taqqut Co-op in Arctic Bay.

Recent changes in ownership and management at **Nanisivik Mines** has caused concern among some participants, as a former mine manager was always the driving force behind the marathon. Time will tell if the new management continues to support this event. Interested participants should contact Nanisivik Mines for details.

Accommodation and Dining

Enokseot Hotel is the only hotel in Arctic Bay. It sleeps 16 guests in eight rooms. Bathrooms are shared. Single rooms cannot generally be reserved, especially during the busy summer months. Cafeteria-style meals are served in a small but comfortable dining room. There is also a very small common lounge with a television, and a public telephone in the lobby. Hotel rooms do not have phones or TVs. The room rate is $130 per person per night; meals are an additional $70 per day.

There is no formal campground in Arctic Bay, although good camping sites abound. Inquire at the **hamlet office** before you set up your camp.

There is no restaurant in Arctic Bay. With sufficient notice, however, Enokseot Hotel can provide meals for non-guests.

Services

The **Health Centre** is staffed by resident nurses. Walk-in clinics are from 8:30 a.m. to 12 p.m., and health clinics are from 1 to 5 p.m., Monday to Friday. They are also on call after hours for emergencies.

DIRECTORY

The 819 and 403 area codes change to 867 on Oct. 21, 1997.

Accommodation and Dining

Enokseot Hotel
VISA accepted.
Tel.: (819) 439-8811
Fax: (819) 439-8242

Outfitters/Guides/ Tour Operators

Niglasuk Company
Tel.: (819) 439-9949
Fax: (819) 439-8341

Services

Airport
Tel.: (819) 436-8869

Alcohol Education Committee
Tel.: (819) 439-8476
Fax: (819) 439-8767

Churches

All Saints Anglican Church
Tel.: (819) 439-8869

Full Gospel Church
Tel.: (819) 439-8505

Hamlet Office
Tel.: (819) 439-9917
Fax: (819) 439-8767

Health Centre
Tel.: (819) 439-8816
Fax: (819) 439-8315

Hunters and Trappers Organization
Tel.: (819) 439-9949
Fax: (819) 439-8341

Nanisivik Mines Ltd.
Tel.: (819) 436-7502
Fax: (819) 436-7435

Police (RCMP)
Tel.: (819) 439-9966 or (819) 436-7474
Fax: (819) 436-7557

Post Office
Located near Hunters and Trappers Organization.
Tel.: (819) 439-8494

Radio Station (FM 107.1)
Tel.: (819) 439-9922

Schools

Inuujaq
Tel.: (819) 439-8843
Fax: (819) 439-8766

Nunavut Arctic College
Tel.: (819) 439-9913
Fax: (819) 439-8393

Taxi

Arqvartuuq Services
Tel.: (819) 439-8227

Weather Office
Tel.: (819) 436-7554

Stores

Northern Store
10 a.m.–6:30 p.m., Monday to Wednesday; 10 a.m.–9 p.m., Thursday and Friday; 10 a.m.–6:30 p.m., Saturday.
Traveller's cheques, Interac.
Tel.: (819) 439-9914
Fax: (819) 439-8725

Taqqut Co-op
10 a.m.–10 p.m., Monday to Friday; 1 p.m.–8 p.m., Saturday.
Traveller's cheques, VISA, Interac.
Tel.: (819) 439-9934
Fax: (819) 439-8765

NANISIVIK

by Kenn Harper

The Nanisivik townsite was developed as part of the infrastructure of the Nanisivik lead/zinc mine, which opened in 1974.

Population:	287 (Inuit: 37%, non-Inuit: 63%)
Telephone Area Code:	819 (changes to 867 on Oct. 21, 1997)
Time Zone:	Eastern Time
Postal Code:	X0A 0X0
How to Get There:	Possible routes:
	• Ottawa/Montreal-Iqaluit-Nanisivik
	• Kangerlussuaq (Greenland)-Iqaluit-Nanisivik
	• Yellowknife-Nanisivik
	Iqaluit to Nanisivik (1,200 kilometres north) or Yellowknife to Nanisivik (1,700 kilometres northeast) is via First Air. Passengers must stay overnight in Iqaluit or Yellowknife before going on to Nanisivik
Banks:	None
Alcohol:	Alcohol may be brought into Nanisivik, governed only by the provisions of the NWT Liquor Control Act
Taxis:	There is no taxi in Nanisivik, but **Arqvartuuq Services** in neighboring Arctic Bay provides taxi service between the communities and to the **Nanisivik Airport**

Nanisivik is an Inuktitut word that means, appropriately, "the place where one finds things." The ore body was first discovered in 1910–1911 by Arthur English, a prospector on Captain Joseph Bernier's second Canadian government expedition to the High Arctic.

The architecture in Nanisivik is quite different from that of other northern settlements. Many residences have curved exterior walls to fend off the incredible winds that howl through the community. The settlement is dominated by a large white dome that serves as a cafeteria for the mining company. Surrounding it on two sides is a large metal-clad complex known as the Town Centre. This building houses the Northern store, a recreation complex (including one of only two swimming pools in Nunavut), school, day-care centre, post office, fire hall, **RCMP** detachment, **health centre** and government offices. **St. Piren's**, a brightly painted church in Nanisivik, is Nunavut's only multi-denominational place of worship, serving both Anglicans and Catholics.

Tours

This is a mining town. Other than the Midnight Sun Marathon and its mid-winter counterpart, there are no activities for visitors here: no hotel, no outfitters and no organized tours. The town is best visited on day trips from Arctic Bay, although there is not much to do other than hike. No mine tours are offered, except by special arrangement with **Nanisivik Mines**.

If you go, heed the signs identifying West Twin Lake, a pristine-looking body of water to the south of the community off the airport road. Despite its attractive appearance, West Twin Lake is the tailings pond for the mine and as such receives the waste products of ore processing. East Twin Lake is the source of the community's fresh water.

Behind the community is a mountain known locally to non-Inuit as Mount Fuji; Inuit call it *Nasalluganngua q* because of its hat-like appearance. Locals ski or snowboard here.

Down the hill from the townsite, the mountainside is pocked with holes, the result of more than 20 years of underground mining. Ore is stockpiled in a large storage shed on the beach, where it awaits summer shipment to Europe. Nanisivik has the only deep-water harbor on Baffin Island.

Events

In recent years, a group of diehard local runners has organized and participated in the Brain Dead Marathon, a parody of the well-known Midnight Sun summer marathon between Nanisivik and Arctic Bay. The Brain Dead Marathon sees participants run across the snow and ice of Strathcona Sound and back to Nanisivik in the depths of mid-December's cold and darkness.

Accommodation and Dining

There is no hotel or camp site in Nanisivik. Transients may be accommodated in a bunkhouse operated by Nanisivik Mines, although the company's staff takes priority. Except during the Midnight Sun Marathon, visitors are encouraged to stay in nearby Arctic Bay.

There is no restaurant in Nanisivik. Cafeteria-style meals are available in the large dome building operated by the mining company for its employees. Meal hours are limited. Groceries can be purchased from the **Northern store**.

DIRECTORY

The 819 and 403 area codes change to 867 on Oct. 21, 1997.

Services

Airport
For flight and weather information.
Tel.: (819) 436-7554
Fax: (819) 436-7230

Allurut School
Tel.: (819) 436-7350

Arqvartuuq Services
An Arctic Bay taxi company.
Tel.: (819) 439-8227

Health Centre
8:30 a.m.–5 p.m., Monday to Friday.
Tel.: (819) 436-7482
Fax: (819) 436-7495
A nurse is on call for emergencies 24 hours a day.

Nanisivik Mines Ltd.
Tel.: (819) 436-7502
Fax: (819) 436-7435

Northern Store
10 a.m.–6:30 p.m., Monday to Wednesday; 10 a.m.–7 p.m., Thursday; 12–6 p.m., Friday and Saturday.
VISA, MasterCard, Interac.
Tel.: (819) 436-7322
Fax: (819) 436-7477

Police (RCMP)
Tel.: (819) 436-7474
Fax: (819) 436-7557

Post Office
Tel.: (819) 436-7502

St. Piren's Anglican Church
The church is also used by visiting Roman Catholic priests. Call minister in Arctic Bay.
Tel.: (819) 439-8869

POND INLET

by Marian and Mike Ferguson

Traditional Inuit culture thrives in the modern community of Pond Inlet, a bewitching array of past and present at the northern tip of Baffin Island.

Population:	1,154 (Inuit: 94%, non-Inuit: 6%)
Telephone Area Code:	819 (changes to 867 on Oct. 21, 1997)
Time Zone:	Eastern Time
Postal Code:	X0A 0S0
How to Get There:	Possible routes:
	• Ottawa/Montreal-Iqaluit-Pond Inlet
	• Kangerlussuaq (Greenland)-Iqaluit-Pond Inlet
	• Winnipeg-Rankin Inlet-Iqaluit-Pond Inlet
	• Yellowknife-Rankin Inlet-Iqaluit-Pond Inlet
	Iqaluit to Pond Inlet (1,066 kilometres north) is via First Air. Passengers must stay overnight in Iqaluit
Banks:	None. Cash and traveller's cheques are preferable
Alcohol:	Alcohol and alcoholic beverages cannot be purchased in Pond Inlet
	Visitors who want to bring alcohol into the community must first obtain a permit from the community's **Alcohol Review Board**
Taxis:	No. Hotel guests are transported to and from the **airport** by the hotel van

Near a satellite dish that brings southern culture into the community you'll find caribou and sealskins drying for winter clothing, while dogteams bark and howl in the distance.

Inuit and other arctic inhabitants have occupied this area for thousands of years. The people of Pond Inlet and the surrounding area are the *Tununirmiut*, the people of *Tununiq*, "the land that faces away from the sun." This is the area around Pond Inlet and Eclipse Sound — the land to the north. Pond Inlet is called *Mittimatalik*, the place where Mittima is buried. Exactly who Mittima was, however, remains a mystery.

History

Explorer John Ross gave the body of water between Bylot Island and Baffin Island its English name in 1818 when he dubbed it "Pond's Bay" after a British astronomer. Whalers had arrived a year earlier, in search of the valuable bowhead whale. It would be almost 100 years before the area's first shore whaling station was established in 1903, but by then the industry had all but collapsed. By 1912, only one whaling ship attempted a bowhead hunt in the area, with no success. A nearby national historic site commemorates the whaling industry in the eastern Arctic.

In the mid-1800s, a shaman (*angakkuq*) and powerful leader, Qillaq, led some 60 Inuit on a migration from Tununiq to Greenland. Qillaq was apparently fleeing from Inuit who were enemies of his family. The migration by Qitdlarssuaq (Qillaq's Greenlandic name) had a profound effect on the lives of both the Tununirmiut and the Polar Inuit, who had been isolated in northern Greenland for more than 100 years. The newcomers re-introduced important Inuit technology such as the kayak, bow and arrow, and *kakivak* (fish spear) to their Greenlandic brethren. To this day the Polar Inuit and Tununirmiut are closely related.

In 1912, three expeditions arrived in Pond Inlet looking for gold. Although none was found, the expeditions opened small trading posts, and Pond Inlet became a trading centre. The Hudson's Bay Co. arrived in 1921, when they bought out the Arctic Gold Exploration Syndicate.

Pond Inlet became the site of arctic intrigue in 1920, when Robert Janes, an independent trader from the Pond Inlet area, was murdered en route to Igloolik. Inuit apparently greatly distrusted Janes and decided his activities could no longer be tolerated. News of the killing travelled out of the North and the RCMP arrived in 1921 to investigate. In 1923, three Inuit were tried on a ship near Pond Inlet; two were convicted, and one was taken to a penitentiary in southern Canada.

The Anglican and Catholic missions were both constructed in 1922, and served to partially divide some Inuit for years. Elders still recall being told not to visit the other mission, despite their curiosity. The original Roman Catholic mission was recently renovated after a tragic 1994 fire destroyed the previous chapel. The fire took the life of Father Guy Mary-Rousselière, a priest and world-renowned archeologist who had lived in Pond Inlet for 37 years.

A federal school was built in the 1960s, along with residences for some children whose parents lived on the land. Eventually, most Inuit moved into town as the government provided more housing. Today, four families continue to live on the land in what are called "outpost camps."

Pond Inlet: Its Land and Wildlife

Wildlife abounds among the mountains and in the waters around Pond Inlet. You can frequently see caribou in March and April, when they are within sight of town and on Bylot Island. In May, they migrate into the picturesque fiords southwest of Pond Inlet where wolves may also be seen. Caribou with young calves can be spotted in the fiords in August and September. More than 30 species of birds nest and raise their young from May to September.

The fiords and floe edge are favored camping and fishing areas for local families in spring and summer. You may encounter polar bears near the floe edge in spring and almost anywhere during the open-water season. The local renewable resources officer with the Northwest Territories' Department of **Resources, Wildlife and Economic Development** is a good person to talk to for information on avoiding dangerous encounters. The **Mittimatalik Hunters and Trappers Organization** (HTO) can arrange polar bear or caribou hunts.

Seals are seen basking on the sea ice in May and June. With an experienced guide, photographers can approach seals very closely on the ice. Seals, seabirds, polar bears, narwhals and belugas — and even walrus, bowhead or killer whales — may be seen at the floe edge from mid-May through June. Narwhals and seabirds can be readily photographed here. Marine mammals are seen in many places once the ice breaks up.

Tours

A good place to begin your exploration of Pond Inlet is the **Rebecca P. Idlout Library**, in the Nattinnak Centre. The library has extensive information on the area's natural and human history, as well as a collection of historical references and photographs. The **Nattinnak Centre** plans to house several displays featuring the natural and cultural heritage of the area. An elders' group also has a meeting and work area in Nattinnak.

A few minutes' walk from Nattinnak is a *qammaq* (sod house) that was reconstructed by the elders group in 1991 as an example of traditional Inuit homes used until the 1960s. Although the qammaq has not been maintained since being built, visitors can go inside and imagine Inuit life as it was not long ago.

You could also arrange to visit a local carver, enjoy a drum dance or take a guided nature walk.

In addition to several outstanding archeological sites, visitors will find magnificent scenery, intriguing geological formations, abundant wildlife and colorful plants near Pond Inlet. Cross-country skiing, dogsledding, snowmobiling, hiking, kayaking, boating, fishing, hunting and exploring are some activities that visitors enjoy. April and May are the best months for cross-country skiing to a nearby iceberg, always a popular meeting place for picnics and sliding. Whatever your mode of transportation, long distances can be travelled with continual daylight from May through August. Overnight dogsled and snowmobile trips can be booked from April to June through local licensed outfitters. If outfitters are available when you arrive, shorter trips may also be arranged.

Hiking opportunities abound in Pond Inlet. Experienced backpackers can trek to the glaciers and mountains southeast of Pond Inlet in two to five days. Although Janes Creek is not usually passable in July, if you are careful wading across it at other times, you can hike 15 kilometres east of town and then climb a trail up Mount Herodier to enjoy the breathtaking view from its 765-metre peak. You can also pitch a tent at the base of Mount Herodier, where many local families camp during summer.

For a shorter hike, you can go to *Qilalukat* (Salmon Creek), two kilometres west of town, to see the remains of a Thule village. En route you will see examples of land patterned by permafrost along the coastal escarpment. In July and August, you can fish for arctic char along the coast towards Salmon River, two kilometres west of Qilalukat.

Pond Inlet is becoming a popular destination for experienced arctic kayakers. Outfitters can take you to the floe edge in May and June, but always exercise caution in your kayak. Whales can appear unexpectedly from under the ice, and drifting floes can move quickly with changes in wind direction. Ice conditions are unfavorable during July, making progress very slow. August is the best month for kayaking. Even so, severe winds — although infrequent — can keep you pinned in a safe harbor for a day or so.

Char fishing is best done through frozen lakes in April or May, or along the coast in August. Fishing trips can take one or more days, or fishing can be mixed with other activities. Fishing licences must be obtained from the renewable resources officer.

Tagak Outfitting Services, **Polar Sea Adventures** and **Toonoonik Sahoonik Outfitters** offer a variety of guided tours. Most outfitters prefer groups of four to eight persons with most trips lasting five to nine days. They will customize trips to the needs of their clients, however. You can book your trip directly with an outfitter, or through **Tununiq Travel**, which markets and sells tours for local outfitters.

Visitors planning to travel on the land, ice or water occasionally encounter delays of hours, and perhaps a couple of days. Guides know the dangers that a seemingly innocuous wind or snowfall may foretell. You should remain patient, and trust your guide's judgment as he attempts to take you to your destination without risking your life.

Shopping

Several Inuit produce fine sculptures of soapstone, ivory, whalebone and marble. Both green and red soapstone come from local sources. Beautiful wall hangings, pencil drawings and caribou-hair tuftings are also produced by local artists. Toonoonik Sahoonik Co-op has display cases filled with excellent examples of these products and other souvenirs.

The **Toonoonik Sahoonik Co-op** and the **Northern store** both sell a wide variety of hard goods, groceries and country foods. Both stores get fresh produce, dairy products, bread and meats from southern Canada once a week.

Events

Country foods, like caribou, arctic char, seal and *maktaaq* are still the staples of the Inuit diet. On special occasions, these foods are offered at community feasts, which are open to visitors. You need a permit to take certain country foods out of the Northwest Territories, so check with the renewable resources officer.

Accommodation and Dining

Operated by Toonoonik Sahoonik Co-op, the **Sauniq Hotel** has 17 guest rooms with double occupancy, each with cable television and private bath. The price is $155 per person per night, not including meals. With meal plan, the price is $230. Guests can chat or play cribbage in the sitting room. Laundry facilities are available.

From May through September, some visitors camp on the tundra north of the airport or along the beach west of the hamlet. There is a territorial camping area with picnic tables and tent platforms at Qilalukat.

The **Arctic Research Establishment** has accommodations and other facilities for researchers holding scientific research licences and permits. The Nunavut Research Institute in Iqaluit provides advice on obtaining research permits.

If you want to stay with an Inuit family, arrangements can be made through the **hamlet office**.

The Sauniq Hotel's dining room serves three hearty meals daily at set hours, but reservations are required if you are not a hotel guest. Subject to change, breakfast costs $20, lunch $25 and dinner $30. The Toonoonik Sahoonik Co-op operates a **restaurant** that is open during its store hours, and on Sunday from 3 to 7 p.m.

Services

At the **Health Centre**, near **Ulaajuk School**, nurses provide out-patient services by appointment between 9 and 11:30 a.m., Monday through Friday. For emergencies, you can call the centre at any time. For non-medical emergencies, call the local **RCMP** detachment.

DIRECTORY

The 819 and 403 area codes change to 867 on Oct. 21, 1997.

Accommodation and Dining

Sauniq Hotel
VISA, MasterCard, American Express.
Tel.: (819) 899-8928
Fax: (819) 899-8364

Toonoonik Sahoonik Restaurant
10 a.m.–8 p.m., Monday to Friday;
1–8 p.m., Saturday; 3–7 p.m., Sunday.
VISA, MasterCard, American Express, Diners Club/enRoute.
Tel.: (819) 899-8912
Fax: (819) 899-8770

Outfitters/Guides/ Tour Operators

Mittimatalik Hunters and Trappers Organization
Tel.: (819) 899-8856
Fax: (819) 899-8095

Nattinnak Centre
Hours change seasonally; open daily with extended hours during tourist seasons. Check posted hours at library, stores and hotel.
Tel.: (819) 899-8225
Fax: (819) 899-8246

Polar Sea Adventures
Tel.: (819) 899-8870
Fax: (819) 899-8817

Tagak Outfitting Services
Tel.: (819) 899-8932

Toonoonik Sahoonik Outfitters
Tel.: (819) 899-8366
Fax: (819) 899-8364
Web site: www.pondtour.com

Tununiq Travel
Tel.: (819) 899-8994
E-mail: tununiq@netcom.ca

Services

Airport
Tel.: (819) 899-8882

Alcohol Review Board
Tel.: (819) 899-8984

Arctic Research Establishment
Tel.: (819) 899-8823
Fax: (819) 899-8926

Churches

Roman Catholic Mission
Tel.: (819) 899-8083

Saint Timothy's Anglican Church
No phone.

Hamlet Office
Tel.: (819) 899-8935
Fax: (819) 899-8940

Health Centre
Tel.: (819) 899-8840
Fax: (819) 899-8997

Police (RCMP)
Tel.: (819) 899-8822
Fax: (819) 899-8832

Post Office
In the former hamlet office.
Tel.: (819) 899-8343

Radio Station (FM 105.1)
Tel.: (819) 899-8884

Rebecca P. Idlout Library
Hours change seasonally. Check posted hours at library, stores and hotel.
Tel.: (819) 899-8972

Resources, Wildlife and Economic Development
Speak to the renewable resources officer.
Tel.: (819) 899-8819
Fax: (819) 899-8711
E-mail: George_Koonoo@gov.nt.ca

Schools

Nunavut Arctic College
Tel.: (819) 899-8837
Fax: (819) 899-8960

Ulaajuk School
Tel.: (819) 899-8964
Fax: (819) 899-8780

Weather Office
Tel.: (819) 899-8873

Stores

Northern Store
10 a.m.–8 p.m., Monday to Friday; 1–6 p.m., Saturday. Closed Sunday.
VISA, MasterCard, Interac.
Tel.: (819) 899-8848
Fax: (819) 899-8954

Toonoonik Sahoonik Co-op
10 a.m.–8 p.m., Monday to Friday; 1–8 p.m., Saturday. Closed Sunday.
VISA, MasterCard, American Express, Diners Club/enRoute, Interac.
Tel.: (819) 899-8912
Fax: (819) 899-8770

BYLOT ISLAND

by Marian and Mike Ferguson

Perched 700 kilometres north of the Arctic Circle and 600 kilometres west of Greenland in the High Arctic, Bylot Island is one of the richest wildlife habitats in all of Nunavut.

Every summer, the island and surrounding waters play host to hundreds of thousands of birds, as well as 21 species of marine and land mammals.

Established in 1965 as a migratory bird sanctuary, negotiations are under way so that Bylot Island will soon become the centre of a new national park protecting adjacent regions of north Baffin Island. North Baffin National Park will cover almost 23,000 square kilometres, including most of Bylot Island and parts of Oliver Sound and the Borden Peninsula. Although new facilities are not expected in the park for at least several years, excellent guiding, outfitting and information services are already available in the nearby community of Pond Inlet.

Pond Inlet offers an unparalleled view of the rugged mountains, extensive ice fields, intricate glaciers and productive wetlands of Bylot Island. This sight is one of many reasons more and more visitors are drawn here every year. Think twice before setting out for the island on foot, though. Although Bylot's mountains may seem just a short jaunt across the sea ice of Eclipse Sound, they are actually 25 kilometres north of Pond Inlet.

The Land and its Wildlife

More than 18,000 square kilometres in size, Bylot Island is dominated by a Precambrian mountain range rising 2,000 metres out of Baffin Bay. Ice fields are pierced by peaks and ridges, producing numerous glaciers flowing to the sea. Much of the island drops into the water off sheer cliffs, broken occasionally by steep-walled valleys that act as solar collectors. Although more than 360 plant species are found on the island, vegetation is sparse on the moraines of retreating glaciers and in eroded sandstone valleys.

Bylot's distinctive hoodoos (columns of strangely shaped rocks) are formed by the erosion of sandstone around a harder "cap" rock that eventually produces 10- to 15-metre pillars of sandstone. At the bases of some sedimentary cliffs, you may also find sandstone spheres (*ġugisak*) that can be as large as baseballs.

On the island's uplands you'll find prostrate shrubs, flowering herbs and lichens. In addition to arctic foxes, weasels, arctic hares, collared lemmings, snowy owls and gyrfalcons, you may also see caribou, which have recently begun to winter here after an absence of several decades. Most caribou migrate south to Baffin Island in April and May, but some males may remain during summer. According to Inuit elders, the caribou will eventually devastate the upland vegetation, causing them to seek wintering areas elsewhere. The southwest corner of the island is a 1,300-square-kilometre rolling plain of lush wetlands covered by cotton grass, willow and moss. This is the seasonal home of the world's largest colony of greater snow geese (*kanguq*), one of 30 species of breeding birds found here. In 1993 the colony numbered 75,000 adult geese, a 300 per cent increase over the previous decade.

The Sea and its Wildlife

A large polynya — an area of year-round open water — lies in Baffin Bay east of Bylot Island. The resulting floe edge is an important feeding area for a host of marine animals. The island's northeastern coast is also an extensive denning area and summer retreat for polar bears. Along the floe edge in spring, and almost anywhere during summer, visitors may encounter these majestic carnivores along with walruses, beluga whales, bowhead whales, killer whales, narwhals and five species of seals.

The cliffs along this coast are the summer homes of more than 300,000 thick-billed murres (*akpa*) and 80,000 black-legged kittiwakes (*nauluktu-apik*). You can watch these curious birds feeding at the floe edge and nesting on cliffs at the southeast corner of the island.

The People and their History

Abundant wildlife has drawn people to Bylot Island for 4,000 years. Archeological sites on the island offer testimony to the prehistoric lives of Inuit and their predecessors. Several such sites are concentrated on the southeastern part of the island within sight of the floe edge.

Robert Bylot, a British sea captain, and William Baffin, another British navigator, are believed to be the first Europeans to see the island, arriving here in 1616. In the 1800s, bowhead whalers frequented these waters until the industry collapsed in the early 1900s. J. E. Bernier of L'Islet, Quebec, claimed Bylot Island for Canada in 1906. Traders arrived in 1912, and missionaries followed 17 years later. In the 1960s Inuit gradually settled in government-sponsored homes in Pond Inlet. Today, Inuit continue to subsist on the mammals and birds of the area.

Planning a Visit

The island is accessible from Pond Inlet year-round, except during breakup (July) and freeze-up (October and November). Once the ice is solid enough, you can travel to the island by dogteam or snowmobile. If you choose to ski to the island, be wary of open water along the shore in June. In August and September, guides can take you to Bylot by boat. You could also kayak to the island, but always keep a close eye on the weather.

In any season, weather on Bylot Island can differ greatly from that in Pond Inlet. Don't be surprised if on a clear, calm day your guide refuses to leave town, especially if fog obscures the bottom of Bylot's mountains. This "fog" may be snow or sea spray blown into the air by high winds.

To arrange a trip to Bylot Island, contact a local licensed outfitter. Outfitters have permits to enter the sanctuary. Independent travellers to the island must first obtain a permit from the **Canadian Wildlife Service** in Yellowknife, which monitors human activity on the island. Allow at least 45 days for a reply.

For general information on Bylot Island and the Pond Inlet area, contact the **Nattinnak Centre** in Pond Inlet.

DIRECTORY

The 819 and 403 area codes change to 867 on Oct. 21, 1997.

Canadian Wildlife Service
5204 50th Ave., Box 2970, 3rd Floor
Diamond Plaza
Yellowknife NT X1A 2R2 Canada
Tel.: (403) 920-6056
Fax: (403) 873-8185
E-mail: kevin.mccormick@ec.gc.ca
Web site: www.mb.ec.gc.ca

Nattinnak Centre
Tel.: (819) 899-8226
Fax: (819) 899-8246

Polar Sea Adventures
Tel.: (819) 899-8870
Fax: (819) 899-8817

Tagak Outfitting Services
Tel.: (819) 899-8932

Toonoonik Sahoonik Outfitters
Tel.: (819) 899-8366
Fax: (819) 899-8364
Web site: www.pondtour.com

CLYDE RIVER

by Beverly Illauq

Sometimes called the "Gateway to the Great Fiords," Clyde River is on Baffin Island's east coast in the shelter of Patricia Bay, off Clyde Inlet — a fiord that stretches west almost to the tip of the Barnes Ice Cap.

Population:	708 (Inuit: 95%, non-Inuit: 5%)
Telephone Area Code:	819 (changes to 867 on Oct. 21, 1997)
Time Zone:	Eastern Time
Postal Code:	X0A 0E0
How to Get There:	Possible routes:
	• Winnipeg-Rankin Inlet-Iqaluit-Clyde River
	• Yellowknife-Iqaluit-Clyde River
	• Ottawa/Montreal-Iqaluit-Clyde River
	• Kangerlussuaq (Greenland)-Iqaluit-Clyde River
	Iqaluit to Clyde River (about 750 kilometres north) is via First Air
Banks:	None. Cash and traveller's cheques are preferable
Alcohol:	Alcohol and alcoholic beverages cannot be purchased in Clyde River.
	Visitors who want to bring alcohol into the community must first
	obtain a permit from the community's **Alcohol Education Committee**
Taxis:	No

In fact, *Kangiqtugaapik*, the Inuktitut name for Clyde River, means "nice little inlet."

Perched on a flood plain, Clyde River is the contact point for travel into Sam Ford Fiord and the other deep fiords of central Baffin that have become internationally renowned for their soaring walls and spectacular scenery. Glaciers and icebergs abound in the region, and there are 10 fiords within a 100-kilometre radius of the hamlet.

Most Clyde River families are involved in traditional hunting and camping activities. Skin clothing is still made and worn, and many families depend on the animals harvested throughout the year for food. Family camping remains a major activity, especially in spring and summer. There is a mass exodus from the communities in early June, as soon as school finishes, and families travel by snowmobile and *qamutiit* over the cracks of the sea ice to traditional family camping sites that dot the shores of the fiords. Many of these locations are ancient, and a visitor with a keen eye for history can find three or more styles of dwellings and landmarks, some dating back 2,000 years or more.

With the decline of the sealskin and fur markets, government jobs and handicrafts have become the most important sources of income, but subsistence hunting remains a central aspect of life for Clyde River. The tourism industry is seen by many as a way of showing others the importance and strength of traditional Inuit culture, and has become a key economic focus for the community.

Most residents here over 40 speak very little English, as do children nine years old and under. Young people communicate quite easily in English, and at least one person in Clyde River speaks French.

With the coming of Nunavut, the community has become very politically active. Another important issue has been the development of the Igaliqtuuq (Isabella Bay) Biosphere Reserve, an area world-renowned for the significant eastern Arctic bowhead whale population that summers and breeds in the vicinity. However, travel is along an exposed coastline, making access difficult, so tourism in this area is restricted.

History

Vikings may have arrived here 1,000 years ago. Norwegian explorer and author Helge Ingstad considers Cape Aston to be the *Helluland,* or Flat-Stone Land of Norse sagas. Six centuries later, in 1616, British explorers Robert Bylot and William Baffin mapped the area.

Inuit families have been migrating through this area for generations, travelling from as far away as Repulse Bay and the Iqaluit area to seek spouses and keep in touch with relatives. Groups of Inuit scoured the fiords' headlands in winter and spring, searching for marine mammals. In summer they walked miles inland, following caribou and living in lightweight skin tents that the dogs carried on their backs.

In 1818, Clyde River was given its English moniker by British explorer James Ross during his visit here. Beginning in 1820, whalers — particularly Scots — regularly crossed from Greenland to Baffin Island via Melville Bay and searched south along the Baffin coast for bowhead whales. There were few Inuit on this part of the coast, and many left to trade with whalers at more popular shore points to the north and south.

As whaling declined early this century, trading increased. In 1924, a Hudson's Bay Co. trading post was established at Clyde River. Inuit began to make tri-annual visits — at Christmas, in the late spring and when the ice first formed — to trade furs for supplies and exchange news. During the Second World War, a US Coast Guard weather station was erected at Cape Christian near Clyde River. A small federal school was built in 1960. Between 1967 and 1970, the community was moved to a new site across Patricia Bay to take advantage of a better water supply and a good airstrip location.

Clyde River: Its Land and Wildlife

At times, high winds prevent water travel during summer and fall. In the winter and early spring, there may be whiteout conditions with blowing snow. Blizzards usually last between 24 and 48 hours. From the end of May and through June, water on top of the ice can be a problem. Travellers should bring a good, warm pair of boots. Due to the mountainous terrain, weather conditions may vary dramatically within five kilometres of land or water.

Clyde River's "dark season" begins about Nov. 23 when the sun sets, and ends when it rises again about Jan. 18. During this period, peak light occurs at 11:15 a.m. with varying degrees of twilight between 9 a.m. and 2 p.m. By April, Clyde River is flooded with sunshine, and from May 21 until July 21, there is continuous, 24-hour-a-day sunlight.

Seals (ringed, harp, bearded and hooded) live here and the polar bears that prey on them can be seen year-round. Narwhals can be spotted right in Patricia Bay, but are more often seen in Clyde Inlet. Bowhead whales have been seen in Patricia Bay as well, but you'll have a much better chance of spying them around Cape Christian or along the coast on a trip to their breeding grounds in Isabella Bay.

Caribou may be glimpsed in nearby fiords. Hares, arctic foxes and lemmings are also common. Nearby are nesting grounds for arctic terns, Greater Snow geese, Brant's geese, king eiders, gyrfalcons, snowy owls and a variety of gulls, waterfowl and shore birds. Ravens and ptarmigans are the only birds that stay through the winter. Arctic char populate lakes and rivers as well as the fiords and bays. Arctic cod and sculpin are fished by children throughout the summer months and there is a small turbot fishery. Greenland sharks and killer whales inhabit area waters.

No hiking trails have been laid out, but several good hikes can be plotted using topographical maps. You may need to travel by boat to the end of a fiord to access a more interesting trail. Drinking water can be in short supply in July and August after the snow has melted. Sawtooth Mountain, a hike of about 15 kilometres, is a fine vantage point for the breathtaking scenery. If birding is a passion, see the waterfowl nesting sites to the north of the community in August. Hiking along the Clyde River is beautiful from June to September. But keep in mind that hiking on the tundra can be very difficult during wet summers if the ground is soggy.

Adventure travellers, or anyone intending to be alone outside Clyde River without a licensed outfitter, should register with the local RCMP and fill out a wilderness travel registration form. (See "Adventure Travel," chapter 11, for more important travel advice, including information on HF radios, personal locator beacons and global positioning system receivers.) The local search and rescue team requests that all expeditions carry a battery-powered HF radio. Rental is about $100 per week.

HF radio channels 5210 and 5031 are monitored constantly by Inuit hunters and outpost camp residents. Although many of these people do not speak English and fewer still speak French or other European languages, they can contact officials in each community who can communicate with visitors by HF radio, should it be required. Don't hesitate to break into the Inuktitut chatter of 5031. Channel 5210 is supposed to be the emergency channel, although it is used casually. Personal locator beacons and global positioning system receivers work well in this area, but M-Sat radios do not function well this far north.

Fishing for arctic char is particularly good from mid-July to mid-August. Some rivers would appear to be good fly-fishing sites, but few people have been successful.

Local residents hunt seal, caribou and small game year-round, and some hunters are willing to take visitors with them on a hunting trip. Each season has its own interesting method of hunting seal and caribou. An outfitter or the **Resources, Wildlife and Economic Development** officer can tell you what's in season.

Seal dens can be viewed in late April and May, young seals are on top of the ice in June.

Between August and October, hungry polar bears frequent the community and camp sites along the fiords. They're waiting for the sea ice to form that will enable them to again hunt seals. In April and other times of the year, you'll see bears hunting seal pups.

Polar bear hunting season begins in March for local hunters and at the end of April for sport hunters. Five bears are reserved for out-of-town sport hunters. Arrangements must be made well in advance through the Clyde River **Hunters and Trappers Organization** (HTO). Polar bear skins can sometimes be purchased from individual hunters.

Tours

Visitors can take part in Inuit cultural tours, and view wildlife and the dramatic scenery of the eastern fiords from November through May by dogteam travel with an outfitter. Camping at a traditional camp site is another popular outing. Skin clothing for winter travel is highly recommended. It can be borrowed or purchased custom-made if at least one month's notice is given to the HTO or an outfitter. Prices run about $75 for mitts, $200 for *kamiit* (sealskin boots), and $800 for caribou skin suits.

Depending on ice conditions, people can travel by boat from the beginning of August through to mid-September to view summer scenery and wildlife, and hunker down at traditional camp sites in the fiords. All licensed guides and outfitters must supply visitors with floater suits. Lifejackets are inadequate for the Arctic. Clyde River's many fiords and inlets provide challenging sea kayaking, and big wall climbing and mountaineering in Sam Ford Fiord has recently attracted a lot of international interest.

Prehistoric Thule and Dorset period tent rings, stone houses, fox traps and storage bins can be viewed at Cape Hewitt, about 32 kilometres from the settlement. Some artifacts left by European whalers and early Inuit inhabitants distinguish other camp sites. Another interesting day trip is to the abandoned Cape Christian U.S. air navigation base, about 16 kilometres by snowmobile or all-terrain vehicle. Either take a rifle as protection from the bears that frequent this site, or hire a guide who is trained to use a rifle. He will act as a bear monitor, to watch out for you.

There are three active outpost camps within about 32 kilometres of the settlement. You can arrange to visit them through an outfitter.

Newcomers are also welcome to visit **Quluaq School**, the **hamlet office** and the Resources, Wildlife and Economic Development office. The school has some artifacts on display, including three historic kayaks.

Shopping

Clyde River carvers work in whalebone, soapstone, granite, antler and ivory. The **Manimiut Store** has a small gallery of carvings and crafts. The Northern store also has some high-quality, pricey carvings, along with souvenirs and Clyde River's largest selection of dry goods, clothing, and food. An outfitter can lead you to carvers, artisans and traditional sewers to witness stone and ivory carving, and the making of traditional tools and skin clothing.

Qayaakut has a small selection of sewing and handicraft supplies. Shoppers can also place orders for cloth parkas or *amautiit* (woman's parka-cum-baby carrier).

Accommodation and Dining

The **Qammaq Hotel** has 12 beds in double-occupancy rooms at $192.50 per night (meals included), with bathroom, shower and laundry facilities. Meals alone can be obtained by non-guests if advance notice is given: breakfast is $16.50, lunch is $22, and dinner is $27.50. There are no restaurants in Clyde River.

Room and board with local residents can be arranged either through the **Visitors Centre** or an outfitter (the latter can also arrange for meals alone at a private residence).

A local outfitter can set you up in a tent or igloo, either in the settlement or at a traditional camp site. Four cabins located at remote camp sites are on a first come, first served basis. Would-be campers should contact an outfitter before arriving in the community.

The **Northern** and Manimiut stores both sell groceries. The Manimiut Store also has hot microwaved snacks, and visitors may cook their own meals at the Visitors Centre. Open during the day as an information centre, the Visitors Centre also houses a small display of local handicrafts, laundry facilities, telephone services, a small library and a TV/VCR. User fees are from $35 per person per day.

Kaukittuq, located beside the Resources, Wildlife and Economic Development office, sells "country food" at various times, including frozen arctic char, *maktaaq*, smoked fish, dried fish and dried caribou meat. Make an appointment with the HTO to purchase food from here.

Services

First Air has four passenger flights in and out of Clyde River weekly. Chartered flights into Clyde River can be arranged through First Air, or through Air Nunavut.

A nurse is always on call for emergencies at Clyde River's health centre. For regular medical attention, make an appointment sometime between 8:30 and 11:30 a.m. weekdays.

Other visitors have arrived in Clyde River via dogteam, snowmobile, boat and kayak. It's wise to contact a local outfitter, the secretary/manager at the hamlet office, the **RCMP**, or Resources, Wildlife and Economic Development to advise them of your arrival, to ensure that someone is waiting for you who can help make arrangements during your stay.

You'll find fax services through the Visitors Centre, Manimiut Store and the Northern store. A modem will be available at Apitak Corporation by Sept. 1, 1997.

CBC Northern Service broadcasts in Inuktitut and English on the **radio**. Every day between 12 and 12:30 p.m., 5 and 6 p.m., and 10:30 and 11:30 p.m., the volunteer-run local radio society broadcasts, too. Announcements requesting a tour, clothing to be made, or any other kind of help can be placed by phoning in a request in English.

DIRECTORY

The 819 and 403 area codes change to 867 on Oct. 21, 1997.

Accommodation and Dining

Qammaq Hotel

VISA, Interac.
Tel.: (819) 924-6201
Fax: (819) 924-6282

Outfitters/Guides/ Tour Operators

Hunters and Trappers Organization (HTO)

9 a.m.–5 p.m., Monday to Friday.
Tel.: (819) 924-6202 or 924-6191
Fax: (819) 924-6197
On Saturdays, call either Inutiq Iqaqrialu at (819) 924-6278 or Killiktee Jaypetee at (819) 924-6470.

Qullikkut Guides and Outfitters

Seven experienced Inuit hunters show visitors their land, arctic wildlife and the Inuit lifestyle. Custom or package tours by dogteam, snowmobile or boat. Support services for hiking and other adventure expeditions.
Cash, VISA.
Tel.: (819) 924-6268
Fax: (819) 924-6362

Visitors Centre

VISA accepted.
Tel.: (819) 924-6034
Fax: (819) 924-6362

Services

Airport

Tel.: (819) 924-6365

Alcohol Education Committee

Tel.: (819) 924-6339

Churches

Anglican Church of the Redeemer

No telephone.

Pentecostal Church

No telephone.

Hamlet Office

Tel.: (819) 924-6220
Fax: (819) 924-6293

Health Centre

Tel.: (819) 924-6377
Fax: (819) 924-6244

Library

Located in the Ilisaqsivik building.
3–6 p.m. daily.
Tel.: (819) 924-6266

Police (RCMP)

Tel.: (819) 924-6200
Fax: (819) 924-6276

Post Office

Located beside the office inside the Northern store.
10 a.m.–5 p.m.
Tel.: (819) 924-6465

Radio Station

Tel.: (819) 924-6265

Resources, Wildlife and Economic Development

Tel.: (819) 924-6235
Fax: (819) 924-6356

School

Quluaq School

Tel.: (819) 924-6313

Weather Office

Tel.: (819) 924-6344

Stores

Kangiqtugaapik Qayait Rentals

Kayak rentals.
Cash, traveller's cheques.
Tel.: (819) 924-6278

Kaukittuq

Located at the community freezer beside the Resources, Wildlife and Economic Development office. 9 a.m.–5 p.m., Monday to Friday. Cash only.
Tel.: (819) 924-6202

Manimiut Store
VISA, Interac, certified cheques.
10 a.m.–12 p.m., 1:30–10 p.m., Monday to Friday; 1:30 to 10 p.m., Saturday; 2:30–5:30 p.m., 9–11 p.m., Sunday.
Tel.: (819) 924-6201
Fax: (819) 924-6282

Nammautaq
Sells hunting equipment and ammunition. Operated by the HTO, it's located beside the community freezer.
9 a.m.–12 p.m., 1–5 p.m., Monday to Friday. Cash only.
Tel.: (819) 924-6202

Northern Store
VISA, Interac, certified cheques.
10 a.m.–12:30 p.m., 2–6 p.m., Monday, Tuesday, Wednesday and Friday; 10 a.m.–5 p.m., 6–8 p.m., Thursday; 1–5 p.m., Saturday.
Tel.: (819) 924-6260
Fax: (819) 924-6386

Qayaakut
Open by appointment at any time. Ask for Lydia or Ezekiel Qayak.
Cash sales.
Tel./Fax: (819) 924-6224
Tel.: (819) 924-6405

AUYUITTUQ NATIONAL PARK RESERVE

by Bruce Rigby

Set aside in 1972 by the government of Canada, Auyuittuq National Park Reserve, or "the land that never melts," was the first national park north of the Arctic Circle.

The area was given "reserve" status to denote that the identified lands were subject to a land claims process. Although the park area was modified by the 1993 Nunavut Land Claims Act, it is still termed a park reserve until an Inuit Impact and Benefits Agreement is successfully completed. These negotiations are ongoing.

Located on Baffin Island's breathtaking Cumberland Peninsula, Auyuittuq (pronounced "ow-you-ee-tuk") covers 21,500 square kilometres of deep mountain valleys, dramatic fiords, ancient glaciers, and spiny peaks. Most visitors travel in Akshayuk Pass (formerly Pangnirtung Pass), although the remote northern section of the park holds its own mysteries as well.

Akshayuk Pass is a mystical valley system bordered by mountains and cliffs that runs between North and South Pangnirtung Fiords. The pass, which splits the line of mountains along Cumberland Peninsula, is a popular year-round transportation route through the park. Skiers and hikers traverse its 97 kilometres in spring and summer while residents of Broughton Island and Pangnirtung use it for snowmobile travel between their communities in winter. The part of Akshayuk Pass most frequented is the section between Overlord Mountain and Summit Lake.

In stark comparison to Akshayuk Pass lies the north side of Auyuittuq, a remote mosaic of brittle glaciers and deeply incised fiords. This region contains areas of historical interest and provides excellent opportunities for viewing marine life. More difficult to access in summer, the north end of the park is best seen during spring. Few visitors venture into this distant part of the park.

A large part of Auyuittuq's north side is the rarely accessed Penny Ice Cap. This brooding vestige of the last Ice Age occupies approximately 5,100 square kilometres and reaches some 2,100 metres in elevation. With ice as thick as 300 metres in places, the ice cap provides an excellent record of past climates and has been the base for several major scientific studies into climatic change and global warming. The ice cap also has an uncanny effect on local weather conditions: passing winds become cooler and increase in velocity as they descend through nearby mountain passes.

Entering/Exiting the Park from the South

The southern part of Auyuittuq comprises the land between Overlord Mountain and Summit Lake; Akshayuk Pass is the most common route between the two. This part of the park is usually travelled in spring and summer. The season begins in March, as groups of mountain climbers tackle some of the most challenging terrain in the world. Other spring visitors plan on skiing Akshayuk Pass, only to find that the brutal winds of winter have peppered the snow with sand and gravel. Those willing to hike with skis on their backs will find many excellent pockets of snow in protected valleys, however.

Most visitors enter Auyuittuq through the park's southern entrance at Overlord, a 25-kilometre trip from the community of Pangnirtung. Local outfitters will take you there by either snowmobile or boat, depending on the season. There are alternate routes to the southern end of the park through smaller passes in the region that can be accessed by boat or plane. The $75 per person fee for travel to the park (minimum two people) is set by the Pangnirtung Outfitters' Association. It may seem steep, but it represents the costs of maintaining and operating vehicles in a remote environment.

Note that from roughly mid-June to mid-July, ice conditions in South Pangnirtung Fiord are unsafe for snowmobiles and preclude the use of boats. Visitors must therefore enter the park by foot, about a two-day walk from Pangnirtung. The same holds true for the autumn, although travellers rarely visit Auyuittuq this late in the season.

The rudimentary camp sites at Overlord are grouped among the boulders around the warden cabin and shelter. The site has an outhouse; fresh water can be obtained from a nearby stream. Remember that the water contains high levels of glacial sediment, so let it settle before drinking. Also remember that the estuary of the Weasel River is affected by tides. What appears as an expansive mud plain when the tide is out can quickly turn your tent into an impromptu waterbed. Stay well back from the shore. From Overlord a well-marked trail enters the park, continuing into Akshayuk Pass.

The trail loops to Summit Lake and back, a total distance of about 66 kilometres. Few groups hike the entire pass in this direction, mainly because summer ice conditions between North Pangnirtung Fiord and Broughton Island are erratic and make trip planning difficult. There have been instances where hikers have arrived at North Pangnirtung Fiord only to find it impossible to be picked up. The subsequent 97-kilometre trek back to Overlord is a long one. Plan your trip well.

The trail is clearly marked in several ways. In some areas rocks are lined along the path to give a clear definition of a route. In other locations, *inuksuit* provide guides to the trail. Simple rock piles are also used. Many streams have some form of footbridge. The Weasel River has both a suspension bridge and suspended "breeches buoy"-type chairs for crossing. (The latter is a cable crossing with a harness. The hiker sits in the "breeches buoy" chair, which is secured to the cable, to get across.)

There are quite a few streams that you'll have to ford, though. Look for small piles of rocks on either side of the stream. These indicate shallow areas.

Entering/Exiting the Park from the North

The northern half of Akshayuk Pass can be accessed through North Pangnirtung Fiord from Broughton Island by foot, skis, snowmobile or boat, a distance of approximately 40 kilometres. Since Broughton Island is indeed an island, this end of the pass is not accessible by foot during breakup and freeze-up. The fiord usually becomes ice-free in August, although local wind conditions may occasionally push ice back into the fiord, causing unexpected delays in drop-offs and pickups.

The rest of northern Auyuittuq is best seen during spring and in the company of outfitters from Broughton Island. Dogsled or snowmobile trips can be arranged, and opportunities for wildlife viewing abound. Remote fiords create a splendid backdrop for viewing seabird colonies and marine mammals such as polar bears, seals and whales. Exploring northern Auyuittuq on foot is only for seasoned backcountry travellers who are experienced in arctic travel.

Unlike Pangnirtung, outfitters in Broughton Island negotiate their own fees. Be prepared to pay somewhere around $200 per person to get into the park. Contact the park office to obtain a listing of licensed outfitters and their current rates.

A word of warning: The north end of the park is frequented by polar bears at various times throughout the year, so special precautions should be taken. Park officials may find it necessary to close parts of the park when the number of bears is high and the risk of a "negative encounter" great. If you wish to plan a trip into the north part of the park, contact park officials well in advance to avoid unpleasant surprises.

The Glacial Landscape

With its excellent examples of past and current glacial activity, Auyuittuq is a geologist's dream. Icy tendrils of glaciers hang ominously overhead; loud explosions rattle through the pass as house-sized chunks of Precambrian granite crash to the valley floor. Glacial debris litter Akshayuk Pass, and erratics (large boulders) can be found balanced or perched in interesting and unusual positions. The work of water and wind is also evident, creating large deposits of sand and glacial moraines, and carving sinuous patterns in the landscape.

The horns, cirques and polished pinnacles of Auyuittuq offer more evidence of glacial activity. The scoured surface of Mount Thor is the tallest uninterrupted cliff face on the planet, attracting climbers from around the world. The truncated twin peaks of Mount Asgard can be seen from the Summit Lake area. Visitors may recognize Asgard from the James Bond film *The Spy Who Loved Me*.

Glacial processes are still very active in the park. This can be seen in Auyuittuq's mountain streams, which are best crossed in the early morning before melting glacial ice increases their flow dramatically. Wind erosion is also present, and gales carrying sand particles have been known to strip paint from buildings and machinery and pit the heavy windows of the wardens' cabins. For these reasons, care should be taken at all times. There are many examples of active rock and glacier slides, and flash flooding can occur in periods of heavy rain. On one occasion, a park warden was obliged to dump his pack and run to avoid being overtaken by a landslide. Avoid camping in areas bare of vegetation or lichen, or which look cleaner than others around them, as they may still be an active slope or subject to active erosion.

Vegetation

Because of the extremely slow growth and recovery rate of arctic vegetation, the most frequently visited parts of the park lack the showy displays of vegetation found in other areas of Nunavut. Plants grow low to the ground and are predominately made up of lichens, mosses, sedges, dwarf willows or smaller patches of flowering plants. Cotton grasses can be found in lower lying areas, and the eastern version of fireweed — the broad-leafed willow herb — can be found in sandy areas along stream beds.

Birds and Mammals

The timing of your visit, the length of your stay and your location within the park will all affect the types of wildlife you see in Auyuittuq. Wildlife tend to avoid the more well-travelled areas at times when higher concentrations of visitors are present. Those travelling in off seasons and in smaller groups should see more wildlife. The following birds have all been seen in the park: snow buntings, peregrine falcons, redpolls, ptarmigan, ravens, red-throated loons, glaucous gulls and Canada geese. Land mammals that visitors are most likely to see include lemmings, ermine (weasels), foxes and arctic hares. Caribou have also been seen in the park, but in areas not usually seen by most visitors. Unlike the large herds of caribou in other parts of Nunavut, there are relatively few caribou in the park.

Planning a Visit

The majority of Auyuittuq's visitors come in July and August and spend most of their time in the southern part of the park. While Auyuittuq has much to offer, anyone looking for a wilderness experience with extensive solitude may wish to reconsider visiting the park during this time, or make arrangements to visit a less heavily travelled region. Park staff and outfitters will both be happy to assist in planning your visit.

As with other Canadian national parks, Parks Canada now charges an entry fee to Auyuittuq. The fee is $15 per person for a single day, $40 per person for up to three nights, and $100 per person for more than three days. The fee provides access to other national parks in the Northwest Territories. Parks Canada has also instituted other measures for cost recovery, such as for search and rescue.

DIRECTORY

The 819 and 403 area codes change to 867 on Oct. 21, 1997.

Auyuittuq National Park Reserve
P.O. Box 353, Pangnirtung NT,
X0A 0R0 Canada
Tel.: (819) 473-8828
Fax: (819) 473-8612
E-mail: nunavut_info@pch.gc.ca

Pangnirtung Outfitters' Association
Contact the outfitters directly or
call the Angmarlik Visitors Centre
in Pangnirtung.
Tel.: (819) 473-8737
Fax: (819) 473-8685

KEKERTEN HISTORIC PARK

by Mike Vlessides

Like many other historical sites in Nunavut, the legacy of Kekerten Island is born of the often-checkered relationship between Inuit and the British and American whalers that pillaged arctic waters in the 18th, 19th and 20th centuries.

Located on the north shore of Cumberland Sound some 50 kilometres from Pangnirtung, Kekerten was once the hub of whaling activity in the sound.

Today, Kekerten Historic Park is a fascinating destination for visitors to Pangnirtung wishing to make a day trip into this turbulent world. Here you'll find the remnants of a bygone era described by signage along an interpretive trail. Among the many features of the site are the foundations of three storehouses built in 1857 by Scottish whalers, large cast-iron pots once used for rendering whale oil, blubber-hauling pins and the remains of a whaleboat slip.

The Foundations of Whaling

Commercial whaling did not enter Canadian Arctic waters until 1820, when British whalers ventured north from their traditional territory off southeast Greenland into the area around Pond Inlet and Lancaster Sound. They were not disappointed. These untested waters were rich with their principal quarry, the bowhead whale, and for the next two decades became the primary destination of the British whaling fleet. Indeed, the new-found region proved so fecund that between 1820 and 1840, more than 13,000 whales were slaughtered here.

But for all its profitability, bowhead whaling was an uncertain undertaking. During these two decades, the ravages of arctic weather took a heavy toll on the whalers, resulting in hundreds of deaths and dozens of lost ships. In 1830 alone, 19 ships were lost and myriad others damaged.

As a result of these dangerous conditions — as well as a rapidly decreasing bowhead population in the immediate area — the whalers were forced to consider alternative methods of performing their livelihood. The prevailing sentiment was that a permanent whaling settlement in more southerly waters would provide the refuge so badly needed by both men and ships.

The answer came by way of a rumor. For years, whalers had heard tales of a large southerly bay that not only abounded with bowheads, but was also free of ice until well into January. Inuit called this place *Tenudiackbik*. In the spring of 1840, Scottish whaler William Penny decided to find the legendary body of water. He elicited the aid of a young Inuk named Eenoolooapik, who directed the whaler into the mouth of what is now known as Cumberland Sound. British whaling was resuscitated. Within a few years, both British and American whaling ships were visiting the sound with increasing regularity.

In 1852, a group of American whalers aboard the vessel *McLellan* became the first group to spend the winter in Cumberland Sound, setting a precedent that was soon to become standard practice for most whalers in the region. Five years later, Penny established a permanent station in the sound when he erected a station house at Kekerten for the Arctic Aberdeen

Company. The Americans soon followed suit. The establishment of these wintering stations created a permanent foundation for contact and trade between Inuit and non-Inuit; neither group would ever be the same.

Attracted by a culture rich with material items of which they were enamored, Inuit flocked to the whaling stations to perform services that would get them the items they so desired. Among other things, Inuit transported blubber between the floe edge and the harbor, rendered whale oil, and worked as whaleboat crews. They also supplied the whalers with fresh meat and fur clothing. In exchange, the whalers gave Inuit a host of manufactured items, including rifles, telescopes, knives, needles and kettles. Inuit also got dry goods such as biscuits and tobacco.

And while much good came of the relationship that was forged between the two cultures, Inuit suffered desperately for their newly found ties with the whalers. Inuit were highly susceptible to the alien diseases of the Europeans and Americans, and viruses ravaged native settlements. By 1857, some 17 years after their initial contact with the whalers, the 1,000-strong Inuit of Cumberland Sound had seen their population reduced to less than 350. To exacerbate the problem, working with whalers drastically altered traditional Inuit subsistence patterns, and many failed to cache adequate food stores for times of shortage, often resulting in needless starvation.

An Industry at its Peak

The late 1850s and early 1860s were the golden years for bowhead whaling in Cumberland Sound. As many as 30 ships visited the area each autumn; about a dozen regularly spent the winter in the vicinity of Kekerten, or Penny's Harbour as it was known to the whalers. By 1860, stations at Blacklead Island (on the south shore of the sound) and Cape Haven (near the mouth of the sound) joined Kekerten as permanent whaling posts.

It was in this same year, however, that American whaling ships first ventured into Hudson Bay and discovered it to be a fertile whaling area. Most of the American fleet would concentrate on the area for a number of years, spending summers there and wintering in Cumberland Sound. It would only take five years for bowhead stocks in these new waters to shrink precipitously, so ships began returning to the sound.

They were met with a similar situation. Cumberland Sound was yielding fewer whales each year, the result of two decades of intense exploitation. The Arctic Aberdeen Company sold its stations, effectively ending William Penny's participation in the whale fishery. After 1864, the "discoverer" of Cumberland Sound never set foot in the Arctic again.

By 1870, the number of ships visiting the sound had declined to only half that of a decade earlier. But despite the relative dearth of whales, Cumberland Sound was still the location of choice for a dwindling industry. A few ships from each nation overwintered there until the late 1870s. By 1882, American involvement in Eastern Arctic whaling was practically nil. The only permanent station still operating was at Kekerten.

Other Options

As bowhead populations shrank, whaling companies looked to other mammals to fill the void in their pocketbooks. As early as 1872, an American company was netting beluga whales at the head of the sound. More attention was paid to seals, however, which boasted enormous populations in the sound. The 1870s saw increasing trade for sealskins and seal blubber.

As a result of this novel demand for seal products, Inuit returned to preferred sealing grounds across the sound, where they would await the arrival of whaling companies and the products for which they traded. Within 20 years, the seal population had been thoroughly decimated, leaving local Inuit with little food sources to see them through the winter. This probably caused many Inuit to move back to the stations in large numbers in the late 1800s. By the waning months of the 19th century, both Blacklead and Kekerten were home to a few hundred Inuit and a handful of non-Inuit whalers.

When the price of whalebone dropped 17¢ per kilogram in 1912, the fate of the bowhead fishery was sealed. After 1913, no whaling ships left for the Arctic. Nonetheless, Inuit at Blacklead and Kekerten continued to hunt whales there for five more years; by this time the whale fishery had become an important part of their culture. Both Kekerten and Blacklead served intermittently as trading posts, but were abandoned in the mid-1920s and late 1930s, respectively. Today, whaling is but a fading memory in the minds of a few Pangnirtung elders. Etooangat Aksayook, one of the last Inuit whalers, passed away in late 1995.

Your Trip to Kekerten

Trips to Kekerten are best arranged in Pangnirtung through the Angmarlik Centre, the local visitors centre and museum. Inquire about the different outfitters and services offered. Outfitters recommended by the Angmarlik Centre stay with visitors while at the park and provide interpretive tours. They also supply meals.

In late spring — early May to mid-June — most people reach Kekerten by snowmobile, although those with ample time and energy can ski. Regardless of your mode of transportation, always prepare for unexpectedly cold temperatures and winds that eat through several layers of clothing. Note that during the latter weeks of June and early July, travelling on the ice is an uncertain proposition and best left to Inuit who are well versed in pre-breakup travel.

Summer travel to Kekerten is usually by Lake Winnipeg boat or freighter canoe. Don't plan a seaward trip for earlier than July 15, since ice often lingers this late in the year. Once the ice clears, boat trips to the park are possible until late September, when the waters slowly begin to congeal once again. Dress warmly, even on the balmiest days. It's also worth carrying waterproof clothing, including rubber boots. Your licensed guide or outfitter will provide a survival suit for boat travel. If travelling without an outfitter, rent a survival suit somewhere in town. Pangnirtung Fiord is subject to tremendous tides and will dictate your departure and arrival times.

Aside from ski excursions, a round-trip to Kekerten — with time out to enjoy the park — takes about 12 hours. You won't be spending the evening there, since camping is not permitted. A cabin at the park provides shelter in case of emergency; ask your guide if he or she carries survival gear before you embark. If you plan to ski there, then plan on camping for the night somewhere outside the park.

PANGNIRTUNG

by Kenn Harper

Pangnirtung — "the place of the bull caribou" — is located on a narrow coastal plain against a spectacular backdrop of high mountains and a winding river valley.

Population:	1,243 (Inuit: 92%, non-Inuit: 8%)
Telephone Area Code:	819 (changes to 867 on Oct. 21, 1997)
Time Zone:	Eastern Time
Postal Code:	X0A 0R0
How to Get There:	Possible routes:
	• Ottawa/Montreal-Iqaluit-Pangnirtung
	• Kangerlussuaq (Greenland)-Iqaluit-Pangnirtung
	• Winnipeg-Rankin Inlet-Iqaluit-Pangnirtung
	• Yellowknife-Rankin Inlet-Iqaluit-Pangnirtung
	Iqaluit to Pangnirtung (297 kilometres northeast) is via First Air, Air Nunavut, or Kenn Borek
Banks:	None. Cash or traveller's cheques are preferable
Alcohol:	Alcohol and alcoholic beverages are prohibited
Taxis:	Yes

Legend says a hunter named Atagooyuk gave the place its name well over 100 years ago when caribou had not yet changed their patterns as a result of the incursions of man.

History

Cumberland Sound, the large body of water Pangnirtung Fiord opens into, has been a traditional home of Inuit for more than 1,000 years. Here, they and predecessors of the Thule and Dorset cultures lived in small hunting camps along the shore. Their survival depended on the seals, walruses and beluga whales that populated the waters of Cumberland Sound, and on the magnificent bowhead whale that also frequented these waters.

Englishman John Davis was the first non-Inuk known to have entered Cumberland Sound, although it is probable that Norse from Greenland occasionally visited the area as well. Davis, an explorer in search of a northwest passage to the presumed riches of the Orient, navigated the sound in 1585 and again in 1587. The sound was not re-entered by Europeans until 1840.

In 1839, a Scottish whaler named William Penny took a young Inuk man, Eenoolooapik, to Scotland to spend the winter. The following spring Eenoolooapik guided Penny into the mouth of Cumberland Sound. What ensued was 80 years of exploitation by whalers and free traders. The effect of whaling on the Inuit was cataclysmic. Traditional settlement patterns

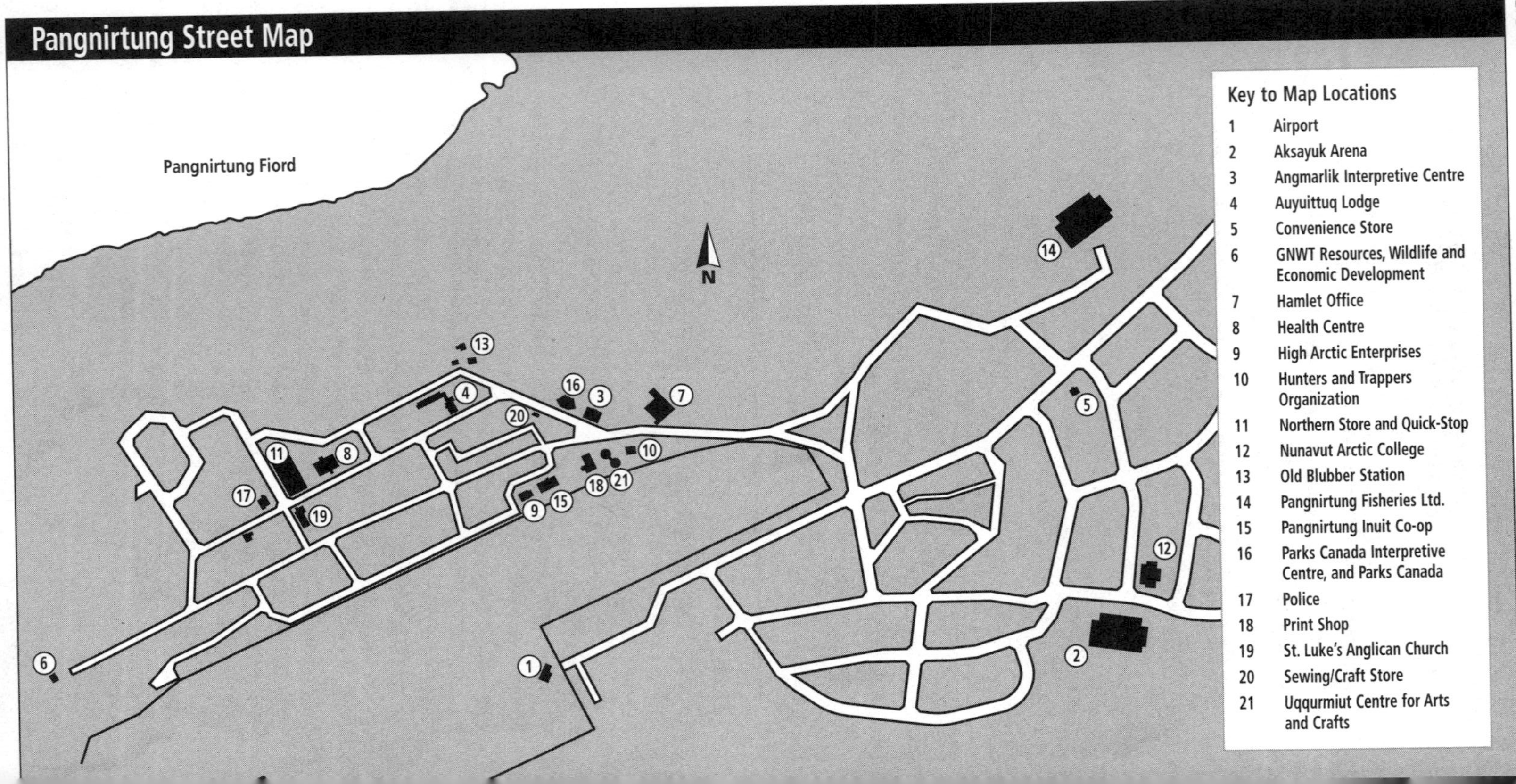
Pangnirtung Street Map
Pangnirtung Fiord
N
Key to Map Locations
1 Airport
2 Aksayuk Arena
3 Angmarlik Interpretive Centre
4 Auyuittuq Lodge
5 Convenience Store
6 GNWT Resources, Wildlife and Economic Development
7 Hamlet Office
8 Health Centre
9 High Arctic Enterprises
10 Hunters and Trappers Organization
11 Northern Store and Quick-Stop
12 Nunavut Arctic College
13 Old Blubber Station
14 Pangnirtung Fisheries Ltd.
15 Pangnirtung Inuit Co-op
16 Parks Canada Interpretive Centre, and Parks Canada
17 Police
18 Print Shop
19 St. Luke's Anglican Church
20 Sewing/Craft Store
21 Uqqurmiut Centre for Arts and Crafts

changed as many abandoned their hunting camps to congregate at two main whaling stations: Blacklead Island off the south coast of the sound, and Kekerten off its north coast. Although whaling brought access to guns, ammunition and wooden boats, many Inuit succumbed to diseases to which they had no immunity.

In 1894, in the declining years of the bowhead industry, an event of paramount importance to the people of Baffin Island occurred: The Church Missionary Society of London, England, established a mission station at Blacklead Island under the pioneering leadership of Reverend Edmund James Peck, a veteran of almost two decades of mission work in northern Quebec. Peck brought with him the gift of a written language, for he promoted the use of the syllabic writing system — adapted from the Cree system — for the Inuit language. Inuit learned the syllabic system quickly, and passed knowledge of it up the coast to camps that had never seen a missionary. Peck produced biblical material in syllabics; this material also spread quickly throughout the region. After the last missionary left Blacklead Island in the early 1900s, Inuit catechists kept both religion and literacy alive.

When whaling declined, Inuit returned to life in camps scattered throughout Cumberland Sound. The establishment of a trading post by the Hudson's Bay Co. in 1921 was followed two years later by a detachment of the RCMP. In 1929, St. Luke's mission hospital was established under Dr. Lesley Livingstone. Until the 1960s, most Inuit continued to live in traditional camps, although a few opted for Pangnirtung and employment. Jim Kilabuk, who worked for the Hudson's Bay Co. for 45 years, was a competent traveller and guide — the mentor of many young traders who came and went during his tenure. Nookiguak was the special constable who assisted the RCMP by guiding their patrols of the sound and the east Baffin coast; after his death in 1949, he was replaced by Joanasie Dialla, who held the position for more than 20 years. Etuangat, who died in his mid-90s in late 1995, was the last of the Inuit whalemen. He also spent many years guiding doctors stationed in Pangnirtung to camps throughout the region. These are the unsung heroes of the three establishments — traders, police and medical workers — that formed the foundation for the modern town of Pangnirtung (pronounced "pang-near-tung").

The history of Pangnirtung would not be complete without mention of William Duval, namesake of the mountain to the east of the community and the river that flows between it and the town. Sivutiksaq, as he was known to Inuit, was a German-born American whaler who came to Cumberland Sound as a young man in the 1870s and spent his life in the Arctic. He is the grandfather or great-grandfather of any Pangnirtung resident with the surname Akpalialuk. Duval died at Usualuk camp in Cumberland Sound in 1931.

In 1956, the federal government sent its first teacher to Pangnirtung, and in 1962 it established an administrative office. That same year, a disastrous distemper epidemic killed most of the dogs in Cumberland Sound, threatening Inuit livelihood. A number of families moved into the community of Pangnirtung from the land. The resulting change in lifestyle was an abrupt one.

The last few decades, though filled with promise, have also been fraught with difficulties for the people of Pangnirtung. This was a seal-hunting community, and when sealskin prices declined precipitously in the 1970s and 1980s, hunting became uneconomical. At the same time, improved health care dramatically increased life expectancy. These two factors, combined with a high birthrate, made for a rapidly increasing population with high unemployment; the social problems that accompany such a situation soon followed. With substantial government assistance, the community currently operates a turbot fishery. The government has also encouraged development of arts and crafts, including Pangnirtung's unique weaving industry.

Pangnirtung: Its Land and Wildlife

The beauty of Pangnirtung is largely born of its backdrop, the lofty mountains of Cumberland Peninsula, where some peaks reach 2,200 metres. The peninsula is bisected by both Akshayuk and Kingnait passes, providing an overland route from Cumberland Sound to Davis Strait. The central part of the peninsula is dominated by the massive Penny Ice Cap, from which many glaciers flow to the sea. Most of the better-known peaks in Cumberland Peninsula were named during a 1953 expedition of the Arctic Institute of North America.

Marine life has been important in the history of Cumberland Sound. Large numbers of beluga whales may be seen at their calving grounds in Millet Bay near the head of the sound; they sometimes wander into Pangnirtung Fiord. Walruses can be seen in the sound; occasionally, so can bowhead whales. Polar bears, which frequent the sea ice near the mouth of the sound, are rarely spotted close to Pangnirtung. Ringed seals are found throughout the sound and the fiord.

Caribou are typically found a considerable distance from Pangnirtung, in the hills past the head of Clearwater Fiord or inland from the south coast of Cumberland Sound, toward Nettilling Lake.

The Pangnirtung area has always been well known for its arctic char fishing. One camp currently operates at Kingnait Fiord. This is a hard business and the season is short, so many camps do not survive. It is best to contact the Angmarlik Interpretive Centre, the local visitors centre, before booking a fishing trip.

Tours

"Downtown" Pangnirtung is a living testimony to the community's history. The Angmarlik Interpretive Centre functions as a community museum, library and elders' centre. Displays represent traditional Inuit and whaling life in Cumberland Sound. Elders are often present during the afternoon, either playing cards, knitting or just reminiscing with each other. You may have an opportunity to chat with some of them, if the staff are free to act as interpreters.

Next door is the **interpretive centre** operated by Parks Canada, which houses displays and exhibits to help interpret the varied nature of nearby Auyuittuq National Park Reserve. **Parks Canada** has its office in the same building.

To the other side of the Angmarlik Centre is a small, old building painted bright yellow. Although originally on a different site, this was the home of the community's first doctor.

In the middle of downtown Pangnirtung stands the former St. Luke's mission hospital and associated church buildings, most of them clad in the drab grey shingles typical of Anglican buildings in the Arctic. The old hospital now houses the Arthur Turner Training School, where Inuit catechists from throughout the diocese of the Arctic are trained.

Behind the **church** stands the shortest two-storey house imaginable. This is where Jim Kilabuk lived and raised his family. A cluster of buildings behind the Northern store were the former Hudson's Bay Co. buildings. The remains of a small rail track can be seen near the beach in this area; on it supplies were hauled up from the beach at shiptime (at that time, the supply ship only pulled into port once a year). On a high rock near the shore is a small black cannon that was only fired at shiptime. On the beach near Auyuittuq Lodge are the buildings of the old whaling station, operated by the Hudson's Bay Co. until 1964. They have been refurbished in recent years; a traditional whaleboat complements the scene.

For those not ready for the challenge of hiking in Auyuittuq National Park Reserve, there are a few good hiking trails that start just outside Pangnirtung. The Ukuma Trail skirts the Duval River and heads toward Kingnait Fiord, which parallels Pangnirtung Fiord over the mountains behind the community. You can also spend a day climbing Mount Duval, but exercise caution, especially when snow covers the ground. A few years ago, a doctor ventured too close to the sheer face of this mountain and plunged to his death. In the 1950s a clerk from the Hudson's Bay Co. fell from the top, and slid, bounced and scraped his way to the bottom. Inuit found him unconscious, but he had miraculously suffered no broken bones and lived to tell the tale.

Hikers needing gasoline and naphtha should contact **J. R. Peyton Enterprises**, the local fuel distributor. Their depot is in a small building beside the tank farm on the beach. Hours are limited.

There is an ever-changing number of outfitters in Pangnirtung. Over the years, the most reliable has been **Alivaktuk Outfitting Services**, operated by Joavee Alivaktuk. Others may be contacted through the Angmarlik Interpretive Centre. Summer visitors can arrange for boat tours to Auyuittuq National Park Reserve or Kekerten Historic Park. Snowmobile tours may be arranged in spring. As of this writing, nobody offers tours by dogteam, but this could change.

Southern-based tour operators also bring groups of tourists to Pangnirtung for activities both in the community and the wilderness beyond. In 1996, **Arctic Odysseys** of Seattle, Washington pioneered Twin Otter-based skiing in the mountains of the park and Cumberland Peninsula; participants reported world-class descents of more than 1,200 metres per run.

Shopping

The **Uqqurmiut Centre for Arts and Crafts** is a locally owned business that is primarily a tapestry studio, print shop and craft gallery. The unique design of this building, reminiscent of a cluster of tents at a traditional camp site, makes it a warm and friendly place for artists to work in, and is equally inviting to visitors. A small shop sells tapestries and prints, as well as crocheted hats, soapstone and whalebone carvings, brooches, and pins by many local artists. The weaving shop also produces blankets, scarves and sweaters.

Weaving was introduced to Pangnirtung almost 30 years ago as Inuit searched for ways to create an economic lifestyle after the wholesale move from traditional camps to Pangnirtung. Don Stuart, an artist from southern Canada, moved to the community and taught local women his craft. Each tapestry bears the name of both the artist who created the scene and the weaver. At the front desk you will be able to arrange a tour. The shop's friendly weavers are mostly monolingual Inuktitut speakers, so unless you speak Inuktitut, conversation will be limited. Those wishing to take pictures are encouraged to leave a donation.

Pangnirtung is also well known for its prints. A new collection is produced each year, to be marketed in southern Canada. Artists typically focus on legends, whaling and traditional activities. The interactions of whalers and traders with Inuit are often the subjects of these colorful productions.

Carving is also important to Pangnirtung. A small but dedicated group of local carvers produces objects in stone imported from Cape Dorset and Kimmirut. Whalebone carvings are still made, although the ready supply of whalebone at traditional sites in Cumberland Sound has been largely exhausted. It is important to note that the whalebone used in carvings is not the same 'whalebone' of whaling literature. Whalers referred to the long and valuable strips of baleen from the mouth of the bowhead as whalebone; the whalebone used by artists is actual bone, usually of the bowhead's vertebrae or skull, cream-colored and very porous. Carvings can be purchased in the Uqqurmiut Centre. Many artists also visit the hotel during mealtimes to sell their wares; this is a time for barter or shrewd bargaining.

Three stores sell groceries in Pangnirtung: the **Northern store**, **Pangnirtung Inuit Co-op**, and **High Arctic Enterprises**. Basic foodstuffs are always available, but the vagaries of plane schedules determine whether fresh, imported items like milk, eggs, bread, fruit and vegetables are in stock. The Northern also runs a small **convenience store** in the east section of the community.

Accommodation and Dining

There's only one hotel in town. **Auyuittuq Lodge** is in the downtown area of Pangnirtung, a stone's throw from the fiord. Its lounge provides a spectacular view of surrounding peaks, the tidal flats and the comings and goings of local hunters and fishermen. The lodge has 44 beds in 22 double rooms. Count on sharing your room with another guest in the peak summer season. None of the rooms have private baths, but there are central washrooms on each floor. The room rate is $120 per person per night without meals. With the meal plan, the cost per night is $185. Meals are $15 for breakfast, $20 for lunch, and $30 for supper.

The menu is fixed. If you have any food prohibitions or allergies, advise the manager well in advance of meal time. Meal times are well posted. If you plan on skipping a meal, advise the manager in advance or you will be charged for it. With advance notice, the staff can prepare box lunches for hikers. If you are not a guest in the lodge, make a reservation if you wish to dine at the hotel.

At Auyuittuq Lodge you will rub shoulders with construction workers, prospectors, accountants, engineers, people on meetings and courses, and many others — a random sampling of those who make the northern economy tick. The lodge is almost entirely Inuit staffed. Auyuittuq Lodge is one of few hotels in Nunavut offering separate lounges for smokers and non-smokers. The lodge offers group rates.

Campers can stay in the Pisuktinu Tungavik Territorial Campground on a raised area just above the beach past the Duval River. There is no charge to use the campground, which is open from June until September. Services are minimal. There is no shower, and many trekkers use the washroom facilities at Auyuittuq Lodge for a small fee. High winds can rise spontaneously in Pangnirtung at any time of the year, so campers should have very strong tents. Be careful not to leave any valuables unattended at the camp site, or even outside your tent while you sleep at night. Like many northern communities, Pangnirtung has a great deal of petty theft and vandalism, a result of the high unemployment and unrealizable expectations of today's youth.

Fast food has recently come to Pangnirtung. The Northern store's **Quick-Stop** offers selected items from Pizza Hut and Kentucky Fried Chicken as well as other snacks, but no burgers or sandwiches.

Services

The Pangnirtung **Health Centre**, next to the Northern, operates a medical clinic from 9 a.m. to 12 p.m. weekdays. Public health sessions run from 1 to 5 p.m. Emergencies are handled as necessary. There is also a **dental clinic** in town, as well as an **RCMP** detachment.

Pangnirtung is currently served by three airlines. **First Air** has served the community the longest and with the most reliability. **Air Nunavut** and **Kenn Borek Air** also provide passenger and freight service. They are all based in Iqaluit. Depending on the day of the week, their schedules may allow connections from Pangnirtung and Broughton Island.

DIRECTORY

The 819 and 403 area codes change to 867 on Oct. 21, 1997.

Accommodation and Dining

Auyuittuq Lodge
VISA, MasterCard, Diners Club/enRoute.
Tel.: (819) 473-8955
Fax: (819) 473-8611

Outfitters/Guides/Tour Operators

Alivaktuk Outfitting Services
Tel.: (819) 473-8721
Fax: (819) 473-8721

Angmarlik Interpretive Centre
For outfitter information.
9 a.m.–5:30 p.m., Monday to Friday.
Tel.: (819) 473-8737
Fax: (819) 473-8685

Arctic Odysseys
Tel.: (206) 325-1977
Fax: (206) 726-8488
E-mail: arctic4u@aol.com

Services

Airport
Tel.: (819) 473-8907/8746

Church

St. Luke's Anglican Church
Services at 9:30 a.m., Sunday (English); 11 a.m., 6:30 p.m., Sunday (Inuktitut).
Tel.: (819) 473-8014
Fax: (819) 473-8383

Hamlet Office
Tel.: (819) 473-8953
Fax: (819) 473-8832

Health Centre (and dental clinic)
Tel.: (819) 473-8977
Fax: (819) 473-8519

Parks Canada Interpretive Centre, and Parks Canada
Tel.: (819) 473-8828
Fax: (819) 473-8612
E-mail: nunavut_info@pch.gc.ca

Police (RCMP)
Tel.: (819) 473-8833
Fax: (819) 473-8915

Post Office
In former hamlet office.
Tel.: (819) 473-8940

Radio Station (FM 105.1)
Tel.: (819) 473-8975

School

Nunavut Arctic College
Tel.: (819) 473-8923

Taxi

Tiriaq Taxi
Tel.: (819) 473-8050
Fax: (819) 473-8305

Weather Office
Tel.: (819) 473-8907

Stores

Convenience Store
Tel.: (819) 473-8306

High Arctic Enterprises
10 a.m.–12:30 p.m., 2–6 p.m., 7–10 p.m., Monday to Friday; 2–6 p.m., 7–10 p.m., Saturday. Closed Sunday.
VISA, MasterCard, Interac.
Tel.: (819) 473-8648
Fax: (819) 473-8993

J. R. Peyton Enterprises
10 a.m.–12 p.m., Monday and Thursday; 1–6 p.m., Tuesday and Wednesday; 1–6 p.m., and 7–9 p.m., Friday; 1–5 p.m., Saturday.
VISA, Interac.
Tel.: (819) 473-8896
Fax: (819) 473-8924

Northern Store
10 a.m.–6 p.m., Monday to Thursday; 10 a.m.–8 p.m., Friday; 10 a.m.–6 p.m., Saturday. Closed Sunday.
VISA, MasterCard, Interac.
Tel.: (819) 473-8935
Fax: (819) 473-8610

Pangnirtung Inuit Co-op
10 a.m.–10 p.m., Monday to Friday; 1–10 p.m., Saturday; 1–5 p.m., Sunday.
VISA accepted.
Tel.: (819) 473-8936
Fax: (819) 473-8657

Quick-Stop
10 a.m.–9 p.m., Monday to Saturday; 1–7 p.m., Sunday.
Tel.: (819) 473-8026
Fax: (819) 473-8610

Uqqurmiut Centre for Arts and Crafts
9 a.m.–5 p.m., Monday to Friday; Saturday by appointment.
VISA, MasterCard, Interac.
Tel.: (819) 473-8870
Fax: (819) 473-8634
E-mail: inuitart@nunanet.com
Web site: www.uqqurmiut.com

BROUGHTON ISLAND

by Don Pickle

Frequently called "the iceberg capital of the North," Broughton Island sits off the coast of Baffin Island some 96 kilometres north of the Arctic Circle.

Population:	488 (Inuit: 95%, non-Inuit: 5%)
Telephone Area Code:	819 (changes to 867 on Oct. 21, 1997)
Time Zone:	Eastern Time
Postal Code:	X0A 0B0
How to Get There:	Possible routes: • Ottawa/Montreal-Iqaluit-Broughton Island • Winnipeg-Rankin Inlet-Iqaluit-Broughton Island • Yellowknife-Rankin Inlet-Iqaluit-Broughton Island • Kangerlussuaq (Greenland)-Iqaluit-Broughton Island Iqaluit to Broughton Island (470 kilometres northeast) is via First Air or Air Nunavut
Banks:	None. Cash and traveller's cheques are preferable
Alcohol:	Alcohol and alcoholic beverages cannot be purchased in Broughton Island. Visitors who want to bring alcohol into Broughton Island must first obtain a permit from the community's **Alcohol and Drug Education Committee**
Taxis:	No

Though only approximately 16 kilometres long and 12 kilometres wide, its Inuktitut name — *Qikiqtarjuaq* — means "Big Island."

Hunting and fishing are still important parts of daily life here, and families will often spend much of their time "on the land" during spring and summer. Inuktitut is the language of choice in Broughton Island, although an increasing number of people speak English. Children are taught in Inuktitut until Grade 4, when some English instruction begins.

History

The area around Broughton Island may have been inhabited as many as 4,000 years ago. Approximately 1,000 years ago, people of the Thule culture entered the region from northern Alaska. Today's Inuit — including those in Broughton Island — are direct descendants of the Thule. Evidence of this culture around Broughton Island dates back almost 800 years and can be seen at a Thule camp site approximately 90 minutes from town by boat.

John Davis was the first European to explore the area; he named nearby Cumberland Peninsula in 1585. Kivitoo, about 60 kilometres northwest of Broughton Island, and Padloping Island, roughly 90 kilometres to the south, soon became important stops for bowhead whalers. Kivitoo was abandoned in the mid-'20s, although the iron vats used for rendering whale blubber were left behind. These relics, as well as a small graveyard, can still be seen today.

In 1955, construction began on a DEW Line site at Broughton Island, attracting Inuit from Clyde River, Pangnirtung, Kivitoo, and Padloping Island, who came to Broughton in search of employment. The site became fully operational in 1957; a Hudson's Bay Co. store was established three years later. By 1968, the federal government's Department of Indian Affairs and Northern Development had relocated residents from Kivitoo and Padloping Island to Broughton Island. On Aug. 31, 1979, Broughton Island obtained hamlet status.

Broughton Island: Its Land and Wildlife

Scores of oddly shaped icebergs can usually be found in the waters around Broughton Island, hence the community's nickname. Outfitters will take visitors on snowmobile and boat trips to see icebergs. If travelling by boat, exercise extreme caution around these behemoths, as they are always shifting and breaking apart. Don't ask your guide to get dangerously close to an iceberg, since they can unexpectedly flip, smashing your boat to splinters.

The island and the surrounding area are also home to spectacular land forms and wildlife. Nearby lies the massive Penny Ice Cap, the largest ice cap on Baffin Island, and the many glaciers it has sired. Waters abound with walruses, polar bears, seals, narwhals, belugas, and even occasional bowhead whales.

The area is also home to a bounty of birds. In fact, discussions are taking place regarding the development of a bird sanctuary at Cape Searle and Reid Bay, the largest fulmar-nesting area in the eastern Arctic.

Tours

There are a number of good hiking trails on Broughton Island. Information can be obtained from the economic development officer with the GNWT's Department of **Resources, Wildlife and Economic Development**, or the manager of the Tulugak Co-op. Be sure to file your intended route and expected return time with someone in the community before heading out on the land. You should also check with the renewable resources officer about the proximity of polar bears, which frequent the area in summer and autumn.

The primary tourist seasons are spring and summer. Guided trips by boat, dogteam, or snowmobile can take you along the Baffin Island coast. Snowmobile and dogteam trips are possible from January through July; boat travel starts in August and continues through November. Visitors may also ski or backpack in **Auyuittuq National Park Reserve**.

Shopping

Traditionally, whalebone carving was most common in this area, but contemporary carvers primarily use stone and ivory. Although carving is not as predominant as it once was, there are still noted artists in Broughton Island. Local crafts and carvings are available from the **Sijjamiut store** or **Minnguq Sewing Group**. The sewing group is renowned for its excellence in traditional sealskin and caribou-skin clothing. Artisans there specialize in sealskin boots (*kamiit*), pants and parkas. You can also ask the economic development officer to assist you in contacting local artists.

Groceries are available from the **Northern store**, but selection is seasonal and availability is dependent upon flight service.

Accommodation and Dining

There are two hotels and one hostel in Broughton Island. The **Tulugak Co-op Hotel** is a 10-room, 20-bed hotel with private bath and cable TV in each room. Its cafeteria-style restaurant has a set menu, although requests for traditional foods and special diets will be accommodated, with sufficient notice. The cost is $185 per person per night, including meals, and $120 per person per night without meals. Visitors not staying at the hotel can still dine there, but they must give ample notice.

The **Siku Hotel**, with eight beds in four rooms, is adjacent to the main river on Broughton Island, allowing for a babbling-brook atmosphere in spring. You can cook your own meals in the kitchen or eat at the Tulugak Co-op Hotel. The cost is $100 per person per night, or if you choose to prepare three meals daily in their kitchen, it's $120.

The **hostel** has 10 beds in an old Quonset hut (a prefabricated metal shelter like a half-cylinder on its flat side) with a wood stove and no running water. It costs $20 per person per night.

There is also a campground outside town, overlooking the community. Here you'll find tent platforms, an outhouse, drinking water, and little else. The campground is free, but rapid weather changes and polar bears sometimes make you wish you'd paid to stay elsewhere.

Services

Broughton Island's **health centre** is staffed by two registered nurses. Walk-in service is available Monday to Friday from 8:30 to 11:30 a.m. In the afternoons (between 1 and 4:30 p.m.), visitors must first make an appointment. Emergency service is always available. There is also a local **RCMP** detachment.

DIRECTORY

The 403 and 819 area codes change to 867 on Oct. 21, 1997.

Accommodation

Siku Hotel
Tel.: (819) 927-8111 or (819) 927-8112

Tulugak Co-op Hotel
VISA, Diners Club/enRoute.
Tel.: (819) 927-8874 or (819) 927-8833
Fax: (819) 927-8124

Tuniq Shelter
Hostel. Traveller's cheques, Interac.
Tel.: (819) 927-8390
Fax: (819) 927-8404
E-mail: icebound@nunanet.com

Outfitters/Guides/Tour Operators

Auyuittuq National Park Reserve
Warden.
Tel.: (819) 927-8834
Fax: (819) 927-8454

Iceberg Outfitting
Ask for Stevie Audlakiak.
Tel.: (819) 927-8459
Fax: (819) 927-8296

Nauyak Outfitting
Ask for Allan Kooneeliusie.
Tel.: (819) 927-8427
Fax: (819) 927-8120

Pikaluyak Outfitting
Ask for Pauloosie Kooneeliusie.
Tel.: (819) 927-8390
Fax: (819) 927-8404
E-mail: icebound@nunanet.com

Services

Airport
Tel.: (819) 927-8873

Alcohol and Drug Education Committee
Tel.: (819) 927-8428
Fax: (819) 927-8120

Churches

Katisivik Full Gospel Church
Services: 11 a.m. and 7 p.m., Sunday; 7:30 p.m., Wednesday.
Tel.: (819) 927-8852
Fax: (819) 927-8344

St. Michaels and All Angels Anglican Church
Services: 11 a.m. and 6:30 p.m., Sunday.
No telephone number available.

Hamlet Office
Tel.: (819) 927-8832
Fax: (819) 927-8120

Health Centre
Tel.: (819) 927-8916
Fax: (819) 927-8217

Police (RCMP)
Tel.: (819) 927-8967
Fax: (819) 927-8309

Post Office
In hamlet building.
No telephone.

Radio Station (FM 107.1)
Tel.: (819) 927-8971 or (819) 927-8855

Resources, Wildlife and Economic Development
Ask for the economic development officer or the renewable resources officer.
Tel.: (819) 927-8832
Fax: (819) 927-8120
E-mail: pickle@nunanet.com

Schools

Inuksuit School
Tel.: (819) 927-8938
Fax: (819) 927-8067

Nunavut Arctic College
Tel.: (819) 927-8847
Fax: (819) 927-8219

Weather Office
Tel.: (819) 927-8792

Shopping

Minnguq Sewing Group
Shop opens according to customers' needs. Call to set up an appointment.
Tel.: (819) 927-8885
Fax: (819) 927-8318

Northern Store
10 a.m.–noon, 1–6:30 p.m., Monday to Friday; 1–6:30 p.m., Saturday. Closed Sunday. VISA, Interac.
Tel.: (819) 927-8917
Fax: (819) 927-8070

Sijjamiut Store
6–10 p.m., Monday to Friday; 1–10 p.m., Saturday. Closed Sunday. Cash only.
Tel.: (819) 927-8102
Fax: (819) 927-8019

IQALUIT

by Alootook Ipellie and Carol Rigby

If Mexico City is the largest metropolis on Earth, then Iqaluit easily gets the same designation within the new territory of Nunavut.

Population:	4,220 (Inuit: 62%, non-Inuit: 38%)
Telephone Area Code:	819 (changes to 867 on Oct. 21, 1997)
Time Zone:	Eastern Time
Postal Code:	X0A 0H0
How to Get There:	Possible routes:
	• Ottawa/Montreal-Iqaluit
	• Winnipeg-Rankin Inlet-Iqaluit
	• Yellowknife-Rankin Inlet-Iqaluit
	• Kangerlussuaq (Greenland)-Iqaluit
	Ottawa to Iqaluit and Montreal to Iqaluit (both about 2,100 kilometres north) are via First Air, which also serves the Greenland route.
	Rankin Inlet to Iqaluit (about 1,200 kilometres east) is via Air Canada, Canadian Airlines, or First Air
Banks:	Yes — the Royal Bank of Canada and the Bank of Montreal
Alcohol:	Alcohol and alcoholic beverages cannot be purchased in Iqaluit, although licensed restaurants, bars and private clubs serve alcohol. Visitors who want to bring alcohol into the community must first obtain a permit from the **NWT Liquor Commission** in Iqaluit
Taxis:	Yes

When you arrive at the bustling Iqaluit Airport, you might feel as though you've entered a frontier town. In several ways, you have. Iqaluit is the transportation hub to other Baffin Island communities, as well as to Greenland. And in December 1995, it was selected in a Nunavut-wide plebiscite to be the capital of the new central and eastern Arctic territory. That historic day arrives on April 1, 1999.

The main portion of Iqaluit (pronounced "ee-kal-a-wheat") overlooks Koojesse Inlet, which has some of the country's longest stretches of exposed area at low tide. At one time, these beaches were dotted with clusters of Inuit huts. Later, as modern houses, shops and public buildings were constructed, this little village grew to reflect its increasing population and impending importance as a government town. A decentralized government that will add jobs to almost half of all Nunavut communities is expected to bring almost 100 jobs to Iqaluit alone, and private enterprises built around this public sector growth are burgeoning as well. Iqaluit's population too is a mix: a mix of cultures (only about two-thirds of residents here are Inuit, compared to other communities that are more than 90 per cent Inuit) and

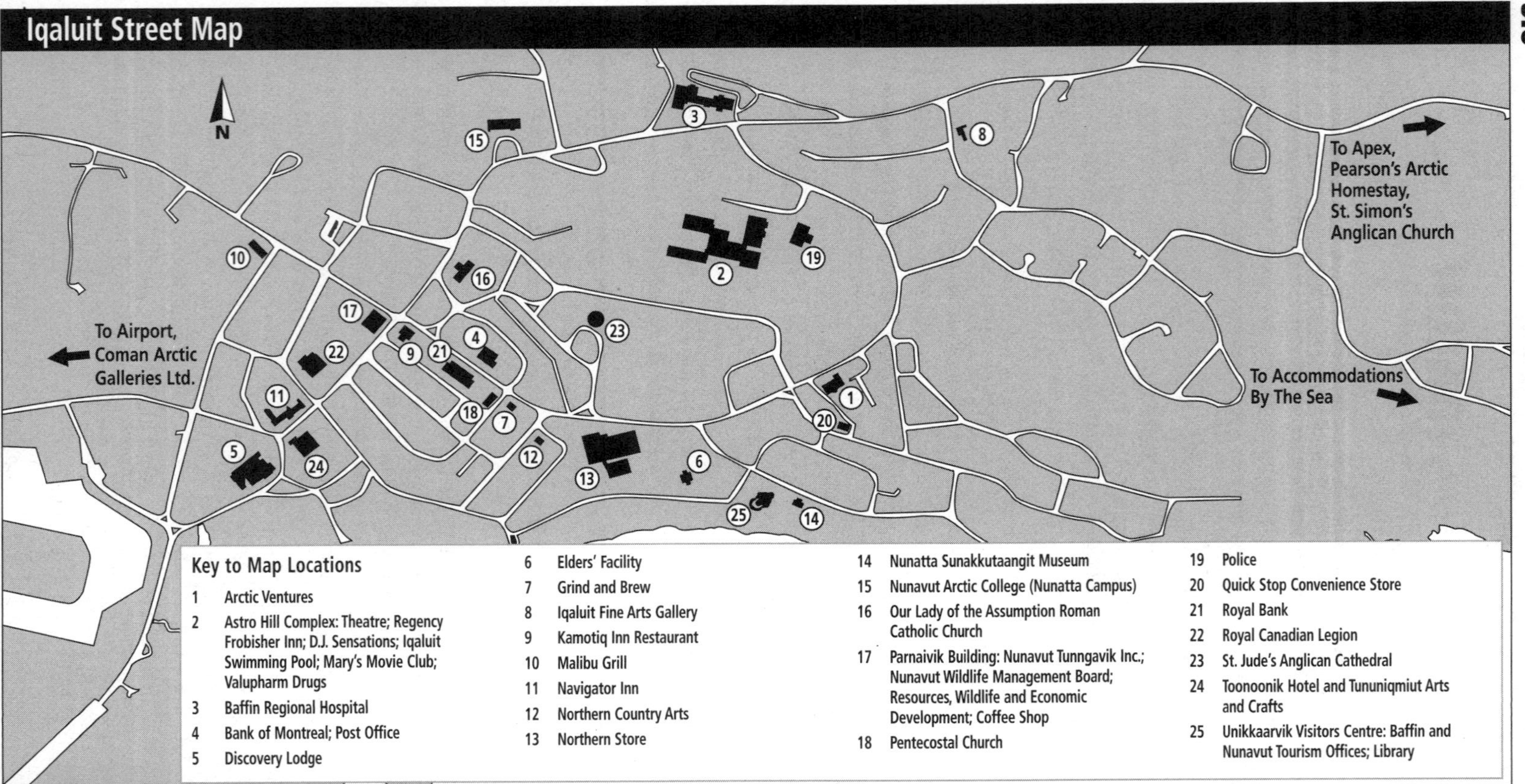
Iqaluit Street Map
N
To Airport, Coman Arctic Galleries Ltd.
To Apex, Pearson's Arctic Homestay, St. Simon's Anglican Church
To Accommodations By The Sea
1
2
3
4
5
6
7
8
9
10
11
12
13
14
15
16
17
18
19
20
21
22
23
24
25
Key to Map Locations
1 Arctic Ventures
2 Astro Hill Complex: Theatre; Regency Frobisher Inn; D.J. Sensations; Iqaluit Swimming Pool; Mary's Movie Club; Valupharm Drugs
3 Baffin Regional Hospital
4 Bank of Montreal; Post Office
5 Discovery Lodge
6 Elders' Facility
7 Grind and Brew
8 Iqaluit Fine Arts Gallery
9 Kamotiq Inn Restaurant
10 Malibu Grill
11 Navigator Inn
12 Northern Country Arts
13 Northern Store
14 Nunatta Sunakkutaangit Museum
15 Nunavut Arctic College (Nunatta Campus)
16 Our Lady of the Assumption Roman Catholic Church
17 Parnaivik Building: Nunavut Tunngavik Inc.; Nunavut Wildlife Management Board; Resources, Wildlife and Economic Development; Coffee Shop
18 Pentecostal Church
19 Police
20 Quick Stop Convenience Store
21 Royal Bank
22 Royal Canadian Legion
23 St. Jude's Anglican Cathedral
24 Toonoonik Hotel and Tununiqmiut Arts and Crafts
25 Unikkaarvik Visitors Centre: Baffin and Nunavut Tourism Offices; Library

languages. Iqaluit, due north of the province of Quebec, is also home to about 400 francophones and a French-language radio station.

The United States (US) airbase to the north of town used to be separate from the main village, with a road linking the two sites. What was once wide open country is now one large urban development. About eight kilometres to the south lies the small suburb of *Niaqunngut*, or Apex as it's officially called. Built by the Canadian government as a model community in 1955, it used to be the main centre of activity, with a public school, nursing station, community and fire hall. The Hudson's Bay Co. store and warehouses were also built nearby.

History

Thousands of years ago, when Iqaluit, like the rest of the Arctic, was still uncharted wilderness, the ancient explorers of the Dorset and Thule cultures hunted and camped on this pure and silent land. The lands and waters here were prime hunting and fishing grounds; local vegetation provided edible plants and berries in season. These nomadic hunters would remain as long as there was game, then move on to other areas where animals were more plentiful.

In 1942, during the Second World War, the US Air Force, with the blessing of the Canadian government, selected Iqaluit as an ideal site to build an airstrip. It was to be long enough to handle large aircraft transporting war materials from the United States to its European allies. During this time, many Inuit from surrounding hunting camps were recruited to help construct the airstrip, aircraft hangars and related buildings.

These hunters and their families had no choice but to begin building year-round huts on the beaches of Koojesse Inlet, using wood discarded from the airbase and the local dump. The Inuit referred to the little village that grew here as Iqaluit, meaning "a school of fish." Fish, especially arctic char, abound here in spring and summer, after their swim down the Sylvia Grinnell River, two kilometres west of the village. They reappear in droves in autumn, when it's time for them to swim back up to Sylvia Grinnell Lake for the winter.

Before long, the village — together with the airbase and Apex Hill (its previous name) — appeared on official government maps as Frobisher Bay. And this is how it came to be known to the outside world. The name was in honor of Martin Frobisher, the English sailor who "discovered" the bay in 1576 while searching with his crew for the Northwest Passage to the Orient. Frobisher made three voyages to the bay, mainly to mine black ore from Kabloona ("White Man") Island at the mouth of the bay. Frobisher believed the island contained gold. Several skirmishes with local Inuit ensued; in one incident, Inuit took five of Frobisher's men hostage. They were never heard from again. In other instances, Frobisher captured four Inuit whom he took back with him to England, presumably to display to the Royal Family and to the curious English public. The Inuit did not live long in that strange land.

In another clash with Inuit, Frobisher was stabbed in the buttocks by an arrow, earning him the dubious distinction of being the first Englishman known to have been wounded by an Inuk. As for the precious ore he and his men carried to England, it turned out to be fool's gold! Thus ended

Frobisher's quest for polar gold and his explorations of the lands and waters beyond the bay that later bore his name.

In the 18th and 19th centuries, other explorers and whalers from Europe and later, North America, embarked on similar northern expeditions. The impact of western culture intensified in south Baffin Island when missionaries arrived, spreading the Christian religion that would replace centuries-old Inuit shamanistic rituals and beliefs.

Like other Inuit communities throughout the North, Iqaluit couldn't escape westernization of its traditional culture and heritage. The Hudson's Bay Co. trading post, for example, moved to Iqaluit in 1950 from Ward Inlet, almost 50 kilometres south on the north coast of Frobisher Bay. In 1955, activity further escalated when supplies and workers arrived in Iqaluit as construction of the eastern section of the DEW Line began. By 1957, Iqaluit had a population of approximately 1,200, of whom 489 were Inuit.

The United States turned over its airbase to the Royal Canadian Air Force after the Second World War. By 1963, the Americans had gone, and Iqaluit was to become the Canadian government administration, communications and transportation centre for the Eastern Arctic. This coincided with Canada's efforts, during these Cold War years, to claim sovereignty in the Canadian North.

Since its early days as a village, Iqaluit has been home to many strong Inuit leaders. Simonie Michael is one who comes to mind. A carpenter by trade, Simonie became chairman of the Sisi Housing Co-op in Apex Hill. In that position, he was one of the first community leaders to make decisions affecting both Inuit and Euro-Canadians. By the mid-1960s, he became president of Inook Ltd., the first Inuit-owned company in Iqaluit and in Canada. Simonie was also president of the Frobisher Community Council and a member of the St. Simon's Anglican Church Council.

Abraham "Abe" Okpik, a MacKenzie Delta Inuk who became chairman of the Apex Hill Community Association in 1963, was the first Inuk to be appointed to the GNWT, at a time when the federal government alone chose representatives for that assembly. He also served, in 1979, as the head of Project Surname, a plan that required all Inuit families to select a surname to replace the disk-numbers previously assigned to them as identification by the federal government.

Another able leader was Simonie Alainga, an inspirational hunting and traditional games instructor to many young Inuit. Simonie was the thread connecting many Inuit community dwellers to the land and to their hunting traditions. In the early 1960s, he was among the first to encourage those having difficulty with community life to return to the land if they chose. His memory has endured as a comfort to Inuit caught in the clash between western and traditional values.

Anakudluk was another traditionalist who became a lay reader in the Anglican ministry. He was always a source of great spiritual strength to a community in transition. Arnitook Ipeelie, too, became a lay reader and was among the first Inuit to teach youngsters to read and write Inuktitut syllabics. He was a respected orator and a powerful singer, as well.

Inutsiaq was one of the first of Iqaluit's leaders to organize Inuit games during festive seasons. A deeply spiritual man, he was a wonderful storyteller who often told his tales over the radio. He was also famous for his childbirth carvings, sought by collectors from across Canada and abroad.

Then there are Iqaluit's eccentric Euro-Canadians! Scotsman Bill MacKenzie, a long-time resident who came here as a Hudson's Bay Co. clerk, will always be remembered as the first, and perhaps last, farmer in the eastern Arctic. Former mayor and GNWT Legislative Assembly member Bryan Pearson, whom Inuit know as "Sudluq," the skinny one, is the Brit who could be pretender to Frobisher's fame in these parts. If you want to hear a good yarn about Iqaluit in the early days, "Sudluq" is your man!

Another respected resident is Gordon Rennie, the smiling, long-time manager of the Northern store, who's fluent in Inuktitut. Fred Coman, too, as an art dealer and businessman, has contributed much to the community through his entrepreneurship and volunteer work over many years.

Iqaluit: Its Land and Wildlife

In summer, you can follow a well-worn foot trail from Iqaluit along the water's edge to Niaqunngut, where you can enjoy the region's many delicate plants and flowers. You're also likely to discover an *inuksuk* or two — those legendary stone markers that Inuit traditionally built as landmarks on many parts of the tundra. Some *inuksuit* were built to resemble humans, to help hunters lead caribou into lakes where they could be more easily killed from a kayak. You'll probably see the enigmatic black scavenger bird of the North, the raven. If you're hiking in mid-summer, be sure to bring mosquito repellent or appropriate protective gear, to avoid being stung by blood-thirsty arctic "vampires"!

The majestic landscape around Iqaluit and Apex is a major feature of the area. You can take a short hike out of town to get to the tundra or head towards Sylvia Grinnell Territorial Park on the banks of the Sylvia Grinnell River. A government-operated camp site here provides picnic tables, enclosed outdoor toilets, a foul-weather shelter and garbage receptacles. If you wish to camp, you're best to do so here, unless you have connections in town who can suggest other camp sites. You can also arrange a visit with a licensed local outfitter to nearby Qaummaarviit Historic Park. Licensed outfitters in Iqaluit include: **Eetuk Outfitting**, **NorthWinds Arctic Adventures**, **Purlaavik Outfitting**, and **Qairrulik Outfitting Ltd**.

Iqaluit's **Unikkaarvik Visitors Centre**, located on the beach between the Pairijait Tigumivik Elders' Facility and the Nunatta Sunakkutaangit Museum, provides brochures describing day hikes in the vicinity of town. Recent building development in some areas, however, has caused a few trails to disappear — such as the one along the shoreline to Apex. When you do leave the beaten path, you'll discover a wide variety of lovely arctic wildflowers. They're at their best in July.

Tours

Essential early stops for any visitor to Iqaluit or to the Baffin Region should be at the Visitors Centre and the museum, conveniently located side-by-side on Iqaluit's beachfront.

The **Nunatta Sunakkutaangit Museum**, housed in a renovated Hudson's Bay Co. trading post building, is a compact but excellent museum whose permanent collection of artifacts relates to the history of south Baffin Island. It also maintains temporary displays of artwork.

Next door is the Unikkaarvik Visitors Centre and the offices of **Nunavut Tourism**, as well as the Iqaluit Centennial Library. The Visitors Centre displays spectacular artwork, including a life-size marble carving of a drum dancer crafted by Inuit carvers under the watchful eye of renowned Canadian sculptor George Pratt.

At the **Iqaluit Centennial Library**, visitors will discover the Thomas Manning collection of polar books, the personal collection of respected biologist Thomas Manning.

Located on the beachfront, the **Pairijait Tigumivik Elders' Facility** was designed to convey the feeling of a traditional *qamṃaq*, or sod hut. As it's really for elders whose enjoyment may be spoiled by too many visitors, call first to arrange an appropriate time to visit. When you go, take an interpreter with you, as most elders speak little or no English.

To see a real qammaq, visit Apex. Here you'll find a traditional sod hut used by local women for social gatherings, traditional sewing, and other activities. Alicee Joamie is the contact at this **Elders' Facility**. As she speaks Inuktitut only, you're best to call the **Town of Iqaluit's recreation department** to arrange a visit.

Shopping

Iqaluit, like many of Nunavut's communities, is paradise for lovers of art and fine crafts. Among the stone carvings by local Inuit artists, you'll see depictions of arctic animals, some in dancing postures, as well as human and legendary heads and figures. The sculpture is generally realistic, and always well-finished. The stone, an even-textured grey-green stone and a brighter green stone that has the look of marble, is the same as that used by artists in Kimmirut and Cape Dorset. Miniature carvings in antler and ivory are also available.

In addition to the arts and crafts displayed in the museum, you'll find several commercial art outlets that sell graphics, paintings and other crafts. The following dealers have reputations for carrying quality artwork: Arctic Ventures, **Coman Arctic Galleries Ltd.**, **Iqaluit Fine Arts Gallery**, **Northern Country Arts**, and **Tununiqmiut Arts and Crafts**. Try to shop around to compare prices. Some stores, like **Arctic Ventures** and **D.J. Sensations**, both located in the Brown Building, sell jewelry made from traditional materials, silver and other metals, plus small carvings. Here you may also find hand-sewn, knitted, and crocheted crafts such as duffel socks and tuques, and seal or caribou skin mitts and boots. The **Arts and Crafts Centre**, located in Nunavut Arctic College, displays artwork from the Baffin Region; although it doesn't sell to the public, it will refer you to local galleries that do. Of the non-Inuit artists who work in Iqaluit, some have gallery or display space in their homes. Contact the Unikkaarvik Visitors Centre for further information.

Events

Since 1964, Iqaluit residents have celebrated the coming of spring with their annual Toonik Tyme festival, held for a week sometime in the last two weeks of April. The festival attracts tourists from around the world who come to enjoy Inuit traditional games, snowmobile and dogteam races, entertainment and community feasts. Since it's organized each year by a volunteer committee, it's wise to confirm in advance the dates of festivities.

The festival is named after the *Tuniit*, those people whom legend claims were living in the land that's now Greenland and the eastern Canadian Arctic when ancestors of today's Inuit arrived from the West about 1,000 years ago. Many archeologists think the Tuniit were people of the so-called Dorset culture. Inuit stories describe their almost superhuman strength and stamina. Legends also say the Tuniit slept with their feet above their heads to make them better runners! Around Iqaluit, some elders believe that ghosts of the Tuniit can still be seen, dressed in caribou skins, moving across the hills near the community in spring.

Traditional Inuit games are one of the festival's biggest attractions. Local residents look forward to the fishing and hunting contests, while tourists gather to watch igloo-building, bannock-making and harpoon-throwing competitions. The snowmobile, which has largely replaced the dogsled, is featured in the annual heart-stopping hill climb and in the long-distance race to the community of Kimmirut and back, run every few years. In 1990, Johnny Mikijuk set a new record for the 156.9-kilometre round-trip, completing it in four hours and 17 minutes. An Iqaluit town councillor, Jimmy "Flash" Kilabuk, won his nickname from his record-breaking time in that race a few years earlier. Evenings at the festival feature indoor entertainment — dances, talent shows and concerts.

Temperatures during Toonik Tyme generally range from –20° C to –10° C. Daylight in late April is beginning to stretch into the evening and the sky is usually sunny and bright. It's still parka and boot weather, though, and visitors are advised to bring warm clothing. Sunglasses, sunscreen and lotion for dry skin are also recommended. Unusually warm weather or spring blizzards can wreak havoc with scheduled events; they may cause festivities to be cancelled! If possible, events are usually rescheduled. Everything in the North depends on the weather, so try to be flexible.

Accommodation

Iqaluit offers visitors more choice in accommodation than anywhere else in Nunavut. Depending on your preference and budget, you can choose from full-service hotels, bed and breakfasts (known as "tourist homes" in Nunavut), or the local campground. Unlike other communities in Nunavut, it's almost unheard-of in Iqaluit to share hotel rooms with strangers.

Book ahead, as rooms may be hard to find during busy summer months. Many lodges and hotels cater primarily to summer construction crews, so tourist accommodation isn't always a high priority.

The **Regency Frobisher Inn**, located in the Astro Hill Mall, is a 50-room hotel offering single and double occupancy. It accommodates at least 150 people. Rooms have private bath, telephone and cable TV. Suites are available, as are laundry and room service. They'll also freeze fish caught by anglers staying at the hotel. There is a licensed dining room, banquet room and cocktail lounge, as well as conference facilities for up to 60 people. The room price doesn't include meals. Airport pickup is available on request. Rates per night are: regular — $160 to $170; corporate and tours — $140 to $150; government — $130 to $140.

The **Discovery Lodge**, renovated in 1993, is a 37-room facility that accommodates at least 61 people. Single, double and executive-suite occupancy are available. All rooms have double beds, private bath, cable TV, radio and direct-dial telephone. A fax machine is provided for guests, as well as laundry service and complimentary airport shuttle service. The lodge has a restaurant, but meals aren't included in the room rate ($170 per night, or $140 with a corporate discount). The hotel is close to the airport.

The **Navigator Inn**, near the airport, accommodates 51 people in 35 rooms. Rooms are equipped with private bath, cable TV, radio and modem-ready telephone. The hotel has conference and translation facilities for up to 125 people, and provides a fax machine, photocopier, and access to e-mail and the Internet. It also has a banquet hall, licensed lounge and dining room, a coffee shop and food take-out service. Rates per night are $139 for single, and $154 for double rooms. The room price doesn't include meals.

The **Toonoonik Hotel** is an 18-room, full-service hotel that accommodates up to 35 people. It's recently undergone renovations to its licensed dining room. All rooms have private baths, cable TV and telephone; laundry facilities are also available. Single rooms are $99.95, doubles are $124.95. Meals are not included. The hotel is located between the tip of Koojesse Inlet and the airport.

Pearson's Arctic Homestay, located on the road to Apex, is owned and operated by Iqaluit's former mayor, Bryan Pearson. Arctic Homestay can accommodate up to six people. Rates are $100 per person per night, including breakfast. Special rates are offered for families and cots are available for children. A shuttle service is available.

Accommodations By The Sea is a six-bedroom facility located in the new Tundra Valley subdivision in Iqaluit. The bathroom facilities are shared. There is phone and cable TV service. Use of kitchen and laundry facilities can be arranged, as can an optional meal service and special group rates. Rates per night (including breakfast) are $95 for single, and $110 for double rooms. Arrangements can also be made to use the facilities for conferences or banquets. A shuttle service to and from the airport is available.

Restaurants

Because of its size, Iqaluit also offers more choice in dining than do other communities. Several Iqaluit establishments offer full-course meals, some including "country food" such as arctic char, caribou, muskox or *maktaaq*. Meals are expensive. A family of four having hamburger platters and drinks — two drinks for the parents — may easily pay $80. Meals at all major hotels and restaurants are of reasonable quality. The cooking can even be excellent, although quality varies according to the staff of the moment. Ask around to find out where the food is best at the time of your visit.

The following dining establishments are also licensed to serve alcoholic beverages.

The recently renovated dining room at the **Toonoonik Hotel**, open from 7 a.m. to 9 p.m., offers lunch and dinner specials, with an emphasis on "country food."

The Discovery Lodge's well-appointed **Granite Room** serves breakfast, lunch and dinner. Menus feature international cuisine, with some arctic foods available. Daily specials and Sunday brunch are also offered. Banquets, weddings and special events can be held here. This is one of the more expensive places to eat in town, but the quality is usually very good. You're advised to make reservations.

The dining room at the **Regency Frobisher Inn** specializes in arctic foods on both its lunch and dinner menus. Northern offerings include arctic char (smoked, poached or grilled), scallops, Greenland shrimp and caribou. Standard North American fare is also available, as is an all-you-can-eat Sunday brunch (11 a.m. to 2 p.m.), and a Monday-to-Friday buffet (11 a.m. to 1:30 p.m.).

The **Kamotiq Inn Restaurant** has two dining rooms: an igloo-shaped dome and a café-style room with the look of a northern patio, right down to the umbrellas. Daily luncheon buffets are available. There is an all-you-can-eat brunch on Sundays. The Kamotiq offers steaks, seafood, arctic cuisine, ribs, and some Mexican dishes.

The dining room at the **Navigator Inn** is a favorite with local residents for its pizza on Friday nights and its all-you-can-eat pizza buffet on Saturday nights. There is also a smorgasbord on Sunday (5 to 9 p.m.). Book ahead on those days. There are separate menus for breakfast and lunch, although the dining room is closed for breakfast and lunch on Sunday. The dinner menu has a wide range, from standard North American fare to arctic specialties like char and caribou. Daily hot and cold specials are offered. Reservations are recommended.

The **Royal Canadian Legion** offers everything from snacks to full-course hot lunches and has a cocktail lounge. You must be a member of the Legion or come as the guest of a member.

The **Malibu Grill** opened for business in 1996. It advertises "a taste of the south up north" and offers such fare as elaborate burgers, giant fries, chicken wings, and Mexican-influenced foods. It's the only restaurant in town where the staff wear shorts and Hawaiian shirts. So far, the potted palms in the lobby seem to be surviving the Iqaluit weather! This is a place to find casual food rather than a fancy dinner.

Several places in town sell snacks and fast food, but like the restaurants, they are expensive compared with their southern counterparts. At **Arctic Ventures** you can pick up sandwiches, drinks or the makings for a picnic. Arctic Ventures also operates a combined snack bar/gift and convenience store at the Iqaluit Airport. **Kanguk** is a convenience store in the **Astro Hill complex**. The **Northern store** has a stand-up coffee shop and snack bar just off its lobby that sells sandwiches, snacks, hamburgers, and the like. The Navigator Inn, in addition to its dining room, has a sit-down coffee shop where you can buy quick snacks to eat there or take out. Open daily, the shop's menu includes breakfast and lunch items.

The Snack offers a large eat-in or take-out menu, including several kinds of pizza, burgers, submarine sandwiches, fried chicken and French-Canadian specialties such as *poutine* — french fries smothered with melted cheese and gravy. The Snack offers a 24-hour free delivery service. The **Quick Stop Convenience** store is Iqaluit's licensed outlet for Pizza Hut and Kentucky Fried Chicken, but with prices that make visitors blanch! They also offer other convenience foods.

The **cafeteria at Nunavut Arctic College** is open during college hours.

The **Grind and Brew** offers freshly brewed specialty coffees and desserts. The coffee shop area is very small, with just a couple of tables, but the coffee is good. There's also a **coffee shop in the Parnaivik Building**.

Campers can pick up groceries at the **Northern** and Arctic Ventures stores.

Entertainment and Recreation

Iqaluit is the only community in the Baffin with a bit of a "night life." Your night on the town may be limited, though, to a meal in a restaurant, a visit to a hotel lounge, a movie, or dancing at the Royal Canadian Legion — if you have visiting privileges or know a member who can sign you in. The new **Astro Hill Theatre**, located in the Astro Hill Complex, offers two first-run movies each week. If you're in the mood for a video and have access to a video cassette recorder (VCR), you can choose from several video rental outlets: **Mary's Movie Club**, **Quick Stop Convenience**, and **Video Shack**, upstairs in the Arctic Ventures main store.

Other sources of entertainment are Friday night bingos, held at varying times and locations to raise funds for service groups, and the occasional concert or dance. Notices for these events are usually posted on bulletin boards in places like the **post office** (located in the same building as the Bank of Montreal), the Visitors Centre, and banks; they're also announced on local radio shows. Although Iqaluit's entertainment may appeal to local citizens more than to visitors, you'll find occasional performances by local artists interesting. Community residents get most excited when southern musical groups such as the Barenaked Ladies come to town!

Recreation facilities in town include a **skating arena** and a **curling rink**, used in the winter. The local **swimming pool** may be closed during summer for repairs, so call ahead if you wish to swim. (Campers will also find showers here.) Several school gymnasiums are often booked by local groups for activities such as badminton, karate, fencing, and indoor soccer. The Town of Iqaluit's department of recreation offers programs at these facilities as well; call for more information. Several clubs and groups also provide a variety of activities such as karate or aquafitness that usually run from September to June. Again, contact the town's recreation department for details. The **Frobisher Racquet Club** has squash and racquet ball courts, a fitness centre, pool tables, darts, shuffleboard, curling facilities, and a licensed bar and restaurant. To use these facilities, you must be signed in by a member.

Services

The **Baffin Regional Hospital** in Iqaluit handles most local health-care needs. For emergency medical attention, patients should get themselves to the hospital if they can. If an ambulance is required, call the emergency phone number and one will be sent. The municipality provides **ambulance service** 24 hours a day. If possible, call ahead and talk to the nurse-in-charge on emergency duty. For non-emergency medical care, contact the outpatient clinic at the hospital to make an appointment.

Although there's no resident eye doctor in Iqaluit, an ophthalmologist visits every three or four months. Inquire at the hospital. You can purchase eyeglasses at **Baffin Optical**, although you'll need to be in town for a week or two as glasses are made up in Yellowknife. The outlet can also make minor repairs for missing screws, bent arms, etc. If staff are dispensing glasses in other Baffin communities, Baffin Optical can be closed on any given week. A notice to this effect is usually posted. The **Iqaluit Dental Clinic** is located in Iqaluit House. The only drugstore on Baffin, **Valupharm Drugs**, is located in the Astro Hill Complex.

St. Jude's Anglican Cathedral, next door to the Nakasuk Elementary School, is an architectural gem. Shaped like an igloo with a spire on top, the church was designed and built by members of the congregation. Inside you'll see beautiful wall hangings behind the altar, depicting Inuit traditional life and church activity. Other unique furnishings include altar rails made from *qamutiit* turned on their sides, a *qamutik* pulpit, sealskin kneeling pads, an altar cross made of narwhal tusks, and a soapstone font dedicated by Queen Elizabeth II. The church is usually open during the day, but if it's closed, inquire at the Anglican mission house. Although there's no charge to see the church, donations are gratefully accepted. St. Jude's holds separate Sunday services in English and Inuktitut.

Services are also offered in Inuktitut at **St. Simon's Church** in Apex. Established more than 30 years ago, it was the first Anglican church in the area, and is typical of churches in the small communities. Services at **Our Lady of the Assumption** Roman Catholic Church are delivered in a combination of English, French and Inuktitut. Iqaluit also has a **Pentecostal Church** and a **Baha'i House**. Consult the community calendar section of the local weekly newspaper, ***Nunatsiaq News***, for up-to-date listings of church schedules and activities.

Among Iqaluit's service groups are the **Elks**, the **Rotary Club** (which offers lunches Wednesdays at noon in the Frobisher Inn), and the **Royal Canadian Legion**. **L'Association francophone d'Iqaluit** (The Iqaluit Francophone Association) offers programs to promote the cultural and social life of Iqaluit's French-speaking residents. The Scouting movement is active here, as are several other community service groups that vary from year to year. Contact the Town of Iqaluit's recreation department for details.

DIRECTORY

The 819 and 403 area codes change to 867 on Oct. 21, 1997.

Accommodation

Accommodations By The Sea
Traveller's cheques accepted.
Tel.: (819) 979-6074/3344 or 979-0219 (leave a message)
Fax: (819) 979-3410
E-mail: BytheSea@VEmail.net

Discovery Lodge
VISA, MasterCard, American Express, Diners Club/enRoute.
Tel.: (819) 979-4433
Fax: (819) 979-6591

Navigator Inn
VISA, MasterCard, American Express, Diners Club/enRoute, Interac.
Tel.: (819) 979-6201
Fax: (819) 979-4296
E-mail: navinn@nunanet.com

Pearson's Arctic Homestay
VISA, traveller's cheques.
Tel./Fax: (819) 979-6408

Regency Frobisher Inn
VISA, MasterCard, American Express, Diners Club/enRoute, Interac.
Tel.: (819) 979-2222
Fax: (819) 979-0427
E-mail: frobinn@nunanet.com

Toonoonik Hotel
VISA, MasterCard, American Express.
Tel.: (819) 979-6733
Fax: (819) 979-4210

Churches and Service Groups

Association francophone d'Iqaluit
Iqaluit Francophone Association.
Tel.: (819) 979-4606
Fax: (819) 979-0800
E-mail: AFI@nunanet.com
Web site: www.nunanet.com/~afi

Churches

Baha'i House
Tel.: (819) 979-6580

Our Lady of the Assumption Roman Catholic Church
Services: 10 a.m., Sunday mass.
Tel./Fax: (819) 979-5805
E-mail: cathmiss@nunanet.com

Pentecostal Church
Services: 11 a.m., 7 p.m., Sunday;
Bible study: 7:30 p.m., Wednesday.
Tel.: (819) 979-5779
E-mail: wmoore@nunanet.com
Web site: www.nunanet.com/~wmoore

St. Jude's Anglican Cathedral
Tel.: (819) 979-5595
E-mail: rbriggs@nunanet.com

St. Simon's Anglican Church (Apex)
No telephone number.

Elks
Tel.: (819) 979-5791

Rotary Club
No telephone number. Luncheons held Wednesday at Regency Frobisher Inn.

Royal Canadian Legion
Tel.: (819) 979-6215

Entertainment and Recreation

Astro Hill Theatre
Tel.: (819) 979-3500

Frobisher Racquet Club
Tel.: (819) 979-0020
Fax: (819) 979-0051

Iqaluit Arena
Tel.: (819) 979-5621

Iqaluit Curling Rink
Tel.: (819) 979-5622

Iqaluit Department of Recreation
Tel.: (819) 979-5600
Fax: (819) 979-3712

Iqaluit Swimming Pool
Tel.: (819) 979-5624

Mary's Movie Club
Tel.: (819) 979-5722
Fax: (819) 979-5757

Video Shack
In Arctic Ventures store, upstairs.
Tel.: (819) 979-1351

Medical Services

Baffin Optical
Tel.: (819) 979-4300

Baffin Regional Hospital
General inquiries:
Tel.: (819) 979-7300

Emergencies:
Tel.: (819) 979-7350

For appointments:
Tel.: (819) 979-7352

Iqaluit Ambulance
Tel.: (819) 979-4422

Iqaluit Dental Clinic
8:30 a.m.–5 p.m., Monday to Friday.
Tel.: (819) 979-4437

Outfitters/Guides/ Tour Operators

Eetuk Outfitting
Tel.: (819) 979-1984
Fax: (819) 979-1994

NorthWinds Arctic Adventures
Tel.: (819) 979-0551
Fax: (819) 979-0551
E-mail: plandry@nunanet.com
Web site: www.nunanet.com/~plandry

Nunavut Tourism
P.O. Box 1450, Iqaluit NT,
X0A 0H0 Canada
Tel.: 1-800-491-7910 (for Canada and the United States)
Tel.: (819) 979-6551
Fax: (819) 979-1261
E-mail: nunatour@nunanet.com
Web site: www.nunatour.nt.ca

Purlaavik Outfitting
Tel.: (819) 979-6094
Fax: (819) 979-4070

Qairrulik Outfitting Ltd.
Tel.: (819) 979-6280
Fax: (819) 979-1950

Unikkaarvik Visitors Centre
Tel.: (819) 979-4636
Fax: (819) 979-1261
E-mail: nunatour@nunanet.com

Restaurants/Snack Bars/Fast Food

Arctic Ventures
Tel.: (819) 979-5992
Fax: (819) 979-4207

Astro Hill Complex
Tel.: (819) 979-4781
Fax: (819) 979-4729

Cafeteria, Nunavut Arctic College
Call in the morning.
Tel.: (819) 979-1260

Discovery Lodge's Granite Room
Tel.: (819) 979-4433

Grind and Brew
Tel.: (819) 979-0606
Fax: (819) 979-7081

Kamotiq Inn Restaurant
VISA, MasterCard, American Express, Diners Club/enRoute.
Tel.: (819) 979-5937
Fax: (819) 979-3098

Kanguk Convenience
Tel.: (819) 979-4781
Fax: (819) 979-4869

Malibu Grill
Tel.: (819) 979-0220

Navigator Inn
Tel.: (819) 979-6201

Parnaivik Coffee Shop
Tel.: (819) 979-2860

Quick Stop Convenience
Tel.: (819) 979-0657 or 979-2961

Regency Frobisher Inn
Tel.: (819) 979-2222

Royal Canadian Legion
Tel.: (819) 979-6215
Fax: (819) 979-4687

The Snack
Tel.: (819) 979-6767

Toonoonik Hotel
Tel.: (819) 979-6733

Services

Airport
Tel.: (819) 979-5046

Baffin Regional Chamber of Commerce
Tel.: (819) 979-4653
Fax: (819) 979-2929

Iqaluit Centennial Library
Tel.: (819) 979-5400

Iqaluit Chamber of Commerce
Tel.: (819) 979-4095
Fax: (819) 979-2929

Iqaluit Town Office
Tel.: (819) 979-5600

Iqaluit Trade and Promotion Office
Tel.: (819) 979-3156
Fax: (819) 979-2929

Nunatsiaq News
Tel.: (819) 979-5357
Fax: (819) 979-4763
E-mail: nunat@nunanet.com
Web site: www.nunanet.com/~nunat

NWT Liquor Commission/ Iqaluit Liquor Warehouse
Tel.: (819) 979-5918
Fax: (819) 979-5836

Police (RCMP)
Tel.: (819) 979-5211
Fax: (819) 979-1842

Post Office
In Iqaluit House.
Tel.: (819) 979-5864
Fax: (819) 979-1842

Radio Station (AM 1230)
Tel.: (819) 979-6100

Schools

Baffin Divisional Board of Education
Tel.: (819) 979-5236

Inuksuk High School
Tel.: (819) 979-5281
Fax: (819) 979-4380

Joamie Ilinniarvik School
Tel.: (819) 979-6206
Fax: (819) 979-0686
Web site: www.nunanet.com/~joamie

Nanook School
Tel.: (819) 979-6597

Nunavut Arctic College
Tel.: (819) 979-4100
Fax: (819) 979-4119

Weather Information
Tel.: (819) 979-6448

Shopping

Arctic Ventures
Main store:
10 a.m.–10 p.m., Monday to Saturday;
1–10 p.m., Sunday.
VISA, MasterCard, Interac.
Tel.: (819) 979-5992
Fax: (819) 979-4207
E-mail: keisses@nunanet.com

Airport outlet:
7:30 a.m.–6 p.m., Monday.
7:30 a.m.–3:30 p.m., Tuesday and Thursday. 7:30 a.m.–5 p.m., Wednesday. 7:30 a.m.–7 p.m., Friday. 10 a.m.–3 p.m., Saturday. 12–3 p.m., Sunday. VISA, MasterCard, Interac.
Tel.: (819) 979-0043

Arts and Crafts Centre
Part of Nunavut Arctic College.
Tel.: (819) 979-7265

Coman Arctic Galleries Ltd.
9 a.m.–5 p.m., Monday to Saturday. Phone first for other times; will open upon request. VISA, MasterCard.
Tel.: (819) 979-0222
Fax: (819) 979-6854
E-mail: icerick@aol.com or
sculptures@aol.com

D.J. Sensations
9:30 a.m.–6 p.m., Monday to Thursday;
9:30 a.m.–6:30 p.m., Friday;
10:30 a.m.–5:30 p.m., Saturday.
By appointment on Sunday.
VISA, MasterCard, Interac.
Tel.: 1-888-979-0650 or (819) 979-0650
Fax: (819) 979-0045
E-mail: dj@nunanet.com

Iqaluit Fine Arts Gallery
8 a.m.–6 p.m., Monday to Saturday.
By appointment Sunday evening.
VISA, MasterCard, American Express, Interac.
Tel.: (819) 979-5748
Fax: (819) 979-6092

Mary's Movie Club
1–11 p.m. every day except Christmas and New Year's Day.
VISA, MasterCard, Interac.
Tel.: (819) 979-5722
Fax: (819) 979-5757

Northern Country Arts
10 a.m.–6 p.m., Monday to Friday.
1–6 p.m., Saturday and Sunday.
VISA, Interac.
Tel.: (819) 979-0067
Fax: (819) 979-5330
E-mail: northart@nunanet.com
Web site: www.nunanet.com/~northart

Northern Store
Main store:
10 a.m.–8 p.m., Monday to Friday;
10 a.m.–6 p.m., Saturday. VISA, MasterCard, American Express, Interac.
Tel.: (819) 979-5277
Fax: (819) 979-6635

Quick Stop:
10 a.m.–11 p.m., Monday to Saturday;
12–11 p.m., Sunday and holidays. VISA, MasterCard, American Express, Interac.

Kanguk Convenience Store:
8 a.m.–8 p.m., Monday to Friday;
8 a.m.–7 p.m., Saturday; 12–6 p.m., Sunday. Closed holidays. VISA, MasterCard, American Express, Interac.

Tununiqmiut Arts and Crafts
Located in the Toonoonik Hotel.
9 a.m.–9 p.m. every day.
Will open on request.
VISA, MasterCard, American Express, Discovery, Interac.
Tel.: (819) 979-3511
Fax: (819) 979-4210

Valupharm Drugs
10 a.m.–1 p.m. and 2–6:30 p.m., Monday to Friday; 1–5 p.m., Saturday. Closed Sunday.
VISA, MasterCard, Interac.
Tel.: (819) 979-0655 or 979-3055
Fax: (819) 979-0654

Tours

Elders' Facility (Qammaq in Apex)
Tel.: (819) 979-5626

Nunatta Sunakkutaangit Museum
Tel.: (819) 979-5537
Fax: (819) 979-4533
E-mail: museum@nunanet.com

Pairijait Tigumivik Elders' Facility
Tel.: (819) 979-5626

QAUMMAARVIIT HISTORIC PARK

by Bruce Rigby

Qaummaarviit (pronounced "cow-mar-veet") is one of three territorial parks around Iqaluit, but the only one dedicated to preserving a cultural site of historic importance.

Called "the place that shines" in Inuktitut, the site has long been of interest to residents and visitors alike; well over 750 years of intermittent occupancy are evident here. Qaummaarviit was made a historic park by the GNWT in 1985.

History

The narrow island on which Qaummaarviit sits is part of a small group of islands adjacent to Peterhead Inlet at the north end of Frobisher Bay. The island is only one-quarter square kilometre in total area. Archeologists generally agree that no more than 25 people lived here at any one time.

The site preserves a record of the Thule people, who originated in Alaska some 1,000 years ago and slowly spread across the Canadian Arctic to Greenland. Scientists aren't sure what precipitated this migration, although many feel the Thule were taking advantage of improved weather conditions to expand their harvesting area and travel to regions they were previously unable to reach.

Thule culture is distinguished from others that resided in Nunavut by its reputation for inventiveness and adaptability. In addition to using traditional modes of transportation such as the dogsled and *qajaq* (kayak), the Thule are also credited with developing the *umiaq*, or "women's boat." The umiaq was a large, skin boat capable of holding entire families and their belongings. The umiaq was generally paddled by women, as men travelled in the faster and more mobile qajaq. The Thule were adept at hunting all forms of land and sea mammals, including the mammoth bowhead whale.

Upon their arrival here, the Thule discovered they were not alone. Already resident were the Dorset Inuit, or *Tuniit*, who had occupied the eastern Arctic for approximately 1,500 years. The Tuniit are still a popular folklore topic among Inuit. Elders tell stories of the giant-like people who produced intricate artwork, only to disappear after the arrival of the Thule. Some archeologists feel the demise of the Tuniit was precipitated by their inability to adapt to changes in wildlife and climate. Although there is no evidence that the Tuniit occupied Qaummaarviit itself, tools and implements have been found that show they used the area.

Although the Thule are generally understood to be a marine culture, the location of Qaummaarviit presents many questions to researchers, as it is located on one of the innermost inlets of Frobisher Bay and more than 100 kilometres from the normal winter location of the floe edge. However, the great variety of animal bones found at the site indicates it was likely chosen because of its proximity to abundant land species, which were used for both clothing and food.

Evidence shows that Qaummaarviit was occupied until approximately the end of the 18th century, when it was abandoned as a permanent site. Scientists have suggested that just as the expansion of the Thule into this region may have corresponded with a warming climatic period, the departure from the site roughly corresponds with a period termed the "little ice age," a period of global cooling that began around AD 1400.

What to See and Do

Qaummaarviit is comprised of a variety of features. In the summer, luxuriant patches of vegetation scattered throughout the park seem out of character with the rocky landscape around them. This is caused by the decay of buried organic materials that collected at the site over many years. Known by archeologists as "middens," these areas are usually rich with materials and artifacts for analysis. Thousands of tools have been recovered, as well as the remains of animals such as ringed and harp seals, caribou, walruses, bowhead whales, beluga whales, foxes, wolves, dogs and birds.

Central to the site are the remains of 11 semi-buried sod houses. These houses are more permanent versions of the snow *iglu* still occasionally used across Nunavut. And although sod houses used whalebone, sod and stone as their building materials, they exhibited many characteristics similar to the traditional snowhouse. As with the snow iglu, a sod house's entryway was constructed lower than the main living area to trap cold air and prevent it from entering the dwelling. Sod houses, like *igluit* (three or more igloos; two are *igluuk*), also used a "sleeping platform" from which daily activities were directed. Visitors will also notice that care was taken to align the dwellings in a southeasterly direction to maximize light and heat received from the sun. Several tent rings also indicate Qaummaarviit was used in summer.

As part of the excavation and development of the site, two house foundations have been left open for viewing. A $3 guidebook available from the Unikkaarvik Visitors Centre in Iqaluit provides good background information and describes some of the sights along the island's well-marked trail. The trail winds its way from a small cove on the south end of the island and terminates at a series of grave sites, tent rings and meat caches. Interpretive signs explain features of interest at length.

Getting There

Qaummaarviit is accessible by ski, dogsled or snowmobile in the winter months, and by boat during the open-water season. However, since the park is approximately 12 kilometres from Iqaluit, it is recommended that visitors take advantage of local outfitting services, many of which provide on-site interpretation and a snack. Arrangements can be made through the Unikkaarvik Visitors Centre.

If you hire an outfitter, try to go by dogteam, one of the most enjoyable ways to get to the park during the lengthening days of spring. Such trips can take place well into June, as the sea ice remains several metres thick and safe for travelling, despite a rather unsettling layer of surface water. If travelling this late in the season, don't be alarmed to find your excursion scheduled well into the evening hours to take advantage of the cooler temperatures that make sled-pulling easier for dogs. You may also find that your outfitter has dressed his or her dogs with colorful booties; these protect the animals' feet from the sharp edges of granular snow and sea ice. As the season progresses, cracks of open water will widen, eventually making it unsafe to travel to the island until breakup is complete.

If dogsled is your chosen mode of transportation, allow yourself the better part of a day to travel to and explore Qaummaarviit. Travel by snowmobile and *qamutik* is much quicker, and will significantly decrease the length of your trip. Skiing to the park takes a good day, depending on your experience and ability. Also, remember that Frobisher Bay is subject to tides of up to 15 metres, which can also affect travel in any season. Earlier in the season this simply means there is a greater expanse of rough ice to climb to get to the island. Later in the season, tides affect both the amount of surface water on the ice and the amount and location of open water near the shore.

Whether travelling in winter or summer, visitors should dress warmly. New, high-tech gear has a lot to offer, but you'll find many locals opt for heavy parkas when on the bay. The air temperature here is generally cooler than on land, and the lack of any high topography or vegetation will ensure that even the lightest breeze will have a significant cooling effect. A general adage used by residents is "dress for the worst, enjoy the best," so make sure you have foul weather gear, warm mitts or gloves and a woolen tuque. Good quality sunglasses are also a must to prevent snow blindness in spring and reduce the reflection of sunlight off the water in summer.

Breakup in the north end of Frobisher Bay usually takes place around mid-July. Remember that in the early open-water season there is usually ice still floating in the bay. Strong onshore winds can trap even the most experienced boaters. Most local outfitters use 22- or 24-foot freighter canoes or Lake Winnipeg boats. These boats are designed to transport heavy loads over long distances and are powered by outboard motors. Boat travel to Qaummaarviit takes from 30 to 45 minutes, depending on tidal conditions and wind. Camping is not permitted.

For help in planning your visit to Qaummaarviit Historic Park, phone Visitor Services at the Unikkaarvik Visitors Centre in Iqaluit at (819) 979-4636 (fax is (819) 979-1261), or e-mail them at nunatour@nunanet.com. Web site: www.nunatour.nt.ca.

SYLVIA GRINNELL TERRITORIAL PARK

by Colleen Dupuis

Set on the outskirts of Iqaluit, Sylvia Grinnell Territorial Park is 148 hectares of natural beauty bound to make an impression on any visitor. Bring your camera; photo opportunities abound!

As its name suggests, the park's most popular features are the gentle falls and crystal waters of the Sylvia Grinnell River, named for the granddaughter of one of the financiers of American explorer Charles Francis Hall. The lower part of the river — from the falls to nearby Koojesse Inlet — is part of the tidal system of the inlet and only navigable at high tide. During extremely high tides these gentle falls all but disappear, becoming an extensive series of rapids.

Getting There

From the centre of Iqaluit, it's an easy 30-minute walk to the park; new signage will help visitors find their way. From the three-way stop by the gas station, proceed north to the Aeroplex Building, number 1084. Turn left and continue past the yield sign, until you see the sign for Sylvia Grinnell Territorial Park. Turn right and follow the signs. This route will take you past some interesting local attractions, including an area near a stream where a local dogteam is kept for the summer. Feel free to take pictures, but be careful not to get too close to the dogs. If you don't want to walk, the short cab ride to the park is $5 per person. There are no phones in the park, so don't forget to make arrangements to be picked up later.

Facilities in the park include a parking area with two nearby outhouses, barbecue pits and a recently constructed viewing platform. There is no fee for either day use or camping. Vehicle use in the park is not encouraged, although you may encounter the odd all-terrain vehicle.

What to See and Do

In addition to being a favorite picnic site, Sylvia Grinnell Territorial Park is also a popular fishing spot. In the past, the river had an abundance of large arctic char. It is still a great place to catch smaller, pan-sized char. Remember to get a fishing licence before you drop your line.

Camping at the park is also quite common, although there are no tent platforms or running water. Small plateaus on the riverbank provide some shelter for campers. Future plans call for a short-term camping area about one kilometre upriver of the falls/viewing platform, just above the tidal flats at the foot of the bank.

The park is an ideal spot to spend a day exploring. Flora and fauna are varied and abundant. Several species of rare plants have been identified here, including the woodsia fern, one of the rarest plants in the country. In the summer the tundra floor becomes a carpet of mountain avens — the cream-colored flower of the Northwest Territories — arctic heather, saxifrages, arctic poppies and other wildflowers. The subtle colors and delicate foliage are a photographer's delight.

Wildlife sightings are not uncommon, either. Caribou frequent the area in winter and spring; a few remain throughout summer. Arctic fox dens are also located within the park, so keep your eyes peeled for mother foxes returning to feed their young.

Southern Baffin Island is an area of major bird activity during summer, and the park is no exception. As many as 40 species can be found here during the balmy days of June and July. This area is the most southerly breeding ground of the elusive common ringed plover. Other commonly sighted species include the Lapland longspur and the snow bunting. Avid birders should also be on the lookout for the Northern wheatear. Rarely seen in North America south of the Labrador coast, this bird nests in the park before its winter migration to Africa and India.

Once you've descended the steep riverbank, walking is relatively easy at Sylvia Grinnell. Nonetheless, the rocky tundra terrain is not the place for tennis shoes, so wear sturdy hiking boots. No formal trails exist in the park, but an old military road runs near the river. It traverses prime birding and wildlife-viewing areas before doubling back around the north end of the airport, an approximate 10-kilometre hike. The scenery is spectacular. Don't forget your binoculars, lunch and sunscreen.

The entire area around the park was gouged by massive glaciers; deposits are plentiful in the Sylvia Grinnell Valley. The new viewing platform, perched some 55 metres above the falls, offers a commanding view of the work of these ice-age behemoths. Here you can easily trace the path of the receding glaciers and the deposits they left behind. It's also a great place to watch the sunset.

If you are interested in archeological sites, there are also a few stone cairns and Thule ruins in the park. One of the best is just south of the falls on the east side of the river. Even in the absence of defined trails, navigation is easy: the river is to your right as you head south and to your left as you head north. Future development plans call for a footbridge across the river. Until the bridge is constructed, however, don't attempt to cross on your own. Sylvia Grinnell River may look relatively benign, but fording it is difficult and dangerous at the best of times. You may be able to make arrangements with local licensed outfitters to take you to the far side by boat during high tides. Outfitters are not always available, however.

Enjoy your visit to the park, but always keep in mind that although just outside Iqaluit, going for a hike here means going out on the tundra. Use caution not to disturb flora any more than necessary; signs of your passing will remain long after you're gone. Carry out your garbage, too. And remember to let someone know your plans since there are no phones in the park.

KIMMIRUT

by Robert Jaffray

Take a stroll through this seaside community and you'll quickly notice how differently things are done here.

Population:	397 (Inuit: 92%, non-Inuit: 8%)
Telephone Area Code:	819 (changes to 867 on Oct. 21, 1997)
Time Zone:	Eastern Time
Postal Code:	X0A 0N0
How to Get There:	Possible routes:
	• Ottawa/Montreal-Iqaluit-Kimmirut
	• Winnipeg-Rankin Inlet-Iqaluit-Kimmirut
	• Yellowknife-Rankin Inlet-Iqaluit-Kimmirut
	• Kangerlussuaq (Greenland)-Iqaluit-Kimmirut
	Iqaluit to Kimmirut (121 kilometres south) is via First Air
Banks:	No. It is preferable to bring cash and traveller's cheques
Alcohol:	Alcohol and alcoholic beverages are prohibited
Taxis:	No, although the Co-op, which owns the Kimik Hotel, will meet planes and ferry guests around in their trucks

Houses usually face the water instead of the street so residents can keep an eye on the comings and goings of hunters and fishermen. Children play "Inuit baseball," where the runner runs the opposite direction from southern-style baseball and can be tagged out by a thrown ball. Young girls attend to baby siblings by carrying them in an *amauti,* a hooded woman's parka.

Most Kimmirut residents are carvers, an industry worth approximately $800,000 to the local economy. You can often watch them make their living with grinder and file outside their homes. Many also work in the wage economy for one of the local retail stores, the hamlet, or the territorial government. Virtually everyone participates in the traditional economy of hunting and fishing, a vital link between old and new.

History

There is a long history of human presence in the area around Kimmirut (pronounced "kim-mi-root"). Archeological remains indicate people have occupied the region for some 4,000 years; evidence of Thule, Dorset and Pre-Dorset cultures is scattered throughout the area.

First contact with Europeans came in the 17th century when Hudson's Bay Co. supply ships travelling through Hudson Strait began trading with Inuit. Contact intensified in 1860 with the arrival of American and Scottish whalers. When Robert Kinnes of the Scottish-owned Tay Whale Fishing Company established a mica mine nearby, it drew Inuit to the area. In 1900, the Anglican Church established its second mission on Baffin Island, building a mission house across the bay from today's community. Hoping to capitalize on the abundant white fox population and the growing dependence of Inuit on non-traditional goods, the Hudson's Bay Co. erected Baffin Island's first trading post here in 1911. An RCMP post was established on the east side of Glasgow Inlet in 1927.

Until a US army base arrived in Frobisher Bay in 1945, Kimmirut (known until recently as Lake Harbour) was the administrative centre for the south Baffin. RCMP officers from the Lake Harbour post patrolled as far north as Pangnirtung, west beyond Cape Dorset, and all the camps around the Hudson's Bay Co. post of Frobisher Bay. After the runway was built at Frobisher Bay (now called Iqaluit), focus began to shift away from Lake Harbour and toward Nunavut's future capital, Iqaluit.

The community continued to grow, however. A federal school was established in the 1950s, and a government-administered nursing station soon followed.

Kimmirut: Its Land and Wildlife

Kimmirut is situated beside the ocean at the northern extremity of Glasgow Inlet. About 60 metres across the water lies the landmark for which the community is named — a *kimmirut* (heel), a rocky outcrop that resembles a human heel.

Visitors to Kimmirut will get a crash course in tidal action if they are here for more than a few hours. Tides here, which are sometimes greater than 11 metres, are strikingly apparent as the water level rises and falls along the sheer rock face of the heel. In winter, very low tides sometimes pull the ice down far enough to reveal a dazzling ice wall over 10 metres high.

The bulk of the town stretches along the narrow strip of land that runs north/south along the ocean. Recent housing additions dot surrounding hills. Most of the community's commercial ventures are in the older section of town. Here you'll find the hamlet administration, school, retail stores, and visitor services. A few businesses are located 'uptown,' including a gift shop and convenience store (both operate on an irregular basis, though).

It is not uncommon to walk within minutes of the community and see a caribou lope across your path. Equally common are tiny lemmings that dart from rock to rock. Seagulls frequent the area; ravens talk to you from their perches overhead. On a calm summer day, a seal may pop its inquisitive head out of the water or a beluga whale may find its way into a nearby bay. Further afield you may see a fox, arctic hare, or even a wolf, at a distance. On rare occasions, polar bears have come into the community.

Throughout the community and the surrounding hillsides you'll find abundant and varied flora. Dwarf fireweed, white heather and arctic poppies add a delightful touch of color throughout summer. You may even see dandelions in some areas, their growth fostered by a climate warmer than any other on Baffin Island.

Tours

The best place to start exploring is the **Katannilik Territorial Park Interpretive Centre**, located in the white and green building at the crossroads of the community. Scheduled for completion in June 1997, the Centre will have displays on the park, local geology, community history, traditional lifestyles and climatic anomalies, among others. The Centre will also boast a resource centre, video theatre, and working waterfall.

The Interpretive Centre is also the place to pick up a community brochure, containing a detailed map of Kimmirut, local sites of interest, and a short history of the surrounding area. Added touches like a syllabic chart (Inuktitut, the language of Inuit, is often written in syllabics) and a concise list of useful phone numbers make it a good reference document.

You may want to hike to the top of the hill behind the runway for a great view of town and the surrounding area. To the south lies Hudson Strait. On clear days you can sometimes see *Qikiqtarjuaq* ("Big Island") to the southwest, the largest island on the south coast of Baffin Island.

Hike due west of Kimmirut to get to the reversing falls, where Soper Lake drains into the ocean. Try to time your hike with the high tide of a full or new moon and watch the ocean reverse this drainage and flood Soper Lake with sea water. You can also walk east from the town around the end of Glasgow Inlet and visit historic sites such as the original RCMP post and the site of the Anglican mission house. Here you can also climb on to the kimmirut. Longer treks can be made into Katannilik Territorial Park Reserve, which is a minimum six-hour round trip.

Two outfitters are currently registered in Kimmirut. The **Mayukalik Hunters and Trappers Organization** arranges ocean day-trips to view wildlife, icebergs, waterfalls and sea mammals — usually ringed and harp seals, but occasionally walrus and beluga whales. They can also arrange community tours for individuals and groups ($30 per person), and offer shuttle service to and from Soper Lake for travellers arriving by canoe from Katannilik Park. **Qayaq Nunavut** also handles ocean trips, and arranges canoeing and hiking trips in the Soper Valley.

Shopping

Kimmirut's two largest retail stores are both located in the older section of town. The **Kimik Co-op** carries a good variety of groceries, as well as dry goods and hardware. It is also the only place in town that sells naphtha. The **Northern store** carries a similar selection of goods, but carries more clothing and fewer groceries. Both stores have a selection of souvenirs.

The **KTJ Convenience Store** is located near the airport and has a basic selection of convenience items. Be advised, though, that it operates irregularly throughout the year. At press time, it was closed.

Events

Special events are sometimes held in the community centre, called the **Akavak Centre**. Contact the hamlet recreation co-ordinator for more details. When no events are scheduled, the centre hosts a variety of sports activities.

Accommodation and Dining

The **Kimik Hotel** is located above the Co-op store. Sixteen people can stay in eight rooms, each with its own washroom, for $185 per person per night, including meals. The price per person without meals is $125. Summers can be especially busy for the hotel, so it is necessary to phone ahead to make arrangements. Ask for a room facing the water; they offer great views of Glasgow Inlet and the area across the harbor. Sometimes seals and even whales can be seen from this vantage point. If your room doesn't face the water, you can still enjoy the view from the hotel's restaurant and coffee shop.

If you would prefer to stay with a local family for a few nights, you can contact the Hunters and Trappers Organization to participate in the community's unique Home Stay Program, in which a local family will host you for the night. The cost is $120 per person per night and includes both breakfast and a large traditional daytime or evening meal. Most home stay families can only accommodate two people, so larger groups will be divided throughout the community. These parties can still arrange to have their evening meal together, however.

Although there is no campground in Kimmirut, plans are in the works to designate one. Check at the Interpretive Centre for the best locations to pitch your tent or latest developments in a designated campground.

The hotel restaurant is open to the public, but serving hotel guests is their first priority. You can stop by any morning or afternoon for coffee; a muffin or piece of pie may also be available. If you're looking for a full meal, inquire with the cook or hotel manager. They will often allow you to dine with hotel guests, or even provide a second sitting, but give them a few hours' notice. Breakfast is $10, lunch is $20, and supper is $30. Local families also prepare meals for visitors and serve traditional foods such as caribou stew, char chowder, bannock (a traditional fried bread), berries and tea. Arrangements can be made through the Hunters and Trappers Organization, given at least a day's notice. The cost is currently $22 per person.

Services

Kimmirut's **Health Centre** is located beside the Northern store. Drop-in clinics run from 9 to 11:30 a.m. weekdays. Two resident nurses handle all medical situations, most of them on site.

DIRECTORY

The 819 and 403 area codes change to 867 on Oct. 21, 1997.

Accommodation and Dining

Kimik Hotel
VISA, Interac.
Tel.: (819) 939-2093
Fax: (819) 939-2005

Outfitters/Guides/ Tour Operators

Mayukalik Hunters and Trappers Organization
Tel.: (819) 939-2355
Fax: (819) 939-2112

Qayaq Nunavut
Tel.: (819) 939-2307
Fax: (819) 939-2119

Services

Airport
Tel.: (819) 939-2250

Akavak Centre
Community centre.
Tel.: (819) 939-2113

Church

St. Paul's Anglican Church
No phone.

Hamlet Office
Tel.: (819) 939-2245
Fax: (819) 939-2045

Health Centre
Tel.: (819) 939-2217
Fax: (819) 939-2068

Katannilik Territorial Park Interpretive Centre
Usually open 8:30 a.m.–noon and 1–5 p.m., Monday to Friday. May have some evening and weekend hours, which will likely be posted.
Tel.: (819) 939-2084
Fax: (819) 939-2406
E-mail: rjaffray@nunanet.com

Police (RCMP)
Tel.: (819) 939-2333
Fax: (819) 939-2146

Post Office
Located on 1st floor of Kimmirut Hamlet Office Building.
10 a.m.–noon; 1–2 p.m., Monday to Friday. No phone.

Radio Station (FM 107.1)
Tel.: (819) 939-2126
Fax: (819) 939-2380

Schools

Aqiggiq School
Tel.: (819) 939-2221
Fax: (819) 939-2334

Nunavut Arctic College
Tel.: (819) 939-2414
Fax: (819) 939-2299

Weather Office
Tel.: (819) 939-2045

Stores

Kimik Co-op
9 a.m.–noon, 1–6 p.m., Monday and Tuesday; 9 a.m.–noon, 1–8 p.m., Wednesday; 9 a.m.–noon, 1–9 p.m., Thursday and Friday; noon to 6 p.m., Saturday. Open for tour ships (even on Sundays). VISA, MasterCard, American Express, Diners Club/enRoute, Interac.
Tel.: (819) 939-2322
Fax: (819) 939-2005

KTJ Convenience Store
Operates on an irregular basis through the year.
7 p.m.–midnight, Monday to Saturday;
1 p.m.–midnight, Sunday.
Accepts cash only.
Tel.: (819) 939-2100

Northern Store
10 a.m.–noon, 1:30–6 p.m., Monday to Wednesday; 10 a.m.–noon, 1:30–8 p.m., Thursday and Friday; 1–5 p.m., Saturday. Closed Sunday. VISA, MasterCard, Interac.
Tel.: (819) 939-2242
Fax: (819) 939-2353

KATANNILIK TERRITORIAL PARK RESERVE

by Robert Jaffray

Spanning the Meta Incognita Peninsula in southern Baffin Island, Katannilik Territorial Park Reserve — "the place of waterfalls" — is a surprisingly fertile arctic oasis tucked in the middle of an ancient and unforgiving landscape.

Central to the park is the Soper River Valley, some 110 kilometres of meandering wilderness punctuated by countless cascades. Along the river itself, on its many tributaries, and in the streams and rivulets flowing down the sides of the valley, these waterfalls echo the recurring theme of the park.

Katannilik stretches northward from the top of Pleasant Inlet along the coast of Hudson Strait (just outside the community of Kimmirut) toward the south shore of Frobisher Bay, following the Soper Valley and a traditional overland trail called the *Itijjagiaq*. The park's eastern and western boundaries follow a series of rivers, lakes and hills on the plateau above the river valley. Known locally as *Kuujjuaq* — "big river" — the Soper was designated a Canadian heritage river in 1992 for its cultural significance in the lives of Inuit, its natural beauty and its countless opportunities for recreation.

Getting to the Park

Katannilik is one of the most accessible parks in Nunavut; there are three ways to get there from Iqaluit. The simplest is to take a scheduled flight with First Air to Kimmirut, which flies four days per week much of the year. Additional flights are often scheduled in the summer by Kenn Borek Air. Those travelling in large groups may want to consider chartering a plane to Kimmirut.

The park is only minutes from Kimmirut, although it will take you a good three hours to hike into the Soper Valley. For those more eager to get into the valley, boats can be hired in Kimmirut to take you across Soper Lake to Soper Falls at the south end of the valley. These services are offered by the **Mayukalik Hunters and Trappers Organization** and **Qayaq Nunavut**.

You can also get into the park by chartering a flight to Mount Joy or the Livingstone River confluence, the two designated landing strips in the Soper Valley. This is the most popular method of getting into Katannilik. The strip at the Livingstone is on the west side of the river, though, and should only be used if you plan on taking some form of boat in with you. Both First Air and Kenn Borek have Twin Otters that can land on these strips. The cost varies from year to year but should be around $1,000.

Some Iqaluit outfitters, such as **Eetuk Outfitting** and **NorthWinds Arctic Adventures**, offer package tours of Katannilik Park that fly visitors in or transport them by dogsled in winter. As part of the tour, visitors are taken across Frobisher Bay to the Itijjagiaq trailhead, where they can hike southwest to the Soper Valley and eventually Kimmirut. Book in advance. It's often not possible to book outfitters by the day.

Topography

A complex series of folds, plunges and shears dating from the formation of the Earth make Katannilik rich with a variety of rock formations and exposed geological domains. The park is comprised of three distinct landscapes.

The first starts at the south shore of Frobisher Bay, where the Itijjagiaq Trail begins. Rising 670 metres from sea level to the plateau of the Meta Incognita Peninsula, the landscape is a playground of deep gorges and sloping valleys. Increasing elevation means shelter becomes scarce as the topography flattens out. It also means a corresponding decrease in vegetation, as temperatures drop.

The plateau of the Meta Incognita Peninsula has changed little since the last glaciers receded. Glacial scars are readily discernible, and the shallow, rolling topography is testament to the force of these frozen behemoths. Rocks and boulders scattered across the smooth surface of the plateau look like they've fallen from the sky in a rock shower.

The third region of the park is the Soper Valley, a product of receding glaciers, water erosion and the existing thermal oasis. Over the millennia, the water level of the river has fluctuated, leaving terraces throughout the valley floor. These terraces range from three to 30 metres above the current height of the river. The river valley is most impressive at its northern end. To the south, the valley walls start to diminish as the topography rolls gently toward Hudson Strait.

Vegetation

Plant life in Katannilik varies from virtually nil in some areas to astoundingly abundant in others. Where conditions are inhospitable, such as the plateau, you can still often find plant life within millimetres of the ground. You won't need to look so diligently in the abundant Soper Valley, however, where summer temperatures average some 5° C higher than nearby Kimmirut, itself the warmest community on Baffin Island.

In 1930, naturalist Joseph Dewey Soper, after whom the river was named, explored the area while working for the Canadian government. Soper catalogued much of the valley's plant life, including willow trees as tall as 3.6 metres, the tallest in the region. Uncommonly large willows still grow in well-protected areas of the valley.

Four communities of vegetation have been identified in the valley, each composed of plants with common nutritive needs. The dwarf shrub/heath tundra community is primarily made up of willow, dwarf birch, Lapland rosebay, Labrador tea, and arctic heather. This community, which needs more warmth than others, is found in moist areas below 210 metres in elevation.

The grassland tundra group, with its characteristic tussocks of moss surrounded by shallow water, is the one you want to avoid hiking across. The group includes sedges, arctic cotton, sphagnum moss, bistorts and willows, and is usually found along bodies of water in the river valley.

The bedrock/hill summit community is in exposed areas that are neither wet nor warm. Generally lacking good soil, this community is characterized by large amounts of lichen, but also comprises purple saxifrage, arctic poppy, mountain avens, broad-leafed willow herb, and chickweed, all of which tend to grow close to the ground and form a mat of color as they bloom.

The snowpatch community is aptly named for its penchant for late-thawing areas where drifting has slowed the seasonal development of plants. As the snow melts, it permits arctic heather to grow first, followed by dwarf willows, mountain sorrel and finally, mosses. This regimented pattern results in rings of vegetation that distinguish the community.

Mid-July to late August is the best time to see Katannilik's vivid arctic bloom, starting with purple saxifrage, and followed by bluebells and dwarf fireweed. In late summer and early autumn, berries carpet the park. Inuit from Kimmirut flock to the valley to harvest blueberries, crowberries, mountain cranberries and bearberries as they have done for millennia.

Wildlife

Where there is vegetation you'll find wildlife. With a terrain as rich as any in the Baffin Region, the Soper Valley is no exception. With any luck you should be able to spot caribou, lemmings, hares, foxes and wolves. And while polar bears could enter the valley at any time, their preference for seals keeps them in coastal areas to the north and south.

The most common animal in the park is the caribou. These caribou do not undertake the long overland migrations of the mainland variety, but circulate throughout south Baffin Island, and the Meta Incognita Peninsula in particular. In summer and autumn, caribou prefer the lush vegetation of the valley. Winter and spring sees them moving to the uplands, where wind blows the ground free of snow and exposes lichens.

Wolves and foxes are also abundant throughout the park. Observant summer visitors may find fox dens in well-drained, rolling terrain throughout the valley; evidence of these winsome creatures is easier to spot in winter, as their tracks zigzag across the valley. Katannilik is home to both arctic and red foxes. The number of wolves in the park fluctuates with the availability of prey, though they are not as numerous as foxes.

Lemmings and hares are a favorite food of many larger predators and tend to make themselves scarce when creatures of the two-legged sort are in the vicinity. With some careful observation, however, you may be rewarded with a glimpse of one or both. Hares favor the protection of rocky hillsides. Lemmings can sometimes be seen darting from one tunnel to another.

Peregrine falcons and gyrfalcons are both present in Katannilik. Peregrines are found closer inland while gyrfalcons favor the coast. They are joined in the valley by two other predatory birds: the snowy owl, easily recognizable by its white plumage and unmistakable eyes, and the rough-legged hawk, one of the most common birds of prey in the Arctic.

The most common birds in Katannilik are the rock ptarmigan and snow bunting. The ptarmigan, which resides here throughout the year, is never easy to spot. In summer their mottled brown plumage blends in perfectly with the surroundings; in winter they are pure white. The snow bunting, a member of the finch family, spends all but winter in the area. Black and white males are more easily spotted than brownish females.

Migratory birds such as Canada geese and red-breasted mergansers frequent marshy areas of the river valley, while snow geese can be seen as they migrate in the spring and fall. All three species of loons are often present closer to the coast at the southern end of the park, as are other shorebirds such as murres, terns and black guillemots.

Although there are generally no char in the Soper River, they can sometimes be found at either Soper Falls or at the reversing falls, where Soper Lake drains into the ocean. Landlocked char can be found in the lakes on either side of the Soper Valley, but are not usually eaten because they may contain tapeworm cysts.

Three varieties of cod can be found in Soper Lake: Arctic, Greenland and Atlantic. Inuit catch these in summer and throughout the winter. They are easy to catch, and though they are eaten, the activity is considered mostly a form of recreation.

Geology

Minerals in Katannilik are as plentiful as they are varied. Exposed bedrock reveals diopside, marble, low-quality garnet and various other semiprecious gems. Apatite can be found in blue, green and rose hues. Bands of crystalline limestone transect the valley and the river.

Mining has been attempted sporadically in the Soper Valley since 1900, when a Scottish company extracted mica from a number of locales in and around the river. Graphite was also mined in the early 20th century. Outcrops of both are still easy to find.

A deposit of lapis lazuli, a brilliant blue gemstone found in only a few locations in the world, is also located in the valley. Though the stones here are of poor quality, their color and rarity make them worth seeking. It too was mined, but abandoned in the early 1970s. The mica and lapis lazuli deposits are located on parcels of Inuit-owned land within the park boundaries and require special permission to access.

Activities

With careful planning, anyone can have a safe and enjoyable visit to this arctic oasis.

The mainstay of summer activity in Katannilik is hiking, and options are virtually limitless. You can enjoy a casual discovery walk along the river terraces or perhaps tackle the entire trip from Kimmirut to Frobisher Bay, a 10- to 12-day trek across the Meta Incognita Peninsula.

Complementing Katannilik's hiking opportunities is the accessibility of much of the park by water. You could combine the two modes of transportation and spend a week hiking along the Soper River while a guide transports your gear by boat and prepares your meals. Another option is to raft down the Soper for a few hours each day, leaving you ample opportunity to explore the surrounding hills.

The Itijjagiaq Trail is part of a route travelled for centuries by Inuit venturing north to the Nettilling Lake area to hunt caribou and meet with relatives from as far away as Pangnirtung. Although it is part of the park, Itijjagiaq is nonetheless a wilderness trail and should not be undertaken without careful consideration. The route is not marked, so hikers contemplating it should be experienced in backcountry travel, first aid and map reading. The trailhead on the south shore of Frobisher Bay can be reached by boat from Iqaluit. The **Unikkaarvik Visitors Centre** there has a list of licensed outfitters that provide this service.

Seven emergency shelters are located along the 120-kilometre trail. A heated cabin in the Soper Valley will accommodate larger parties. It has a table, counters, sleeping platforms, and washrooms. The park master plan includes building some park maintenance facilities, a second group facility, and installation of signs along hiking trails.

Hikers planning on tackling the trail should look into buying the *Itijjagiaq Trail Guide*. The guide provides a detailed description of the trail, including contour maps, emergency shelters, and points of interest. Park protocol and regulations are also included. It can be purchased for $15 from the **Katannilik Territorial Park Interpretive Centre** in Kimmirut or the Unikkaarvik Visitors Centre in Iqaluit.

From Kimmirut, the cooling effects of the Arctic Ocean quickly fade as you hike into the park. As you approach the south end of the Soper Valley, where the river flows into the lake at Soper Falls, you'll find the first of several camping areas. Facilities here are limited to washrooms and tent platforms with windbreaks. Terraces further along the valley also provide good spots to set up camp. Day-hike possibilities from these areas abound.

As its name suggests, Katannilik is full of waterfalls. The largest is Soper Falls, where the emerald green Soper River flows into Soper Lake through a white marble chasm. Farther upstream, just before the Livingstone River flows into the Soper River, is Livingstone Falls; slightly further north, an easy day-hike up the Cascade River brings you to Cascade Falls, the highest waterfall in the park.

The *Soper River Guidebook* is a good resource for anyone travelling on the river. It provides detailed descriptions of points of interest along the river, the location and class of various rapids, and recommends a course through some of the trickier sections, all of which is referenced on accompanying maps. Available from the same sources that carry the *Itijjagiaq Trail Guide* mentioned earlier, the *Soper River Guidebook* also includes useful park protocol and interpretive information.

In winter and spring, Katannilik is used by recreational snowmobilers, cross-country skiers, and dogsledding enthusiasts. Guided dogsled trips between Iqaluit and Kimmirut take about four days; on snowmobile it only takes some six hours. Dogsled trips are currently offered by NorthWinds Arctic Adventures in Iqaluit. Snowmobile rentals are available from Eetuk Outfitting Equipment Rentals, also in Iqaluit. Both outfitters rent clothing and other equipment for winter and summer excursions.

Planning Your Visit

If you're planning a trip to Katannilik Territorial Park Reserve, start by contacting **Nunavut Tourism** staff at the Unikkaarvik Visitors Centre in Iqaluit or the Katannilik Territorial Park Interpretive Centre in Kimmirut.

DIRECTORY

The 819 and 403 area codes change to 867 on Oct. 21, 1997.

Eetuk Outfitting (Iqaluit)
Tel.: (819) 979-1984
Fax: (819) 979-1994

Katannilik Territorial Park Interpretive Centre
Tel.: (819) 939-2084
Fax: (819) 939-2406
E-mail: rjaffray@nunanet.com

Mayukalik Hunters and Trappers Organization (Kimmirut)
Tel.: (819) 939-2355
Fax: (819) 939-2112

NorthWinds Arctic Adventures (Iqaluit)
Tel.: (819) 979-0551
Fax: (819) 979-0551
E-mail: plandry@nunanet.com
Web site: www.nunanet.com/~plandry

Nunavut Tourism
P.O. Box 1450, Iqaluit NT,
X0A 0H0 Canada
Tel.: 1-800-491-7910 (for Canada and the United States)
Tel.: (819) 979-6551
Fax: (819) 979-1261
E-mail: nunatour@nunanet.com
Web site: www.nunatour.nt.ca

Qayaq Nunavut (Kimmirut)
Tel.: (819) 939-2307
Fax: (819) 939-2119

Resources, Wildlife and Economic Development
Includes the Katannilik Park office.
Tel.: (819) 939-2416
Fax: (819) 939-2406
E-mail: rjaffray@nunanet.com

Unikkaarvik Visitors Centre (Iqaluit)
Tel.: (819) 979-4636
Fax: (819) 979-1261
E-mail: nunatour@nunanet.com
Web site: www.nunatour.nt.ca

CAPE DORSET

by John Laird

Along the northwest shore of Dorset Island, surrounded on one side by rocky hills and on the other, by Hudson Strait, lies Cape Dorset — a community that, since the 1950s, has come to be known as the Inuit art capital of the world.

Population:	1,118 (Inuit: 92%, non-Inuit: 8%)
Telephone Area Code:	819 (changes to 867 on Oct. 21, 1997)
Time Zone:	Eastern Time
Postal Code:	X0A 0C0
How to Get There:	Possible routes:
	• Ottawa/Montreal-Iqaluit-Cape Dorset
	• Winnipeg-Rankin Inlet-Cape Dorset
	• Yellowknife-Rankin Inlet-Cape Dorset
	• Kangerlussuaq (Greenland)-Iqaluit-Cape Dorset
	Iqaluit to Cape Dorset (395 kilometres west) is via First Air, Air Nunavut or Kenn Borek. Rankin Inlet to Cape Dorset (almost 800 kilometres east) is via First Air
Banks:	None. Cash and traveller's cheques are preferable
Alcohol:	Alcohol and alcoholic beverages cannot be purchased in Cape Dorset. Visitors who want to bring alcohol into the community must first obtain a permit from the community's **Alcohol Education Committee**
Taxis:	Yes

In the distance are the jagged outlines of islands, and the inlets of Baffin Island's southern coast. Like most other settlements in Nunavut, Cape Dorset is a modern community, with winding gravel roads, small wooden houses, schools, stores, hotels, a nursing station, government offices, and churches. But it is Cape Dorset's outstanding artists and their printmaking and stone-carving shop that have earned the town renown.

Each year, art lovers and naturalists flock to Cape Dorset to enjoy the treasures of the West Baffin Eskimo Co-operative and to chat with the acclaimed artists who work here. In 1995, German Chancellor Helmut Kohl made the visit with Canadian Prime Minister Jean Chrétien. Visitors come, as well, to absorb the rich heritage of local Inuit, and to tour the breathtaking arctic landscape with its abundance of wildlife. The Mallikjuaq Historic Park Visitors Centre, due to be completed in late 1997 or early 1998, display artifacts portraying the history of Dorset and Mallikjuaq islands.

History

"Since long ago," Cape Dorset elder Qupapik Ragee says of his community, "our ancestors called it *Kingait*." Kingait is the Inuktitut word for "high

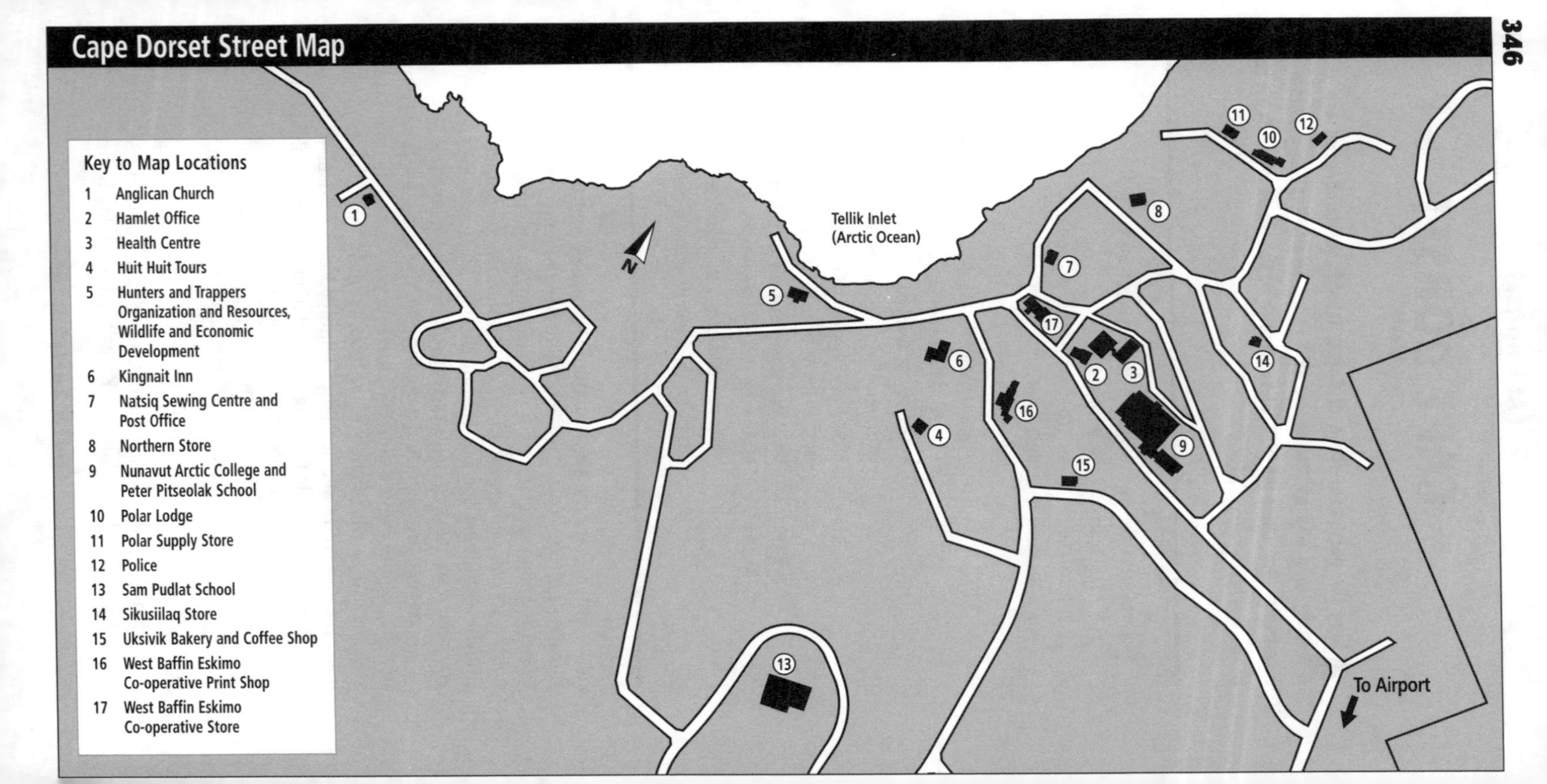
Cape Dorset Street Map
Key to Map Locations
1 Anglican Church
2 Hamlet Office
3 Health Centre
4 Huit Huit Tours
5 Hunters and Trappers Organization and Resources, Wildlife and Economic Development
6 Kingnait Inn
7 Natsiq Sewing Centre and Post Office
8 Northern Store
9 Nunavut Arctic College and Peter Pitseolak School
10 Polar Lodge
11 Polar Supply Store
12 Police
13 Sam Pudlat School
14 Sikusiilaq Store
15 Uksivik Bakery and Coffee Shop
16 West Baffin Eskimo Co-operative Print Shop
17 West Baffin Eskimo Co-operative Store
Tellik Inlet
(Arctic Ocean)
N
To Airport

mountains," describing the steep, rocky hills that overlook the town. The Inuit here are direct descendants of the Thule, who inhabited this region in small groups more than 1,000 years ago. You can explore remnants of their culture — such as stone foundations of their houses — at several sites on Dorset and Baffin islands. In 1925, Diamond Jenness became the first archeologist to identify the remains of an even earlier civilization, that of the Dorset, who lived here from about 800 BC to AD 1300. Other researchers have since discovered artifacts dating back 3,500 years to the pre-Dorset, and even earlier, cultures.

European explorers who arrived on these shores in the 17th century were relatively recent visitors. They named the Foxe Peninsula (Dorset Island lies off the south coast of this peninsula) after the English explorer, Luke Foxe. And they named Dorset Island to honor his benefactor, the Earl of Dorset. From 1850 to the early 1900s, whalers and missionaries visited the area. In 1913, the Hudson's Bay Co. set up a trading post here. Between 1938 and 1953, two churches, a school and a few houses were constructed. By the mid-1950s, Inuit began to build permanent homes in the area. This marked a major change in their lives, as now they increasingly felt the influence of government.

In 1947, the *Nascopie*, the supply ship that brought goods to the region from the South, ran aground off the coast of Dorset Island. Before she sank, the resourceful Inuit salvaged supplies, fuel, and even wood from the ship. They used this wood to construct their homes in Cape Dorset and along the coast of Dorset Island.

Today, most local Inuit are engaged in the same activities you might find in any small community in Canada: running businesses, working in offices, and attending school. If you walk the 1.2 kilometres from one end of town to the other, you'll see a blend of modern and traditional Inuit culture — snowmobiles and all-terrain vehicles parked outside homes; caribou and polar bear hides hanging from railings; arctic char fillets drying on racks; and perhaps a frozen seal or two resting on a doorstep. Children laugh and play in the streets, chattering in a steady stream of Inuktitut.

Cape Dorset: Its Land and Wildlife

Information and maps for day trips on Dorset and Mallikjuaq islands are included in the *Mallikjuaq Historic Park Guide*, available from the **Hamlet of Cape Dorset's community development department** and Nunavut Tourism. The Mallikjuaq Historic Park Visitors Centre, located next to the Kingnait Inn, contains displays and interpretive information on the archeology and trails on both Dorset and Mallikjuaq islands. Mallikjuaq Historic Park holds such archeological attractions as Thule houses, kayak stands, a fox trap, *inuksuk*, and meat caches, all within a two-hour hike around the island. You can take a boat to the island or hike there at low tide. Check with the community development office for information on tides, and referrals to licensed tour operators providing boat rides. Costs for outfitters vary. Day trips (per person) are $75 to $150 for a boat ride, and $150 to $200 for a dogsledding excursion. Some outfitters provide custom-designed trips for three to seven days that cost $300 per day and up.

On Dorset Island, you'll find several interesting hikes. The waterfall route takes you from the south edge of town, past a little waterfall to the beach. The pipeline route goes to "T" Lake, the source of Cape Dorset's drinking water, then winds up into the hills to a lookout whose view fans the south end of Dorset Island, other distant islands, and Hudson Strait. Another hike takes you east past the tank farm (where fuel shipped to Cape Dorset is stored in house-sized tanks) and over the tundra and gravel, to the beach at Apalooktook Point. If you're walking with a guide, he or she will point out archeological sites on the island, such as Thule houses, caches, and burial sites. Although there are no camping or picnic facilities on the island, staff at the community development office will tell you of suitable locations for camping. Be sure to bring your camp stove; there's no firewood.

While there are many hills and rocky areas on Dorset Island, you can find accessible routes to most areas. Hiking will require stamina — no problem for those who exercise regularly. Wear sturdy, waterproof boots for trekking over the spongy, sometimes wet, tundra. As weather may be variable, wear clothing suitable for rain and cold. In summer, be sure to bring your insect repellent.

From March to May, daily hours of sunlight increase, although temperatures remain moderate. Because light reflected from the snow is intense, you're wise to wear sunscreen and sunglasses. Between late May and early August, hours of daylight continue to increase, reaching a maximum of 20 hours of light in June and July. Summer temperatures, however, are generally cool, with an average high of 7.2° C, dropping to a few degrees below zero at night. Between October and February, hours of daylight decrease, with a maximum of five hours of light on the shortest days in December. Winter temperatures drop to between –25° C to –35° C and even colder. From December to late June, the ocean is frozen around the community, and people travel over the ice with snowmobiles or dogteams. Land travel to other regions is impossible in October and November, when the ocean is freezing, and again in June and sometimes in early July, during breakup.

In many areas of Dorset Island, you'll discover caribou, walrus and seals, as well as a variety of arctic shore and migratory birds. In spring and fall, you might see migrating beluga whales and the odd bowhead whale pass near the community. Find out the best season for viewing wildlife. Remember that in spring and fall, polar bears may roam around the island; they're dangerous, so take a licensed guide to act as a bear monitor on your outings. For information on wildlife, and hunting and fishing licences, contact the GNWT's Department of **Resources, Wildlife and Economic Development**.

Tours

Huit Huit Tours has tailored different tours to different palates. A community tour stops in at the West Baffin Eskimo Co-operative where stonecut prints are made. A cultural evening in town features storytelling by elders, throat singers, and tea with artists.

Huit Huit also has on-the-land tours that introduce you to traditional seasonal activities of local Inuit — jigging for fish on the lake ice, seal hunting, the list goes on. There are also custom-designed outings, such as camping in an igloo or tent, fishing and hunting, as well as trips to the floe edge, to archeological sites, and to the hosts' cabin. Co-owner Kristiina Alariaq says prices vary according to the activity and number of people involved. Costs must be shared by a group.

Seekuu Outfitting provides summer boat trips along the coast of Baffin Island. Visitors camp, eat "country food" and see archeological sites, wildlife, and icebergs. In Cape Dorset, visits are arranged to meet local artists and to tour the West Baffin Eskimo Co-operative. The cost, about $1,200 per person per week, includes accommodation at the Cape Dorset home of tour operator Jimmy Manning.

When cruise ships arrive in July and August, the Municipality of Cape Dorset organizes tours of the town, the West Baffin Eskimo Co-operative, and archeological sites on Mallikjuaq Island. Elders dress in traditional clothing and demonstrate the hunting lifestyle that has served them and their families for generations. Tea and bannock (fried bread) are served, and translation is provided. More information can be obtained from the community development department.

Shopping

The West Baffin Eskimo Co-operative is a centre for stonecut printing, lithographic printmaking, etching, and Inuit sculpture. Many artists who work here are known by name in the global art community, and have exhibited their work in public and private galleries throughout Canada and abroad. Traditionally, Inuit carved small sculptures from ivory, bone and wood. The era of modern Inuit art began in 1948, after art school graduate James Houston returned from a trip to the Arctic and convinced the Canadian government that the small sculptures being produced by talented Inuit artists were marketable. Later, Houston, working as a government employee in Cape Dorset, helped bring about a local printmaking industry after an Inuk artist asserted Inuit could create such artwork. By 1961, the Co-operative was incorporated, housing studios and marketing artwork for the benefit of the entire community.

The Co-operative sales outlet is located in the Stonecut studio and is open year-round. Visitors can purchase soapstone, bone and marble carvings, etchings, lithographic prints and postcards. Printmakers work in the studios from September to June, taking time off in summer. The Co-op will package and ship the art for you. For tours, contact the Co-op or the guides listed in this chapter.

You'll also find carvers at work outside their homes or in a small shed nearby. Although they appreciate your interest in their work, you'd be courteous to ask permission before taking their photographs. As some Inuit speak only Inuktitut, hire a guide who can interpret for you.

The **Natsiq Sewing Centre** offers courses in traditional activities such as sewing skin clothing, and throat singing — a unique form of Inuit music that sees two people face each other with mouths close together, quickly repeating different sounds that emanate from deep within the throat. Natsiq also sells duffel parkas, socks, and packing dolls, as well as traditional clothing made from caribou and seal.

The **Polar Supply Store** sells Inuit carvings, snacks and a few groceries. They'll also repair and rent equipment, snow machines and trucks.

The **West Baffin Eskimo Co-operative Store** sells groceries and also includes the services of a mechanic, Yamaha and Home Hardware dealerships, and a gas station. Inuit prints and carvings are sold in the **print shop** across the road.

The **Northern store**, according to its manager, supplies everything from toothpicks to snow machines. That includes groceries, dry goods and hardware.

Finally, the **Sikusiilaq Store** is a convenience store selling snack foods and some groceries and clothing.

Accommodation and Dining

Renovated in 1995, the **Kingnait Inn** has 17 rooms, each with two single beds, TV, toilet and washbasin. Eight of these rooms also have showers, while in remaining rooms, showers are shared. Although single accommodation is available, when the hotel is fully booked, you'll have to share a room. Laundry facilities are available for guests after 5 p.m. There is a pay phone in the hall. Rates are $200 per person per night with meals or $150 without meals. The dining room is open from 7 a.m. to 8 p.m. seven days a week; guests eat at specific times. Box lunches are available for $12 to $15; notify the cook the night before you require them. Guests are met at the airport.

The eight rooms in the **Polar Lodge** have two single beds per room as well as a telephone and TV. Washrooms and showers are separate from rooms. On request, guests will be picked up at the airport. Rates are $175 per person per night with meals, or $135 without meals. The dining room is open from 7 a.m. to 7 p.m. Monday to Saturday, and 7 a.m. to 10 p.m. on Sunday.

Huit Huit Tours offers accommodation for nine people at their beach and guest houses. Each have fully furnished kitchen, living and dining room, TV and laundry. Guests prepare their own meals. Rates are $135 per person per night. Guests are met at the airport.

The **Uksivik Bakery and Coffee Shop**'s baking days are over — it now only provides coffee and light meals for lunch and supper.

DIRECTORY

The 819 and 403 area codes change to 867 on Oct. 21, 1997.

Accommodation and Dining

Huit Huit Tours
Cash, traveller's cheques.
Tel.: (819) 897-8806
Fax: (819) 897-8434

Kingnait Inn
VISA, traveller's cheques.
Tel.: (819) 897-8863
Fax: (819) 897-8907

Polar Lodge
VISA, MasterCard, Interac.
Tel.: (819) 897-8335
Fax: (819) 897-8055

Uksivik Bakery and Coffee Shop
4:30–7 p.m., Monday; 11 a.m.–7 p.m., Tuesday to Friday; 2–7 p.m., Sunday. Closed Saturday. Cash only.
Tel.: (819) 897-8548

Outfitters/Guides/ Tour Operators

Aiviq Hunters and Trappers Organization
Tel.: (819) 897-8978
Fax: (819) 897-8214

Hamlet of Cape Dorset, Community Development Department
For tourism information.
Tel.: (819) 897-8996
Fax: (819) 897-8475

Huit Huit Tours
Tel.: (819) 897-8806
Fax: (819) 897-8434

Seekuu Outfitting
Cash, traveller's cheques.
Tel.: (819) 897-8198
Fax: (819) 897-8186

Services

Airport
Tel.: (819) 897-8938 (First Air)

Alcohol Education Committee
Tel.: (819) 897-8915
Fax: (819) 897-8495

Churches

Anglican Church
Sunday services are at 11 a.m. and 7 p.m. Wednesday service is at 7 p.m. Services in Inuktitut (with occasional bilingual services).
Tel.: (819) 897-8312

Baha'i
For information on meeting times, contact Thelma Perry.
Tel.: (819) 897-8851

Pentecostal Church
Sunday services at 11 a.m. and 7 p.m. Services in Inuktitut.
Tel.: (819) 897-8966

Hamlet Office
Tel.: (819) 897-8943
Fax: (819) 897-8030

Health Centre
Tel.: (819) 897-8820
Fax: (819) 897-8194

Police (RCMP)
Tel.: (819) 897-8855
Fax: (819) 897-8324

Post Office
Located in the Northern store.
11 a.m.–1 p.m. and 2–5:30 p.m., Monday to Wednesday;
1–5:30 p.m., Thursday and Friday.
Tel.: (819) 897-8811

Radio Station (FM 105.1)
Tel.: (819) 897-8875

Resources, Wildlife and Economic Development

Tel.: (819) 897-8932
Fax: (819) 897-8475

Schools

Nunavut Arctic College

Tel.: (819) 897-8850
Fax: (819) 897-8244

Peter Pitseolak School

Tel.: (819) 897-8826
Fax: (819) 897-8919

Sam Pudlat School

Tel.: (819) 897-8332
Fax: (819) 897-8405

Taxi

Polar Taxi

Tel.: (819) 897-8340

Weather Office

Tel.: (819) 897-8330

Stores

Natsiq Sewing Centre

Usually open 1–5 p.m., Monday to Friday.
Tel.: (819) 897-8212

Northern Store

10 a.m.–6 p.m. daily, except 10 a.m.–7 p.m. on Wednesday. Closed Sunday.
VISA, MasterCard, Interac.
Tel.: (819) 897-8811
Fax: (819) 897-8832

Polar Supply Store

1–10 p.m. daily.
VISA, MasterCard, Interac.
Tel.: (819) 897-8969
Fax: (819) 897-8055

Sikusiilaq Store

12–10 p.m., Sunday to Thursday;
12 p.m. to 12 a.m., Friday and Saturday.
Cash only.
Tel.: (819) 897-8009
Fax: (819) 897-8907

West Baffin Eskimo Co-operative Print Shop

9 a.m.–5 p.m., Monday to Friday.
VISA, Interac.
Tel.: (819) 897-8944
Fax: (819) 897-8049

West Baffin Eskimo Co-operative Store

9 a.m.–6 p.m., Monday and Tuesday;
9 a.m.–7 p.m., Wednesday to Friday;
9 a.m.–5 p.m., Saturday. Closed Sunday.
VISA, cash, traveller's cheques.
Tel.: (819) 897-8997
Fax: (819) 897-8000

MALLIKJUAQ HISTORIC PARK

by John Laird

Mallikjuaq means "big wave" in Inuktitut, an appropriate name for an island where rounded rock hills and low tundra valleys resemble giant rolling waves.

But while Mallikjuaq Historic Park derives its name from its topography, it gets its spirit from its human history. A 45-minute walk from the community of Cape Dorset, you'll find excellent archeological sites and stone structures here dating back some three millennia.

About 1,000 years ago, the people of the Thule culture lived on Mallikjuaq in low, stone houses framed with whalebone ribs and covered with hides and sod. The east arm of the island boasts the remains of nine winter houses with stone foundations still in place. Scattered throughout the area are the bones of whales, seals and walruses, a vital resource for the Thule. Archeological evidence indicates that people from the Dorset culture — predecessor of the Thule — also inhabited the island. The point of access to these winter houses is the southeast shore of Mallikjuaq Island. From the beach, walk on to the tundra toward a large pond where the houses are.

The northwest coast of Mallikjuaq Island boasts a number of more contemporary, though no less interesting, stone features. Tent rings, fireplaces and meat caches here date back between 50 and 200 years. The ingenuity of arctic inhabitants is illustrated by the many self-supporting stone structures they created, such as kayak stands and *inuksuit*. Other stone piles here represent fox traps and burial sites. Local Inuit elders ask visitors to respect their heritage by not disturbing the sites, which are currently protected under Northwest Territories legislation.

What to See and Do

Mallikjuaq's archeological sites are easy to reach and can be thoroughly toured in about two hours. The gentle slopes of the island's east end offer excellent views of the undulating landscape as well as Hudson Strait. The steep rock hills in the southwest corner of the island are less easily scaled. Sandy beaches can be found among the island's more common offering of gravel and rocky shorelines; these make excellent places to camp. You can also kayak around nearby coves and islands.

Wildlife is plentiful in summer, and you may see caribou, arctic hares, peregrine falcons, snowy owls, ptarmigans and ducks. Polar bears roam the coast in spring and fall, an exciting yet potentially dangerous visitor. To avoid any unexpected encounters, travel with an experienced, licensed guide who can act as a bear monitor for you. Seals may appear at any time; beluga whales migrate through nearby waters in October and April. If you are very lucky you may even spot a massive bowhead whale, although they are infrequent visitors. Fishing for arctic char is popular in nearby bays.

The best time of year to visit Mallikjuaq is in July and August, when warm temperatures and abundant sunshine bring tundra wildflowers briefly to life. Large patches of tundra are covered with these colorful, ground-hugging plants. Autumn starts in late August, when patches of tundra turn a vibrant red and yellow.

The *Mallikjuaq Historic Park Trail Guide* offers clear directions to the island and interprets the park's many features. You can obtain a copy from **Nunavut Tourism** or **Cape Dorset's hamlet office**.

Getting There

In summer, local outfitters will take groups of up to three people on the 10-minute boat ride across the inlet for about $75. For an additional $75 or so, your guide will throw in a tour of the island's historic sites, wildlife and plants, as well as tea and bannock. If you ask, your guide may also supply local foods such as caribou, char or seal. Make arrangements well in advance of your arrival to Cape Dorset. Finding a guide on short notice is sometimes difficult. Your ideal guide is one who not only has a good understanding of the history of the island, but who also likes to tell stories about Inuit culture.

You can also hike to Mallikjuaq, a 45-minute trek from Cape Dorset to the northwest tip of Dorset Island and across the tidal flats of Tellik Inlet. This hike — which is only possible at low tide — is recommended for agile walkers prepared for slippery, algae-covered rocks and innumerable puddles. If foot is your chosen mode of transport, make sure you check tide times before heading out, or you may find yourself spending an evening on the island, alone and without food and shelter. The community's economic development officer is happy to talk to visitors about tides and walking trips to Mallikjuaq. If you hike without a guide, inform someone of your travel plans, such as the local RCMP detachment or the hotel, if you are a guest. Guides offer walking tours for $50 to $75; information is available from the Municipality of Cape Dorset.

In winter, the landscape of Mallikjuaq takes on a completely different appearance as snow creates a variety of patterns on the rock hills. Archeological sites and vegetation will be covered by snow, although you may be lucky enough to see a caribou or arctic hare. Cape Dorset residents occasionally build igloos on the island.

At this time of year you can walk directly across the ice to Mallikjuaq or hire a guide with a snowmobile to take you. Expect to pay $75 to $150, depending on the service provided. A great way to travel is by dogteam, bundled in caribou skins on a *qamutik* and listening to the quiet crunch of the snow as you glide over it. A day trip by dogteam costs $150 to $200 for a group of up to three people, including lunch. It is not possible to cross to Tellik Inlet during breakup and freeze-up, which occur in June and October. A late breakup may delay crossing until early July.

Be Prepared

Even though the area enjoys almost 20 hours of sunlight in summer, the temperature averages a high of just 7.2° C and can drop below zero any time. Winter temperatures can plummet below –40° C between December and March. The shortest days of December yield about five hours of sunshine.

Regardless of the season in which you travel, always be prepared for the unexpected, as weather conditions can vary throughout the day. Even in summer, you'll need warm and waterproof clothing, a hat, and mitts. Rubber boots are best for getting to shore from a boat; sturdy, waterproof hiking boots work best on the spongy and sometimes soggy tundra. Insect repellent is a worthy companion, as bugs can be voracious, especially on calm days. In winter, insulated clothing such as parkas, snow pants, mitts and boots are essential. Bring sunglasses and sunscreen in any season. In summer they'll protect you from long hours of sunlight. In winter and spring they'll guard against the bright sun reflecting off the snow.

Though Mallikjuaq is a territorial park, it remains untouched. There are no services or facilities on the island. Local people will drink water from the island's many streams and ponds, although it is recommended that you bring your own drinking water or boil water collected on the island. To preserve the park, carry out your garbage and leave the island as you found it. Groceries and some camping supplies can be purchased in Cape Dorset at the Co-op and the Northern store. The Kingnait Inn will provide a boxed lunch for about $15.

DIRECTORY

The 819 and 403 area codes change to 867 on Oct. 21, 1997.

Cape Dorset Hamlet Office
Tel.: (819) 897-8943
Fax: (819) 897-8030

Cape Dorset Hunters and Trappers Organization
For information on local outfitters and guides.
Tel.: (819) 897-8978
Fax: (819) 897-8214

Economic Development Office
Tel.: (819) 897-8996
Fax: (819) 897-8142

Nunavut Tourism
P.O. Box 1450, Iqaluit NT,
X0A 0H0 Canada
Ask Nunavut Tourism or the Cape Dorset Hamlet Office (above) for a copy of the *Mallikjuaq Historic Park Trail Guide.*
Tel.: 1-800-491-7910 (for Canada and the United States)
Tel.: (819) 979-6551
Fax: (819) 979-1261
E-mail: nunatour@nunanet.com
Web site: www.nunatour.nt.ca

SANIKILUAQ

by Miriam Fleming

Nunavut's southernmost community, Sanikiluaq, is located on the Belcher Islands in southeastern Hudson Bay, about 150 kilometres off the coast of Quebec.

Population:	631 (Inuit: 95%, non-Inuit: 5%)
Telephone Area Code:	819 (changes to 867 on Oct. 21, 1997)
Time Zone:	Eastern Time
Postal Code:	X0A 0J0
How to Get There:	Possible routes:
	• Montreal-Kuujjuarapik-Umiujaq-Sanikiluaq
	• Iqaluit-Sanikiluaq
	• Winnipeg-Montreal-Kuujjuarapik-Umiujaq-Sanikiluaq
	• Kangerlussuaq (Greenland)-Iqaluit-Sanikiluaq
	Montreal to Sanikiluaq (almost 1,500 kilometres north) is via First Air and Air Inuit. Iqaluit to Sanikiluaq (about 1,000 kilometres south) is via Air Nunavut
Banks:	None. Visitors should bring traveller's cheques, cash or money orders
Alcohol:	Alcohol and alcoholic beverages are prohibited
Taxis:	Arrangements can be made with Amaulik Hotel to pick up and deliver hotel guests from the airport

Although more than 1,100 kilometres south of the Arctic Circle, the islands are distinctly arctic. No trees grow here and except in valleys, only a thin layer of soil covers the ground. The islands' peak is 155 metres above sea level; some cliffs rise from 50 to 70 metres.

Fly on a clear day into Sanikiluaq via Umiujaq, Quebec, and you'll see a unique clutch of 1,500 islands. Spread out over almost 3,000 square kilometres, these are the Belcher Islands, the largest group of islands in Hudson Bay. The main group of the archipelago forms an S-shaped pattern whose long, narrow peninsulas are separated by clearly defined channels.

Although Sanikiluaq (pronounced "san-ee-kil-a-wak") is the only permanent settlement here, many Inuit live and camp throughout the archipelago during spring and summer. Sanikiluaq lies on the main group of islands, on a narrow piece of land near the north end of Flaherty Island, bounded by Eskimo Harbour to the northwest and by Sanikiluaq Lake to the south.

In a world that's being resculpted by industrial developments, Sanikiluaq residents have worked hard to ensure that traditional knowledge has a place in modern environmental management.

An ongoing, long-term study has amassed traditional knowledge from 28 Inuit and Cree communities around Hudson Bay, James Bay and Hudson Strait so that in the face of northern Quebec's Great Whale hydroelectric project, the traditional knowledge of native people would be used in the region's environmental assessment. The research has resulted in a forthcoming book, *Portrait of the Bays: The Land, The Waters and People of Hudson Bay and James Bay* (Toronto: University of Toronto Press), as well as a 1995 award from the Friends of the United Nations, citing Sanikiluaq as one of 50 exemplary communities worldwide committed to building a sense of common unity. The study's headquarters are in the **Hudson Bay Office** in Sanikiluaq.

History

The Inuit have inhabited the Belcher Islands for centuries. While some ancestors of present-day inhabitants migrated here from northern Quebec, others came when the Thule culture was declining between AD 1200 and 1400. Earlier occupation is evidenced in the archeological sites of the Dorset culture from 500 BC to AD 1000.

The islands first came to the attention of outsiders after Henry Hudson spotted them in 1610. More than 230 years later, Thomas Wiegand, a servant of the Hudson's Bay Co., led an exploration party from Fort George (Chisasibi, Quebec) to the Belcher Islands. It was another 60 years before the first *qallunaat* wintered here. The sailors of the day survived by using the wood from their ship for fuel.

The Inuit survived in this sometimes forbidding land through their ingenuity. In the late 1800s when caribou disappeared from the islands (possibly due to icy conditions that made foraging impossible), women began sewing winter parkas from eider duck skins. The men were renowned for their knowledge of ice fields and their kayaking skills. They were respected, as well, for two-person kayaks which they navigated adeptly through the rough waters of the bay. Their dogs were prized as items of trade during annual trips to mainland posts.

A Hudson's Bay Co. trading post, constructed in 1928, operated sporadically. It was relocated from Tukarak Island to Eskimo Harbour in 1961. That same year, the federal government built a school in the southern part of Flaherty Island. During the 1960s, two communities existed in the islands: North Camp, where the trading post was located, and South Camp, where the school was built.

The community of Sanikiluaq wasn't established until 1971, when the federal government centralized its services and moved the buildings and inhabitants of South Camp to North Camp. Today, Sanikiluaq is a growing, modern settlement whose economy is based on hunting, fishing, tourism and soapstone carving.

Sanikiluaq: Its Land and Wildlife

Most of the small islands in the archipelago provide breeding grounds for several species of ducks and geese. Rocky crevices, lakes and ponds are summer home to many other migrating birds. Most of the species that nest in the Belcher Islands or visit here are water birds, including common eider, red-throated loon, common loon, arctic loon, Canada goose, Brant, merganser, black guillemot, arctic tern and gulls. There are also a few land birds such as rock ptarmigan, rough-legged hawk, peregrine falcon, snowy owl, horned lark, Lapland longspur and snow bunting.

Arctic char are found in the rivers, lakes, and offshore waters, while whitefish swim in the lakes. Coastal waters are a source of cod, capelin, lump fish, and sculpin. They're also home to ringed seal, bearded seal, harbour seal, beluga whale, walrus and polar bear. On the tundra, fox, reindeer, arctic hare, and lemming may be seen. Reindeer were introduced in 1978 about 100 years after the caribou disappeared.

Sanikiluaq, anchored in Hudson Bay, has weather that can be blustery and unpredictable. The islands are surrounded by open sea, and high winds and storms can arise suddenly. Information on daily temperatures and wind conditions can be obtained from the observer/communicator at the local **airport**.

Tours

In the Sanikiluaq area, you'll find many trails that are great for both walking and driving all-terrain vehicles (ATVs). One trail that's visible from the **Mitiq Co-op** — one of Sanikiluaq's two major stores — is an easy walk to a small bay three kilometres from the community. This is the site of a former mussel farm.

The trail continues about two kilometres, then crosses a river. Once across, you can hike up a gentle valley slope to a point overlooking *Kattak* (Entrance). In July and August, this is a lovely spot for a picnic. The tundra here is carpeted with arctic flowers, and the panorama of Eskimo Harbour, Tukarak Island and the Baker's Dozen Islands is superb.

Eight kilometres from the settlement, you'll find Dorset and Thule archeological sites near *Kingaaluk* (Big Mountain) and *Katapik* (Small Entrance) on the west side of Eskimo Harbour.

Another good spot for a picnic is Katapik, which you can reach easily by ATV, boat, or snowmobile. It's also Sanikiluaq's favored destination for gathering mussels, sea urchins, and sea cucumbers. On weekends, when the weather is fine, community picnics are often held here.

The best camp site in Sanikiluaq is the gravel beach just north of the harbor and east of the old boats. The view from the beach is marvellous. Check with the **hamlet office** to find out if camping permits are required, and remember that winds here can be strong. You should have a sturdy tent that can be secured to large rocks.

Inuit-made canvas tents can be rented from the **Sanniit Co-operative Ltd**. To rent other camping gear, snowmobiles and ATVs, call the **Hunters and Trappers Organization** in advance of your visit. Few tourists travel to Sanikiluaq. The Inuit here worry when they see visitors venture out on the land or water without a guide. For their peace of mind — and your safety — please inform the RCMP of your destination. (You can also obtain emergency locator beacons from the hamlet office.) While Sanikiluaq does not currently have any licensed outfitters, local people do organize boat trips to Wiegand Island (*Tungasitik*) and to the soapstone mines on Tukarak Island, 40 kilometres away.

To hunt and fish in the islands, you'll need a licence. Access restrictions exist on Inuit-owned land as a result of the 1993 Nunavut Land Claims Agreement, so if your hunting and fishing plans lead you to such private property, contact the Nunavut Land Administration Office (Baffin Region) in advance of your trip for permission to cross onto the land. See Chapter 11, "Adventure Travel," for more information. To obtain a territorial wildlife export permit, contact the municipal liaison office.

Sanikiluaq Lake, on the south side of the community is the settlement's main source of drinking water. All activities, including fishing or kayaking, are discouraged on the lake.

Shopping

The soapstone carvings of Belcher Islands and Sanikiluaq, treasured in offices and homes around the world, are usually realistic portrayals of the animals and birds found here. A large selection of carvings is available at the Mitiq Co-operative, as are groceries and dry goods.

Two other stores in Sanikiluaq are Sanniit Co-operative Ltd. and the **Northern store**. Sanniit sells eiderdown outerwear and duvets, ideal for arctic camping. The Northern store sells a range of goods, including groceries, clothing, hardware and compact discs.

Accommodation and Dining

Sanikiluaq's only hotel, the **Amaulik**, is owned and operated by the Mitiq Co-operative Association. The timeworn building, however, will soon be relegated to another use; the Co-operative plans to open a new eight-room (double occupancy) hotel by the spring of 1998, complete with a gift shop, meeting room, 49-seat dining room and private washrooms and televisions in all hotel rooms.

Meanwhile, the current hotel accommodates 20 people in eight rooms, with a mininum of two beds per room. Rooms with three or four beds have a private washroom. The television lounge and washrooms for double-occupancy rooms are shared. Prices are $140 per person per night (without meals), or $190 with meals. Non-guests can also eat at the small cafeteria-style dining room if they make prior arrangements with the manager. On occasion, they may also arrange, through the manager, to share a traditional meal with an Inuit family. If given prior notice, the kitchen staff prepares bagged lunches.

Services

The **health centre**, open weekdays from 8:30 a.m. to 12 p.m. and from 1 to 4:30 p.m., has two registered nurses and a community health representative who treat routine medical problems. Nurses are on call for emergencies, and can be reached by calling the health centre.

NorthwesTel provides poor telephone service to Sanikiluaq. If you have difficulty making a long-distance call or if the line goes dead, you'll know why. Sanikiluaq isn't yet hooked up to the Internet. To send or receive a fax, contact the hamlet office. A small fee applies.

To help orient you while in Sanikiluaq, you can obtain a community map from the hamlet office.

The local **Nuiyak School** welcomes visitors to attend classes in history, cultural and environmental studies. Call the school principal for an invitation.

If you'd like to do some research while in town, browse through the Hudson Bay Office's reading room. You'll find works on the Hudson Bay, James Bay and Hudson Strait marine, coastal and riverine areas.

Finally, if you feel inclined to volunteer your services while you're here, contact the community economic development officer at the **hamlet office** before you arrive in Sanikiluaq. The experience may provide you with a calibre of travel stories few can equal.

DIRECTORY

The 819 and 403 area codes change to 867 on Oct. 21, 1997.

Accommodation and Dining

Amaulik Hotel
VISA, MasterCard, American Express, Diners Club/enRoute, traveller's cheques.
Tel.: (819) 266-8821 or (819) 266-8909
Fax: (819) 266-8727 or (819) 266-8844

Services

Airport
8 a.m.–6 p.m., Monday to Friday.
Tel.: (819) 266-8824 or (819) 266-8874

Church

St. Philip's Anglican Church
Services: 10 a.m. and 7 p.m., Sunday, in Inuktitut; 7 p.m., Wednesday.
Tel.: (819) 266-8832

Hamlet Office
Ask for the community economic development officer or municipal liaison officer.
Tel.: (819) 266-8874
Fax: (819) 266-8903

Health Centre
Tel.: (819) 266-8965
Fax: (819) 266-8802

Hudson Bay Office
Tel.: (819) 266-8980
Fax: (819) 266-8837

Police (RCMP)
Tel.: (819) 266-8812
Fax: (819) 266-8952

Post Office
Located in the Northern store.
10 a.m.–12 p.m., 1:30–5:30 p.m., Monday to Friday.
Tel.: (819) 266-8945

Radio Station (FM 106.1)
Operated by Sanikiluaq Broadcasting Society. Interactive radio bingos frequently held on weeknights.
Tel.: (819) 266-8893 or (819) 266-8833

Sanikiluaq Hunters and Trappers Organization
Tel.: (819) 266-8709
Fax: (819) 266-8131

Schools

Nuiyak School
Tel.: (819) 266-8816 or (819) 266-8817
Fax: (819) 266-8843

Nunavut Arctic College
Tel.: (819) 266-8885

Shopping

Mitiq Co-op
9 a.m.–6 p.m., Monday to Saturday. Closed Sunday. VISA, MasterCard, American Express, Diners Club/enRoute, traveller's cheques.
Tel.: (819) 266-8909 or (819) 266-8821
Fax: (819) 266-8727 or (819) 266-8844

Northern Store
9:30 a.m.–6 p.m., Monday to Thursday;
9:30 a.m.–7 p.m., Friday;
9:30 a.m.–6 p.m., Saturday. Closed Sunday. VISA, MasterCard, Interac, traveller's cheques.
Tel.: (819) 266-8836
Fax: (819) 266-8840

Sanniit Co-operative Ltd.
8:30 a.m.–12 p.m., 1–5 p.m., Monday to Friday. Cash, traveller's cheques.
Tel.: (819) 266-8920
Fax: (819) 266-8920

CONTRIBUTORS

John Amagoalik of Iqaluit is chief commissioner of the Nunavut Implementation Commission, the public institution helping design Nunavut's government.

Laisa Audlaluk is recreation co-ordinator for the Hamlet of Grise Fiord, and is also involved in the suicide prevention program. During the summer she works at Ellesmere Island National Park Reserve.

Larry Audlaluk of Grise Fiord is president of the Grise Fiord Inuit Co-op Ltd., vice-president of Qikiqtani Inuit Association, and a board member of Nunavut Tunngavik Inc. Audlaluk says he enjoys his work with the Nunavut land claim, and is very interested in the political development of Nunavut and the impending Nunavut government. Audlaluk was among those who were moved by the federal government, from Inukjuak, Quebec, to Grise Fiord in 1953; he has been involved in the High Arctic relocation issue as a result.

Mike Beedell is an internationally published photographer, adventurer, and guide who suffers from a chronic case of arctic fever. He is the author of *The Magnetic North* and his work is regularly featured in fine magazines throughout the world. Beedell runs custom photo tours to many outstanding areas north of 60.

Jennifer Bernius is a writer and editor who lives in Ottawa. During the 1970s, she worked with Inuit Tapirisat of Canada, writing and editing stories for ITC's magazine, *Inuit Today*.

George Bohlender moved to the Northwest Territories from Toronto in 1985, working in retail management and consulting in Iqaluit and Pangnirtung, and as an economic development officer for the GNWT in Arctic Bay. He now lives in Taloyoak with wife Madelaine and daughter Gina. An employee of the Kitikmeot Economic Development Commission since July 1995, Bohlender serves as the community economic development officer for Taloyoak, Pelly Bay, and Gjoa Haven in the Kitikmeot Region.

Colleen Dupuis of Iqaluit is a communications consultant and a member of the advisory committee overseeing developments within the Sylvia Grinnell Territorial Park.

Michael P. Ellsworth teaches a senior class at Quqshuun Illihakvik School, Gjoa Haven. Although hired to teach, he willingly acknowledges the fact that it is he who continues to do much of the learning. He moved to Gjoa Haven in August 1996, along with his wife Jan, a fellow teacher. Ellsworth is originally from Prince Edward Island and enjoys his stay on another of Canada's great islands, King William Island.

Peter Ernerk of Rankin Inlet is a cultural activist and freelance writer specializing in Inuit culture and northern political developments. Currently a member of the Nunavut Implementation Commission, Ernerk was minister of Social Development, Economic Development and Natural and Cultural Affairs with the government of the Northwest Territories between 1975 and 1979, and is a former director of Tungavik Federation of Nunavut.

Judy Farrow has lived in the Northwest Territories since 1971 and for 15 years made Iqaluit her home. In 1980, she received a Canada Council Grant to research Inuktitut names and traditional uses of arctic plants. Farrow currently lives in Yellowknife, working for the Métis Nation.

After living in Iqaluit for seven years, **Marian Ferguson** has resided in Pond Inlet since 1988. She is a freelance writer and travel consultant who designs adventures for arctic travellers.

Mike Ferguson, a wildlife biologist, has travelled in most remote parts of Baffin Island over the past 16 years and has authored several scientific publications on Baffin caribou.

Freelance writer **Lyn Hancock** of Lantzville, British Columbia has travelled to almost every community in Nunavut and written extensively about her experiences in magazines and newspapers. The author of several books about the Canadian North, including *There's a Seal in My Sleeping Bag*, Hancock's most recent effort is *Winging It In the North*.

Iqaluit's **Kenn Harper** is a historian, linguist and businessman who has lived 30 years in the Arctic. He is the author of *Give Me My Father's Body: The Life of Minik, the New York Eskimo*.

Beverly Illauq arrived in Clyde River in 1983 to teach school for one year, married a local hunter, and is now deeply involved in education, community development and managing Qullikkut Guides and Outfitters.

Formerly from Iqaluit, **Alootook Ipellie** is a freelance writer and illustrator now living in Ottawa. He is the author of the book *Arctic Dreams and Nightmares.*

Robert Jaffray of Kimmirut works for the government of the Northwest Territories as an economic development officer, and has lived in the Baffin since 1989. He and his wife have four young children.

Terry Jesudason owns and operates High Arctic International Explorer Services Ltd. in Resolute. She has more than 25 years experience in the High Arctic in the tourism industry, operating a guest home for travellers and providing support for polar expeditions.

Robin Johnstone of Edmonton is a wildlife biologist, ecotourism guide, and freelance photojournalist. He came to Canada from his native New Zealand to study peregrine falcons at Rankin Inlet for his PhD.

Darren Keith is a Yellowknife resident who takes his holidays on the tundra. Since graduating from the Native Studies Program at the University of Alberta, his passion for the North and its people has resulted in many journeys by boat and snowmobile in the Kivalliq Region of Nunavut. Keith is a writer, researcher and planner with Parks Canada. He has conducted research to record Inuit oral history and traditional placenames, and has completed community-based management plans for Arvia'juaq and Caribou Crossing National Historic Sites.

A biologist and author of 14 books on hunting and fishing, **Jerome Knap** of Almonte, Ontario has worked since the late 1970s with the Ojibwa of Northern Ontario and the Inuit of the Northwest Territories to help develop and market hunting and fishing tourism endeavors.

Ulrike Komaksiutiksak came north 10 years ago to work for the NWT Aboveground Swimming Pool Program, working a summer in Normen Wells and the following two summers in Rankin Inlet, this time under the auspices of Municipal and Community Affairs. Here, she says, she met her "arctic souvenir" — husband Jerry. Since marrying, they have lived in Yellowknife, Fort Smith, Iqaluit and Whale Cove, and together are raising their three children.

Millie Kuliktana of Kugluktuk is an educator and consultant with the Kitikmeot Board of Education, focusing on culture and language preservation. She is also a wife and mother of three children, a hamlet council member, and a community volunteer at large.

John Laird is a park planner and landscape architect, living in Yellowknife. Over the last eight years he has worked as a consultant visiting many communities and scenic areas in Nunavut and throughout the Northwest Territories.

Karen LeGresley Hamre is a landscape architect who has been based in Yellowknife since 1983. She has done designs for numerous parks, trails and interpretive sites across the North, including the Meliadine River Territorial Park, Sylvia Grinnell Territorial Park and Mount Pelly.

Olav Loken studied physical geography in Norway and Canada. Over a span of 25 years, he held several federal government positions, always with a "northern connection." He is now a consultant in Ottawa, specializing in Antarctic issues.

John MacDonald makes his home in Igloolik where he is co-ordinator of the Igloolik Research Centre. During the past 38 years he has lived and worked in various Inuit communities in the Northwest Territories and in Arctic Quebec.

A journalism graduate from Nunavut Arctic College, freelance writer **Ann Meekitjuk Hanson** of Iqaluit grew up "on the land" in the traditional Inuit lifestyle. She later attended school in Toronto, and subsequently worked as a broadcaster for the Canadian Broadcasting Corporation, airing cultural programming, current affairs, histories, and lifestyles programming in Inuktitut.

Former teacher **Steven W. Metzger** of Pelly Bay specializes in research, writing and computer consulting. Interested in developmental, educational and cultural issues, Metzger also has a universal love of land and landscapes. His motto, he says, is "to work hard, but never hurry."

Jimi Onalik is currently the regional youth co-ordinator for the Kivalliq Inuit Association in Rankin Inlet, his home since 1983. Throughout high school Onalik worked as a tour guide, and has since travelled throughout Canada, the United States, Denmark and Australia.

Freelance interpreter/translator — and now writer — **Joe Otokiak** of Cambridge Bay has lived in the Kitikmeot Region of Nunavut most of his life, and is married with five children and one grandchild. He says he just enjoys life and tries to be active as much as possible, traditionally and otherwise.

Photojournalist **Terry Pearce** of Iqaluit is a longtime backcountry skier who has travelled extensively in all seasons throughout Nunavut.

Broughton Island's **Don Pickle** has lived in the North since 1994, working in both the Kitikmeot and the Baffin regions as a senior administrative officer for the hamlets of Taloyoak and Broughton Island. He enjoys spending time on the land. Despite his capacity to get lost, Pickle says he has always made it home thanks to the strong abilities of the Canadian Rangers.

George Qulaut, a hunter from Igloolik, worked for many years with the Igloolik Research Centre where he was instrumental in starting the Igloolik Oral History Project. He is currently a commissioner with the Nunavut Implementation Commission.

Bruce Rigby of Iqaluit came north in 1978 as part of a geologic mapping party with the Geological Survey of Canada. Since then he has been actively involved in the development of the Baffin tourism industry as guide, outfitter and tourism instructor, chairman of the Environmental Technology Program of Nunavut Arctic College, and district superintendent for Parks Canada. He is currently science advisor to the Commissioner of the Northwest Territories and executive director of the Nunavut Research Institute.

Carol Rigby moved north in 1986, in husband Bruce's wake, with toddler and infant in tow. Since then she has taught business communications at Nunavut Arctic College, worked as an editor and writer with Nortext Multimedia Inc., including production work on the now-defunct *Arctic Circle* magazine, and as a freelance writer, producing visitor guides to Iqaluit and the Baffin. A major contributor to *The Baffin Handbook*, Carol now works as the library technician for Baffin Regional Library.

Sue Rowley of Pittsburgh, Pennsylvania is an archeologist and ethnohistorian. She is also a research associate of the Nunavut Research Institute.

Iqaluit's **David Serkoak** graduted from the Teacher Education Program in Fort Smith in 1978, moving to Arviat to teach there until 1989. A curator at the Museum of Mankind in London, England for the "Living Arctic" exhibit prior to coming to Iqaluit, Serkoak has since taught at Nunavut Arctic College, Inuksuk High School and now, at Joamie School. He is married to Lesley and has three daughters. Serkoak, who makes Inuit drums as a hobby, drum dances with his youngest daughter, Karla.

Writer/editor **Marion Soublière** of Ottawa first became a devotee of northern issues through work with the Beverly and Qamanirjuaq Caribou Management Board, Nunavut Tunngavik Inc. and other northern groups. The highlight of her time as managing editor of *The Nunavut Handbook* has been really getting to know the people of Canada's North.

For 25 years, **Dave Sutherland** of Yellowknife worked in the field of Inuit art with the government of the Northwest Territories, rising to the head of the art and crafts division. He has been a private consultant since 1986.

Shirley Tagalik has lived in Arviat since 1976. She works as an educator, and enjoys hunting, fishing, and taking pleasure from the community's rich diversity with her husband and three daughters.

Louis Tapardjuk is from Igloolik where he is actively involved in programs promoting Inuit traditional skills and values. In 1996 he was appointed executive director of the Inuit Social Development Council.

Hunter **Andrew Taqtu** of Arctic Bay was born near Pond Inlet. He has worked at different jobs, and has been an outfitter for 12 years, taking out all kinds of people who do different things. "If they are divers I go diving with them," he says. Taqtu has taken tourist guide courses to level III.

Since 1991, outdoorsman, naturalist, and writer/editor **Mike Vlessides** has spent most of his time living in the Arctic, although he has been known to make the occasional foray to his homeland of New York City. His two years in Nunavut proved to be the most fascinating of his life. Now living in Canmore, Alberta, Vlessides most recently served as editor of *Up Here* magazine.

Tracy Wallace has lived in Chesterfield Inlet, Rankin Inlet, Winnipeg and the surrounding area, Scotland, and Ottawa. She considers each one to be home just as much as the other. Now a proud mother of two, she lives in Rankin Inlet where she works in the field of commercial development for the Department of Transportation.

Renee Wissink, presently working in Haida Gwaii (Queen Charlotte Islands) in British Columbia, lived in Nunavut for 15 years and worked as a teacher, consultant, and national park warden. He also headed the 1986 Qitdlarssuaq Expedition, retracing the 19th century Inuit migration from Baffin Island to Greenland led by the shaman Qillaq — who later became known as "Qitdlarssuaq" or the great Qitdlaq.

GLOSSARY

amauti ("a-mau-tee"); a woman's parka in which a baby is carried in the hood. An *amauti* is often pristine white and colorfully trimmed

ATVs all-terrain vehicles

Baffin Region includes Sanikiluaq, Iqaluit, Kimmirut, Cape Dorset, Broughton Island, Pangnirtung, Nanisivik, Clyde River, Pond Inlet, Arctic Bay, Grise Fiord, Resolute, Igloolik, and Hall Beach. Total population: 12,948 (1996 Census of Canada)

cache meat that is stored outdoors on the land for future use

DEW Line the Canadian government, pressed by the United States and urged as well by the Royal Canadian Air Force to install an arctic early-warning chain in the midst of the Cold War, began construction of a 22-station DEW Line in 1953. It stretched along the Arctic Coast from Alaska to Baffin Island

Dorset the Dorset culture appeared around 2,700 years ago when the Nunavut climate cooled and the Paleoeskimo lifestyle underwent a period of rapid transition. The Dorset people had a rich artistic tradition, carving miniature masterpieces from ivory and antler for ceremonial and decorative use

Eskimo a Cree Indian word that means "eaters of raw meat," *Eskimo* is considered a derogatory term that is no longer used to describe the Inuit of Nunavut

floe edge the place where open water joins land-fast ice; where still waters meet waters propelled by currents

GNWT government of the Northwest Territories

GPS Global Positioning System. This handheld receiver uses satellite information to identify your current location

GST the Goods and Services Tax is a seven per cent federal tax that consumers must pay. Non-residents of Canada are entitled to a refund on goods and accommodation, provided they stay less than one month at that accommodation

HF radio high frequency radio is used to communicate in emergencies and other situations, especially by hunters and people travelling or living on the land. The most common version is the Spillsbury SBX-11, sometimes called the radiotelephone

hoodoos columns of strangely shaped rocks formed by the erosion of sandstone around a harder "cap" rock that eventually produces 10- to 15-metre pillars of sandstone. Found on Bylot Island off north Baffin Island

HTO Hunters and Trappers Organization. HTOs, based in almost every community in Nunavut, serve the interests of local hunters and trappers. They are an invaluable source of information about wildlife in the area, and the lay of the land

ice pans year-round sea ice that occasionally occurs. Ice pans floating in and out on the tides are common in summer

iglu igloo

Inuk ("ee-nook"); a person of Inuit descent. Two such people are *Inuuk*; three or more are *Inuit* ("ee-neu-eet"). Note that the plural is never used with an "s" (i.e. the Inuits)

inuksuit ("ee-nook-soo-eet"); rock cairns often shaped in the form of a human, these landmarks established where Inuit had travelled. The singular of the word is *inuksuk* ("like a human"). The anglicized version of the plural, *inuksuks*, is often heard

inuktitut ("ee-nook-tee-tut"); the language of Inuit

kamiit ("cam-eet"); sealskin boots. The anglicized version of the plural, *kamiks*, is often heard

Keewatin the previous name for the Kivalliq Region. Since this name change has only recently taken place, many people still refer to the "Keewatin"

Kitikmeot Region includes Pelly Bay, Bathurst Inlet, Taloyoak, Kugluktuk, Gjoa Haven, Cambridge Bay and Umingmaktok. Total population: 5,067 (1996 Census of Canada). While the nearby community of Holman is currently part of the Kitikmeot, it has opted not to become part of Nunavut when the new territory forms in 1999

Kivalliq Region includes Repulse Bay, Arviat, Coral Harbour, Whale Cove, Rankin Inlet, Baker Lake, and Chesterfield Inlet. Total population: 6,868 (1996 Census of Canada)

leads patches of open water found during spring breakup of sea ice

maktaaq ("muk-tuk"); whale skin, considered a delicacy by Inuit

nanuq ("na-nook"); polar bear

Nunavut ("new-na-voot"); our land

NWT the Northwest Territories, which until April 1, 1999, comprises the central and eastern Arctic area that will become Nunavut, plus the western Arctic, which has yet to be renamed

outpost camp isolated camps where families of Inuit hunt, trap and fish to feed and clothe themselves and their families according to their traditional subsistence lifestyle

polynyas places where there is regularly no, or very thin, sea ice; these conditions may be caused by a combination of winds and upwelling ocean currents. Polynyas are important for wildlife

qajaq kayak

qallunaat ("ka-bloo-na"); white people

qamutik ("ka-ma-tik"); a long, slatted wooden sled pulled by dogteam or snow machine. The plural is *qamutiit* ("ka-ma-teet"); the anglicized version, *qamutiks*, is frequently used, though

qulliq ("coo-lik"); a soapstone oil lamp in the shape of a half-moon, its carved-out hollow contains the fat and wick

RCMP the Royal Canadian Mounted Police is Canada's national police force

snow machine a snowmobile

Thule about 1,000 years ago, a new group of people emigrated from northern Alaska into what is now Nunavut. Archeologists believe the Thule ("too-lee") to be the first of two Neoeskimo subgroups

Tuniit the *Tuniit* ("too-neet") occupied Nunavut before the ancestors of Inuit arrived. Although there were intermarriages between the two groups, there were also fights, and the Tuniit removed themselves from areas occupied by the Thule. Eventually the Tuniit disappeared

weathered out a local expression meaning bad weather has set in and thrown a wrench into plans